Semper Anticus

Rita Kirchgassner

Inspiring Voices®

All opinions on family and military history are mine unless otherwise noted. Many are speculation based on history. Any errors in transcribing the primary records were not intentional. Jared Leiker authored the blogs documenting our journey to Europe in 2013. Mark Kirchgassner and Krista Kirchgassner also offered thoughts and memories from the journey.

Inspiring Voices books may be ordered through booksellers or by contacting:

Inspiring Voices
1663 Liberty Drive
Bloomington, IN 47403
www.inspiringvoices.com
1 (866) 697-5313

ISBN: 978-1-4624-1123-8 (sc)
ISBN: 978-1-4624-1124-5 (e)

Library of Congress Control Number: 2015906673

Print information available on the last page.

Inspiring Voices rev. date: 10/17/2016

For John Schweisthal,

lest we forget that without his heroic deed our journey
in 2013 would not have come to pass.

John Schweisthal

Preface

2016

THE FIRST PRINTING OF *SEMPER ANTICUS* was completed in June of 2015. After reviewing the book this past year, I made some additions and corrected spelling errors that were unintentionally missed. Thanks to my brother John and Hugh F. Foster III for their assistance during this time of revision. Hugh provided additional information on the soldiers who served in Company C during World War II.

As you read this book, please know that it is not meant to be an analysis or an intellectual insight to the Forty-Fifth Infantry Division's role in World War II. It is just a daughter documenting what she discovered during her years of research. I can only hope that all who read about my father's life experience will be as in awe as I am.

Semper Anticus is transalated as "Always Forward," and was the motto of the Forty-Fifth Infantry Division. Today, it becomes my motto also. I want to ensure my father's story always goes forward—to his descendents.

Acknowledgments

THANKS GO FIRST TO MY SAVIOR, Jesus Christ. He has blessed me abundantly throughout my life, especially with family and friends, who have shared in my dream to bring this manuscript to completion.

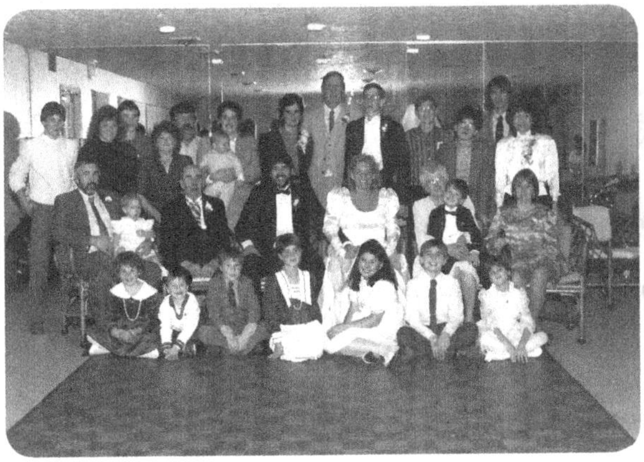

Kirchgassner Family 1987

Sharon Decker, Kathy A. Klump. (1st Row) 2nd Row: Rita Kirchgassner, Kathy Hartman, Sally Wells, Kathy Schmeltzer, Roseann Fuernstein, Bernadette Lewis. (2nd Row) Kathy Klump, Rita Klump, Cindy Hilty, Mary Booker, Skip Henlein, Lisa Nobbe and Kristen Hartman. (3rd Row)

Without their support as I worked through the material, this manuscript would not have come together. Thanks to Floyd Trossman, Essie Adams, the John Schweisthal family, and Phyllis Dealy. Their editorial advice came at a time when I did not know if I could do my part of the project. They offered encouragement when I needed it most, easing my doubts. Thanks also to Zac Wyse for the prayer support and Brooke Livingston, a student at Lawrenceburg High School in Indiana, who helped me type the manuscript. She is a natural collaborator, and without her assistance I would not have met my personal deadline.

"Co-workers and students who assisted me during this project."

Left to Right: Steve Johnson, Daniel Backus, Angie Rowlett, Tyler Schwarz, Paul Terle, Shawn Lightner, Adam Oyler, Brooke Livingston, LeAnn Ambs and Bill Snyder.

I am grateful to Anne Seppala Kirchgassner for rechecking the facts from the National Archives in the manuscript. I do not think she knew what her husband, Mark, volunteered her for, but she said yes without hesitation. Robyn Kirchgassner, Rachel Mersmann, and Megan Swales assisted by typing and editing in the homestretch, making this a family affair. Denise Kirchgassner generously shared her artistic talent with the family and did the cartography. Lastly, John Grathwohl for investing in my latest adventure. (Remember Alaska?)

In reading the history of the Forty-Fifth Infantry Division, you will see many locations identified only with numbers. Lt. Col. Hugh F. Foster III, US Army (Ret.), noted one problem: during World War II the US military used a map of France from the 1920s. I didn't have time to research for something more specific, so I am leaving that task to the next generation of Kirchgassners. Maybe with future advances in technology, they will be able to find the exact coordinates.

Special thanks to Lieutenant Colonel Foster, Dave Kerr, the Lilly Endowment, and Dr. Lise Pommois. All generously assisted with this project.

Any proceeds from the sale of this book will go to the Anna Jo Kirchgassner Memorial Fund, which supports many local not-for-profit organizations or charities, All Saints Parish, including the Kitchen Mission.

The Kitchen Mission comprises of a group of volunteers who donate soup, breads and desserts for delivery to those in the surrounding communities who are ill, elderly or just to say hello. (My grandmother, Dorie Nordmeyer, fed anyone who came to her home, especially during the time of the Depression. Grandma always reminded me that any stranger could be an angel of God and not to turn anyone away. Her example and that of my mother, Anna Jo Kirchgassner, who also cooked food for others, primarily the parish priests, are the ones who have inspired me to volunteer my time to the Kitchen Mission.)

Volunteers for Kitchen Mission: Left to right-Tom Peters, Whitey Widolff, Bev Graf, Mary Bittner, Denny Gaynor, Floyd Trossman, Gerri Stutz, Skip Henlein, Theresa and Mark Widolff, Cindy Hornbach, Rita Klump, Amy Graf and Connie Heil.

Dan and Judy Kirchgassner's family
Mark and Krista's Wedding
June 2014

The Yorkville Boys

My dad was an Indiana farm boy.
Depression raised, and like his childhood friends,
Left the lean times in Yorkville
To fight in a war for other people's freedom.
From tractors to tanks,
Fishing boats to battleships,
They served on all fronts with honor.
All gave a lot; several gave all.
Home from the war
They married, raised families, and lived in Faith.
They never seemed to replay the war,
but it left a large scar deep into their souls.
As they fade one by one into the sunset,
And the last Taps is played,
It begs the same old question:
Where have all the good men gone?

-Dan Kirchgassner
January 13, 2015

Introduction

[MAYBE I HAVE BEEN driven to research and record family history for the past forty years because I was the only one in my family not named after a relative. My mother would never divulge why I was called Rita Kay, a name not in the family heritage. I guess since I could never point to a family member whose given name I shared, I at least wanted to find out more about my surname. My siblings and I had that much in common.

My brothers and sisters have supported my research over the years, but they will admit that I follow a different trail and probably inherited a rare combination of family genes. Or maybe I am different due to my allergies. My mother told me that as an infant I was raised on goat's milk, the only substance my body would tolerate without side effects. Even today, I'm still looking for ways to account for who I am.

Sometimes my siblings are not eager to discuss the family lineage with me. As the family story unfolds, maybe you will understand the hesitancy. But family history has helped define who I am today, and I want to entrust this inheritance to my descendants. Then I can be sure that this history will not dissipate and may be expanded upon by the next generation.

Kirchgassner family with John Grathwohl and Rita
February 1986
Anne, Dad, Mom, Rita, John, Essie and John. (1st Row)
John, Carmen, Mark, Judy, Dan, Mary and Floyd. (2nd Row)

My desire to research and write this book, *Semper Anticus* ("Always Forward," the motto of the Forty-Fifth Infantry Division), has deep roots. As far back as I can remember, I have loved tales from history. I was always enthralled by stories of Christian martyrs, ancient Greece and Rome, the medieval period, and the patriots of the American Revolution. I could never read enough about the heroes or the heroines, real or mythical, who defied the odds or maybe even the gods to complete a quest for the sole purpose of defending their native lands or upholding family honor.

The stories I most treasure raise questions. For example, I always wonder if I would have been as courageous as Antigone, who felt it was her duty to bury her brother with all rites due him, even though by doing so she faced death. The same with Perpetua and Felicity who bravely faced the lions rather than denounce Christianity. Or would I have been as brave as King Leonidas, the leader of three hundred Spartans who, against overwhelming odds, defended Thermopylae against Persian invaders? Leonidas preferred to be returned home dead on his shield than to live a long life in defeat. And who could not enjoy reading about the hero Ulysses? He spent ten years after the Trojan War trying to return to his beloved wife, Penelope, and to his kingdom, Ithaca. Only love of family and country would give a man the tenacity to survive all of the trials Ulysses endured.

My favorite above all, though, is the story of Nathan Hale, a schoolteacher and a patriot from Connecticut. Heading to the gallows after being found guilty of spying on the British during the Revolutionary War, he said he regretted that he had only one life to give for his country. I get goosebumps when I consider how a man facing certain death could remain fearless in the cause of winning freedom for others.

I put my dad, Robert Kirchgassner, on the same pedestal as the heroes of bygone days. He would be abashed by this, since he never wanted attention. He can rest in peace. My goal is not to irk my dad but to preserve his story for future generations of Kirchgassners. I want his descendants to know the enormous odds he overcame, never once complaining about the cards he was dealt (unless he was in a poker game). Like Nathan Hale, my father was a patriot willing to sacrifice his life so that others could enjoy the right to life, liberty, and the pursuit of happiness. My father was one of many soldiers during World War II who deserve recognition. Maybe some of their children, like me, will preserve their record of service for future generations. After all, how we ever thank them enough for answering when destiny called?

Dad cooking.

When I graduated from college in 1975, my father gave me permission to research the two facets of his life that have intrigued me since I was a child. These were the absence of his biological father from birth and his service in the army during World War II. Dad served in Company C of the 157th Infantry Regiment in the Forty-Fifth Infantry Division from the invasion of Sicily in July 1943 until he was critically wounded in battle in France on October 27, 1944.

Like so many of his generation, my father did not readily share his war experiences. In 1976, I traveled to San Diego, California, with a college friend, Pat Arcady, and met one of Dad's comrades, G. W. Allen, who had undergone basic training with my dad at Camp Wolters in Texas. He was eager for news about my father, since they had not seen each other for more than thirty years. We did not discuss the war.

Researching these two life-changing events was a complicated task. First of all, I was attempting to trace a person who had disappeared in 1917. Social Security numbers did not exist then, and it had been more than fifty years since his last confirmed sighting. This made finding leads difficult. Even after doing many interviews with contemporaries, documenting different theories, and researching for many hours, I have not discovered what happened to my dad's biological father in September 1917. But that has not discouraged me from continuing my research. I ponder different scenarios. Did he deliberately leave Yorkville, Indiana, or was he the victim of foul play or an accident? Perhaps he perished in the flu epidemic of 1918. I hope someday to discover the answer that has eluded my family for four generations. Not all of my relatives share this passion to find my grandfather, and I respect their reasons.

Retrieving Dad's personnel file from the army proved to be just as challenging as looking for a missing person. More than 80 percent of army personnel records from

World War II were destroyed in a fire at the National Personnel Records Center in St. Louis, Missouri, in 1973. For a time, this limited my research to general rather than specific information. However, about seven years ago a series of events changed the direction of my research and gave me access to invaluable information about Dad's service.

These turns of events began when my nephew Mark Kirchgassner joined the faculty at Lawrenceburg High School where I am employed. For years we had collaborated on World War II research as we were in awe of Dad's service. In fact, our desire to learn more about his wartime experiences led both of us to study the social sciences in college. Working closer together, we now had time to expand our research on the Forty-Fifth Infantry Division.

The next step forward came when Jared Leiker arrived from Kansas to take a position at Lawrenceburg High School. Jared shared our enthusiasm for gathering information about the Forty-Fifth Infantry Division's role in World War II. With Jared's technology skills, we located fellow researchers Dave Kerr and Hugh F. Foster III. The resources and information that Dave and Hugh shared enabled us to piece together where Dad had served. Dave spent hundreds of hours researching at the National Archives and provided copies of all after-action reports for the 157th Infantry Regiment along with United States Army Signal Corps photos from the time the 157th was engaged in battle. Without the information that Dave and Hugh obtained, a life-changing event would never have come to pass.

Mark, Rita and Jared at the Berlin Wall.

In October of 2012, Mark and I submitted an application through the Teacher Creativity Fellowship Program sponsored by the Lilly Endowment to visit some of the places in Europe where the 157th Infantry Regiment had fought. We proposed to document what had occurred at a certain site, such as Anzio, Italy, in 1944, and what it was like there almost seventy years later in 2013. We were awarded the grant in February 2013. After many hours of planning an itinerary (aided immeasurably by Jared's technology skills), Mark and I, Jared, and Mark's fiancée, Krista Wuestefeld, departed on June 1, 2013. The trip took us to nine sites where the 157th Regiment had fought and in some instances had liberated people from the Nazi regime. Our blogs documenting the journey are included with the reports from Company C of the 157th Infantry.

What follows is the story of my father and other men who served their country in the 157th Regiment, Company C.—Rita Kirchgassner]

"For human beings this is impossible,
but for God all things are possible."
(Matthew 19:26)
New American Bible

Prologue

[In April of 1917, the United States entered World War I to support its allies in Europe. Yorkville, Indiana, a small village nearly smack dab in the center of America, consisted of about twenty-two homes; a few businesses and a new church under construction were in the main area, with farms surrounding. Thirty-two men from Yorkville volunteered and departed for Europe to serve their country: Joseph Ege, Theodore Fuchs, Joseph Fuchs, Joseph Kuebel, William Kuebel, Roman Kuebel, Frank Krieger, Otto Miller, Michael Steinmetz, Edward Widolff, Frank Widolff, George Kuebel, Edwin Dumont, John Fuchs, Tony Fuchs, George R. Miller, Michael Zerr, Edward Gardner, Julius Zerr, Anthony Hornbach, Julius Miller, George N. Miller, Frank Roell, Theodore Schantz, Lawrence Joerger, Otto Neurohr, Raymond Hornbach, Joseph Trossman, Joseph Joerger, Otto Steinmetz, Michael Miller, and Clemens Steinmetz. All of these men were members of St. Martin Catholic Parish, in Yorkville.

Construction of the new church began in 1914 and finished in 1917 while the men were away serving their country. (Parishioners had paid the total cost of fifty-five thousand dollars by 1922.) Fr. Sonderman was the parish priest and St. Martin School was in operation.

[In the early and late teens of 1900, Yorkville had a saloon owned by Charles Zerr. A blacksmith shop owned by John Miller with Nicholas Zimmer owning a farm equipment store. There were three grocery stores, two of which were owned by Charles Hornbach and George Widolff. A post office was in Widolff's store and Joseph Mason was the mailman. Dr. John C. Elliot took care of the ill. Around 1924, the first cars came to Yorkville.—Floyd Hornbach]

In 1917, nineteen-year-old Dorothea Henrietta Nordmeyer, who lived a short walk from the church, was with child. She probably sat on her front porch and watched the church being built in the spring. Horse-driven huckster wagons loaded with bricks for the new church made the journey from the train station in Guilford, Indiana, one hill and about five curvy miles from Yorkville. The delicate stained-glass windows from Austria that adorn the church to this day were delivered in the same way over the same country road. The Kirchgassner, Hoffmeier, and Nordmeyer families (my ancestors) together donated $340 toward the construction. They also hauled a total of 163 loads of material to the church site.

This was an era when the Catholic Church and the local priest had great influence in the lives of parishioners. Vatican II with all of its sweeping changes would not have seemed even a remote possibility at the beginning of the twentieth century. The church and the society would not have been a comfort to Dorothea and her family. The sin of being pregnant without a husband would have weighed heavily on Dorothea's conscience and might have been viewed as a punishment by some.

Though she attended Mass daily and tried to follow the rules laid out by the Catholic Church, my grandmother believed in the superstitions from the old country. I still remember the stories she told of hexes, of a deceased priest sighted at night offering unsaid Masses, and of a mysterious light in the sky over Yorkville. Though my siblings and I would be scared, Grandma Dorie would always reassure us that ghosts had never been known to hurt anyone. It helped that Dad would add the disclaimer that ghosts were usually sighted when spirits were involved. Also, Grandma Dorie was fearful that robbers would come to the farm. She always kept her doors locked. Dad alleviated my child like fears once again, by saying, "If robbers come, I will help them to look for money because we can use some."

I'm sure many whispered about Dorothea's appearance as the baby inside her grew. It would have been difficult for Dorothea not to notice the looks or to hear the murmurs as she attended Mass or walked about in the village. Even worse, perhaps she was shunned.

Given her predilection for supernatural tales, the weather from around May 27 through June 1, 1917, must have seemed eerie to my grandma. Low pressure spawned a record number of tornadoes. Seventy-three in total—fifteen in the F4 or F5 category—wreaked havoc throughout the Midwest and the Southeast. One tornado traveled 290 miles from Illinois into Indiana. The northern section of the small town of Mattoon, Illinois, was completely destroyed by a tornado on June 1. My dad's father traveled to that farming community every year to help harvest crops. Mattoon lost fifty-three people and 496 homes.

(In 1976, Mary Lieland Trabel and Cathy Lough traveled with me to Mattoon, Illinois, to do research on my missing grandfather. In the early '80s, Maggie Seitz Gloss, Mary Lieland Trabel, and Sharon Fox Hoerst accompanied me to Washington, D.C., to do family research. Neither journey was successful.)

Mary Lieland Trabel

Cathy Lough, Christina Harris and Ryan Berner

The father of the child was to marry Dorothea in September of 1917, but he did not come to St. Martin's rectory at the arranged time for the vows to be exchanged. Father Sonderman, the parish priest, contacted his parents, but they did not know where he was or when he had left the family farm. The priest and the family attempted to locate the father for many years without success. There were rumors that he had enlisted in the army to fight in World War I, perished during the flu epidemic of 1918 or that he had a family elsewhere. Only speculation, no official documentation has ever been located to confirm what happened to him.

With no husband, in early November of 1917, Dorothea traveled by train to Cincinnati, Ohio, to stay with relatives, possibly her brother, until the birth of her child. More than likely she bundled herself as best as she could so her advanced pregnancy would not be as noticeable. The bare ring finger on her left hand would have been harder to conceal. A single pregnant woman was not always a welcome member of polite society.

At 10 p.m. on November 19, at the City Hospital on West Ninth Street in Cincinnati, Paul H. Rowe, M.D., delivered a male child. The mother was listed as "Dorothy Nordmeyer, unmarried," and her occupation as "doing housework." No one celebrated the birth of a healthy male child that night. A lonely single mother with an infant would have looked out of the hospital window and seen only a few lights from candles or electric lamps flickering across the dark city. Grandma Dorie probably pondered how she was going to manage bringing a child back to her hometown. If the neighbors did not know she was pregnant when she left, the cries of a small babe would alert anyone passing by that a new member of the family had recently arrived.

The Nordmeyers lived in the center of Yorkville next to Widolff's General Store, one of two general stores in town. The other was operated by the Hornbach family. These stores were the town's social centers. The new baby in Yorkville would not have been neglected in some of the conversations when residents visited these establishments for staples and news.

What courage my grandmother showed when she decided to raise her child as a single, unemployed mother and return to the village of her birth. She could have put him up for adoption, gone to work, or started over in Cincinnati, creating a new life for herself. Little did she know that when she chose her son, she also chose me, my brothers and my sisters. Her Catholic faith and her love of family and of Yorkville, Indiana must have helped her make such a brave decision in her darkest moments.

Before leaving Cincinnati for Yorkville, Dorie (her preferred name) brought her child, Robert Lee Nordmeyer, to St. Francis Seraph Church on December 2, 1917, to have him baptized. The Reverend Francis Schaefer baptized Robert, with George and Catherine Nordmeyer, brother and sister-law-serving as sponsors.

Shortly after the baptism, Dorie and Robert returned to Yorkville to live with Dorie's parents. The journey home would have been snowy and bitterly cold. On December 8, 1917, a blizzard struck the Cincinnati area, dropping eleven inches of snow in one day. The cold weather and snow persisted, and by January 1, 1918, the Ohio River was frozen from shore to shore.

Herman and Mary (Folzenlogel) Nordmeyer were Dorie's parents, and she had ten siblings. Her father eventually built two homes in Yorkville, supporting his family by crafting and selling shoes and baseballs in addition to running a molasses mill. Herman was also responsible for bringing a post office to Yorkville. Dad had many fond memories of his grandparents, especially the protectiveness of his grandmother. Once when his biological father's family paid a visit, his grandmother scooped him up and took him into the house. He never knew what was said outside that day.

Dorie married Michael Joseph Kirchgassner on November 30, 1920, in a small ceremony at St. Martin's rectory, shortly after Robert had turned three. Andrew Kirchgassner, Michael's father, had arrived in the United States on February 20, 1885, at age twenty-three. He had sailed from his birthplace of Baden, Germany, on a ship called the ***Waesland***, disembarked in New York, and made connections in Tippecanoe, Indiana. He met and married Barbara Brichler and moved to Yorkville to be with her family. Nicholas Brichler, Barbara's father, had arrived in New Orleans from Le Havre, France, on May 12, 1843, on the ship the ***Forrester***.

Not long after Dorie's marriage to Michael, the family of the biological father sold its farm in Yorkville and moved to Lawrenceburg, Indiana.

Grandma Dorie on her wedding day

On October 18, 1929, Dorie and Mike bought a farm on Leatherwood Road, not far from family, and it became Robert's childhood home. Dad grew up farming like his grandfather Andrew and registered as a Kirchgassner when he entered first grade at St. Martin's School. While society at the time did not smile on chidren who were born illegitimate, Robert thrived with the Kirchgassner family. Michael's two brothers, Aloysius and Isadore, and his sister Mary treated Robert as their own. The brothers moved back to Tippecanoe from Yorkville to farm and to raise families. They spelled the family surname "Kirchgessner." Every summer the brothers and their families would come to Yorkville for a visit.

Grandpa Mike and Dad

Growing up with Dad were his cousins Esther Detzel Klein and Leona Feist Miller, nieces of Dorie who were with him at many family gatherings and became his lifelong friends. Being an only child on a farm limited his time for play, socialization with other kids, and relaxation. Dad never did have siblings. Grandma Dorie had one miscarriage and never became pregnant again.

Dad and Esther Detzel Klein

Dad and Leona Feist Miller

After completing the eighth grade at St. Martin's School, Dad attended Guilford High School in Guilford, Indiana. Dad played center on the basketball team and earned a varsity letter. His senior year, 1935–36, the team lost by three points to Vevay High School in the final sectional game. The high school annual said that "while the team won only 8 of the 18 games played, they were one of the most dangerous aggregations that has ever represented the school." The annual also stated that Robert "has been the center for the basketball team for the past year and [is] a bashful fellow with a great deal of general knowledge." (Today, the Kirchgassners pride themselves on their knowledge of history and geography.)

John Taylor on the far right. (1st Row)
Maurice Miller, Dad third from left, Norbert Wiedeman. (2nd Row)

After his graduation from high school in 1936, Dad went to work on the family farm for his father for twenty dollars a week. On his US Army separation record in July of 1945, Dad described his work experience:

> "Farmhand–General:
> Plowed, planted, cultivated and harvested corn, wheat, rye, oats and hay on 100-acre farm. Drove a tractor and two-horse team. Used riding plows, cultivators; also used a check-row corn planter, and binder. Milked 6 cows and fed cows, hogs and horses. Raised vegetables for own use."

On March 18, 1941, Dad enlisted in the army at Fort Thomas, Kentucky, and was given serial number 35101920. Dad had been appointed leader of a contingent of men from Local Board Number 1 of Dearborn County, Indiana. He was charged with enforcement of Selective Service regulations governing these men enroute to induction stations during the journey from Lawrenceburg, Indiana, to Louisville, Kentucky, that day. All men in the contingent were directed to obey his orders. He completed basic training at Camp Wolters in Mineral Springs, Texas, and advanced training at Pine Camp in New York.—Rita Kirchgassner]

Dad at Camp Wolters

Dad at Pine Camp

[Dad was assigned to the 157th Infantry Regiment of the Forty-Fifth Infantry Division. The motto of the 157th was "Eager for Duty."

The Forty-Fifth Infantry Division (Motto-Semper Anticus) included: The 157th, 179th, and 180th Infantry Regiments, the 158th, 160th, 171st, and 189th Field Artillery Battalions, the Forty-Fifth Signal Company, the 700th Ordnance Company, the Forty-Fifth Quartermaster Company, the Forty-Fifth Reconnaissance Troop, the 120th Engineer Combat Battalion, and the 120th Medical Battalion.]

[Hugh F. Foster III provides the following description of a regiment during WWII such as the 157th Infantry:

*Regimental Headquarters Company-regimental and company headquarters sections.
*Regimental Cannon Company-a company headquarters section with six 105mm howitzers.
*Regimental Antitank Company-a headquarters section, two platoons with 157mm antitank guns, and one mine platoon.
*Regimental Medical Detachment-regimental aid station, battalion aid station sections, litter bearers, and platoon medics—to be attached to the battalions and rifle platoons.

First Battalion Headquarters Company:
*Battalion and company headquarters sections, ammunition and pioneer platoon, communications platoon, intelligence and reconnaissance platoon.
*A (Able), B (Baker), C (Charlie) Companies- the rifle companies. Each rifle company consisted of a headquarters section, three rifle platoons, and a weapons platoon, which had two light machine-guns and three 60mm mortars.

[*Dad was in Company C, Charlie Company, Fourth Platoon. He was mortar section chief. His separation record noted that he was responsible for eighteen men and three mortars in a combat unit in African, Italian, and French campaigns. He saw that his men were cared for in the best possible manner. He directed camouf lage and concealment and also the fire of the three mortars.*—Rita Kirchgassner]

*D (Dog) company: heavy weapons. This company consisted of a headquarters section, two platoons of heavy machine-guns (water-cooled), and one platoon of six 81mm mortars.

Second Battalion Headquarters Company:
E (Easy), F (Fox), G (George) Companies- rifle. H (How) Company-heavy weapons

Third Battalion Headquarters Company:
I (Item), K (King), L (Love) companies-rifle. (J was not used due to its possible confusion with the letter *I* when handwritten.)
M (Mike) company-heavy weapons.]

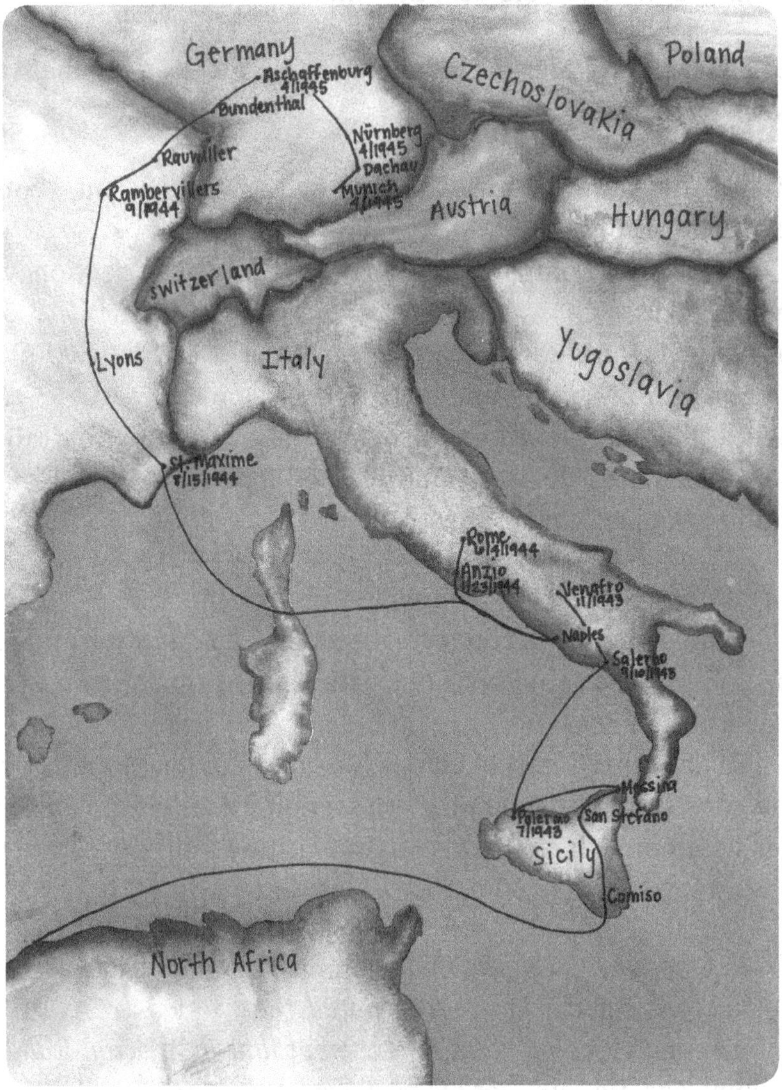

Route of the 157th Infantry
By Denise Kirchgassner

[The men who served in the Fourth Platoon, Company C, 157th Infantry Regiment of the Forty-Fifth Division after October 1, 1943 (when John Schweisthal joined), and before December 2, 1943 (when Roscoe Prince was killed in action), were the reason for our travels and for this book.]

Company C, 4th Platoon

[When this photo was taken, Company C included (?) Anderson, James W. Barkley*, Leo J. Blanchette*, Hanzel Blair, Joseph C. Brossett*, John A. Chorba*, Anthony Czerpak*, Anthony Dumont*, Raymond M. Emig*, Angelo Ficuciello*, Phillip Gellar, Virgil Green., George Hicks, Tillman Holder*, Teton Hurtado* Roman Jozefowicz*, S/Sgt. Max L. Johnson*, George Kiewiet*, Sgt. Robert Kirchgassner*, Peter A., Howard Lynch, William J. Mutchler*, Ray Neitz*, Roscoe Prince*, Edward A. Schemansky, John J. Schweisthal, Harold N. Scott, Leland J. Scott, Horace Simon*, Quienton Steele, Lt. Richard Stone*, Byron Timmons*, Alfred Vigliante*, and Jerry M. Wolfe*.

*Deployed with the 157th Infantry in June 1943.

Robert Kirchgassner is in the center; Alfred Vigilante is next to him on the left; Roscoe Prince and John Schweisthal are second and third from Robert on the right. Richard Adams, Richard Badgett, Thomas Briggs, and Robert Rodenbaugh, who joined Company C at a later date, are mentioned in the epilogue.--Rita Kirchgassner]

[The Thunderbird, the symbol of the Forty-Fifth Infantry Division, is the major deity for many Native Americans, especially in the Southwest. The thunderbird is the harbinger of rain, thunder, and lightning. Lightning strikes when the thunderbird flashes its eyes, and thunder rolls when it flaps its wings. This proved to be the case during the Italian campaign. Some of the worst storms in modern history hit the Italian peninsula in 1943 and 1944. Since most of the fighting was in the mountains, the rain wreaked havoc on the troops. Dad said army mules and vehicles got stuck all the time, and the weather slowed the advance toward Rome.—John Kirchgassner]

My brother John Kirchgassner with his son Rob,
the namesake for Dad.

Chapter 1

Seventy Years Later

The die is cast.
—Caesar

Jared, Krista, Rita and Mark-June 1, 2013

[IT IS JUNE 1, 2013, IN the late afternoon, and an overcast sky greets us as we gather in a hangar in Charlotte, North Carolina. Jared, Mark, Krista, and I are waiting to board a plane that will take us across the Atlantic Ocean to begin our journey. We will travel twelve thousand miles to see where S/Sgt. Robert L. Kirchgassner served during World War II. That is the objective. We have been planning this journey since February 20 when my coworker Laura Hartman notified me that we had been awarded a Teacher Creativity grant by the Lilly Endowment.

At the hangar, I barely reach my assigned seat in time after failing to hear the boarding announcement. I guess the excitement of the trip entranced me. I had to run (yes Zak Kirchgassner I can run)—well, maybe it was a fast walk—to the gate, finding my seat and buckling my safety belt just minutes before the door was shut. I listen to safety instructions by our f light attendant. As our jet accelerates and becomes airborne, I look out the window and take in my final vision of America as my father did almost seventy years ago to the day. My trip is obviously benign compared with his, but departing the land of my birth always produces a ref lective moment for me. I try to process many things past, present, and future. I think of my last look at Yorkville, Indiana, in the morning when I dropped off my car at Daniel and Robyn Kirchgassner's farm at the end of Leatherwood Road. Now I am on a nonstop f light to Rome, Italy, and cannot fathom what adventure awaits me there.

At the Kirchgassner farm with Elizabeth, Samuel, (1st Row)
Rita, Joseph, Krista and Mark. (2nd Row.)

This is not my first trip across the pond, (as my father would say), but it is my first tour of places where my father served during World War II. My father is all I can think about as the plane reaches cruising altitude. He has been gone for almost twenty years, but the wisdom that he shared still affects me deeply. Memories of Dad rush into my consciousness as I recline in my seat, shut my eyes, and listen to the rhythm of the engines. I attempt to sleep before we touch down in Rome, since my internal clock will be six hours behind on Indiana time. When the plane lands and my feet hit the tarmac, I want to adjust quickly to my new surroundings and have plenty of stamina. After all, I am at least two decades older than my companions and prior to departure had nightmares about being left behind. Mark is not known for his patience or for his endearing words.

Sleep, however, continues to elude me as memories fill my mind. I recall one Christmas Eve when I was around eight and Dad gave me my first rod and reel. I was so enthusiastic about the gift that I begged him that night to teach me how to cast. Our small house on Burtzelbach Road was not the right place for a young girl to wrangle with a rod and reel. I had always fished with a cane pole. Now I had a real fishing pole. To hone my skill, I spent the rest of the winter casting it in the bedroom that I shared with my sisters Essie and Mary. It is a wonder I did not break the pole or hook one of them. Spring could not come soon enough. I was eager to show the other kids my new rod and reel while fishing at Miller's Pond.

Kirchgassner Family circa 1960
Rita and Mark (1st Row)
Mary, Dan and John (2nd Row)
Mom and Essie (3rd Row)

My mind drifts to other memories. Jared tries to help pass the time by asking questions, since he knows I am restless and cannot wait to start the journey. I am down to one plane ride and one train ride to Anzio, Italy. My hyperawareness of the moment almost puts me in shock, and I am nearly speechless, which, if you know me, would be hard to believe. Here I am on the brink of living what I could only dream. How can I ever give enough praise to our Lord for allowing me this season in my life?

Jared pours over the itinerary with me, checking to make sure that we have not forgotten any details. He knows how much this trip means to Mark and me, and he does not want us to be disappointed. Jared put the itinerary together. How many travelers have their journey charted on an interactive Smart Board?

As I try to fall asleep again, I calm myself with the thought that regardless of what happens on this journey, I will be able to stand on the beaches in Italy and France where my father came ashore to dig in and prepare for battle to free Europe from the Axis powers. Treading on the sand, breathing in the sea air, and looking upon the expanse of water stretching out from those beaches will surely touch the innermost corners of my soul. My goal of an eternal connection with my father will be met, and future generations will know his story. That is my greatest desire.

When I stride upon those shores, I wonder what emotions I will encounter, knowing that my father and so many others set foot there to strike back at oppressors occupying countries by force and spreading their ideology of hate. I take with me the pride in knowing that my father did not hesitate and was willing to sacrifice his life to free people he had never met. My journey is intended to honor him, his service and to give thanks to John Schweisthal for his self-less act of courage for love of a wounded comrade.

The plane lands in Rome on schedule and without fanfare, and I emerge from my dreamlike sleep and disembark. We collect our baggage and secure transportation to our hostel, the Hotel Texas. It is worth every one of the seventy euros it cost. We realize our adventure has begun as we see ancient aqueducts along the way. We are not jet lagged, but ready to check out the eternal city of Rome. After unpacking, we gather in the hostel's communal area, pick up city maps, and receive advice from our host on where to find the best cuisine Rome has to offer. We do not let on that Mark is looking for a McDonald's— his primary choice anywhere, anytime. Talk to his six siblings—Barbara, Daniel, Michael, Rachel, Zak, and Megan. Their motto is that if you are considering eating at a new place, don't! When in doubt, eat at McDonald's. It is a Kirchgassner thing. Turns out that Mark will not starve while in Rome. There is a McDonald's a short walk up the street.

Mark, Zak, Rachel. (Row 1)
Daniel, Michael, Barbara holding Megan. (Row 2)

Another Kirchgassner trait is being a history enthusiast—no slackers permitted. Dad's yearbook noted this trait in him. Mark, who is the king (King#46-is his nickname. He was co-captain of the East Central High School State Championship Football Team in 1994. His jersey number was "46." He is king of the family when it comes to history, is set on seeing the Colosseum first for multiple reasons. The ten-minute walk from the Hotel Texas to the Colosseum seems like a lark, and we are confident that we will be able to navigate the streets of Rome with ease. We depart from the fourth floor—the hostel is on the top level above offices—and descend several flights of marble steps. These steps lead to an inner courtyard on the first floor that opens onto the streets.

After taking my first step on the marble stairs, for some reason I am catapulted into the air and do not make contact with the second or third steps. I land on my tailbone several steps down, almost reaching the first landing. Krista does not think I fell that far down the stairs, but I remember having to crawl up several steps to get back to the top. Of course, Mark reminds me that he was at the top of the staircase, holding out a helping hand as I returned, crawling to the top.

After the fall, I recall my friend Rita Klump's pre-departure warning not to wear the new flip-flops that an Internet advertisement said were made for walking. "You cannot believe all that you read on the Internet," she said. I guess I should have taken her advice; when I return home, X-rays show a hairline fracture in my back. My companions help me up between fits of laughter and Krista's offers of assistance. We return to the common area and assess my situation. Our host wants me to seek medical attention, but I choose not to; there is no time in the itinerary for a hospital visit. We have been in Rome for less than three hours!

Kathy and Rita

Our itinerary was arranged before we departed Indiana, and any deviation from it would affect what we plan to do and see. I am down to one train ride to Anzio, and I am determined to follow the schedule. We wait to see if the pain in my back subsides after I take a couple of Aleve. Then we attempt to leave again. This time, however, we take the elevator down. If I fall again, Mark won't recover from the laughter.

When we reach the courtyard, I push the electronic button to open the heavy wooden windowless door. Sunlight brief ly blinds us, and our journey back to the European theater of World War II begins.--Rita Kirchgassner]

[Jared's blog: June 1, 2013
Dayton/Charlotte

Now: Made it to the airport on time. So excited to go! We f ly out of Dayton at 12:23 p.m. to Charlotte, North Carolina. The Kirchgassner family dynamic has already started. Made from Dayton, Ohio to Charlotte, North Carolina, for our layover safe and sound. Rita and I have been rereading all about the Forty-Fifth Infantry and the 157th Regiment on our f light. We have started to work on our "then" posting for tomorrow. We are going to provide background information on training and battles that occurred before Anzio. Anzio is the first place we will catch up with the Forty-Fifth Infantry.

Today we begin our journey to follow those who kept us free. Thanks to Sarah Leiker for getting us to the airport.—Jared Leiker]

Jared and Sarah Leiker

[Then (beginning in June of 1943): After training for more than two years, Robert was one of the many thousands of enlisted men in the convoys of 1943 that totaled more than two thousand ships sailing for Europe. The war had been raging for almost four years in Europe, commencing with the invasion of Poland in September of 1939. Britain and France responded by declaring war on Germany after the invasion.

The following are a few of the events that led to the invasion of Europe.

- May of 1940–Winston Churchill becomes prime minister of Britain.
- June 1940–France signs an armistice with Germany after the Germans enter Paris on June 14, 1940. Charles de Gaulle becomes the free French leader. Also, during that month, Italy declares war on France and Britain.
- July 1940–The Battle of Britain begins, and the Germans bomb many cities.
- September 1940–Germany, Italy, and Japan sign the Axis Pact.
- November 1940–Franklin D. Roosevelt is reelected president of the United States.
- June 1941–Germany attacks the Soviet Union.
- December 1941–Japan attacks the United States at Pearl Harbor, Hawaii. The United States and Britain declare war on Japan. Hitler then declares war on the United States.
- January 1942–The Allies hold a conference at Casablanca and plan the invasion of Europe. Churchill believes that an invasion of Sicily will draw attention from troops training to cross the English Channel to invade France. This decision puts the Normandy invasion on hold for about one year. Germany and Italy would send troops to thwart the invasion of Sicily, thus taking the focus off of the Allied troops training in England.

[When the United States entered World War II, after the attack on Pearl Harbor by Japan, the Germans and Italians declared war on the United States. The Roosevelt Administration decided to make the war in Europe the priority. The reason for this was that the Germans were superior in arms to Japan. The plan was to fight in both the European and Pacific Theaters but to send the majority of the American Forces to Europe. After the defeat of Germany and her allies, then the US would concentrate solely on Japan.

The first action of the United States in World War II against the Axis Powers occurred in North Africa. The Germans were trying to take control of North Africa and the Middle East from the British to control the oil fields. The Germans were defeated in North Africa in November of 1942.

The Forty-Fifth Infantry Division was sent to Europe and landed at Oran in North Africa on June 22, 1943. The Prime Minister of England convinced the US to send troops sooner than later. The United States wanted to stockpile material and build up forces, but Winston Churchill and the British Allies wanted the US to invade Sicily and Italy. This would give the Allies time to get ready for a massive assault in Northern France that was in the planning stages and would not commence until June of 1944.

The invasion of Sicily, Operation Husky, commenced on July 10, 1943.—John Kirchgassner]

Dad, Leona Feist Miller and Maurice Miller

To assist in reading:
Dad was in the First Battalion, Company C

All United States Army Signal Corps pictures from World War II that are used in this manuscript were provided by Dave Kerr. Other World War II pictures are used with permission from the 45th Infantry Division-World War II Reenactors and Venturing Crew. www.45thdivsion.org

On June 8, 1943, a US convoy left from Hampton Roads, Virginia, and set sail across the Atlantic Ocean. Dad would write later in life that the troops didn't learn of their destination until they were at sea. He took one look back at the land of his birth, knowing that some of the men would not return. --Rita Kirchgassner]

From the narrative of the 157th Infantry in the National Archives:

[Describing the journey of the 157th Infantry departing America and sailing across the sea.]

It was on June 5th that the troops of the 157th Infantry Regiment of the 45th Infantry Division, under the command of Colonel Charles M. Ankcorn, boarded the ships that were going to take them on the greatest adventure of their lives.

The week preceding had been spent at Camp Patrick Henry, Virginia, their Port of Embarkation, and the men were not unhappy to leave. Since their arrival May 25th–26th from Camp Pickett, Virginia, where for five months they had undergone rigorous training for combat duty overseas, the troops had engaged in zeroing rifles, witnessing training films and making speed marches. They had been limited to special areas within the camp, had lived in overcrowded quarters and had been bored generally.

So it was with something of renewed interest in life that the men boarded the transport ships that were to carry them to foreign shores. Close of embarkation day found the regimental ships anchored in Hampton Roads Harbor.

For four days they remained there while perspiring troops underwent debarkation exercises, listened to lectures and stood rifle inspections. To the relief of all, the ships set sail at 0800 hours, June 8. First battalion and the Regimental Staff rode the U.S.S. Charles Carroll; 2nd battalion the U.S.S. Thomas Jefferson and 3rd battalion the U.S.S. William Biddle while the U.S.S. Susan B. Anthony and U.S.S. Procyon bore "Q" battalion and the remainder of the regiment.

The trip across the Atlantic Ocean was uneventful aside from the fact that enemy submarines threatened the convoy continually. Troops basked in the sunshine, played cards, read books, wrote occasional letters, sharpened bayonets and underwent a regular training schedule consisting of calisthenics, care of equipment and debarkation and abandon ship drill. Occasionally a destroyer created some excitement by dropping depth charges, but even that became routine to the troops after a time. Chief question in their mind was, "Where are we going?" and Army officials yielded no information.

On June 21st the convoy came within sight of the Rock of Gibraltar. By that time, the men determined that they were headed for North Africa, and on June 22 at 10:30 hours, the ships arrived in Oran.

Three days spent in the harbor at Oran were devoted to much the same routine that had been followed throughout the journey across the Atlantic and into the Mediterranean Sea. Though desiring to test their land legs once more, the men were not allowed to leave the ships, despite the allure of the shores of Africa not more than three hundred yards away. Enviously, the troops watched sailors on shore leave climb into landing craft that would take them across the short stretch of water between ship and shore.

June 25th the regiment and the division participated in a ship-to-shore exercise which was to prepare the men for events to come. Troops debarked from ships in pitch dark and in the early hours of the morning, landed on the shores of Africa near St. Cloud, Algeria. They were opposed in the landing by the men of the 36th Division, who had fought in the North African campaign and were detailed to train incoming combat organizations.

The regiment spent the next five days undergoing rigorous training, the purpose of which was to harden leg, arm and shoulder muscles grown soft in the long trip across the Atlantic. The men practiced street fighting with live ammunition, ran combat courses under fire, took long hikes and ran the usual obstacle courses. Here they began the mode of life which was to become unpleasantly familiar in the months to follow: sleeping on the hard, cold ground, eating "K" and "C" rations and standing guard for lonely hours in a land still harboring dangerous enemies. Thoroughly fatigued, they returned to their respective ships on July 1st.

Until July 5th, the ships remained anchored in Oran Harbor while the troops wondered what was happening at the many conferences among regimental, battalion and company officers. On that date at 1630 hours, the ships made their pre-invasion sortie from the harbor of Oran and the same day the men were issued the "Soldiers Guidebook to Sicily," an issuance that left no doubt that the 157th was to take part in the invasion of that island.

Chapter 2

Sicily: The Sword of Damocles

[The largest island on the Mediterranean Sea is Sicily. Unfortunately, because of time and transportation constraints, our itinerary did not include a visit to this island. The Allies' invasion of Europe began with the landing on Sicily. Operation Husky commenced on July 10, 1943, and the 157th Infantry landed at Gela, Sicily.

For the interesting account of how mob members Meyer Lansky and Charles "Lucky" Luciano assisted the Allies' invasion of Sicily, check out *The Day the Thunderbird Cried* by David L. Israel.—Rita Kirchgassner]

Sicily

[GOAL: TO CONQUER SICILY AND TO commence the invasion of Italy from the south. We wanted to show that we were engaging the enemy. Italy was considered the "soft under belly" of Europe by Prime Minister Winston Churchill. America wanted to help Russia as an ally and also to assist with the impending invasion of France off the coast of Normandy which took place in June of 1944.—John Kirchgassner]

From the 157th Regiment Journal, Morning Reports, and After-Action Reports of Company C, 1943 (National Archives)

Sicily

[The invasion began at 4 a.m. in southern Sicily at Gela Beach with army air force and navy destroyers shelling the beaches. The 157th's first objective was to reach San Croce, which it did with little resistance. The next town of Ragusa was taken, and the men continued to march to the north. When we reached Termini Immense, we cut the island in two. We were now getting into the mountain country. The enemy was blowing up bridges and slowing our advance. –Robert Kirchgassner]

Axis Planes drop bombs Signal Corps Photo-Lt. Longini

View of Gela and Scoglitti Signal Corps Photo

July 1-Company C–Pvt. Leo J. Blanchette and Pvt. James W. Barkley are promoted to private first class.

July 9–At sea. At approximately 2300 hours, the regimental ships along with the other ships of the American Seventh Army and the British Eighth Army, comprising the largest amphibious force ever to invade a hostile shore, dropped anchor on the southern and eastern coasts of Sicily, the stepping-stone to Continental Europe.

Enlisted men accounted for from Company C: 190.

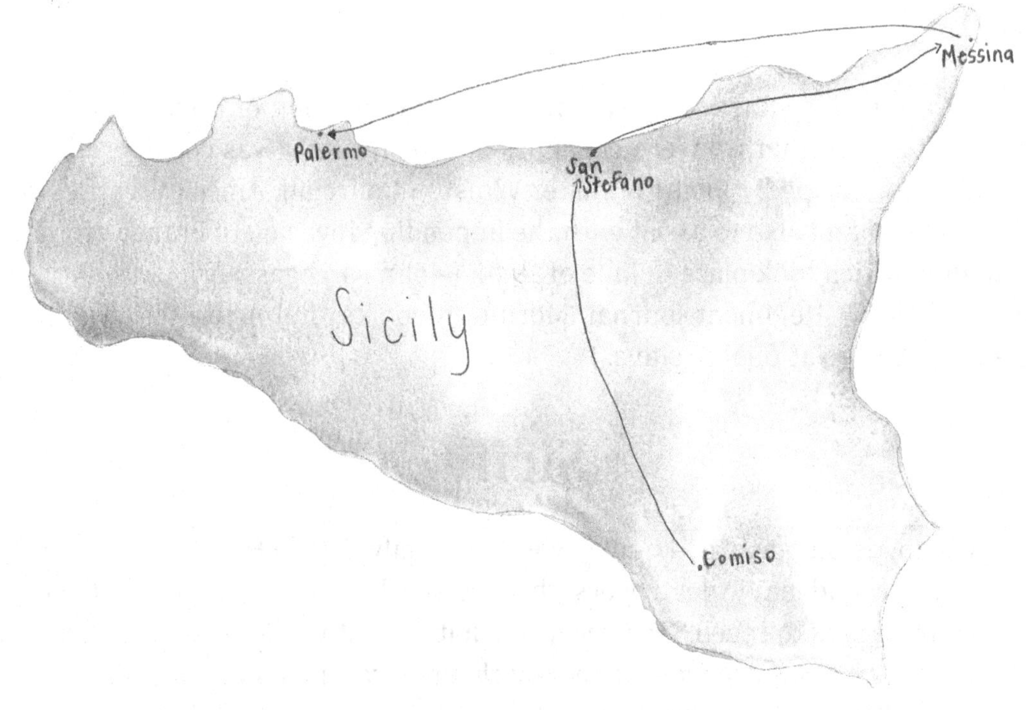

Map of Sicily
Denise Kirchgassner

July 10–Debarkation for the assault got under way at midnight in an unusually rough and unfriendly sea, coupled with enemy aerial bombardment. The disembarking proceeded behind schedule, and the original "H" hour of 0245 was set ahead to 0345. At that time, supported by heavy naval and aerial bombardment, the initial waves of the First and Second Battalions assaulted the beach three miles south of San Croce Camerina. The Third Battalion followed as reserve.

The sector of the beach upon which the regiment landed apparently had been considered naturally impregnable by German and Italian military authorities. It was composed of jagged rocks, and only in certain areas had it been supplemented by barbed wire and gun emplacements. A small garrison of Italians guarded the area.

The enemy garrison offered little resistance when the regiment landed, but the heavy surf and the rocky beach took a toll of more than 50 percent of the landing craft, with a loss of twenty-seven lives throughout the regiment. Company F and Company E were hit particularly hard when two of the invasion boats collided and were swept headlong and out of control into a craggy cove, where the rough sea smashed them against projecting rocks. One of the crafts overturned, but a few men from it reached shore safely.

The regiment with the support of the 158th Field Artillery, moved inland rapidly and by 1300 hours, the First Battalions, commanded by Lt. Col. Preston J. C. Murphy, occupied commanding terrain above its first objective, the town of San Croce Camerina. The Italian garrison of the town made an attempt at resistance but was disheartened by an artillery barrage and at 1545 hours the objective fell without the loss of American life. The initial landing day ended with the regiment occupying positions in and around San Croce Camerina. The regiment captured 500 enemy soldiers and much military equipment.

July 10-11–On the night of July 10 and the morning of July 11, the Second and Third Battalions advanced to the north shore toward Comiso and the strategic airport of Comiso, a distance of about twenty miles. Under the command of Lt. Col. James Chester, at 1000 hours the Third Battalion entered the city. Meanwhile the Second Battalion, under the command of Lt. Col. Irving C. Schaefer, seized a high mountain overlooking Comiso and the Comiso airport. The Third Battalion attacked the airport in the early afternoon and encountered German troops and German mechanized forces. Several German tanks and artillery pieces were destroyed at 1700, and the airport fell into Allied hands. Approximately a hundred enemy planes were captured or destroyed on the ground during the operation.

Company C-Leslie Anderson Jr., PFC John W. Dean and Pvt. Jon Nebelecky are WIA.

On July 11, elements of the 45th Cavalry Reconnaissance Troops, attached to the regiment, entered the city of Ragusa. Forward elements of the First Battalion took over the city late that evening. The regiment captured 450 enemy soldiers during the day. Regimental causalities were light.

Company C-PFC William Baldassari, Pvt. Georges A. Baynes, Pvt. Earl Duff are WIA.

July 12–Tired troops were afforded an opportunity to rest this morning but despite the fact there was little activity, the regiment captured enemy soldiers during the day. Canadian troops entered Ragusa during the morning and made contact with First Battalion. During the afternoon, the regiment, less the Third Battalion, which remained at the Comiso Airport, moved east toward Ragusa then north to Chiaramonte, a distance of 15 miles. In the late evening, the Third Battalion started a march toward Licodia, north of Comiso.

Company C-Pvt. Constantine L. O'Neill is WIA. Morale excellent.

July 13–The regiment swung northeast toward Monterosa, First Battalion on right flank, and Third Battalion on left flank, and Second Battalion in the center. First Battalion overcame steady small-arms fire and captured the Italian garrisons at Elmo and Monterosa, then proceeded north toward the main highway between Vizzini and Licodia. Near the highway, the First Battalion met bitter German resistance.

Despite stubborn small arms resistance, Third Battalion entered Licodia at dusk. Twenty American soldiers lost their lives and approximately forty men were wounded during the day's action, several casualties accounted for by German snipers and armored vehicles. Using a flame thrower, German troops completely destroyed one half-track, burning to death five of its occupants.

That evening the British Fifty-First Highland Division passed through the 157th Infantry on the way to Vizzini. During the night the First Battalion and Third Battalion out-posted the high ground to the northeast and northwest of Licodia, respectively. Second Battalion occupied Monterosa and surrounding ground. It was learned that the enemy garrisons of Elmo, Monterosa, and Licodia had netted 1,100 prisoners.

July 14–The entire regiment was assembled at Licodia by dawn. The British attacked Vizzini on the right while First Battalion, after an all-night march through mountainous terrain, launched a drive on the highway west of the city. Heavy German artillery and f lak fire inflicted many casualties on the First Battalion, which made little progress. The British were unsuccessful at Vizzini, and the situation remained static throughout the day and night. The First and Third Battalions continued to hold their positions north of Licodia while the Second Battalion remained in reserve south of the city.

Company C–First Lt. Adrian B. Caldwell, WIA, was awarded the Silver Star for gallantry in action near Vizzini on July 14. Also WIA, Pvt. Frank Mitrowski, Sgt. Richard A. Simmons, PFC William G. Singleton and PFC Charles G. Yanulaitis. First Lt. Ainse Spears becomes company commander. One enlisted man, Pvt. Anthony J. Miranda, was KIA. (Killed in action on July 13, 1943. Corrected on morning report.)

July 15–In the early morning, elements of the First Canadian Division passed through the regiment, bound for Grammichele, which was captured that night. At 0930 the British took Vizzini. Elements of the First Battalion, Company A, commanded by Capt. Leo Markrud, had previously pushed on the outskirts of Vizzini and engaged heavy enemy opposition; 88's and MG's, inflicting several causalities. Captain Markrud received a fractured right arm. Elements of the British Eighth Army continued to pass through the regiment throughout the day. The battalions remained in position and captured eighteen German snipers. At 1900 the troops were alerted for a motor move to a bivouac area near Riesi, distance of 90 miles west of their present location.

July 16–Marked the end of the first phase of the campaign for the regiment. In six days the command had marched more than a hundred miles of enemy-held hills and highways, captured more than three thousand enemy soldiers and had taken all important objectives in its zone of action.

July 17–The regiment moved by motor to a bivouac area near Riesi on the left flank of the American Second Corps, and it was ordered to continue northward to Pietraperzie. The regiment moved forward as the leading element of the Forty-Fifth Division in a column of battalions with the Third Battalion leading and the First and Second Battalions following. The movement was rapid and the troops marched continuously from the morning of July 17 until the evening of July 18. During those two days they hiked thirty-two miles, meeting little opposition, although artillery duels were frequent. The regiment captured 110 enemy soldiers during the period.

Company C–Enlisted men: 188

July 18- Company C–One enlisted man, Pvt. Thomas J. Quinn, died from fever of unknown origin.

July 19–Tired and worn troops were relieved by the 180th Infantry and were bivouacked near San Caterina. First Battalion received heavy shelling, and Third Battalion uncovered an enemy ammunition dump containing 3,680 rounds of 88mm shells.

Company C–A private is in the hands of military authority on rape charges. Awaiting court- martial.

July 20–Near Caterina. Morale of the troops is very good and the weather is hot.

July 21–Left Caterina at 1300 and marched twenty miles to arrive at Vallelunga at 2000 hours.

July 22–An alert to move at 0700. With Second Battalion leading and First and Third Battalions in the rear, the regiment set out under the cover of darkness to establish roadblocks at a railroad junction near Cerda. With the objective but a mile away, Second Battalion walked into an ambush. Enemy machine-gunners concealed in pillboxes strategically located on the surrounding slopes opened fire with tracers and ack ack on the highway down which the troops marched, pinning the men to the ground. Enemy mortar crews fired effectively into positions that had been registered hours before, and in the midst of all the activity, the Germans blew up a large bridge nearby, scattering jagged chunks of cement and dirt over the heads of the prone men. Regimental artillery and mortar fire saved the situation, and men of the Second Battalion withdrew successfully, reorganized, and then pushed on to cut the highway. Several casualties resulted from the ambush.

July 23–The regiment occupied Cefalu and again was relieved by the 180th Infantry. Guards were established against an attack from the sea, and over the next two days, several naval engagements were reported to have taken place within striking distance of the beaches of Celalu.

July 24–27–Company C–Cefalu, Sicily. Guard duty.

July 28–Moved by truck from nine miles west of Cusa Marina and attacked the hill one mile east of Cusa. Worst battle of the Sicilian campaign. In the Forty-Fifth Division, the conflict is known as the ***Battle of Bloody Ridge***.

First Battalion attacked Castel Di Tusa and succeeded in reaching its objective at 1840 hours in spite of serious opposition. Third and Second Battalions, meanwhile, moved in support of First Battalion.

Company C–Two enlisted men KIA: Sgt. Robert F. Hanna, Jr., and Cpl. Wilford L. Henry.

July 29-Enemy troops made a determined stand for the city of Motta D'Affermo, located on a high ridge overlooking all surrounding areas. First and Third Battalions, attacking the city, suffered many casualties when they encountered heavy machine-gun and artillery fire. German snipers, using silencers on their rifles, also took their toll. Night found the men of the First Battalion tired and hungry, partially reorganized, and low on ammunition but in possession of the high ground northwest of Motta D'Affermo. Second Battalion, which had taken Pettineo that morning, moved forward to assist in the battle, but met heavy artillery fire and was forced to delay its advance. Casualties suffered by the regiment during the day totaled 108, fourteen of which were listed as KIA.

Recognizing the seriousness of the situation and beset with the problem of supplying the weary troops with food and ammunition, the battalion commanders borrowed pack mules from the natives, and under the cover of darkness, volunteer mule skinners led, pushed, and prodded their beasts of burden up the steep hills to deliver supplies from the rear areas. In many cases, the weary men outlasted the mules. Burdens that mules had been carrying often were transferred to the backs of laboring soldiers.

Determined troops of the battered First Battalion continued the attack the next day and succeeded in repulsing several strong German counterattacks despite continued casualties. During the day, the enemy withdrew from Motta D'Affermo to Retina, and the battalions of the regiment consolidated to continue the advance. Late in the night, the Second Battalion moved east cross country to Retina Ridge and gained control of the coast road to San Stefano.

Company C-Pvt. Dean W. Terry and First Sgt. Elmo F. Cromer were awarded the

Silver Star for gallantry in action near San Stefano. Sgt. Robert M. Huckabay KIA. Pvt. Philip T. DiTomaso and Pvt. Dean W. Terry are WIA.

July 30–31–Moved from hill east of Cusa Marina to Motta El Alena by foot and bivouacked for the night.

July 31–At 0715 hours the First Battalion occupied San Stefano, but suffered a number of casualties when the troops walked into a well-laid anti-personnel mine field. Relieved by the Third Division. Marched from Motta El Alena to Tusa Marino and loaded trucks to Termini Imerese for rest.

* * *

So ended the Forty-Fifth Division and the 157th Infantry's first twenty-one days of combat in World War II. Weather conditions during the period had been excellent, although the troops were unaccustomed to the Mediterranean climate. For the regiment, the Battle of Bloody Ridge had been the costliest engagement, but the men had proven themselves capable of overcoming a serious situation, more of which were to come within a few short months.

For extraordinary heroism in action during the first day of that battle, five enlisted men of Company A received the Distinguished Service Cross posthumously. The men were members of two light machine-gun squads which steadfastly held their positions in the face of a fierce German counterattack and overwhelming odds. Men who received the Awards were Sergeant Willard R. Hight, Brighton, Colorado; PFC William B. Olsen, Harrisburg Pennsylvania; PFC George A. McGee, Philadelphia, Pennsylvania; PFC Wesley F. Howe, Yampa, Colorado; and Pvt. Luis Blanco, Phoenix, Arizona.

Colonel Chas. M. Ankcorn, the Regimental Commander also received the Distinguished Service Cross for Extraordinary Heroism in the Battle of Bloody Ridge.

Regimental casualties during the first twenty-one days of combat totaled 263. Of that number, fifty-six enlisted men and two officers were killed in action, thirty-three enlisted men and two officers were seriously wounded, and 165 enlisted men and three officers were lightly wounded. Sixteen enlisted men are missing in action.

> [We continued along the coastal road beyond the town of Cefalu, and the fiercest battle we had fought to date took place—the Battle of Bloody Ridge where we suffered many casualties. After that battle we advanced to Messina. By then the enemy had finally fled across the straits into Italy. Sicily was ours. Our first step home.--Robert L. Kirchgassner]

Panoramic view of Cefalu
Signal Corps Photo -Wever

157th Infantry in Messina 8/17/1943
Signal Corps Photo

[When Dad was in Sicily, communication broke down and he was assigned as a runner. He had to carry a message to headquarters and run through an open field. He said it seemed like the entire German army was shooting at him. He ran faster than he ever had in his life and was lucky that he was not hit.—John Kirchgassner]

August 1–Termini Imerese. Rest period. On alert to defend coast. Men spent their time writing letters, washing clothes, bargaining with the Sicilians, eating the then new 5-in-1 ration and generally enjoying themselves.

[The first time I read "on alert to defend coast," I pondered for days what Dad was envisioning. In fact, every time I see this phrase, I pause and ref lect. My heart palpitates a little as I consider the meaning of these five words. My dad was ever on duty, a constant sentinel looking out at a vast sea. In such a short time how much his life had changed—a different normal. As a farmer, he lived a life in which weather dictated his daily activities. Now, as a soldier, his life hung in the balance at every moment. His experience in Sicily for me recalls the story that was told by Cicero: *The Sword of Damocles.*—Rita Kirchgassner]

August 4-The regiment received its first group of replacements, 123 enlisted men and nine officers.

August 6–A detachment from the Second Battalion moved to a new bivouac area from where guard units operated near an airfield and a number of bridges. The First and Third Battalions underwent a light training schedule of hikes, firing exercises, and combat problems.

Company C–PFC Alfred Vigilante is evacuated to the hospital and returns to duty on August 8. Enlisted men: 178.

August 14–At midnight the regiment was alerted for an amphibious attack behind enemy lines.

August 15-Troops embarked at Termini Imerese. The landing was effected on LST's and LCI's.

August 16–Approximately two miles west of Termini Bagni. But the regiment struck friendly shores because the Third Division that night had advanced through and beyond a landing point. An accident at sea, when a pulley wire snapped as a landing craft which had been rail loaded with men was being lowered into the water, brought about the deaths of eleven men from the First Battalion, the only casualties of the landing.

That afternoon First Battalion traveled forward by truck to Spidafora.

Company C–One private has hemorrhoids, another has bronchitis, and Tech 5/Sgt. Frank Corsaro has malaria. The following men are listed as MIA: Pvt. Roy C. Buhrman, Pvt. Nicholas Dalessandro, Pvt. Robert S. Dowds, Pvt. John C. Edwards, PFC Manuel M. Federico, Pvt. Leonard A. Gorecki, Cpl. Hugo W. Jackson, Pvt. William S. McClung, PFC John F. Mueller, Sgt. Ray A. Peck, and PFC Clarence Riley, Jr.

August 17– Second and Third Battalion rested in the vicinity Termini Bagni, First Battalion advanced toward Messina to assist in the immediate capture of that city.

Company C–One private first class has colitis.

August 18–At approximately 0400, the First Battalion advanced toward Messina to assist in the imminent capture of that city. The First battalion marched into the city in advance of the Third Division, Rangers, and the British Eighth Army. It was the first Allied unit to enter the city, capture of which marked the close of the Sicilian campaign. The troops were subjected to regular shellfire from the shores of Italy across the Straits of Messina during their advance, but casualties were light.

Late that night the regiment was alerted to move by land and sea from the bivouac area to the beach at Marchessana Latina and boarded landing crafts which took them to Palermo.

Company C–Sgt. Robert L. Kirchgassner is hospitalized with malaria.

August 19–Left Brolo at 0300 and marched to the Gulf of Patti and embarked on USS LCI 219 at 0400. Moved out to sea at 0730 and landed at Palermo at 1530. Moved by truck from Palermo at 1800 to bivouac area outside Trabia, Sicily, and arrived at 2145.

The end of the campaign in Sicily brought to the troops of the 157th Infantry approximately three weeks of deserved rest. The men witnessed moving pictures, listened to musical programs, and once were entertained by Bob Hope and Frances Langford, Hollywood stars of radio and screen. Troops were issued baseball, volleyball, and other sports equipment. They listened to radios and phonograph records, read books, wrote letters, and for the first time in Sicily, attended regular church services. A battalion at a time, the regiment visited Palermo, the capital of Sicily.

Training continued, however. The men took leg-conditioning marches, practiced squad, platoon, battalion, and regimental tactics, and conducted one dry landing practice. Meanwhile, they were re-equipped for coming operations.

August 24–Company C–PFC James Barkley is missing at 0600 hours on August 23 and returns to duty at 1130 hours on this date.

August 25–In Trabia, Sicily, during rest period and usual camp duties, officers, noncommissioned officers, and selected privates heard a speech by Lt. Gen. George "Blood and Guts" Patton, commander of the American Seventh Army, who praised the division for its battle discipline during the campaign in Sicily.

Company C–Pvt. Bryon Timmons and Pvt. Teton Hurtado are promoted to private first class.

August 26–Company C–Pvt. Leland A. Scott joins Company C, Fourth Platoon.

August 27–Company C–PFC James Barkley returns to being a private.

August 31–Company C–Pvt. Hanzel Blair joins Company C from 158th Field Artillery Battalion. Enlisted men: 189

September 1–4–The Forty-Fifth Division is transferred to the Fifth Army under the command of Lt. Gen. Mark W. Clark.

Company C–Pvt. William Mutchler has malaria.

September 5–Company C–Sgt. Robert L. Kirchgassner and Pvt. William Mutchler return to duty.

Bill Mutchler and Dad (1st Row)
with their wives behind them circa late1960's.

September 7–The regiment began preparations for a move from the bivouac area, and throughout the day troops and vehicles were loaded onto landing crafts in the harbor at Termini Imerese.

September 8–Convoy at sea by 0430 and joined by larger convoy in the afternoon. Flares dropped at night by enemy planes. At 1830, convoy totaling a hundred ships sailing north, and at 1930 hours turned east toward mainland; estimated position about fifty miles from Naples.

Company C– 2nd Lt. Richard M. Stone is promoted to first lieutenant.

Chapter 3

Italia: Omnes Viae Roman Ducunt (All Roads Lead to Rome)

Salerno

[Operation Avalanche September 1943: Salerno, Italy.

Three Allied Divisions landed at Salerno and fought against six German Divisions. This was a fierce battle as the Allies had the sea literally right behind them and the Germans goal to drive them back into the sea.

When the Operation Avalanche commenced, it was broadcast that Italy had surrendered. Mussolini had been voted out in July of 1943. The Allies hoped that it would meet little resistance from the Germans, but the war in Italy would continue and would not end until 1945.

Today, 2013, Salerno is a beautiful city that lies along the Amalfi Coast, south of Naples, Italy. Houses are nestled in the mountains that encase the city on three sides. The day we were there, the city was bustling with activity, especially at the harbor. We enjoyed a seafood lunch while admiring the harbor and coastline. Any trace of war that took place there some sixty plus years ago was almost non-existent. However, there is a memorial on the beach at Salerno thanking all who helped in the liberation. This memorial touched me personally as I knew that Uncle Vic's resting place was in the Bay of Salerno—Rita Kirchgassner]

Map of Italy
Denise Kirchgassner

FROM THE JOURNAL OF THE 157TH Regiment, Morning Reports, and After-Action Reports of Company C, 1943

September 9–Stood all day in sight of the island of Capri, approximately five miles offshore from Paestum.

June 5, 2013 Salerno--

[Southern Italy has mountainous terrain. As soon as we got to Salerno, the mountains filled with rain clouds, but we never got rain. After seeing how treacherous the terrain is, I wonder why the Allies picked this spot to land. Kirch suspects it's because the place was not heavily guarded by the enemy. The Germans were able to take out a lot of soldiers from high atop the hills. After securing the beachhead, a far superior American army couldn't advance because of the terrain. Here in Salerno, Victor Hoffmeier (Kirch's great-great uncle) died at sea. His boat was hit by a bomb and then a torpedo during the landing. Leaving from the train stop, we spotted an old German gun port on a hillside.

After taking pictures at the beachhead and soaking it in, we decided to take the three-hour train ride back to Rome. On the train we met a retired doctor from Akron, Ohio, who grew up south of Salerno. He was fourteen in 1944. He told us that when the Germans occupied his town, most of the soldiers were nice to him and his family. They would tell the family when to stay in and when to leave. He said he was excited to see the Allies come. He said the Germans didn't have anything compared with America. His family stayed south of the fighting. He said the terrain slowed the army, but everyone knew the war was over when the Americans came. The doctor said his family and others were starving because war ravaged all their farmland and supplies. He said they ate well and had a lot of support when the Allies landed. It was a crazy coincidence that we met this eighty-three-year-old man on a train while he was visiting Salerno. He ended up coming to America and becoming a doctor in the air force.

Salerno pictures with the phone camera didn't turn out great due to the weather. Too many Pompeii pictures to post them all now. Another awesome day. Tomorrow we will relax in Rome.—Jared Leiker]

[The invasion of Salerno took place on September 9, and our regiment was held in reserve. I wished that we were on land, for every night the Germans would fly over and drop bombs on us. Luckily the ships were dispersed and they never hit too many.—Robert L. Kirchgassner]

[This is a part of the war that Dad mentioned many times—when politics entered into decisions being made. For example, the Forty-Fifth Division was held in reserve to let other Allied divisions take the lead. Richard Adams concurred with Dad's reaction to this. Dad was serious about his mission and wanted to get the job done so he could go home. As an infantryman, being in reserve was misery for dad, especially if he was on water.—Rita Kirchgassner]

September 10–At 1630 regiment started landing at Beach Green near Paestum (Pesto), Italy. Only two LSTs were unloaded on this date due to a misunderstanding of orders by the navy. The LST's contained the Transportation and some personnel of the "Q" and Third Battalions. Set up Regimental Command Post 14 Kilometers south of Battipaglia. 158th Field Artillery opened fire on Altavilla Silentina at 2315.

[Unknown to Dad, his future wife's uncle and a fellow resident of Yorkville, Indiana, was killed in action on this date. Victor W. Hoffmeier, motor machinist mate first class in the United States Navy, was on a boat in the bay of Salerno that was bombed by the enemy. He is still listed as MIA, as his body was never recovered.

Leroy Seevers a lifelong resident of New Alsace, Indiana, served in the United States Navy at the same time as Uncle Vic. He served at Salerno, on a patrol boat that was one hundred and ten feet long and sixteen feet wide with a crew of twenty-eight men.

After Uncle Vic was killed in action, Leroy happened to meet the cook on the ship that Uncle Vic served as a machinist. Somehow, Uncle Vic knew that Leroy was patrolling the beach at Salerno. The cook stated that the first bomb that hit the ship fell in the engine area and Uncle Vic died instantly. As the ship was being escorted ashore, it hit a mine and sank.—Rita Kirchgassner]

Victor Hoffmeier

September 11–0800-First and Third (remainder of Third) Battalions started landing about 4 miles north of Paestum.

First Battalion moved 3 miles inland along Sele River. Enemy fire encountered at Bivio Golfi. Company C encountered fire at 1615. First Battalion blocked highways leading to beach to allow rest of regiment to move inland.

[The German soldier was tough. They tried to drive us off the beachhead. We made a stand along the Sele River and stopped them cold.—Robert L. Kirchgassner]

[I came across a recommendation from Maj. Gen. John P. Lucas proposing a citation for Maj. Gen. Troy M. Middleton for heroism in action. On the night of September 14–15, the enemy made a determined attempt to cut the beachhead in two and impede the American offensive. Middleton, at great personal risk and with complete disregard for danger to himself, organized the stubborn resistance and directed counterattacks that decisively influenced the outcome of the battle. Twice during the night he visited each front-line unit and adjusted the defense. His courage and initiative were examples of superior leadership.

However, Lt. Gen. Mark W. Clark said he carefully reviewed and considered the facts set forth in the recommendation and found them insufficient to justify the award of the Distinguished Service Cross to Middleton.—Rita Kirchgassner]

Mark and Krista at Salerno Bay

Pillbox at Salerno

[The terrain was rugged and steep hills surrounded the Salerno beachhead. We could understand how the US Army became bogged down and could not readily advance. We can read all the books we want about the war, but we will never fully comprehend the impact it had on our soldiers. We have heard many stories about Uncle Vic, but the reality hit home when we saw his final resting place in the Bay of Salerno and saw his name on the wall for the missing in action at the Anzio-Nettuno Military Cemetery.—Mark and Krista Kirchgassner]

September 12–Regiment was opposed by strength of a full Panzer Battalion support and 88 mm guns. First Battalion attacked toward Persano at 0655.

1045-First Battalion had reached the bridge at Persano on the outskirts of town. First Battalion was pinned down by enemy tank, artillery and small arms fire. In the late afternoon, Third Battalion was moved to the left flank of First Battalion. All Battalions on line in front of Tobacco Factory. Third Battalion, 36th Engineers in reserve as riflemen.

On the night of September 12th, First and Third Battalions tried to move forward but were held up by enemy fire.

Company C-Pvt. Eugene L. Benson, 2nd Lt. Austin E. Buell, Pvt. Claude Iron Hawk, Pvt. Wallace L. Jordan, Pvt. LeRoy S. Meekins, PFC Bernard D. Pieczynaki and Pvt. Sylvester S. Winemaker are WIA. Second Lt. Louis Peluso and Cpl. Fred L. Vogel are KIA.

September 13–At 1530 enemy opened heavy counterattack on First Battalion, preceded by about twelve Mark IV tanks, and withdrew about a half mile to stronger defensive positions. By 1700 this attack had developed along entire front of First and Third Battalions. One platoon of First Battalion had been cut off and enemy had advanced on our right flank between First Battalion and the 36th Division. Thirty-six Division artillery fire fell on the First Battalion during the battle. Lines were driven back about one-half mile by flanking threat.

At 1900 First and Third Battalions attacked to recover position and were halted one-half kilometer southwest of tobacco factory.

> [The tobacco factory changed hands four times on September 12, and the First Battalion was at one point surrounded by the Germans. The 189th and 158th Artillery Battalions stood in the way, stopped the Germans, and saved the beachhead.—Hugh F. Foster III]

Company C–Enlisted men: 177. Pvt. James C. Brooks (fate unknown to date, listed as MIA but not confirmed), PFC Richard D. Glavaz and Pvt. George H. Robinson are KIA. PFC Michael Callahan, PFC Eugene Drennen and Pvt. Sidney Zuckerman are WIA.

The following become POW's: Pvt. Ernest L. Andrechick, Pvt. John H. Archambeau, Pvt. Robert T. Banar, Pvt. Joseph Bilinski, Pvt. Joseph P. Bolduc, Pvt. Hymie L Brown, Pvt. Elmer Brumbelow, PFC Frank Corsaro, Pvt. Edmund J. Couturier, PFC Leo H. Crispo, 1st Sgt. Elmo F. Cromer, Pvt. Kenneth D. Davis, Pvt. James DiNino, Pvt. Pedro M. Dominguez, Cpl. Milton Drazen, PFC Eugene Drennen, Pvt. Michael J. Duggan, T/5 Alfred B. English, Pvt. John L. Freeman, Pvt. Paul L. Garcia, PFC Kenneth L. Grundon, Sgt. Martin J. Herburger, Pvt. Edgar W. Johnson, S/Sgt. James H. Jones, Pvt. Chester Kadlubowski, Pvt. Robert T. Katan, Pvt. Michael J. Kennedy, Pvt. Nathan N. Kissell, PFC Harry G. Kotsch, Daniel J. Leger, Pvt. Charles T. Maneri, Pvt. William P. McInerney, Cpl. Edwin F. Michaelis, Pvt. Merle T. Minear, PFC Laverne Moore, Pvt. William Mycawka, Cpl. Constantine O'Neill, PFC Stanley J. Papst, PFC William O. Pilius, Pvt. John Rebovich, PFC Louis A. Renfrow, Pvt. George J. Riccardo, Sgt. Cletus W. Roach, PFC Leland E. Scout, PFC Rollo W. Shaffer, Pvt. James J. Twohey, 1st Lt. Richard P. Van Syckle, PFC James J. Whalley, Sgt. Hugh E. Widmier, Cpl. John W. Williams Jr., and PFC Albert L. Willis.

September 14-0215-Message that the 36th Division had broken on our right; confirmed by Colonel Ankcorn. RLT (Regimental Landing Team) withdrew headquarters to RR crossing by Canal and RJ, 1 mile south west of Tobacco Factory. 1045-Enemy counterattack with eight tanks broken up by our artillery fire, 158th Field Artillery. On this date inclusive, three Batteries of the 158th Field Artillery delivered continuous artillery fire and on two occasions broke up tank and troop concentrations massing for attack on against us.

Company C-Pvt. Raymond L. Grabus is WIA. Sgt. Gilbert Aragon and PFC Joseph C. Pellegrino are KIA.

September 15–16–Maintained positions unchanged. Continuous artillery fire and counter-fire. Our artillery prevented two counterattacks from massing during the daylight on September 16. Company C-Pvt. Cecil P. Denton is WIA on September 15th. The following men became POW's on September 16th: Pvt. Charles Bruyere, PFC Frank Kuzina and Pvt. Paul E. Wagner.

September 17–At 1230, the 179th Infantry moved to our right flank. First Battalion of the 179th was attached to the 157th RCT (Regimental Combat Team), under Colonel Ankcorn's command. Artillery fire throughout the day again prevented enemy attempts to mass for counterattack. At about 1700 enemy tried to develop motorized counterattack. Eight of its vehicles were blown up in a minefield hastily laid the preceding night by the First Battalion with engineer support.

Company C-PFC Thomas Garcia is KIA.

(Note) The following units were attached to the RLT upon reaching the beach: Company B, 191st Tank Battalion, Companies B and C, 2nd Chemical Battalion; Battery A 106th C. A. Battalion and Company C, 645th Tank Destroyers Battalion.

[Regimental "teams" such as RLT's and RCT's are temporary organizations for very limited operations. Once the RLT was ashore, that "title" was abandoned and the regiment reverted to 'regiment.'—Hugh F. Foster III]

Mountain Advance Phase

September 18–1100–Ascertained that enemy had withdrawn. Battalions moved up to high ground commanding beach.

Second Battalion landed and was placed in Division Reserve.

September 19–Near Eboli, Italy, reached the tobacco warehouse. Organized to advance north to Contursi.

[The high command called for a push to Naples.—Robert L. Kirchgassner]

[The seaport of Naples was needed by Allies.—John Kirchgassner]

September 20–Second Battalion entered Campagna leading regiment. Route of advance generally east through Contursi, then north through mountains in the center of the Italian peninsula, toward a pass near Lioni. Movement up the national highway in columns of battalions—First, Second, and Third. Regiment supervised civilian medical aid in Campagna, procured further aid from the division.

September 21–RCT moving forward; Second Battalion in advance. Third Battalion moved abreast of Second Battalion on right flank; contacted recon units of British Eighth Army. Movement was up floor of valley from Contursi to core objective: to command high ground. Encountered artillery fire; found all bridges on main highway blown by enemy; had to be bypassed by deep cuts. The 120th Engineers hard at work to facilitate forward movement.

Company C–Pvt. Ray Neitz is evacuated as he is sick with fever of unknown origin.

September 22-RCT with 180th Infantry on left flank move through Contursi. Regiment moving on main highway on Column of Battalions-Third, Second and First. One hundred and eighth Infantry moved on flank on another highway it rounded an intervening mountain.

September 23–Near Contursi, Italy. Fifty-seven men join Company C. Troops resting, morale is good, and weather is fair.

Company C-Pvt. Jesse L. Wright is WIA.

[The regiment's first Medal of Honor recipient, Cpl. James D. Slayton of Company K, earned the medal by wiping out three machine-gun nests with rifle fire, hand grenades, and his bayonet. —Hugh F. Foster III]

Regiment given holding mission to east of Oliveto, while the 179th Infantry which had relieved 180th Infantry advance to Oliveto. Regiment covered right flank of 179th and advanced with Second Battalion forward. 2300-Third Battalion moved up to right flank of Second Battalion.

September 24–Second Battalion ordered to keep moving forward and take high ground above Valva. 0900–Colonel Ankcorn wounded by mine explosion while going forward in car for reconnaissance two miles north of Oliveto. 1300 hours–Colonel Church arrived in command post to command regiment. 1900-Second Battalion had taken the high ground above Valva and Third Battalion was ordered forward to relieve Second Battalion.

September 25–Third Battalion attacked toward Castelnuovo. 1300 hours–Regiment advance halted by artillery, mortar, and machine-gun fire. Battalions dig in for the night. Patrols found bridges forward blown and highway covered by artillery and mortar emplacements. Requested air mission to clear road ahead.

Company C– Pvt. Douglas A. Bibb joins.

September 26– 0600–Air mission undertaken, but most of the bombs fell in Second Battalion area due to error by Air Corps. During the afternoon the Third Battalion occupied and organized the high ground along the Corps objective. The Third Battalion was relieved by the First Battalion after darkness.

Company C-Pvt. Harvard E. Olinger is WIA.

September 27-Battalions still halted south of Castelnuovo. Repair of enemy demolished bridges and clearing of mined roads delayed general forward movement of regiment, however Third Battalion moved forward and organized defensive position northwest of Castelnuovo commanding crossroads. First Battalion relieved Third Battalion at 1800 hours.

September 28–Remained in the defensive position and patrolled to the front. Morale is good. Continued reconnaissance and repair of roads, mostly creating bypasses around blown bridges. Regiment now in position on high ground—Mountain Pass—northwest of Castelnuovo. This was Corps objective.

Company C–Pvt. Virgil H. Green, serial number 37247915 and military occupational specialty (MOS) 745, is assigned.

September 29-Another day of patrols and road construction.

September 30–Troops in rest area in Lioni, Italy. Enemy is retreating fast, and regiment lost enemy contact. Regiment moved from Mountain Pass to one mile west of Lioni.

Company C–Cpl. Angelo Ficuciello is evacuated to 38th Evacuation Hospital, Gesualdo, Italy, with fever of unknown origin.

October 1–Battalions reorganizing at Lioni. Division is out of contact with the enemy. Payday today. At 1600, the regiment is ordered to move forward tomorrow morning.

Company C–Pvt. John Schweisthal (MOS 745) joins Company C along with Pvt. Edward Schemansky (MOS 745) and Pvt. Quienton Steele (MOS 745).

[This would begin the friendship between my Dad and John Schweisthal that would be suspended only temporarily in death.—Rita Kirchgassner]

Lioni, Italy-Citizens greeting the157th Infantry.
City where Dad and John meet and become comrades.
SC Photo

October 2-At 0600 regiment moved forward in column of Battalions-order of March, Second, First and Third. Objective: Benevento. Reached Gesualdo at 1600.

October 3–North of Benevento, Italy. Regiment moved in column by motor to San Giorgio. Third Battalion ordered to lead advance into Benevento tomorrow morning.

October 4–0900–Third Battalion entered Benevento and was halted north of town by enemy artillery. Regiment command post established at 1830 in Benevento. Second and Third Battalions moved forward and occupied high ground northwest of Benevento.

Company C–PFC Ray Neitz returns to duty. Enlisted men: 196.

October 5-Movement toward Ponte delayed by artillery fire and destruction of bridges. First Battalion advanced at 0600 and encountered heavy artillery fire from Fragneto. First Battalion reached high ground above Ponte by assault. Enemy artillery operating from Hill 481. First Battalion took Hill 481 at 1900. At 1730, Third Battalion attacked toward Vitulano. Second Battalion moving along the main road to Ponte.

October 6–Third Battalion has outflanked and enveloped Germans behind Fragneto and Ponte. This was to the left of Calore River across mountains. Second Battalion moving up along main valley highway. Object: High ground north of the river of Ponte.

[Company E was hit by an enemy counterattack and was reduced to forty-five men.—Hugh F. Foster III.]

October 7–First and Third Battalions run into heavy enemy fire on the road by Calore River. Regiment is following the 180th Infantry forward. Second Battalion moving on left flank through high ground to Torrecusso.

Company C-PFC Andrew J. Sojak, Jr. is KIA. Sgt. Max L. Johnson becomes staff sergeant.

> [We were fighting from hill to hill in some of the worst fighting I had ever seen. The weather was bad; the rain and mud were terrible. The only way we got rations and ammo was by men bringing these things up in the hills on the backs of mules at night. Then they would take the dead and the wounded to the rear. When winter arrived, we were dug in, doing patrol duty and holding our positions in the mountains.—Robert L. Kirchgassner]

October 8–At 0230-Third Battalion jumped off in attack in lead of the regiment going west. Third and First Battalions moved forward, through Ponte and along Calore River finding bridges blown, highways mined. Regiment in Division Reserve at approximately 1300. Companies in bivouac area to west of Ponte. Regiment command post in Ponte-Casalduni RR Station.

Company C–PFC Roman Jozefowicz is promoted to corporal.

October 9-Battalions were passed through by the 179th Infantry last night.

October 10-Regiment resting along Calore River. First and Third Battalions two miles west of command post at Ponte-Casalduni. Second Battalion one and one half miles east of command post. Intermittent artillery fire fell during the day on bypass one and one half miles east of command post and on First and Third Battalions. Bombing and strafing attack on road two miles south east of command post at 1700. One prime mover (one wire truck) destroyed; 5 reported killed.

October 11-Battalions resting at same location. Intermittent artillery from about five miles northwest still falling to west of Ponte Casalduni about two miles.

October 12–Battalions resting at same location. Air raid at 1030-Captain Sparks injured by 40 mm AA shell which exploded in Second Battalion area. Third Battalion sent forward to reinforce 180th Infantry which had received counterattack during the afternoon. Much enemy aircraft active during the night. Weather fair.

Company C–One officer WIA.

October 13-Field Order #16 from Division received at 1900. Regiment along north bank of Calore River at Ponte-Casalduni. Third Battalion still with the 180th Infantry. At 2030 command post moved seven miles west along Calore River; one mile north of River; two miles east of Telese. At 2200 the 157th Infantry going through 180th Infantry in direction of Faicchio. Order of March; First, Third and Second Battalions. Weather rainy and cold.

October 14-Much small arms fire to north at 0400. Battalions moving in column of battalions through Telese and northwest to Faicchio. One Hundred Seventy-Ninth Infantry on right flank-to Faicchio via San Lorenzello. First Battalion through Telese and San Sarafino in morning. Tanks and mortar opposition. Part of Third swung south through Ambrosia. One Hundred Seventy-Ninth coming around right flank. Third Battalion moved up behind First Battalion tonight. First Battalion attacked at 2335 toward RJ at Faicchio.

October 15–At 0235-First Battalion halted. At 0600 First Battalion attacked to Faicchio. Second Battalion moved up behind First Battalion and Third Battalion moved into reserve. First Battalion through San Salvatore and around mountain Acero toward Faicchio. Third Battalion ordered to go around left flank tonight. Third Battalion ran into strong resistance at Faicchio after crossing Titerno River and advancing to junction southwest of Faicchio.

October 16–At 0900 Third Battalion supported by 191st Tank and 645th Tank Destroyers again attacked around left flank and moved beyond Faicchio. Second Battalion relieved Third Battalion and moved around Faicchio then west, to Massanti Viscari and northwest to Gioia. Fifty-two enemy soldiers taken. Dive bombing using Lemon Squeezers in afternoon on First Battalion southwest of Faicchio.

Company C-Pvt. Howard Lynch (MOS 745) joins.

October 17-Second Battalion one fourth mile west of Fiora. Third Battalion one and one half mile east. First Battalion three and one half miles south east of Gioia. Regiment command post and artillery moved up. Intermittent artillery fire.

October 18–Second Battalion moving northwest from Gioia. Third and First Battalions moving behind Second. Second Battalion moved to three miles northwest of Gioia. Third Battalion relieved Second Battalion at 2400. Opposition: Small arms and artillery fire.

Company C–Cpl. Angelo Ficuciello returns to duty. Pvt. Paul F. Duff is WIA.

October 19-At 0800, Battalions same position. Regiment objective high ground five miles northwest of Gioia (Castello D Alife). Battalions moving along high ground 1500 yards east of highway. Third Battalion completed relief and moved out at 0630. Third Battalion reached Castello D Alife and Second and First Battalion moved up behind it.

October 20–Battalions going into assembly areas south of Castello D Alife at base of mountains. Patrols comb east west range. 2000 hours 4 Italian Colonels in command post. Are taken to division. Had come from Rome. Regiment in Corps Reserve.

October 21-Usual rest-period duties, weather warm, and morale good. Bivouacked along foot of mountains 2 miles south of Castello Di Alife and one half mile east of Piedmont. Thirty-Fourth Division advancing north across valley and across our left front. Much mortar (6 barrel) and machine-gun fire to front three miles.

October 22-Battalions in bivouac two miles south of Castello Di Alife. Regiment command post moved to one half mile west of Piedmont. Intermittent artillery fire in front. Air raid to south of Naples.

October 23-Ato 0930 General Middleton talked to Battalion and Company Commanders. Numerous (15 or 20) escaped French, English and Italian soldiers in command post. Intermittent artillery fired in front five miles. Air raid to south (Naples).

October 24–Regiment in same area. Barrack bags brought forward. Cpl. Jerry Wolfe has fever of unknown origin.

October 25–Regiment in bivouac. Practice firing machine-guns and bazookas.

October 26–Regiment in bivouac. Practice firing machine-guns and bazookas. Thirty-Fourth Division artillery opened fire to west at 0515.

October 27–Regiment in rest area in vicinity of Piedmont. Practice firing of all weapons. Movies provided for troops in Piedmont Cinema Theatre by special services. Doughnuts brought to personnel of regiment by Red Cross workers (female).

October 28–Regiment still in rest area. Practice firing of weapons continues. Special services activities continue. Show with cast drawn from regiment entertaining troops and natives in the division area.

October 29–Regiment in rest area. Test firing of weapons continues. Anti-personnel mines (more than thirty of them) found in the Second Battalion bivouac area. Some had already injured animals and natives before Second Battalion undertook removal in p.m.

October 30–Further test firing of weapons. Special services entertainment being provided for personnel—stage show and doughnuts Company C–Cpl. Jerry M. Wolfe returns to duty.

November 1–Recon party from the 157th to check area between 238037 and Raviscania 199098 to set the regiment in preparation for move after dark this p.m. The base point for initial phase of commitment 1005. Battalions started moving, order, First, Second and Third at 1500 hours.

November 2–Recon party from regiment ordered out preparatory to closing in on 179th and 180th Infantries. Committed units. Reconnaissance completed by 1400. Regiment marched nine miles to the vicinity of San Angelo, Italy. Order of March: First, Second and Third.

Company C– Enlisted men: 202.

November 3–Vicinity of San Angelo, Italy. No enemy contact.

Company C–Pvt. Tillman Holder, Pvt. James W. Barkley, Pvt. Scott Leland, and Pvt. George Kiewiet Jr. are promoted to private first class.

November 4–Received orders to close regiment on leading elements for possibility of commitment. All troops fed by 1630 and moved out under the cover of darkness. All battalions closed in their areas by 2230. No enemy contact.

November 5–Left bivouac area in vicinity of San Angelo at approximately 2400. Marched thirteen miles to bivouac area near Venafro, Italy (two miles southwest of Ailano). No enemy contact.

November 6–Two miles south of Ailano. Regiment alerted-Second and Third Battalions at 1705 for possibility of counterattack this p.m. No enemy contact.

November 7–In vicinity of Venafro. At 1030 hours regimental commander called meeting of battalion commanders and designated general routes of march for battalion movements. The 157th Infantry ordered by division to pass between the 179th and 180th and continue attack to the northwest. Battalions moved out at dark; First Battalion on the line. Command post moved 1 mile north east of Venafro. Battalions closed in specified areas at 2130. Will push attack at daylight.

Venafro, Italy. Smoke screen-shell thrown by a unit of the Forty-Fifth. SC Photo

[On this date the Chaplain sent Grandma Dorie the following form letter:

Dear Friend,

Over here we realize how much it means to hear from your loved ones at home and in turn for you folks to receive word from your soldier boy overseas.

Although conditions vary greatly, Mass has been celebrated from time to time in olive groves, on mountain tops, in dry river beds and in old churches. It will be a great comfort for you to know that Bob is often present and receives the Sacraments regularly. Not only is he faithfully serving America, but he likewise has proved to be a true soldier of Christ.

This Christmas season will find us far from home on foreign soil, but I'm sure we will be closer in spirit than ever before. Please continue to keep all our boys in your prayers. Wishing you a Holy Christmas and a New Year bright with the hope of peace on earth. I remain,

Home address:	Sincerely.
Univ. of Notre Dame	Joseph D. Barry Chaplain
Notre Dame, Indiana	157th Infantry APO 45
	% Postmaster, N.Y., N.Y.

[Every time the First Battalion was on the line, Father Barry was at the medical aid station. He was a lively character. Even though I was not Catholic, he let me attend Mass and receive communion.—Richard Adams]

November 8–In vicinity of Venafro. First Battalion led off at daylight—order of the March, A, B, C. General Middleton orders battalions to remain in depth as there is a definite threat of counterattack. AT (Antitank) protection put in on Venafro-Isernia Road. Area of regimental command post shelled intermittently by mortars and artillery. Only enemy contact is made by Company B; small arms fire from top of Hill 1025. First Battalion asked for twenty mules this morning. Regiment said it would have them at Venafro at noon. First Battalion took one POW from Ninth Panzer Grenadier Regiment. Vigorous patrolling on all fronts.

November 9-Vicinity of Venafro. Upon receipt of orders from commanding general, First Battalion held positions on Hill 1025. Company A encountered patrol at 1700. Killed four; took five enemy soldiers. Request one rifle company from Second Battalion to support Company B. Vigorous patrolling on all fronts.

November 10–In vicinity of Venafro. Company B moved back slightly to out posted position. Italian Major and prisoner of war report 150 Germans planning to attack Company A and retake high ground. Company B reports its position is not good. Regimental commanding officer determines to reinforce First Battalion with one company from Second Battalion. Company E called upon for reinforcement. Company E cleared on way to join First Battalion at 1020. Captain Aff ley, commanding officer of Company C, KIA. First Battalion took three POWs of 676th Motorized Regiment. First Battalion ordered to move at daylight. Company C leading and Company E to support in depth; elements moving to Hills 759 and 750. Company C to defend ridge, and Company E to attack Hill 850, then organize and defend. Both companies to attack at Hills 1040 and 1010.

Company C-Captain Frank W. Affley, Pvt. Ronald J. Bombard, Pvt. Robert C. McBride, Jr., and PFC Arnold B. Waefler are KIA. Pvt. Frank J. Eoviero and PFC Lawrence E. Kantola are WIA.

November 11–Armistice Day. Company C took three POWs from 67thPanzers, 26th Panzer Division. Company C jumped off at dawn. Company E left First Battalion command post at 0600 for support position in vicinity of Company A. Company B received heavy counterattack from west, at 1330. Attack repulsed at 1525. One platoon of Company E and one platoon of Company C moving up Hill 759 at 1615 meeting resistance. Third Battalion committed on north edge of regiment sector. One platoon of Company G attached to Company B upon suggestion of First Battalion S1. Third Battalion moving to new assembly area; will attack at daylight.

Company C–First Lt. Anse H. Speairs lightly wounded in right hip, Sgt. Leo E. Hamblin and 2nd Lt. James M. Newton are WIA. Pvt. Clifford M Lawson and Pvt. Medford Booker are KIA.

November 12–In vicinity of Venafro. Company C achieved objective, Hill 759. Lt. Neugebauer, Company A killed in action. Company C and Company E received small arms and mortar fire on Hill 759. Germans withdrew, leaving Company C and Company E clear of enemy. Our airplanes bombed and dropped propaganda leaf lets at 1330 hours. Enemy hit one of our artillery prime movers about one mile south of Third Battalion Command Post. Third Battalion meeting steady resistance from bottom of Hill 640.

Company C–In the barrage of fighting on the twelfth, PFC Byron Timmons and Cpl. Jerry Wolfe were wounded in action. Timmons suffered a wound to the right thigh and Wolfe to the left arm and ankle. Both were evacuated to the 94th Evacuation Hospital. Pvt. Phillip V. Angelastro, PFC Robert J. Baldridge, Pvt. Ronald A Butts, Cpl. George Dudics, Pvt. Frederick E. Horn, Pvt. James D. Hughes, Pvt. William H. Laible, Pvt. Vincent D. Masucci and Sgt. William P. Weis are WIA. PFC Anthony Czerpak, Pvt. Virgil Scott were KIA on this date. Cpl. Roman Jozefowicz and PFC James Barkley suffered injuries to the left and right shoulder, respectively. Cpl. Jerry Wolfe and Cpl. Jozefowicz do not return during the war.

November 13–RCT's advance was held up and its positions dominated Hill 769 which the 179th tried to take throughout the day, but which was strongly defended by artillery and small arms. Commanding officer ordered all but essential vehicles be withdrawn from the regimental rear area, near which enemy shells fell twice during the day. The enemy was shelling communications and installations to north (Pozzilli) and west (Venafro) of regimental rear. First Battalion reinforced by Company E and one platoon of Company G on right of regimental sector; continued to mop up Hill 759 and extend flank to south to include Hill 750. Fired numerous artillery missions on enemy to front with good results. Third Battalion placed in line to cover right portion of regimental sector, due to readjustments of sector. Third Battalion attack at daylight Hill 460 to its front-captured 10 enemy soldiers in this vicinity; enemy had good observation of this hill and shelled it severely shortly before noon and twice counterattacked causing about thirty-five casualties. Counter attacks repulsed. Company L withdrew to a more favorable position slightly to rear. Hill 460 appears to be impossible for either side to occupy in any force. Orders from division were received to hold positions for time being until Thirty-Fourth Division advances further on the right of division sector. Estimated causalities for regiment, thirty-four wounded and four killed. Enemy causalities considerably more including fifteen enemy soldiers taken on this date.

Company C–Pvt. Richard R. Dennehy, Pvt. Hubert A. Morin, PFC Victor F. Staley (injured also), and 2nd Lt. Robert F. Wiley are WIA.

November 14–First Battalion with the exception of Company B, was being relieved from position on the hill at 0130 by Second Battalion and moved back to the outskirts of Venafro. Weather rainy and cold.

November 15– First Battalion with the exception of Company B remained in Regimental Reserve. Company B remained on line, sending patrols out during the day, as Second and Third Battalions also did from their forward positions. Enemy artillery interdicted the roads near Pozzilli and Venafro continuously after dark. Company C five miles northeast of Pozzilli, Italy, and moved out of bivouac area at 2400. Marched through Pozzilli for five miles to relieve Company L. First Battalion ran into enemy mine laying.

Company C–Weather rainy and cold. Morale good. In defensive position. One sergeant was demoted to private and transferred to Company L. Pvt. Vincent J. Daschke is WIA.

November 16–Company B remains on the line with Second and Third Battalions. Second Battalion reported civilian information that many enemy were quartered in buildings in Viticuso. Our heavy mortars fired on the enemy during daylight and received return artillery fire without causalities therefrom. The 157th and 179th Infantry on the right of the 157th was informed that enemy patrols of eight to twelve men were trying to work down the Ridge 675 toward Pozzuoli. The 157th Infantry requested air mission against enemy positions when visibility makes this possible. The enemy continued interdicting the Venafro Road, near First Battalion bivouac area and the Pozzuoli Road.

November 17–First Battalion was moving up from its bivouac area at the close of the period to relieve Third Battalion. Company B was replaced by Company L. Second Battalion remained on the line through the day receiving some mortar and artillery fire and informing that enemy patrols were very active along our front. Third Battalion reported that our artillery was effective in interdicting approach of enemy self-propelled guns toward its position. One platoon of AT Company was ordered up as rifleman to support First Battalion's relief of Third Battalion.

November 18–At 0345, First Battalion completed relief of Third Battalion which had begun in previous period. First Battalion took over patrolling of front line and ran into enemy minelaying at approximately (009221). Both patrols withdrew from that ground. Beyond patrolling, the First Battalion's only other action was when Company A fired with good effect on the enemy which our artillery drove from cover on Hill 769. The enemy placed artillery and mortar fire on First and Second Battalion fronts through the period continuing interdicting approaches to Venafro and Pozzouli.

Due to rain in the p.m. an aerial bombing on Viticuso was not executed.

November 19–First Battalion, occupying front-line positions throughout the period, continued patrolling. Company A patrol found blown bridge in need of much repair when we advance. Second Battalion was heavily shelled from 1145 to 1245 and in the afternoon while on the line with First Battalion.

November 20–First Battalion continued in front line position, patrolling throughout the period. First and Second Battalions were under artillery and mortar barrages throughout the period. First Battalion believed enemy guns were located west of Hill 769.

November 21–First Battalion remained on the front and patrolled throughout the period. First Battalion patrols sent out on previous night returned with negative reports. Company C patrolled along both sides of the stream before our lines to its bend.

November 22–First Battalion, on regimental front, patrolled during dark hours. Reports of patrols returning in the early morning hours indicated the enemy was establishing field fortifications on the high ground above the blown bridge before our lines. Company C noted small-arms fire and an enemy motorcycle near the blown bridge.

Company C-Pvt. Raymond Emig evacuated to the 56th Evacuation Hospital with jaundice; does not return to war.

November 23–First Battalion on front throughout the period, patrolled to its front during darkness of the period, both to reconnoiter and in an endeavor to capture prisoners of war. Reported difficulty of capturing enemy soldiers owing to darkness and noise and rocky terrain.

November 24–First Battalion, on front-line positions, patrolled to its front before dawn and after sunset, but made no enemy contacts and was unable to take any POWs, owing to poor visibility. Second Battalion in Regimental Reserve. The enemy continued harassing and interdictory fire throughout the period, hitting C, L, and M Companies and Third Battalion command post. In the p.m. of the period requested air mission was carried out against Concacasale.

Company C-Pvt. Robert B. McChesney and PFC Byron J. Oswald are KIA.

November 25–Patrols of First and Third Battalions, on the front in period, return negative reports of enemy contacts. Second Battalion was in process of relieving First Battalion before daylight, November 26, at the close of the period.

Our artillery was unusually inactive in most of the period in our sector, seeming to devote most attention to First Rangers, on the 157th's left flank.

November 26–First Battalion relieved from defensive positions by Second Battalion by 0435. Marched back to village above Venafro to rest area. Made no enemy contacts but had located booby traps and mine fields.

[Grandma Dorie kept the following newspaper article:

Germans Think Indian Troops are Cannibalistic

Allied Headquarters, North Africa November 26—(AP)—When things were tough around Salerno the Allied strategists moved in a tough outfit to take care of them it was revealed today.

"This was the Fighting Forty-Fifth" Infantry Division, which had won its battle spurs in Sicily and its impact helped roll back the Germans when the Nazis for a few critical days stalled the troops which had made the original American landing on the Italian mainland at Salerno.

The Forty-Fifth is made up largely of troops from Colorado, Oklahoma and New Mexico including more than a thousand Indians, although it contingents from several eastern states.

The Germans have a special dread of the Forty-Fifth's fighting quality because some of them believe the Indians are cannibalistic. The Indians enjoy this hugely, and one of the Indian Sergeant conducts his own "war of nerves" by gesturing toward his month every time newly captured prisoners are brought in his directions.

PROMOTES CANNIBAL RUMOR

It is one of the most colorful in the Army, but what is more important, it is rated as one of the hardest-hitting outfits under the flag.

It made it battle debut in an amphibious assault against Sicily after only a short pause in Africa en route from the United States and its performance under fire caused the ranking officers at Allied headquarters to hail it as a complete vindication of the American training program.

"This division's outstanding record is proof that our training camps are graduating troops full-fledged and ready for combat," said one general.

In the Sicilian campaign the Forty-Fifth was the first to wedge through to the north coast and cut the island in half, returning to the battlefront late in the campaign for Messina.

After smashing ashore along an 18 mile strip of Gela, the Forty-Fifth captured a thousand square miles in three weeks. These troops also marched 140 miles in 14 days while fighting continuously, captured more than 6,000 Italian and German enemy soldiers, took the Comiso and Biscari airports, too the towns of Vittoria and Caltanissetta, knocked out eight giant Tiger tanks and a number of smaller enemy mechanized units, and captured huge stores of enemy ammunition, food, clothing and medical supplies.

POACHED ON CANADIANS

The lads were so anxious for action in the early days of the Sicilian campaign that they even poached on Canadian territory.

A platoon of 30 men captured the town of Ragusa, which the Canadians had been assigned to take—and where holding an Italian garrison of 250 men prisoners when the Canadians arrived. They then turned over the prisoners to their allies and returned to their own division.

Many members of the division take the greatest pride, however, in the job they did dislodging the Germans from "Bloody Ridge," east of San Stefano on the North Sicilian coast.

It took three charges up an almost perpendicular rocky hill to gain the summit, but they made it. A hundred and 50 German bodies at the top testified to the stoutness of the resistance they overcame.

In that engagement, Sgt. Herb Fish of Canyon City, Colorado, killed eight Nazis with eight bullets from a Garand rifle after one enemy had plugged him through the helmet. A young Mexican sergeant from Denver killed five Germans after one of his men had been shot in the last spectacular charge of the ridge. --Hal Boyle]

November 27–Company C in Regimental Reserve. Turned in reports of being sniped at. An air support bombing mission at 1200 against Concacasale met with no enemy fire.

November 28–Second and Third Battalions were on the front, First Battalion in regimental reserve area. Third Battalion located a road running from Viticuso to Concacasale along which heavy enemy vehicles were moving.

Company C-PFC Robert R. Sucher died from being WIA on November 13th.

November 29–Second and Third Battalions were on the front at the beginning of the period. Patrols of both Battalions also located several enemy machine-gun positions. Third Battalion was being relieved by First Battalion at the close of the period.

Company C–S/Sgt. Max L. Johnson is evacuated to 56th Evacuation Hospital with fever of unknown origin. Pvt. Cecil G. Brewer is injured.

November 30–First Battalion was relieving Third Battalion at the beginning of period. Relief was accomplished just before dawn. First Battalion signal operating instructions reported missing at 1830. The missing instructions found at 0300 hours the following day.

December 1–First and Second Battalions were on the front throughout the day. Its patrols made no enemy contact. Second Battalion on front throughout the period, moved a platoon between Hills 460 and 470; discovered enemy on Hill 460, attacked and forced enemy to withdraw; both Battalions on front sent out patrols after sundown. In p.m., twelve planes that dropped bombs east and southeast of the 157th Infantry Regimental Command Post were found by Second Battalion to be ours from propaganda leaflets dropped. The Field Artillery 158th, in support, fired mission on enemy troops in Concacasale.

Company C–Pvt. Douglas A. Bibb is promoted to private first class. Pvt. Leonard Decker is injured.

December 2–First and Second Battalions were on the front again. Third Battalion was in Regimental Reserve. First Battalion patrolled before dawn and after sundown. Patrols in the a.m. found suspected enemy on Hill 770 and found Germans on Mount Fialla. First Battalion observers directed support artillery fire on a group of houses, possibly command post of supply installation. First Battalion also noted enemy fire beginning when green flare went up over Hill 1052 and ceasing on white flare. First Battalion further noted enemy firing machine-guns from Hill 769 toward end of period. Artillery support of the 157th Infantry was active all through period. Our aircraft were very active over enemy lines in direction of Cassino until dusk.

Company C–PFC Leo Blanchette and PFC Leland Scott are promoted to corporal. Cpl. Roscoe Prince is KIA; Sgt. Robert Kirchgassner is WIA. Weather is rainy.

[A Purple Heart was awarded to Sgt. Robert Kirchgassner on this date with injury to left hand as documented on the back of his Honorable Discharge papers.—Rita Kirchgassner]

[Read Jared's blog in chapter 5 about the day Corporal Prince was killed. Prince had been with Dad since advanced training at Pine Camp, New York. They had become good comrades, and his death was a terrible blow to Dad. Essie, my sister, remembers Dad taking her to meet Prince's family in West Virginia after the war had ended.—Rita Kirchgassner]

45th Infantry Mule Pack Train.
Pozzouli, Italy in background.
SC Photo-Lapidus

Rita at Cpl. Roscoe
Prince's Grave

December 3–First Battalion patrols to Hill 750 and Mount Fialla—both unoccupied. Found activity on Hill 770—Cannon Company fired on this hill the rest of the night. Plans for First Battalion patrols to take prisoners and find a new route to Hill 460. At 1600-#610 radio was captured intact by the enemy; contained Army "A" and Wisdom channels.

December 4–First Battalion patrols went south of 770-heard no activity-another patrol went west of Mount Fialla, heard a probable German patrol of 5 men-made no contact with it. Third Battalion completed relief of Second Battalion at 0400. Second Battalion returned to Regimental Reserve. 504th Infantry paratroopers patrol heard digging and chopping by the enemy to lead patrols into an ambush near 000208. Wire strung just above ground running around a hundred to 150 yards with TNT attached.

At 1300 Third Battalion received heavy artillery barrage was followed by infantry attack. Attack was repulsed. Battalions received artillery fire during the night. Four Axis enemy soldiers taken during the period.

December 5–Third Battalion received enemy mortar fire at 0845, about fifty rounds. At. 0940, fifteen more rounds enemy mortar fire on Company B. No damage done. Commanding General, Forty-Fifth Division, visits regimental headquarters, discussing situation with commanding officer of regiment. At 1700 enemy artillery shells fall into regimental command post area. At 2155, Third Battalion contact patrol from Company E contacted Company A-Patrol from Company K returns with information that a gap in fill in road will have to be bridged-gap blown about twenty feet across.

December 6–The regimental position remained virtually the same—First Battalion holding the left flank of the regimental sector and Third Battalion on the right. Action on whole line limited to recon at night. Mine field put in by First Battalion at 012239. Fifteen rounds of 150mm artillery fell in the regimental command post at 0923. Numerous color flares observed during night.

Company C–PFC Bryon Timmons and Cpl. Roman Jozefowicz are dropped from the rolls due to injuries from being in action. Enlisted men: 165.

December 7–Troop dispositions remained same with night combat and recon patrols working in front-west of Battalion areas. Truck vehicles were heard on Viticuso-Concacasale Road. The Second Battalion was ordered to relieve the First Battalion by daylight, December 8. Company C received mortar fire and artillery fire intermittently; during morning more than a hundred rounds fell on their positions. Second Battalion moved out at dusk to relieve First Battalion.

Company C– PFC Teton Hurtado is evacuated after being WIA. PFC Carl J. Vroman is KIA.

December 8–Relief of First Battalion completed at 0345 by Second Battalion, which returned to regimental reserve. At 1400 eight A-36's attacked Viticuso. At 1710, Second Battalion received fifty rounds of artillery. Probably 150 mm-Enemy horse mounted recon troops reported in this sector.

December 9–Early in the morning Company L was fired upon by machine-guns, machine pistols and mortar. At 1130 bombing missions on Casale and Viticuso. Normal interdictions on both fronts by enemy artillery and mortar.

Company C-Pvt. Michael R. Gueli is WIA.

December 10–Information from POWs stated that four Germans dressed as monks would try to infiltrate through our lines and blow up rear installations. At 1440 hours, a flight of twelve American aircraft bombed Casale.

Company C-Troops rested and cleaned up. Morale good.

December 11–A contact patrol working reported trails and road to Concacasale mined and booby trapped. First Battalion at 1900 to relieve Company L on Hill 460 by daylight on December 12. At 1730 enemy shelled Hills 460 and 470 and occupied Hill 470. All available mortars, chemicals, and artillery shelled Hill 470 until 2400. Continued to hold defensive position and usual combat duties. A fifteen-man raiding party from First Battalion will hit Hill 470 at 2400 following a thirty-minute preparation by artillery and mortar.

Company C-Pvt. Harold Scott (MOS 603) joins Company C.

December 12–Reports from recon patrols enemy is well dug in and determined to hold ground in front of regimental sector. Increase of artillery fire on both battalions, time, 0515, 0845, 1210, 1305, 1325, 1340, 1410, and 1700. Four enemy soldiers were taken by outposts and security patrols.

Company C-Cpl. Ross L. Baker, Pvt. John B. Chavez, Pvt. William V. Feinberg and 2nd Lt. Stephen M. Messineo are WIA. Pvt. Calvin L. Cahoon and Sgt. Wilbur H. Craig are injured.

December 13–Raiding party from Company C attacked at 0100. Got to the top of Hill 470. Received rifle and machine-gun fire from positions on Hill 470. Withdrew to Hill 460 and again attacked at 0440 with twenty-five men and engaged in a firefight until dawn. Again withdrew to Hill 460. Other patrols from First Battalion working Hill 769 found mines and trip wires at 025255. Observed artillery fire was delivered on enemy's command post and troop concentrations during the day. Staff conference at 1400 to discuss details of corps attack ordered for December 15 at 0630.

Company C–Sgt. Robert Kirchgassner is evacuated to the 38th Evacuation Hospital for acute cellulitis in left hand. PFC Teton Hurtado is WIA and Pvt. Sylvester A. Tencza is KIA.

December 14–Company B sent strong combat patrols to Hill 460 and Hill 470. Following a firefight, the outpost on Hill 460 could not be contacted, and it was assumed that it was captured. Four men from Company B were observed lying wounded on Hill 470 and could not be reached due to enemy mortars and artillery firing from west slope of Hill 831.

Company C-Cpl. Jose Padilla, PFC Wesley L. Lusk, Pvt. Robert M. Metz, PFC Victor C. Seidler are WIA. Pvt. Henry P. Narozny is injured.

December 15–The Third Battalion (less Company K) moved from their reserve position along road approximately 200 yards above regimental command post to await orders to be committed. Later they were returned to their former assembly area. Regiment attacked at 0630. Company C jumped off for Hill 470 at 0845 and withdrew for Hill 470 at 2000 after suffering casualties.

Company C–Pvt. Nelson L. Harvey, PFC John Nebelecky and PFC Frank J. Wachter and PFC Walter A. Nagel are WIA. Victor Staley is injured. PFC Eugene Benson, PFC Anthony Jose, Pvt. Hubert A. Morin, PFC Joseph W. Pawlik, Sgt. Harold R. Sayhouse, and PFC William G. Singleton are KIA.

The following soldiers became POWs on this date: Pvt. James H. Diehl, Pvt. Michael R. Gueli, Pvt. Joseph E. Koziol (escaped), Pvt. Chester G. McCoy (escaped), Pvt. Stephen J. Michelek, Pvt. Haskel T. Millwood, 2nd Lt. Louis A. Morgenrath (DOW), SSgt. Richard A. Morris (escaped), Pvt. Wilbert V. Rolves, PFC John H. Tourtilotte (escaped) and Pvt. Paul E. Wagner.

December 16–Company G attacked Hill 770 at 0340, encounter heavy opposition and was forced to withdraw to Hill 759. Company E reoccupied Mount Fialla during night, and at noon was counterattacked and forced to withdraw under smoke, suffering heavy casualties.

Company C–Pvt. Alfred R. Bombard and PFC Frederick D. Pape are WIA. Cpl. Angelo Ficuciello is evacuated for a self-inf licted wound. Does not return during the war.

December 17–Patrols started from each battalion to gain contact with enemy. Reached assigned objectives and reported positions vacated and enemy equipment strewn around in great quantity. Numerous dead both our own and Germans on hills involved in the past two days of fighting. Only artillery from fairly long range falling on the front. At 1600 hours regimental commanding officer ordered positions vacated by enemy occupied by our forward elements and patrols pushed out to contact enemy. Patrols reported enemy on high ground generally west of the Viticuso-Acquafondata Road.

December 18–Both battalions moved up on all positions abandoned by enemy—Hills 680, 831, 760, 580, and 770. Consolidation of positions and reorganization of companies occupied most of the day. Withdrawal seems to have been general along entire front. Harassing long-range artillery still falling in the vicinity of Hills 460 and 470. Five Axis enemy soldiers taken.

December 19–Near Viticuso, Italy. After contacting enemy forces on Hill 990, First Battalion pushed off at 1200 for Mount Cavallo and occupied it. Resistance was offered in way of small arms and artillery. Contact was again established by flank units.

Company C–Two enlisted men MIA as of the fourteenth returned to Company C.

December 20–At 0100 Company A received attack on Mount Cavallo from direction of 990. Estimated fifty enemy. Attach was repulsed but ammunition supply running low. Considerable heavy artillery and mortar fire dropped in saddle-Cavallo-Hill 850. Third Battalion ordered to relieve Second Battalion in daylight on December 21.

December 21–Second Battalion relieved by Third Battalion reverts to Regiment Reserve at 048217. Enemy very active, with mortar and artillery probably coming from the vicinity of Acquafondata. Night patrols limited by total blackness—no moon. Germans make extensive use of Pyrotechnics to direct and regulate artillery fire at night.

December 22–At 0700 Company B pushed off in attack on Hill 990-progressed satisfactorily. Received long range machine-gun and artillery fire. Point reached 992246 when they were hit from north and west by force of approximately 100 enemy that seemed to be moving to attack Cavallo. Company A to the south attacked to west to relieve some pressure on Company B. Company B forced back on Mount Cavallo and was replaced by Company K to reorganize. Companies A and C placed together under Lt. Ostrander-interdictory fire placed on Mount Cavallo with mortar and artillery fire by the enemy.

Company C–2nd Lt. Edward N. Kemper is WIA. Pvt. John A. Fischer Jr., serial number 33600528 (MOS 603), joins Company C. Pvt. Howard Lynch is assigned to the hospital for recurrent exhaustion. Does not return during the war.

December 23–All enemy contact is lost. Regiment spent day consolidating forward positions and moving mortar ammunition to forward gun positions as the lot it had was defective, and no preparation could be fired for Company B attack on the twenty-second. Visibility was limited by fog. No enemy were encountered either in town or in the general vicinity. Did not go to Monastery Ridge to west. Division reports all contact lost along the entire front except in the French sector to the north.

Company C- First Lt. Richard M. Stone is wounded in the left leg by shell fragment. PFC Stephen Mucha is WIA.

December 24–Patrols ordered out to gain contact. Hill 990 found empty and occupied by Company K platoon-Hill 1040 also deserted and occupied by our troops. Third Battalion reported seeing Germans on Hill 1130. Shortly before noon about twenty-five rounds of light artillery fell on Company K position. After that barrage, the entire front remained quiet. After dark 158th Field Artillery interdicted Viticuso and Acquafondata.

Company C–S/Sgt. Max L. Johnson returns to duty.

December 25–Third Battalion started relief of First Battalion at 0400 with Second Battalion taking over rear position of Third Battalion when relief was completed. Several rounds of heavy artillery fell on Company L in vicinity of Mount Cavallo. An escaped British POW passing through the lines reported that the Germans have dammed the river and are f looding Cassino Valley to the west.

Army commander visited and had dinner at the command post.

Company C–The fifteen enlisted men who were listed as MIA are dropped from the rolls. Near rest area in Viticuso. Pvt. Neil S. Anello, Forty-Fifth Division mule pack train, is evacuated for exhaustion (12/16/1943.)

December 26–Patrol from Company I ordered to Hill 1130 started across southeastern slope 990 were bracketed by mortars. Returned and tried northeast side. Second Battalion sent patrol to south of Hill 1130, became disoriented and wound up in a skirmish with enemy outpost. Knocked out machine- gun manned by two men. Third Battalion received several rounds of mortar and artillery on reverse south slope of Mount Cavallo.

Company C–PFC John A. Chorba and Pvt. Edward A. Schemansky are evacuated to the 38th Evacuation Hospital for trench foot.

December 27–Third Battalion patrol saw enemy outpost on Hill 1060. Patrol ran into more enemy personnel estimated at twenty men and engaged in a fire fight-two were killed and two wounded. Second Battalion patrols went to Hill 960 and found it unoccupied. Moved on to Hill 1020 and found enemy dugouts and moved over to Hill1130. Found several dugouts with guns pointing southwest and did not engage them.

December 28–Second Battalion started relief of Third Battalion at 0400. First Battalion took over positions of Second Battalion patrols. Three inches of snow on the ground showed no tracks. Town of Viticuso deserted—encountered only one civilian. Remained there till 1500. Artillery fire on enemy troops and reported command post. Few rounds of enemy fire fell on both Battalions during the night. Moved from Venafro area back to hill at 1205. In defensive position; morale is good and weather is cold.

December 29–Second Battalion patrols operating and occupy Hill 990 meeting no resistance. Plans underway for attack by Second Battalion at dawn, December 30. Second Battalion to attack northwest toward Hill 1130 to keep Germans in that region unoccupied so that they can't reinforce the enemy units which will be under the attack of the 180th on the right. First Battalion was inactive.

December 30–Second Battalion attacked at dawn, Company G in advance, bulk of Company G reaches Hill 1040, encountering a heavy shell barrage upon moving through draw in vicinity of

Cavallo. A patrol was ordered to move through Viticuso if possible to determine where or not the Germans had withdrawn. Patrols reached Hill 911 and reported seeing enemy movement across the valley on Hill 1005. Patrol went no further. A second patrol went out on same mission tonight. Second Battalion prepares to return to rest area. Third Battalion resting, alerted to move up December 31.

December 31–Patrol returns at 0230 hours and reports having reached Viticuso without opposition. Third Battalion moves up and Second Battalion returns to rear. Patrol moves into Viticuso where civilians reported having seen 300 men on ridge west of the town four days ago. Patrol moves to ridge and finds abandoned equipment.

Patrol from First Battalion moves to southeast slope of Hill 1130 and encounters small arms fire from top of hill. Patrol attempts to move up on the hill from three different positions, but draws fire each time. Enemy shells land in Pozzouli and Venafro.

Morale good. Weather very cold. Some snow. The operations during the past month were carried out on difficult terrain, with high mountains, a lack of roads, and poor, muddy, icy trails making the supply most difficult. In addition to this, rain fell during most of the month, which increased the causalities considerably due to long periods of exposure while wet. Many evacuations were avoided by bringing in to battalion aid station for short periods. The men most affected by the weather and warming them as well as providing dry socks.

> [Knowing the inclement weather the Forty-Fifth encountered during these months in combat is the reason Jared Leiker, when we experienced inclement weather during our journey, called it "thunderbird weather."—Rita Kirchgassner]

Company C–One enlisted man goes AWOL, and PFC Teton Hurtado is dropped from rolls due to wounds in battle. S/Sgt. Max L. Johnson is evacuated for being ill.

The following men were WIA in 1943, but the exact date of each is unknown: Pvt. Ronald MacDonald, Cpl. Wesley V. Miller, Pvt. Sidney Pollock, Pvt. William J. Schreibeck, S/Sgt. Charlie P. Wahl and Sgt. Clyde H. Wren.

Chapter 4

Hades

You haven't been to hell until you've been to Anzio.
—American GI

Operation Husky-

[Because of the stalemate by Monte Cassino, it was decided to go behind enemy lines in order to trap the Germans. It was also a practice run for Operation Overlord- Normandy invasion. The invasion took the Germans totally by surprise. -John Kirchgassner]

From the 157th Regiment Journal, Morning Reports, and After-Action Reports of Company C, 1944 (National Archives)

January 1, 1944–Holding defensive positions. Morale good, weather cold. Snow is making operations difficult. Visibility limited to fifty feet. First and Third Battalions on the line. Two men from Company D hit by a mine and taken to aid station. From the regiment, Lt. Jean M. Unterberger and Pvt. R. J. Groeger designated as men to attend intelligence school in North Africa. Near Viticuso, Italy.

Company C-Pvt. Virgil Green, Pvt. Quienton Steele, Pvt. William Mutchler, Pvt. Peter E. Krawczel, and Pvt. John Schweisthal are promoted to private first class. Cpl. Leo Blanchette is evacuated for being sick.

January 2–Active patrolling through the day. One prisoner taken. First and Third Battalions still on the line. Held position on Hill 1040; Company C sent out patrols to Hill 1060 thought unoccupied by received rifle fire from that hill when they try to move up it later in the day. Division artillery pours concentration on Mount Molino, an enemy strong point. First Battalion two-man patrol observed enemy and drew mortar fire from vicinity of 963242. Plans underway for patrols from both battalions to operate under the cover of darkness.

January 3–Enemy artillery units active through early morning hours. Had heaviest causalities since December 21. Our artillery concentrates on Mount Molino again. Company C marched to rest area; arrived at 2330. Usual bivouac duties. Enemy aircraft overhead.

Company C– PFC Quienton Steele is evacuated for being sick.

January 4–Second and Third Battalions on the line. Plans under way for a dawn attack on Hill 1130 by Third Battalion on January 5. The FSSF (First Special Service Force, the Devil's Brigade commandos), made up of American and Canadian soldiers, assist the 157th Regiment in battle. Plan to hold hill until relieved by Fifth Army. Plans made anew when General Eagles issues counter orders. Commanding general does not want hill occupied. Regimental forces are to divert attention from FSSF when it attacks at dawn. Patrols to operate between FSSF troops and regimental troops.

[The History Channel has a documentary on the Devil's Brigade attack on Mt. Mayo.—Rita Kirchgassner]

Company C–Cpl. Leo Blanchette and PFC Douglas A. Bibb are evacuated to 38th Evacuation Hospital for trench foot. Pvt. Ray Neitz is promoted to corporal.

January 5–Second and Third Battalions on the line. Artillery active as Third Battalion twenty-six man patrol locates enemy atop Hill 1130. Firefight ensues. Enemy driven out. Division orders troops to hold Hill 1130 and await further orders. At 1800 troops on Hill 1130 ordered to withdraw and await further orders. First Battalion moves up to relieve Second Battalion and Second Battalion to relieve Third Battalion before daylight January 6.

January 6–First and Second Battalions on the line. Snow and ice hampering patrolling. FSSF will attack Mount Mayo at dawn January 7.

January 7–First and Second Battalions on the line. Regiment to operate small combat patrol on Hill 1130. While FSSF attacks Hill 1005 and continues to objective. At 0930 FSSF occupies Hill 1239. Regimental troops also reach hill. Enemy counterattacks FSSF on Hill 1239. Our troops there receive mortar fire. Patrol to 1146 fired upon by machine patrol. Patrol bypassed firer and moved to within 300 yards of top of the hill. Enemy outpost being changed was observed. Company still in position on Hill 831. French officers were shown positions.

Company C–Weather cold. Two enlisted men of Company C who went AWOL are sent to Naples pending trial.

January 8–First and Second Battalions on the front-line positions. Day quiet with patrolling limited. Preparations were being made for relief. Artillery active. Forward observers see FSSF moving to Mount Mayo.

January 9–French troops relieve regiment and occupy all front-line positions. Close command post and move to rest area. Open new command post at 373997. All passed inspection at 0800 and moved from positions on Hill 831 at 0830. Arrived at assembly area at 0930. Moved out of assembly area near Pozzilli at 0930. Entrucked near Venafro at 1300. Detrucked at 1515 in rest area, Gioia, Italy.

Company C–Usual rest-period duties; bivouac near town. Morale very good, weather fair.

January 10–Last elements leave command post. Second Battalion in rest area in last of group troop movements. Troops cleaning up and resting; weather excellent. Received 241 replacements in the regiment, many noncommissioned. No causalities.

[The regiment had been on the line for seventy-two continuous days of combat.—Hugh F. Foster III]

January 11–Company C–Hyman Miller, serial number 33000443, returns to duty. Missing entries of assignment and evacuation.

January 1–20–This marks the first time in more than four months that the regiment had not been engaged in attacking the enemy. More than five hundred replacements were received, and the regiment was almost back to its total authorized strength. The time was spent in rest, care and cleaning of equipment, small unit problems, and firing of weapons. Through the special services section, movies were presented nightly, and there were personal appearances by Joe E. Brown and Humphrey Bogart. The troops were trucked twice to Piedmont to take advantage of the shower units located there. Some officers and men from the regiment attended a mountain training school where they tested mountain equipment and communications in deep snow and near-zero weather.

Company C–Morale very good, weather fair.

January 13–S/Sgt. John R. Clements is assigned to Company C. Company C is now in Telese, Italy.

January 14–Company C–Sgt. Robert Kirchgassner is ill and dropped from rolls. No reason given. **[Hugh F. Foster III states: "Your dad was probably dropped while still hospitalized with his cellulitis."]** Pvt. Horace Simon Jr. is promoted to private first class.

January 15–Company C– Pvt. Edward Schemansky is dropped from rolls.

January 16–Company C– PFC James W. Barkley returns to duty.

January 18–Thirty-two enlisted men assigned to Company C. Sgt. Robert L. Kirchgassner returns to Company C.

January 21–Alert to move. Troops readying for journey to staging area near Naples.

Company C–First Lt. Anse Speairs returns from a period of hospitalization.

Loading onto LST, before Anzio
163rd SC Photo-Blau

January 22–Still awaiting orders to move. Word received that Allies landed unopposed this morning on a beach south of Rome (Anzio).

Company C–Cpl. Quienton Steele is dropped from rolls.

January 23–Still on alert. Tentative date for H-Hour is 1400, January 24. Usual bivouac area duties, making preparations to move, and morale is good.

Company C–Pvt. Howard Lynch is dropped from the rolls. Two enlisted men who went AWOL are in the Fifth Army stockade and awaiting trial. Enlisted men: 217

January 24–At 2200 moved about sixty miles by truck to the vicinity of Casapuzzano, Italy. Order of March 3-2-1-Q.

Company C–PFC Virgil Green is promoted to corporal.

January 25–Division and regiment authorized second star for two campaigns in Mediterranean Theater. Plans under way for loading of troops and vehicles aboard LCIs and LSTs on January 26. Arrive at Casapuzzano at 0130 hours.

Company C–Sgt. Robert L. Kirchgassner becomes staff sergeant. PFC Douglas A. Bibb is ill; no reason given. Cpl. Ray E. Neitz and Cpl. Leland Scott are promoted to sergeant.

January 26–Left bivouac area and arrived at another bivouac area at 1200. Await orders to embark. (No. 3 staging area.) (Troops move to Crater and Nicita staging areas near Naples.)

January 27–Left staging area at 1530 and marched three hours to the Port of Naples. First Battalion embarked on LCI 33 at 2000.

January 28–Entire regiment aboard landing crafts and under way at 1800 hours. At sea. Company C–PFC John Chorba is dropped from the rolls, and Cpl. Virgil Green is promoted to sergeant.

Anzio

January 29–157th Infantry arrives at deserted and battered port of Anzio at 0900 and debarked. Unloading of troops and equipment begins at that time and continues until 1355. Marched to bivouac area six miles from harbor north of Nettuno. Regiment receives three air attacks during the day. Receive corps alert as to the possibility of enemy paratroopers being dropped. All battalions notified. One officer from each battalion ordered out on road reconnaissance in case of possible commitment tonight to protect flanks.

Anzio Harbor-February 1943
163rd SC Photo-Bonnard

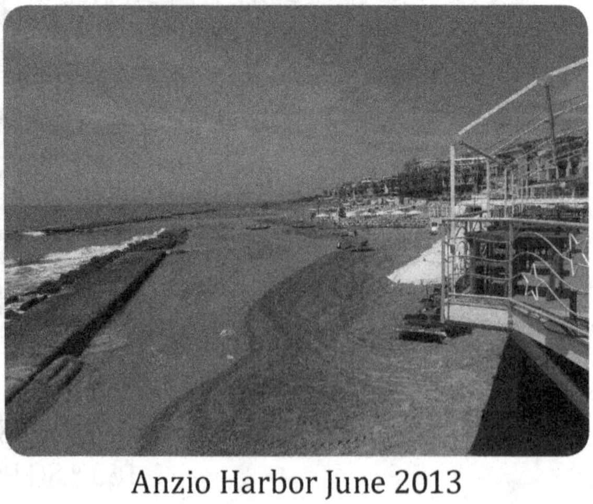

Anzio Harbor June 2013

January 30–158th Field Artillery reports nine twenty-seven enlisted men wounded and three officers wounded, result of last night's bombing raid. Commanding general orders one company on reinforced alert (one hour) for possible parachute attack. Company C designated as mobile alert unit by commanding officer, First Battalion time 1445: regiment on one-hour alert. At the end of the month the regiment was holding a line, defending the beachhead from attack down the coast from the north.

Company C-Bivouac area near Anzio. Enlisted men: 217.

January 31-At 0800 all battalion commanders were called to the command post for instructions on the 45th counter attack. Battalion commanders were alerted to move to area, and conduct reconnaissance of the area. At 1100, unit commanding officers returned and troops started movement in order 1, 2, 3, Q.

First and Second Battalions to move out at 2000 and 2130 respectively.

Summary: The last few days the regiment spent in action against the enemy in the mountains north of Venafro were marked by bitter cold and driving snow which hampered operations and increased our losses to frost bite and trench foot. At the close of January, the regiment as holding a line, defending the beachhead from attack down the coast from the north.

February 1–At 0355, First Battalion completed relief of Second Battalion, Thirty-Sixth Engineers. At 0420, Second Battalion completed relief of Third Battalion, Thirty-Sixth Engineers. First Battalion observed enemy troops at 775315.

At 1105 one platoon of mine sweepers attached to First Battalion for mine laying detail.

At 1545, 894th Tank Destroyer Battalion, two companies attached to regiment, already in position. Fire defense plan of First Battalion and unit dispositions of Second Battalion sent to division.

Second Battalion ordered to move up immediately to limiting line instead of planned time at 2130.

February 2– Two seven-man patrols one from Company G and one from Company F were sent out by Second Battalion after midnight. The patrol from Company G encountered small arms and automatic weapons fire and scattered. Three men were reported missing but returned to their unit.

Difficulty arose in coordinating right boundary of the British brigade on the right. Telephone communication used to secure contact with an officer of the British North Staffordshire Regiment with the left flank.

Orders received to keep civilians from passing through the areas.

Patrol from First Battalion sent out during the night reported that some empty German foxhole were found.

At 1040 artillery fell on part of Company C, Second Battalion command post and Companies E and F. At 1650, twelve enemy planes f lew over area. Report came in by phone from Lieutenant Russell, G Company, that while marching east on highway to rejoin company, one platoon was bombed and strafed, causing seventeen casualties—one killed and sixteen wounded.

An enemy reconnaissance in a force of about sixty men armed with automatic weapons appeared in front of Company A's sector at 1700 and fired artillery on it. Company A fired with small arms, dispersing the enemy troops and inflicting several casualties. Communications Officer Lieutenant Elliot reported that a bomb fell in the old command post area just vacated and wounded the switchboard operator at central switching there.

Company B observed an eight-man German patrol at 1855. Artillery fired upon the patrol and a platoon followed up the barrage and captured one German. The German was found to be a paratrooper. He was the first enemy soldier captured by this regiment on this beachhead.

February 3–In position on left side of the coast road northwest of Anzio. The period opened with continual enemy patrol in our sector. An enemy patrol worked into positions of Second Battalion and fired flares. Patrol withdrew.

Enemy shelled positions five times during the daylight hours. Enemy patrols were active on the front at night and used extensive flares along the front.

Our troops were told not to fire on C-47 aircraft f lying over our area throughout the daylight hours.

Second Battalion was ordered to be relieved by Third Battalion after dark. Second Battalion reverted to Regimental Reserve.

One platoon of Company A, 120th Engineers assisted First Battalion laying wire across their front during the night.

Regiment was warned of possible tank attack between eighty-two and eighty-eight grid line on front line. All AT and TD (Tank Destroyer) personnel were warned.

Company C–S/Sgt. Robert Kirchgassner evacuated for furuncle on the back of the neck. Pvt. Catarino A. DeLeon is WIA.

February 4–At 0245, the Third Battalion completed the relief of Second Battalion. During the day Third Battalion was subjected to some artillery fire. This evening Third Battalion reported a six-barrel mortar firing on it, the first report of the use of this weapon in this sector. The First Battalion sector was quiet during the day, and battalion plans to move to command post in the morning.

February 5–Northwest of Anzio. At midnight, a heavy infiltration of German forces was made in Company L's area and was stopped by light machine-gun fire. A Company I outpost of four men were jumped by an enemy patrol and the men scattered in the dark. One man was hit and failed to return. He could not be located by a searching party which was sent out later.

Held positions as enemy increased shelling. First Battalion reported at 1230 hours that one of our planes was shot down over enemy territory and that the pilot bailed out. A patrol went out to try to rescue him, but he had landed behind enemy lines.

Organization of the battalions was continued and mine fields laid and plotted. One squad of engineers from Company A was sent to each Battalion after dark. Scattered artillery fire continued to fall in the Third Battalion area. Enemy patrolling limited tonight.

Company C–Morale of troops is good.

February 6–Active patrolling, brief brushes with the enemy, and interdictory artillery fire marked the early hours. The enemy continued to feel out the line, pressing forward slightly on the regiment's right flank, but was driven back by small-arms and mortar fire. At dawn the Luftwaffe attacked the harbor but departed amid an intense barrage of anti-aircraft fire.

Forward observers reported the enemy massing tanks and troops in several areas but there was no indication of an attack in force. First and Third Battalions on the line received several heavy shellings during the day and in the afternoon. Eleven US planes miscalculated their targets and bombed and strafed our troops, killing one and wounding two others. Company E relieved these troops at 2130 and moved to reserve position three miles away.

Company C-Morale is good.

February 7–A few minutes after midnight, Lieutenant Patterson reported that one platoon of Company F was captured. Second Battalion verified the breakthrough. At 0045 the regimental commander ordered Second Battalion to counterattack and restore the position. By 0100 hours, the battalion reported that Company F's commander believed his platoon was still intact and he was restoring the position. The Second Battalion commanding officer reported that the enemy had made a diversionary attack on the left platoon of Company F and when the support was sent forward, the enemy withdrew.

Enemy artillery was falling heavily along the entire regiment front line by 0210. By 0305 hours an estimated seven hundred rounds had fallen in this sector, with the major portion of the barrage on the left flank. A large amount of small-arms fire was being directed at First Battalion at 0350. Company I's right flank received artillery air bursts in the vicinity of 900338 and 8933. Enemy troops were fired on at 0420 hours. At 0600 our regiment reported to Division G-3 that the sector had quieted down. We were warned that radar had picked up a concentration of enemy vehicles in the Cisterna-Littoria area. Second Battalion reported five causalities at 0605 hours as a result of an artillery barrage during the night.

The daylight hours were quiet. All units were warned not to fire at a C-47 passing over at 1000 hours. The North Staffordshire regiment on our right reported that through a prisoner it had learned that there was enemy armor at 880355 and also that a paratroop drop might be expected.

By 2040 hours enemy shelling was general throughout the regimental sector. Third Battalion reported a heavy enemy attack between Company L and North Staffordshire was developing. The troops were receiving heavy artillery fire and small arms fire. Company E also received small arms fire.

The British reported armor moving at 865350. The Third Battalion sector still was under control at 2115 but the troops were receiving concentrated machine-gun fire. At 2154, Third Battalion received heavy firing believed to come from tanks in the vicinity of the main road in front of the British.

The German attack continued to develop, and at 2158 hours, Third Battalion called for all the artillery fire that could be mustered. One platoon of Company K, in the Battalion reserve, moved over to Company L's right flank at 2219 hours in the vicinity of 8437. The enemy pushed developed between Company L and the British North Staffs. The British reported that more than fifty enemy had infiltrated through the lines and could not be located. The North Staffs reported sending troops down the draw to regain their original position. Part of one platoon of Company K moved over as further reinforcement for the right flank troops of Company L.

Three green Very pistol flares, followed immediately by two more, went up in front of Company I at 2235. All fire except for a few machine-guns, had virtually ceased. Company I was reported for a possible attack.

By 2251 hours, the front had quieted. The unit of Company K, which had moved up to Company L's right flank was ordered back into Battalion reserve. Third Battalion still maintaining its original position, was reorganized for a possible attack. Company L, which was in close contact with enemy in the fire fight, called for litter bearers at 2310.

Artillery fire, probably from tanks, began falling in Company H's area at 2317 hours. Maj. John G. Boyd, 2nd Battalion Commander, was killed almost instantly by an enemy shell. His orderly was seriously wounded. Capt. Merle M. Mitchell assumed command of the battalion.

Second Battalion reported a frontal attack starting on Company F at 2340 in the same place as the night of February. The enemy continued to press but the situation remained well in hand. Company I reported two men missing in action and one heavy machine-gun lost. Company L reported a section of HMG's knocked out and six causalities. At midnight the situation of both forward battalions was serious, not critical.

Company C-Pvt. Woodson Herring, Pvt. William J. Otter and S/Sgt. Jose Padilla are WIA.

[Third Battalion was hit hard that night, especially Company L.
— Hugh F. Foster III]

February 8–At midnight, the German pressure on Company I had forced the troops out of part of their positions on the right flank and they were counterattacking to regain lost ground.

All small arms fire in the Second Battalion sector had stopped by 0015 and only some long range artillery still fell there. Small arms fire started again in Company L's sector at 0036. At 0117, the Third Battalion commanding officer reported another group of enemy approaching from the rear. Company F sent a platoon at 0136 hours down the draw to clean it out so that the company could return to its positions.

A group of enemy soldiers broke through the British line and roamed at large behind their front. One company of the Irish Guards went out to head off the group, but missed it.

Division was informed at 0216 that the enemy had penetrated to 861322 and one company of the 504th Paratroops was to attack in the advance of their battalions in an effort to gain new ground. Enemy artillery began firing on Company E at 0218.

Company K cleaned out the pocket in the center of the Third Battalion sector and captured two

Germans from the Fourth Company, 145th Regiment, and Sixty-Fifth Division. The regiment executive officer notified the Third Battalion commanding officer that the raid which had been planned in front of the Battalion would be carried out on schedule if possible.

Division was notified at 0245 hours that lost positions of Company I had been retaken and all companies reorganized; double guard had been placed in the rear installations. Patrols were operating in rear areas.

Small arms fire was again falling on Companies I and L at 0322. A report from the Third Battalion from the North Staffs on our right stated that one platoon was without automatic weapons of any kind and that there was a gap between them and the next right flank unit. The rumbling of tanks could be heard in the vacant sector.

Enemy tanks previously reported on the right began firing on Third Battalion at 0400. The North Staffs on the right of the Third Battalion reported they had seventy men in danger of getting encircled so attached them on agreement to the Third Battalion. The Third Battalion was ordered to swing its reserve to the right flank to meet the threat from the east.

By 0420, Division G-2 reported that the British unit on the right reported a gap in its line between the Second North Staffs and the Grenadier Guards, with enemy coming through, although not in great numbers.

Third Battalion reported twelve enemy tanks and infantry at 841326. The regimental commanding officer ordered the Third Battalion to move its reserve to the right flank if not being hit elsewhere. Also, Third Battalion commanding officer requested permission to move Company L back from the high ground which was under artillery fire, to along the stream bed. The permission was granted with the limitation that he was not to move back to the final beachhead line unless absolutely necessary.

Sixth Corps at 0450 verified the breakthrough and stated it extended as far as the main north-and-south road. Suggested moving back to the final beachhead line if necessary. Third Battalion ordered to reconnoiter the final beachhead line at 0516. The British were reported as moving up reserves to counterattack to regain their positions in the vicinity. By 0555, Company L was receiving some machine-gun fire from the right and the front and had started falling back to the stream bed as planned. Third Battalion requested artillery fire on the position vacated by the British to protect the withdrawal of Company L.

A 2½-ton truck from Service Company, loaded with six hundred rounds of 81mm mortar ammunition, hit a mine and blew up at 0630 hours. The driver, thrown clear by the mine, took shelter behind a stone wall before the main explosion and was uninjured.

Division reported at 0650 hours that the British were going to make a recon along the road inside our right boundary and warned us not to fire there unless absolutely necessary to protect our right flank from attack. At 0755 the Twenty-Fourth British Guards informed us that they had reconnaissance out and were going to attempt to regain the area lost. By 0830, Third Battalion reported seeing the British had reached the coordinating point on our right boundary and the commanding officer of the Third Battalion was ordered to contact them. British armored cars continued to travel the unimproved road just inside our right boundary and drew much heavy artillery fire on Companies K and L. G-3 was asked to contact the British to ask them to cease using the road.

Company E of the 179th Infantry was moving up to the switch position in rear of Third Battalion and completed occupation of its position by 2220 without incident.

A small enemy group was reported to be infiltrating into the Second Battalion are in the same region that similar group had attempted entry the night before. The enemy failed to accomplish its mission.

The contact patrol from the Third Battalion found the only enemy located in the vicinity of the coordinating point. The command post of the Forresters was unable to give definite information as to the location of the left flank troops so the commanding officer of the Third Battalion was ordered to remain in his present position until the British left flank was definitely located. Company I captured two enemy soldiers, both Poles. At midnight, the regimental sector was relatively quiet and all troops in the same position as before.

[Once again the beachhead was in danger. Artillery rained down on the Germans—twenty-four thousand rounds in a single 2½-hour period—and Third Battalion's mortars poured out an incredible 9,200 rounds. The German attack was stopped. The regiment was relieved by British forces and moved to the center of the Allied line, taking positions forward of the overpass along the Albano-Anzio highway.—Hugh F. Foster III]

February 9–Company L was still being shelled heavily at 0020. Division G-2 reported that the enemy had made a slight break in the British sector and reached the bridge at 8632 by 0105 hours. The enemy attack, begun during the night in the British sector, resumed during the morning, the German troops supporting tanks. Division G-2 reported that the drive from the northwest had reached 8533 and the attack from the northeast in the area had reached 886333. Third Battalion reported at 1103 that the enemy now occupied the former positions of Company L. A large formation of our bombers flew over at 1710 hours toward the factory area and beyond, unloading their sticks. First Battalion began the relief of Third Battalion at 1815. Heavy artillery was again falling on Third Battalion at 2231. Activity was concentrated mainly near the main road and factory area during the day.

Company C-S/Sgt. Robert B. Whitworth is WIA.

[The Germans launched a tank-supported attack against the regiment. Company E was destroyed and Company G held its ground only after the company commander called artillery fire on his own positions. The Second Battalion adjutant, Capt. Felix L. Sparks, was sent forward to take command of the remnants of Company E, but the enemy attacks were so fierce and concentrated—the Germans drove right up to the foxhole line in tanks and fired the main guns directly into the holes—that only Sparks and two men survived from the company.—Hugh F. Foster III]

February 10–By 0205 hours, the relief of Third Battalion had been completed without incident. Our sector continued to be quiet. In the afternoon, word reached regiment that the Thirty-Sixth Engineers would take over the left half of our sector, now occupied by Second Battalion and Forty-Fifth Reconnaissance Troops. A limiting point at 811310 was agreed upon, reconnaissance of positions made and warning orders issued.

At 1630, Company E of the 179th Infantry was notified that it would be relieved at dark by Company I.

The Thirty-Sixth Combat Engineer Regiment began the relief of the left flank troops in the regimental sector at 1830 and opened their command post at 1900 hours. Our Antitank guns remained in position until the engineers could move theirs into the sector.

At midnight, the relief still was being effected and the entire front at 2400 was extraordinarily quiet.

Company C-PFC Maurice Curtis and Pvt. James R. Reames are WIA.

February 11–Completion of the relief of the Second Battalion by the Thirty-Six Combat Engineer Regiment was accomplished at 0157. Our sector remained quiet during the day.

Division G-3 reported that the 179th Infantry, attacking in the factory area, had not encountered too much resistance. From 1700 to 1900 hours, the First Battalion was heavily shelled, especially the A and C Company areas. Small arms fire was exchanged in front of Company A's position at 2027.

February 12–Northwest of Anzio. Held defensive positions. The night into February 12 was quiet in the regimental sector. Division reported that the 179th Infantry in the factory area to the east of us had taken possession there without too much difficulty, using two companies supported by tanks.

The Thirty-Sixth Combat Engineer Regiment on our left was placed under control of the commanding officer of the 157th Infantry.

At 1317, regiment received the report that a 10-man German patrol had infiltrated through the lines of the Thirty-Sixth Engineers at 792318, captured an outpost of two men, a caliber .50 machine-gun with two man crew, and three men from a 37mm AT gun, during daylight subsequent patrolling failed to locate any of them still within the position.

The entire front was lighted by enemy flares at 2110 hours working the front lines and then the Luftwaffe attacked the British sector and other targets to our rear. First Battalion received a heavy shelling at 2311, and Germans shelled other positions, adding small-arms fire. The latter was reduced considerably by our artillery fire. By midnight, virtually all enemy activity had ceased along the front of this sector and shifted to the British sector. Some infiltration of the enemy suspected near our right boundary.

February 13-Soon after midnight, the order from the corps was received to organize the beachhead line or switch position in rear of our front battalion, which had been started previously by the 179th Infantry, occupied in the past by its Company E and now manned by Company I. Company A reported capturing a an enemy soldier at 0285 hours. The German was brought to the POW enclosure for questioning.

The British Third Infantry Brigade, on our right, reported at 0715 hours that their left flank company had been attacked and the attack repulsed with a loss to the enemy of 18 men killed and four enemy soldiers captured. Plans for relief of the British Third Infantry Brigade by the 157th were started; in turn the 157th would be relieved by the British Fifty-Sixth Division.

The entire front was lighted up by f lares at 1900 but they proved to be dropped by our own aircraft and not German f lares as we had last night, preceding the enemy night bombings. Just before midnight the 45th Cavalry Reconnaissance Troop, less one platoon, was released and ordered into bivouac near 9323. Our platoon will continue to patrol the coastal road February 14. The sector was quiet during the night with only mild artillery interdiction.

Company C–S/Sgt. Robert Kirchgassner returns.

February 14–Only slight artillery and no patrol activity was reported after midnight. Division stated that the 179th Infantry had relieved its First Battalion with the Second Battalion.

At 1030, the staff officers from the British Fifty-Sixth Division arrived, were oriented and went forward to reconnoiter the positions. Additional tactical wire was laid by First Battalion in the forward position and Third Battalion in the switch position.

The front was quiet through the day. The relief of the 157th Infantry started at dark, and by midnight most of the units were off the front.

Company C–PFC Hanzel Blair is evacuated with fever of unknown origin. T/Sgt. James B. Trainor is injured and Pvt. Stanley J. Zielinski is WIA.

February 15–At 0345 hours the British relieved the First Battalion. The regiment yielded its front-line positions to the 167th British Brigade. The new regimental command post opened at 876275.

Company C–Sgt. Leland E. Scott is WIA, not hospitalized. Also WIA, Cpl. Ross L. Baker, Pvt. Calvin L. Cahoon, Pvt. John B. Chavez, Sgt. Wilbur H. Craig, Pvt. William V. Feinberg and 2nd Lt. Stephen M. Messineo. Pvt. Lawrence E. Mendel DOW (died of wounds) received on February 14, 1944.

February 16–Heavy artillery barrages covering the entire front gave warning early in the day that the enemy probably would attempt a breakthrough. At dawn the enemy attacked, hitting the left flank of the Second Battalion with infantry and tanks, giving way occasionally in the face of our small arms, mortar and artillery fire but continuing to press forward. At 1015 hours forward artillery observers reported that Company E's right flank had been completely overrun by tanks and that the enemy was in the Company E foxholes. The tanks led the German infantry in the attack, and when the infantry struck the line, fierce fighting ensued. The enemy successfully drove Company E out of position and captured many enemy soldiers in doing so.

Meanwhile, forward observers reported seeing several concentrations of tanks and other vehicles and inquired into the possibility of an air mission. On the left two British companies also had been overrun.

Successful in the initial phase of their breakthrough in the regimental sector, the Germans began to infiltrate between the Second and Third Battalions which were on the right, three kilometers to the rear in the gap between Second Battalion and the 179th Infantry. The commanding general ordered that a strong combat patrol be sent into the gap to drive out the infiltrating enemy at a point between the overpass and Second Battalion.

Company E in the meantime was receiving small arms fire from both flanks and tank fire from the right rear and the left rear.

In the 179th sector to the right the enemy launched another attack with seven tanks and infantry, heading straight down the road from the factory area. Assisting in the drive for the beach was the German Luftwaffe which strafed the front lines during the afternoon and made several attempts through the day to bomb artillery pieces in the rear. Intense ack ack fire and allied air umbrella kept the enemy planes from doing much damage in their daylight missions.

As nightfall approached, front-line observers could see reinforcements being brought to the front. The Germans were believed to be starting one last determined effort to drive the Allied forces off of the beachhead and would spare neither men nor equipment in doing so. Under cover of darkness, patrols began extensive operations, attempting to contact adjacent units as well as attempting to locate enemy troops and vehicle concentrations and locations. Second Battalion was alerted for a renewal of the attack, expected to be made the following day by a new outfit.

At 2030 hours AntiTank Company reported that thirteen enemy tanks at 315 on the main highway had knocked out one section of 57mm guns. At midnight contact was made with the Oxblood Battalion of the Oxford Buckinghamshire Regiment on the left of the regimental sector; it was found that only sixty-six men remained and the enemy was but fifty yards away from their positions.

Installations in the rear meanwhile were being subjected to heavy night bombing, part of the enemy air effort G-2 reported, the maximum the Germans could produce.

February 17–Shortly after midnight, Company E reported that the enemy was moving forward again, apparently coming from the right of the railroad yards at the f lyover-866326. Company E also reported the enemy infiltrating between the platoons.

Artillery and mortar fire was placed on the attacking troops in the vicinity of the RR yards and the enemy dispersed.

At 2200 hours the AT company commander reported the capture of two German soldiers who were digging in behind the Second Battalion Command Post. A combat patrol from Third Battalion was ordered to clear out other enemy who had infiltrated through the lines. The patrol was to operate along the sides of the north-south road.

Battery and counterbattery fire was continuous through the night. At 0340 hours, the regiment received word that the corps had granted the request for a strong air mission. Shortly after dawn several squadrons of bombers f lew across the lines and bombed enemy troop and vehicle concentrations as well as installations.

Communication with the forward battalions was poor, and only scattered reports came through to headquarters. At 1035 hours, Second Battalion reported repulsing an enemy attack in the vicinity of 858314. At 1040 hours, the Luftwaffe bombed the front lines and dropped anti-personnel bombs in the regimental command post area.

Our artillery continued to fire upon troop and vehicle concentrations.

At 1330 hours, the enemy bombed the command post, completely disrupting communications. There was little contact by wire or radio with forward battalions throughout the day. First Battalion moved closer to the front at 1410 and arrived at 1600. At 1635 hours, Third Battalion reported an undetermined number of enemy 400 yards in front of Company K and behind Second Battalion.

At 2015 hours, Second Battalion, almost completely cut off, reported all quiet. At midnight the Germans bombed the beach and all its sectors with anti-personnel bombs. The enemy's bombs were coming to be a regular occurrence.

Company C–S/Sgt. John Clements wounded in the right cheek and thigh from shell fragment. PFC Horace B. Simon Jr. wounded in the right elbow and thigh from bomb fragment. Does not return during the war. PFC John Schweisthal was WIA but not hospitalized. Pvt. Donald A. Coleman is WIA. Pvt. John Fisher is evacuated sick.

February 18–Continuous patrolling and artillery duels marked the early morning hours, but since communication was virtually at a standstill, the regiment found it nearly impossible to learn the situation on the front. The Second Battalion of the Sixth Armored Infantry was attached to the regiment and moved forward.

At 1050 hours, message through division artillery-Second Battalion, 157th Infantry expressed urgent need for three light mortars, two light machine-guns, two heavy machine-guns and ammunition.

At 1140 hours, the regimental commander ordered Third Battalion to close on Second Battalion and for the two units to establish contact with both flanks. Second Battalion was encountering the heaviest artillery fire it had ever been under and was being subjected to small-arms and tank fire from all directions. The battalion reported heavy infiltration in all areas of the sector but could not estimate the enemy strength in those positions. At 1807, the Third Battalion was ordered to attack with units of the Sixth Armored Infantry and to establish the line between Second Battalion and the 179th Infantry. The Second Battalion of the Sixth Armored Infantry was ordered to hold the old Third Battalion positions after the attack started.

At 1843, hand-to-hand fighting was reported at the overpass, the area occupied by Company I. The company held its ground and drove off the attackers. At 2130 hours the enemy attacked Second Battalion command post down the draw from the blacktop road. The attack was repulsed but the enemy continued to press his advantage. After dark, the Germans dropped anti-personnel bombs in all the sectors once again. First Battalion moved to forward positions on the right to take over front-line position. Began digging in at 2015 and took over front lines at 2400.

Company C: 2nd Lt. Stephen M. Messineo is KIA. PFC Robert J. Baldridge and Pvt. John E. Pass are WIA.

February 19–The activity of enemy personnel and tanks to the front gave indication of an early morning attack on Second Battalion. Front positions along road. Enemy shelled positions with heavy artillery. From 0400 to 0600 hours, the Second Battalion was subjected to continuous artillery fires. Then the shelling ceased abruptly, and tanks and infantry swung into action, breaking through in the 179th sector and cutting the Second Battalion and its companies off from the rear. At 0715 hours, twenty enemy planes bombed and strafed the Third Battalion near the overpass. Battalion maintained position. First Battalion took German enemy soldiers. During the morning the regimental command post moved back to the First Battalion command post. Regiment received reports that British Loyals were attacking enemy positions on the left flank of the 179th in effort to destroy the German foothold there.

At 0737 hours, Second Battalion call for outside help. The Sixth Armored Infantry was moved into a position between Second and Third Battalion. Division meanwhile, committed First Battalion to action with the 179th Infantry. At 1230 hours the regimental command post moved once again; this time to vicinity 842237. Through the remainder of the day only sporadic reports reached headquarters of troop and vehicle concentrations. After dark, Germans dropped anti-personnel bombs in all sectors once again.

Company C–Sgt. Hyman Miller WIA in the right buttock and right foot from a shell fragment. Also WIA is Sgt. Wilbur H. Craig.

February 20–Northwest of Anzio. Shortly after midnight Second Battalion reported it expected heavy infiltrations, although at that time it was quiet. Throughout the early morning hours the battalion reported hearing the sounds of equipment moving in the German sector.

At daybreak, Third Battalion called for fire on houses at 863292 and 862297. The fire drove the enemy out of the buildings and relieved slight pressure on Company I, which was being subjected to machine-gun fire from those positions. At 1540 Third Battalion reported six Tiger tanks and infantry at 9031 and enemy moving toward 887286. At 1700 hours, company reported the enemy smoking the east-west lateral road above the overpass. Information as to just what was happening on the front was difficult to get, and little could be learned of the general situation. At night, the Germans bombed once again.

Company C-Pvt. Claude A. Iron Hawk and Sgt. Lee A. Sylvester are WIA.

February 21–Northwest of Anzio. Heavy shelling by enemy. Usual patrolling and artillery duels marked the early morning hours although about 0400 hours an enemy tank slipped in on the right flank of Company K and opened fire. Artillery fire was placed on it and it ceased to bother the troops. There was no concerted effort to break through although the fighting throughout the day let up but little. The enemy's main effort apparently was one of infiltration. Second Battalion rear command post reported hand-to-hand fighting to the front. Last report on the front line activity came through at 1920 hours when regiment learned that the enemy was attacking down the draw at 860309. The Germans again bombed the beach after dark. The Third Battalion was relieved by the Scots Guards.

Anzio Harbor.
Pvt. Robert J. Schneider, Cpl. Laurence F. Williams
SC Photo-Leibowitz

February 22–At 0330 hours the report reached the regiment that enemy infiltration was so heavy that the British could not relieve Second Battalion. The British refused to take command until the situation was cleared, and it was apparent that the Second Battalion troops would have to fight their way out or all be captured. Throughout the day, reports drifted back through radio interceptions of tanks and enemy infantry hitting the line in many sectors, but there was no serious breakthrough. At 1750 hours the enemy laid a smoke screen at 855304, and enemy troops took advantage of it to infiltrate the area. The Second Battalion rear command post reported hearing Germans talking all over the draw. Little could be learned of the general situation.

Company C-Pvt. George D. Gates is injured. PFC John B. Chavez, PFC Peter F. Krawczel, and T/Sgt. Jack S. Miller are WIA.

February 23–Early in the morning the Twenty-Seventh Queens Battalion took over the Second Battalion's position, but little could be learned of the whereabouts, the strength, or welfare of the Second Battalion itself. The Second Battalion had reported that the artillery forward observer was surrounded by snipers and machine gunners, but that was the last word from the battalion until almost dawn. At 0425, Colonel Brown reported that he evacuated what was left of the Second Battalion to the rear command post and would proceed from there. At 0600 hours the regiment received the report that the Second Battalion had been cut in two by machine-gun fire from a house six hundred yards from the main highway (852302). Shortly after daylight what remained of the Second Battalion reached the reserve area, and through the day, men straggled back from the front. At 1307 hours the forward echelon of the regiment moved to the new command post at 905243. For a change the Germans failed to bomb the beach.

Company C-S/Sgt. Jose Padilla is WIA.

February 24–Company C northwest of Anzio. Heavy shelling continues. The entire regiment minus the First Battalion, which was attached to the 179th Infantry, went into Corps Reserve and began the process of rebuilding. Second Battalion came off the line with fewer than two hundred officers and enlisted men, and the remainder of the month of February was given over to transferring experienced soldiers from the First and Third Battalions to the Second and to furnishing new men for the entire regiment.

Second Battalion began an extensive training program consisting of squad tactics, gun drill, and firing of weapons. Second Battalion had been commended for its action on the front during the period from February 16–23 by the Sixth Corps headquarters, although few of the old men remained to know about it. Second Battalion, in contact with the 179th, had been left stranded when the 179th withdrew under heavy enemy pressure. Company E had taken the brunt of the first heavy enemy attack, when it was hit by tanks and infantry, but had held its ground for a full day before running low on ammunition, being overrun by tanks. Many of its men were forced to surrender or be killed. What was left of the company had withdrawn under intense fire to a knoll five hundred yards away west of the north-south road, and the battalion built up its line of defense in that vicinity.

The battalion command post had been set amid a series of tunnels called the "caves." The caves were subject to heavy fire at all times, and on several occasions the Germans moved in so close that they could throw grenades into the openings. With the 179th withdrawn, the Germans infiltrated straight down the north-south road between the Second and Third Battalions and behind the Second Battalion, all but surrounding those troops. The Third Battalion, positioned in line with the overpass on the north-south road, beat off several attacks during the day and at one time engaged in hand-to-hand combat with the enemy. The Third Battalion even attempted an attack to re-establish contact with the Second Battalion but could make little progress. The distance separating the two Battalions was approximately three kilometers. The Second Battalion of the Sixth Armored Infantry had been attached to the regiment for support and eventually took up a position in the gap between the Second and Third Battalion.

The Second Battalion meanwhile, was receiving fire from all directions and suffered many causalities; many captured. On the relief of the British on February 23, the Battalion was split in two by machine-gun fire at 852302 and had suffered further causalities. The British, who relieved the

Second Battalion on the twenty-fourth, gave up the position and had only twenty men left to tell of the fighting that had taken place there during the day they held the ground. Also on the twenty-fourth, it was reported that Captain Hugo Fieldschmidt, a dentist in the 157th Medical Detachment had taken a party of medics and litter bearers into the lines to bring out the wounded. The captain and all in his party were captured. That day, except for occasional artillery shells which fell in the reserve area, the 157th Infantry sector was quiet, although the 179th and the 180th reported opposition.

Company C-Morale good in Company C. S/Sgt. Max L. Johnson returns to Company C. Pvt. Richard M. Badgett, serial number 35698261 (MOS 745); Pvt. Burnice Auldridge, serial number 38454963 (MOS 745), and Pvt. Frank H. Bietta, serial number 32851422 (MOS 745), are assigned to Company C. PFC Alexander Taksony is WIA.

February 25–Company C–PFC Peter Krawczel is dropped from rolls.

February 26–Northwest of Anzio. Received heavy shelling. The Third Battalion began preparation of defense position No. 3, laying wire and building gun emplacements; Second Battalion, meanwhile, reorganized and re-equipped its men and made plans for the practice firing of weapons.

Company C-S/Sgt. John Clements returns to Company C. Pvt. Will Huffman, serial number 35726559 (MOS 504), is assigned to Company C.

February 27–Northwest of Anzio. Enemy shelled positions. First Battalion of the 157th, Division G-3 announced, would be relieved before dawn on March 1.

Company C–Pvt. Anthony Dumont is evacuated with a scalp shell fragment. S/Sgt. Earl Duff DOW received on February 22nd. Pvt. Robert W. Groh is KIA.

February 28–Northwest of Anzio. In reserve position; relieved by Company A at 0130 and moved back to receive replacements. Enemy shelled positions.

February 29–Although the regimental sector was relatively quiet, the enemy launched a counterattack against the 509th Parachute Battalion in the vicinity of 315 and one company was pushed back to the southeast road. The 509th counterattacked at dusk that night, but at midnight the situation was obscure. The enemy offensive centered on the Cisterna front, and pressure was being maintained along the whole sector.

Company C-Pvt. Edwin R. Kishbach is KIA. Pvt. John F. Kontros is WIA.

March 1–The regiment, less First Battalion, was in corps reserve. First Battalion, minus Company C, was in division reserve and under division control to be committed in the event of a breakthrough anywhere in the division area. Second Battalion continued to reorganize and to train its many new replacements. The regimental sector was quiet. Meanwhile, the enemy continued to exert pressure on Allied front line units.

Company C–First Lt. Anse Speairs becomes company commander. PFC Teton Hurtado returns to duty.

March 2–The regimental sector remained quiet throughout the day. Second Battalion continued its training program. First and Third Battalions rested and made further preparations for combat. Throughout the morning, Allied planes bombed enemy gun positions in the strongest display of air might the regiment had yet seen. On the front, the Third Division and the British reported minor brushes with the enemy.

Company C-Pvt. Jesse L. Wright is WIA.

March 3–During the early morning hours, the Germans bombed the beach, setting one gas dump afire. Otherwise the regimental sector remained quiet. The Battalions continued preparations for combat. The commanding general of the division suggested that the Second Battalion be committed with the 180th to give the new men necessary battle experience. The Second Battalion was alerted to relieve the Second Battalion, the 180th the night and morning of March 5-6. The battalion was on line from twenty-four to forty-eight hours.

Company C–PFC Teton Hurtado evacuated for right knee wound in battle.

March 4–The 157th Regiment, less First Battalion, is in Corps Reserve. Third Battalion continued to improve defense areas three and four and fired machine-guns and mortars for training purposes. Second Battalion continued re-equipping and training while battalion officers made reconnaissance and plans for relief of the Second Battalion, 180th Infantry, to take place the night of March 5-6.

First Battalion is in Division Reserve and made reconnaissance and plans for the relief of the Second Battalion, 180th Infantry. Regimental staff continued liaison and coordination with the First Armored Division regarding counterattack plans.

Company C–Pvt. Harold Scott promoted to private first class.

March 5–Northwest of Anzio in reserve position. The regiment, less the First Battalion, was still in Corps Reserve. First Battalion continued care and cleaning of equipment while officers made reconnaissance of routes in accordance with corps counterattack plans.

Third Battalion continued to improve defense areas three and four and fired machine-guns and mortars for training purposes. While Second Battalion continued re-equipping and training while battalion officers made reconnaissance of routes for counterattack plans. Second Battalion, of the 157th Infantry relieved Second Battalion, 180th Infantry. The relief was completed on the 5th of March at 2330. The period ended with the regiment, less the Second Battalion, in Corps Reserve. The Second Battalion became attached to the 180th Infantry upon completion of ref lief. The 157th sector remained quiet throughout the day.

Company C– PFC Tillman Holder and PFC James W. Barkley are assigned to E Company. Pvt. Edward J. Kowalski is WIA.

March 6–Northwest of Anzio. The regiment, less the Second Battalion, remains in Corps Reserve. The Second Battalion is attached to the 180th Infantry. The First Battalion continued care and cleaning of equipment. Officers of the First Battalion met with tank commanders of the First Armored Division for the purpose of planning tank and infantry coordination in counterattack plans. The Third Battalion improved defense positions three and four and fired machine-guns and mortars for training purposes. The regimental sector again was quiet.

Company C-PFC Bryon Timmons returns.

March 7–The 157th Regiment less the Second Battalion remained in Corps Reserve. Second Battalion attached to 180th Infantry and occupies the position of their reserve battalion. First Battalion continued to improve its area and prepare for further combat. Battalion staff made reconnaissance for firing machine-guns and mortars for training purposes. Third Battalion continued to improve its defense areas and finished the firing of machine-guns and mortars by replacements. The regimental sector was quiet except for some scattered artillery fire throughout the area.

March 8–The 157th Regiment, less the Second Battalion, in Corps Reserve. Second Battalion attached to the 180th Infantry. The First Battalion continued to prepare for combat and conducted small-arms firing for recruit training. Third Battalion improved defense positions three and four. Plans were made for the Second Battalion to be relieved of attachment to the 180th Infantry and return to our control the night of March 9 or 10. Reconnaissance was made and an area chosen to locate the Second Battalion. The commanding general conferred with company commanders and executive officers of the 157th and 179th Infantry at the 157th Infantry command post. Possible plans of attack were discussed. Later presented to the 157th Infantry staff by Lieutenant Colonel Manhart. The regimental sector was quiet except for scattered artillery fire throughout the day.

March 9–The period began with the regiment less the Second Battalion in Corps Reserve. The First Battalion continued preparing for combat and fired machine-guns and small arms for training purposes. The I &R (Intelligence and Reconnaissance) platoon leader made reconnaissance or OP's near the command post, 915283. He was ordered to establish an OP that could cover the ground along the diagonal road northwest of that point in order to observe the ground cover which we expect to attack. Third Battalion made plans to relieve Second Battalion, and relief was completed by 2157 hours at which time the Second Battalion reverted to control of the 157th Infantry. Third Battalion became attached to the 180th Infantry. The regimental sector was generally quiet.

March 10–The 157th Infantry less the Third Battalion was in Corps Reserve. Third Battalion is attached to the 180th Infantry and occupies positions as their reserve battalion. The regiment continued preparing for commitment while training replacements as individual companies directed. Regimental and battalion staffs made up map and terrain reconnaissance for completed attack plans. The regimental sector was quiet except for scattered artillery fire throughout the day.

Company C-PFC Douglas A. Bibb returns. S/Sgt. Max L. Johnson promoted to tech sergeant. PFC Alexander A. Matlavage is WIA.

March 11–Northwest of Anzio. Usual bivouac duties. The First Battalion, Headquarters, Second Battalion, G Company, and part of E Company took showers. The remainder of the regiment, less Third Battalion, which continues in Corps Reserve, will take showers March 12, 1944.

Regimental and battalion officers continued reconnaissance and made further plans for contemplated attack. Special attention given to Plan Panther. The regimental sector was quiet except for light scattered artillery fire throughout the day.

March 12–The regiment less Third Battalion continued in Corps Reserve. Training and preparation for combat were carried on under company control. Regimental and battalion staffs continued plans for Panther operation. Colonel Arnot from division artillery gave the artillery plan to the regimental commanding officer.

Rain prevented the Second Battalion from taking showers. Clouds and rain prevalent throughout the day. Visibility poor. The regimental sector was quiet except for scattered artillery fire throughout the day.

March 13-The regiment less the Third Battalion was in Corps Reserve. Specific plans for Panther operation were outlined at a meeting of regimental officers and of officers of attached units. After dark the regiment was alerted to be on the lookout for fifty enemy paratroopers reported to have been dropped in the Sixth Armored Infantry sector. Lieutenant Lemon of the Second Battalion was killed investigating a butterfly bomb dropped in Second Battalion area the previous night. The front remained quiet although the British fired a heavy artillery concentration after nightfall.

March 14–The regiment, still in Corps Reserve, continued preparations for the attack. Third Battalion, on the line with the 180th Infantry, reported a few casualties suffered in enemy shelling, which occurred during the early morning hours. First and Second Battalions continued training under company control. Second Battalion began preparations to relieve Third Battalion in the 180th sector tonight. First Battalion, located in the vicinity of 9025, reported a few causalities from the early morning German shelling. At approximately 0700 hours the Germans raided the beach with about fifteen planes. Otherwise, the regimental sector remained quiet. At 2300 hours, Second Battalion relieved Third Battalion.

Company C-PFC John Vounatso is injured.

March 15–The 157th Infantry, less Second Battalion, continued in Corps Reserve. Second Battalion was attached to the 180th Infantry. Training and re-equipping the regiment for combat continued through the day. Regimental and battalion staffs continued reconnaissance and planning for Panther operation. The contemplated forward command post has been dug in. Lieutenant Elliot reports that plans for wire and radio communication are complete, but wire will not be laid until specific orders are given for the attack. Enemy activity confined to harassing artillery fire in our sector.

Company C-T/Sgt. Lloyd E. Marsh is WIA.

March 16–The regiment less the Second Battalion in Corps Reserve. The First and Third Battalions carried out small unit problems under company control. Both the First and Third Battalions sent out small groups with the 179th and 180th Infantry patrols to camouf lage themselves with the terrain over which they are to attack. Regimental and battalion staffs continued plans for the contemplated attack. Light artillery fire throughout our sector was the extent of enemy activity. Weather was clear and warm with visibility good.

March 17–The regiment less the Second Battalion in Corps Reserve. Small unit problems were carried on under company control. Plan Panther was changed to Plan Centipede, and definite D-Day for the attack was announced for March 19. Regimental and battalion staffs held conferences and made necessary changes in their plans of attack. Division order for the attack was reviewed, and the regimental order was sent out through message center at 2230. The regimental sector was quiet except for scattered harassing artillery fire. The Third Battalion sent two reconnaissance patrols from the 180th Infantry front lines to establish enemy positions along the route of attack.

Company C-Sgt. Rudolph Kustra is WIA.

March 18–With the Second Battalion still on line with the 180th, the 157th remained in Corps Reserve. The regimental sector remained quiet throughout the period. Final arrangements for the attack were made, and during the afternoon the forward echelon of the command post moved into location at 930273. That night the attack was postponed.

[Mt. Vesuvius erupted on this date in 1944 and has not been active since.—Rita Kirchgassner]

Woman cries as the lava flows toward her home in San Sebastiano, Italy. 163rd SC Photo-Rooney

Mt. Vesuvius-June 2013

March 19–Northwest of Anzio. The 157th, less the Second Battalion, still was in Corps Reserve. Usual training duties. Attack called off; orders rescinded. The forward command post moved back to its former position to await further orders regarding the contemplated attack. In the afternoon, the Second and Third Battalions received air artillery bursts, which produced three casualties. The forward command post moved back to its former position to await further orders regarding the contemplated attack. Morale very good. Weather fair.

March 20–Regiment, less Second Battalion, still was in Corps Reserve. Training and preparation for combat continued under company control. Regimental S-2 and S-3 [intelligence and operations] contacted the Thirtieth Infantry Regiment, making reconnaissance and plans for the contemplated relief of the Thirtieth Infantry by the 157th Infantry. Our sector remained quiet throughout the period with some scattered artillery fire.

March 21–The 157th Infantry, less the Second Battalion, was in Corps Reserve. Training and preparation for combat carried under battalion and separate company control. Preparations were made to relieve the Thirtieth Infantry Regiment in position the nights of March 22–24. The Thirtieth Infantry Regiment has two battalions in line. First Battalion of the 157th will relieve the left battalion of the Thirtieth Infantry the night of March 22–23. Third Battalion will relieve the right battalion of the Thirtieth Infantry the night of March 23–24. Second Battalion, 157th, will revert to Regimental Control as Regimental Reserve.

Staffs of the regiment, First and Third Battalions made reconnaissance of their respective sectors, and the platoon leaders of the First Battalion, 157th Infantry, will remain in position of the Third Battalion until Thirtieth Infantry relief is completed. Enemy activity was confined to light harassing artillery fire.

March 22–Northwest of Anzio. Half mile west of Carona, Italy. One enlisted man of Company C is transferred from the Fifth Army stockade to the hospital for psychoneurosis. Three enlisted men arrested. Company C alerted to relieve Company I, Thirtieth Infantry. Left bivouac area at 1715 and completed relief by 2300. Second Battalion remained in its present position in Regimental Reserve. Third Battalion positions remained unchanged.

March 23–At 0220 hours the First Battalion, 157th completed its relief of the Third Battalion, Thirtieth Infantry. During the morning, plans to coordinate fires between the 157th and the 180th Infantries were placed in effect. In the afternoon, General Pascal ordered that the Second Battalion of the 157th place two companies in position of the 180th front right flank, relieving Companies I and E of the 180th Infantry.

The new regiment command post opened at 934253 at 1800 hours. As midnight approached, First Battalion reported encountering long-range machine-gun fire, but suffered no casualties. In general the front remained quiet.

March 24–Third Battalion completed its relief of the right battalion of the Thirtieth Infantry at 0400 hours and at the same time Company F of the Second Battalion moved into position formerly occupied by Company B Thirtieth Infantry. First Battalion, already on the line, sent patrols out in the vicinity of the stream near 942320 and the house at 926319 where they found considerable activity. Plans for Second Battalion, less Company F, to relieve two companies of the 180th were placed in effect and the relief began at 2000 hours. Generally the front remained quiet during the day, although Second Battalion suffered casualties from shellfire. Colonel Meyer, the new Regimental Commander, reported for duty during the afternoon.

At approximately 2100 hours, Company I received heavy shelling, but encountered no infantry. A platoon of Company L, located in the cemetery, was attacked by infantry and was shelled heavily. A number of casualties resulted.

March 25–Shortly after midnight, Company L platoon withdrew from the cemetery, evacuating its casualties. At 0300 hours, Second Battalion relieved the two companies of the 180th Infantry. First Battalion continued its patrolling activities, and six men of that unit, carrying a bazooka, a Browning Automatic Rifle (BAR), rifles, and rifle grenades, captured House No. 70 at 926319. With the exception of intermittent shelling, the front remained quiet during the day, and the troops merely watched and waited. During the afternoon, Colonel Church, former regimental commander, arrived at the command post to take charge of the regiment once more. Division ordered that Colonel Church assume command and that Colonel Meyer be attached on special duty.

Shortly after midnight, a patrol from Third Battalion moved to the vicinity of the cemetery and heard the enemy digging in around the walls. The enemy continued his interdictory fire on the CR (cross roads) at 925284 and at 950296.

March 26–Through the early morning hours, the enemy continued his harassing and interdictory fire, concentrating particularly on the crossroads at 925284. First Battalion again sent patrols in the vicinity of the stream junction at 94139 and the demolished buildings at 945324. The men who occupied House No. 70 pulled back during the morning of March 25, and in trying to return to the building on March 26, they met opposition. During the morning, the regimental S-2 conferred with First, Second, and Third Battalion S-2s on patrolling to be done by those units during the night. Minor patrol action marked the day. Both enemy and Allied forces engaged in battery and counterbattery fire as usual.

March 27–Shortly after midnight, Company C captured an enemy soldier who was French and had been drafted by the Germans. The POW had a sketch of his company's fire plan and stated that our front lines were to be shelled heavily at dawn. Through interdictory shellfire, First and Third Battalion patrols operated during the early morning hours. One Third Battalion patrol moved into the vicinity of the cemetery and found it occupied. The patrol fired rifle grenades and automatic weapons at the area, but received no return firc. Another Third Battalion patrol moved again into the vicinity of the fork of the stream (963326) and found trip wires. In a field, patrol also found booby-trapped shell holes.

First Battalion patrol with a mission to capture a POW moved within fifty yards of guards at 940319–941320 but could not close in on them because our own artillery was landing too close. The German guard had doubled since the night before. Only minor action occurred during the daylight hours, although the artillery units of both forces remained active. Tank fire was directed against a number of enemy occupied houses and several direct hits were reported. One tank was engaged by an antitank gun, but we the shelled German position in the vicinity of 920324 and the enemy firing ceased. Plans were outlined for two patrols from Second Battalion to operate under cover of darkness and protective fire to capture an enemy soldier and to make investigation of House No. 4 on which mortar had been placed on through the day. Colonel Brown, commanding officer of Second Battalion asked that plans be made for Company F to relieve Company E in near future so that each company would have only six days on the line. Commanding officer Third Battalion proposed a night combat patrol from his unit to go to the cemetery in the wake of bingo fire to drive the enemy out of there. Another Third Battalion patrol planned to move to 95853285 to knock out an enemy machine gun nest. After nightfall, German artillery registered a heavy barrage in the vicinity of the Second Battalion Command Post and continued its usual interdictory fire in the regimental sector. The patrol from Company E left on schedule, but got only fifty yards from the line into own protective wire when it was fired on by machine-gun pistols and artillery which accounted for two causalities. Company G patrol sent out to investigate House No. 4 to within twenty five yards of the building and observed four enemy in the house. The patrol reported probable dug in positions to the rear of the house.

March 28–Near Anzio. Enemy shelling all day. Enemy interdictory fire continued to harass troops and vehicles as dawn approached. First and Third Battalions continued patrolling. The Third Battalion combat patrol found the cemetery unoccupied, but another patrol operating in the vicinity of 958327 encountered rifle grenades and heavy machine-gun fire from around 955329 and 961329. The patrol suffered two casualties and one man was MIA.

During the morning, Lieutenant Colonel Manhart was assigned to the 180th Infantry. First Battalion reported that litter squads carrying a flag with the insignia of the Geneva Red Cross were being fired upon by enemy artillery. Second Battalion reported setting afire a haystack near House No. 4 and uncovering a probable ammunition dump. When the haystack began to burn, two men ran out of the house; one was believed killed by our snipers.

Later in the day, two more men attempted to crawl from the house, but were killed by snipers. Second Battalion reported that Company F would relieve Company E the night of March 29-30, instead of tonight as planned. In general the front remained quiet during the period although the enemy continued his interdictory fire. During the night, Company I killed one German who carried papers identifying his unit as First Company, 956th Regiment, 362nd Division.

Company C–S/Sgt. John Clements evacuated for spastic colitis, cause unknown. One enlisted man court-martialed and transferred to disciplinary training center, North Africa. T/Sgt. Jack S. Miller was WIA and Pvt. Sidney J. Tyrrell was injured.

March 29–Regimental patrolling continued through the early morning hours. A patrol from the First Battalion went to Houses Nos. 69 and 70 where it heard sounds of digging as well as movement in the vicinity of House No. 6. Two patrols from Second Battalion moved in vicinity of the cemetery but could locate nothing. A patrol from Company I moved toward 954327 and failed to return last evening.

Through the daylight hours, division and enemy artillery batteries continued their constant firing. Company E received heavy artillery during the afternoon. Second Battalion planned to relieve Company E with Company F between 2300 and 2400 hours. Third Battalion planned a combat patrol to clean out the cemetery if it was occupied by the enemy. Continuous battery and counterbattery fire marked the day's activities.

Shortly before midnight the patrol from Company I returned. Reported that one officer and enlisted men were killed in a small-arms fight. The patrol had stayed under cover during the daylight hours, unable to move without drawing fire.

Company C-PFC Dominick Mondora is WIA.

March 30–Just after midnight, First Battalion reported receiving long-range machine-gun fire at frequent intervals and expressed the belief that the enemy was attempting to cover his movements. Enemy planes also dropped flares above the First Battalion area. At 0325 hours Company F relieved Company E without incident and Third Battalion continued its patrolling but uncovered nothing. Through the early morning hours the enemy continued to harass the First Battalion with machine-gun fire, and division artillery shelled three enemy machine-gun positions. Second Battalion also received machine-gun fire. The enemy effectively shelled the chemical mortars and the positions occupied by Companies F and G as well as the crossroads at 915284. Division artillery shelled several enemy tank positions. Second Battalion was assigned the task of driving the enemy out of House No. 4 with a patrol of one officer and fifteen enlisted men. The engineers made preparations to build a new supply route under the cover of darkness. Plans were laid for two tanks to fire on Houses Nos. 8 and 66. The firing, originally scheduled for the night of March 29, has been postponed because Company F was relieving Company E and it was believed certain that the tanks would draw fire on the moving troops.

At 1920 hours, Third Battalion reported approximately one company of enemy infantry in front of Company I, moving from west to east. Artillery, mortar, and machine-gun fire was placed on the German troops, and the enemy dispersed, leaving a number of casualties behind.

At 2205 hours, Third Battalion reported having observed 105 enemy at 965355. The Germans moved south to the stream at 954340. Then at 954339 our artillery and mortars engaged them and inflicted heavy casualties. The enemy f led to the woods at 955345 where artillery placed interdictory fire. Throughout the period there was no decrease in enemy artillery.

March 31–Shortly after midnight the enemy increased his artillery fire along the entire front, and patrols from First and Second Battalions engaged in brief skirmishes with the Germans. A patrol from Second Battalion reported that on the right side of House No. 4 the enemy had placed four machine-guns and that inside the building were three or four more. The patrol estimated there was a reinforced platoon of enemy dug in around the house. The patrol saw approximately thirty men approach the house, then became engaged in a brief firefight, suffered one casualty, and retired.

Patrols from the Third Battalion operated north along the fence line to 951332 and in the cemetery once again. They located no enemy, but came under interdictory fire several times.

The front again remained generally quiet throughout the day. Supporting tanks fired sporadically at enemy occupied houses. A platoon from First Battalion reported sighting a Nebelwerfer [rocket launcher] in the vicinity of House No. 114 (914316). After midnight, the regiment started patrolling once again. Second Battalion reported small-arms fighting in front of Company F.

April 1–Half-mile west of Carona, Italy. Enemy continues to shell company position with mortar and artillery. Regiment continued patrolling in the early morning hours. An outpost from Company G received some mortar fire or grenades on its position after midnight and reported hearing what it took to be an enemy patrol nearby. A short time later, tanks fired on House No. 4 and when the barrage had ceased, the outpost could see enemy soldiers going back toward the house. Company G opened fire with mortars and machine-guns. The enemy continued to interdict the crossroads at 915284 and First Battalion received small-arms fire from house at 78679.

Before daybreak, Company G established an outpost in House No. 4, which had been badly damaged by our tanks. The outpost reported locating an enemy outpost a hundred yards left of the house. There was no decrease in enemy artillery. Third Battalion located an enemy dugout at 96153254 and called for artillery and mortar fire upon it. The artillery drove fifteen enemy into the open.

Later, ten more Germans soldiers emerged from the dugout under the artillery fire. At 2100 hours, two enemy tanks came to within four hundred yards of Company B outpost. The artillery fired upon the tanks and they withdrew.

Company C-Pvt. Harold J. McCue and Pvt. Charles F. Schulte Jr., are WIA.

April 2–More enemy in the cemetery. Through the early morning hours the enemy continued his constant harassing fire while the regiment patrolled actively. A patrol from Third Battalion went to the deep ditch at 94253235 and found fresh tracks there. The patrol saw one enemy digging in at that point. It is believed that there may be a machine gun position or observation post in that area. Third Battalion also reported an unestimated number of enemy digging in at 962325, 958328 and more enemy in the cemetery. The artillery fired on the German soldiers in the cemetery and they withdrew. A Third Battalion patrol to the cemetery later found nothing. A patrol from First Battalion went to 96321 and heard mortars firing in the vicinity of House Nos. 76 and 77 as well as a 50mm mortar or rifle grenades being fired from house at 938322. During the morning hours, Second and Third Battalions received artillery fire in their positions.

In the afternoon, Company I observed enemy in the dugout at 96153254 and placed machine-gun and mortar fire on the position. The enemy waved a white f lag and tried to come into our lines, but went back under fire. Later, one enemy soldier started toward our lines, but someone shot at him, wounded him, and he went back into the dugout. The men of Company I yelled at him to surrender. Company I then received mortar fire, but the mortars were silenced by our artillery.

At sunset, Third Battalion observed approximately twenty enemy digging in at 970338 and called for artillery fire on that position. The fire inflicted an unestimated number of casualties on the enemy. In the early evening supporting tanks fired upon House Nos. 4, 5, 6 and 7 and Company G reported that House No. 5 badly damaged. At 2128 hours a self-propelled gun in the vicinity of House No. 8 opened fire on Company G and the tanks that were shelling houses. Heavier artillery units also opened fire on the company and tanks. The tanks withdrew and the artillery followed them.

April 3–A patrol from Second Battalion went to House No. 4 and found no enemy. It located mortar positions north of the house and other dug-in positions south of the house. Another patrol from First Battalion found House No. 70 occupied. One enemy surrendered to the Second Platoon of Company B in the vicinity of 939314. Listening posts from Third Battalion heard sounds they took to be the enemy driving wire stakes into the ground northwest of the cemetery and heard digging in at 941322. The patrol received machine-gun fire from the north. The patrol could not locate the gun. The men found a dead German in a foxhole seventy-five yards south of the cemetery.

During the morning, plans were made for tanks to occupy positions at 942315 and 945317 during the night so that they could combat the tanks that come down each night to fire on Company B. It was planned that before daylight the tanks would pull back. A twenty-four-man raiding party from Company C planned to attack House No. 70 and the positions in that vicinity. During the day the artillery, as always, remained active. The commanding officer of First Battalion requested an air mission on 927363 where tanks had been located. The First Battalion also reported centers of enemy activity at 915650, 933350, and 955345. The day was generally quiet, although after dark, enemy planes bombed the front and the rear areas. It was believed that the Germans dropped bombs in their own areas.

Company C-Pvt. Winthrop E. Annetts is WIA.

April 4–Shortly after midnight, First Battalion reported that a tank was firing from the vicinity of 933338 and that machine-guns were firing from Houses Nos. 76, 77, and 78. Company B reported that the enemy dropped anti-personnel bombs in his own area. Third Battalion observed eight enemy soldiers enter the cemetery at 949326 and called for artillery fire on them.

Just before daybreak, Company B received machine-gun fire from House No. 78 and called for tank fire on the position. The raiding party from First Battalion found House No. 70 unoccupied, but received machine-gun fire from an outhouse. The machine-gun was silenced by the patrol's fire. Company E relieved Company G without incident. Company I captured a prisoner. During daylight hours, regimental personnel attended division intelligence school at division headquarters. Lt. Col. James Maloney was assigned to Third Battalion. The artillery fired upon a tank at 90863488 and scored a direct hit. The battalions laid plans for the night's patrolling, and the scheduled tank shoot was postponed until April 5.

That night the enemy registered heavy interdictory fire on the road from Padiglione north to 918307 as well as more than three hundred rounds of artillery on the road between Houses Nos. 1 and 2. The enemy also dropped anti-personnel bombs in the same area.

Company C-2nd Lt. Victor I. Minahan Jr., is WIA.

April 5–Shortly after midnight, a patrol from Third Battalion reported the enemy setting up machine-guns in the southeast corner of the cemetery and estimated that a platoon of enemy was dug in 150 yards on each side of it. Shellfire was placed on the cemetery. First Battalion received enemy artillery fire between midnight and 0200 hours, while Third Battalion exchanged small-arms fire with the enemy troops in the cemetery. Company F reported enemy tank activity in front of its right platoon. Because of the bright moonlight, patrolling was difficult.

A patrol from First Battalion moved to within a hundred yards of House No. 70, but saw nothing. The patrol heard sounds of digging from the direction of Houses Nos. 67, 68, and 69. Another patrol moved up the ditch to 940319 and found the ditch occupied. The patrol observed a mortar firing from a position between the right fork and a haystack. Third Battalion patrols reported considerable activity in and around the cemetery.

During the daylight hours, the regiment and the 191st Tank Battalion made further plans for the scheduled night's tank shoot, while artillery remained active, firing on tanks and troop concentrations and targets of opportunity.

First Battalion received artillery, mortar, and machine-gun fire at 2100 hours, and an hour later Second Battalion also received artillery and small-arms fire. Both First and Second Battalions saw enemy moving north in the vicinity of 913305. The tanks' fire fell on House Nos. 4 and 5 and answering fire fell on Company G. After the tanks had pulled back, a heavy concentration of enemy fire fell in the positions they had occupied.

Company C–Pvt. Will E. Huffman evacuated. PFC Clifford E. Merchant and PFC Alfred C. Miller are WIA.

April 6–Enemy artillery fire increased shortly after midnight, and First Battalion encountered small-arms and machine-gun fire from the vicinity of House No. 70. At 0350 hours, Third Battalion reported receiving considerable artillery, mortar, and small-arms fire. At 0345 hours, Company F received an attack from the direction of House No. 5 and the draw to the north, but by 0429 hours, almost all firing ceased. The company saw no enemy personnel and suspected that the firing had come from an enemy outpost in the vicinity of 915305. Company E reported machine-guns firing from House No. 4 and mortar and machine-guns firing from House No. 5. Direct hits by mortars silenced the enemy firing from the houses. A patrol from Third Battalion went to a point three hundred yards south of the cemetery and opened fire with a BAR. The patrol received return fire from the southeast and southwest corners of the cemetery and rifle-grenade fire from the northwest of the cemetery. Through the day, all artillery units, as usual, remained active. Third Battalion made plans for being relieved by the First Battalion of the 180th Infantry. The regiment resumed patrolling.

April 7–Shortly after midnight, Company F reported the details on the attack it had received at approximately 0300 hours on April 6. Company F reported its left and center platoons had been attacked by two platoons and one squad of enemy. One platoon came in at 916302 and the other 915305. A squad came in from the north of the diagonal road, 915311, down the fence line and several snipers came down the main draw 917312. A patrol from Third Battalion returned at 2400 hours and reported seeing two enemy driving stakes for wire at the southeast corner of the cemetery and hearing digging southwest of the cemetery. A patrol from Second Battalion went to 915303 and found an enemy outpost in the same position as before.

Before daylight, Third Battalion was relieved by First Battalion of the 180th Infantry, which came under regimental control at that time. Through the day, the artillery continued to fire on enemy positions, but for the most part the front remained quiet. Company F was shelled with propaganda leaf lets, believed to be our own. Personnel from the regiment attended a division reconnaissance school while the battalion on the line made plans for night's patrolling. After nightfall, tanks moved into position in the Second Battalion sector. One of the tanks got to within seventy-five yards of House No. 4 and opened fire, then was hit by shells from an antitank weapon. The tank crew escaped under the protective fire of Second Battalion machine-guns. As midnight approached, the enemy continued harassing fire on troops, roads, and ammunition dumps.

April 8–A patrol from First Battalion of the 180th Infantry returned shortly after midnight. The patrol went up the draw to the cemetery and left a machine-gun and a BAR team in the draw to fire on enemy machine gunners. The patrol encountered no opposition going into the cemetery and thoroughly investigated it without meeting the enemy. One man went around the cemetery and at the northwest corner found enemy barbed wire running in a northwest direction. He rejoined the rest of the patrol at the southwest corner of the cemetery. Shortly, the patrol received machine-gun fire from the northwest along the wire. Machine-guns also fired from a haystack west of the cemetery and from a lone tree three hundred yards east of the cemetery. On the way back, the patrol received mortar fire, which accounted for two causalities.

Before daylight, Companies E and F were subjected to self-propelled or tank fire from the rear. This day, both forces continued battery and counterbattery fire while infantry activity remained at a minimum. A two-man patrol left First Battalion at 0850 hours to move up the draw in front of Garibaldi's tomb. Shortly before noon, Allied planes dive-bombed enemy positions in the vicinity of 916317. As dusk approached, Company F observed enemy movement around the outpost position at 915302 and opened fire on the position with mortars. In a few minutes, two enemy medical aid men appeared in the area, carrying a white f lag. At 2030 hours, the First Battalion 180th Infantry reported that Houses Nos. 124 and 125 were receiving enemy artillery fire at the rate of about one round per minute. The battalion also reported suspected enemy tank movement in the vicinity of 955345. After dark, the regiment and First Battalion of the 180th Infantry began patrolling once more while artillery units of both forces maintained constant interdictory and harassing fire. First Battalion received machine-gun fire from the cemetery and called for artillery fire on the enemy positions. In the Second Battalion sector, Company G began the relief of Company F. Company C-Pvt. Irving Blumengold, Pvt. Robert A. Heath and Pvt. Raymond B. Tapley are WIA.

April 9–At 0155 hours, Second Battalion reported its relief completed with three casualties in Company G as a result of mortar fire. A patrol from First Battalion of the 180th Infantry went to the draw south of the cemetery and dug in. Another patrol from that unit left the dug in positions and went to a point fifty yards south of the cemetery where the men located an enemy machine-gun to the right of the graveyard. One man from the patrol started toward the position, but the machine-gun opened fire. The patrol also observed a company of the enemy northwest of the cemetery and moving toward it, so the men returned to the dug-in position and placed fire on the Germans. A 2½-ton truck came down the trail from the north of the cemetery and pulled up behind it. Artillery firing continued to mark the daylight action while the battalions on the line made plans for patrolling. There was little decrease in enemy artillery fire. After dark and shortly before midnight Second Battalion reported seeing an estimated thirty enemy in the vicinity of House No. 4 as well as a tank firing from near House No. 5. Mortar fire dispersed the enemy troops and artillery fire drove the tank away from House No. 5. The vehicle withdrew about five hundred yards north of the house and shut off its motor.

During the night Colonel Sears, an ordinance officer, moved into the line with Company E. His objective: to kill a German before his retirement six months from this date.

April 10–Same position. A patrol from Company E had followed the draw northwest to 922304 and encountered no enemy activity. A four-man patrol from the Forty-Fifth Recon left the First Battalion and went up the drainage ditch northeast from House No. 151. The patrol found four slit trenches on the north side of the ditch extending southwest from the tree at 943318. One slit trench contained a raincoat, a second contained a booby-trapped can and a cement mine, a third a mattress, and a fourth a gas cape.

A patrol from First Battalion, 180th made contact with Company B, 157th Infantry. Another patrol of the 180th Infantry reached a point of 150 yards south of the cemetery and observed a machine-gun about fifty yards south of the cemetery firing into the First Battalion of the 157th Infantry. The patrol located an enemy mortar position at 95453320. Throughout the early morning hours, the enemy continued shelling of positions, and enemy aircraft dropped bombs over the area. Tank fire scored a direct hit on the kitchen in the rear command post and wounded two guards. An enemy soldier from the Fifth Company, 29th Panzer Grenadier Regiment, deserted to Company E. As usual, artillery firing marked the daylight activity. At approximately 1030 hours, Company E received mortar fire from the vicinity of House No. 5, and artillery was placed on the enemy positions.

During the afternoon, Second Battalion reported one dead enemy in front of Company E, killed by a sniper, Colonel Sears. At 1922 hours, Second Battalion reported receiving a concentration of air bursts, and an hour later the enemy placed heavy artillery and mortar fire on Companies E and G. Later First Battalion reported heavy shelling. As midnight approached, the Germans shelled the rear extensively. A command post in front of the First Battalion, 180th Infantry, reported 20 enemy dead in the area of 963328.

Company C–PFC Byron Timmons is promoted to corporal.

April 11–Shortly after midnight there were reports of scattered machine-gun fire over the entire front and interdictory fire on the crossroads at 918284. G-3 instructed regiment by radio that between 2015 and 2115 and between 2300 and 2400 all artillery pieces would remain quiet so that friendly air protection could bomb all gun flashes seen during those periods of time.

A patrol from First Battalion, 180th Infantry, with a mission to go to 955326, moved as far as the lone tree east of the cemetery (949326) and was fired upon by a machine-gun pistol. The patrol returned fire and then received machine-gun fire from weapons approximately a hundred yards east of the cemetery and from other guns west of the cemetery. After a brief exchange of fire, the patrol returned.

A patrol from the First Battalion went to 93653190 and reported locating two machine-guns at 94353185 and a mortar position just to the north of the machine-guns, which at the time were firing into the regimental sector. Before dawn, the enemy increased artillery fire and shelled the rear areas, the regimental command post, and the Second Battalion command post.

First Battalion of the 180th Infantry reported observing a smoke screen in front of the First Battalion of the 135th Infantry. The report was confirmed by the 135th Infantry, which reported the smoke screen was laid to cover the withdrawal of a working party that had one KIA and three MIA.

Again artillery marked the daylight hours. At 1100 hours, First Battalion reported fire at vicinity of 9032 near House No. 71. A tank was firing on Company A at the rate of six rounds every ten minutes. Regiment began preparations for its relief by a unit of the Third Division. During the day, plans were made as usual for night's patrolling.

At 1845 hours, First Battalion, 180th Infantry, reported heavy shelling and that the enemy guns could not be observed. The firing ceased a short time later when the artillery shelled a tank at 903323. Gun flashes also were observed at 898343. At 1940 hours, G-3 reported to the regiment that the scheduled bombing mission had been canceled. At 1945 hours, Second Battalion reported receiving heavy artillery concentration, most of which landed on Company G and Second Battalion command post. The enemy artillery buried a mortar and two men, but the men were rescued.

After dark, the battalions on the line started patrolling once again. Observation posts reported tank activity around House No. 66 and House No. 8 as well as mortar positions of House No. 4. First Battalion reported observing thirty enemy in the vicinity of House No. 78. There was no decrease in enemy artillery fire, and during the night the front was continually lighted up by flares that the enemy set off.

April 12–After midnight, two patrols from First Battalion returned to their sectors of operation. The first patrol went up a ditch, turned right just below stream junction 941319, and then went to 943317 where it found unoccupied positions. From there, the patrol went to the wire at 942318 and found positions from the ditch to the wire unoccupied. The patrol observed two enemy on the other side of the wire and on its way back encountered an enemy crawling down the ditch toward it. The men challenged him and he got up and ran; he became caught in the wire and the patrol opened fire on him. He threw a hand grenade at the men, and when they looked again, he was gone. The second patrol went up the ditch to the wire at 938318 and saw enemy equipment in the ditch—field glasses, pack, and belt. They did not touch it since they encountered machine-gun fire; they could progress no farther, so returned.

A patrol from the First Battalion, 180th Infantry, returned to report encountering no enemy, but having directed artillery fire on three machine-gun positions with good results. The positions were in the south corners of the cemetery and at the lone tree east of the cemetery.

As dawn approached the enemy laid a smoke screen in front of the First Battalion, which brought all its machine-guns, mortars, and artillery support into play, receiving little return fire. However, at 0630 hours, First Battalion reported its Company B had received a hundred rounds of mortar fire. During the morning, G-3 reported to the regiment that the air corps plan, which had been canceled the previous night, would be carried out tonight. Plans also were made for a tank show to be directed against strong point No. 62.

The battalions reported observing German litter bearers at 935331 and an ambulance at 932345, believed to be the personnel carrier, with a white flag attached. In the afternoon, First Battalion engaged in a brief exchange with the enemy. Thirty-four enemy planes raided the beach at approximately 1915 hours but were driven off by intense ack-ack fire. At 2010 Third Battalion began its move to the new area. Once more, after dark, patrols began operations while the enemy continued his harassing and interdictory fire.

Company C-PFC Quienton Steele returns.

April 13–At approximately midnight, the enemy raided the entire regimental sector, bombing the rear areas, the regimental command post, the guns, and the front-line troops in an extensive air assault. The bombings did little damage.

A patrol from Second Battalion worked its way up to the wire twenty-five yards south of House No. 4. Then enemy planes dropped flares. Exposed, the patrol received rifle grenades from the house and withdrew. The men reported that the planes dropped many bombs between Houses Nos. 5 and 6.

Through the early morning hours both forces continued battery and counterbattery fire. Third Battalion closed in the area at approximately 0040 hours. A reconnaissance patrol from First Battalion went to 936317 and picked up some German equipment. The patrol found two antitank mines on each side of the ditch.

Again artillery activity marked the daylight hours. Regiment was informed that the air corps would continue its night bombings between the hours of 2300 to 2400 and 0400 to 0500, but in the afternoon, the plan again was canceled. Second Battalion planned a two-man patrol, one member of which spoke German, which would go up the draw to 921315, where two enemy were seen digging in during the morning. The men were to attempt to get the enemy to surrender. However, Company A fired a mortar barrage on the enemy soldiers, and one of them jumped out of the hole, ran north about fifty yards, and jumped into another ditch.

Company C–Pvt. Will E. Huffman returns. Pvt. Clarence E. Moody, Pvt. Woodrow W. Thomas, Cpl. Paul H. Valdez and Pvt. Robert C. Carnahan-all became POWs on December 15, 1943 and were executed on this day. PFC Tom Bryant is WIA.

April 14–Enemy continued to shell positions. At approximately midnight, a German patrol of unestimated strength attempted to drive through the lines at the left platoon of Company G, but was driven away in a brief firefight. By 0300 hours the action had subsided.

A patrol from Second Battalion went to 921315 and found at least a squad dug in at a draw at 92003155 and an outpost of two men at 92053155.

By 0145 hours the Second Battalion of the Thirtieth Infantry had relieved the First Battalion, 180th Infantry, which was on its way back to a rest area. At 0415 hours, the Second Battalion of the Thirtieth Infantry reported a platoon of enemy pinned down between Companies E and G. The enemy withdrew.

Scattered artillery firing marked the daylight hours, and troops observed considerable activity around the houses.

After dark, the Third Battalion, Thirtieth Infantry, began the relief of our First Battalion.

April 15–By 0420 hours, First Battalion had been relieved, and the Third Battalion of the Thirtieth Infantry was in command of the sector. Through the early morning hours, enemy artillery continued to harass the troops and interdict roads.

Through the day, the front remained generally quiet, but by nightfall the enemy was laying heavy fire on the troops. Second Battalion, relieved by the First Battalion of the Thirtieth Infantry, began the move back to the staging area. The forward regimental command post during the afternoon had moved into the rest area.

April 16–26–By 0425 all of Second Battalion and Cannon Company had been relieved. First Battalion was in the rest area, and Second Battalion moved into the staging area.

During the day, the regiment set up beach defense, and by midnight, Second Battalion had closed in the rest area. During this period, the regiment was in rest area in the large wooded area five miles east of Nettuno. This time was partially spent on reorganization, re-equipping, and training. A varied program of athletics and recreation, which occupied the rest of the time, was conducted by the regiment's special services section. A softball tournament was held, and the regimental championship was won by Headquarters Company, Third Battalion, which defeated AT by a score of 7-3. Movies and variety shows were held nightly. All troops were given two opportunities to visit the showers operated by the 120th Engineers.

Combat infantryman's badges were received, and 1,361 of them were awarded to qualified members of the command.

[S/Sgt. Robert L Kirchgassner received his badge that day, April 24, 1944. According to General Orders 1, HQ, 157th Infantry Regiment, dated 24 April 1944, S/Sgt. Robert Kirchgassner, ASN 35101920, was awarded the combat infantryman badge, effective 1 January 1944, for "exemplary conduct in action against the enemy."—Rita Kirchgassner]

PFC Raymond R. Wagner of Company L was selected to fire in the corps snipers contest; he did not, however, place in the contest. Near the end of the month, 155 general replacements for the entire regiment.

April 16-Company C-Pvt. Ryan D. Baker is WIA.

April 20–Company C–No change in position. S/Sgt. John Clements returns to Company C.

April 23–Company C-Near Anzio. Richard Adams, serial number 32958105 (MOS 745), and PFC Thomas Briggs (MOS 745) join Company C.

April 24-Company C-PFC Teton Hurtado is WIA.

[At Anzio, we did not come out of the foxhole during the day. At night, two men in a foxhole, took turns doing two hour shifts of guard duty. —Richard Adams]

April 27–Near Anzio. Usual rest duties. Preparing to move. Made final preparations in the a.m. Left area by truck at 1935, detrucked at 2035, and marched to division reserve positions; First Battalion took over former position of Second Battalion of the Fifteenth Infantry Regiment at 27237227B. Arrived at 2115.

The 157th Infantry relieved two battalions of the Fifteenth Infantry plus Antitank, Cannon, and Headquarters Companies without incident. First Battalion, 157th Infantry completed relief of Second Battalion, Fifteenth Infantry at 272327. Second Battalion completed relief Third Battalion Fifteenth Infantry at 272215. Third Battalion of the 157th Infantry remained in rest and training area, manning interior guard and beach defenses. Regiment made plans for the Third Battalion to relieve Second Battalion, Seventh Infantry the night of April 28-29.

April 28–Command of the sector passed from the command of the Fifteenth Infantry to the command of the 157th Infantry on April 28th at 0050 hours. Interdictory and harassing artillery fire fell throughout the sector on Third Battalion of the 157th Infantry during its movement. Security motor patrol of the regimental area conducted by I & R platoons as anti-paratroop measure. Enemy aircraft dropped personnel bombs in the regimental command post area.

Company C-Pvt. Anthony Dumont returns.

April 29–The 157th Infantry remained in Division Reserve position. Counterattack plans were made up and distributed to all units concerned. Plans for regimental training school under the direction of Major Reeves were completed. I & R Platoons continued to maintain anti-paratroop patrol in rear areas. Second Battalion, 180th Infantry, continued under the control of the 157th Infantry and occupied the beachhead line. Intermittent enemy artillery fire throughout the area.

April 30–Division reserve position; troops took showers. All troops continued to improve their positions, and four hours were spent in training. I and R Platoons continued anti-paratrooper patrol of the regimental area. Second Battalion of the 180th Infantry reverted to control of the 180th Infantry at 0101230.

Company C–Morale very good.

May 1–Reserve position near Anzio. Throughout the period, the regimental sector remained quiet, although artillery batteries for both forces were active, interdicting roads and firing targets of opportunity. During the morning, the Second Battalion, 180th Infantry, under the command of the

157th Infantry reverted to the control of its own regiment. Plans were made for the 157th Infantry to relieve the 179th Infantry in three or four days. Tentatively, First Battalion would hold the left flank, Second Battalion would occupy the central sector, and Third Battalion would protect the right flank.

After dark, there was a marked increase in enemy artillery fire.

Company C–Pvt. Richard Badgett, Pvt. Frank H. Bietta, and Pvt. Will E. Huffman are promoted to private first class.

May 2–During the early morning hours, the regimental command post reported continuous small-arms fire along the front, and at 0400, it reported heavy artillery fire heading in both directions. At daylight the action quieted.

Through the morning the regimental sector was subjected to spasmodic artillery fire, a few rounds of which fell in the M Company area. Regiment made plans for practice firing bazookas. During the afternoon, Col. H. A. Meyer, on special duty with the 157th Infantry, was relieved of assignment to take command of the 179th Infantry.

At 2245 hours, enemy planes made a raid on the beach, bombing the front line and rear areas intensely. Two of the planes were reported shot down, and the regiment suffered no casualties.

May 3–At 0400 hours, enemy planes again raided the beach, dropping anti-personnel bombs and heavy bombs throughout the regimental sector. The raid lasted thirty minutes. No casualties reported. Through the day, the sector remained quiet. Regiment asked division ordinance to remove several dud bombs that fell in the Third Battalion area during the raids.

May 4–At 0330 hours, the regiment command post reported heavy artillery and small- arms fire in the British sector to the left, but the 157th sector remained quiet. At dawn, the 179th Infantry reported having received a counterattack, following an unsuccessful attempt to take some ground in the vicinity of the windmill. The 179th reported that a company of enemy, supported by machine-gun, mortar, and artillery fire, assaulted its Third Battalion, but the attack was repulsed.

Throughout the day, further plans for the coming attack were made by regimental and battalion staffs. After dark, enemy artillery fire increased once more, and approximately a hundred rounds fell in the area occupied by Company D. No casualties reported.

Company C–In Division Reserve. Usual bivouac training. Troops took showers.

May 5–Shortly after midnight, the enemy laid an artillery barrage in the Second Battalion area, many of the shells landing in the vicinity of headquarters and Company G. No casualties reported.

Through the day, the regimental sector remained quiet. Plans for the coming attack were furthered, and the roster of regimental personnel who would attend the engineers' school was forwarded to G-3. The battalion prepared for the relief of the 179th Infantry.

After dark, Third Battalion moved forward to relieve Third Battalion of the 179th Infantry, but encountered artillery and tank fire in attempting to effect the relief. Three Second Battalion officers, advance detail for the battalion, were wounded while with the Second Battalion of the 179th Infantry.

There was a marked increase in enemy artillery fire, many of the shells landing in the rear as well as the forward areas.

* * *

[Dad wrote Mom the following letter on this date:

Somewhere in Italy
Dearest Anna Jo,

I have written to you every day for the past two weeks. I have never heard from you for a few days. How is my girl this evening? All right, I hope. Do you go to many shows? Did you ever see anything about Italy in the news reel? Say, how is the election coming back home? I sure would like to be back home arguing with those Democrats. But I guess I will stay here and fight the Germans. Did you ever get those poems I sent you? I make a $120.00 a month over here. I can sure save money. A fellow doesn't get to spend any. I send almost all of mine home. When I get home, I hope to buy a farm. Well, this is all I know for now. Hoping you are well and in good health.

To the sweetest girl I know,
Lots of Love,
Bob]

May 6–Anzio. Shortly after midnight, Third Battalion reported its relief of the Third Battalion of the 179th Infantry being held up by enemy artillery fire, but at 0130 hours the relief had been completed except parts of Companies I and L. The battalion reported having suffered several casualties.

An hour later, Third Battalion reported the relief was completed, with one squad of Company L unable to move into position. The squad remained off the line until the following night. At dawn, the Third Battalion casualties had mounted to fourteen wounded as enemy artillery and mortar fire raked the area.

Generally the front remained quiet until noon. Company L reported observing three enemy vehicles at 882309, but before artillery fire could be laid on them, the enemy obscured them with smoke. The artillery fired on enemy personnel at 882309 a few moments later, and Third Battalion reported good results were obtained.

At dusk, the enemy increased his artillery fire, shelling ammo dumps in the rear areas as Second Battalion moved forward to relieve a unit of the 179th Infantry. By 2300 hours, the squad from Company L moved into position. Two German soldiers surrendered to Company K. By midnight, Second Battalion had relieved the Second Battalion of the 179th Infantry without incident, and the command passed to the commanding officer of our unit.

May 7–Throughout the early morning hours, the enemy spasmodically subjected Second and Third Battalion troops to machine-gun, mortar, and artillery fire and kept the front alight with amber, green, and white f lares. Shortly before dawn, intense enemy artillery fire fell on the right flank of the Third Battalion and Companies F and G of the Second Battalion. Company F suffered two casualties, bringing the total wounded to four. During the day, the front remained generally quiet, although the enemy subjected Second Battalion to intermittent shellings. Plans were made for evening patrols, and in the afternoon, the regimental staff moved to a forward command post at 91752665.

After nightfall, First Battalion made ready to move to front-line positions to relieve 179th Infantry. Left reserve positions at 1915, marched to company assembly area, and proceeded to relieve Company C of the 179th Infantry by platoons. At 2100 hours, Company L received heavy shellings throughout its sectors, with some indication of enemy infantry action to the immediate front. By midnight, one company of First Battalion had succeeded in relieving one company of First Battalion, 179th Infantry.

May 8–Shortly after midnight, Second Battalion reported that Company E had suffered one killed and one wounded when a contact patrol from that unit attempted to reach Company L. Communications between the two companies had been disrupted by enemy artillery fire.

At 0050 hours, Third Battalion reported its recent action was against an estimated platoon assembled in a draw in the vicinity of 900295, from which groups of six or seven men from time to time probed the front line near Company L's position. The S-3, 179th Infantry reported that the same action occurred almost every other night. By 0145, First Battalion, 157th Infantry, had completed its relief of the First Battalion, 179th Infantry. The command of the sector passed to the regimental commander, 157th Infantry.

Through the early morning hours, the battalions received intermittent artillery fire and machine-gun fire. Company C engaged the enemy in sporadic firefights while Third Battalion placed artillery and mortar fire on enemy personnel and mortar emplacements in front of Company L.

During the morning the enemy placed mortar fire on Second Battalion and succeeded in knocking out one light machine-gun belonging to Company E. In the afternoon, First Battalion fired artillery and mortars on an operation post in House No. 5, and Second Battalion reported it believed that the suspected observation post near the well at 904310 had been knocked out by artillery. Plans were made for the regular evening patrols.

After dusk, the enemy continued to harass the troops with artillery fire, and sporadic firefights broke out on the line. A company outpost suffered one man killed. Shortly after midnight, Company F received about ten rounds of mortar fire, landing at a rate of one a minute.

Company C-Pvt. James R. Adams was KIA. Cpl. Bernard Pieczynaki is WIA.

> [John Schweisthal was the gunner and I was his assistant. The ground was soft and didn't realize that the plate holding the mortar gun was sinking. Next thing we know is that we hit a tree close to us and we were showered with debris.—Richard Adams]

May 9–During the early morning hours, short firefights broke out on the front. Company L received intermittent mortar fire for several hours. A Second Battalion patrol went to 906298 and reached a point twenty yards from the windmill. The patrol reported a machine-gun firing at 90453005 on an azimuth of 165 degrees. Another Second Battalion patrol went to 913306 and the end of the draw and found evidence of personnel at that point. The patrol reported a machine-gun firing from the vicinity of 91253075 on an azimuth of 220 degrees. Companies F and G reported Nebelwerfers firing from House No. 26 or House No. 28.

In a brief firefight, Company K captured two enemy soldiers, members of the Ninth Company, Eighth Panzer Grenadier Regiment, Third Panzer Grenadier Division. A contact patrol from the 180th checked in with the left company of Second Battalion at 0410 hours.

During the morning, questioning of the prisoners revealed that the first platoon of their unit was located at 896295, the second platoon at 897297, and the third platoon on a hill at 894297. Mines and concertina wire were in front of the Ninth Company. The minefield was marked. The prisoners reported that the men carry gas masks and take gas mask training regularly.

Through the day, the enemy continued to harass the troops with artillery fire and mortar fire, which landed in Company F area, knocked out a heavy machine-gun, killed two men and wounded three. Supporting artillery fired upon targets of opportunity and upon suspected enemy observation posts. Enemy artillery pounded the Second Battalion command post at Padiglione.

After nightfall, enemy artillery fire increased and the battalions engaged German foot troops in prolonged firefights. Company L received a heavy concentration of artillery fire, and the enemy received shellings in return. The First Battalion reported receiving tank or antitank fire from House No. 5. By midnight, the action had quieted, although firefights broke out occasionally. Second Battalion, having engaged the enemy in a firefight for approximately 1½ hours, received fire from a self-propelled gun to the rear of House No. 27 after small-arms firing had ceased.

Cpl. Leo Blanchette returns along with PFC Hanzel Blair to Company C. Blanchette is evacuated sick in the line of duty and does not return during the war.

May 10–Anzio. Parties from Company B, 180th Infantry, arrived at position. Germans, active in small numbers, put mortars, artillery, and small-arms fire on positions. Shortly after midnight, Third Battalion reported that an estimated four thousand rounds of artillery fell on its positions between 2230 and 2400 hours. The battalion reported that the enemy action started by smoking Company L's left platoon and part of the center platoon. They covered both flank platoons with small arms fire and started moving it toward the center platoon. Third Battalion countered with artillery and mortars, and the enemy returned like fire with 170mm and 50mm shells.

First Battalion engaged ten or fifteen enemy, observed digging a position at 91953135, with mortars and machine-guns. The fire killed one enemy soldier, and the enemy withdrew. A patrol from Company C moved out to investigate a small group of enemy digging in at 92283128, got to within fifteen yards of the group, and was fired upon. The patrol exchanged fire with the enemy, but results were undetermined.

A patrol from Second Battalion went to 912306 and ran into double concertina wire running southwest from 91253060. Two men went through the wire and at that time saw four enemy jump into a hole fifteen yards behind it, with nine more coming up the wire from the southwest. The patrol opened fire with a BAR and received return fire from three machine-guns at 91253060, 912310, and 906303. The machine-gun fire wounded four men, one seriously. The patrol withdrew while one man returned to Company G outpost and returned with a blanket to get the badly wounded man. Two of the other wounded men disappeared and were presumed captured.

Throughout the day the artillery batteries of both forces remained active. Just at dawn, an unidentified plane was shot down over enemy territory. At 1130 hours, First Battalion reported seeing Red Cross f lags on both sides of House No. 5.

Plans for the approaching attack were furthered, and the regimental staff conferred with staff members of the 191st Tank Battalion concerning the clearing of paths for tanks with Bangalore torpedoes.

After dark, the Second Battalion, 170th Infantry, began the relief of the Second Battalion of the 157th Infantry. Corps told the regiment that it expected the enemy to fire an artillery concentration, and plans were made for counter-battery shoot. Sporadically, the enemy shelled the troops on the line, and again brief firefights broke out in the battalion sectors. By midnight, the Second Battalion, 179th Infantry, had half completed the relief of the Second Battalion, 157th Infantry.

Company C–Pvt. Thomas A. Schill is WIA and PFC Walter Wilson is injured.

May 11–Anzio. Receiving enemy fire of all types. Shortly after midnight, Second Battalion reported its relief by the Second Battalion, 179th had been completed and the sector now was under the command of that unit. Second Battalion closed in the reserve area by 0145 hours. Through the early morning hours the front remained generally quiet, although brief skirmishes broke out in the First and

Third Battalion sectors and the enemy continued to interdict roads and to shell the front-line troops spasmodically. At dawn, Company L placed mortar fire on a group of enemy located at 899294 and later reported seeing four casualties evacuated from that position.

During the morning, corps issued orders that all vehicles would use blackout lights on any night move, that MPs would carry flashlights that glowed red, and that MPs with a thorough knowledge of the routes would be stationed at all crossroads.

The front remained generally quiet throughout the day and the forward troops received only intermittent shellings.

May 12–Shortly after midnight, Third Battalion reported that its relief by a unit of the 179th Infantry had been completed. Through the day the front again remained generally quiet, although some machine-gun and mortar fire was reported in the First Battalion sector.

Regimental and battalion staffs furthered attack plans. By midnight, AT Company completed the relief of three guns of the 180th AT at Camp Morto.

Company C-Pvt. Earl T. Weicht is KIA.

May 13–Shortly after midnight, Second Battalion reported having completed the relief of the Second Battalion, 180th Infantry. The Second Battalion at that time came under the control of the 180th Infantry.

At 0100 hours, First Battalion reported its relief by the First Battalion, 180th Infantry, had been completed. By 0130 hours, the battalion had closed in the reserve area.

During the morning, plans were made for First Battalion to take tank and infantry training on May 15. So that the First Battalion might take training, Third Battalion was scheduled to relieve it the night of May 14–15. On the night of May 15–16, First Battalion would move back into its original position, relieving Third Battalion.

Second Battalion, on the line, made plans to send two reconnaissance patrols into the forward areas after dark. Regiment scheduled a conference at Third Battalion headquarters between S-2, 120th Engineers; commanding officer, Company A, 120th Engineers; commanding officer, Second Battalion,

135th Infantry; commanding officer, First Battalion, Armored Infantry; commanding officer, Sixteenth Engineers; Third Battalion, 157th Infantry, and the regimental staff.

Second Battalion, on the line, encountered sporadic artillery fire as well as intermittent machine-gun fire. The Second Battalion called for artillery on a tank at 951333 and on troops at 956352, who were moving southeast. At 2047 hours, the regiment opened its new command post at 932254.

May 14–Throughout the morning hours, the Second Battalion sector remained quiet. A patrol went to 952323, where it found single strand of concertina wire of our own with three trip wires in stream bed in front of the concertina. Another patrol left from 951322 and went north approximately 500 yards. It found no wire or mines. A machine-gun fired from a point further north, but the patrol could not locate it. A bombing raid in the rear area wounded three men in the regimental training school area. During the morning, G-3 informed the regiment that the machine-gun range would be at the disposal of the 157th troops the morning of May 15.

Throughout the day, the regimental sector remained relatively quiet. Plans were made for the two Second Battalion patrols to investigate the battalion front in search of mines, wire, and enemy installations. There patrols were to be accompanied by members of the AT mine clearing platoon. Further plans were made for fifteen regimental officers to make reconnaissance f lights in the field artillery planes. Other plans were made for troops from the regiment to attend engineers' school on May 15. At dusk, the entire front line staged a "turkey shoot." Before midnight, Third Battalion had relieved First Battalion. First Battalion went to reserve position.

May 15–Shortly after midnight, the enemy opened machine-gun and machine pistol fire on the Third Battalion of the 180th Infantry, part of the fire falling on the left company of our Second Battalion. At 0240 hours, an unidentified plane dropped a parachute with a bundle attached in the 168th Infantry sector.

A patrol from Second Battalion moved up the stream to 954327 and found no wire or mines. It located one dead German in the stream at 952323. Since there was no path, the patrol waded up the stream in knee-deep water. A second patrol left 949320 and went west 100 yards, then north 200 yards. From there it moved to a point 150 yards southeast of the cemetery, then went east 200 yards, veered north to the stream and followed it back to position. The patrol located a two-man outpost at 949321 at the lone tree. The patrol found no wire or mines.

At dawn, corps artillery loosed a fifteen-minute concentration on the German troops. A patrol from Company E picked up the parachute and bundle at 958322.

Through the day, sporadic artillery concentrations fell on the Second Battalion troops and in the rear areas. Corps announced the times of its artillery shoots scheduled for May 16 and 17. Plans for Second Battalion patrols were the same as they had been the previous night.

May 16–After midnight, Second Battalion informed regiment that the cylinder that been dropped to the ground by parachute contained propaganda leaf lets. Second Battalion patrol left from 951322 and went up the draw to 952323. There it turned west and started to cross the field. It moved about fifty yards before encountering machine-gun fire at 953330. Another patrol heard an undetermined number of enemy in the draw at 955328. Enroute it cut three trip wires. The patrol was fired upon by a machine- gun at 953330. It reported hearing an underdetermined number of enemy in the draw at 955238.

Twice, enemy f lat-trajectory fire landed in the area occupied by Company D. Corps announced plans for another all-gun shoot. Second Battalion made plans for one man who understood German to go behind enemy lines. He would carry a sound power phone with him.

Company C–In Division Reserve….troops showered and prepared to move to former position by Mussolini Canal. Enemy artillery fired three barrages left of Company C position. After dark, left area at 2115, marched to position by Mussolini Canal, and arrived at 2210. Relieved Second Battalion on the battle handover line. The enemy continued to interdict roads and to shell the front and rear areas.

May 17–Shortly after midnight, Second Battalion reported that patrols from Company F had reached the First Battalion, 168th Infantry, and the Third Battalion of the 180th Infantry. The German-speaking man from Company G moved into position a hundred yards south of the cemetery.

A patrol from Second Battalion accompanied the German-speaking soldier as far as 948325. Then the leader moved forward to a point approximately twenty-five yards below the west edge of the cemetery, where he was halted by a sentry. He remained there, listened for a while, and then returned.

Another patrol went up the draw from 951321 and at point 200 yards up the stream observed three machine-guns, one directly north, one on an azimuth of 337 degrees and another on an azimuth of 272 degrees. One hundred yards farther up the patrol located three trip wires, which the men marked. The patrol also located concertina wire, which had been pushed aside.

Through the day, the situation remained generally static. Once again, corps announced its plans for a daily all-gun shoot and requested targets. Second Battalion made plans to continue its patrolling activities and reported its one-man outpost, still in position, had located enemy machine-guns at 958436, fifteen men and a machine-gun at 946323, and 50mm mortar positions at 953324. After dark, the man on the outpost returned. Enemy artillery fire increased, and fifty rounds of 170mm landed in the Company B area. Shortly before midnight, enemy aircraft raided the beach.

May 18–Normal artillery fire and frequent exchanges of machine-gun fire marked the early morning hours. Several patrols from Second Battalion moved to different vicinities, but did not contact the enemy.

At 0900 hours, corps opened one of its daily shoots, pouring fifteen-minute artillery concentration on enemy lines.

The regimental sector remained quiet throughout the day, and troops received only the normal enemy artillery concentrations. Further plans were made for the coming attack, and the regiment was informed that division units would use the sniper range on May 22–23. Second Battalion laid plans for its evening patrols and corps announced that it would stage another shoot May 19 at 2145 hours to 2200 hours. All Second Battalion weapons were ordered to take part.

May 19–Throughout the early morning hours, the front remained generally quiet. At 0250 hours, Second Battalion reported a sharp increase in artillery fire. A patrol from Second Battalion left Company G, right platoon, and went up the east bank of the Carano stream where it located an enemy outpost at 953323 in a small depression. The patrol heard movement and talking in the vicinity of 955328. It entered the draw and returned down the stream bed. The patrol reported a machine-gun firing from the vicinity of 953324.

At 0400 hours, corps staged another of its fifteen-minute all-gun shoots.

Through the day, the situation remained static. First Battalion planned to send a recon patrol to 942317 to find the width and depth of the ditch and to determine the steepness of its slopes. Second Battalion planned to send a recon patrol and ambush patrol of six men, who would operate in the vicinity of 95253245.

The regimental commander scheduled a meeting in the command post between battalion commanders and the commanders of the Antitank and Cannon Companies and attached units. The meeting was to take place at 1000 hours, May 20.

Again after dark, the enemy increased his artillery firing, and heavy concentrations fell in the First Battalion sector. Two men were wounded.

At 2200 hours, Company C relieved Company B, but as Company B began to move from the area, it received forty rounds of artillery fire, believed to have originated in the factory area.

May 20–Shortly after midnight, First and Second Battalions reported that neither of their patrols had located anything. Enemy mortar fire landed in Company E sector and killed two men.

Through the early morning hours, brief skirmishes broke out on the line, but by dawn, all was quiet. During the morning, the regimental commander met with unit commanders to discuss the current attack plans. The engineers' school was discontinued indefinitely.

Through the day, the artillery was active, firing upon troops and upon vehicle concentrations with good results. Third Battalion planned to send two patrols up the stream after nightfall.

After dusk, the enemy subjected the regiment sector to normal artillery concentrations. G-3 informed regiment of a change in plans for the commitment of the division in the current attack, but the regimental commander ordered regimental units to continue their scheduled activities for the night. By midnight, part of the Second Battalion had been relieved by the Third Battalion.

Company C-PFC John Chorba returns.

May 21–By 0100 hours, the relief had been completed. Brief skirmishes broke out on the line in front of the Third Battalion.

One Third Battalion patrol attempted to go up the Carano stream but came under supporting artillery fire so had to withdraw. A second patrol went to the vicinity of the cemetery and established a listening post. It reported MP (Machine Pistol-German sub-machine gun, the MP 38 or MP 40) firing from the cemetery, a machine-gun firing north of the cemetery, and a machine-gun firing from the vicinity of House No. 134.

During the morning, the regimental commander ordered that all personnel carry gas masks. Artillery firing marked the day's activities and supporting batteries fired with good results on troop and vehicle concentrations. Plans for the coming attack were furthered.

At 2100 hours, corps staged another fifteen-minute shoot. The commander of the AT Company was given permission to remove three of his guns from the 179th sector to the regimental sector.

Company C–Anzio. Reserve position. A few enemy artillery shells coming in.

May 22–Through the early morning hours the front remained extraordinarily quiet. One Third Battalion patrol moved up the Carona stream and found nothing. Nor was anything found when another patrol went to the cemetery.

At 1745 hours, the division commander informed the regimental commander that Plan Buffalo would proceed as ordered, and the regiment began final preparations for the attack to be launched the following day.

After dark, First Battalion moved forward to a position from which it planned to jump off with Third Battalion in the morning. The Third Battalion, 180th Infantry, moved into the original position occupied by the First Battalion of the 157th Infantry.

[On January 22, 1944, troops hit the Anzio-Nettuno Harbor. The landing was a success. The enemy was taken by surprise. Patrols even advanced to the outskirts of Rome. Then the Germans counterattacked and fierce fighting continued until we held a small perimeter of seven miles. Due to the lack of supplies, men were driven back. The Germans threw everything that they had at us, wanting to drive us into the sea. The winter was long and we held our position. The Germans could shell us anywhere on the beach. They even shelled the ships that brought in supplies. The ships had to unload at night or lay a smoke screen in the daytime. We lay in foxholes from January to May, protecting our positions, going on patrols, and repulsing attacks by the Germans. At last on May 23, the order came for us to move out. We were on our way to Rome.—Robert L. Kirchgassner]

[It was difficult to imagine that this quaint town of Anzio was the setting for a major battle of World War II. We were standing on a rooftop, looking out over the Mediterranean Sea, envisioning what the place must have looked like the day of the invasion.

I was trying to put myself in my grandfather's shoes and to imagine what he must have been thinking, but I realized I could not fully comprehend the feelings that he was experiencing.—Mark Kirchgassner]

Chapter 5

Roma Pax

Jared's Blog:

[June 4, 2013. Today was a pretty powerful day. All morning, Rita kept saying, "I've come five thousand miles and I'm only a train ride from Anzio." (Americans say "an-z-o," and Italians say "on-cee-o," by the way.) After an hour-long train ride south, we arrived in Anzio. There we toured a museum devoted to Anzio's role in World War II. I learned that American and British troops were unable to penetrate the Gustav Line, which was north of Salerno and stretched across Italy from the west to the east. The Allies fought fierce battles, but a combination of terrain and German troops frustrated their campaign to liberate Italy. At that point the Sixth Army (which included the Forty-Fifth Division and the 157th Infantry) went to sea, coming back ashore on a twenty-two-kilometer stretch between Anzio and Nettuno.

The plan was to get behind the line and split German forces. We visited this beachhead today. The Allies caught the Germans off guard, but got held up at Anzio beach until reinforcements arrived. By then they had weakened and stretched the German forces so much that liberation was inevitable, though not without a great fight. Unfortunately, we were not able to take pictures inside the museum. I did get pictures of the building, the staff, a monument marking the location of the landing and commemorating the soldiers lost, and a building said to have been a barrack after the landing. We sat on a rooftop for some time, envisioning what the invasion looked like. Near the beachhead, rock was being blasted at a quarry. It was as if we could hear the men and the artillery from that eventful day.

Leaving Anzio, we visited the American World War II cemetery in Nettuno. We could see the graves of soldiers lost on the beach. There was also a monument to soldiers who lost their lives but whose bodies weren't recovered. More than thirty thousand troops gave their lives at Anzio.

That number represents thirty thousand young men. And that brings me to the special story of H24.

That letter and number will remain forever in my mind. In grave H24 lies the body of Roscoe Prince. He was a young man whom Sgt. Robert Kirchgassner first met at Camp Pine, New York. There they became great friends. Roscoe was from the hills of West Virginia and had just been married before he was sent to war. He served in the same infantry regiment as the sergeant. The two had shared a tent for months. Every so often, they had to shake the dirt from the blanket/rug covering their hole. One day the two flipped a coin to decide who would do it. Roscoe lost and just as he began the chore a mortar hit. The shell fragment killed him instantly. Robert was hit in the hand, but not seriously wounded. Until today no one from the Kirchgassner family had ever been to visit Roscoe. Robert was a coin flip away from being the one in that cemetery. Roscoe was a great young soldier with a promising life and dreams.

Returning after this powerful experience, we decided to stroll around Rome and take in some sights. We ate gelato on the Spanish Steps, saw the Pantheon, and enjoyed the scenery at the Piazza Novano. At night, storm clouds rolled in. Vendors were selling ponchos and umbrellas everywhere. We didn't buy any. We felt like the Forty-Fifth Infantry's thunderbird was flying overhead to say thanks for visiting. It never did rain. What a great day. Tomorrow we head to Pompeii and to Salerno, the Allies' first landing site in Continental Europe.—Jared Leiker]

[The train ride from Rome to Anzio was a blur. The landscape rolled by as I sat and stared out of the window. I don't know if I spoke a word on the way, as I was humbled to be in that place at that time. I didn't let my aching back ruin the moment. After disembarking from the train, the first thing we did was to walk to the Anzio museum.

When we arrived at the museum, we were greeted by the curator and the staff, who were pleasant even with a language barrier. We were not permitted to take photos inside, but seeing the mementos of the past was riveting. Photos, letters, and artifacts from the battle filled the room. We stayed a couple of hours and had the opportunity to watch original footage of the landing at Anzio.

As we prepared to leave, one of the curator's friends, who spoke a little English, directed us to the harbor where the Palace of the Sea is located. Along the way we noticed that many buildings in Anzio carried plaques commemorating the battle. There were also many monuments thanking those who liberated the city. By the time we reached the Palace of the Sea, we had seen miles of the seashore where the Allies disembarked and dug in for battle. The owner of a café on the shore let us go up to the roof where we sat in the warm sunshine and took pictures as we looked out over the harbor. What a beautiful view and an enjoyable afternoon! The seriousness of the day was lightened when I made a faux paus. You can read about it in Jared's blog. Mark could only say, "Remember, Daniel doesn't want you to embarrass the family."

I know there has been much discussion about the error the Allies made by landing at Anzio and digging in instead of advancing to Rome. The Allied advance had been stymied at the Gustav Line, and British Prime Minister Winston Churchill proposed the landing at Anzio. Operation Shingle began on January 22, 1944. Maj. Gen. John Lucas was in charge of the operation. When the Allies landed, they found the area fairly quiet. Instead of advancing, the Allies dug in with thirty-six thousand men and secured a two- to three-mile-deep beachhead. The Forty-Fifth Infantry Division came ashore on the second day.

This is where the speculation arises. Major Gen. Lucas should have advanced that first night toward Rome, but he did not. He chose instead to secure the beachhead even further. Another stalemate began and the Battle of Anzio ensued.

German Field Marshal Albert Kesselring took immediate action after hearing of the landing at Anzio, and within forty- eight hours he had more than forty thousand soldiers in place. Within a month, Gen. Mark Clark replaced Lucas, who paid for his hesitation with General Lucian Truscott.

The Allies were dug in for four months, and though they were outnumbered one hundred thousand to seventy-six thousand at one time, the Allies held the line. The Germans could not drive them back to the sea.

I believe that if the Allies had failed to hold the line at Anzio, the landing at Normandy would not have been as successful. The Allies fought many divisions of German soldiers that otherwise would have been dispatched north to thwart the landing at Normandy. Operation Shingle is the forgotten D-Day, and I do not believe that history has given the men who served at Anzio enough credit for their tremendous courage.

The 157th Infantry received a presidential citation for its defense of the left shoulder of the beachhead, but sister divisions serving at Anzio were not acknowledged.

The Forty-Fifth Division was supposed to receive a presidential citation for the performance of its regiments in the Battle of Anzio. On July 1, 1947, General Clark approved a recommendation for the division to receive the award. The citation never came through. (Col. John Embry, US Army (Ret.), Monograph No. 8)

I decided to take this case to the commander in chief. With so many of our veterans passing every day, I felt that there was no time to procrastinate or to follow the chain of command. (Ask my friend Kathy Hartman, and she will tell you that this is how I operate and is always volunteered to assist me.) So upon my return to the States, one of the first things I did was to write to President Obama. I enclosed documentation showing that the Forty-Fifth Infantry Division had never been honored for its efforts. To date, I have not received a response. That won't deter me; ask my girlfriends, and they will tell you that I will pursue this request.

One last reflection from Italy: I find it interesting that Mount Vesuvius erupted while Company C was in Anzio and has not been heard from since. Jared got it right when he coined the phrase *thunderbird weather.* — Rita Kirchgassner]

[Every cobblestone street corner in Rome seems to be home to another stunning Roman Catholic Church. People here have tremendous pride in these historic buildings, which remain in pristine condition. The Romans had to have remarkable creativity and ambition to build these churches, some nearly two thousand years old. Words cannot describe the breathtaking size, architecture, and beauty of St. Peter's Basilica in Vatican City. Being this close to the heart of Catholicism made me reflect on my spirituality and grow stronger in my faith.—Krista Kirchgassner]

Jared's Blog:

June 2, 2013 Rome-

[Finally got to our hostel in Rome, Hotel Texas. We saw so many beautiful sights on the drive in. Headed out to get some fresh air and a bite to eat.

We spent the day walking around and getting accustomed to the city. On our walks we were able to see several beautiful churches. We saw the chains that held St. Peter. We had dinner at a café right outside the Colosseum. Our day ended with a trip to Fontana de Trevi. Auto correct hates Italian names.—Jared Leiker]

June 4, 2013 The Vatican-

[We began the day with a European breakfast and a Vatican tour. The Vatican and all its glory were breathtaking. Headed for a tour of the Colosseum this afternoon. We will post more about our day this evening, but here are just a few pictures from this morning. Sorry, but no pictures are allowed in the Sistine Chapel.

Stat of the day: if you looked at each piece of artwork for one minute on the seven-kilometer walk through the Vatican Museum, you would take about forty years to finish.

The Colosseum has been my favorite tour so far. Colosseum is actually a nickname. The real name is Flavian Amphitheater. From there we walked through the ancient ruins and the Forum along Holy Road.

Tomorrow is the start of our journey with the Thunderbirds of the Forty-Fifth Division. We will meet up with them after a short train ride from Rome.

With orders to attack, hold, and advance, the Forty-Fifth moved toward the northern coast of Sicily, liberating towns. Once troops hit the northern coast, they moved east to Messina and completely controlled the island.

We'll get an early start to the day, June 5, with a two-hour train ride south to Naples and then to Pompeii for the morning. After that we'll head to the beachhead at Salerno. During the battles, Italians had accused the Forty-Fifth of war crimes. They claimed the Forty-Fifth never stopped to sleep or to eat. In a speech to the Forty-Fifth, General Patton said, "Your division is one of the best, if not the best division, in the history of American arms."

An American GI said, "You haven't been to hell until you've been to Anzio."

The Forty-Fifth Division landed at Salerno first in September of 1943. The division then broke off from the army and went back to sea to storm the beaches at Anzio. This was a tactical maneuver to get behind the German line. For logistical reasons, we will visit Anzio today and Salerno tomorrow.

Good night, America. Ciao.]

June 5, 2013 Pompeii--

[European showers are getting pretty old. Our shower is eighteen by eighteen inches. My shoulders touch the walls when I shower. Also, there is no temperature regulator, and the water supply is limited. If anyone turns on a sink faucet, the shower turns to the temperature of steaming hot coffee. You have to jump out of the shower before you get burned. After another miserable shower, we visited Pompeii. It was a really neat place. Most Americans know the story that Mount Vesuvius erupted in AD 79, burying the city in volcanic ash. The amazing thing people don't know is how large the city was. It was home to more than twenty thousand people living on sixty-six hectares. Vatican City is only forty-four hectares. I'd guess that's three hundred US acres or more. Pompeii is a giant ancient city. It was so cool to walk around and see how life was. I'm still amazed at how advanced civilization was that long ago. Mount Vesuvius last erupted in 1944, and that was when the Thunderbirds were in Italy. — Jared Leiker]

June 6, 2013 On to Rome

[After long, hard fight in Salerno and Anzio, the troops pushed north to Rome. From there, the Forty-Fifth finally reached Rome, which had already surrendered. Like the Forty-Fifth, we used Rome to relax, recoup, and recover.

I got up early for a long jog in a huge park. It's essentially the Italians' Central Park. Who else can say they saw ruins, a castle, and a zoo on their morning run? I must add, though, that Rome is a lot hillier than Greendale, Indiana.

We visited the Liberation of Italy Museum, which was fascinating. Everything was in Italian, but we had a guy translate roughly for us.

This afternoon, we returned to the Vatican. We wanted to check out St. Peter's tomb, climb the basilica dome, and see a few other things we didn't have time for earlier. Climbing to the top of the dome was the best thing I've done here so far. It is 551 tough steps one way, but the sights along the way are amazing.

We thought of Dave Kerr as we visited the Liberation Museum, the museum in Anzio, and the Nettuna cemetery. We wanted to thank him for being instrumental in getting us a lot of information about Sgt. Robert Kirchgassner. Rita is excited to find information for Dave about the 157th Infantry.

So again, thank you, Dave, for helping make all this possible.—Jared Leiker]

From a foxhole in 1944, Anzio, Italy:

I Hope

I hope when this is over
I hope I'll be around.
I hope I won't be left here
Underneath the ground.
I hope I'll keep on going.
I hope I'll see it through.
I hope that I'll be coming home.
I hope that I'll see you.
I hope they keep on missing.
I hope my luck holds out.
I hope that I can take it
And keep a-sweating 'em out.
I hope I'll keep on living.
I hope all this is true.

I hope that I'll be coming back.
I hope that I'll see you.
I hope that you'll still be there.
I hope that you're still my gal.
I hope that if you ain't
At least you're still my pal.
I hope it isn't someone else.
I hope it's no one new.
I hope that it will still be me.
I hope that I'll see you.

—S/Sgt. Max L. Johnson
Anzio, 1944

[Excerpt of a letter written by S/Sgt. Max L. Johnson to Anna Jo Hoffmeier in May, 1944 from Anzio.

Anna Jo Hoffmeier
732 Considine Ave.
Cincinnati, Ohio

Dear Anna Jo,

I read your swell letter. I am glad you like the poems. I know that you must be a really swell girl. Cause that is all Bob talks about. He thinks the world and all of you. But he won't tell anybody. I know how he feels. I was married and my wife died at childbirth along with the baby.

A better guy than Bob they just don't make. He is really a fighting man, the best Staff of the Company. Well Anna Jo there isn't much I can tell you. I am glad that you did write. I really didn't think you would. Don't worry about Bob. He will be O.K. I would enjoy very much hearing from you again.

Sincerely,
Max]

* * *

[The only way out of Anzio was to run from shell hole to shell hole. On the morning of May 23, our artillery and groups of fighter planes bombed, shelled, and strafed the German positions. But the shelling and the bombing would not destroy the mine fields that lay ahead and would wipe out the attacking infantry. The Germans were prepared for us to move. They had tanks and infantry dug in. We suffered a lot of casualties. After about ten days of fighting, on June 2 we captured the high ground and the town of Velletri. We looked down on Anzio. The German resistance was broken and we were on our way to Rome.

I walked on the Appian Way—built by the Romans two thousand years ago. On June 4 we entered the outskirts of Rome. On June 6 we heard the news that the Allies had crossed the English Channel and had landed in France. Men were jubilant and morale was high. We thought that the war would soon be over.—Robert L. Kirchgassner]

May 23–At 0123 hours, the regiment opened its forward command post at 938297. First and Third Battalions reported that they were in position and that their fronts were quiet.

At 0411 hours, the British, on the left, opened a demonstration, attacking a strong point on the Albano-Anzio highway with an entire division. A platoon from Company I infiltrated up the stream, suffering two men killed by mines.

At 0545 hours, the thirty-five-minute pre-attack artillery concentration began, and at approximately 0625 hours, First and Third Battalions jumped off in the midst of light rain. Visibility was limited to three hundred yards. At 0655 hours, Third Battalion ordered the artillery to lift its fire to the 334th grid line; at 0700 hours, it ordered fire on the 337th grid line and at 0710 hours, it ordered fire lifted to the 341st grid line, evidence that the attack was progressing satisfactorily. At 0715 hours, the regiment was informed that the Third Battalion troops were three hundred yards beyond and north of the cemetery and that the company had lost contact with the 135th Infantry on the right and was attempting to regain contact. The battalion reported having captured several enemy soldiers from the Sixth Company, 362nd Regiment. First Battalion reported having taken its first objective and that at 0724 hours. Company A had moved through Company B and was pushing on, meeting little resistance. The Battalion reported contacting Company G, 180th Infantry on the left.

At 0730 hours, the regiment learned that the 180th Infantry had occupied Houses Nos. 76 and 77, and at 0738 Third Battalion called for a lift of artillery fire to the 345th grid line.

At 0745 hours, Third Battalion request regiment to contact the 135th Infantry on the right and to ask its regimental commander to move his troops abreast of Company I.

The Third Battalion reported that Company I now was five hundred yards north of the cemetery. Company L, moving through the cemetery, received friendly artillery fire and asked that it be lifted so that the company could keep advancing.

By 0750 hours, the 180th had taken Houses Nos. 78 and 79. Two friendly tanks hit mines in the 1st Battalion sector and were used for pill boxes.

At 0752 hours, reports reached regiment that First Battalion had captured eighteen enemy soldiers while Third Battalion had captured twelve, most of them from the 956th Regiment. The battalions reported meeting only light resistance and that casualties were light.

At 0807 hours, Third Battalion reported having captured approximately fifty enemy soldiers and informed regiment that Company I had reached the south edge of the woods. The first sergeant of Company I was six hundred yards south of the woods, and the left flank element of the 135th Infantry was on the line with him. At 0830 hours, First Battalion reported it was sending fifty prisoners back to the canal.

By 0842 hours, Company I had reached its final objective and was Hill No. 76. It was receiving machine-gun fire from the right flank, Third Battalion reported. Regiment urged the 135th Infantry to move up on the right on line with Company I, which was six hundred to one thousand yards in advanced. Company L continued its advance on the left of Company I was reported six hundred yards north of the cemetery.

At 0847 hours, Third Battalion reported it had committed one platoon of Company K on the right of Company I to help fill the gap between the Third Battalion and the 135th Infantry. Company I reported it was dispersing its machine-guns and was receiving some fire from House Nos. 139, 140, and 141. Third Battalion reported it was holding up its advance until the unit on the right had moved up on the line.

Company L continued to push forward, moving slowly because of mine fields. At 0915 hours, First Battalion reported its tank support had hit a new mine field near House No. 68 and asked that eight litter bearers be sent forward. First Battalion continued its advance, meeting slight resistance. Its tank support was slowed by mine fields in the vicinity of the end of the road above the cemetery. At 0854 hours, Third Battalion asked that all artillery directed south of the railroad on its sector be stopped. Through the remainder of the morning, First Battalion continued to advance and Company A moved to within seven hundred yards of House No. 78.

At 1315 hours, First Battalion reported it had suffered an estimated thirty casualties, most of them from mines. There was a marked increase in enemy artillery fire, and at 1420 hours, the forward artillery observer reported six to eight tanks moving down the railroad bed toward Company I. Company I called for fire to be placed on the tanks. At 1435 hours, the air observation post reported twenty-four Mark VI tanks moving down from 950355. At 1501, Third Battalion called for immediate TD and tank support as part of Company I had been cut off. At 1509 hours, Third Battalion reported three enemy tanks in front of L Company at 930323.

At 1511 hours, Third Battalion reported that Company I and two platoons of Company K had been cut off and that Company L had withdrawn to the Carona stream. At 1514 hours, regiment dispatched messengers to First and Third Battalions to inform them that TD support was on its way forward. At 1536 hours, Third Battalion reported that corps was directing artillery on the tanks and that the action was quieting. First Battalion reported that Company C would relieve Company B so that Company B could reorganize.

At 1638 hours, First Battalion informed regiment that Company C was counterattacking to try to regain House Nos. 140, 141, and 142. The First Battalion also reported a gap of five hundred yards existed between it and the 180th and that two platoons from each unit were going to close the gap.

At 1651 hours, Second Battalion was alerted for an after-dark move. At 1749 hours, Company I reported having pulled back to the railroad bed because friendly artillery fire was falling on the company position. Regiment ordered Cannon and Antitank Companies to move guns forward after dark. Second Battalion began its move into position.

After dark, Third Battalion received heavy caliber artillery fire, thought to be friendly. No friendly guns were firing into the area, however, so the fire was believed to originate in the factory area. The 135th Infantry moved forward in line with Company I beyond the railroad tracks.

First Battalion suffered two hundred casualties, among them Captain Caldwell, Company D, who had lost part of his leg when he stepped on a mine. Third Battalion had no estimate of its casualties. It was learned that Lieutenant Barker of Company L had lost part of his leg when he stepped on a mine.

By 2137 hours, both First and Third Battalions were on their objectives, attempting to tie in with the flank units, the 180th Infantry and the 135th Infantry, respectively. Second Battalion began is move into position.

Enemy soldiers taken during the day totaled ninety-six.

At midnight, only scattered artillery harassed troops in the regimental sector. Second Battalion, in reserve position, reported finding a number of First and Third Battalion men in the slit trench area.

Company C–Anzio. Enemy shelled company assembly area in ditch by Carona stream. Morale good. Pvt. Harry R. Loria is injured. Pvt. Leonard F. Decker, 2nd Lt. Alexander J. Forbes, Pvt. Howard McIntyre, PFC Dominick Mondora, PFC William F. Seeman and 1st Lt. Thomas J. Slade Jr. are WIA.

[The regiment was in the forefront for the kickoff for Rome with First and Third Battalions in the attack. The regiment's second Medal of Honor was earned on this day by an NCO platoon leader in Company I, Tech Sgt. Van T. Barfoot, who destroyed three machine-gun positions, knocked out a German tank and shot down its escaping crew, blew up a German artillery piece, and then escorted two wounded men 1,700 yards to safety. One platoon of Company B was trapped in a ditch and was virtually wiped out by German tanks. The attack continued down the Cisterna-Campoleone road.—Hugh F. Foster III.]

[Hugh met Van T. Barfoot, and I have a letter from him.—Rita Kirchgassner]

"Awarded: Medal of Honor for his heroic actions at Anzio.
Lt. Van T. Barfoot. May 23, 1944.
SC Photo

May 24–First and Third Battalions regained contact, and the Third Battalion also contacted the 135th Infantry on the right. Antitank Company reported having removed fifty mines from the road leading to House No. 139 and at 0350 hours reported further that its four guns on the way to Third Battalion had hit a mine field and that they could not be taken further. At 0400 hours, Third Battalion reported that Company I was receiving heavy caliber artillery fire, while First Battalion also reported receiving shellings along its front. At 0455 hours, Third Battalion was alerted to move. At 0530 hours, the 135th Infantry, on the right, jumped off.

At 0840 hours, Third Battalion reported it was receiving artillery concentrations on its position, three to four hundred yards in front of the railroad tracks. Third Battalion was informed that a company of tanks and a recon party from the CCA was moving into its area.

Through the remaining morning hours, the regimental sector was subjected to only scattered artillery fire. Company I received friendly fire in its position, so pulled back to the railroad tracks.

During the afternoon the situation remained static, while the enemy shelled the front line heavily. Third Battalion planned sending patrols to the northwest to establish contact with the enemy. Corps announced that its patrol to the south had moved down as far as the lakes, where a salient from the Eighty-Eighth Division had met it. CCA was ordered to enter Cisterna.

At 1840 hours, First Battalion reported it was sending twenty-one POWs to the rear. Patrols from Companies A and C were ordered to move northwest to make contact with the enemy. First Battalion estimated its casualties at seventy-five wounded, twenty-five killed, and twenty-five missing.

At 2105 hours, the 180th on the left reported it was being counterattacked. And a few moments later First Battalion reported receiving heavy shellfire on its position.

At 2145 hours, division announced that the unit on the right of the Third Battalion would attack at dawn the following morning and ordered that the 157th be prepared to send in two battalions to positions north of the railroad tracks.

Artillery supporting the regiment fired in front of the 180th Infantry troops to help them stop the counterattack they were encountering at 2250 hours. Reports reached regiment that the action had quieted. It was believed that the skirmish had been caused by a 12 man patrol supported by tanks.

Just before midnight, both First and Third Battalions were harassed by friendly artillery fire falling short. Regimental patrols probed enemy lines and made contact with the flank units.

Company C–PFC Alfred Vigliante (MOS-506) is promoted to corporal southeast of Carano, Italy.

May 25–Just after midnight, reports reached regiment that a platoon from Company B had filled the gap five hundred yards between Company C and Company L. Company A reported having suffered approximately sixteen casualties from small-arms and artillery fire during the enemy attack in front of the 180th Infantry the day before at 2250 hours. By 0315 hours, most of the casualties had been evacuated.

Through the early morning hours, the enemy subjected the troops to normal artillery barrages. A three-man enemy patrol came in on Company I, and in a brush, one man was killed; the other two escaped. Regimental patrols could locate no enemy. At 1055 hours, Third Battalion reported that a thousand-yard gap still existed between it and the 135th Infantry. The regimental commander ordered the Second Battalion to reconnoiter that sector, since it would probably move into the gap.

Throughout the daylight hours, the regimental sector remained generally quiet. The 135th Infantry closed the gap between it and the Third Battalion to five hundred yards but began pushing north in the face of slight resistance to increase the gap once more. A recon patrol from the division moved between the two units.

First and Third Battalions were ordered to send out patrols to the northwest to attempt to contact the enemy, believed to have withdrawn. At 1658 hours, Second Battalion reported it had completed its reconnaissance and was ready to move.

At 1800 hours, First Battalion was alerted to attack to the northwest to seize the stream running from 929347 to 935362. Patrols from both battalions probed the ditch at 94153410, which they found mined. The patrols received tank fire from 938358.

After dark, regimental patrols extended their operations. The regiment was to attack at 1100 hours May 26 with the division. The division objective was the ground from 8637 to 825385. Second Battalion, with attachments, was to lead the regimental attack.

Company C–3.3 miles north of Carano. Sent patrols north of railroad bed. Patrol contacted enemy outpost, killed two. Pvt. Edward Schemansky returns to Company C. Company B occupied company's position for jump-off May 26.

May 26–At 0200 hours, the regimental commander gave the battalion commander the details on the proposed morning attack. The 157th Infantry would be on the right of the division and would have the Second Battalion, 179th Infantry, and Company B, 157th Infantry, under its control. Our Second Battalion would pass through the Third Battalion and push forward, maintaining contact with the 133rd Infantry on the right and the 180th Infantry on the left. Third Battalion would hold its position until the 133rd Infantry had passed through the position and then on order would follow Second Battalion. First Battalion was in Regimental Reserve.

At 0230 hours, the jump-off time was changed to 1000 hours. At 0455 hours the advanced echelon of the regimental command post moved forward to 954342. The rear echelon was moved to a new command post at 940289. At 0900 hours, the jump-off time was changed again to 1100 hours. The battalions were informed.

The attack opened on schedule, and Second Battalion encountered slight resistance, which slackened as the troops pushed forward. On the right the 133rd Infantry moved up but at 1135 hours, it was two thousand yards to the right rear of the Second Battalion and a large gap existed between the two units.

At 1210 hours, Second Battalion reported it had captured five enemy soldiers from the Fifth Company, 956th Regiment. At 1219 hours, the Second Battalion reported that Company F was being attacked by two tanks in the vicinity of 9235. A few moments later, reports reached the regiment that Company F was receiving heavy small-arms fire from the 133rd Infantry sector and that the 133rd Infantry was not yet on the line with our regimental troops.

At 1314 hours, Second Battalion sent back a call for medics for Companies B and F. Third Battalion, following Second Battalion, encountered small-arms and artillery fire. At 1320 hours, Second Battalion reported its troops had reached Castel Nuova, but were meeting stiffening resistance. Second Battalion had suffered thirty casualties.

At 1341 hours, the battalion reported that Companies B and F had reached the objective. Third Battalion moved forward, and the companies echeloned five hundred yards apart.

At 1346 hours, Second Battalion reported that Companies B, G, and F were being held up at 935360 and asked for additional tank support along the railroad. No tanks could be secured. At 1432 hours, Company K moved forward, but received concentrations of mortar and machine-gun fire from the north. At 1507 hours, Third Battalion reported that Company K was immediately behind the reserve company of Second Battalion and the company was receiving tank fire.

At 1600 hours, regiment received reports that the unit on the right had been stopped by enemy fire. Second Battalion was ordered to continue its advance, and the Thirty-Fourth Division unit on the right flank was ordered by the corps to move forward. Third Battalion moved into position on the objective and protected Second Battalion's right flank.

At 1912 hours, Second Battalion reported that Company E was at 924361, Company B at 923356, Second Battalion at 933362.

The division commander ordered the regiment to continue its attack at 0615 hours the following morning, and plans were made for the Third Battalion to move through the Second Battalion. At dusk, regimental patrols began once more. Losses for the day were placed at thirty-eight wounded and twenty-four killed. At 2100 hours, Company C began its move into the Second Battalion sector to relieve Company B. The enemy harassed the troops with normal artillery fire, and brief skirmishes broke out on the line.

Company C–Same positions in ditch three-quarters of a mile from Carano. Enemy shelled positions very heavily. Pvt. Richard Messick and Pvt. Henry J. Sponder are KIA.

May 27–At 0235 hours, the regiment received reports of the Second Battalion casualties. It was estimated that Company F had suffered eleven KIA, sixty-seven WIA, and two MIAs; Company G, twenty WIA; Company E, twenty WIA; Company H fifteen WIA. Reports also came back that the enemy had twelve tanks across the railroad at 9237. The engineers postponed building a bridge at 915326 until the regiment had pushed forward, allowing them to work in daylight.

At 0620 hours, Second Battalion reported that it had jumped-off on time and at 0745 hours, it sent back word that Companies G and B were advancing, but Company E was held up by enemy armor. At 1053 hours, Second Battalion reported that it would like the Thirty-Fourth Division to place artillery fire on tanks at 920373. The fire was not forthcoming, and at 1325 hours, regimental artillery fired the mission. At 1355, the regimental commander ordered Third Battalion to follow directly behind. Third Battalion was ordered to move through Second Battalion once its objective was taken and to push forward from there. Company C was to be attached to Third Battalion and First Battalion was to follow Third Battalion.

Second Battalion jumped off at 1500 hours, and at 1555 hours, it reported that Company E and Company G had reached the objective. Company E suffered heavy casualties from mines and small arms.

At 1645 hours, Third Battalion began the move through Second Battalion and at 1850 hours, it reported it had reached the LD. **[Line of Departure is a geographical place from which an attack commences. –Hugh F. Foster III]** At 1930 hours, Company F reported to have only eleven men left with no officers. Second Battalion reported it had forty-one prisoners and First Battalion had twenty-six prisoners.

At 2050 hours, Third Battalion had moved through Second Battalion and had reached Spaciassi Creek. At 2055 hours, Third Battalion reported that Captain Austin of Company L had been killed. At 2100 hours, the regimental commander ordered Third Battalion to hold up its advance on the 89 Northing and to push forward at 0615 hours. Patrols continued to probe enemy lines, and the enemy shellings marked the remaining hours.

Company C: Pvt. Vincent C. Oeschger is KIA. This company echeloned to right rear to protect flank at 2400. First Lt. Richard Stone is reassigned from First Battalion headquarters. Pvt. Philip V. Angelastro and PFC William R. Broome Jr., are WIA.

> [A German counterattack again decimated the reconstituted Company E, driving the men into a mine field where the commander, all but one officer, and NCO leaders became casualties.—Hugh F. Foster III.]

May 28–Through the early morning hours, regiment and battalions made contact with the adjacent units and furthered plans for the morning attack. Third Battalion reported that Company I near the railroad track, had received direct tank and machine-gun fire. The Thirty-Fourth Division recon troops moved in the gap between the Third Battalion and the 133rd Infantry. At 0514 hours Second Battalion reported an increase in its strength from the preceding night. Company E now had fifty men and Company F had fifty-five. At 0610 hours, Third Battalion reported that it would jump off at 0700 hours and that the preparatory artillery fire would begin at 0640 hours. Company K was to move southwest to try to gain action with the 180th, which had jumped off and was meeting no resistance on the left.

Third Battalion attacked on schedule and met with only slight resistance. Part of Company K was pinned down at 0750 hours by small-arms fire. At 0945 hours, Third Battalion reported that it had reached the west branch of Spaciassi Creek, where it was receiving heavy artillery and machine-gun fire.

Third Battalion informed regiment that the troops were in need of tanks and that regimental armored units were unable to cross the deep creek. Third Battalion troops had moved forward only two hundred yards from the jump-off point and were unable to advance against the heavy fire they were receiving. Three tank destroyers and five tanks were sent forward to assist the troops.

The division commander planned to send one battalion of the 179th Infantry to the northwest and the Third Battalion on the right. At 1244 hours, Third Battalion reported that Companies I and L were going to attempt to advance to the 89th grid line. With the TDs in position to fire, the two companies jumped on our right at 1250 hours.

At 1400 hours, Third Battalion reported it again was being held up by heavy fire. Regiment was informed that the Second Battalion, 179th, would jump off on our right at 1700 hours.

At 1658 hours, Third Battalion reported that Company C had jumped off once more, supported by tanks. By 1719, Company C had advanced approximately five hundred yards. At 1855 hours, Third Battalion reported it was across the eighty-ninth grid line. By 2017 hours, Company C had tied in with the 180th Infantry and Third Battalion was receiving small-arms, tank, and artillery fire.

At 2030 hours, Third Battalion reported that enemy infantry was infiltrating behind its right rear company. Company A was moved forward to stop the infiltration. At 2054 hours, Company K received an enemy counterattack, and at 2105 hours, Company C was ordered to fall back to the west fork of Spaciassi Creek.

Through the remaining hours the situation was static. First Battalion took up position in the north fork of Spaciassi Creek. The First Armored Infantry prepared to move through the regiment to continue the attack. Replacements (126) were sent forward to the battalions on the line.

Company C-Continued attack. Heavy fire of all types.

Cpl. Alden L. Abbott, 1st Sgt. Joseph D. Allee, PFC Leonard Kapica, PFC Ramon Manny, PFC Norman H. Meyers and Pvt. Edwin H. Nickels (Nickles) are KIA.

PFC James C. Howard, Pvt. Thomas A Schill and PFC Henry J. Wild are WIA.

May 29–Shortly after midnight, Antitank Company reported its minesweepers had contacted the 180th right flank and had found Companies C and K in the Spaciassi Creek. Third Battalion reported the loss of Captain Evans, Company I commander, who was believed captured. Companies I and L had been hit hard in the previous day's action. The regimental commander ordered the Third Battalion to patrol to the west to keep the road open on the 89th grid line. First Battalion was ordered to move up behind Third Battalion and at daybreak move into the east fork of the Spaciassi Creek. Antitank Company informed regiment that it was placing guns in the gap between the 179th and 157th Infantries.

First Battalion closed its command post at 0445 hours to move forward to its new position, and at 0730 hours, Third Battalion reported armor was moving through. At 0840 hours, Third Battalion reported armor was making good progress and meeting only a little artillery fire.

During the morning, Companies A and C reverted to the First Battalion control, and through the remainder of the day, men drifted back to the Third Battalion. Only sporadic artillery fire harassed the troops.

At 1700 hours, First Battalion was alerted to move, and at 1930 hours the regimental command post opened anew at 934362. Shortly before midnight, the 179th reported two of the battalions had moved through the First Armored Division and were meeting heavy resistance.

Company C–In reserve position north of Carano in the vicinity of the railroad bridge; morale good. Sgt. Ray Neitz is evacuated for a sprained ankle. PFC Harold Roth, serial number 36104675 (MOS-745); Pvt. Andrew M. Ondrik, serial number 34734845 (MOS-745), and PFC Nick Pavelich, serial number 35573860 (MOS-745) are assigned to Company C.

Pvt. John C. Belo, PFC Stanley J. Lata, Cpl. Roy J. Morris, Pvt. Charles F. Schulte Jr. and S/Sgt. Victor F. Staley are WIA.

[The regiment was relieved, and many of the stragglers took shelter under a ledge, which was toppled by artillery fire. Many men were killed and wounded. One-hundred-sixty were evacuated, and several were buried under the collapsed ledge.—Hugh F. Foster III]

May 30–Through the morning hours, the regimental sector remained generally quiet. During the morning, the regiment was ordered to outpost the First Armored Division after dark. In the afternoon, regiment was informed that two battalions of the 179th were being subjected to heavy small arms and artillery fire.

At 1610 hours, the regiment was ordered to move immediately to relieve the Sixth Armored Infantry and to attack in a column of battalions the following morning. The regiment was to pass to the control of the First Armored Division at that time. The 158th Field Artillery would be relieved of attachment to the 157th Infantry. Battalions were alerted to move at 2000 hours. Artillery fire fell in Company I area and accounted for eleven casualties.

Unit commanders met with the regimental company commander at 1900 hours and received orders as follows:

First Battalion would lead the morning attack astride the railroad. Third Battalion echeloned to the left rear.

Second Battalion, five hundred yards behind, ready to move left or right.

Tanks would attack through the infantry, and the regiment would jump off as soon as the tanks had passed their first objective.

The battalions began the move at approximately 2000 hours. First Battalion receiving artillery enroute. Regiment informed the battalion that the tanks would move through at 0530 hours, then fan out. First Battalion was to follow them in the advance. Shortly before midnight, the regiment received in replacement ten officers and 251 enlisted men.

Company C-Left reserve position and marched north along railroad 4½ miles to area for attack. One sergeant goes AWOL. Pvt. Israel Hoffman, serial number 31051520 (MOS-745), and Pvt. Rudolph Hodges, serial number 34878936 (MOS 745), are assigned to Company C.

Pvt. Edwin R. Connell, S/Sgt. Lawrence Criss, S/Sgt. Norman C. Foss, PFC Theodore E. Miles, PFC Raymond L. Wehner and Sgt. Walter A. Worth are WIA.

May 31–At 0045 hours, the regiment opened its forward command post at 903378. First Battalion relieved Third Battalion, Sixth Armored Infantry, at 0219 hours. By 0230 hours, all units had moved into position, and the regiment was under the command of the First Armored Division.

First Battalion jumped off behind the tanks at 0450 hours and passed the first phase line 854400-867410, meeting slight resistance. At 0733 hours, Company A was pinned down by machine-gun and mortar fire. By 0747 hours, one platoon of Company C was on phase line three. By 0820 hours, all of Company C had reached phase line three, while Company A was on phase line two.

At 0905, First Battalion reported that enemy resistance was lessening and that the troops were progressing. The battalion command post was moving to the cave at 858399. Second Battalion was in Marano Creek, vicinity of 867392. Third Battalion was moving to the vicinity of 861399.

At 1027 hours, Second Battalion moved into the positions formerly occupied by Third Battalion. At 1055 hours, regiment learned that twelve enemy tanks were located at 855414 and that artillery, tanks, and tank destroyers were firing on them. Company A was forced to pull back to 854408 because of artillery and small-arms fire from the southwest. The tanks had stopped because of antitank guns in the vicinity of 356412.

At 1130 hours, First Battalion was returned to regimental control with a company of light tanks attached. At 1200 hours, a platoon from Company B assaulted the hill at 856395 under orders to clear it of enemy and to organize the positions. At 1240 hours, the regiment learned that it would return to Forty-Fifth Division control at 2000 hours. First Battalion was to remain in position; Third Battalion was to organize its position and to prepare to counterattack to the left and front. Second Battalion was ready to counterattack either to the left or right.

First Battalion came under heavy artillery fire and reported at 1805 hours that it had suffered approximately a hundred casualties. Through the remaining hours, the enemy artillery batteries directed fire on the entire regimental sector, much of it falling on the First Battalion. The regiment received sixty-eight replacements.

Company C–Near Campoleone, Italy. Attacked at 0530 along railroad approximately four miles north of Campoleone. PFC William Mutchler and PFC George Kiewiet are AWOL at 0700 hours, but missing entry of return to duty from AWOL. PFC Burnice Auldridge is evacuated for a scalp wound. PFC James D. Hughes, PFC Efird E. Love, Sgt. Herbert J. Mayo, PFC Frank Mitrowski, Pvt. James Moore, Cpl. Cephus G. Newton, Pvt. Guiodo G. Pallozzi, Pvt. Fred S. Phillips, PFC Sidney Pollock, Pvt. James R. Reames, PFC John R. Saul, PFC George V. Tillman, T/Sgt. James B. Trainor, Pvt. Frank J. Wachter and Pvt. Saul Weinstein are WIA.

Pvt. James H. Johnson, PFC Ralph E. Lipps and PFC Luther R. Wilson are KIA.

June 1–Through the early morning hours, the situation remained static. First and Second Battalions reported receiving artillery and mortar fire. Regiment was informed at 0815 hours that the 180th Infantry had jumped off in attack at 0530 hours and was meeting only slight resistance. The 179th also reported meeting only slight resistance.

At 1055 hours, the regiment learned that the town of Velletri had been taken. During the afternoon, the regiment was alerted to move beyond Velletri with the Thirty-Sixth Division. Plans were made for a unit from the 180th Infantry to relieve First Battalion of the 157th Infantry.

Battalions were alerted to move and were informed that the entrucking and assembly area for the regiment would be at 897352. First Battalion was scheduled to move the following morning, but Second and Third Battalions were to assemble at 2200 and 2300 hours, respectively.

At 2238 the regiment opened a new command post at 0038, and plans were made for troops to jump off with the Thirty-Sixth Division in the morning, serving as an assault regiment.

Company C–Near Campoleone, Italy, in defensive position. Small amount of artillery and mortar fire coming in. PFC Joseph Brossett is evacuated sick on this date. Missing entry of return to duty.

Pvt. Thomas L. McGuire, PFC Robert D. Mitchell, Pvt. Joseph R. Shutack, PFC John Vounatso and Pvt. Herbert D. Wensley are WIA.

June 2–Shortly after midnight Second and Third Battalions arrive in bivouac areas west of Highway 7. At 0730 hours the Thirty-Sixth Engineers reported that all resistance had been cleared from Velletri and that the roads had been swept for mines and vehicles could pass. Regimental troops began moving at 0745 hours, preparing for the morning infantry attack, which was to follow in the wake of tanks. The 157th Infantry was under the control of the Thirty-Sixth Division.

At 1030 hours, the regiment opened its forward command post in Velletri, and at 1300 hours, Sixth Corps ordered First Battalion to disregard objectives seven and eight and to take nine. First Battalion entrucked to move forward, and at 1335 hours it passed through Velletri. At 1550 hours, Second Battalion reported receiving artillery from the right flank and that the tanks supporting it were unable to move. At 1655 hours, Second Battalion reported that one platoon of Company F had reached Hill 517 (934445).

At 1800 hours, First Battalion reported that Company A was moving west at 942434 and that Company B was following but was receiving mortar and small-arms fire.

At 1920 hours, Second Battalion reported that the hill at 935445 was a strong point, that one platoon of Company F and all of Company G were pinned down along the 935th grid line, but that Companies A and G were tied in.

At 2045 hours, the regimental commander ordered First Battalion to stop its attack and to dig in for the night and alerted Third Battalion to move through Second Battalion the following morning. The attack was at 0700 hours. Second Battalion was ordered to stop its attack and to organize the ground in the vicinity of 935445.

Company C–Pvt. John Fisher returns to duty. Cpl. George J. Stengel and Sgt. Walter A. Worth are WIA.

[My brother, Loran, was a medic in the 85th Division coming in from the east to Rome was killed in action on this day.—Richard Adams]

June 3–Through the early morning hours, contact was made with the Thirty-Sixth Engineers, who were on the right flank, although not joined. The orders of the regimental commander were that at 0700 hours the Third Battalion would attack in the direction of Genzano with its left north of Highway 7. The Second Battalion to follow the axis Highway 7 in regimental reserve. The orders of the regimental commander were changed at 0630 hours when he went forward and found out during the night the bulk of the enemy forces had moved to the west and that resistance was light. The regimental commander immediately changed the order and instructed each battalion to attack at once in a column of companies: third on the right, north of Highway 7; second astride Highway 7, and first, with a platoon of tanks attached, south of Highway 7. The attack moved rapidly and troops encountered only light resistance, mostly in the form of artillery and mines. By 0930 hours, the leading Company L on the right had seized the high ground at 916448. Genzano was at this time held by the enemy. The Second Battalion, Company G leading, had reached a point at 920443, and the First Battalion was in the vicinity of 920430. The regimental commander, then at 920443, ordered the Third Battalion to occupy the hill at 916448 to protect the regimental right flank. The remainder of the Third Battalion was to push to the southwest and to seize and occupy the right (north) portion of the objective (Hill 415). The Second Battalion was to occupy the left (south) part of the hill. The First Battalion was to remain in Regimental Reserve.

In the afternoon, the enemy had withdrawn from Lanuvio (916-420), which allowed elements of the Thirty-Fourth Division in that vicinity to push north. One regiment had reached a point just south of the Second Battalion of the 157th Infantry. Another battalion (100th of the Thirty-Fourth Division) was pushing to the northwest around the southern slope of Hill 415. This movement caused some intermingling of units.

At 1140 hours, the corps commander, General Truscott, visited the command post and was oriented on the ground we held. At 1145 hours, word arrived from corps headquarters informing regiment that the 157th Infantry was now under the control of the Thirty-Fourth Division which ordered us to attack and seize Genzano. Thus, the regiment was disposed in an entirely different direction and had a different objective. The Sixth Corps and the Thirty-Fourth Division were so notified and the order was canceled. By 1300 hours, the regiment was near the slopes of Hill 415 with the 100th Battalion of the Thirty-Fourth Division.

Orders were received to push on to the west and seize the new objective. However, from that time until 2200 hours, the troops were under artillery and mortar fire from Genzano (enemy held) and heavy friendly firing from the vicinity of 895400, the sector from which the First Armored Division was pushing north. The commanding general of the Thirty-Fourth Division visited the command post at 1330 and conferred with the regimental commander, at which time other movements and ours were coordinated. At 2000, the regiment moved to the west in a column of battalions to seize the new objective.

The Thirty-Fourth Division attacked to the north to seize Genzano. Movement was slow in the rough country but progressed without opposition. By 2400 hours, the leading elements had reached 899435 and were moving northwest. The object of the cross-country movement was to force out or trap the enemy, who was opposing our forces, which were attacking north. It was entirely successful.

Company C–2½ miles north of Velletri, Italy. Moved by truck to assembly area to Velletri, detrucked and marched 1½ miles out of town. Small amount of enemy artillery and mortar fire in vicinity. PFC Hanzel Blair is evacuated due to exhaustion and does not return during the war. Sgt. Leland Scott is treated for laryngitis.

PFC Robert J. Bloomfield, PFC Calvin L. Cahoon and Pvt. Morris M. Marcus are WIA.

June 4–Through the early morning hours, the regiment continued its advance, meeting no resistance whatsoever. At 0345, it had reached its first objective and had notified the Thirty-Fourth Division of that fact. At that time the 157th Infantry came back to the control of the Forty-Fifth Division.

Regiment was ordered to assemble its troops and await further instructions. By 0800 hours, Second Battalion was on Hill Cecchini, 874448, First Battalion at 879454 and Third Battalion at 883448. At 0810 the regimental command post began its move to 8763448. At 1715 hours, the command post opened anew at 833475. The battalions moved into assembly area on the 8,347th grid line. During the evening hours, regimental patrols probed the forward areas but could locate no enemy troops, and it was reported that the Forty-Fifth Division had reached the Tiber River.

Company C-Marched from vicinity of Velletri north approximately 4½ miles to assembly area.

Cpl. Wallace Moffitt Jr. is WIA.

June 5–It was reported that the 180th Division had crossed the Tiber River.

Company C-Shuttled by truck and marched fourteen miles to assembly area south of Rome.

[After Anzio, the American army I believe, became the first army ever to conquer Rome from the south. Dad entered Rome in an ambulance. Since he had a short time in Rome before the Forty-Fifth Infantry Division had to get ready for another invasion, he took advantage of the opportunity to see the ancient city. He wanted to see the catacombs, and when he entered the underground tombs, he quickly became lost. It took him a while to find his way out.

Dad had fond memories of the civilian population in Italy and France. He said that they were extremely grateful for being liberated from the Nazi nightmare. The civilians would thank the liberators by giving them wine, bread, or any food that they had.

Even though the Forty-Fifth Infantry Division helped to conquer Southern Italy and liberate the city of Rome, fighting continued in Northern Italy—John Kirchgassner]

* * *

Jared's Blog,
June 6, 2013 Rome--

Then: There was no more fighting in Italy for the 45th Infantry Division. The 157th set up camp about fifteen miles north of Rome. There the troops relaxed and got passes to go explore the Eternal City. They made the most of their time. From the book *Eager for Duty*: "The city was probably given a jubilant working over by the 157th." They were tough guys to say the least, and that might be part of the reason they were such great soldiers. Sounds just like his grandson, Mark Kirchgassner—ten feet tall and bulletproof.

Today was a pretty relaxed day. We went to visit the oldest church in Rome this morning. On the way back, we walked through a f lea market. I could have bought a Rolex for twenty-five euros (I'm sure it was real), but who needs a Rolex when you can sport a Timex? In the afternoon, we split up to soak in Rome however we liked. Kirch and Krista went on a lovers' stroll through the park, Rita got knickknacks for her family, and I exercised in the park. It was a good day, but we didn't take many pictures.

To keep you entertained, I'll note some bloopers from our trip so far. We nearly missed our plane in Dayton. On our first night here, Rita slipped on the stairs and busted her butt. The ladies have more blisters on their feet than Rome has churches. The front-desk worker thought Kirch was Russian. (That is a first.) Rita pulled an alarm trying to flush the toilet while at a restaurant in Anzio, causing restaurant workers to run. Racing

Kirch up the stairs, I wiped out on a rug that was clearly not secured down. There were too many other incidents to mention. Great times.

Tonight we went out for our final taste of Rome. Had a great bowl of pasta while we watched the waiter and the cook get in a fight that spilled out into the street because Mark's order was messed up. Someone put mushrooms on Mark's cheese pizza. Mark eat fungi? I don't think so. From there, we said good-bye to the Colosseum and the Vatican. More of an excuse to see them all lit up at night. Thank you, Rome.—Jared Leiker]

[The Thunderbirds were the first of the armed forces to reach Vatican City, crossing the Tiber River on June 4, 1944. Rome had surrendered, and the troops used the city as a place to get some R&R. The 157th Infantry Regiment's breakout for Rome took place on May 23, 1944. S/Sgt. Robert Kirchgassner wrote later that the only way out of Anzio was to "run from shell hole to shell hole." It took the regiment about twelve days to reach its objective—Rome.

Seeing Rome almost seventy years later, Company C would recognize the historic buildings, especially the Colosseum, and would be happy to know that after liberation, Rome continues to thrive as an ancient city in a modern world. We loved Rome. The history, the culture, the cuisine, and the friendly people made our visit to the city a wonderful experience. We think the Thunderbirds would appreciate the fact that some traits of American life, like visiting McDonald's for lunch, are deeply embedded in Rome. Lines were long to order the coveted Big Mac.

We spent a good part of one day in the World War II museum during our time in Rome. Many of the displays were dedicated to those who gave their lives resisting the occupation of Rome by the fascists. Also on display were the insignias of the first American troops to enter Rome. The city had been spared the scars of war, since the infrastructure was considered off limits. Rome did not undergo continual bombing as London and other cities did. The curator explained to us that the Allies used Catholic pilots so that the Vatican and historical churches would not be bombed. The Axis powers controlling Italy did not want to damage the valuable art displayed in many of Rome's churches.

As the Allied troops marched through the streets of Rome in June of 1944, the Italians showered them with f lowers and shouts of joy. Liberation had finally come. Gen. Mark Clark led the American troops through the city . The euphoria was shor t-lived as the invasion of France had begun on the Normandy coast on June 6, 1944. The GIs who had battled the best of Hitler's military while living in foxholes in Anzio for four months were quickly forgot ten when the news of D-Day hit the radio throughout the world. The Fort y-Fifth Division did not rest long, because the invasion of France from the south was being planned for August. The troops had to complete training for the mission to succeed.

I received a phone call early in the morning from my daughter, Spec. Abigail Grathwohl Weber of the US Army. She had read on the Internet that the Archbishop of Indianapolis was recommending that St. Martin Parish be closed in the near future and combined with other parishes. That news was a tremendous disappointment to me. I had traveled more than five thousand miles to honor my father, who, like my mother, had served St. Martin Parish. My dad was a member of the Holy Name Society. Their families had served the parish since the 1850s.

Owen, Grace, Kate, Harper, and David. (1st Row)
Elizabeth, Sam, Noah and Hayden. (2nd Row)
Hoping that St. Martin Parish will not be closed in the future.

As I toured the Vatican and saw all the marvels the popes had preserved from the ancient world, I wondered if my church would preserve the history of my family and other families who were members of the parish. The veterans of World War I donated the side altars of St. Martin Church in gratitude to God for their safe return. What will happen to the altars if my parish closes? Will the statue of the Infant of Prague, in memory of my uncle Vic Hoffmeier, who died in World War II, stay by the side altar for all to remember his sacrifice? What about the bricks and mortar that every family donated for the church to be erected in 1917? If my dad were still among us, he would see the closing of the parish as something more than the loss of a building. This church is a witness to the faith of so many who have worshiped there, and now their living testament may be forgotten in the future.—Rita Kirchgassner]

June 6–Company C-Southwest of Rome in assembly area.

June 8–Company C-Five miles west of Rome in rest and training area. (From June 8 to June 19, the regiment remained in a reserve area, rested and prepared for future operations. On June 11, awards were presented in a formal regimental decoration ceremony and on June 15, Second Battalion received its citation as a distinguished unit likewise in a formal ceremony. Throughout the period, regimental troops, battalions one at a time, visited Rome.

Company C-Sgt. Stanley P. Granger DOW received on May 31st.

[It was June 9 and we came to a stop north and west of Rome. We were in a rest area now and given passes to Rome.—Robert L. Kirchgassner]

Sgt. George V. Marangoni hoisted the American f lag in Rome.
SC Photo

45th Infantry Division marching past the Colosseum.
Used with permission from the 45th Infantry Division WWII Reenactors

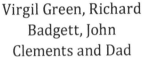

Virgil Green, Richard Badgett, John Clements and Dad

Colosseum-June 2013

June 10–Company C-Five miles west of Rome. T/Sgt. Max L. Johnson is evacuated due to exhaustion and does not return during the war.

PFC Douglas A. Bibb, 1st Lt. Anse H. Speairs and Pvt. Sylvester Winemaker are WIA.

[Dad never saw Max again, but at Dad's wake, Johnson sent f lowers and a card that read, "To a good soldier."—Rita Kirchgassner]

June 12–Company C–PFC Harold Scott is evacuated due to tonsillitis.

June 13–Company C–PFC Hanzel Blair is dropped from rolls. T/4 Orville E. Leek is WIA.

June 14–Company C–T/Sgt. Max L. Johnson is dropped from rolls. Sgt. Leland Scott returns to duty.

June 15–Company C–Second Battalion receives its Citation as Distinguished Unit in a formal ceremony. Throughout the period, regimental troops were able to visit Rome. PFC Burnice N. Auldridge returns.

June 16–Company C–PFC Burnice N. Auldridge is evacuated for being sick.

June 19–Company C-Moved by truck from vicinity of Rome to vicinity of Anzio, arriving at 2030 where units began boarding the LCI's and LST's that were to carry them to Salerno. Other units were to travel overland.

June 21–Company C–Anzio, Italy. At sea. Company received order to move to port at 1600, left area by truck at 1700, loaded on LST at 2000.

June 22–Company C twelve miles south of Salerno. Second lieutenant has scabies.

June 23–The entire regiment closed in the areas in the vicinity of 755270. Through the remainder of the month the regiment remained in the area near Salerno. The troops began amphibious training, took hikes and swims.

Company C-Sgt. Ray Neitz returns to company. PFC Harold N. Scott returns to duty. Pvt. C. J. Lampasso DOW received on May 23rd.

PFC Karl R. Connor is WIA.

June 27–Company C-Twelve miles south of Salerno. Lt. Anse Speairs is promoted to captain.

June 28–Company C–A private is sent to the regimental stockade. Two privates have fever of unknown origin.

June 30–Company C–Report of a self-inf licted gunshot wound by private who went AWOL is apprehended.

July 1–Company C-Twelve miles south of Salerno. Pvt. Joseph C. Brossett, Pvt. Richard Adams, Pvt. Thomas Briggs, Pvt. Rudolph Hodges, and Pvt. Andrew M. Ondrik are promoted to private first class.

July 2–Company C–Pvt. Clarence Pierce is promoted to private first class.

July 4–Company C-Twelve miles southeast of Salerno. Sgt. Leland Scott is promoted to staff sergeant. Three enlisted men are AWOL. Enlisted men: 266.

July 9–Company C–PFC Harold Scott is assigned to the 32nd Field Hospital.

July 10–15–Practice by companies and battalions; the men made practice landings and learned the handling of Bangalore torpedoes. Regiment moved to a rest camp near Agropoli on July 12.

Company C–Agropoli, Italy. Usual rest-period duties and training. Sgt. Virgil Green is ill due to a penile lesion, and PFC George Kiewiet Jr. has a fever of unknown origin. PFC Harold N. Scott and Sgt. Hyman Miller return to duty.

> [To the newly joined members of the 157th Infantry, Col. John H. Church wrote in a welcoming pamphlet: "On July 10, 1944, the 157th Infantry has been in combat for one year during which time it participated in three major amphibious operations and played an important role in two campaigns. It has spent with the 45th Division approximately 246 days on the front lines. In pivotal battles, it has suffered great casualties, and today the number of original members who assaulted the beach at Sicily is extremely limited within the Regiment. With the constant f low of replacements, hailing from all sections from the United States, it remains an essential part of one of the strongest and most renowned Infantry Divisions in the American Army."]

July 16–Company C–Usual rest-camp duties. First Lt. Richard Stone is released from assignment and assigned to the 7th Replacement Depot. Does not return during the war.

July 19–Company C–Troops made fifteen-mile march from 0300 to 0600. Getting ready to move. PFC George Kiewiet is ill. Sgt. Virgil Green returns to duty.

July 20–Company C-Near Naples, Italy. S/Sgt. Robert Kirchgassner assigned to hospital for acute frontal sinusitis.

July 21–Company C-Near Naples, Italy. Moved by truck from rest area near Agropoli to training in the area of Naples. Usual camp duties. PFC George Kiewiet Jr. returns to duty. PFC Thomas M. Briggs has fever of unknown origin. PFC Joseph Brossett is evacuated, being ill, and does not return to war.

July 22–Company C–S/Sgt. Robert Kirchgassner returns to duty.

July 26–Company C-Sgt. Ray Neitz is absent due to not-yet-diagnosed illness manifested by pain in both feet. Reclassified for assignment and does during the war.

July 27–Company C-Near Naples, Italy. Pvt. Israel A. Hoffman, assigned to 2nd Replacement Depot, is released from duty due to lunar cartilage in right knee, and assigned to 262nd Station Hospital.

July 28–Company C–PFC John A. Chorba is evacuated for being sick and does not return to war.

July 29–Through the month the regiment continued amphibious training and took hikes for physical hardening purposes.

Company C-Near Naples, Italy.

August 1–There could be no doubt but that the month of August would see the Forty-Fifth Division and the 157th Infantry in action against the enemy once more. Off the line since a few days following the capture of Rome, the division had had the longest rest of its combat history. Speed marches, long hikes and extensive amphibious training through the months of June and July had kept the 157th Infantry in excellent condition, however, and physically the troops were prepared for any future operation.

August 4–The regiment, during the first six days of August, was bivouacked in the "dust bowl" area in the vicinity of the town of Giuigliano, where the men engaged in general training and sought recreation at moving picture and stage show provided by special services.

Company C-Near Naples, Italy. Sgt. Virgil Green is reduced to private.

August 5–Company C near Naples, Italy. S/Sgt. John Clements is promoted to tech sergeant, PFC Quienton Steele is promoted to corporal, and Pvt. John A. Fischer Jr. is promoted to private first class.

August 6–Company C–PFC Thomas W. Briggs returns to duty.

August 7–Command post at 066573 closed; troops move to vicinity of Pozzuoli, Italy. Boarded LCIs and LSTs for practice amphibious exercises at Salerno. Command post opens aboard LCI 952 in Pozzuoli.

August 8–10–The morning of August 8, the 157th Infantry with the other units of the Forty-Fifth Division, stormed the stretch of the beach between Salerno and Agropoli for an H-hour exercise called Thunderbird. The commander of the Sixth Corps halted the exercise before noon that day, and the troops returned to their ships. On August 9, they debarked in the Nevada Staging Area (for LCIs) and Texas Staging Area (for LSTs) near Pozzuoli to await further orders.

Two days in the staging area and the regiment boarded landing crafts for the second time, the LCIs setting sail for the Salerno Harbor, while other ships remained anchored near Naples in the shadow of Mount Vesuvius.

Company C–Naples, Italy. Staging area. Pvt. Virgil Green is transferred to 262nd Station Hospital with fever of unknown origin.

August 10–Company C–PFC George Kiewiet Jr. transferred to 182nd Station Hospital for unknown reasons. S/Sgt. Leland A. Scott is transferred to 225th Station Hospital.

August 11–In harbor. Regular ship duties.

> [By this time, it was common knowledge among those serving in Company C, 4th Platoon, where Dad was, so was John. It was a mutual friendship. — Richard Adams]

August 12–14–Left harbor at 1630 for future operations vicinity of St. Maxime. At sea. The following morning, the regimental convoy began the journey, which was to take the troops to the coast of southern France, where they were to assault the beaches in the vicinity of the town of St. Maxime. First and Third Battalions were to make initial landings while Second Battalion was to remain in regimental reserve.

At 1445 hours on August 13, orientation on future operation in southern France by Colonel James for troops on LCI 520; D-Day, August 15; H-hour, 0800.

On August 14, the convoy passed between Corsica and Sardinia at 0700 hours, traveled north along the coast of Corsica, and then swung northwest toward France at 1730 hours. First waves of troops were scheduled to strike the beach at 0800 hours the following morning, and every man had seen maps showing the 157th landing points and had been provided with all available information concerning enemy installations and strength in that sector.

[The regiment had finished training. Then the footrace began to keep up with the German army, retreating to its own border. The regiment participated in the rapid push up the valley of the Rhone, meeting stiff resistance here and there but advancing rapidly.—Hugh F. Foster III]

Bagnoli, Italy. Equipment loaded day and night
for the invasion of France.
SC Photo-Lapidus

Chapter 6
Gaul

A hammer is merely a swinging weight without an anvil to strike steel upon.
—Unknown

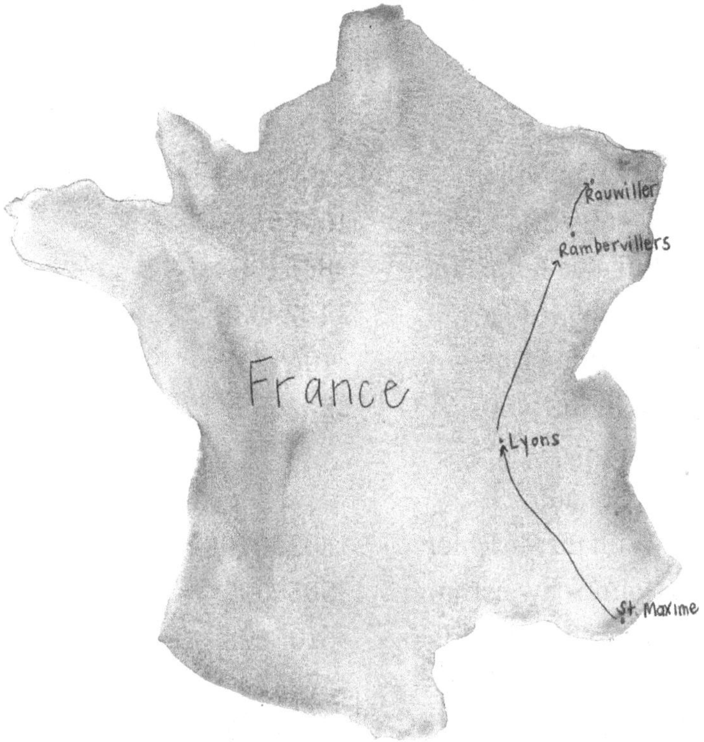

Operation Dragoon (a k a Anvil)
Plan De La Tour, France

[After the liberation of Rome, the Forty-Fifth Division was taken out of the fight in Italy to prepare for the invasion of Southern France in August of 1944. The reason for this invasion was to relieve pressure on Allied forces that had landed in Northern France, the famous D-Day invasion of June 6, 1944. The long awaited crossing of the English Channel and troops invading Southern France would hopefully speed up the liberation of France and the end of the war.

The plan in the invasion of Southern France was that the American and Allied Forces would proceed up the Rhone River and join the forces that had invaded from the north.—John Kirchgassner]

DAD HAD CARRIED A SMALL NOTEBOOK in his pocket, recording the names and serial numbers of the men who were with him during the invasion of France.

First Squad:	
Sgt. Virgil Green	37247915
PFC Nick Pavelich	35573860
PFC Richard Badgett	35698261
PFC Richard Adams	32958105
Pvt. Israel Hoffman	31051520
Pvt. John Fischer	33600528
Second Squad:	
Sgt. Hyman Miller	33000443
PFC George Kiewiet	16086521
Pfc Burnice Auldridge	38454963
PFC Rudolf Hodges	34878936
PFC Anthony Dumont	31069237
PFC Will Huffman	35726559
Third Squad:	
Sgt. William Mutchler	13020870
PFC John Schweisthal	35051605
PFC Harold Roth	36104675
PFC Andrew Ondrik	34734845
PFC Douglas Bill	33627507
PFC Clarence Pierce	17010733

[The invasion of southern France proved to be one of the most successful amphibious operations in history. The following is a timeline of the invasion: --John Kirchgassner]

August 15–D-Day Journal:

0400-The Air Corps bombed the coast, striking at German gun positions and troop and vehicle concentrations.

0700-0730-Heavy bombers concentrated on the sector which the 157th was to assault and at approximately the same time the Navy's battle wagons loosed a tremendous forty minute bombardment gun fire along the coast.

0749–Assault boats filled with infantrymen.

0755–Short-range rocket fire on beaches.

0800–H-Hour and in contact with First Battalion and division by radio. It was observed that assault troops of first wave landed on Red and Green Beaches. Message sent to division: no fire observed on troops. First and Third Battalions, the regimental assault units, moved through the gaping holes in the barbed wire and crossed the six-foot seawall without suffering a casualty. Resistance was short-lived. German gun crews and riflemen made their way down the hills to surrender.

0810-Third Battalion radio first and second waves ashore.

0823-Third Battalion reports third wave ashore.

0825–First Battalion reported ashore.

0835-Company B, First Battalion on initial objective.

0900–Regimental forward command post landed on Red Beach, 510225.

0905–Command post at First Battalion (503229).

0920-Navy reports slight mortar fire on all beaches. Regimental command post at 497227.

0922–First Battalion has captured twelve POWs.

0930–First Battalion: no resistance or mines encountered on the beach. Companies B at 490234 and C at 492235 are in contact. Regimental command post at 4972273. POWs state no mines or infantry in the area.

0950-All Second Battalion has landed.

1005–Rear-echelon regiment command post leaves LCI 520 to land on Green Beach.

1010–Radio message to division: Red Battalion, approximately Company B, at 485237. Company C-White Battalion at 490240; all landed, moving to first phase line.

[It was pretty much standard in the US Army of the time to "color code" the battalions, for simplicity in documenting things. The American colors were used to that the Red was 1st Battalion, White was the 2nd Battalion and Blue was the 3rd Battalion. Regiments and divisions were also "coded"; in the 45th the division was "Power" and the 157th was "Poison."—Hugh F. Foster]

1016-Radio message-First Battalion command post at 491229.

1030–From S-2: First Battalion, Companies B and C, are on objective; Company A at 477245.

1035–First Battalion reports at objective; resistance slight.

1040–Elements of 158th Field Artillery passing command post.

1045–Major Barr in command post takes our information and gives us 180th information.

1120–Captain Slyter to S-3 reports Company I moving to St. Maxime. Civilian reports five hundred Germans in St. Maxime moved out at 0600.

1255–Colonel Perry in command post.

1300–Civilian report: barbed wire, and bridge mined on both sides at 460231.

1320–First and Second Battalions report situation and location of front-line troops.

1325–Lieutenant Boesel, part of the rear command post, reports that First Battalion neutralized roadblock at 470232.

1325–Messenger from Third Battalion: moving into St. Maxime.

1326–Inform me immediately when St. Maxime is captured: G-3, Forty–Fifth Division.

1327-Request dispositions of all battalions.

1350–Message, First Battalion Company A at 463238: no resistance.

1400–General Eagles calls Poison 6 (regimental commander) for situation.

1415-Company A at 463238; Company B and C at 465250.

1415–Captain Carroll reports Company E at 457214. Company I at 478205. Company L following Company I. Artillery falling on troops at 478205. Pillbox at St. Maxime knocked out. Company K fighting for hotel. A mile inland regimental infantrymen captured an entire battery of heavy artillery. A Third Battalion unit uncovered a camouflaged dugout that enemy soldiers evacuated only minutes before, leaving on the stove a pot of hot coffee and a cauldron of boiling water. The men drank the coffee and used the boiling water for shaving.

1431–Message to division: First Battalion has objective A, Hill J; Second Battalion, Company F, last reported at 466218; Company G leading. Companies E and F moving on objective at 425213.

1455–Elements of Cannon Company unloaded and passing regimental command post.

1515–General Pascal in command post with Colonel Reynolds.

1525-Message from Third Battalion-St. Maxime cleared out leaving two squads of Company K.

1525–Paper diary and overlays taken by Third Battalion taken to division by Major Bishop. Town of St. Maxime has been captured by the Third Battalion.

1530-First Battalion command post at 463238.

1540–Message from commander of the 157th to commander First Battalion: give situation and location of companies.

1545-Commanding officer of Second Battalion to commanding officer of the 157th: How far has axis road been cleared?

1550–Message S-3 to 157th to commander of the Second Battalion: 117th Recon troops reported to be in Plan De La Tour; road apparently unmined.

1620–Major Carr: road okay to point 445230. Patrol stopped him at that point and stated that they were going one thousand feet further-patrol from headquarters First Battalion.

1656–Lieutenant Boesel reports Company A at 445240, Company B at 430255, and out of communication with Company C as of 1660.

1715–General Church leaves for division and forward command post.

1725-In contact with the Eighty-Third Chemical Battalion.

1830-Message to G-3 (Operations Officer), Forty Fifth Division, 157th command post at 423238 at 1810.

1845–Captain Tinkle from the 158th Field Artillery reports that the 117th Cavalry Recon has been in Plan De La Tour and Valauris and has not contacted anything.

1900–First Battalion: twenty enemy reported digging in from 400230-411232. Will send a platoon to investigate.

1901–Captain Elliot reports to Third Battalion command post.

1925–Message from Sixth Corps: clear beaches and St. Maxime as soon as possible; advance to Fresha Valley as soon as possible. Expect to land CCI (French) over your beaches.

1927–Gas, rations, water, and ammo dump two hundred yards down road on left side reported by S-4 (Supply Officer.)

1930–First Battalion: civilian reports bridge at Vidauban blown.

1940–Captain Riggs in command post: no information in addition to above.

2020–General Pascal in command post reports Thirty-Sixth Division having rough time and hasn't landed yet.

2030–Major Sparks in command post: ordered to hold tonight, jump off at 0600.

2045–Lieutenant Boesel reports to lead elements of Second Battalion at 260290.

2046–General Church orders Lieutenant Boesel to Second Battalion with instructions for tomorrow: jump off at 0550 and advance to final objective; wait there for further orders; report hourly.

2050–Capt. Clay Barnes in command post reports AntiTank Company two hundred yards up road on the left-hand side.

2245–Telephone–Commanding general, Forty-Fifth Division, to commander of the 157th Infantry: have First and Third Battalions go to Vidauban and Lorgues. Have Second Battalion go on to Le Luc. Use shortest and best route.

2255–General Church sends orders to be sent to Second Battalion with order to go on to Le Luc as fast as possible, using stream bed and rails as route. Do not use Plan De La Tour road.

2256–Major Mitchell in command post. General Church orders him with his battalion to go to Plan De La Tour and follow axis of communication road so he can follow either First or Second Battalions. Send out motor patrol to Grimaud and St. Tropez to see if the route is clear. When they return, move battalion to Plan De La Tour and report. Major Mitchell reports Third Battalion at 4418 at 2200, objective D.

Company C-Made an assault on southern France from St. Maxime.

Jared's Blog:
[June 24, 2013 Nice--
St. Maxime is about an hour and a half west of Nice along the Mediterranean coast. It's situated between Nice and Marseille. This was the site chosen for Operation Dragoon. The Forty-Fifth would make its fourth and final amphibious assault on Europe here. Boats pulled in near the beach in the harbor. The Thunderbirds didn't meet nearly the resistance that they had in their other invasions.

I found this a disappointing day because of our trip to St. Maxime. First, public transportation, as usual, was a complete nightmare getting to St. Maxime from Nice. That wasn't as disappointing as what we found when we arrived. The only clue that the Forty-Fifth was there was a small statue of a naked mermaid with the date of the landing that sat in the middle of a sidewalk. The harbor is full of small boats and tourist shops, with a small beach that looks out to St. Tropez Island. My heart was slightly broken that there was little marking the site of such a significant event in world history. But maybe that's why they did it— so people could be free to do as they please and to move on with happy lives.

Although the tribute to the invasion was a disappointment, the day wasn't. Just to walk the same beach as heroes of the greatest generation was a treat. We spent the remainder of our day on the beach at Nice. This is our final day in Europe.—Jared Leiker]

[This day was the only time on the journey when I knew that Jared was frustrated with me. The day was not going as planned. The buses were delayed. When we finally arrived in Nice, we went to a tourist kiosk, looking for information. I asked the worker about World War II, but she was not fluent in English. I kept trying, but Jared broke in, saying, "Snoop (the nickname my nephews gave me long time ago), she does not understand and does not care about your words. Let's go!" So we did and found the marker.—Rita Kirchgassner]

[The bus ride from Nice to St. Maxime was long and full of anticipation of seeing where the Forty-Fifth Infantry landed in France. As I traveled, I could only wonder if the soldiers' anticipation of landing at St. Maxime was anything like mine, though I knew their journey had far greater consequences.—Mark Kirchgassner]

Rita at St. Maxime-June 2013

Mark at St. Maxime-June 2013

August 16–By dawn the morning of August 16, the regiment was on the move once more. Preceded by motorized patrols, First Battalion pushed forward by truck to Vidauban, and after a short firefight, neutralized an enemy roadblock in that region. The battalion moved through the town and occupied the high ground. General Church ordered motorized patrols toward Lorgues.

At 1140 hours, First Battalion destroyed enemy material: forty-two light machine-guns, five potato mashers, five drums of ammo, and one mine.

At 1341 hours, First Battalion reported Company C in Vidauban. At 1450 hours, Captain Edwards reported First Battalion encountered enemy point of resistance in vicinity of 312342. A strong point in town was knocked out and town occupied at 1330.

At 1730 hours, Lieutenant Farley reported that at 1200 hours, Company C surprised the Germans, who were getting ready to evacuate Vidauban. The Germans f led along the Le Luc road, fighting a delaying action as they left. This action cost the Germans more than twenty-five men and about twenty-five POWs. There was still sniper fire in Vidauban at 1700 hours.

Second Battalion, shuttling toward Le Luc, encountered two enemy strong points during the afternoon but with the aid of tanks, drove the Germans from their positions. The fighting lasted until 2300 hours when the enemy troops withdrew.

Company C-Pvt. Frank McCarthy and PFC George V. Tillman are WIA.

[Company C–PFC John Schweisthal is shot through the ear by a German sniper during a house-to-house search near Lorgues, France. John is sent to the ship *Acadia* for medical treatment. PFC Richard Adams remembers that John and he were conducting a house-to-house search when they were pinned down by a sniper with a machine-gun. They were standing in an 18 inch recess of a house with 80 pound packs on their backs. In between bursts is when John peered out for a look.-Richard Adams]

August 17–First Battalion moved to Lorgues, reaching the city late in the afternoon. Second Battalion jumped off in attack at Le Luc at dawn and met resistance immediately. Supported by tanks, the companies closed in on the town from the surrounding high ground, moving slowly along the ridges. Twice during the morning, the German defenders turned back infantry attacks. Continuous pressure drove the enemy from the town late in the afternoon. The troops, advancing to the high ground north of town, found that nine enemy trucks and five tanks had been destroyed in the attack.

At 1832 hours, First Battalion telephoned command post to report two hundred to three hundred enemy in vicinity of 209358 and high ground southwest.

At 1930 hours, First Battalion reported the French Forces of the Interior (FFI) chief sent a message: "Urgent to send men and ammo as soon as possible. At Salernes estimated seventy Germans setting up roadblock two kilometers before Salernes."

At 1950 hours First Battalion reported that it captured two hundred enemy soldiers in Lorgues plus twenty wounded in a hospital there. Twenty-five German soldiers are dead.

At 2100 hours First Battalion received a message from a French civilian and it stated, "The FFI Chief at Barjols says Germans are bringing in two hundred fresh troops into his town." Company C-Pvt. Burnice N. Auldridge is reassigned.

August 18–At 0620 hours, with the Second Battalion in regimental reserve and the Third Battalion in support, the First Battalion attacked toward Salernes, preceded by motorized patrols from the regimental intelligence and reconnaissance platoon. First Battalion arrived in Salernes at 0945 with troops just on the other side. It met no resistance, and during the afternoon it shuttled into Tavernes, which it found unoccupied. Attempting to push on to Varages, however, motorized patrols from the battalion and from the regiment encountered an enemy roadblock in a steep walled valley, strategically placed. This roadblock held up the advance of the battalion for an hour. The enemy succeeded in capturing on jeep and damaging another. By 1700 hours, the Germans had withdrawn. Company C began moving into Varages, while Company A approached it from the north. Company B, moving through the town, cut the highway running south.

At 1830 hours, General Church returned to command post; stated First Battalion mopping up town. Company C was held up by roadblock this side of Varages.

Third Battalion, the support unit, sent one company with a platoon of tanks attached toward Barjols, where the FFI (French Forces of the Interior) were waging a losing battle. Enroute the company met the 179th Infantry, which had been ordered to take the town, so the unit returned to the battalion.

August 19–With relief units from Third Battalion under its control, First Battalion began the push west. At 0600, the First Battalion began its push west toward the day's regimental objective, Rions. Shuttling forward in trucks, the troops captured the towns of St. Martin and Esparron without a shot being fired. Approaching Rions at approximately 1200 hours, however, they encountered an enemy roadblock, which they cleared after a two-hour firefight.

[First Lieutenant Donald Waugh who commanded the mortars and machine guns in Company C was killed in action.-Richard Adams]

Meanwhile, Second Battalion, in regimental reserve, sent one company southeast toward Barjols to contact Company B, 179th Infantry. Another company moved north to help the Forty-Fifth Reconnaissance troops capture La Verdiere. The town fell at 1680 hours.

A runner reported at 1040 hours: Company C at 8150 and still advancing.

As the regiment moved inland, the assistance of the partisan French became increasingly noticeable. Armed with M-1 and automatic rifles and weighted to the full with ammunition and grenades, they returned from the front cheering the Americans, shaking hands all around, and relating their experiences in voluble French. Patriot patrols accompanied the battalions on marches forward, and small FFI groups searched the mountain passes and valleys, flushing Germans from their scattered hiding places. Information from the Marquis proved invaluable to the rapidly moving regiment.

Though the men were tiring, their morale was high and the French people did much to keep it so. As troops moved through the town, the entire populace lined the streets, saying "Viva Americano," waving, and extending their fingers in the sign for victory. Typically, the plodding doughboys were most impressed with the pleasant and high-spirited Mademoiselles and the French wines. The study of the French language became an increasingly important part of each man's daily routine.

Company C-KIA: S/Sgt. Norman C. Foss, Pvt. Paul T. Martin and Pvt. Frank J. Wachter.

August 20–First Battalion became regimental reserve while Second Battalion moved forward to cross the Durance River, a tributary of the Rhone. The lead elements succeeded in fording the river by 0800 hours, and motorized patrols traveled toward Pertuis, Moulin Du Pas, and Beaumont. Shortly after midnight, Companies E and F reached the city of Pertuis, where Second Battalion remained for the night. The Germans had destroyed the main bridge, which crossed the Durance River, and other regimental units were delayed several hours before an engineers' structure was completed. By evening, all troops made the crossing.

At 1900 hours, S-3 (Operations Officer) stated that Company C will occupy St. Paul Les Durance, placing roadblock on road running northeast from there and one on road running southeast from there.

Company C–Rions, France. Capt. Anse Speairs is relieved of his duties due to illness.

August 21–The 179th Infantry pushed through First Battalion. A motorized patrol made reconnaissance in Apt and found it occupied by enemy infantry and armor. Third Battalion remained in position on the high ground southeast of Moulin Du Pas.

At 1155 hours, Captain Carroll stated that General Church had ordered First Battalion to area in vicinity of La Bastide Jourdans and to close assembly area before dark tonight.

Company C-Remained in Rions until it was shuttled to St. Paul Les Durance for the night. Set up roadblocks southeast and northeast of the town. Weather clear.

August 22–Company A, with heavy weapons, three platoons from Cannon Company, one platoon of tanks, and two tank destroyers attached, moved toward Apt to clear the town of resistance. By midafternoon the enemy had withdrawn and Company A had set up roadblocks.

August 23–Activity was limited, although Company B relieved four roadblocks that had been established by the 179th Infantry. Shortly before midnight the 157th Infantry came under corps control.

Company C-Captain Speairs returned to duty.

August 24–The regiment was relieved by the Seventh Infantry of the Third Division, and the following day it shuttled to the vicinity of the town Serres. During the afternoon, Third Battalion, with a platoon from AntiTank and Cannon Companies, moved to Nyons to contact the Thirty-Sixth Division, coming under the command of Task Force Butler at that time.

August 26–The regiment shuttled to Crest. At 1440 hours, Company F, reinforced, jumped off in the attack on the town of Allex. Second Battalion, sweeping into town from the high ground, met stubborn resistance and engaged the enemy in the narrow streets. Fighting flared up in all sections of the town, and shortly before midnight, Second Battalion patrols were ordered to clear the enemy from the southwest part of Allex, utilizing hand grenades and tommy guns. The patrols were not successful.

Company C-PFC Rudolph Hodges is assigned to the 120th Medical Battalion.

August 27–At dawn, the regiment received word from Second Battalion that fifteen Mark IV Tanks, entering Allex from the south, had swung in position a thousand yards west of town.

Company C was in reserve on the east side. General Church ordered that another platoon of Company A be placed in right rear of Company C roadblock almost due north of Crest.

At 0630 hours, following a fifteen-minute artillery and mortar barrage that swept Allex from east to west, Second Battalion attacked. At 0735 hours the town had been cleared of enemy and the companies were establishing roadblocks. At 1000 hours, Company G passed through Company E and launched an assault on the high ground northeast of Livron, where the battalion was to intersect the road running north along the Rhone River. At 1110 hours the Sixth Corps commander ordered the attacked stopped because of possible strong resistance from the north. Third Battalion is still attached to Task Force Butler.

At 1237 hours, Lieutenant Farley returns from FFI headquarters. He states that there are a thousand FFI to the east of our positions ready to accompany us on our advance to Valence.

At 1910, Lieutenant Kambeitz says that Third Battalion cut road at 9464 but enemy had come in on both sides of them. Thirty-Sixth Division troops finally came upon their flanks.

Company C–Weather is rainy and visibility is poor in the morning.

August 28–At 0845 hours, Captain Carroll said that the Thirty-Sixth Division will furnish transportation to return the 157th to the Forty-Fifth Division. Shortly after noon, the Second Battalion renewed its attack on the high ground northeast of Livron. It met immediate resistance, encountering artillery, tank, and small-arms fire, but pressed forward slowly. Company E was pinned down by three Mark VI tanks at 1355 hours. Following a three-hour battle, the battalion took time to reorganize, then reopened its assault at 1745 hours. Company G reached the objective three hours later.

At 1845 hours Captain McGinnis stated that Companies B and C were relieved and Company A would be relieved after dark.

Little was reported on the welfare of the Third Battalion, attached to Task Force Butler and fighting in conjunction with the Thirty-Sixth Division in the vicinity of Loriol, south of the Rhone

River. It was learned that the Third Battalion was meeting bitter resistance and that Company K had been hard hit, but details were not available.

August 29–Shortly after midnight, the regiment was relieved by the 142nd Infantry of the Thirty-Sixth Division, and after daylight the regiment was shuttled to the vicinity of the town of Voirons, a trip of more than a hundred miles.

It was reported that Third Battalion, still attached to Task Force Butler, had captured five hundred enemy and knocked out, with the aid of the 191st Tank Battalion, hundreds of enemy vehicles, which jammed a convoy in a mountain pass. One Mark VI tank, men from the Third Battalion reported, had been set afire and destroyed by machine-gun tracer bullets, which hit either a gas can or a camouf lage net.

At 2100 hours, the regiment returned to corps control.

Company C-Furnished thirty riflemen to go to Bowig with four light tanks. PFC Rudolph T. Hodges returns to duty.

August 30–Col. Walter P. O'Brien assumed command of the 157th Infantry, relieving newly appointed Brig. Gen. John H. Church, who had received a new assignment. In the afternoon, Third Battalion returned to regimental control.

The regiment moved once more, bivouacking during the afternoon in the vicinity of the town of Les Abrets.

Company C relieved the roadblock of the 179th Infantry at 1600 hours, while Company B sent a motorized platoon on patrol from Chamoux to Grenoble with a mission to contact the French. Third Battalion was still attached to Task Force Butler.

Company C–PFC Harold L. Roth evacuated to the 120th Medical Battalion.

August 31–Company C sent a strong recon patrol to Beautepiere early in the morning. Third Battalion entrucked at 0630 hours and moved to the vicinity of Les Abrets. At 0700 hours Second Battalion set out by truck for the same area. By 1840 hours, the regiment, less First Battalion, had closed in the area.

First Battalion's roadblock at 355424 was relieved by the Fifteenth Infantry at 1830 hours. Replacements in the regiment: 192.

There were bets waged in the regiment that the month of September would see the end of the war with Germany. News reports indicated that the forces on the western and Russian fronts were moving forward with speed equal to that of the American and French troops pushing inland from the south of France. September, some said, was "Victory Month"—survive it for thirty days and chances were excellent one would survive the war.

> [The invasion of France was the Sicily-Salerno pattern all over again, bombing the beaches and shelling by naval guns. Our landing was perfect. Casualties were light. Third Battalion captured the town of St. Maxime. We continued to push north to the Durance River. Crossing it, we met opposition. We moved up the Rhone Valley. The enemy set up roadblocks at almost every town. The FFI were very helpful to us, telling us where the Germans were. The FFI fought alongside of us. The farther north we got, the more the Germans were fighting to hold us back. We were getting close to their homeland.—Robert L. Kirchgassner]

September 1–The regiment moved by truck to the vicinity of the city of Lagnieu. First Battalion at 1351 hours started moving to 2695. At 1855 hours First Battalion cleared the bridge at 249049 and was going toward the town of Meximieux to aid the 179th Infantry. Company F of that unit received heavy casualties. At 1351 hours, the First Battalion began moving forward to assist the virtually surrounded 179th Infantry and artillery men who were being hit from all sides at Meximieux. By nightfall the First Battalion reached the edge of town, applying pressure from the east. At 1955 hours, Company B was on the edge of town, receiving small-arms and mortar fire. Company C was committed to the north to enter the town from that direction.

At 2335 hours, First Battalion sent a patrol north to Villieux and one south to 035205.

At 1620 hours Second Battalion sent a patrol along the river Ain from Les Barrieres to Gevrieux. Company C–Enlisted men: 206.

September 2–The First Battalion patrol to Villieux made physical contact with the 179th Infantry, and the battalion remained in the vicinity of Meximieux through the morning hours. Resistance was cleared from the town at 0350 hours. Ten German tanks were destroyed.

Second Battalion at 0200 hours moved forward to an area in the vicinity of Chateau Gaillard from where it had started an attack across the Ain River. By 0620 hours the Second Battalion had made the crossing and was meeting no opposition. The battalion continued to attack north. Third Battalion followed Second Battalion.

First Battalion moved from Meximieux to Priay and relieved Third Battalion roadblocks at 1416. At 1445 hours, a motorized patrol from the First Battalion traveled from Priay to Chalamont, encountering roadblocks at 260160. At 256160, the patrol was fired upon by a German dressed in an American uniform and in charge of an American vehicle. The patrol returned at 1745 hours. Later the First Battalion sent a patrol to the vicinity of Chalamont to contact the Fifteenth Infantry.

Second Battalion continued its attack to the north. At noon, Company F in the lead and Companies G and E following in respective order attacked from Montbeque and at 1416 closed in on Donsonnas. There Second Battalion received long-range tank fire. Supporting artillery returned the fire. At 1525 hours Second Battalion received fire from Certines. At 1720 hours, Company G started to attack Franciere and an hour later encountered direct tank fire. By 2110 hours, Company G had reached the north side of Franciere and was receiving small arms fire. Second Battalion remained in the vicinity of Franciere throughout the night.

Third Battalion continued to follow Second Battalion in its attack. Company I engaged in a brief skirmish with two enemy patrols which approached its position.

Company C–T/Sgt. John R. Clements evacuated to the 120th Medical Battalion.

September 3–Second Battalion continued to attack to the northwest at 0630 hours in columns of Companies F, E, and G. At 0809, patrols moved toward Certines without meeting opposition. Second Battalion attacked the town late in the morning, Company F leading the assault while Company G moved in from the west and Company E pushed between them. Companies E and F encountered all types of fire coming from Certines and northwest but Company G advanced against only slight resistance. The men observed a large enemy ammunition dump, estimating two companies of German personnel, tanks, and vehicles in the woods at 246296. Company G called for artillery fire to be placed on them. At 2135 the ammunition dump blew up, the explosions resulting from friendly artillery shellings. Company G, which was a thousand yards southeast at the time, was pulled back to relieve Company A on a roadblock.

Third Battalion followed Second Battalion in the morning's attack. In the afternoon, Third Battalion assembled and attacked in a column toward Montagnat on the right of Second Battalion.

First Battalion, minus two platoons of Company A, which were manning roadblocks in the vicinity of Priay, closed in an assembly area in the vicinity of 278250 at 1511 hours. Company A's two platoons were released at 2047 hours. Company A minus two platoons, relieved Company I road block at 266241 at 1641 hours. Company B, with a section of HMG's, placed a road block at 273268. The Ranger Battalion and A and P Platoons were placed at La Trancier for tank protection.

September 4–Company G relieved the road block manned by Company A 366241 at 0220 hours. First Battalion assembled, passed through Second Battalion at 0410 hours against no opposition, and attacked a designated objective just south of Bourg. It gained its objective at 0725 hours and placed roadblocks at 218374, 213352, and 237350. Companies B and C sent strong patrols into the center of Bourg to contact Third Battalion and the 180th Infantry patrols. Patrols reached the center of town by 0915 hours.

Second Battalion cleared Certines at 0235 hours, reorganized, and sent a motor patrol to Les Rippes; it met no enemy. Upon its relief by First Battalion, the Second Battalion assembled in the vicinity of Chateau De Gemaud. Company G was released from its roadblock at 0845 hours and the battalion assembled in the vicinity of 26344.

Third Battalion, encountering no resistance, took Montagnat at 0204 hours. At 0935 hours, a Third Battalion patrol contacted First Battalion and 180th Infantry patrols in the center of Bourg. Through the morning Third Battalion remained assembled in the vicinity of Montagnat. During the evening, Third Battalion entrucked and shuttled toward Mantry.

Company C–PFC Harold L. Roth returns.

September 5–First and Second Battalions entrucked shortly after dawn and reached the vicinity of Mantry at 0930 and 1020 hours, respectively.

September 6–During the morning the regiment remained in the area near Mantry, but in the afternoon elements began the long shuttle to the vicinity of Cote Brune.

Company C–T/Sgt. John Clements returns to duty.

September 7–Last elements of Second Battalion closed in the vicinity of Cote Brune during the morning. First Battalion placed roadblocks at 068578 and 085619. A recon patrol from First Battalion went to Landresse, Laviron, Pierrefontaine, and Varcel. Third Battalion relieved 180th Infantry roadblock at 945571. Company K established contact with the Third Division with patrols. The regiment was still in division reserve.

September 8–First Battalion in the morning moved from the vicinity of 008574 to 110679, closing at 1830 hours. The battalion sent motor patrols to Provechere and all roads running north, east, and south from 110679. The patrols made no contact with the enemy.

Second Battalion moved from the vicinity of 995367 to 097677, closing in at 1842 hours.

Third Battalion moved by motor from vicinity of 006578 to the vicinity of Clerval, closing in at 2000 hours. Company I moved across the river to a position at 136747, giving protection to an engineer bridge building crew. The battalion placed roadblocks in the vicinity of 155755, 160737 and 160730.

Company C–PFC Teton Hurtado is transferred to the United States. Does not return during the war.

September 9–First Battalion moved to Randevillers to put in roadblock, closing in at 0800 hours. The battalion established contact with the French on the right and patrolled to the east and northeast of Randevillers. At 1707 hours the First Battalion, minus one company, was ordered to Chaux Les Clerval to relieve roadblocks maintained by Second Battalion at 155753, 164739, and 163730. Company C remained in the vicinity of Randevillers and continued to maintain roadblocks.

Second Battalion started foot movement to Chaux Les Clerval at 1000 hours and during the afternoon relieved the roadblocks in the area. At 1700 hours the Second Battalion was ordered to cross the Daubs River and move in the area of Fontaine, relieving Company I roadblock at L'Hopital.

At 0930 hours, Third Battalion moved to Gondenans-Montby in Companies L and K. A small group of enemy moved into Gondenans-Montby from the west, and Company K at Fontaine sent a platoon into the neighboring town to drive the Germans out. After being relieved by Company F, Company I on road block, reverted to battalion control.

The 157th Regiment received two hundred enlisted men as replacements.

Company C-Pvt. Edward Beattie, serial number 31447668 (MOS-745), joins Company C. Pvt. Harold Scott is evacuated sick.

September 10–At 0630 hours, Third Battalion, Company I leading, attacked toward Uzele, where it met spasmodic resistance. By 1410 hours, Company L was at 090835, and Company I, passing on the right, reached a position at 095848. Company K placed roadblocks in the vicinity of Uzele, now clear of the enemy.

Second Battalion followed Third Battalion in the attack during the morning and at 1620 hours was committed on the right. The battalion moved from Gondenans-Montby to 123854, where it remained for the night.

First Battalion remained in Clerval, manning roadblocks on all roads to the east. At 1630 hours Company C relieved roadblocks of Company K at 084818, 0858244, and 097818. Remainder of the battalion, less one platoon of Company B, toward midnight moved in the direction of 090795.

Company C– S/Sgt. Leland Scott returns to duty.

September 11–First Battalion reached the vicinity of 090795 at 0850 hours, and at 0900 hours the platoon from Company B, holding the roadblock at L'Hopital, was relieved and reverted to battalion control.

At 0430 hours, Company C relieved Company K on the roadblocks in the vicinity of Uzele; at 0630 hours, Company K moved northeast to 120835 at Aubenas, meeting no resistance.

Second Battalion jumped off at 0630 hours, moving toward Fallon, Melecey, and Georfans. Company F at noon was at 140862, Company E was attacking Bournois from the south, and Company H was at 133854. Company E cleared Bournois at 1445 hours and moved north through the town to 132880. Company F was still held up by fire. At 1850 hours, Company F reported tanks and infantry attacking from the right rear. Company G was moved northeast to assist Company F. By 1935 hours, the resistance at the rear of Company F was cleared by artillery fire. Second Battalion held up and organized its positions.

Company K of the Third Battalion cleared the town of Aubenas by 1435 hours, moving in from the southeast. The company placed roadblocks east and west of the town. At 1635 hours, Company K was at 094869; Company L at 084857; and Company I at 102878. At 2026 hours, Company I and L received an enemy attack from the northwest. The attack was repulsed by artillery fire. Third Battalion organized its position and remained there for the night. The battalion reported the loss of Maj. Merle Mitchell and Capt. Henry Huggins.

First Battalion was in Regimental Reserve, holding roadblocks in the vicinity of Uzele. At 1415 hours, Company A moved to 095847 and Company B to 090837. At 1745 hours, Company C moved to the vicinity of Cubry, placing roadblocks there after pulling the roadblocks at Uzele. At 2200 hours, Company C sent a patrol from Cubry to 078868, then to Cubrial and to Cubry, making no contact with enemy or friendly troops.

Company C–PFC Andrew Ondrik is evacuated to the 120th Medical Battalion.

September 12–By 0645 hours, First Battalion had passed through Third Battalion and following a five-minute artillery preparation, attacked toward the northwest. The battalion attacked in columns of Companies A, B, C. Company A received spasmodic small-arms fire as it advanced.

Second Battalion continued its attack at 0630 hours. Companies F and E encountered fire from the front and right, while Company G, advancing toward Fallon, also encountered resistance. Third Battalion during the morning cleared the woods in the vicinity of 0988 of enemy resistance.

With Companies B and C in the vicinity of Cubry, Company A continued to attack northeast, meeting spasmodic resistance. By 1345 hours, Company A had reached 078867 and was joined on the left by Company C, 180th Infantry. There the company held up its advance for nearly two hours until tank support came forward. At 1530 hours, the battalion jumped off once more, moving to 098891 against slight resistance. At approximately 2030 hours, the enemy assaulted Company A from the left flank and succeeded in separating the two assault platoons from the reserve and weapons platoons, which captured several enemy soldiers. Through the night, First Battalion was out of contact with Company A.

Second Battalion also continued its attack to the northeast but could make little progress against the intense fire it received from the woods in the vicinity of 145864 and the hill at 140874. During the afternoon Third Battalion remained in the vicinity of Aubenas, manning roadblocks. At 1910 hours Company L coordinated its attack with Company A and assaulted Hill 392, taking the objective at 2120 hours. Company I shifted to a position 085870-095870 while Company K continued to man roadblocks.

Company L sent a patrol to 120880 to get observation on Melecey.

September 13–First anniversary of the 157th's famed "Black Monday" stand on the Salerno beachhead in Italy, and the regiment jumped off in attack once more.

At 0700 hours Company B began its attack from the vicinity of Aubenas, going to the north to 100890, which it gained at 0920 hours. A patrol from Company A found the bodies of Maj. Merle Mitchell and Capt. Henry J. Huggins. The remainder of the First Battalion followed Company B in the attack. The company continued to press forward, passing through Villers La Ville with a platoon of medium tanks and infantry about noon. At 1505 hours Company B placed a platoon on the road at 115919, and the remainder of the unit established roadblocks at 114910. Company C, in position at 115900, sent a patrol to 124907 and south to Melecey. Company B sent a patrol to contact the 180th Infantry on the left.

In the Second Battalion sector, Company G jumped off at 0945 hours and pushed forward slowly against bitter opposition. Companies E and F coordinated with Company I, 179th Infantry, on the right, and attacked toward the northeast, advancing along the high ground against intense small-arms, mortar, and tank fire. By noon, Company G had gained the hill at 138874 and in mopping up had taken many prisoners. The company also had called for artillery fire on an estimated two companies of enemy and horse-drawn artillery in the vicinity of Grammont. At approximately 1600 hours, one platoon from Company G with a platoon of medium tanks left hill 138874 and went to Company F's left flank, which was marked by smoke. The platoon and its supporting tanks cut off a large number of Germans and in a brief skirmish captured them. Infantrymen assaulted the woods with bayonets and drove out other enemy soldiers. The battalion during the day's action captured approximately 210 enemy soldiers. By 1800 hours, Companies E and F had cleared the enemy resistance in their sector, and the battalion took up positions for the night.

Third Battalion, with Company I as the assault unit, attacked to the north. By 1300 hours Company I had reached 873115, and tanks and infantry were clearing the enemy from Fallon. The battalion established roadblocks and remained in Fallon for the night.

Company C–Enlisted men: 194.

September 14–Drizzling rain and poor visibility hampered the day's operations. The boundary in the 157th and 180th sectors had been changed, and Company B of the First Battalion as a result was in the 180th Infantry sector. Because of poor visibility, the artillery preparation for the battalion's attack was postponed until 0850 hours, and at 0920 hours, Company C jumped off, followed by Company B, which had been relieved by the 180th Infantry, and Company A. The battalion met no resistance and pushed on to Senargent. At 1240 hours, Company C sent patrols to Hill 835, while Company B established a roadblock in the vicinity of St. Ferjeux and Company A took up a position near Villargent. The battalion remained in position until approximately 2000 hours when it was relieved by a unit from the 180th Infantry. At that time, the battalion moved forward to relieve the Third Battalion. The relief was completed at 2320 hours.

Second Battalion jumped off in attack at 0700 hours in a column of Companies G, E, and F. By 0820 hours, a platoon from Company G with an attached platoon of tanks had reached Grammont, where it encountered sporadic small-arms fire. The town was cleared by Company G at 0907 hours, and the company took up a position northeast of there. It sent a patrol to Courchaton and on to Hill 533. The battalion continued its attack northeast toward Hill 385, three miles distant.

Third Battalion jumped off at 0700 hours, attacking in a column of Companies I, K, and L. By 0745 hours Company L had cleared Melecey and moved northeast. Company I moved north of Melecey to the woods at 127887. The Third Battalion took the high ground in the vicinity of 172903 and remained in position until relieved by the First Battalion, at which time the unit reverted to Regimental Reserve. The battalion assembled in the vicinity of Fallon.

[The regiment's third Medal of Honor was earned on this day near Grammont, France. Lt. Almond E. Fisher led his platoon in a predawn attack against heavy resistance. Fisher knocked out five automatic weapons, and although he had wounds in both feet, insisted on staying in command until his platoon's position was consolidated and secure.—Hugh F. Foster III]

September 15–Throughout the day the battalions remained in position. A patrol from the First Battalion, consisting of one officer and twenty-five enlisted men, moved to the woods at 148912 and found a disabled enemy vehicle there. It continued to the crossroads at 156918 and heard enemy movement en route. Upon its return, the patrol directed artillery fire on those areas.

A patrol from Company F moved toward Courchaton and engaged enemy troops in a brief firefight. It returned at 2345 hours.

September 16–The battalions again remained in position throughout the day. Second Battalion sent a patrol to Courchaton and established a listening post near the town. Third Battalion sent a combat patrol to Mignafans where the men heard enemy movement. The patrol then went to Senargent where it contacted no enemy. It then moved to the rear of Hill 385 where it heard vehicles moving on a trail and saw six enemy vehicles parked at 162907.

Company C–PFC Burnice Auldridge reassigned. One private went AWOL. In reserve.

September 17–Throughout the day the regiment held its position and maintained contact with the enemy. Second Battalion sent a listening post to Courchaton at 1700 hours. The post made no contact with the enemy. Sporadic tank fire harassed the troops during the day.

September 18–At 0900 hours Antitank and Cannon Companies and Third Battalion began moving to Cubrial in preparation for the relief of the regiment by the French.

First Battalion, still on the line, sent a patrol of one officer and five enlisted men to Vellechevreux at 1300 hours. The patrol returned at 1420 hours to report the town unoccupied by the enemy. At 1430 hours a reinforced platoon from Company A left to take the town. Another patrol ventured to Secenans but found enemy there. A third patrol went from Grammont to Courchaton and to Foret De Courchaton, where it located no enemy but reported seeing Germans in outlying districts. A three-man recon patrol from Company C went to Hill 385 and saw enemy moving between Secenans and Grange Le Bourg.

At 2030 hours, Company C relieved Companies F and G on position. Second Battalion moved to vicinity of Cubrial.

September 19–First Battalion relieved by French troops at approximately 0930 hours and moved to assembly area in the vicinity of Cubrial. Third Battalion shuttled to the vicinity of 8211 north of Bourguignon.

September 20–The 157th Infantry shuttled toward the town of Darnieulle. Third Battalion sent a recon patrol through Baines Les Baines. The 157th Infantry spent September 19 and 20 shuttling approximately eighty miles down the extreme left flank of the Seventh Army, moving through Baines Les Baines to the vicinity of Darnieulle. Occupying a key position between General Patton's Third Army and General Patch's Seventh Army, the regiment began crossing the rain-swollen Moselle River on September 21.

September 21–After stopping overnight in the vicinity of 035445, First Battalion moved by truck to vicinity of Darnieulle, arriving there at 0930 hours. A motorized patrol from the First Battalion was sent to Darnieulle, north to Fomeroy, Gigne, Mozelay, and Frizon to check the river crossing at Chatel. Another patrol from the battalion traveled from Uxegney and went north to Oncourt and Igney to check for river crossings on either side of the town. A foot patrol from the First Battalion was sent from Uxegney to check the fords northeast of there and to Galby to check for a river crossing.

Third Battalion moved toward Oncourt during the morning. It sent recon patrols to Igney and Thaon in an attempt to find crossings over the Moselle River. It also sent a platoon of tanks and a platoon from Company L into Thaon. The tanks and infantry reached the canal where they fired upon enemy roadblocks, which had been reported by civilians. They withdrew under the cover of darkness, and a short time later Thaon was shelled by the enemy. Throughout the remainder of the night Third Battalion sent patrols into Thaon at two-hour intervals.

First Battalion, during the afternoon, sent a platoon from Company C, reinforced, to Epinal through Darnieulle and Les Farges. It reached 015549 at about 1800 hours and engaged the enemy in a firefight. It was ordered to break contact with the enemy and return to the battalion. At 2100 hours, the First Battalion, with two platoons of tanks, one platoon of 57mm, and one platoon of Cannon Company attached, then moved by motor across the Moselle River at Chatel and detrucked. It then marched to the assembly area at Vaxamcourt.

Second Battalion, in position in the vicinity of 921573, sent a motor patrol to Uxegney, Domevre and west to Fomerey.

September 22–With Company B leading, First Battalion attacked to the southeast to gain objective

050590, 080540, jumping off at 0750 hours. By 0845 Company B was in a firefight in the vicinity of 027654. A platoon of tanks was sent forward to help clear resistance from the woods. Company B, unable to advance, withdrew at 1415 hours and placed artillery, mortar and cannon fire on the enemy. It then attacked again and two hours later was making slow progress against intense enemy fire. Company A was committed on the right and attacked east down the road from 027660. Both companies began to receive fire of all types from the east and south, so ceased attacking and dug in for the night.

Second Battalion moved to Chatel by motor and followed First Battalion to Vaxamcourt. During the afternoon it established roadblocks at Zincourt and Fallegney. Company G sent a patrol to Domevre Sur Durboin, which reported hearing enemy activity in and around town.

Third Battalion, during the morning, moved to Igney, where it began crossing the river. So that the battalion would have armor support, a platoon of tanks and a platoon of infantry moved acrossed the bridge at Chatel and joined the battalion on the east side of the river at Igney. A contact patrol moved from Domevre to Les Forges to meet units of the 180th Infantry. By mid-afternoon the entire Third Battalion had crossed the river and was attacking south in column. Company L, leading the attack, met determined resistance shortly before nightfall and received fire from all sides. At 1930 hours the enemy attacked the left flank of Company L. The company attacked south, then east while Company I moved in on the left, inflicting heavy casualties on the enemy. Resistance had slackened by 2200 hours.

Company C–In Reserve. Pvt. Israel Hoffman returns to duty.

September 23–At 0630 hours Company C passed through Company B and the First Battalion attacked with tanks in support, the two companies abreast. At the same time, Company L attacked south and gained the edge of the woods, contacting Company C on the left. Company A moved forward slowly, still meeting heavy resistance from the vicinity of 037659. Company C sent a platoon of infantry and a platoon of tanks into that area to assist Company A.

Attempting to clear the woods, Company C and Company L encountered fire of all types and could make only limited progress. Company B began moving up between Company A and Company C. By 1435 hours, Company C had cut the road at 038644 and attacked southeast toward Hill 375. Company A, moving slowly, still was receiving intense fire.

During the afternoon, Company C sent a patrol to the high ground northeast of Girmont, while Company A began to bypass the pocket of resistance at 038655. At 1730 hours Company B and Company C renewed the attack on Girmont, clearing the woods of enemy personnel and capturing many enemy soldiers. Company A, still meeting heavy resistance, reported suffering heavy casualties. Receiving fire from Hill 375, the First Battalion dug in for the night.

Second Battalion, in regimental reserve, manning roadblocks at Pallegney and Zincourt, moved into line during the afternoon with Company F in advance attacked southeast toward Domevre Sur Durboin and southwest toward Girmont with a platoon of tanks attached. Moving through Pallegney, Company F received heavy artillery fire, but continued on to Domevre Sur Durboin. On the outskirts of town, Company E was committed. It reached northwest edge of Domevre Sur Durboin at 2158 hours and sent patrols into the town.

Third Battalion throughout the day supported First Battalion in its attack and protected regimental right flank.

Company C–WIA: PFC Thomas M. Briggs, Pvt. Edward Schemansky, PFC William Mutchler and Sgt. Bryon Timmons. Timmons does not return during the war.

KIA: PFC Lucian Mills.

September 24–At 0700 hours, Company C attacked Girmont but was held down by fire from hill 375. Company B, attempting to take the hill, met bitter resistance. At 0715 hours, Company K, with two platoons of tanks and supported by Company I, attacked through Company L toward the west side of Girmont, encountering only light resistance. Second Battalion attacked the town of Domevre Sur Durboin again at dawn, moving in from the west and north. Company G, manning roadblocks at Pallegney and Zincourt, sent a patrol into Domevre Sur Durboin that encountered no enemy. Company E, with a platoon of Company G, a platoon of tanks, and two tank destroyers attached, moved in on the town from the north. The battalion met stubborn resistance, encountered all types of fire, and was unable to enter the village. Late in the afternoon Company E withdrew from the north side of Domevre Sur Durboin and moved to the west side to aid Company F. Unable to advance, the battalion dug in for the night and sent a platoon from Company G into the town on patrol. The patrol failed to return.

Company B, attacking Hill 375, was engaged in a firefight with enemy personnel who were attempting to pass over the northwest slope from Girmont. The company reported destroying a large number of Germans. Company C made slow progress against artillery and small-arms fire coming from the vicinity of Girmont. With the aid of Company I and tanks, it started into Girmont in mid-afternoon, clearing the town by 1800 hours. Company C placed roadblocks on the two roads running east of the town.

Third Battalion attacked south in a column of companies and passed the western edge of Girmont.

Company C-Pvt. Virgil Green returns. PFC John M. Fisher Jr. is lightly wounded. Enlisted men: 171.

September 25–At 0700 hours First Battalion attacked Hill 375 and made good progress against sporadic resistance. By 1435 hours the hill had been cleared of resistance, and Company B organized its position on that ground. Company A gained the woods in the vicinity of 063627. Company C, during the afternoon, relieved Company B on the hill. Company B then motored to the vicinity of 073599.

At 0710 hours, Second Battalion again attacked Domevre Sur Durboin, Company E finally clearing it of resistance at 1651 hours. The battalion then organized that vicinity for all-around defense. Third Battalion continued attacking northeast, bypassing Dogneville and meeting little resistance. By nightfall the battalion was within striking distance of Sercoeur, upon which Company L placed artillery fire.

Company C-Pvt. Israel Hoffman is WIA and Pvt. John F. Kotai is KIA.

September 26–At 0700 hours Third Battalion continued its attack to the northeast, clearing Villoncourt at 0900 hours, advancing on Sercoeur. With Company K and Company I on high ground overlooking Sercoeur, Company L attacked the town. Company K gained the main road at 116636 and continued to the northeast, with Company I following. Shortly after noon, firefights broke out in the northeast and southern sections of the town. By 1400 hours the town was cleared of enemy, and the Third Battalion moved northeast toward Padou. The battalion moved through Padoux and occupied positions in the vicinity of the town for the night.

First Battalion followed Third Battalion in attack, taking over the roadblocks between Bayecourt and Villoncourt, Villoncourt and Sercoeur. Second Battalion shuttled to the vicinity of Dogneville and followed behind Third and First in Regimental Reserve. It closed in the vicinity of Fort De Longchamp.

Company A, placing a roadblock northwest of Villoncourt, sent a patrol to Bayecourt. Company B relieved Company L in Sercoeur at 1400 hours. Company C took up a position northeast of Sercoeur during the afternoon.

Company C–PFC Richard Adams (tree bursts-seven pieces of fragment in his arm), PFC Hyman Miller, and Pvt. Rudolph Hodges WIA, not hospitalized. PFC Andrew Ondrik returns to duty.

September 27–The 157th Infantry, on the left flank of the Forty-Fifth Division, continued to attack northeast, moving forward through drizzling rain. First Battalion moved to Padoux to relieve the Third Battalion positions there. A patrol from Company C ventured to Hill 353 and found it unoccupied. Company C entered Bult and found it unoccupied. Other patrols worked toward Badmenil and met no resistance.

Third Battalion continued its attack toward Vomecourt during the afternoon, meeting only light resistance. The objective was taken at 1740 hours, and the battalion blocked the roads leading northwest to Rambervillers Forest. The Pioneer Platoon cleared two roads of felled trees leading from Vomecourt to Bult. Security patrols operated on roads leading northwest from Padoux-Vomecourt axis.

Second Battalion, in Regimental Reserve, moved from the Fort Du Longchamp area to Sercoeur, taking over the First Battalion roadblocks; 112 replacements in the 157th Infantry.

Company C–Lt. Philip Geller is assigned.

September 28–At 0715 hours First Battalion was ordered to pass through Third Battalion and continue the attack to St. Gorgons. Company C sent a patrol toward the town. Second Battalion moved to Padoux and sent Company G to Bult. A mine squad removed antitank mines and demolitions from the road between Bayecourt and Villoncourt.

First Battalion, in a column of Companies A, B, and C, pushed northeast toward Rambervillers, clearing St. Gorgon of slight resistance by 1400 hours. Company B, occupying the high ground, sent three patrols into Rambervillers where they encountered the enemy. Company C sent a patrol to St. Helene and it contacted elements of the 180th Infantry. The First Battalion blocked all the roads leading south from Rambervillers and established its positions for the night, sending patrols into the town and northeast of it during the hours of darkness.

Company C–PFC Will E. Huffman is evacuated to 120th Medical Battalion.

September 29–At dawn a strong patrol from First Battalion moved into Rambervillers. Third Battalion remained in Vomecourt.

Patrols from First Battalion covered all the roads to the south of the town and to the northwest, contacting the FFI at 173702. At 1445 hours, Company B reported enemy mining the road between Jeanmenil and Rambervillers. Tank destroyers and mortars fired upon them. All patrols were called in early in the afternoon when French armor attacked Rambervillers from the northwest. A patrol from Company A was ordered to 197717, but engaged in a firefight and withdrew at 2025 hours. During the night the enemy placed artillery, rockets, and mortars on St. Gorgon.

Second Battalion remained in Regimental Reserve.

Company C–Bult, France. PFC John Schweisthal returns to duty.

[S/Sgt. Robert L. Kirchgassner was awarded the Bronze Star for heroism in battle. Two of the men in squad three were reduced in rank that day, but that order was rescinded days later. Dad would never tell us why he got the Bronze Star.—Rita Kirchgassner]

September 30–First Battalion continued its attack to the northeast at 0700 hours, moving forward in the wake of a fifteen-minute artillery preparation. Second Battalion at 0840 hours moved toward St. Gorgon, supporting First Battalion in its attack, while Third Battalion reverted to Regimental Reserve.

First Battalion, moving through Rambervillers at approximately noon, encountered sporadic small-arms and artillery fire but pressed on to cut the road junction at 189720. There machine-gun crews from Company C knocked out five enemy vehicles that were trying to escape northeast to Menil Sur Belvitte. At 1355 hours, Company A passed through Company C and continued to the northeast edge of town where the battalion established its position for the night. Heavy artillery, Nebelwerfer, and mortar fire fell on the town throughout the night.

Second Battalion, supporting First Battalion, remained in a column of companies and sent patrols to Bru. The patrols engaged in a firefight in the town and withdrew. A patrol from Company G, attempting to contact 180th Infantry, also encountered the enemy, engaged in a brief firefight, and withdrew.

Company C-Pvt. Clyde Ashe, Sgt. John E. Boggs, PFC Robert A. Miller and 1st Sgt. Syd Stogel are WIA.

> [By now it was September. We had a lot of small towns to take and the terrain was getting hilly. We were to attack Rambervillers, a strategic railroad center. It was a hard battle, but we finally took the town.—Robert L. Kirchgassner]

October 1–October heralded the approach of another winter, the second in which the 157th Infantry had engaged in combat. As rain increasingly hampered operations, the regiment prepared to hold its positions on the outskirts of Rambervillers and overlooking the towns of Jeanmenil and Bru. Ammunition, particularly for mortars and artillery pieces, was rationed although supply for tanks, tank destroyers, and 90mm guns was adequate for support in any normal encounter with the enemy. As the days passed, the front-line infantrymen, situated in densely forested areas, dug deeper into the ground and with timbers built dugout roofs that would protect them from tree bursts, the cause of most of the woods-fighting casualties. Patrols probed the enemy lines daily, engaging in brief skirmishes as they sought out German mine fields, wire and gun positions. Mission of most of the patrols was to capture enemy soldiers, but as always, the enemy proved wary.

Third Battalion relieved First Battalion on position and continued the attack to the northeast, encountering numerous mine fields and booby traps. Since a change in boundaries gave half of the sector to the Fifteenth Corps, the Third Battalion switched direction of its move and advanced toward Bru to the east. The regiment continued to protect the left flank of the corps.

At 0700 hours, Second Battalion jumped off in attack on Jeanmenil and supported by tanks and tank destroyers, made steady progress against small-arms and artillery fire. Company E, moving into position at 215715, suddenly encountered fire of all types coming from Jeanmenil. Company F committed to the right with a plan to circle the town and attack it from the southeast side, while Company G, at 210697, furnished protection for the regimental right flank. Against bitter resistance, the Second Battalion gained ground slowly but still was short of the town by nightfall when it dug in its positions.

Third Battalion, attacking Bru, gained the wooded ridge at 217740 but throughout the rest of the day could make only limited gains against stubborn opposition.

First Battalion reverted to Regimental Reserve and set out road blocks.

Company C-In Regimental Reserve and set up roadblocks. Cpl. Quienton Steele is evacuated to the 120th Medical Battalion.

October 2–Second and Third Battalions resumed their attacks during the morning but were unable to gain ground. By noon, however, Company E had reached the edge of Jeanmenil where it received enemy machine-gun fire, while two squads of Company G, moving east, reached 226697. At 1425 hours the enemy pinned the two squads to the ground and threatened to encircle them from the southwest. The squads withdrew under the cover of a supporting artillery concentration. The battalion remained where it was and patrolled to Jeanmenil.

Third Battalion remained on the high ground north and west of Bru and placed a mine field at 201722. It cut Bru-Rambervillers road with antitank fire.

Patrols from the regiment maintained contact with the French on the left.

October 3–During the morning Company F moved up to 218706 and dug in on the southwest edge of Jeanmenil. First Battalion continued to man roadblocks at 189720, 186728, and 182731 and sent contact patrols to Donciers and Reville to meet the French. Company C maintained contact patrols to Second and Third Battalions. The enemy shelled Rambervillers from 0945 hours until 1000 hours, killing and wounding many civilians who had taken shelter in city hall. (Fifteen civilians were killed.) Throughout the afternoon the battalions made no change in positions. Company F tied in its left flank with Company E right flank after nightfall and sent a contact patrol to the 180th Infantry. (205868) Company I of the Third Battalion mainlined contact with 117th Recon Troop on the left.

The highway was lined with civilians making their way to the rear. Ninety-eight replacements in the 157th Infantry.

October 4–First Battalion remained in Regimental Reserve, manning roadblocks at 195728, 183731, and 186728. At 1440 hours Company B reported enemy artillery falling in the company area. At about 1600 hours, First Battalion made a reconnaissance of the Third Battalion position, which was to be relieved the night of October 5–6.

Second Battalion remained in position and placed tank destroyer fire on an enemy observation post in the church in Jeanmenil. Throughout the night, patrols maintained contact between companies, and shortly before midnight Company E sent personnel to occupy a knocked-out friendly tank at 221709.

Third Battalion also remained in position. During the afternoon, Company K sent a patrol to the house at 224744, where the men located fifteen enemy dug in west of the building. Third Battalion placed mortar fire on the position.

October 5–Beginning on this date (until October 20), the regiment remained in position on the left flank of the division sector as patrols each day probed deep into enemy territory. Sporadically, the enemy shelled the line and on one occasion fired rockets into the center of Rambervillers where the regimental and reserve battalion command posts were located. During this time the enemy had established defenses for the first time since the landings in southern France on August 15. The enemy built camouflaged dugouts in the dense woods, established strategically located machine-gun nests, laid mine fields, and set out barbed-wire entanglements. Commonly, German infantrymen laid down heavy concentrations of coordinated artillery and small-arms fire in what became known as "turkey shoots." Doughboys returned from the front to report having killed German snipers who were firing from the tops of trees.

Most to be feared were the tree bursts, but with the men secure in dugouts, regimental losses were limited. With pouring rains, however, inevitably came seepage and self-made living quarters had to be bailed. As often as possible, company kitchens furnished the men on the line two meals a day, but in many instances, carrying details could feed no more than a reserve platoon.

Daily, fifty men came off the line and were sent to the newly established regiment rest center, located in the huge German barracks on the outskirts of Rambervillers. There they were afforded the luxury of a hot shower, clean clothes, and a bed. As time passed, moving pictures became available and a snack bar served the best drinks obtainable. Not surprisingly, the men spent a major portion of their time writing letters, reading, and listening to the radio.

Well-defined enemy strong points were the towns of Jeanmenil and Bru and the woods that surrounded them. Time and again chemical mortars fired into Jeanmenil, setting the town ablaze. At night, men engaged in patrolling often were exposed to the enemy view by light from the f lames. Dead cows and horses lined the streets, and every building had gaping holes in it. A main target in the town was the church steeple, which the Germans had used for an observation post, until nearly the entire building was battered to the ground by artillery fire.

Not since the days of Anzio beachhead had regimental patrolling been so extensive. Skirmishes were commonplace as patrols sought prisoners of war in enemy positions. The forests proved a distinct advantage to the Germans because to reach them, patrols had to cross over open pastured areas that lay under constant observation. The patrols, however, frequently located enemy positions without being observed and upon return called for artillery fire to be placed upon them.

First Battalion continued to man roadblocks throughout the morning, and at 1710 hours began moving out to relieve Third Battalion on the high ground north and west of Bru (2274). By 1850 hours the relief had been completed, and Third Battalion reverted to Regimental Reserve. A patrol from First Battalion headquarters moved along the secondary road south of the Bru-Rambervillers Road and as far as the west edge of Bru (214725). The patrol heard enemy vehicular activity in town.

Sporadic enemy artillery fire fell on the Second Battalion sector throughout the day. Enemy movement was heard in Jeanmenil, and at 1910 hours chemical mortars fired a concentration on the town, starting a fire in the northwest section that burned throughout the night. A patrol from Company G made a limited-objective attack to 226710, but was driven off by intense small-arms, mortar, and machine-gun fire. Chemical mortars fired a barrage on the enemy positions, and the platoon attacked again, reaching its objective and digging in. Throughout the night, Second Battalion received sporadic artillery and small-arms fire.

October 6 –At 0300 a platoon of Company E relieved the platoon of Company G, which staged the attack while local patrols from Company G worked between the positions of Company E and Company F every two hours. A patrol from Company G also contacted the 180th Infantry at 208685.

Throughout the day the battalions remained in position, Third Battalion in Regimental Reserve, manning roadblocks at 195728, 183731, and 186728. A ranger patrol from First Battalion left the forward command post at 1800 hours with a mission to go to 215738, 216733, to Bru, and to woods 216731. At 2153 hours, the patrol returned and reported an enemy outpost at 213732, an enemy machine-gun at 215730, and vehicles and tanks moving in that vicinity. Throughout the night Cannon Company placed interdictory fire on those positions and on the town of Bru, where enemy vehicles were reported. At 2300 hours, the artillery placed a time-on-target attack on Bru.

At 2250 hours, Company G relieved Company E on position.

Company C– PFC William Mutchler returns to duty, becomes a corporal, and receives a new MOS, 653. PFC Buckner Morris is WIA.

October 7–Enemy artillery fire fell on Company G position at 0212 hours. At 0600 hours, artillery, chemical, and 81mm mortar fire was placed on Jeanmenil, and at 0830 hours Second Battalion placed chemical mortar fire on enemy personnel and vehicles in the town. The chemical mortars started two fires in the town.

Patrols from both Companies G and F worked toward Jeanmenil with the mission of securing a prisoner of war, but they were unsuccessful. The patrols reported seeing many Germans in the town. Company E maintained contact with the 180th Infantry on the right.

First Battalion at 1105 hours sent a patrol to the clearing at 224744. The patrol moved east three hundred yards along the 220th grid, then encountered thirty to forty enemy dug in. After an exchange of fire, the patrol withdrew. The artillery fired upon the enemy located at 230790.

Company C–Pvt. Edward A. Schemansky is promoted to private first class, Pvt. Virgil H. Green becomes a corporal and has a new MOS of 653, and Tech Sgt. John R. Clements becomes first sergeant.

October 8–The 157th Infantry remained in position on the left flank of the Forty-Fifth Division and with patrols maintained contact with the 180th Infantry on the right and with the 117th Recon on the left. During the early morning hours, the Second Battalion's A and P Platoons placed twelve antitank mines at 219713 and booby-trapped the knocked-out tank in front of the Second Battalion position. Spasmodically the enemy interdicted Rambervillers and the vicinity of the town with artillery fire.

First Battalion remained in position on the high ground north and west of Bru. A patrol of ten men left the battalion at 1330 hours from 218740 and went to the edge of the woods at 213740. The patrol moved through the woods to 221740 where it saw enemy positions, but they were unoccupied. The patrol returned at 1748 hours.

Second Battalion sent a patrol from Company G to the south edge of Jeanmenil to determine if the town still contained enemy. It left at 2100 hours and moved to 224710. The men heard enemy movement in town and were fired upon by enemy riflemen, so withdrew. A patrol from Company F moved southeast to 217690 with a mission to occupy the house at 219688. When the patrol reached

217690, it heard enemy on both flanks and rear so withdrew without engaging the German forces. Company E throughout the day maintained contact with the 180th Infantry.

Third Battalion made reconnaissance of the Second Battalion positions in preparation for the relief scheduled for the night of October 9–10.

October 9–Throughout the day the regiment continued to hold its positions and to reinforce them. First Battalion maintained physical contact with the 117th Recon troop on the left of the regimental position and established a warning system of white phosphorus grenades at 216745. After nightfall, Third Battalion began moving forward to relieve Second Battalion in the vicinity of the town of Jeanmenil. The battalions encountered spasmodic small-arms fire and artillery fire throughout the day.

Company C–Pvt. John Fisher returns to duty.

October 10–Third Battalion completed its relief of Second Battalion at 0230 hours. Company I moved into position at 2016 hours, Company K at 2239 hours.

Throughout the day the regiment held its position. The battalions made plans to send out reconnaissance patrols and to establish outposts. Mission of the patrols was to capture POWs.

Company C-T/4 Orville Leek is WIA.

October 11–Because of rain and overhanging clouds, visibility was poor throughout the morning. During the afternoon the weather cleared and provided good visibility for observers.

First Battalion remained in position on the high ground north and west of Bru on the 2,174th grid line. The battalion patrolled north, east, and south. One patrol of six enlisted men ventured to 224745 and located enemy, who were building a dugout. The patrol returned and mortar fire was placed on the enemy position. The Germans dispersed. A ten-man patrol left the Company B position, 218742, and moved along the south edge of the woods to the road at 225728, where it observed fifty enemy. Some were in the woods, digging in and improving their positions.

A reconnaissance patrol of eight men left at 0900 hours from position 210747, moved along the north edge of the woods, east to 219746, then north along west edge of woods to 223749. At this point, two hundred yards into the woods at 223749, the enemy fired rifles and machine-guns at the patrol and pinned it to the ground. The patrol located enemy dug in along the west edge of the woods at 223749. A fifteen man patrol tried to cut off the Americans, but was unsuccessful.

A patrol of four men from Company C left at 1300 hours from 212735, went across woods 215733, and continued through to next patch of woods to two houses at 21757305. The patrol combed the houses and found that they had been evacuated hastily. The men then moved into a patch of trees at 217729 and observed one German moving around house near the road at 217728. The man was in the open, so the patrol made no effort to capture him.

Third Battalion also patrolled the forward areas aggressively. Company K sent a patrol, consisting of one officer and eight enlisted men, to the vicinity of the starch factory at 221707, from where the men moved to the highway at 234707 in an attempt to capture or ambush one or more enemy. The main body of the patrol remained in that area while the patrol leader and two men went to the road junction at 232710 to investigate the houses. From there they observed for one hour large fires in the town of Jeanmenil, making further investigations inadvisable. The men were unable to locate any signs of the enemy.

A patrol from Company K, accompanied by two men from the mine platoon of Antitank Company, investigated the road from 221707 to within a hundred yards of Jeanmenil. No mines were located. The patrol left at midnight and returned at 0330 hours.

A patrol of one officer and five enlisted men from Company L left from the railroad station at 213705 and proceeded along the tracks to the house at 218691. The patrol then went to the road and the stream in the vicinity of 225697, making no contact with the enemy. The patrol left at midnight and returned at 0245 hours.

Second Battalion remained in Regimental Reserve in the vicinity of the town of Rambervillers and manned roadblocks.

Company C-PFC John J. Lepore Jr., Cpl. Theodore E. Miles and PFC Stanley W. Wyrostek are WIA.

October 12–Throughout the day the regiment engaged in patrolling the forward areas and in strengthening its defensive positions. At dawn eighteen rounds of Nebelwerfer fire fell in Rambervillers, the regimental command post location.

At 0100 hours a Company C outpost drew small-arms fire from 218733 and withdrew to 217731. Artillery fire was placed on the enemy at 228731 during the morning.

A patrol from Company A left from 214746 moved north 350 yards and found unoccupied enemy positions. A patrol left at 0800 hours. It then moved further north fifty to seventy five yards and heard enemy talking to the north. It returned at 1045 hours.

The ranger patrol was sent to a reported enemy machine-gun position at 223749 and found unoccupied positions. A raiding patrol left 214733 at 1610 hours, went to the houses at 216731, and found one enemy dead there. The patrol moved an outpost to 216732 and at 1930 hours sent three men to search the enemy dead for identification. The men searched the dead men but found nothing.

At 1630 hours, Companies A and B opened fire with machine-guns upon enemy patrol. The enemy ran in front of Company B, which placed mortar fire on the German soldiers.

In the Third Battalion sector, a patrol from Company I returned shortly after midnight and reported that it observed for thirty minutes from 220720 and had seen sixteen to seventeen enemy moving from Bru. The patrol moved to the vicinity of Bru and was fired upon by an enemy machine-gun. The patrol heard digging at 223705 and found unoccupied enemy positions at 218723 and 219722.

A patrol from Company K returned at 0430 hours and reported having heard two enemy trucks in Jeanmenil and having established an ambush at 228712, which remained in position for five hours. The men heard and saw nothing.

Other patrols that were sent out to capture enemy soldiers were unsuccessful. At 2205 hours a patrol from Company L contacted the Thirty-Sixth Engineers.

Company C-PFC Thomas M. Briggs is MIA and later listed as KIA.

October 13–Ammunition became increasingly available, and the regiment at prearranged periods of each day coordinated its artillery, anti-aircraft, mortar, and small-arms fire, concentrating on known enemy positions. For half-hour periods, the front would flare up as the Germans released an intense counter fire; then all would be quiet again.

The regiment continued to hold its position on the north flank of the Forty-Fifth Division and maintained contact with the 117th Recon on the north and Second Battalion, Thirty-Sixth Engineers, on the south.

First Battalion, occupying the high ground north and west of Bru, maintained close contact with the enemy through patrols. The artillery and mortars laid concentrations on known enemy positions. At 2200 hours, enemy artillery shelled the Company C positions for fifteen minutes.

A nine-man recon patrol from Company B left position at 217744 at 0945 hours and went through the edge of the woods to the clearing at 225740, where the men located four enemy in dug-in positions. The patrol returned shortly before noon.

A Company B patrol of nine men left at 1330 hours and went through woods to edge of clearing 223742, where it saw one enemy. The patrol fired upon him and at the same time saw two enemy soldiers cross the small clearing at 224741 and go toward the high ground. The patrol then turned left and went along the edge of woods at 224747, returning to the parent unit at 1531 hours.

At 1715 hours Company B sent a combat patrol of thirty-two men into a position east of the road at 220741. There the patrol waited for the scheduled fifteen-minute artillery barrage on the enemy positions in the vicinity of 225700. The artillery lifted at 1730 hours, and the patrol jumped off immediately. It received small-arms fire from the enemy positions. One of the positions was a small patch of woods at 226743, another the small clearing in the main part of the woods at 224740. The patrol attempted to move to the right of the enemy positions, but was unsuccessful. The patrol saw four enemy running toward the house at 224744 in the clearing. The men fired upon the enemy and reported killing or wounding three of the German soldiers. An enemy patrol attempted to approach the Americans, so the patrol withdrew at 1800 hours.

In the Third Battalion sector, Company L completed the relief of Company K at 2145 hours. Second Battalion remained in Regimental Reserve in Rambervillers and manned roadblocks on the outskirts of town. The battalion completed reconnaissance of the First Battalion positions in preparation for relief of October 14.

Company C–Captain Speairs is relieved of assignment and assigned to regimental headquarters. PFC Will E. Huffman returns to duty.

October 14–During the early morning Second Battalion moved forward and completed the relief of First Battalion at 1315 hours. At 1500 hours Company E sent a patrol east from the company position to 220743 and then to 218746. The patrol reached 224743, found unoccupied positions, observed twelve enemy in vicinity of 224742 and two enemy at 242738. The patrol found an enemy bomb at 242738 and returned at 1810 hours.

At 1530 hours a patrol from Company F left 218741 and went to 222740, where it encountered two enemy soldiers, whom the men captured. After returning to the command post with the POWs, the patrol, with five additional men, left for 224739 and encountered one enemy soldier. The men killed him with rifle fire. The men then observed thirty to forty enemy at 226740, placed mortar and small-arms fire on the Germans, and withdrew to the company position at 1720 hours.

Third Battalion remained in its defensive position and sent one platoon of Company K to make a raid on a house at 231710 with a mission to capture a POW. The patrol left at 1845 hours and had not yet returned by midnight.

October 15–First Battalion remained in Regimental Reserve throughout the day and manned roadblocks in the vicinity of Rambervillers. At 1700 hours, Company B, with one section of heavy machine-guns and one section of 81mm mortars attached, began shuttling to St. Helene. The company arrived there at 1825 hours and was placed in division reserve under division control.

Second Battalion set up a warning system of White Phosphorus grenades to trip wires in the vicinity of 213742. Throughout the afternoon and night, sporadic artillery and mortar fire fell upon the battalion position. A patrol from Company E left 216746 at 1300 hours and went to 223746. Here the patrol saw ten enemy soldiers 100 yards to the front. The patrol fired on the enemy patrol and withdrew to 224745. The patrol, from that position, saw an enemy patrol approaching from the flank, so withdrew at 1515 hours.

A patrol from Company F left 217741 at 1300 hours and went to 224744. At that point the men observed four enemy at 226744 going south toward the house at 224743. The patrol placed 60mm and 81mm mortar fire on the house, then moved to 215725 where it located unoccupied enemy positions. The patrol returned at 1530 hours.

The Company G outpost at 216732 was forced from position at 2025 hours by the enemy. A squad, in attempting to retake the position was forced to withdraw because of grenades and machine-gun fire.

In the Third Battalion sector, the raiding patrol from Company K returned at 0130 hours. The patrol reported that when it had reached a point within seven hundred yards of the road at 234707, the enemy fired illuminating flares from Jeanmenil. A German machine-gun fired upon the patrol from 233707 and other positions in that vicinity. The enemy then placed mortar fire on the patrol.

The patrol reported that it had observed two enemy tanks at 237703 firing into the Company L position. The men heard hammering coming from the houses at 238709, but were unable to get to the houses, so they returned.

Company L sent an ambush patrol of one squad to search the woods south of Company L and to 232698 to take enemy under fire or capture any passing the position. At 2100 hours Company I sent an ambush patrol to 217721.

October 16–The regiment maintained its position as rain and cold made operations increasingly difficult. Company B at 1430 hours was released from division control and motored to 182732 where it relieved the roadblock established by the Ammunition-and-Pioneer and Ranger Platoons. The battalion staff and company commanders made reconnaissance of the Third Battalion positions preparatory to relieving that unit the night of October 17 and 18.

Second Battalion remained in position on the high ground north and west of Bru at 220726. The outpost, which had been driven off position by the Germans the previous night, reoccupied the ground at 0055 hours. At 0830 hours the battalion, in a coordination of artillery, anti-aircraft, mortar, machine-gun, and small-arms fire, placed a concentration on known enemy positions in the vicinity of Bru. The enemy returned a heavy counter fire.

At noon a patrol from Company E, consisting of one officer and six enlisted men, left at 218845 and followed the edge of the woods to 222746. The patrol saw several small groups of enemy and proceeded to 222747, where the men saw five enemy enter a dugout twenty-five yards to the northeast. The patrol started closing in on the dugout when enemy started coming out of it. A firefight ensued and at least two enemy were hit. The patrol returned at 1445 hours.

At 1230 hours a patrol from Company F proceeded to 225743. Part of the patrol was left at that point as a listening post, while the remainder of the patrol continued to 223744. There the men saw thirty enemy moving northwest into the woods and carrying mortars. The patrol returned at 1530 hours.

At 1930 hours an ambush patrol from Company E went to 216755.

In the Third Battalion sector, the coordinated fire brought an increase of enemy artillery and small arms, which continued for more than an hour. Company I sent a ten-man ambush patrol and listening post to 218721. The men remained in position until dawn, but made no contact. Company L sent an ambush patrol to listening post 232698 but made no contact with the enemy.

Company C–PFC Rudolf T. Hodges is lightly wounded in the right hand; not hospitalized.

October 17–Operating in drizzling rain, patrols from the regiment maintained contact with enemy in the vicinity of Jeanmenil and Bru. First Battalion remained in Regimental Reserve until 1830 hours when it began the move forward to relieve Third Battalion. The relief was completed by 2100 hours.

In the Second Battalion sector, Company F at 1330 hours sent a thirty-three man patrol from 218740 to the enemy strong point in the vicinity of Bru at 226740 to make a raid and take prisoners. At 224739 the patrol ran into trip-wired booby traps that exploded. One of the lead scouts was blown high into the air and killed immediately. Warned by the explosions, the enemy opened fire. The patrol then received machine-gun and rifle fire from 224742. The men returned the fire but were unable to determine the exact enemy locations. The patrol withdrew to the lines at 1544 hours. A seven man patrol left 216737 at 2000 hours with a mission to go to 224736 and on to the road junction at 222732, making reconnaissance for enemy positions and roadblocks.

During the morning from 0750–0800 hours, the artillery coordinated with the mortars and rifles on the front in placing fire on the enemy lines. Second Battalion received fire of all types in return.

Patrols from Third Battalion, prior to the time it was relieved, encountered no enemy in establishing ambushes near the Bru-Jeanmenil road and along the Colline Des Eaus stream.

Company C-In defensive position in Jeanmenil, France. Enemy shelling heavy. PFC Edward Schemansky is evacuated sick.

October 18–The regiment, with the First and Second Battalions on the line, continued to hold its positions in the vicinity of Jeanmenil and Bru. Third Battalion, in Regimental Reserve, was alerted to move to the 179th Infantry sector. At 1415 hours, elements of the "Q" Battalion relieved the Third Battalion positions and roadblocks at 195738, 1837131, and 186738.

> ["Q" Battalion was a local use to identify an ad hoc battalion-size organization (several company size units.)—Hugh F. Foster III]

In the First Battalion sector, Company C suffered casualties from enemy machine-gun and mortar fire, which the Germans placed on the position at 0645 hours. At 2030 hours, a five-man reconnaissance patrol from Company A left the lines. It had not returned by midnight.

Second Battalion received sporadic artillery fire throughout the day, forty rounds of 105mm falling on Company F at 1122 hours. A patrol from Company E left 216747, went to 218745, and then to 220745 where it found concertina wire. The patrol followed the wire to 218746, where it saw four enemy. The patrol fired on the enemy and wounded three. The patrol received machine-gun and tank fire while at 218745. The patrol left at 0945 hours and returned at 1155 hours.

Company E sent another patrol of five men from the company position to 219746 where the men found enemy wire. They followed it southeast and saw two enemy in the vicinity of 221745. The patrol followed the wire to its end and then returned to the lines.

A seven-man patrol from Company G engaged in a skirmish with the enemy at 224737. Company C–Cpl. Quienton Steele returns to duty. Pvt. Miles A. Kellner and Pvt. John B. Phillips are WIA.

October 19–The 157th Infantry continued holding its positions on the north flank of the Forty-Fifth Division sector. Third Battalion, under division control, shuttled from Rambervillers at 0530 hours to the vicinity of Grandvillers, where it was attached to the 179th Infantry.

Sporadic artillery fire fell on the First Battalion position throughout the day. A reconnaissance patrol of five men left from Company A at 215706 and went to 244695. The patrol heard enemy movement at 245698 and 246691, then went to 232694 and returned to its parent unit. At 2225 hours, the Germans marked their front line with flares when enemy planes patrolled the areas.

Second Battalion received sporadic artillery and Nebelwerfer fire throughout the day. A patrol from Company F left from 220740 at 1300 hours and went to the edge of the woods at 223745, where the men encountered enemy wire running from the clearing. The wire was three or four feet high. The patrol observed from that point for an hour and then returned at 1645 hours.

A second recon patrol from Company F (four men) left 220740 and moved east to 221740, where it turned northeast and proceeded to the clearing at 223741. The patrol saw no enemy activity and located no wire or booby traps. It returned at 1640 hours.

A seven-man patrol from Company G left 219740 and moved southeast into the edge of the woods at 224737. At the edge of the woods the patrol heard enemy talking and moving about. The men attempted to advance into the woods and cross the road, but the enemy opened fire. After a brief skirmish, the patrol withdrew, returning at 2120 hours.

October 20–The 157th Infantry continued to hold its position on the north flank of the division. During the morning, enemy artillery, estimated to be 105mm fell, intermittently in the southeast section of Rambervillers. Third Battalion, attached to the 179th Infantry, attacked east on the flank of the division sector of operations.

First Battalion, in position on Jeanmenil-Rambervillers Road, received sporadic mortar and artillery fire throughout the day. Plans were made for the relief of Company C by Company B. At 0700 hours tank destroyers fired on enemy Nebelwerfers at 242736.

A five-man recon patrol from the battalion left 218703 and went to 218706, moving then to the fork in the stream at 219705. It then turned north to 231709 where it waited for thirty minutes. The patrol heard movement at La Haye Vaneau (237709) and a tank moving along the road at 230713 toward Jeanmenil. The patrol turned southeast to 237704, then to 236703, then crossed the stream and went south along the edge of the woods to 243696. It returned cross country to 228697 and back to the lines.

Another reconnaissance patrol of five men left 217703 and moved along the road to 220801. From there it traveled southeast toward Housseras to 228695, where the men located rectangular mines dug in on the road. The patrol returned without encountering enemy.

In the Second Battalion sector, sporadic enemy artillery fire fell upon Company G in the morning and again in the afternoon. A patrol located an enemy mortar at 225729, and chemical mortars and tank destroyers fired upon it. Two patrols, one from Company E and one from Company F, left at

1330 hours from 216747. The patrol from Company E went to 218746, while the patrol from Company F ventured to 220745. Both patrols blew holes in the enemy wire approximately fifteen yards wide, using Bangalore torpedoes. Snipers placed in position at both openings remained in position until 1630 hours but saw no one.

A five-man reconnaissance patrol from Company F left 217737 and moved to 224736, where it heard an enemy patrol moving southeast. The men waited until the enemy passed, then proceeded to Hill 372 (225736). The patrol heard digging and movement to the east. It returned at 2130.

Company C-S/Sgt. Russell W. Jones and PFC Harold L. Milliman were WIA and DOW on this day. Pvt. Willoughby G. Hagenbuch, Pvt. Walter N. Howard, Pvt. James Moore and PFC Eustaquio Sallas are WIA.

October 21–Operating in clear, cool weather, the regiment maintained its positions. Third Battalion, attached to the 179th Infantry, attacked on the right flank of the division.

In the First Battalion sector, Company B relieved Cannon Company position, completing the action at 2100 hours. Throughout the day, sporadic small-arms and artillery fire harassed the troops.

At 1930 hours a six-man ranger patrol left 215706, moved to 220705 and to Jeanmenil, then along the edge of the town to 230711. The patrol had not returned by 2400 hours.

A four-man patrol from Company A left the position at dark with a mission to Housseras to look for enemy positions and to investigate the woods. The patrol reached 230694 and heard enemy movement there.

Another four-man patrol from Company A left after dark and went to 2269 to investigate the woods. The patrol found nothing and returned at 2315 hours.

During the morning a patrol composed of men from Company E and from the 117th Recon went to the gaps blown in the enemy wire at 220746. The patrol found that the gaps had not been repaired and blew two more gaps in the wire at 220744. The enemy then opened fire with two machine-guns, and in a firefight, the patrol forced one crew to withdraw while the other abandoned its weapon. The patrol captured one enemy soldier.

Patrols from Company F and Company G, probing the forward areas near Bru, encountered artillery and mortar fire. Second Battalion received sporadic machine-gun fire throughout the day.

Company C–PFC Harold N. Scott is AWOL, missing the past two days.

October 22–During the morning, Third Battalion reverted to the control of the 157th Infantry and assembled at St. Gorgon. Second Battalion was relieved by the Third Battalion of the Thirty-Sixth Engineers as nightfall approached. A Company G outpost at 216732 was attacked from the front in the relief, and the men threw hand grenades at the enemy. The Germans then attacked the outpost from the rear, and again the outpost repulsed the assault with hand grenades. At 2215 hours a squad from the Thirty-Sixth Engineers moved out to help clear the resistance and to relieve the outpost but by midnight had not been able to break through to the trapped men. Companies E and F assembled in the vicinity of St. Helene at approximately midnight.

In the First Battalion sector, the Ranger Patrol that left the lines shortly before midnight October 21 returned at 0145 hours. The patrol reported hearing enemy activity in the vicinity of 223707 and in Jeanmenil as well as locating an enemy machine-gun at 225711 and enemy dug in at 227709.

Enemy artillery harassed the First Battalion troops throughout the day. Patrols probed the areas near Housseras and Autry, investigating the woods for enemy strong points and installations. A five-man ranger patrol reported the bridge at 217703 blown.

Company C–PFC Harold Scott is arrested for going AWOL. PFC Ladislaus S. Dombrowski is WIA.

October 23–During the day the Regimental Command Post moved from Rambervillers to St. Helene at 200663. The Third Battalion, Thirty-Sixth Engineers, which had relieved the Second

Battalion of the 157th Infantry on the north flank of the division sector, was released to its parent organization. First and Second Battalions, Thirty-Sixth Engineers, were attached to the 157th Infantry.

In the First Battalion sector, sporadic enemy artillery and mortar fire harassed the troops. An enemy outpost was located in front of Company A, and a raiding party moved out to close with it. The raiding party had not yet returned at 2400 hours. The First Battalion also attacked for a limited objective, the first few buildings on the west edge of Jeanmenil, but large fires started by chemical mortars gave off too much light. The attack was held up temporarily. A reconnaissance patrol of five men left 214706, moved to 217703, and found a roadblock of three trees. The bridge at 217703 was blown. Near 223700 the patrol encountered enemy digging in and heard the rattling of ammo boxes in woods just to the north.

Second Battalion assembled in the vicinity of St. Helene, the outpost group that was engaged in the firefight during the relief arriving at 0930 hours.

Third Battalion Second Battalion sent out two reconnaissance patrols, one from Company F and one from Company E. Company F patrol encountered machine- pistol and rifle fire from the woods at 241668.remained in Regimental Reserve in the vicinity of St. Gorgon.

Company C– PFC Edward A. Schemansky returns to duty.

October 24–The 157th Infantry remained in assembly areas and made plans and reconnaissance for the attack on October 25. First Battalion remained in defensive positions east of Rambervillers until relieved by elements of the Thirty-Sixth Engineers toward midnight. Effecting the relief, Company B engaged the enemy in a firefight. Throughout the day, First Battalion was subjected to heavy artillery fire.

Second Battalion, in an assembly area near St. Helene, sent out a reconnaissance patrol, which located the enemy dug in near the town of Williams Fontaine.

Third Battalion remained near St. Gorgon.

Company C–Pvt. Israel A. Hoffman is evacuated to the 120th Medical Battalion. Does not return during the war.

October 25–At 0630 hours, the Second and Third Battalions jumped off in attack. Second Battalion moved forward behind a smoke screen laid down by chemical mortars, encountering little resistance in covering the first thousand yards, but meeting intense machine- gun fire in moving across the clearing in the 2,466th grid line. One platoon of Company G moved north, clearing William Fontaine, then with a platoon of tanks in support, moved to the woods in the northeast sector of the 2,466th grid line. The platoon succeeded in knocking out several enemy machine-guns. The remainder of Company G infiltrated into the same group of woods, clearing the sector west of the twenty-fifth grid line. Company F continued pushing east against determined enemy resistance.

Before daylight, Third Battalion moved Company I from Autry toward Housseras, and at 0630 hours Company K and Company L jumped off in attack. Enemy resistance was light until the troops reached the edge of the woods, where they came under machine-gun and mortar fire. The enemy halted the advance of Company L, but Company I, with a platoon of tanks attached, and pushed into Housseras, meeting intense resistance. After a house-to- house battle, the company cleared Housseras of enemy by 1700 hours. Company K and Company L began moving southeast, clearing Les Hauts Pres.

By midnight, the regiment had gained the initial ridge east of the Rambervillers-Autry plain and had established contact with the 179th Infantry to the south. Company C of the Thirty-Sixth Engineers was released to the control of its parent organization.

[Bitter fighting against strong resistance and horrible weather continued until the regiment was withdrawn to a rest area on November 8, 1944.
— Hugh F. Foster III]

October 26–Throughout the day the regiment continued its attack to the northeast, meeting only slight opposition. Second Battalion, with First Battalion following in reserve, jumped off at 0600 hours and shortly before noon gained the objective at 263688. The battalion continued its attack at 1335 hours and at 1620 hours began receiving small-arms and artillery fire. Company G, attempting to cut the Jeanmenil Road, was held up by enemy fire. Company E sent one platoon to cut the Jeanmenil Road at 275695 and established a roadblock there at 2400 hours.

First Battalion, during the afternoon, was committed on the right of Second Battalion.

Third Battalion remained in position until Second Battalion came abreast, when at 0800 hours it jumped off once more, attacking northeast. Company I remained in position at Housseras while Company K, with Company L in support, led the attack. By 1345 hours the two companies had reached the vicinity of 252697, in position for tanks and tank destroyers to fire directly on the Jeanmenil road. Company I, swinging the right flank to the north, received tank fire from Fraipertuis. A patrol from Company L reported being fired upon by unidentified personnel who were wearing American uniforms and carrying M-1 Rifles. The battalion established its positions and prepared to be relieved by the Third Battalion, 180th Infantry.

Company C–PFC John A. Fischer is evacuated to the 120th Medical Battalion.

October 27–The regiment, with the Third Battalion, 180th Infantry attached, continued its attack to the northeast.

First Battalion jumped off at 0700 hours and encountered heavy machine-gun, mortar, and small-arms fire. Company A and Company C made slow but steady progress against increasingly stiffening resistance. Company C, moving around the south flank of Company A, sent a combat group to 298682, where it encountered a strong enemy roadblock. When the enemy saw the group, the Germans evacuated the position, leaving several automatic weapons in place.

Second Battalion, after establishing a roadblock and mine field on the Jeanmenil-LaSalle road at 275695, moved down to within fifty yards of the south side of the road. Throughout the day Companies G and F encountered heavy small-arms resistance from enemy infantry who were dug in on the north side of the road.

Third Battalion was relieved at 1040 hours by Third Battalion of the 180th Infantry.

Company C-Pvt. Phillip V. Angelastro, S/Sgt. Robert L. Kirchgassner, PFC Forest Payton, Pvt. Michael Skowronek and PFC Henry J. Wild were WIA. PFC Charles C. Green is KIA.

[Bob was always in the lead with John Schweisthal right behind him. Bob didn't have to tell us to get down on this day. We were coming out of a wooded area into a clearing when a barrage of enemy gunfire and mortar fire came upon us. We were caught by surprise and had to retreat back into the woods. Bob and Richard Badgett were both seriously wounded. I could hear many soldiers hollering for medics. I can still see John helping to carry the stretcher that Bob was on when he was taken off the battlefield.

John commandeered an Army jeep somehow and got Bob to the battalion aid station quickly. From there (John told me forty years later at a Forty-Fifth Division Reunion,) he rode in the ambulance with Bob to the field hospital which was eight to ten miles behind enemy lines. He said no one questioned him.

Sadly, Richard Badgett did not survive as he died in my arms. Neither Bob or John returned during the war.—Richard Adams]

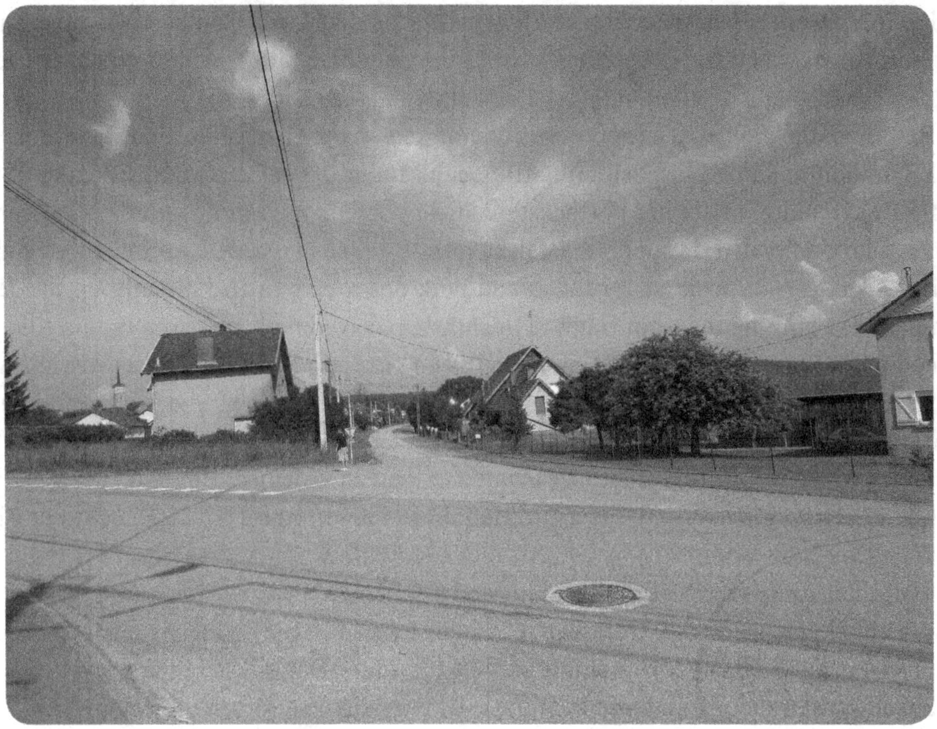

"Jeanmenil"

[After the liberation of Rome, the Forty-Fifth Infantry Division was part of the invasion of France. Dad loved the South of France and the Rhone Valley. The people were helpful and kind to the American troops.—John Kirchgassner]

[Visiting the town where my grandfather fought his last battle of the war stirred a lot of emotions. My grandfather was always my hero, and to be in the place where he almost lost his life produced a feeling I do not know if I will ever replicate. As we got closer to the town, I started getting goosebumps. As I walked around the town of Jeanmenil, I had mixed feelings. I was proud that my grandfather was a soldier, sorrowful at knowing he was wounded, and thankful for him and the other soldiers who served here.—Mark D. Kirchgassner]

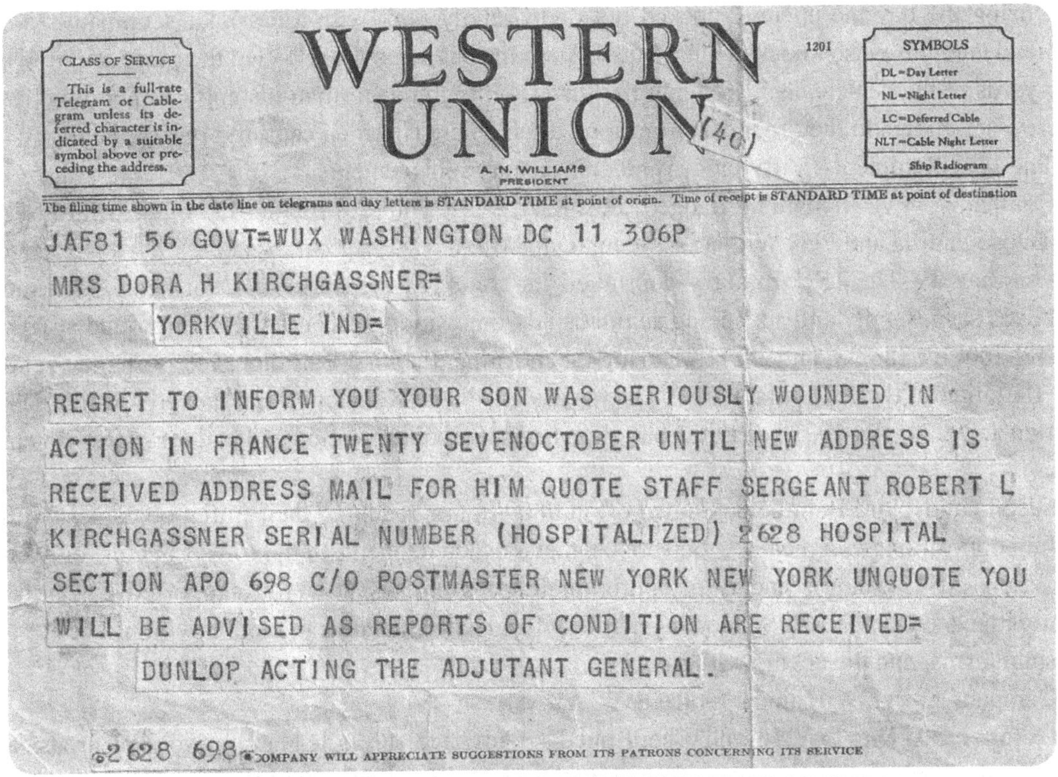

CLASS OF SERVICE
This is a full-rate Telegram or Cablegram unless its deferred character is indicated by a suitable symbol above or preceding the address.

WESTERN UNION (40)
A. N. WILLIAMS
PRESIDENT

1201

SYMBOLS
DL=Day Letter
NL=Night Letter
LC=Deferred Cable
NLT=Cable Night Letter
Ship Radiogram

The filing time shown in the date line on telegrams and day letters is STANDARD TIME at point of origin. Time of receipt is STANDARD TIME at point of destination

JAF81 56 GOVT=WUX WASHINGTON DC 11 306P
MRS DORA H KIRCHGASSNER=
YORKVILLE IND=

REGRET TO INFORM YOU YOUR SON WAS SERIOUSLY WOUNDED IN ACTION IN FRANCE TWENTY SEVENOCTOBER UNTIL NEW ADDRESS IS RECEIVED ADDRESS MAIL FOR HIM QUOTE STAFF SERGEANT ROBERT L KIRCHGASSNER SERIAL NUMBER (HOSPITALIZED) 2628 HOSPITAL SECTION APO 698 C/O POSTMASTER NEW YORK NEW YORK UNQUOTE YOU WILL BE ADVISED AS REPORTS OF CONDITION ARE RECEIVED=
DUNLOP ACTING THE ADJUTANT GENERAL.

2628 698 COMPANY WILL APPRECIATE SUGGESTIONS FROM ITS PATRONS CONCERNING ITS SERVICE

Copy of the telegram Grandma Dorie received.

October 28–The 157th Infantry continued its attack to the north and east, encountering pockets of stiff resistance. First Battalion jumped off at 0700 hours, Companies B and C spearheading the assault. Company C encountered resistance from the eastern slope of a hill at 298694, where the enemy was dug in. Company B maneuvered behind Company C and attacked from the right. By 1415 hours the First Battalion was able to renew its attack and made steady progress.

Second Battalion coordinated its attack with the Third Battalion, jumping off at 0930 hours for the high ground at 279703. Second Battalion met intense small-arms fire in crossing the Jeanmenil highway. At 1330 hours Company F, followed by Company E, gained objective 279699 after a heavy firefight. Company E then moved through Company F and pushed on toward the final objective. By 1545 hours the companies had reached the objective and dug in, with Company E at 282703, Company F at 278703, and Company G on a roadblock at 272696.

During the day the enemy knocked out one friendly tank with a bazooka. Company L's Pvt. Carmen Dalphonse also knocked out a Mark IV with a bazooka. He reloaded the piece, ran to within forty yards of the vehicle, and fired into the turret, killing one German instantly. Other members of the crew scrambled to the ground and ran for a ditch where riflemen captured two of them.

The 157th Regiment—Fifty-eight WIA and seventy replacements.

Company C-Pvt. Richard M. Badgett, Jr. is KIA. 2nd Lt. Paul C. Brockhoff, S/Sgt. Edward Dalton, S/Sgt. Jose Padilla and PFC William F. Seeman are WIA.

October 29–The 157th Infantry continued its attack to the north and northeast, clearing its objectives successfully and advancing against slight opposition to secure the high ground at 293707, 203712, 280712, 286713, and 285717. During the morning, the First Battalion, 179th Infantry, relieved First Battalion of the 157th Infantry, which was assigned a new objective and moved toward the road junction at 292705. By 1925 hours, the battalion had secured its position and had registered defensive fires.

Second and Third Battalions jumped off at 0800 hours, reaching their initial objectives without meeting opposition. Assigned new objectives, they pushed deeper into the forests against only slight opposition. At 1745 hours enemy of approximately a company strength, supported by one tank, counterattacked Company I. Supporting artillery fired a barrage in conjunction with protective fires and small arms, and the enemy withdrew.

Company C-Pvt. William H. Grace is WIA.

October 30–The 157th Infantry continued to advance through heavily wooded areas. First Battalion during the afternoon was relieved by the Third Battalion, 179th Infantry, while Second and Third Battalions, 157th Infantry, jumped off in attack at 0800 hours. Second Battalion reached its objective without difficulty, but after it had established its position it received fire of all types.

In the Third Battalion sector, Company L met determined resistance in spearheading an attack for the high ground at 296725. Company K was committed on the left flank and met resistance at 294717. Tanks were moved forward to knock out the enemy, and the advance continued. At 1150 hours Company K had gained 292718, but met small-arms fire from dug-in positions to the front. At 1230 hours Company L received grazing machine-gun fire that continued until approximately 1415 hours when both Companies L and K began moving against small-arms fire. Before nightfall the battalion established its positions and sent patrols forward to contact the enemy. Some enemy, members of a convict battalion, were trapped between Companies L and I, which captured seventy-eight enemy soldiers. One of the convicts had been sentenced to death for proclaiming publicly that following the war, Adolf would be a barracks orderly in a prison camp in Siberia. Another had been sentenced to nine months' imprisonment for being fifty-four hours absent without leave.

Company C-PFC Buckner Morris, PFC Walter B. Sorensen, Cpl. Quienton Steele and Pvt. William E. Wright are WIA.

October 31–The 157th Infantry continued to attack to the north and northeast, occupying the high ground at 288744 and 294737.

Second and Third Battalions jumped off at 0800 hours, First Battalion following in close support of Third Battalion. Second Battalion advanced against slight opposition across the road to 285733 and 289733, continuing forward from there. At 1630 hours, the enemy launched a counterattack against Company G, sliding southeast of Company F and into Third Battalion. In a heavy firefight, the enemy withdrew but loosed mortar and artillery fire on the line for several hours afterward.

Third Battalion's advance was slow as the companies engaged enemy who were dug in along the 732th grid line. By 1352 hours the enemy had withdrawn and the advance continued.

At 1630 hours the enemy counterattack glanced off Company I and struck Company K before the unit had dug in its position for the night. Heavy fighting, and Company K was driven back a hundred yards before the attack was broken and the enemy dispersed. Company K suffered many losses. A German officer, chancing upon an abandoned .30-caliber machine-gun, directed its fire into the flank of part of a platoon, which was taking cover deep in a trench used by infantry troops during World War I. Grave registration crews later carried twelve American dead from the trench. Throughout the night the line received intense mortar and artillery concentrations.

Company C–PFC Harold N. Scott transferred as a private to Company K. Pvt. Edward Beattie is AWOL. S/Sgt. Edward Dalton, PFC Frank Mitrowski and PFC Guiodo G. Pallozzi are WIA. Pvt. Alfred L. Senape is WIA and later DOW.

[It was October and we were getting into the Vosges Mountains. They were covered in dense woods. The enemy was hard to find with all the dense cover. The enemy artillery would fire at us; the shells would burst in the trees and send fragments over our positions, causing casualties. It was the start of the rainy season. On October 27, in the vicinity of Housseras and Jeanmenil, we were moving up a hill when the Germans threw a mortar barrage on us. I was badly wounded, and one of my men was killed.—Robert L. Kirchgassner]

[Jared's Blog:
June 19, 2013 Epinal--Jeanmenil-- Then:

Epinal, France, is at the base of the Vosges Mountains. The Allies were marching through Europe on their way to Germany. They had the Germans on the retreat, but the enemy now had shorter supply lines, was not overextended, and could continue to fight.

Robert Kirchgassner and the 157th were pushing through the hillside, fighting tough battles in dense woods, liberating small town after small town.

The Germans used hilltops and rivers as key strong points. The Americans had to try to cross a river under heavy fire or work up a mountain or a hill through dense woods as the Germans fired down at them. Once they had secured a hill or a river, the Americans had to repeat the process all over again at the next one. This meant slow going with high casualties. The 157th had spent a lot of time fighting in the area.

This is where Robert Kirchgassner would end his fighting. The 157th had secured a small town east of Epinal named Jeanmenil. The troops were working around a pass between hilltops. Sergeant Kirchgassner and a few other men had entered a clearing when a German mortar suddenly struck. Robert was hit in the chest and abdomen by fragments.

The men scrambled back into the woods, but damage had been done. Richard Badgett of Kentucky, a good friend of Robert's, was killed. Robert was taken to a field hospital, critically wounded. Obviously he would somehow miraculously pull through or we wouldn't be here today, but this was the end of his fighting.

Now:

Today we spent the morning touring the American military cemetery and memorial at Epinal. Like the other military cemeteries, it is very beautiful.

We found the grave of Richard Badgett at the site. Dick Adams had been in contact with Richard's relatives in Kentucky before the trip, but they didn't recall much about him. Our goal was to make sure this fallen soldier was not forgotten.

We met with the cemetery superintendent, a very sharp Vietnam veteran named Dwight Anderson. We told him Richard's story and gave him a picture of Richard taken during the war. Anderson was excited. He spends countless hours trying to put names and stories with the more than five thousand heroes buried at the cemetery.

Anderson then spent a couple of hours recounting the fighting by the Forty-Fifth and the Allies, giving us a tour of the graves, and sharing stories about the soldiers buried in this place. We learned so much about the young men and women who gave their lives for us. We saw the graves of brothers, groups of friends, unknown soldiers, the brother of Dick Clark (*American Bandstand*), Tuskegee airmen, Japanese-American fighters, Chinese-American soldiers, women, Red Cross members, Medal of Honor winners, and even two wrestlers who were on a USO mission. I could have listened to the story of every person in the cemetery.

I can't do justice to Anderson's accounts. He shared a link to one soldier's story, which can be found on YouTube. Wells Lewis was the young son of author Sinclair Lewis. He has a neat but sad story. Check it out.

One symbol at the cemetery that resonated with me was the trees. Lining the middle lawn between the two plots were two rows of sycamore trees, the state tree of Indiana. The tops of the trees were cut off, making them look quite different from what we were used to seeing. The practice has roots in ancient Egypt. When the Egyptians got a new pharaoh, they would begin building his pyramid to entomb him upon his death. If the pharaoh died early, they wouldn't have time to put a top on the pyramid, and a pyramid without a top became synonymous with a life cut too short. Thus many of the American military cemeteries have trees or bushes without tops.

Before the tour, we met one of the smartest people I have ever encountered. Dr. Lise Pommois is an English teacher from France, and her passion is the battles of World Wars I and II. She spends her time writing books, studying battle sites, doing research at the National Archives in Washington, D.C., hosting former soldiers and those interested, and immersing herself in projects related to the world wars. Her depth of knowledge and generosity with her time are unfathomable. At one point during lunch we were asking her so many questions that she said if we wanted to continue we had to let her eat. Lise was one of the biggest reasons for our visit to Epinal. She has also an awesome sense of humor.

After Lise took us to the cemetery in the morning, we spent the afternoon driving all around the French countryside pinpointing the battlefields. The war has been over for sixty-eight years, and the landscape and the environment have changed drastically since then. She took us to the hills and the forest where she has determined that the Forty-Fifth would have fought. Along the way we saw several small monuments to troops from World War II. In the town of Autry, we stumbled across an old abbey that had clearly seen fighting between the Germans and the

157th. We learned that the church's spire and roof had been damaged in bombings. The front door had been blown off, and we found bullet holes in the side of the building.

Bridge over La Moselle River Epinal, France
SC Photo-Lapidus

Military Cemetery at
Epinal, France

From there we spent quite some time trying to find the spot where Sergeant Kirchgassner was wounded and his good friend was killed. Even with the morning reports and the maps, it was not possible to pinpoint the location, but Lise showed us the most likely area. It was neat being there, picturing what our troops saw during the fight for global freedom.

We will spend the day tomorrow learning more about the fighting here and traveling among the battlefields of France. We will hike to find foxholes. Today was extremely educational, and I've covered only the broad highlights and not the details of what we learned. We are so blessed to have a world-renowned tour guide. I can't wait to see what tomorrow holds.—Jared Leiker

Company C arrived on the outskirts of Jeanmenil, France, on October 10, 1944, amid reports of heavy enemy shelling. On October 23, PFC Edward Schemansky suffered a wound in the neck. On October 27, Company C finally took Jeanmenil and set up roadblocks. S/Sgt. Robert Kirchgassner was wounded.

According to the hospital report, Robert was seriously wounded with a blood pressure reading of 0/0 upon arrival. From the morning reports, we know that something also happened to John on that day. His time as an infantryman was over. Yet Robert later said that John commandeered an army Jeep to get him to the field hospital. Back at the battle scene, Richard Badgett died in Richard Adams's arms. As he held his comrade, Richard saw John with a group of men carrying Robert on a stretcher.—Jared Leiker and Rita Kirchgassner]

November 1–As rumors of imminent relief by a new division pervaded, the regiment continued its daily attacks through the densely wooded foothills of the Vosges Mountains. Though inclement weather hampered operations and brought increased losses in personnel, the 157th Infantry made steady progress, overcoming pockets of resistance in a dogged advance through the forests. Enemy opposition fortunately, was limited in the main to small arms and mortar fire, although the troops occasionally received sporadic shellings.

Patrolling marked the action, although Second Battalion launched a limited-objective attack at noon and by nightfall had cut the main road. A contact patrol from Company C, attempting to reach Company L, encountered intense small- arms fire, but the resistance was cleared when a platoon from Company C moved forward and engaged the enemy in a firefight. While the patrol continued its mission, the platoons established a position between Company C and Company L and four times during the day drove infiltrating enemy patrols out of the sector.

Company C-Sgt. Grant Gover is KIA. Pvt. James P. Schuler is WIA.

November 2–At 0800 hours, First and Second Battalions jumped off in attack, First Battalion pressing toward the St. Benoit-Etival highway against heavy opposition. A field of Schu-mines impeded the battalion's advanced, but by 1640 hours, Company A had crossed the highway and had penetrated into the woods on the opposite side. Second Battalion, attacking east, met small-arms, mortar, and self-propelled fire but gained ground steadily. Company G, attempting to capture hill 467, met bitter resistance from German infantrymen well concealed and dug in along the slope. The company lost ground but, supported by artillery and tanks, overran the strong point on the second assault.

Company C-PFC Robert J. Bartley DOW. He was WIA on October 31st.

November 3–Company C-Les Angles, France. S/Sgt. Leland Scott is WIA. PFC George Kiewiet Jr. (WIA) and PFC Rudolph T. Hodges are evacuated to the 120th Medical Battalion. These three soldiers do not return during the war. Pvt. James O. Stephens is KIA.

November 3–4–The infantry continued attacking to the east and northeast, advancing slowly toward the Meurthe River. The companies found the enemy making increased use of mines and booby traps, Third Battalion locating one roadblock of a quarter-mile length, every tree in it wired to explosive charges.

November 4–In the morning they reached high ground two thousand yards west of St. Remy, which patrols found occupied by groups of Germans.

Company C–PFC Edward Schemansky is evacuated sick. Pvt. George S. White and Pvt. William E. Wright are WIA.

November 5–Resistance stiffened as the regiment continued to press through the woods. First Battalion, attacking in a column of companies, met intense machine-gun fire, which held up the advance for three hours before supporting tanks moved forward and knocked out the German positions.

Third Battalion, contacting the 399th Infantry of the newly committed 100th Division, launched an attack toward the east at 1550 hours, meeting resistance from a series of battered houses. At 1615 hours, Company L received an enemy counterattack from the northeast, which delayed the advance for more than an hour. At 1840 hours, Company K became engaged in a heavy firefight, and tanks moved forward to knock out enemy machine-gun positions. By nightfall the battalion had dug in and organized the ground, but throughout the hours of darkness it received a sporadic concentration of artillery and anti-aircraft fire.

Second Battalion, which since October 30 had been under the command of Capt. Charles Edwards in the absence of Col. Laurence Brown, on leave, and Maj. George Kessler, wounded in action, remained in position, awaiting the scheduled relief by a battalion from the 100th Division. Patrols probed the forward areas, engaging in frequent brushes with scattered groups of enemy.

One patrol of three officers and thirty-two enlisted men, moving toward a hill mass, encountered approximately fifty Germans and engaged them in a heavy firefight. Under intense small-arms fire, which brought casualties, the patrol withdrew to more advantageous ground while Company G moved forward to reinforce it. The fighting continued until late afternoon when Company G was ordered to withdraw, and with the remainder of the battalion began the long shuttle to the rest area at Martigney Les Bains.

Company C-First Lt. Phillip Gellar is lightly wounded and evacuated to the 120th Medical Battalion. Enlisted men: 143. Also WIA are Pvt. Thomas A. Campana, PFC Alfred C. Miller and PFC George V. Tillman.

[This letter was written by a German soldier from the 951st Regiment in the Vosges:

Dear Mother,

I want to send you a few lines today. I am still pretty well and I hope the same applies to you. I am again in a new sector of the front, namely in the Vosges in France. The front is very quiet. We are in a house on a hill and the Americans are right across from us in the woods. During the day we cannot leave the house. If we go out, we are shot at. It is the same with the Americans. So everyone stays where he is. We arrived here yesterday morning before dawn. We relieved other companies that had been here for a long time. The comrades left us a butchered pig, a calf, and three rabbits. You can imagine how the cook cursed and how we ate. We would rather eat till we can eat no more than leave it to the comrades of another unit. We also found a lot of preserves, plum, cherries, pears, etc., in the cellar. So now we live again like "God in France." When you look at the enemy with binoculars you can see the type of cigarettes he is smoking, we are so close together.

Now I want to end this letter, dear mother, and I hope to hear from you soon.

Many greetings from your son,

/s/Walter]

November 6–With the First Battalion, 398th Infantry attached, the regiment continued its attack, progressing slowly against stubborn small-arms resistance. Company C launched the initial assault against a well-defended hill mass, but virtually pinned beneath artillery, mortar, Nebelwerfer, and small-arms fire, they finally withdrew to the woods line. Company A started moving along the north slope of the hill mass but received direct fire from enemy machine-guns emplaced along the ridges. Until nightfall every move brought intense fire, and throughout the hours of darkness, First Battalion, now being commanded by Colonel Brown, returned to duty and received sporadic shellings.

Third Battalion, meanwhile, continued its house-to-house fighting up the southeast road to Pajaille, engaging scattered groups of enemy at close quarters. A platoon of Germans counterattacked Company I at 0630 hours, but the enemy dispersed under artillery and rifle fire. At 1500 hours, Company I sent a strong patrol toward the town of Pajaille, but the enemy armed with automatic weapons opened fire from the house on the outskirts of the village. The patrol withdrew under intense fire.

The 398th Infantry confined its activities to patrolling, exchanging a few rounds of small- arms fire with groups of enemy.

Company C-PFC Andrew M. Ondrik is lightly wounded and evacuated to the 120th Medical Battalion and does not return during the war. Also WIA were Cpl. Thomas H. McKay, PFC William E. Metz and PFC Peter B. Scaletta. S/Sgt. Roy J. Morris and PFC Ignatius Schauman are KIA.

November 7–With Third Battalion remaining in position in preparation for its relief, First Battalion jumped off in attack once more, moving forward at 0800 hours. The enemy launched a counterattack against Company A during the morning but fell back under artillery and small-arms fire. At 1400 hours, however, the Germans pinned Company B under intense flanking fire and partially surrounded the unit. Company C moved up on the right, engaging the enemy in a heavy firefight, and by nightfall had cleared Company B's exposed flank of enemy. After dark a few Germans infiltrated between the two companies and were captured.

Shortly after noon, Company I moved forward slowly, attacking the enemy-occupied houses with some success. At 1600 hours elements of the Third Battalion, 399th Infantry, began the shuttle to the rest area in Darney, while the battalion from the 399th Infantry came under regimental control.

Company C-Sgt. Jack Hachett, Sgt. John G. Humenik, S/Sgt. Holly P. Nickell, Pvt. John J. Smith, Cpl. John W. Taylor and T/Sgt. James B. Trainor.

November 8–First Battalion remained in position throughout the morning, awaiting relief, while the First Battalion, 398th Infantry, launched an attack upon the high ground in front of its position. The attackers encountered immediate machine-gun fire and could make no progress. At 1530 hours, First Battalion was relieved by the Second Battalion, 399th Infantry, and began the shuttle to the division rest area.

Company C–Les Angles, France. Relieved by the 100th Division. Enlisted men: 124.

November 9–Company C in Martigney Les Baines, France. Private sent to regimental stockade for going AWOL. Nineteen new enlisted men assigned to Company C. Enlisted men: 124. Cpl. Virgil Green is WIA.

November 9–24–Troops from the 157th Infantry remained bivouacked in and near the towns of Martigney Les Bains and Darney. All men lived in enclosed quarters, three companies from Third Battalion utilizing German barracks near Darney while Second Battalion and two companies from First Battalion occupied the resort hotels in Martigney Les Bains. With the advent of snows and increased rainfall, the crowded living places proved a welcome change from the life the men led for eighty-six days prior to their relief from the front lines.

Always of prime importance, a shower unit situated in Martigney Les Bains operated daily, and with but few exceptions all troops bathed and received new or laundered clothing. Through special services, men were able to attend moving pictures or stage shows each afternoon or evening, and reading or writing rooms were available to all troops. To maintain physical fitness, the companies conducted four-hour training periods each day, engaging in close-order drill or firing problems. The remaining hours were free, and the infantrymen knew how to use them.

Company C-Pvt. Kenneth D. Davis and PFC William J. Klymn become POWs.

November 10–Company C–PFC Edward Schemansky returns to duty. Pvt. Edward Beattie is in confinement in Gray, France.

November 11–Company C–Rest camp duties. Enlisted men: 158. Pvt. Nathen Tucker becomes a POW.

November 13–Company C–Usual camp duties and training. Enlisted: 182.

November 14–In the rain-swept town of Darney, Gen. Alexander Patch, commander of Seventh Army, presented the men of Company I, 157th Infantry, the distinguished unit badges awarded them in a presidential citation commending the organization for its stand at the Flyover Bridge on the Anzio beachhead in February 1944. To close the ceremony, General Patch and Gen. W.W. Eagles, commander of the Forty-Fifth Division, pinned silver oak leaves on the jacket shoulders of Felix L. Sparks, the battalion commander. Battlefield promotion to lieutenant colonel came as a complete and pleasant surprise to the lanky officer, who had received his promotion to major only three months before, August 5, 1944.

November 17–18–Rumors began circulating that the regiment soon would be committed again, and chaplains from the 157th Infantry conducted memorial services for the men of the organization who had been killed on fields of battle in Sicily, Italy, and France. Hundreds of civilians, respecting the occasion and curious to learn what was taking place, voluntarily attended the ceremonies.

Loss of Major Kessler as Second Battalion executive officer brought about changes in the chain of command. Maj. George Cole, executive officer of First Battalion, was assigned to Second Battalion, while Capt. Charles Edwards, regimental intelligence officer, took the vacant executive post. Capt. Robert Slyter, executive officer of Third Battalion, was assigned to regiment as S-2, while Cannon Company commander Capt. John L. McGinnis became executive officer of Third Battalion. First Lt. John Kambeitz took command of Cannon Company.

November 19– Company C-PFC John A. Fisher Jr. returns.

November 20–Division alerted the regiment to move, but final orders did not arrive until the morning of November 23, the presidentially proclaimed Thanksgiving Day. The 157th Infantry celebrated Thanksgiving one day early, company kitchens preparing hundreds of pounds of turkey and the troops consuming the supper meal November 22. The following morning three officers and thirty-five enlisted men traveled to a rest camp in Paris, the first regimental group to visit the capital city of France.

Company C–Pvt. Anthony L. Dumont is promoted to private first class.

November 21–Company C–PFC Edward Schemansky is ill and does not return during the war. Pvt. Edward J. Beattie is in regimental stockade.

November 24–In a drizzling all-day rain, the regiment shuttled from the rest area to the vicinity of the recently captured city of Sarrebourg, a distance of approximately ninety miles. The convoys traveled a roundabout route, crossing flooded, shell-pocked fields marked by dead livestock half covered with mud and continuing through totally destroyed villages where an occasional civilian family gave the men unenthusiastic greetings. As the troops entered Alsace-Lorraine, they found road signs printed in German and talked to local citizens who knew no French. First Battalion that night bivouacked in the vicinity of Langate and set patrols into the forward areas, while Third Battalion moved into areas near Haute Clocher. At 1650 hours, Second Battalion, which had reached Dolving, sent Companies E and F to the high ground on the north side of the wooded area overlooking Oberstinzel. A patrol from the battalion moved to Sarraltroff and contacted elements of the Seventy-First Infantry.

At 1000 hours the following morning, the 157th Infantry was attached to the Forty-Fourth Division and moved to Brouvillers. First Battalion arrived at Brouvillers at 1215 hours, then shuttled to Lixhiem, where the men assembled before advancing toward Rauwiller, a town that the Germans had retaken from a unit of the Forty-Fourth Division in a heavy counterattack. The battalion encountered sporadic small-arms fire, but by 1800 hours, Company A had occupied the shell-battered town. The unit, which had received the initial counterattack, reorganized amid the shambles of Rauwiller and with the First Battalion attached, advanced toward the high ground north of the town.

Company C–Epinal, France. Cpl. Virgil Green, Cpl. William Mutchler, and Cpl. Quienton Steele all are promoted to sergeant. Sgt. Raymond W. Koss is WIA.

November 25–Company C–Epinal France. PFC Richard Adams is WIA (hit with shrapnel in the back) and evacuated. Sgt. Virgil Green and PFC Frank H. Biette are evacuated and do not return during the war. PFC Henry E. Carr, Pvt. Rollin F. Law, T/Sgt. Henry J. Millspaugh, PFC William E. Santerre and Cpl. Walter B. Sorensen were WIA.

> [The regiment returned to combat and the attack. The men pushed through the Alsatian plain toward the German border.—Hugh F. Foster III]

November 26-While the GRS squads cleared American and German bodies from Rauwiller, the First Battalion continued its attack to the north through morning, meeting little resistance in mopping up the surrounding areas. Second and Third Battalions remained in regimental reserve in the vicinity of Brouvillers.

At 0630 hours the 157th Infantry reverted to division control and began shuttling to the vicinity of Neuwiller, Second Battalion attacking toward Wienbourg at 1300 hours. The infantrymen met no opposition until they approached the town. Then scattered groups of enemy offered slight small-arms resistance. The companies blocked all the roads leading out of Wienbourg and established positions for the night.

November 27–28–At 0715 hours Companies E and F attacked toward the east, meeting the first opposition in the approach march to the town of Ingwiller, where an enemy roadblock opened fire upon Company F. In a brief firefight, the company destroyed the roadblock and captured two 75mm guns and eleven enemy soldiers. By 1314 hours, Company E had taken Ingwiller.

While the Third Battalion moved toward the town of Zinswiller against opposition, First Battalion moved forward from the roadblocks at Weiterwiller. Enemy broke into Company B position and overran one machine-gun crew but the company dispersed the Germans and regained the weapon in a thirty-minute firefight.

Company C–Epinal, France. Roadblock at Weiterwiller, France. Enlisted men: 161.

November 29–At 0615 hours, Sgt. James Martin, an anti-tank man from Birmingham, Alabama, noticed six Germans approaching a house in which was located a forward Third Battalion switchboard. Though in the darkness he was unable to identify them definitely as enemy, his suspicions led him to follow them down the road. When one of the group started creeping toward the front door of the house while the five others concealed themselves, Martin raced around to the rear of the building and entered it, stepping quietly past ten sleeping soldiers as he took up a crouched position behind the door. Through the entrance walked a six-foot German, who covered the sleeping figures with a U.S. carbine and yelled, "Handts op!"

Martin swung into immediate action, turning his flashlight full in the face of the enemy soldier and firing ten .45 slugs into the man's chest with a pistol. The German screamed and toppled over dead on the front steps while his five companions scrambled into the woods.

The 157th Infantry, under the command of Lt. Col. Chester James, taking the place of Col. Walter O'Brien, who had become ill the previous night and had been evacuated to a hospital, renewed its attack, meeting increased resistance in the advance toward the northeast. Second Battalion, during the morning, cleared resistance from the town of Bishholtz, receiving heavy concentrations of machine-gun, mortar, and tank fire as it pressed forward throughout the day. Third Battalion, meanwhile, encountered an estimated company of enemy and light armor in attacking Rothback. Supporting tanks engaged the enemy from the south side of the town while the battalion circled and entered the village from the north. By 1300 hours Companies K and L had cleared the town of resistance, and Companies I and K continued toward Offwiller. Company I reported reaching Offwiller at 1530 hours, and Company L, moving forward, occupied positions on the north side of the town. At approximately 2215 hours, an enemy patrol came into the company position, and in the ensuing firefight, the men captured one German officer. Another enemy patrol attacked Company I, which captured five enemy soldiers in the skirmish that followed.

Until relieved at 1512 hours by a battalion from the 397th Infantry, First Battalion remained on roadblocks. In the late afternoon it moved to the vicinity of Rothback and set up its positions for the night. A patrol from Company A moved toward Zinswiller but came under machine-gun and f lak fire, which resulted in eight casualties.

November 30–The regiment continued attacking to the northeast, Company E receiving direct fire from a Mark IV tank at 0840 hours. Artillery fire destroyed the tank on the Offwiller-Zinswiller road at 0930 hours.

Main enemy resistance centered around the Third Battalion position. Shortly after midnight, a strong enemy patrol worked its way along the high ground to the northeast of the battalion positions and engaged Company L in a firefight. The Germans dispersed and at 0200 hours, elements of the patrol approached the Company I position. Company I also dispersed the Germans and succeeded in capturing several enemy soldiers.

By 1000 hours Company I and elements of Company L had reached high ground from which they harassed enemy infantry and armor in the Zinswiller sector. The battalion established a mine field in front of its position.

During the afternoon Colonel O'Brien returned to the organization and resumed command of the 157th Infantry.

December, the regiment's and the Forty-Fifth Division's eighteenth month of combat, saw the 157th Infantry penetrating German soil and engaging the outer defenses of the Siegfried Line after a steady advance over mountainous Alsatian terrain. Contrary to general expectations, December weather remained unusually moderate, although daily rains during the first half impeded operations. As it had the previous winter, trench foot took a heavy toll, and the strain of battle and exposure to the elements forced the evacuation of scores of soldiers. Companies at times operated with strengths as low as fifty-five men. Resistance, though not always intense, remained steady, a tribute to the tactical skills of the retreating Germans, who had demonstrated time and again their mastery of defending important ground with limited troops.

December 1–During the early morning hours, two squads from Company G moved toward the high ground on the Second Battalion front in an attempt to outpost it preparatory to the contemplated day's attack. The ever-alert enemy loosed intense concentrations of 20mm and machine-gun fire upon the advancing men, who continued a stubborn advance along the upward- sloping ground. By 0230 hours, the squads had attained the remaining hours of darkness, and the enemy plastered the slope with heavy artillery concentrations.

At 0800 hours Second and Third Battalions jumped off in attack, advancing generally northeast against stubborn enemy resistance. In the Second Battalion sector, German shellfire pinned the assaulting Company G to the ground, but Company E, on the left, continued to make steady progress. Pushing forward slowly, the company drove the enemy from an orchard to the front and by 1530 hours had gained the battalion objective, the ridge west of the town of Zinswiller. Company F, following in reserve, moved up on the ridge at 1600 hours just as the enemy loosed intense concentrations of rocket, f lak, and artillery fire on the occupying troops. Under fire, Second Battalion dug in its positions for the night along the ridge line.

In the Third Battalion sector, Company L reached the hill northwest of Zinswiller against only slight resistance, but at 1145 hours, enemy of approximately a platoon in strength launched a counterattack. In the midst of the ensuing firefight, Company I moved around to the north of the hill and southeast toward the Company L right flank, mopping up scattered groups of enemy. The battalion established its position on high ground overlooking Zinswiller.

Company C–PFC John A. Fisher Jr. is evacuated to the 120th Medical Battalion and does not return during the war. Pvt. Harold C. Koenig DOW received on November 25th.

December 2–The regiment remained in position on the north flank of the division sector and patrolled to the north and east. A patrol from Company B made its way to Hill 369 and remained in observation there for an hour, contacting a friendly patrol from the 106th Reconnaissance Troop. The two patrols engaged twenty to thirty enemy who were moving south, and under fire the Germans withdrew. Both patrols returned to their respective units, the men from Company B venturing onto the hill once more at 1120 hours. At 1610 hours elements of the Forty-Fifth Reconnaissance Troop began the relief of First Battalion, the relief being completed at 1930 hours.

Protected on the east by a mine field four hundred yards from its position, Second Battalion throughout the day limited its activities to patrolling and to firing upon targets of opportunity. Battalion long-range machine-gun fire and artillery drove an enemy mortar crew out of its position in the cemetery on the outskirts of Zinswiller, and shellfire set burning a German vehicle that was observed moving into the town from the northeast.

At 1045 hours a reconnaissance patrol from Company G moved toward Zinswiller, reaching one point where it received direct tank fire from the north side of the stream. The men found a small bridge across the stream still intact. At 1730 hours another patrol from Company G started toward Zinswiller to secure the bridge, but upon arrival, found that it had been blown.

Meeting sporadic resistance, Company G moved into Zinswiller shortly after midnight December 2, clearing enemy snipers from houses inside the shell-battered town, and began crossing the swift-f lowing stream that ran through it. By 0445 hours the company had occupied part of the town, encountering concentrations of long-range artillery fire. Shelled sporadically, the company continued to press its advantage, two platoons wading the stream before 0800 hours. By 1000 hours, Zinswiller had been cleared of resistance and all roads leading from it had been blocked. Artillery and self-propelled fire continued to hamper the engineers attempting to build a bridge across the stream.

First and Third Battalions, also encountering steady opposition, waded the stream and pushed forward to the high ground on the opposite side, establishing their defensive positions at 1600 hours. Company B and elements of Company I moved into Zinswiller.

Company C–Saverne, France. First Sgt. John Clements reduced to private and then promoted to tech sergeant and transferred to Company D.

December 3–Company C–Saverne, France Sgt. Quienton Steele and Sgt. William Mutchler are slightly wounded and evacuated to the 120th Medical Battalion and do not return during the war.. Cpl. Henry J. Wild is KIA. PFC Donald L. Hayford, Sgt. Raymond W. Koss, PFC Frederick J. Mundt and PFC Frank T. Pullman are also WIA. Pvt. M. A. Skowronek is injured. Enlisted men: 156.

[Mutchler lasted a long time.—Richard Adams]

December 4–Moving toward the northeast, Company A and Company C jumped off in attack shortly after dawn. The troops followed the Oberbronn-Niederbronn road and met little resistance until they attempted crossing open ground and the enemy loosed a tremendous f lak concentration. Exposed under a vicious cross-fire and heavily shelled, the companies remained pinned in positions throughout the remainder of the day. Company B, moving forward, encountered like resistance and could make no progress as Company A and Company C suffered serious casualties.

Third Battalion, meanwhile, jumped off for the high ground on Hill 485, Companies K and L moving along the slopes north of Oberbronn and Company I making a direct assault upon the town. Entering from the southwest at 1240 hours, Company I engaged enemy in house-to- house fighting and cleared Oberbronn of resistance by late afternoon. Company K and Company L, moving through the forests to the north, flanked the town, then moved in from the northeast and captured the crew of three 20mm f lak guns and one 75mm gun. While Company I remained in Oberbronn, Companies K and L continued on to the battalion objective. Second Battalion remained in Regimental Reserve throughout the day.

Company C– Bouxwiller, France. Pvt. Edward Beattie returns to duty. Pvt. Roy H. Hanlin and PFC Walker H. Nickell are KIA. Enlisted men: 140.

December 5–Still meeting stubborn resistance, the First and Third Battalions continued their advance and made slight gains. Company K and Company L reached ground from which they had observation and brought fire upon the road running northwest of Niederbronn. Company K engaged the enemy in grenade fighting at midnight.

Company C-S/Sgt. Hugh H. Brown, Sgt. Thomas L. Cobb, Pvt. Alvie E. Foreman, Pvt. Thomas A. Gunning, Pvt. Richard C. Hallgren, 1st Lt. John J. Hussey, 1st Lt. Robert M. McCurry and Pvt. Daniel H. Norton are WIA.

December 6–7–The 157th Infantry remained in position on the north flank of the division sector of operations, patrolling the forward areas extensively. First Battalion received direct tank fire from the vicinity of Niederbronn while the enemy shelled Third Battalion sporadically.

December 6 –During the hours of darkness, PFC Arnold Robbins of Company A, hearing thrashing in the area to his immediate front, ventured forward and came upon a German who was attempting to strangle PFC Cornelius Noonan Jr. of Pittsburgh, Pennsylvania. Robbins made the best of a ticklish situation. He bounced his M-1 rifle across the Kraut's head, the weapon splitting apart after the third blow. Robbins and Noonan captured the German, who, though groggy, seemed little the worse for wear.

December 7–They marked the third anniversary of the Japanese attack on Pearl Harbor, Hawaii, maneuvering into position from which to jump off the following morning. By late afternoon the three battalion command posts and the regimental command post had moved up to the high ground on the left, preparing to launch an assault at 0730 hours December 8. Sporadically, the enemy shelled Oberbronn throughout the day.

Company C–Oberbronn, France. In defensive position. Enlisted men: 113.

December 8–In the midst of a downpour of rain, the Second Battalion jumped off on schedule, Companies F and G abreast advancing toward the objective, Hill 480. Under heavy shellfire, most of which fell upon Company G, a platoon from Company F moved into the factory on the outskirts of Niederbronn, engaging occupying enemy in a heavy firefight. By 1108 hours, Company G had crossed the road in the woods and Company E had moved into its assault position, though under intense mortar, artillery, and small-arms fire. In the wake of an artillery preparation, Company E and Company G began their slow advance up the west side of Hill 480, while the remainder of Company F joined the platoon still fighting in the factory. From dug-in positions on Hill 480, the enemy placed heavy fire on Companies E and G as the units took ground approximately two hundred yards from the top of the ridge, but by 1425 hours the resistance had been cleared. Following two hours spent on reorganizing the weary men, the two companies began moving forward once more. Company F left the factory area at 1815 hours and advanced along the woods line until 2255 hours when the battalion established its position for the night.

Third Battalion, meanwhile, followed the progressing Second Battalion in the advance, Company L supporting the assault on Hill 480 and Company K entering the factory. Two platoons from Company I blocked the Niederbronn road from the north but were relieved at 1758 hours by Company I of the 179th Infantry.

First Battalion remained in position until 1410 hours when it launched an attack upon Niederbronn, Companies A and C advancing along the edge of the woods and making their way down the main road. By 1655 hours the two companies had reached a position south of the factory, where they received heavy concentrations of mortar fire. They continued forward until darkness fell and they established their positions for the night.

Having cut the Niederbronn-Phillippsbourg Road and having seized the high ground commanding the northeast approached to Niederbronn, the 157th Infantry at 0630 hours launched an attack upon the town proper. Company B moved in from the west, while Company and Company C advanced upon it from the north. Enemy snipers impeded the advance, but in house-to-house fighting the battalion cleared Niederbronn of resistance by 1530 hours. The Germans continued to shell the town at intervals.

Second Battalion mopped up its positions during the morning and sent combat patrols into the forward areas. Northeast of Niederbronn, one patrol cleared a chateau of resistance. Third Battalion, in the interim, limited its day's activities to patrolling, although Company L received a slight attack during the afternoon and a squad from Company K moved out to engage the enemy. The Germans had dispersed by 1530 hours.

Company C-PFC Kenneth L. R. Smith is KIA.

December 10–While enemy artillery batteries and mortars interdicted the Oberbronn-Niederbronn road throughout the day, the 157th Infantry, on the north flank of the division, renewed its attack toward the northeast. Second and Third Battalions jumped off at 0700 hours, but after advancing four hundred yards, they received a heavy counterattack when an established two hundred enemy foot soldiers in a massed assault attempted to drive behind Company E and Company F. Second Battalion, with the assistance of Company I, which entered the battle area from the north, repulsed the attack in a violent firefight.

The advance continued, Company F cutting the road and destroying an enemy roadblock, while Company G to the south forced its way forward under heavy fire of all types.

Third Battalion also encountered steady resistance throughout the day, but by 1700 hours, Company K had reached the outskirts of the town of Jaegerthal and engaged pillboxes located on the north edge of the village. Tank fire destroyed the concrete emplacements, and the infantry pushed through. Enemy shellfire fell upon the company positions throughout the remainder of the night.

With the companies pushing forward over mountainous terrain inaccessible to vehicles, the regiment, for the third time in its combat history, began utilization of pack mules, which each night hauled supplies to the troops under the cover of darkness. Regular army mules handled by experienced Negro mule skinners made up the pack trains, a far cry from those employed by the regiment in Sicily and Italy where all and any available animals were used for supply hauls and "skinners" were drawn from the line companies. Its supplies replenished by the newly committed mule trains and their handlers. Second and Third Battalions renewed their attacks at daybreak.

Company C–Niederbronn, France. In defensive position. S/Sgt. William E. Fry and PFC Harold E. MacFarland are WIA. Enlisted men: 133.

December 11–Second Battalion made steady progress throughout the day, although encountering sporadic resistance in taking the town of Judenburg and occupying the northern section of Langensoultzbach, where patrols probing deeper into the town could locate no enemy. Third Battalion also made steady advances and established its position for the night on high ground, where Company I engaged the enemy in a firefight and captured several enemy soldiers.

In Regimental Reserve, First Battalion protected the 157th Infantry right flank and mopped up behind the advancing Second Battalion. A patrol from Company B reached Neuwiller at noon, making no contact with defending enemy, and by 1500 hours, the company had occupied the town. Company A and Company C established their positions to the northeast.

Company C–PFC Howard Hager is KIA. Nenwiller, France. Present: 150.

Chapter 7
Germania

"The fortress of Aschaffenburg will be defended to the last man."
Major van Lambert
Commander of the German garrison

DECEMBER 12 –AT DAY BREAK, COMPANY G, on the north edge of Langensoultzbach, began moving south and engaged small groups of enemy who were offering resistance from the houses and the woods surrounding the town. As Company E moved into position from the northwest, firefights ensued but by mid-afternoon the town had been cleared of resistance. Company E occupied Langensoultzbach while Company F and Company G moved along the woods line, meeting heavy small-arms, mortar,

and artillery concentrations. Fighting continued throughout the hours of darkness, and the battalion received concentration of long-range mortar and artillery fire.

Third Battalion also jumped off at daylight and engaged enemy infantry in a heavy firefight, which grew in intensity until two platoons of Company K moved west to assist Company I, receiving the brunt of a German counterattack. In intense and prolonged close-in fighting, the companies routed enemy infantry from organized positions, but the stubborn German troops continued to impede the advance throughout the day, making use of open emplacements in the old Maginot Line fortifications. The action continued far into the night while supplies came forward to the engaged companies. First Battalion remained in regimental reserve and followed behind the Second and Third Battalions.

That evening Lt. Col. Dwight Funk, a big, genial Oklahoman commanding the 158th Field Artillery Battalion supporting the 157th Infantry, phoned Col. Walter P. O'Brien, regimental commander, in the forward command post. "Colonel," he said, "From where we are we can lay a barrage across the border. Say the word and we'll toss a concentration into Germany." "What are you waiting for?" queried the colonel good naturedly. "Fire away." "Okay, sir!" came the answer. "On the way."

[One day short of the Forty-Fifth Division's 365th day in battle, 158th Field Artillery Battalion fired the division's first shells into German territory. — Hugh F. Foster III]

December 13–The 157th Infantry suddenly changed the direction of its attack from northeast to north and against light opposition made a steady advance throughout the day. First Battalion, leading the regiment in column, jumped off at 1000 hours, crossing mountainous terrain in a column of Companies C, B, and A and at intervals receiving enemy artillery concentrations. During the middle of the afternoon, enemy small-arms fire pinned Company C to the ground, but Company B, committed on the left, moved into a strategic position on a ridge, cut the road running north, and placed mines upon it. Company C, able to move once more, also cut the road and mined it. That night the battalion was supplied by carrying parties.

Following in the wake of the rapidly progressing First Battalion, Third Battalion protected the regimental left flank throughout the day and during mid-afternoon captured the town of Disteldorf. With Company L occupying the town, the battalion that night was supplied by carrying parties.

Company C–PFC Harold L. Roth, PFC Donald R. Gray and PFC Clarence E. Pierce are KIA near Bouxwiller, France.

December 14–In the advance, it was evident that the enemy had strengthened his defenses in the regimental sector as the 157th Infantry encountered increased resistance in continuing its drive north. The First Battalion began its attack at 0730 hours, infiltrating one platoon of Company C across the Northwest road while Company A established a roadblock to the south.

Shortly after leaving the line of departure, Company C, making its way up a hill, encountered strong resistance from a force of enemy dug in along the slope, and a heavy firefight ensued immediately. In a mountain battle reminiscent of those waged a year previously north of Venafro, Italy, the Germans, from positions on high ground, repulsed the company's attack, and Company B moved across the road and pushed forward on the Company C west flank. Under a swath of fire of all types, neither unit could progress, and Company A, relieved by Company G, 179th Infantry, swung in a wide circle to the east, attempting to flank the German position. The far-reaching enemy defenses proved effective again, however, and Company A came under intense small-arms, mortar, and artillery fire, making only slight progress. At 2000 hours, the enemy plastered the First Battalion position with an artillery concentration, most of which fell upon Company A. While enemy shellfire sporadically fell upon the occupied areas, the companies dug in their positions for the night.

Third Battalion, meanwhile, came under heavy shellfire as it pushed forward, clearing one enemy strong point of resistance by dislodging German infantrymen who were attempting to impede the advance from their positions behind a series of felled trees. Two enemy tanks, dug in on the northeast-southwest road, placed direct fire on the advancing companies, but chemical mortar and artillery fire forced them into withdrawal. At 1930 hours, Company L received an estimated two hundred rounds of artillery and mortar fire, and the tanks returned to harass the unit with direct fire.

Throughout the day, Second Battalion remained in Regimental Reserve, receiving a forty-round artillery barrage before moving forward behind First Battalion at 1115 hours.

Company C-Pvt. Brady O. Ferrell is injured. Pvt. Michael Karacab Jr. and Pvt. R. L. Welch are WIA.

December 15–Closing in on the German frontier, the 157th Infantry renewed its attack to the north shortly after dawn, pushing forward to high ground although encountering steady resistance. By afternoon, 60mm mortars were firing into Germany, but nightfall found the infantry troops still in Alsatian territory.

Company C–Lembach, France. Company in the attack south of town. Pvt. Willis A Hartung and PFC Ernest W. McAnelly are WIA. Present: 135.

December 16–First Battalion jumped off in attack at 0933 hours, supported by armor moving forward from the town of Wingen. Scattered artillery fire fell upon the approaching troops as they forced their way across the German border, where the men from Company A, 157th Infantry, one of the first Seventh Army units to enter the Reich, placed placards on the trees for the signatures of the doughboy "guests" who were lumbering into Germany. One placard invited the infantrymen to "Spit on Hitler," typically substituting an *h* for the *p* in the first word.

At 1430 hours, Company A occupied the German town of Nothwiller on the outer edge of the famed Siegfried fortifications. A combat patrol from Company A and Company C climbed the high, forested hill in the vicinity of Nothwiller and from its vantage point observed an enemy vehicle moving from Nied-Schlettenbach to the town of Bundenthal. The patrol also observed a concrete roadblock, two hundred yards from which lay another roadblock of felled trees, approximately five hundred yards long. The main bridge west of Nied-Schlettenbach had been blown.

Third Battalion, meanwhile, obtained its objective against sporadic resistance, while Second Battalion moved forward in Regimental Reserve.

Company C–Pvt. Edward Beattie is ill. S/Sgt. Daniel Ficco and PFC John F. Geonetta become POWs.

December 17–In a column of companies, First Battalion again attacked toward the north at 0730 hours, making steady progress, so that by noon Company C was approaching the enemy-held town of Bundenthal, destined to play a leading role in regimental activities throughout the remainder of the month. The battalion halted its advance at 1425 hours and sent patrols ahead to investigate the forward areas. One patrol from Company C ventured toward Bundenthal, near which the men located enemy in dug-in positions and captured one prisoner. The battalion established its position for the night on ground overlooking Bundenthal and prepared to renew its attack the following morning.

Second Battalion, committed once more, also opened its attack at 0730 hours and in a column of companies, made steady gains, although impeded by fire from pillboxes that helped to form the outer rim of the German Siegfried Line. Calling for artillery, the observers watched direct hits bounce off the huge concrete emplacements, barely scarring the exteriors. The battalion stopped its advance in the vicinity of a marsh, the result of the Germans damming the south-flowing stream. The German dam was protected by pillboxes, while the marsh, it soon was learned, was covered by grazing fire. Second Battalion troops prepared to attempt a crossing in rubber boats being brought forward over the mountain routes by carrying parties.

Third Battalion throughout the day supported the First and Second Battalions by observation and fire.

Company C–Bundenthal, Germany. Company in the attack, and PFC Douglas A. Bibb is evacuated to the 120th Medical Battalion. First Lt. Phillip F. Gellar returns to Company C.

December 18–At 0255 hours, Company F brought forward five assault boats and attempted crossing the German-created marsh. It was impossible to maneuver the boats in the swamp, so the troops debarked and attempted wading toward the north shore in waist-deep water. The alert enemy opened machine-gun fire from the protective pillboxes and encasements, and the doughboys were forced back to cover. Before dawn, Company F had attempted three times to cross the delaying marsh at different points along the stream line, but on each occasion, the Germans had forced a withdrawal, utilizing mortars and artillery as well as machine-guns. At daylight the companies withdrew to covered positions, and Company E and Company G moved to the northwest to use the bridgeheads established by First Battalion. At midnight, Second Battalion again was preparing to attempt a crossing.

First Battalion began its attack in the pre-dawn dusk of the morning, Company C leading the assault and moving across open terrain south of Bundenthal. Dropping into an antitank ditch, the men crossed the bridge, and two platoons moved into the south edge of the town. Daylight exposed the infiltrating troops to enemy view, and the Germans suddenly loosed intense small-arms and machine-gun fire on the last platoon of Company C and on Company B, following. Pinned under concentrations from all sides, the men remained in their exposed positions throughout the entire day. Supplies reached them at dusk when the fire abated. Meanwhile, the two leading platoons of Company C were trapped in the town of Bundenthal, occupying buildings that the enemy machine-gunned and shelled sporadically.

Third Battalion remained on Hill 485 and patrolled to the flanks and to the front extensively while supporting First and Second Battalions through observation and fire during the day.

Company C-Pvt. William J. Akin, and Pvt. Andrew G. Palkendo are WIA. Pvt. Willis B. Fortson is injured.

December 19–Throughout the early morning hours, patrols from First Battalion attempted to establish contact with the two platoons from Company C, which were cut off in Bundenthal. Unsuccessful, the patrols also tried to reach the remainder of Company C in the cemetery, but small-arms fire drove them back. Company B attempted to push forward at 0500 hours but drew fire from all sides immediately and was forced to remain in position. Sporadic shellfire fell upon the First Battalion troops during the day. Then at nightfall the companies renewed their efforts to reach the trapped men. A patrol contacted the platoon from Company C, occupying the cemetery, and the unit withdrew to the battalion lines.

In the Second Battalion sector, Company G moved toward Bundenthal at 0400 hours and in the vicinity of the cemetery, encountered a heavy concentration of machine-gun fire that split the column. The two forward platoons remained pinned to the ground, while the fire forced withdrawal of the rear elements, which remained in concealment throughout the remainder of the day. With the fall of darkness, patrols ventured forward in attempts to contact the two Company G platoons but met with no success. Toward midnight the battalion assembled and prepared to relieve the First Battalion, 179th Infantry, on its dug-in position on the left flank of the corps sector.

December 20–Patrols from First and Second Battalions attempted to penetrate the outer Siegfried defenses during the hours of darkness, searching for the four platoons trapped in the town of Bundenthal. Small-arms, machine-gun, and mortar fire from the German pillboxes prevented any of the patrols penetrating farther than the cemetery on the outskirts of the town. No trace could be found of the missing men holding out in a town surrounded by enemy-occupied emplacements.

At daylight, Company A and Company B shifted into a defensive position to the southwest, while Second Battalion companies returned to Nothwiller, shuttled and marched to Lembach, and relieved the First Battalion, 179th Infantry, on the outpost positions on the north flank of the Forty-Fifth Division sector. Third Battalion adjusted its position to cover a wider sector.

Company C–Nothwiller, Germany. Company in reserve for reorganization, and Pvt. Edward Beattie returns to duty.

December 21–Lt. Col. Chester James took command of the 157th Infantry once again, relieving Colonel O'Brien, who that morning began a ten-day leave. Patrols from First Battalion during the early morning hours again attempted to reach the platoons in Bundenthal but again were able to penetrate no farther than the cemetery. Little hope remained that the handful of Americans occupying the town would ever reach their own lines again. Daily the Germans pounded the village with artillery fire and machine-gunned the buildings, two of which were set aflame. The First Battalion had no radio communication with the four platoons.

During the morning German artillery fire fell in the town of Nothwiller, where the regimental, First and Third Battalion command posts were situated. One dud shell, 105mm, hit the building in which the regimental command post was located, penetrated the outer wall, smashed through a winding staircase, hit the floor of a room occupied by Maj. James Carroll, regimental S-3 from Lakewood, Ohio, and S/Sgt. Raymond Groeger from Peetz, Colorado, bounced up to the ceiling, and fell on the head of the bed on which the plans and training officer was sitting. Covered with debris, the major and Groeger emerged with only slight scratches.

On the line First and Second Battalions patrolled the forward areas extensively. A patrol from Company E moved into Windstein and encountered no enemy, while a patrol from Company F met no resistance in the town of Niedersteinbach. A patrol from Company G drew machine-gun fire in attempting to move into Schonau.

Company C–Nothwiller, Germany. In reserve position. Private sick to AWOL. Placed in regimental stockade. Pvt. Robert Rodenbaugh (MOS 745) joins Company C, and Sgt. Hyman Miller is evacuated to the 120th Medical Battalion. Enlisted men: 159.

December 22–Throughout the hours of darkness, patrols from First Battalion again attempted to reach the platoons in Bundenthal. The patrols were unsuccessful, but at 0645 hours, two men from Company G, Sgt. William Alter, St. Paul, Indiana, and Pvt. Al Guriel, New Goshen, Indiana, members of one of the trapped platoons, made their way out of the town and back to the lines, reaching safety just before dawn. Taken to the regimental command post, they reported that approximately seventy men from Company C and Company G still stranded in the south edge of Bundenthal, that they were low on ammunition and were caring for several wounded. Medical supplies were exhausted, and the surrounded doughboys were surviving on hog mash and raw potatoes and water. Among the dead, Alter and Guriel reported, were two officers, killed in the shellings the town received frequently. A third officer, Lt. Glenn Terry, Cortez, Colorado, recently promoted from technical sergeant, was seriously wounded but was directing the men's defensive action. Commanding the besieged group was 1st Lt. Carl Byas, Needville, Texas, who also had been wounded slightly. The two infantrymen expressed confidence that the platoons in Bundenthal could hold their positions for another day, and immediate plans were made to rescue the trapped doughboys. Lt. Col. Chester James, acting regimental commander, and Lt. Col. Ralph M. Krieger, First Battalion, commanding the 158th Field Artillery Battalion, proposed making the attempt just after the fall of dusk December 23. Tentatively the artillery batteries would register the pillboxes during the day and that night coordinate concentrated fire with the actions of a First Battalion patrol.

The battalions limited their activities to patrolling the forward areas. A patrol from Company K engaged six Germans in a firefight, was driven back, returned with additional support, and could not again establish contact with the enemy.

December 23–The 157th Infantry again limited its activities to patrolling, while the enemy shelled Bundenthal and Nothwiller. According to plan, the artillery registered the areas surrounding Bundenthal in preparation for the attempt to rescue the men who had fought for existence there since December 18. Two men, attempting to carry medical supplies into the town while under the cover of darkness, were driven back by machine-gun fire.

At 1800 hours, a twelve-man patrol from Company A and Company B started toward the cemetery on the outskirts of Bundenthal. Browning Automatic Rifles and machine-guns poured fire on known enemy positions as the patrol advanced, and the artillery loosed a thousand-round concentration on the German pillboxes. Moving through the path left clear in the swath of fire, Tech Sgt. Warren Haynes of Taconite, Minnesota; PFC Edgar Ingleton, Flint, Michigan; PFC Joseph Long, Washington D.C., and Cpl. Raymond Dwyer, a medic from Elizabeth, New Jersey, hastily made their way into the edge of the town. Haynes contacted the weary troops holding the first house, and runners alerted the remainder of the town's defenders to the attempted withdrawal. Shouldering the wounded and carrying others on blanket stretchers, the men made a dash for the enemy, who were pinned in pillboxes being pulverized under tons of f lying steel. As the haggard doughboys scrambled into the ditch a hundred yards from the edge of town, the Germans loosed defensive fires that were countered by the artillery and by First Battalion automatic-weapons men.

Unshaven and worn, many of the soldiers who had withstood six days of siege in the battered German town of Bundenthal were evacuated to hospitals, while the others were sent to the recently established regimental rest camp in Niederbronn, where they were provided rooms and beds in which to sleep, showered, clothed, and fed the first satisfactory meals they had received in days. They were photographed by news cameramen and interviewed by correspondents, alert to an outstanding Christmas season story.

The four platoons all had been trapped in the same fashion. Entering the outskirts of Bundenthal in the early morning darkness almost a week previously, the men had received machine-gun fire from all sides as soon as dawn exposed them to enemy view. Seeking shelter in the first house on the edge of town, one man from Company G was killed and another wounded. The remainder crept into a barn and surrounding buildings and discovered that two platoons from Company C were holding out in other houses scattered across a large square two hundred yards wide. Flanked on all sides by enemy-occupied pillboxes, the men saw the buildings ripped down around them by machine-gun and artillery fire. On the first day the platoons from Company G occupied Bundenthal, Pvt. Eugene Gates, a rifleman from Kentucky, climbed into the second-story window of one of the houses and fired three rifle grenades through the main slot of a pillbox fifty feet away. Though the pillbox apparently was undamaged, the machine-gun it enclosed stopped firing completely.

While German artillery and machine-guns slowly chipped away at the houses, the men foraged for food and water. Patrols each night made their way about the besieged town, locating a stream at the northern edge, the water from which was stagnant. Usually the patrols had to fight their way back to the buildings. One foraging group chanced upon several penned rabbits and some vegetables, stealing them out from under the guns of a nearby pillbox. The men cooked the food in a rusty bucket, but smoke from the fire drew heavy machine-gun and artillery concentration, so cooking had to be discontinued. In the barn the trapped Yanks located hog meal and half-rotten apples. By mixing the hog meal with water, the men developed a "cereal" and ate it heartily. Water one day was furnished by a Russian forced laborer, but after he returned to the German lines he never came back.

Battling against heavy odds, the weary doughboys engaged enemy infantry in firefights until almost all the ammunition supply had been expended. They stood guard in the upper stories of the buildings, remaining alert and preventing the Germans from closing in on them. One man from Company C fell f lat to the floor of a second-story room, then stood up to find that he occupied a platform supported by fragment-scarred timbers. The shell had torn out the wall beneath him.

Concussion from an exploding shell threw a man from Company G down a f light of stairs. Shrapnel from another shell sheared the igniter cap from the top of a hand grenade Tech Sgt. William Whitaker of Phoenix, Arizona, carried in his breast pocket. The force of the blow threw Whitaker tumbling forty feet and left the imprints of the grenade serrations on his chest. The grenade itself, fortunately, did not explode.

Enemy tracer bullets set fire to the hay in the barn men from Company G occupied, but the hard-put doughboys extinguished the blaze. Tracers also set one of the houses afire in which Company C men were seeking concealment. The blaze out of control, the doughboys ran for another building and were fired upon by snipers who saw them exposed to view by the f lames.

The only communication the besieged men had with the American lines was a small walkie-talkie radio, and on the third day, it went dead. Casualties mounted and on the fourth day, three men volunteered to attempt making a break for the lines, contacting friendly troops, and returning with morphine. They never left the village, for as they stepped from the shelter of the building, a machine-gun opened up on them, and two of the three fell to the street seriously wounded.

No one knew how Sergeant Alter and Private Guriel had fared after they made their early morning attempt to reach friendly lines December 22. No one knew either what was taking place the night of December 23 when the American artillery loosed a forty-five-minute barrage and placed a ring of fire around the town of Bundenthal. Alerted to the attempt being made to rescue them from their trapped positions, however, they readily followed Sergeant Haynes into the antitank ditch south of the town, evacuating their wounded as rapidly as possible. Reaching the lines, they were sent immediately to the regimental rest camp where they enjoyed a Christmas many of them had expected never to see.

Company C soldiers rescued from the town of Bundenthal SC Photo

December 24–The 157th Infantry remained in its defensive position and again patrolled the forward areas extensively. Second Battalion improved its position somewhat during the day. Patrols from the battalion ventured into the towns of Schonau and Niedersteinbach but located no enemy. In the First Battalion sector, an M-12 self-propelled gun placed direct fire on some of the enemy pillboxes to the front. One emplacement was damaged and the aperture of another was destroyed.

The regiment spent Christmas Day still holding its defensive position on the German frontier. Patrols again probed the forward areas. One patrol from Company F went to Niedersteinbach and returned with reports of plastic mines on every curve in the road and concrete roadblocks inside the town. Artillery fire was placed on a house where enemy troops had been seen and on observed emplacements. Shortly before midnight, a four-man unidentified patrol reached the Company A command post, was challenged, and f led. At 2330 hours Company A reported that the patrol had killed one man and wounded another in the foxholes.

Though the 157 Infantry, as it had a year before, spent Christmas on the lines, the men ate Christmas dinner complete with turkey and all the trimmings.

Company C–PFC Burnice Auldridge is promoted to corporal. Pvt. Charles E. Tutt is injured.

December 25–Company C–Nothwiller, Germany. Twenty-five enlisted men promoted from private to private first class. Pvt. Dencil A. Laymon is WIA. PFC Floyd Macauley is injured.

December 26–First and Third Battalions remained in their defensive positions until they were relieved by units from the 180th Infantry. The battalions reached assembly areas at approximately 1600 hours and made preparations for the contemplated attack of December 27. Meanwhile, Company E with the attached Company C, 179th Infantry, and two platoons from the Forty-Fifth Recon, made a limited attack, reaching the objective at 1450 hours without meeting resistance.

Company C–Pvt. Edward Beattie is ill.

December 27–First Battalion jumped off in attack toward the northwest at 0815 hours of the brisk morning, passing through elements of the Second Battalion, which was holding a defensive position on the division's northwest flank. With Company A and Company C abreast, the battalion made steady progress until it reached the east-west valley running through the town of Schonau. Here the assaulting companies encountered intense small-arms fire from dug-in positions at the base of the wooded hill to the front, and attempts to flank the Germans' strong point brought heavy artillery and mortar concentrations. Under fire, the battalion established its position for the night in the areas in the vicinity of the captured town of Hirschthal.

Third Battalion launched its assault at 0830 hours, also passing through elements of the Second Battalion and jumping off from the vicinity of the town of Niedersteinbach. The advancing companies met steady resistance that increased as they closed in on Obersteinbach. Company K and Company L reached the high ground overlooking the enemy-held village, and one platoon from Company K ventured into the edge of town to engage the Germans. Defending every house in the village, the enemy loosed heavy fire from all sides upon the approaching platoon and in the violent fight that followed, all but destroyed the K Company unit. Few of the men succeeded in withdrawing to the lines, and regimental headquarters heard rumors that civilians had come out of the houses and had killed wounded as they lay helpless on the ground. There was no confirmation of the report, however.

While the entire battalion received concentrations of mortar and artillery fire, Company I continued north and engaged an estimated company of enemy in the town of Wencelsbach. Pushing forward slowly, the company occupied the town and held it throughout the night, although the Germans launched four counterattacks in an effort to take repossession. During the hours of darkness, the regimental lines received sporadic shellfire concentrations.

December 28–Holding the ground it had gained the day before, the 157th Infantry remained in positions and again began patrolling the forward areas. In the Third Battalion sector, Company I repulsed regular counterattacks from 0030 hours to 0630 hours, but by daylight the enemy activity had quieted. During the afternoon Company I improved its defense position.

Company C-PFC Richard Adams is reassigned and returns to duty.

> [When I was released from the hospital and sent back to the front, no combat boots were available. I was given old work shoes to wear in deep snow.—Richard Adams]

December 29–Still defending the northwest flank of the division sector, the 157th Infantry limited its activities in the main to active patrolling, while reports reached the regiment the enemy was massing troops in the sectors far to the left. Civilians in the towns of Lembach, Jaegerthal, Langensoultzbach, and others watched uneasily as engineers placed charges of dynamite under the bridges as a precautionary measure and as more and more troops and tanks began moving to the rear. On the regimental front, Third Battalion repulsed three local attacks.

During the early morning hours, ten enemy riflemen and five bazooka teams assaulted the line in the wake of an artillery and mortar barrage, knocking out one 57mm anti-tank gun before retiring under heavy small-arms fire. German artillery batteries and mortars continued to pound the town of Obersteinbach and the surrounding company positions. Then, just before dawn, from twenty to thirty enemy infiltrated between Company L and Company I. The second attack was repulsed with the assistance of the battalion ammunition and pioneer platoon, which had moved into position during the night. Through the daylight hours, scattered artillery fire fell upon the battalion. Then at 1730 hours the enemy launched a third attack, assaulting the west flank of Company I and gaining no ground. By 2130 hours, the position had been restored, the ammunition and pioneer platoon, the Antitank squad, and two light tanks forcing German foot troops to f lee north up the stream bed. Except for occasional artillery fire falling in Obersteinbach, the remainder of the day was quiet.

Sporadic artillery fire also fell upon Second Battalion during the day, and the enemy occasionally interdicted the town of Dambach in the battalion sector.

December 30–Reinforced by the Forty-Fifth Reconnaissance Troop, the 157th Infantry maintained its defensive position, patrolling the forward areas actively. Patrols from the regiment entered the towns of Schonau and Neunhoffen but encountered no enemy. During the morning, Company I was relieved by Company B, 179th Infantry, and moved into a battalion reserve position.

December 31–Colonel O'Brien returned to take command of the regiment, and patrolling continued throughout the day. Patrols from both Second and Third Battalions searched the houses in Obersteinbach but could locate no enemy. Shortly before midnight, a patrol from Company F set up an ambush on the edge of the town of Neunhoffen and watched an enemy patrol enter the town from the woods. The men heard a woman talking, a light flashed, and the patrol entered a house but did not reappear. The regimental infantrymen celebrated the coming of 1945 in their cold foxholes situated on the snow-laden and wooded mountain slopes on the frontier of Adolf Hitler's Third Reich.

Company C-The following men were WIA in 1944 but the dates are unknown: PFC Juan Chavez, Cpl. Raymond W. Koss, Pvt. Wilbur M. Miller, PFC Buckner S. Morris, Sgt. Ray Neitz, PFC Frederick D. Pape and Pvt. Earl T. Weicht.

From the 157th Regiment Journal, Morning Reports, and After-Action Reports of Company C, 1945 (National Archives)

January 1, 1945–Was a clear, cold day, the type of day Americans are apt to call "perfect football weather." An elusive sun peered through the clouds occasionally and warmed the men of the 157th Infantry huddled in their foxholes in the outer defenses of the Siegfried Line. To the men themselves, it was more than just another day. It was separate and important; it was a time for taking stock, a time for remembering. The memories were as varied as the men themselves; they were the personal memories of clerks, truck drivers, farmers, schoolboys; they were the memories of American soldiers far from home who had seen and done much in twelve months. Some thought of home and the hangovers of previous years, the family dinners, and the gatherings of friends that are such a part of the tradition of the holiday in America. They remembered the men who fought beside them, and the cold, miserable weather of Venafro. They remembered the bloody days at the Volturno, the hell that was Anzio, and the capture of Rome. They remembered too the "purple death" wine of Italy and the "white lightning" of France. A lighter note was struck when one doughboy suggested as a replacement for the by-now-worn-out motto "Win the War in '44" a simpler, more realistic "Stay Alive in '45."

It was a cold, clear day this New Year's Day 1945, and inside every man were the knowledge and the satisfaction of a difficult job well done that warmed them more than the intermittent sun overhead. They had gotten up out of their holes on Anzio and walked to Rome against every conceivable weapon of war, against a stubborn, well-dug-in foe looking down their throats. Two successful amphibious landings had been made on Hitler's so-called impregnable Fortress Europe, a nation had been liberated, and GI brogans were planted firmly on the sacred soil of Adolf Hitler's Third Reich. In the mind of each man was the knowledge that this was it, this was the payoff, that the long fight that had started on the beaches of Sicily was nearing its climax. Mostly it was a time of gratitude. It was "perfect football weather" inside the German border, the foe had been driven back, and they were still alive. No infantryman could ask for more than that.

On January 1, 1945, the comparative lull of the sector of the Seventh Army front was broken when the Germans launched a heavy counterattack, supported by artillery fire on the left of the regimental sector. The 275th Infantry of the Seventieth Division was driven back, and heavy fighting was reported in the streets of Phillippsbourg. After committing the First Battalion of the 274th Infantry, the Americans had almost succeeded in reaching their original positions, but the Bitche salient continued to widen. On the sector the First Battalion of the 315th Infantry attached to the regiment on the right flank. The Thirty-Sixth Engineers was on the right of that battalion. The First Battalion remained in its position during the day, improving it.

Several patrols were sent out, and a C Company patrol sent out at dark reported hearing an enemy halftrack and enemy personnel. The patrol returned at 2230, and mortar fire was placed in that area. The Second Battalion reported enemy movement in the vicinity of Obersteinbach. Artillery was placed on the road intermittently with good results. At 0148, F Company engaged the enemy in a small-arms fight to the front. At 0245 much enemy activity was heard in Neunhoffen and artillery was placed there. E Company reported that an enemy patrol came in at 0250, but the men succeeded in driving it back, inflicting heavy losses. At 0800 the Battalion Observation Post sighted approximately three hundred enemy and seventeen horse-drawn artillery pieces in and around Neunhoffen. An air mission was requested on the woods east of Neunhoffen and the town itself. The first mission was unsuccessful, but the second mission around 1200 was declared very successful.

During the late morning First Battalion, 179th Infantry, moved around to the rear of Second Battalion to give support if needed. During the afternoon the sector was relatively quiet, but at 1700 G Company got into a firefight with an estimated thirty enemy troops who came in between G and E Company positions. At 1710, B Company, 179th Infantry, went into position between E and G Companies. One platoon of A Company, 179th Infantry, was sent to Dambach to clear enemy out of there and to swing in between F and G Companies when that mission was accomplished. At 2100, First Battalion, 179th Infantry, minus A Company, reverted to control of the parent organization. During the day the Third Battalion remained in position. I Company relieved B Company of the 157th Infantry. B Company reverted to control of its own battalion. One platoon of the Forty-Fifth Reconnaissance Troop, which was attached to 157th Infantry until 0900, reverted to control of the Forty-Fifth Division. The remaining platoon stayed in positions as regimental reserve.

January 2–The regiment started a retrograde movement to prepared positions on the Maginot Line. The First and Third Battalion sectors were fairly quiet and thus made their withdrawal in an orderly fashion. B Company remained in position to cover the rest of the battalion, while the Ranger Platoon of the Third Battalion did the same for that unit. Our artillery fired on enemy personnel moving in front of the Third Battalion position. Company A of the 179th Infantry placed one platoon in position between F and G Companies, while the remaining two platoons cleared the town of Dambach at 0300 hours. At 0715 a group of enemy determined at a strength of fifteen to twenty men moved toward Company A, 179th, but was dispersed by small-arms fire. At 1035 hours Company F, via a patrol, contacted the 275th Infantry Regiment. That evening enemy patrols of some strength were reported probing the battalion front, but all attempts to penetrate our defenses were broken up by small arms and artillery. With E Company leading, followed by G Company and A Company of the 179th, the battalion started to withdraw to prepared positions. At the close of the period, only F Company remained to be moved. E Company received some artillery fire enroute to the rear.

January 3–The day dawned bright and clear as the troops remained in their Maginot Line positions. The First Battalion took over regimental reserve positions. Because of the heavy enemy attack on Phillippsbourg in the morning, C Company sent a platoon to a wooded ridge several thousand yards southeast of the town as an outpost. Near the close of the period, C Company sent a contact patrol to E Company. The forward observer with Second Battalion called for fire upon thirty-five enemy and twelve handcarts coming into Dambach at about 2200 hours. At 2240 hours an enemy patrol probed the left flank of F Company, situated on the left flank of the battalion, and cut the communication wire. Patrols were sent out to determine the enemy strength and had not returned at the close of the period.

An I Company patrol contacted elements of the 180th Infantry Regiment early in the morning at 0415 hours. At 1000 hours the ammunition and pioneer platoon of the Third Battalion relieved the elements of the 180th Infantry Regiment at Gunsthal. I Company lengthened its frontage to the east. M Company fired its mortars on enemy personnel at 1130. At 1500 a four-man enemy patrol contacted I Company. The veteran doughboys closed in on them and killed the entire group. It made contact with the Third Battalion on the left and the Thirty-Sixth Engineers on the right. The day was quiet and most of the time was spent improving positions.

January 4–The 157th Infantry Regiment continued to man the Maginot Line defenses and improve the positions against any possible enemy counterattack. The First Battalion remained in Regimental Reserve but was alerted at 1100 to a possible enemy counterattack. A, B, and C Companies dug in alternate positions during the day. At 0430 a Company C patrol contacted elements of the Second Battalion. The Second Battalion continued to defend its portion of the Maginot Line. Chemical mortars started several fires in Dambach. At 1100 hours the battalion was alerted to a possible enemy counterattack in its sector, and engineers laid tactical wire in front of the E and G Company positions. At 1800 hours battalion guides moved A Company of the 275th Infantry into position on the left flank of F Company. Considerable enemy activity was reported in the vicinity of Neunhoffen during the daylight hours. The Third Battalion sector remained quiet throughout the day except for a few rounds of artillery that fell in the area during the morning hours. K Company sent a patrol to a high ridge overlooking the Windstein valley but made no contact. To the right of the regimental sector, the First Battalion of the 315th Infantry Regiment continued to defend the Maginot Line. The battalion sent a patrol to Disteldorf and found the town unoccupied.

January 5–The First Battalion continued in Regimental Reserve. The companies continued to improve their alternate positions. At 0400, an F Company patrol contacted A Company, 275th Infantry Regiment, and returned. Another F Company patrol to Dambach returned at 0630 and reported that it had heard enemy moving around in town. The men received some small-arms fire from the town as they went and returned. B Company sent a patrol to observe the Nuenhoffen-Philippsbourg sector at 1045. The patrol returned at 1600 and reported that it had contacted four to six enemy about 1,500 yards east of the Nuenhoffen-Philippsbourg Road. At 1620 the enemy smoked the town of Nuenhoffen, and our artillery placed a *Time on Target* in the town.

["Smoked" means inundating the place with White Phosphorus artillery shells, which produced instant, thick, billowing clouds of white smoke and to obscure sight into and out of the area.

Time On Target is an artillery term for a method of timing a barrage so that all the shells from a number of artillery units land on a particular target at the same instant, thus providing a devastating, enormously destructive multiple impact.—Hugh F. Foster III]

F Company sent a patrol to the town of Dambach where some enemy were reported. Artillery fire was placed at the northern end of the town. G Company received several rounds of medium artillery at the close of the period. L Company of the Third Battalion sent a patrol to a ridge overlooking the Windstein Valley at 1040 hours. The patrol returned at 1635, reporting twenty to thirty enemy in the area. A road intersection in the L Company area received an estimated twenty-five rounds of 105mm artillery at 2200 hours. Enemy artillery fell on this road intersection at the close of the period. The First Battalion, 315th Infantry, sent a patrol to Disteldorf where it got into a firefight. A patrol sent to a high peak northeast of Disteldorf made no contact with the enemy but saw four or five as it returned. The enemy were reported by patrols to be dug in on the eastern edge of Disteldorf. Four enemy were reported on a road east of Disteldorf.

Company C-Pvt. Jennings Huddleston, Pvt. Elmer E. Menefee and Pvt. James Vlaming are WIA.

January 6–The day dawned clear and cold. The First Battalion continued in Regimental Reserve with B Company attached to the Second Battalion in the reserve position. E Company of the Second Battalion sent a patrol through the town of Dambach and to the hill just east of there. The men found nothing and returned. F Company sent a two-man patrol to the southeast edge of Dambach where the men saw ten enemy marching down the street and entering the last house on the southeast edge of town. After dark, 81mm and 4.2 inch (chemical mortars) mortars laid fire in that vicinity. I Company of the Third Battalion sent a patrol to a high hill at the northern edge of the Windstein Valley. It made no contact with the enemy. First Battalion, 315th Infantry, still attached to the 157th Infantry Regiment, sent a patrol to Disteldorf in the morning hours. It made no contact with the enemy nor did a patrol to a high hill 1,500 yards east of Disteldorf. Enemy were reported behind A Company, and at 2200 hours a patrol sent to find them reported no contact after a search of an hour and a half.

January 7–There was considerable enemy activity reported in Dambach. B Company reverted to the control of the First Battalion and relieved F Company at 1930 hours. A Company relieved E Company at 1930 hours. C Company relieved G Company at about 2020 hours. G Company was attached to the First Battalion and occupied the positions formerly occupied by B Company. I Company of the Third Battalion sent a patrol to the two high peaks at the northern edge of the Windstein Valley. It made no contact with the enemy. An I Company patrol to a high peak eight hundred yards east of the Wineckerthal-Herrenhol Road found communication wires there. The patrol contacted three enemy on the northern slopes of the hill whom it tried to capture. First Battalion, 315th Infantry, reported enemy tank activity in Disteldorf during the early morning, but a daylight patrol found no tanks there. The battalion fired mortars at a point in the road eight hundred yards north of Lembach at 1025 hours. Three patrols were sent to forward areas to the north and northeast of Disteldorf.

Company C-2nd Lt. Louis A. Morgenrath became a POW on December 15, 1944 and DOW on this date.

January 8–The regiment remained in position, manning the Maginot Line defenses. The First Battalion reported twelve rounds of 105mm artillery falling in the C Company sector. A patrol from C Company reached the stream west of the town of Wineckerthal and followed it to the outskirts of Dambach. The patrol reported singing and talking in town. Another C Company patrol set up an outpost on the road to Dambach about a thousand yards from town and reported enemy movement on the hill to the north. The Second Battalion remained in Regimental Reserve with G Company still occupying the First Battalion reserve position. F Company sent a patrol to a point five hundred yards south of the Philippsbourg-Neiderbronn road but found no trace of the enemy. I Company, Third

Battalion, and K Company, Third Battalion, sent patrols to the areas on the northern edge of the Windstein Valley but found no evidence of the enemy. The First Battalion, 315th Infantry, remained on the regimental right. A patrol sent to a position about two thousand yards north of Disteldorf reported two enemy there. There was no traffic or movement on the Obersteinbach-Niedersteinbach road or in either of the towns. Another patrol to a high hill eight hundred yards northeast of Disteldorf reported no signs of the enemy. A patrol to a point just off the Lembach road observed a seven-man enemy patrol moving southeast on the Lembach road.

January 9–The First Battalion remained in position. A few scattered rounds of artillery fell in the sector in the morning and again in the evening with some mortar fire coming from the west edge of Dambach. The Second Battalion remained in reserve with G Company in the area behind First Battalion reserve. The Third Battalion also remained in position during the day but sent out several patrols. All patrols returned without contacting enemy. I Company put trip flares in front of its positions, and at 2020 an enemy patrol set off the flares. Machine-guns fired at the patrol, dispersing it to the north. The First Battalion of the 315th Infantry, attached to us, remained in position. Several of its patrols encountered enemy troops and got into firefights. All patrols returned without casualties.

January 10–The First and Third Battalions remained in position. The Second Battalion remained in position until 1415 hours when it moved to Rothbach by motor where it was placed under Forty-Fifth Division control. In the afternoon, enemy artillery scored a direct hit on Pillbox No. 5 but caused no damage. At 2237 hours, heavy enemy artillery fell about Pillbox No. 4 and scored several direct hits, but no damage was reported. A patrol was sent to a stream just south of Herrenhof to set up an ambush. An enemy patrol appeared in front of the pillbox later on, but our artillery fired upon it, causing the Germans to disperse. C Company observed enemy personnel digging in on a densely wooded ridge 2,500 yards northeast of Dambach. Our artillery fired upon them. The Third Battalion reported 88mm fire falling in Jaegerthal at 0415 hours. An L Company patrol covered the ridge line overlooking both the Windstein Valley and the Wineckerthal road. The men reported nothing in the area. An I Company patrol reported enemy tracks in the snow on a ridge at the northern edge of the Windstein Valley. They were going north. The First Battalion of the 315th Infantry received scattered rounds of artillery both at the opening and the closing of the day. A patrol to a ridge line about a thousand yards above Disteldorf reported an estimated platoon of enemy dug in.

January 11–The Second Battalion remained under Forty-Fifth Division control. The First Battalion remained in position. Pillbox No. 4 received some machine-gun fire in the morning. That evening, the engineers placed trip flares between the pillboxes. The ambush patrol returned, reporting that it had reached the stream but could not cross it. The men heard enemy talking and some movement on the road to Dambach. At 1900 hours a raiding party consisting of one officer and eight enlisted men was sent to Dambach with the task of capturing one enemy soldier. At the close of the period, the battalion was in the process of being relieved by Second Battalion, 274th Infantry. Some enemy activity was reported by Second Battalion to its front, and B Company remained in the reserve position until all companies had been relieved. The Third Battalion received artillery fire from an estimated 105mm caliber. Patrols from both I and L Companies made no contact with the enemy. The First Battalion, 315th Infantry, reported its sector as being quiet throughout the day.

January 12–13–The 157th Infantry was relieved of its position in the Maginot Line defenses. The First Battalion was relieved by the Second Battalion, 274th Infantry. Relief was completed on January 13 at 0753, and the battalion moved to the vicinity of Zinswiller, relieving Third Battalion, 276th Infantry, at 1130. The battalion was shelled while going into position. The Second Battalion relieved the positions of Second Battalion, 276th Infantry, at 1045 on January 13 and reverted to regimental control. The battalion received considerable artillery fire on the forward positions during the day. E and F Companies received an estimated 250 rounds at 1400 hours. The Third Battalion was relieved by the First Battalion of the 276th Infantry. The relief was completed by 1203 hours January 13, and the battalion moved by motor to an assembly area and made preparations to attack the following morning through the Second Battalion positions.

January 13–The 157th Infantry faced one of the severest tests in its history. It was more than a test of guns and tactics; it was also a test of an intangible something called "fighting heart" and plain, downright American guts.

After relieving the 276th Regiment of the Seventieth Division on the evening of January 13, 1945, the regiment received a barrage of an estimated two hundred rounds of artillery fire. The enemy was a worthy one. Identified later as the Sixth SS Mountain Division, the outfit had been transported to this sector from Finland. An organization of refreshed, well-trained, fanatical Nazis, they were fighting over the type of terrain they had trained in with the type of weather best suited to their particular brand of warfare.

January 14–The First Battalion of the 315th Infantry was on the left. In the early morning, it jumped off in an attack, and after making a slight advance was counterattacked. The men suffered several counterattacks during the day and were forced back to their original positions. On the right flank of the 157th Infantry Regiment, the Thirty-Sixth Engineers improved their positions during the day and prepared to attack the following morning.

On the 157th Infantry front, the First and Third Battalions began an attack on the right flank of the regimental sector at 0830 on the morning of January 14. Initially, A Company was on the right and C Company on the left. The Third Battalion moved in a column of Companies K, L, and I. Second Battalion was in reserve, but received heavy German artillery fire throughout the day. At 1000, K Company contacted the enemy and was pinned down. Meanwhile, on the First Battalion front, a platoon of B Company passed through the A Company positions and contacted enemy troops. A firefight ensued. Two hours later, at 1430, the platoon withdrew to the B Company positions and placed artillery fire on the enemy. At 1530, L Company had reached its objective with K Company on the left of C Company, 315th Infantry. Both battalions set up defensive positions for the night. After dark, A Company sent patrols northeast down the slope of a ridge where they contacted German troops and got into a firefight. The patrol returned without casualties.

Company C-S/Sgt. Donald R. Anthony, Pvt. Stanley Bakay, PFC Charles M. Best, Pvt. Albert R. Burkley, S/Sgt. Clyde H. Carrick, PFC Elton E. Hutson, 2nd Lt. George W. Jenkins, T/5 Robert T. Jones, PFC Ralph E. Kinkead, PFC James M. Lewis, PFC Silas McCraney, PFC Bradford W. McGibney, PFC William E. Metz, PFC Michael Seaman, Pvt. R. L. Welch, PFC Harold Wenger and PFC Johnny L. Williams are WIA.

January 15–The First Battalion, 315th Infantry, attacked on our left with B Company leading. Advancing two hundred yards the men met with heavy artillery and mortar fire and were forced back to their original positions. On the right flank the Thirty-Sixth Engineers sent two combat patrols to Rehback, both of which were forced to withdraw under fire. They were scheduled to attack during the day but failed to do so.

The attack continued against stiffening enemy resistance. During the early morning hours, ten rounds of 170mm fell in Zinswiller, and the forward positions received heavy and constant artillery fire. At 0800, B Company, under cover of a ground haze, jumped off in the attack. Advancing against sporadic enemy resistance, the men reached their objective at 1124. Meanwhile, A and C Companies remained in position. After reaching its objective, B Company received heavy artillery and small- arms fire. At this point, A Company sent a patrol forward to contact B Company. The patrol ran into a stubborn, well-dug-in foe and was unable to make contact. B Company, finding its position untenable, withdrew to its former position, arriving there at 1230. At 1420, C Company started an attack but was driven back by a stubborn foe who refused to relinquish any ground. At 1950, B Company had made contact with the Thirty-Sixth Combat Engineers on the right, and the battalion set up defensive positions.

During the day, the Third Battalion also continued its attack to the north. At 1200, L Company had reached its objective, followed by I Company. K Company engaged the enemy in a firefight and succeeded in driving the Germans off and at 1330 made physical contact with L Company. K Company then moved to the west and reached its objective on a ridge at 1530. The Germans immediately counterattacked on the right flank. I Company, on the right, aided K Company in an attempt to repulse the enemy thrust. The fight continued for an hour and a half, and many enemy were killed and captured. The enemy failed to dent our line, and a heavy mortar barrage fell into the regimental sector until well after dark. We suffered heavy casualties, and after dark, the battalion and Antitank Platoon was placed with I Company. Throughout the night, heavy shell fire harassed our troops as they sat alert in their wet, cold foxholes.

Company C-Pvt. Devon W. Hancock is KIA. Pvt. William F. Proctor and Pvt. Antonio Rodriguez are WIA. PFC Joseph A. Major is injured.

January 16–The Second Battalion of the 157th Infantry relieved the First Battalion of the 315th Infantry. The 180th Infantry on the left flank, and it remained in position during the day and held its line. On the right flank, the Thirty-Sixth Engineers also held. The only organization in the sector attacking, the 157th Infantry was 1,500 yards in advance of the units to its right and left, and as a consequence its flanks were exposed. To repulse the thrust, the Germans massed their guns and zeroed in on our positions, placing tremendous artillery fire on the regimental troops and particularly upon Third Battalion. At 0900, C Company moved forward toward the right flank of L Company. By

1200 the men had reached their objective and established contact with L Company. At this time, B Company started moving around the left flank of F Company. It then ran into a strong enemy force, and because of the enemy's numerical superiority was forced to disengage itself and move to the west and the north. The men set up positions there and gave support to the Third Battalion during an enemy attack.

At 1330 hours, a First Battalion ration train comprised of three-1/4 ton trucks was ambushed by German riflemen supported by two machine-guns firing cross-fire along the road. Cpl. Alfred Miller of Westernport, Maryland, one of four survivors, said, "I'd just returned from the hospital and I was riding up with the ration truck to rejoin my outfit. We rounded a bend in the road and all hell broke loose! We were fired on by riflemen and machine-guns placed strategically so that they commanded the road. We all hit the ditch on the side of the road. I rolled down the embankment until I found myself in a semi-covered position. After covering the road with small-arms and machine-gun fire, the Germans began firing rifle grenades at the men on the ground. I saw one man take a direct hit in the face and fall over dead. Grenades fell around my position, and I crawled to another position without getting hit. By crawling and running from one covered position to another, I succeeded in getting back to our lines."

During the day, E and G Companies relieved the positions of First Battalion, 315th Infantry. At 1345, G Company with two light tanks attached, attacked the enemy dug in on a hill to the front and succeeded in clearing the position by 1645. The men then moved northeast to make physical contact with K Company's left flank. At 1722, a patrol from G Company reported enemy troops between the

G and K Company positions. A strong force was sent to clear up the situation, and by 1750 physical contact between the two companies had been reestablished. E Company moved forward, and at 1830 made contact with C Company on the right. At 2355, enemy troops were reported between the right platoon and the remainder of the company.

On the Third Battalion front, it was also a day of hard, bitter fighting. At 0300 on the morning of January 16, an enemy patrol attempted to get around the right flank of L Company but was driven off. The Germans continued to shell the front-line troops during the early morning hours. At 1130 machine-gun fire was reported to the right rear of L Company. At 1235 the battalion command post received a direct hit from a rocket. No casualties. At 1330 the Germans launched a large-scale attack against K and L Companies. K Company also reported enemy behind it. By 1540 the enemy was attacking along the entire front. At 1600, enemy had succeeded in infiltrating behind I Company. At 1607, K and I Companies reported that they were completely surrounded. At 1632 the battalion Antitank Company and two light tanks were sent forward in an attempt to contact I Company. This was accomplished at 1713. The companies were supplied with rations and ammunition by 1940. At 1835, the enemy attack had ceased and Third Battalion, with the aid of B Company and a composite company composed of all available personnel in headquarters, started mopping up the enemy behind its position. At the end of the day, Germans remained behind the American lines.

Company C-T/4 Ivan Bean, PFC Robert M. Deppen and Pvt. Clarence J. Sampier are WIA.

January 17–The 180th Infantry tried three times to close the exposed left flank but could make little progress against heavy fire. However, patrols succeeded in contacting our E Company. On the right flank the Thirty-Sixth Engineers again remained in position, holding their line.

In the 157th Infantry sector, enemy artillery pounded our positions in hours-long concentrations. At 0830, B Company began an attack toward the northeast, but because of enemy artillery and small-arms fire was unable to move after repeated attempts. At 1400, A and F Companies jumped off in the attack and failed to gain ground. For the rest of the regiment, the day was spent trying to clear up the pockets of enemy resistance behind the lines. Enemy troops continued to infiltrate to build up a line in the rear, with five machine-guns covering the strategic draw that controlled the avenue of withdrawal open to the American troops. Repeated attempts to supply C Company failed.

In the Third Battalion sector, 2nd Lt. Willis Talkington of Craig, Colorado, ammunition and pioneer platoon leader, attempted to reach the companies in a light tank. Fighting his way through the German line behind his battalion, he succeeded in reaching I Company with food, ammunition, radio batteries, and stretchers for the wounded. He remained with the company overnight and attempted to return at dawn. The tank was hit twice by bazooka fire; the lieutenant was wounded in the face by shrapnel, and the tank driver was killed. Though painfully wounded, the Colorado lieutenant told the remaining tank men to climb out and make a run for it. They refused and Talkington made the break alone. He succeeded in getting back to the American lines safely, and nothing further has been heard from the tankers.

> [In fact, all of the tankers survived and were captured, and they all survived captivity.—Hugh F. Foster III]

At 1720 hours, Colonel O'Brien gave our situation to the division G-3 and requested permission to withdraw the troops from their exposed position, proposing moving them into line with the 180th Infantry on the left and the Thirty-Sixth Engineers on the right. After consulting with the division commander, the division plans and training officer replied that the general said to hold the present line as long as possible because it would show our weakness if he withdrew.

Company C–Pvt. Edward Beattie is AWOL. PFC Andrew G. Palkendo and William E. Santerre are WIA.

January 18–The 180th Infantry again held its position, but on the right flank the Thirty-Sixth Engineers launched an attack. Advancing to within a hundred yards of the objective, Hill 403, they were forced back by a superior enemy force, and the end of the day found them again in their original positions. Our flanks remained open. On the morning of January 18, the 157th Infantry organized a provisional battalion consisting of B Company, F Company, and composite company of Headquarters and Antitank Companies, 157th Infantry, and G Company of the 179th Infantry. With G Company, 179th, on the right and B Company, 157th, on the left, an attack was launched at 0630. B Company was unable to move because of heavy enemy small-arms, mortar, and artillery fire, and G Company was pinned down at 0930. In conjunction with this attack, all available personnel from Headquarters Company, Second Battalion, began an attack in an effort to clean out the enemy behind the forward companies. At 1910 the attack was discontinued due to heavy causalities. At 0915, G Company, 157th, positions were overrun by enemy. There was no physical contact with the companies for the Third Battalion, but radio communication was still intact. Attempts to supply the companies failed.

January 19–Both flanks, 180th Infantry on the left and the Thirty-Sixth Engineers on the right, held. During the early morning hours, the enemy continued to shell the regimental sector with all types of guns, including rockets. A reported total of two thousand rounds of mortar, artillery fire, and rocket fire fell in the regimental area. At 0940, G Company, 179th Infantry, and B Company, 157th, jumped off and were pinned down immediately by severe machine-gun, mortar, and artillery fire. G Company succeeded in advancing six hundred yards, and the enemy came in on both flanks, forcing it to withdraw. The men were forced to leave two 300 radios behind after partially destroying them.

The companies dug in for the night, and patrols were sent out throughout the night to retain contact between them.

Second Battalion of the 411th Infantry was attached to the regiment at 1400. It was moved to an assembly area in preparation for an attack on the morning of the twentieth. At 2020, a hundred rounds of rocket fire and two hundred rounds of artillery landed in Reipertswiller, hitting the chemical mortar ammunition dump and putting the mortars out of action. The men continually radioed back for help, stating that they could not hold out much longer. Radio contact was maintained with the companies of the Third Battalion. During the day, Lt. Col. Felix L. Sparks of Miami, Arizona, commanding officer of the Third Battalion, tried to blast his way through to his companies in a medium tank. On the way up, he saw wounded American soldiers huddling in a ditch. Despite heavy small-arms fire, he personally helped the wounded onto the side of the tank. German artillery fell in the vicinity, and one shell landed close to the tank, partially destroying the gun and the periscope apparatus. Before withdrawing with the wounded men, the tank fired all its ammunition at the enemy, an estimated five thousand rounds of .30-caliber machine-gun ammunition and an undetermined amount of 76mm ammunition.

[Lt. Col. Felix Sparks was awarded the Silver Star Medal-his second-for his exploits in this engagement.—Hugh F. Foster III]

Plans were made to attempt to supply the Third Battalion by air, should the planned attack fail to relieve the position. At 2127 the First Fighter Bomber Aerial Resupply Detachment was alerted by

G-4, Seventh Army. Priorities were established as follows: (1) ammunition, (2) signal supplies, (3) medical supplies, (4) rations, for four hundred men. At 2340 hours, medical and signal supplies arrived and were immediately packed and loaded on trucks in preparation for transportation to the airfield.

January 20–The 157th Infantry continued attacking, although little hope remained that the entrapped companies would be able to break through the encircling German lines. On the left flank the 180th Infantry remained in position, while the Thirty-Sixth Engineers on the right also held. The Germans continued to mass their artillery on our sector, and we received heavy fire and continuous barrages during the day.

At 0725 on the morning of January 20, Second Battalion, 411th Infantry, attacked through First Battalion, 157th Infantry, and received heavy enemy mortar and artillery fire. Reorganizing, it jumped off again at 1015. Again the men received mortar and artillery fire and in addition received cross-fire from enemy bunkers. This attack also failed. Meanwhile, the plans to attempt to supply the besieged men by plane went ahead. The take-off was scheduled for 1245. The weather—cold, driving sleet and snow with little or no visibility—prevented the take-off. At 1500, the containers were unloaded when it was apparent that the mission could not be flown. At 1700, the mission was officially canceled. Plans were made to have the isolated companies of the Third Battalion fight their way back to our lines at 1530. Messages were sent to them to attack to the southwest. At 1630, K Company reported by radio that it was impossible to get back. The men were ordered to attack again.

At 1740, two men from I Company reported into the battalion command post. PFC Benjamin Melton of Wilson, North Carolina, one of the survivors, said, "The wounded men were put into holes with unwounded men so that they could be cared for properly. Some were bleeding severely and needed tourniquets. We made those out of belts and had to loosen them every thirty minutes. We had no medical supplies, no food, and no heat to melt the snow for water. We hunted around and found a box of K rations under the ammunition pile. These rations were given only to the wounded men. At 1530 we were ordered to attack to the rear. Ammunition was scarce, but with the little we had we were determined to make a break for it. Enemy artillery, zeroed in, blew some of the men to bits. I saw one of my officers get a direct hit. I was knocked to the ground several times by the concussion of exploding shells. Luckily I was unwounded. We made no headway and so returned to our holes to surrender.

"I remember reading about the machine-gunning of American prisoners on Malmedy and was damned if I was gonna stay there and be killed in cold blood. We were ordered to lay down our arms. Those who were able stuck white handkerchiefs to their guns and stuck them muzzle down into the snow. The tankers up there tied white handkerchiefs on the muzzle of their light 37mms. Together with Pvt. Walter Bruce and another guy, I made a break for it. We made it but the other fellow was killed. We kept about halfway up the slope of the hill and stayed away from all paths and trails. We saw shoe-pack marks and followed those for a while. Then we saw a shelter half covering a foxhole and waited to make sure it was ours. When I saw a GI pop his head out, don't you know but I was happy." "The enemy artillery and mortar fire up there was the worst I've ever seen. At least 75 percent of the men on the hill had a wound of some kind and some had two or three wounds."

[On January 20, far to the north, the Germans launched the Ardennes Offensive, known in history as the Battle of the Bulge. Allied forces in the south (Forty-Fifth Infantry Division) were just inside France and began occupying the Maginot Line. Just as the 157th Regiment was withdrawing, the Germans initiated Operation Northwind. The Germans launched strong attacks in the south and penetrated the left flank of the Forty-Fifth Infantry Division. The regiment was ordered to move to this area and restore the ruptured line. From January 11 through January 20, the regiment was embroiled in a hot action that saw the Third Battalion and companies from the First and Second Battalions surrounded and overcome by the fresh SS Mountain Infantry Regiment. When the fight ended, 426 men had been captured.—Hugh F. Foster III]

Company C–T/4 George A. Hicks (MOS) 745 is assigned to Company C. PFC Howard Chapman, S/Sgt. William E. Fry, Pvt. Adam Schaff, Pvt. John M. Stafford and Pvt. Alva H. Woodruff Jr. are MIA.

The following became POW's on this date: PFC Richard Adams, PFC Leon N. Anglemyer, Cpl. Donald C. Arvin, Cpl. Burnice N. Auldridge, PFC Vito J. Blanco, S/Sgt. Cleveland Blalock, Cpl. Attilio D. Bregante, PFC Edward A. Blizzard, Cpl. Glen K. Burgess, PFC Roy A. Canter, Sgt. Charles Carter, PFC Isaac F. Caudle, S/Sgt. Thomas Cobb, PFC Coy Cowles, T/Sgt. Victor R. Davy, Sgt. Robert J. Dearden, 2nd Lt. Arthur D. Dewitt, PFC Ladislaus S. Dombrowski, 2nd Lt. Robert B. Dralle, PFC Sam Emanuel, PFC Angelo A. Fiondella, 1st Lt. John E. Floyd, PFC Chester D. Fuller, 1st Lt. Phillip Geller, Pvt. Ralph J. Griebel, S/Sgt, Jack L. Hatchett, PFC William R. Hauser, PFC Francis L. Hubbard, PFC Will E. Huffman, PFC Edward J. Humphreys Jr., Pvt. Claude Jaynes, Pvt. Olen D. Jones, PFC Robert N. Jucoff, Pvt. Alec Karobonik, Pvt. John M. Kilcrease, Pvt. Alfred Kramer, PFC John. J. Lepore Jr., PFC Charles F. Martin, PFC Walter E. McClain, Cpl. Howard R. McIntyre, 2nd Lt. William R. Meigs, S/Sgt. Harry F. Morris, PFC Joseph V. Moscato, Cpl. Robert C. Nash (DOW), S/Sgt. Holly P. Nickell, PFC William L. O'Keefe, Cpl. Cuiodo G. Pallozi, PFC Nick Pavelich, PFC Bliss Peterson, PFC Anthony Posluszny, Pvt. Earl K. Reed, Pvt. Robert C. Rodenbaugh, Pvt. Pedro Romero, Pvt. John A. Santacroce, PFC John R. Sauls, Pvt. Mose O. Scarboro, PFC Okey O. Shafer Jr., PFC Joseph A. Shanno, Pvt. John Siegrist, Pvt. Leonard W. Smith, Pvt. Walter P. Stanlewicz, Pvt. Clyde Stover, T/4 Lester R. Straub, PFC Winston Sutter, PFC Norman E. Tenute, Cpl. Robert H. Thorhauer, PFC Louis E. Tudico, PFC Juan L. Vigil, Pvt. Marion Waugh, Cpl. Cletus Williams and Cpl. Gaylon O. Worthington. Plus five men who were transferred to other companies and became POWs.

[First three days we walked to a train. Fifty of us were put in a boxcar. It was so crowded that twenty-five had to stand while the other twenty-five laid down. One young soldier, Breakfield from North Carolina, had just arrived on the front. Two weeks earlier he was eating a turkey dinner with family in the states and now he is a POW.—Richard Adams]

Dr. Lise Pommois at a foxhole near Reipertswiller

January 21–The sector was quiet during the daylight hours, and the 157th Infantry withdrew through the 180th Infantry and the Thirty-Sixth Combat Engineers. Protected by screening forces, the regiment retired from the field of battle, leaving behind it the Third Battalion rifle companies, elements of Company M, and all of Companies C and G. **[One platoon of Company G was not surrounded and not lost.—Hugh F. Foster III]** By the end of the day, the regiment had arrived in an assembly area in preparation for a move to the rear for reorganization and training.

The screening forces of the three battalions of the 157th Infantry joined their respective organizations in the assembly area near Zittersheim. The First and Second Battalions entrucked in the evening and moved to new assembly areas. The First Battalion moved to Schoenburg and the Second Battalion to Lohr. Except for the battalion command post, which moved to Ottwiller, the Third Battalion remained in Zittersheim.

Company C-Cpl. Alfred J. Vigliante is injured.

[Cpl. Vigliante is the last remaining one of the thirty three members of the 4th Platoon who were photographed in October of 1943 and is still on active duty with his original company.—Rita Kirchgassner]

January 22–Early in the morning, the Third Battalion moved to Ottwiller and spent the rest of the day obtaining bivouac space for the troops. The First and Second Battalions remained in their respective areas.

January 23–Because of change in the corps boundary, the Second and Third Battalions sent reconnaissance parties into neighboring towns to find new quartering space for the troops. The following day, Second Battalion moved to Hangwiller, Third Battalion to Metting, and regimental headquarters to Bust. The First Battalion remained in Schoenburg and began training for future actions.

For the third time in its combat history, the 157th Infantry began extensive reorganization of its companies. Over a three-day period more than a thousand replacements were assigned to separate units throughout the regiment, and the names of thirty new officers were added to the rolls. Nearly two hundred experienced noncommissioned officers and potential noncommissioned officers were transferred in from other combat organizations: the Thirty-Sixth Infantry Division, the 103rd Infantry Division, the Forty-Forth Infantry Division, the Seventieth Infantry Division, and the Sixty-Third Infantry Division. Throughout the remainder of the month, the regimental troops underwent extensive training and gradually became acquainted with each other as the ever-warning rumors began circulating that the 157th Infantry was about to swing into action on the lines once more.

Company C–PFC Anthony Dumont is transferred to 516th Military Police Battalion. First Lt. Phillip F. Geller, Cpl. Burnice N. Auldridge, PFC Richard F. Adams, PFC Will E. Huffman, PFC Nick Pavelich, Pvt. Robert Rodenbaugh are listed as MIA but are POWs.

[Company C total losses: 6 KIA, 26 WIA and evacuated and 71 POWs, one of whom died in captivity.--Hugh F. Foster III]

January 26–Company C–Eighty-seven men are assigned on this date.

January 27–Company C–Cpl. Alfred J. Vigilante suffered a concussion on January 21 and eventually is transferred to Fort Dix, New Jersey, for recuperation.

January 30–Company C–Hyman Miller returns to duty.

* * *

[June 20, 2013--Today started with thunderbird weather. Hail with heavy rain greeted us as we started our way to Reipertswiller. From Epinal to Reipertswiller is a three-hour drive. Our guide Lise Pommois has studied the military history of northern France for decades. As we were making our way to Reipertswiller, she was able to tell us which battalion and/or division liberated the towns and the villages. One of our first stops was outside a village named Viombous. A burnt-out farmhouse still stands where fifty-seven members of the French Resistance perished. British paratroopers were meeting with the members as supplies were being dropped. Someone betrayed both groups and they were surrounded by the enemy and perished. A memorial stands at the site.

By now the rain had left us. We had lunch in the town of Saverne, which has a lengthy history, having been established by the Romans in the first century. We saw the headquarters of the Forty-Fifth Division when General Patch was in command.

Lise drove us to the mountains that overlook Reipertswiller. She could drive only so far. We proceeded on foot for more than an hour, ascending a mountain. We discovered several foxholes that once had been occupied by the Forty-Fifth.

Not long after we were out of the mountains the rain came again.

It has been a thirteen-hour day, and we wish we could listen and learn more from Lise. But we need to arise at 5 a.m. for departure to Switzerland. However, she has promised to come to our high school and speak to our students. We cannot thank her enough for sharing her knowledge with us.—Rita Kirchgassner]

[Off to the French Riviera in the morning. St. Maxime on the French Riviera is the site of Forty-Fifth amphibious invasion of France.—Jared Leiker]

White phosphorus shell
hits Reipertswiller
SC Photo

Reipertswiller
June 2013

Litchenberg
June 2013

February 1945–February—the month that a year before had seen the 157th Infantry receive the brunt of an all-out German drive to break through the defending Allied forces on the Anzio beachhead—was one of the most unexciting periods of combat in which the organization ever had engaged. True, the men were on the line for half a month, occupying a semi-circular position below the battle-torn Reipertswiller sector where the Third Battalion had been lost in January, but this section was limited. In some areas, the patrols probed deep into German territory without seeing signs of enemy, and front-line casualties were light. To improve matters, the weather took a turn for the better, and the number of men evacuated because of exposure to the elements became noticeably less. To prevent trench foot, the infantrymen employed the "buddy system" and at regular intervals massaged each other's feet. One battalion surgeon threatened to have court-martialed the man who let his buddy get trench foot.

February 3–The 157th Infantry relieved the 180th Infantry on position in the vicinity of Wimmenau. By 2115 hours the entire relief had been completed without incident, and patrols began probing the forward areas in the vicinity of Hill 343, Hill 335, and Hill 301, making contact with small groups of enemy, who also probably were engaged in patrolling.

February 4–While Third Battalion remained in Regimental Reserve, First and Second Battalions sent patrols into enemy territory and established observation and listening posts. The regimental front remained relatively quiet throughout the day, most of the enemy artillery fire that fell from the sector landing in the town of Reipertswiller. Men on observation post duty in the town at 1920 hours reported seeing a rocket fired from Hill 301. They reported that they saw the sparks take off.

February 5–Patrolling again marked the day's activities while the regimental front again remained quiet. At dawn the enemy subjected Reipertswiller to sporadic artillery fire and throughout the remainder of the day interdicted the town and its surrounding areas. Patrols from Second Battalion returned to their companies early in the morning after having brushed with small groups of enemy. Second Battalion was relieved by the First Battalion of the 179th Infantry at 2100 hours and moved into an assembly area preparatory to relieving in turn the Second Battalion, Thirty-Sixth Engineers, on the right on the following day.

Company C-S/Sgt. Frank T. Easton is KIA.

February 6–While the front remained quiet, Second and Third Battalions relieved battalions of the Thirty-Sixth Engineers and took up positions in the vicinity of Lichtenburg. The entire relief had been completed by 2120 hours without incident. The regimental lines followed the ridges running generally southeast, First Battalion on the left, Third Battalion, with new troops, holding ground in the center where its flanks were anchored, and Second Battalion on the right.

First Battalion remained in position and patrolled the forward areas actively. One patrol ventured into the small town of Sagemuehl, which lay in the valley immediately in front of the lines, and returned with the information that it had encountered no enemy. As proof, the men offered the cow they'd brought back, claiming if there had been any Germans in the town, the animal would have been a Kraut captive instead of an American one. The cow later was reported to have stepped on a mine, and beefsteak came to the front lines.

February 7 again found the front relatively quiet, and the battalions moved to the top of Hill 301 after spending most of the daylight hours in Reipertswiller. The patrol remained in observation for one and a half hours and returned at 2140 hours after having made no contact with the enemy and after having seen no German activity. A patrol from the Second Battalion ventured into the edge of the old Reipertswiller battleground and found thirteen enemy dead and two American.

Third Battalion continued to improve its positions throughout the day, receiving enemy mortar fire along its entire front at 0930 hours. At approximately the same time, artillery fire fell in Lichtenburg, where the Second and Third Battalions and regimental headquarters men were observing from the ancient castle where reportedly the composer Wagner wrote the opera *Lohengrin.*

During the following eleven days in which the 157th Infantry served on line, the battalions continued vigorous patrolling. Enemy artillery and mortar fire falling on the front-line positions increased sharply, the main impact area the town of Reipertswiller, the position occupied by the forward elements of Third Battalion and the Second Battalion right flank. First Battalion troops on several occasions saw enemy moving about on the east edge of Reipertswiller and directed artillery and mortar fire upon them with good results.

February 12–Almost as active as the regimental patrols were those the enemy sent into the forward areas. A patrol came into the lines and announced to the troops who met it that it came from an adjacent battalion. The men reported they had killed six Germans and had captured one other of an enemy group that supposedly had infiltrated between the two battalions. A check with the adjacent battalion revealed that it had sent out a contact patrol.

On the same day, an enemy soldier tapped a company telephone line and listened to the conversations passing over it for several hours. A German-speaking American conversed with the soldier, but all attempts to capture him failed. The line was not harmed nor could the place of tapping be located.

February 13–A regimental patrol probing in the vicinity of Hill 301 became engaged in a firefight with a small group of enemy who withdrew to prepared positions, then suddenly were reinforced by the additional fifteen or twenty Germans. In brief but heavy fighting, the patrol was forced to withdraw under 50mm mortar fire brought to bear upon it and after a hand-grenade exchange.

February 15–Contact parties from the 232nd Infantry of the Forty-Second Infantry Division moved into position with the regimental troops to remain there until the prospective relief of the 157th Infantry by their organization had been completed. The relief was effected February 17 and had been completed by 2255 hours. As the battalions came back to assembly areas, the troops entrucked and began the lengthy shuttle into the army reserve area in the Rambervillers sector. The remainder of the month was devoted to training and recreation.

February 17–Company C-Pvt. Edward Beattie in confinement at Dijon, France.

February 20–Company C-Pvt. Edward Beattie in regimental stockade.

March 1945–It was mid-March before the 157th Infantry and the Forty-Fifth Division again were committed to action, this time serving with the Fifteenth Corps operating in the province of Lorraine, France. Until March 13 the regiment remained in the army reserve area in the Rambervillers sector and conducted an extensive training program, squads and platoons engaging in small unit problems. Lt. Col. Felix Sparks, the Third Battalion commander, in initiating competitive training, gave a three-day pass to Paris to a full squad from Company K, adjudged the best in the battalion.

March 2-Company C-Cpl. Robert C. Nash DOW received on January 20, 1945.

March 6–The regiment began dry-run training in river crossings, and for the six days that followed, the men learned to paddle boats and practiced embarking, debarking, and assaulting inland by boat teams. On Sunday, March 11, the battalions engaged in a practice crossing of a lake in the vicinity of Hemming. The only accident to mar the day's activities occurred in the evening when a boat loaded with men from Company A overturned, throwing all the occupants into the water. One man drowned and twelve were hospitalized.

March 12–Company C–Pvt. Edward Beattie returns to duty.

March 13--At 1500 hours, the 157th Infantry started movement by motor from the army reserve area and reached an assembly area in the vicinity of Sarregumines by 2245 hours. Throughout the following day, the troops relaxed and made final preparations for the Seventh Army drive scheduled to begin at 0100 hours the morning of March 15, mission of which was to clear all the German defenses in the Seventh Army sector west of the Rhine River, nearly one hundred miles distant. The Thunderbird Division was situated on the left flank of the Fifteenth Corps and was adjoined on the left by elements of the Eleventh Corps, on the immediate right by the Third Division. The Thunderbirds were to attack with the 180th Infantry on the left, the 157th Infantry on the right, and the 179th in reserve. The main sweep through the towns of Obergailbach, Wattweiler, and Homburg and through the Siegfried Line east of the Blies River. The 157th Infantry, supported by five battalions of artillery, was to jump off with the Second Battalion on the left, the First Battalion on the right, and the Third Battalion in reserve.

Information gathered through intelligence sources indicated that enemy resistance throughout the initial phase of the attack probably would be limited. It was expected that the Germans would choose to withdraw to the Siegfried defenses behind them rather than attempt holding the positions they occupied at jump-off time, and it was believed certain that they would fight a delaying action to allow the main body of troops to retire to the famous emplacements. Even the Siegfried defenses, intelligence indicated, would be unable to stop the tremendous attack to be hurled against them, however, unless supporting forces not readily available were rushed forward as reinforcement. Intelligence reported that according to captured enemy soldiers, the Germans in the Forty-Fifth Division sector were receiving no replacements and that some units were receiving personnel from Volkssturm. The noticeable lack of artillery fire indicated that the Germans were conserving ammunition, and it was known, according to intelligence, that the enemy had not more than fifty tanks and self-propelled guns in the Forty-Fifth Division zone south of the division objective. Being used as stationary artillery, the German armor was expected to become active after the attack started, and it was believed certain that lacking sufficient reserves, the Germans would employ the maximum of mines, obstacles, and demolitions.

> [Volkssturm was basically a militia of old men and young boys, drafted into emergency military service.—Hugh F. Foster III]

March 14–As nightfall approached, the regiment began moving into jump off-position. At 1800 hours the regimental command post opened in Woelfing, where the Second Battalion command post also was located, and the battalions moved from their areas in the vicinity of Remelling, Sarreinsming, and Zetting, closing their positions behind forward elements of the Forty-Fourth Infantry Division by 2330 hours.

Company C–Pvt. Edward Beattie is AWOL.

With the First Battalion on the east and the Second Battalion on the west of the regimental sector, the 157th Infantry jumped off in night attack at 0100 hours March 15, passing through the Seventy-First Infantry and 114th Infantry of the Forty-Fourth Division and pushing forward toward the northeast. Progress was slow, particularly in the First Battalion sector, because of the extensive mine fields that lay in front of the advancing troops. Alerted by tremendous concentrations of artillery fire and by the huge searchlights that exposed the entire front, the enemy placed intense 20mm fire from f lak wagons on Company A and Company B, leading the battalion in attack, and men from Company A, unsuspectingly attempting to dig hasty trenches in an anti-personnel mine field, suffered casualties. Company B remained pinned beneath f lak fire until supporting artillery concentrations, pounding the German-held areas, forced an enemy withdrawal and allowed the advance to continue. By 0400 hours, Company B had cleared the woods to its front but again received 20mm fire as well as machine-gun concentrations loosed by bypassed enemy infantrymen, who held positions between the company's reserve and support platoons. Driven out with losses by Company B riflemen, the Germans withdrew, and artillery fell in the woods occupied by other elements of the company.

To assist the hard-pressed First Battalion, tanks were sent forward during the morning, and Company B and Company C jumped off in attack, following in the wake of any artillery preparation. In an advance that cost the enemy the loss of three tanks and probably two others, Company C moved into Obergailbach, but was forced to withdraw under small-arms fire from within the town, heavy f lak and mortar fire from the woods north and northeast of it, and self- propelled fire from the area north of Niedergailbach. Upon withdrawal, the troops found that the enemy had moved around the left flank and occupied positions to the rear. Taken under rifle fire, the Germans withdrew, however.

Supplied with rations, the First Battalion renewed its attack at 2130 hours, and by midnight, Company C had captured Obergailbach and with Company B was pushing north.

Apparently surprising the Germans, Second Battalion, meanwhile, in a column of Companies E, G, and F, made a steady advance in the wake of an artillery preparation placed on the woods to the front. One platoon of Company G swung west preparatory to entering the town of Bliesbrucken, but the remainder of the battalion continued to advance against light opposition. First resistance in strength came at daylight on the edge of the German frontier when Company E became engaged in a firefight with enemy occupying the town of Niedergailbach inside the Third Reich. Heavy fighting also broke out in Bliesbrucken, which the platoon of Company G found well defended, and at 0830 hours, the remainder of the company received a counterattack by an estimated seventy Germans. In a lengthy exchange of fire, the enemy withdrew, suffering casualties, and Company G, less the platoon in Bliesbrucken, moved forward into the adjoining woods. Shortly after noon, the platoon, having fought for three hours against enemy well emplaced on the east slope of the hill northwest of the town, in the orchard to the east, and in Bliesbrucken itself, was ordered to withdraw.

Heavy fighting in the Second Battalion sector continued throughout the remainder of the afternoon while the troops were being provided with rations, and at 1548 hours, At 1930 hours, Company E began moving forward once more, attempting to enter Niedergailbach as Company F and Company G followed in close support. Heavy concentrations of machine-gun, mortar, and self-propelled fire from the west, north, and east forced the company to withdraw to its original position, however, and it established its defenses there for the night.

Initially in regimental reserve, elements of Third Battalion were committed at noon to capture the strongly defended town of Bliesbrucken. Company K moved forward and encountered the enemy. Striking the Germans from the flank, the company killed or took captive every member of the enemy group, then pushed on to jump-off position on the outskirts of Bliesbrucken. The company attacked at 1700 hours, moving in under smoke and entering the town from the northeast while the enemy forces traveled south out of Bliesbrucken, then attempted to swing behind the assaulting unit. While Company L moved into position from which it blocked the flanking movement, Company K engaged the enemy in a three-hour firefight, finally withdrawing to the northeast edge of the town to begin reorganization.

In the day's operations, the 157th Infantry gained approximately 3,500 yards of well- defended ground, captured eighty enemy soldiers, and inf licted serious losses in personnel upon the enemy forces in the sector.

[On March 15, 157th Regiment units were rebuilt and were once again in the attack.—Hugh F. Foster III]

March 16–Continuing its push forward during the early morning hours, the 157th Infantry, situated on the right flank of the Forty-Fifth Division sector, met only light opposition, and the troops in an advance reminiscent of the initial phase of the campaign in southern France, made rapid progress. Obergailbach fell to the First Battalion before dawn, and Second Battalion, in an attack launched at 0800 hours, captured the shell-shattered town of Niedergailbach. Third Battalion, shortly before noon, began moving to an assembly area in the vicinity of Obergailbach, while elements of the 179th Infantry relieved Company K on the northeast edge of Bliesbrucken. Ordered to pass through the Second Battalion late in the evening, the Third Battalion troops entrucked and began shuttling to an assembly area near Seyweiler where at dusk, elements of the regiment were receiving tank fire. During the day, the assaulting companies captured seventy-three enemy soldiers.

March 17–For the second time in its combat history, the regiment contacted the famed Siegfried emplacements, to which the German forces had withdrawn as had been anticipated. At 0300 hours, Company I and Company L passed through Second Battalion and continued to advance until 0700 hours when First Battalion passed through Third Battalion. Moving forward in a column of Companies A, C, and B, First Battalion met no opposition until noon when it drew small-arms and mortar fire from the Siegfried emplacements. One platoon from Company B attempted to clear the town of Hengstbach of resistance but met strong opposition from enemy, who were supported by fire from Hill 32.

In preparation for an attack, Company A sent patrols to the north, then, preceded by an artillery concentration, jumped off in assault during the late afternoon hours. The enemy brought heavy small-arms and shell fire to bear on the attacking troops, and they were forced to withdraw.

Information gained from the attack and from patrol reports indicated that the Germans had installed their outer defenses behind "dragon teeth," which were covered by machine-gun fire from bunkers and pillboxes emplaced to the north. Enemy artillery behind the concrete defenses became active at dusk, and fell on Second Battalion troops in position in the vicinity of Hengstbach brought casualties. At 1930 hours, Company G captured Hengstbach and pushed on toward the high ground to the north.

March 18–The supporting artillery batteries registered the emplacements lying in front of the troops on the line, while enemy artillery sporadically fell in the regimental sector. At 1230 hours the artillery began a thirty-minute concentration of fire upon the concrete emplacements, and at 1300 hours, First and Second Battalions jumped off in attack, crossing the rolling hills to begin the initial breach of the Siegfried Line. In the First Battalion sector, Company C, in the face of heavy small-arms, machine-gun, and artillery fire, passed through the outer ring of "dragon teeth" and supported by a company of medium tanks, assaulted the pillboxes and bunkers to the north. While the tanks moved up to the "dragon teeth" and loosed direct fire upon the ports and apertures of the enemy pillboxes, infantry and demolition teams from the engineers blew a path through which the vehicles followed. Direct tank fire demolished one pillbox, and eight of the emplacements fell to the relentless infantry assault teams. Moving through the breech in the line, Company A came forward to assist Company C in mop-up operations, and an armed bulldozer was brought into the area to fill the antitank ditch so that armor could cross it. As darkness fell, the battalion established its defenses for the night and reorganized its companies.

Heavy artillery fire impeded the Second Battalion advance, but Company F, supported by a company of tank destroyers, gained ground slowly until coming under intense small-arms fire from a concrete fort approximately a hundred yards long. In savage fighting, Company F overran the fort while Company E, moving up on the west flank, knocked out three pillboxes and tied in on the left flank of Company F. While enemy artillery fell in the Second Battalion sector, the companies dug in their positions for the night.

Third Battalion, meanwhile, remained in Regimental Reserve but toward nightfall began moving into position behind First Battalion, preparatory to passing through that unit the following morning.

Company C–S/Sgt. Donald R. Anthony and PFC Donald R. Zauhar are injured. T/4 George Hicks is WIA and does not return during the war. Others WIA are PFC Eugene Beck, PFC Tom R. Caldwell, T/5 Victor V. Castro, PFC Oris H. Crain, 2nd Lt. Beattie M. DeLong, S/Sgt. Dan P. Dougherty, PFC Marvin M. Fritsch, Pvt. Bernard James, 2nd Lt. Henry W. Jones, PFC Harold R. Jordan, Pvt. Michael Karacab Jr. PFC Ralph E. Kinkead, Cpl. Thomas McKay, PFC James Moore, 1st Lt. Alvin E. Ousey, PFC Holice W. Phillips, PFC Floyd G. Rose, Sgt. Sidney J. Sabel, S/Sgt. Lloyd L. Slover, Cpl. Fred P. Sykora, Pvt. James Vlaming, PFC Earl D. Wardrop, PFC William L. Ware, PFC George S. White and S/Sgt. Dennis E. Willingham.

T/Sgt. James W. Dearduff, PFC Frank E Warnock and PFC John S. Weston are KIA.

March 19–Throughout the hours of darkness, the regimental front remained quiet, but at 0619 hours, while the artillery was placing a concentration of fire along the enemy lines preparatory to the morning's attack, the Germans assaulted the First Battalion troops. They were repulsed in a twenty-minute action, and at 0630 hours, Third Battalion passed through First Battalion to begin driving deeper into the Siegfried emplacements. In conjunction, Second Battalion renewed its attack on the concrete defenses at 1015 hours.

Fighting desperately to prevent a breakthrough, the Germans placed intense concentrations of small-arms and machine-gun fire upon the oncoming troops, but were incapable of launching a coordinated counterattack in strength. Pressing forward against fire of all types, the Third and Second Battalions overran thirty pillboxes in the day's operations and penetrated completely the first defense line. Patrols from Third Battalion probed the streets of Wattweiler, while the engineers filled the antitank ditch, which paralleled the "dragon teeth," and permitted armor support to move forward. While German artillery fire fell in the regimental sector, the troops established positions for the night and prepared to renew their attack shortly after dawn the following morning.

In the Second Battalion sector that evening, infantry found a deserted pillbox in which was set up a German switchboard, still in full operation. Exploiting the advantage it afforded, Maj. Robert Slyter, the regimental S-2, sent forward 1st Lt. Fritz Schnaittacher and 2nd Lt. Fred Kaufman, interrogators, to listen to the conversations coming over the wires.

The two officers, both native Germans, remained in the solitude of the huge concrete structures for two hours gathering data, the importance of which they failed to realize until two days later.

"There were many calls going through the board," Lieutenant Schnaittacher reported, "but we were able to hear well on only one line. A German officer, whom we determined to be an SS captain, was issuing orders to the troops occupying the positions in front of us, and we heard him tell them to destroy all the telephones in the bunkers, either with hand grenades or axes, and to gas up all their vehicles in preparation for a move. The trucks were to gas up, he said, at Kleinbunderbach, a town about twenty kilometers distant, and the German troops were to get it by force, if necessary. There would be a control point at Harsbert on the way to Landsturl, he said, and everything left behind was to be destroyed before they moved at 2300 hours.

"We reported what we'd learned to Major Slyter at 2250 hours, and he got in touch with division and air liaison. The last we heard of the whole thing was that night fighters had been sent out and that they'd plastered a German convoy of vehicles which extended three-abreast for miles."

Company C-Pvt. Johnnie B Jones is WIA and later DOW. T/5 Norman L. Eledge, Pvt. Robert D. Green, Pvt. Charles Hirschman Sr., Pvt. Jack H. Patterson, PFC Harvey O. Trygestad and PFC Oress M. Walker are WIA.

March 20–Only a few scattered rounds of artillery and mortar fire fell in the regimental sector during the early morning hours as the Germans broke contact with the attacking forces and attempted to retreat into the depths of the fatherland. It had taken the enemy nine years to prepare the Siegfried defenses that the 157th Infantry and other Seventh Army units had overrun in less than a week, although it had been expected that it might take three months to breach the famed defenses. And the entire operation had been accomplished with but one-third of the casualties the regiment had suffered during the drive across the plains of Anzio nearly a year before when the Allies smashed a less formidable line. Reports indicated that the Third Army, on the left, was branching behind the enemy forces opposing the Seventh Army and pocketing the Germans who lay between.

In the regiment sector, Second Battalion met opposition during the afternoon when the troops received machine-gun, mortar, and Antitank fire from the hills south of Kirrberg, but in a swift advance, the companies brushed the resistance aside and caught the Germans defending the town completely by surprise, capturing nearly 350 enemy soldiers, several artillery pieces, and much equipment in a brief battle.

First Battalion, during the afternoon, suffered the loss of the battalion S-3, Capt. William T. Barnes, who with the acting battalion commander, Maj. Charles Edwards, and several enlisted men was investigating a manned cave where had been placed thousands of liters of gasoline. When one of the men fired into the pillbox, the gasoline exploded and sheets of flame enveloped the group, burning Captain Barnes and three others seriously. Of the four, only one lived.

Thus began one of the most spectacular advances in which the 157th Infantry ever had taken part. Typical infantrymen, nobody wanted to walk, so the advancing doughboys commandeered bicycles, motorcycles, and abandoned trucks to chase the fleeing enemy. Germans attempting to defend the town of Martinshohe were overrun by a tide of battle-weary GIs who had found new spirit in Adolf Hitler's sacred soil where the damage they inflicted now hurt the right people.

Hundreds of German prisoners filed back to the rear for processing, some of the more fortunate ones riding in crowded trucks while others walked. Completely overrun, they surrendered in groups and in many instances appeared disappointed because no one paid any attention to them. Straggling Germans, still wearing their gray-green uniforms and surrender caps, wandered aimlessly about, watching in dazed amazement the flood of troops, supplies, and equipment sweeping past them toward the west bank of the Rhine River. Civilians, the first the regimental troops had encountered in great numbers in Germany, also watched and wondered.

Company C-PFC Angelo F. Zito is KIA. PFC Oliver I. Hurt and PFC Doyle W. Whisenhunt are WIA.

> ["Surrender caps" was a term invented by the GIs to describe the standard field cap, the M-43 cap. Germans were taught that POWs should not be allowed to retain their steel helmets, so most of them donned the cap upon surrender.
>
> By March 20, the Siegfried Line had been penetrated, and the Germans began a withdrawal to the Rhine River. The regiment pursued them at great speed. Its sister regiments, the 179th and the 180th, conducted assault crossings on the Rhine River by March 26.—Hugh F. Foster III]

By March 23 the 157th Infantry with other Seventh Army elements had reached the Rhine and was situated in the vicinity of the city of Westhofen through which Third and Seventh Army convoys continued to pass in an endless stream. While the 157th Infantry outposted the western bank of the river, the remainder of the division prepared to make a crossing in conjunction with the Third Division on the right flank.

March 25-Company C-Sgt. Ortho Taylor DOW received on March 19, 1945.

March 26–At 0200 hours while German aircraft hovered overhead, drawing flak fire that downed two planes, the 179th Infantry and the 180th Infantry launched the Forty-Fifth Division attack against the enemy positions on the east bank of the Rhine River. Crossing the quarter-mile stretch of water in assault boats and with no protective artillery concentration preceding them, the troops took the enemy by surprise, and it was not until the boats had been emptied and were returning to the opposite bank that intense mortar fire fell into the division sector. Though fifty of the boats were damaged, many beyond repair, the main body of assault troops had gained the foothold that doomed the enemy position, and by morning the Thunderbirds had pressed inland from the river nearly two miles. In Division Reserve, the 157th Infantry began crossing the Rhine at 1100 hours, the entire First Battalion reaching the east bank by 1250 hours. By nightfall all the battalions had made the crossing, and Second and Third Battalion were making preparations to launch a coordinated attack the following morning.

The two battalions moved off in attack at 0730 hours March 27 in the wake of elements of General Patton's Third Army, meeting no opposition. White f lags of surrender appeared in the towns of Georgenhausen, Reinheim, and Spachbrucken as the troops pushed through, some walking, others riding tanks and tank destroyers as they had during the drive through southern France. One patrol from Third Battalion observed a train moving into Gr-Biederau and called for tank destroyer fire to be placed upon it. Though the train was unhit, it backed hastily out of the town. The patrol then ventured into Gr-Unstadt and captured a hospital in which were several German patients. By nightfall, patrols from both battalions had reached the Main River, where enemy could be seen on the east bank.

[The "Gr" is an abbreviation for "Gross" meaning "large." Town names are also found with a "KL" as abbreviation: that means "Klein" or small.—Hugh F. Foster III]

At 2130 hours that night, the enemy brought forward a loudspeaking system and began talking to Third Battalion troops who were situated across the river from the town of Reinheim. Impressive caterwauling of "Achtung, Achtung," intermixed with women's screams, however, had little psychological effect on the troops, most of whom couldn't understand what was being said and were too tired to listen carefully anyhow.

[The regiment crossed the Main River on a railroad bridge and found itself involved in close-quarter fighting against bitterly resisting SS troops in the city; all three battalions were committed to the attack. The fierce fighting, including a pitched battle for the town castle, went on until the city fell.—Hugh F. Foster III.]

[June 17, 2013--We stayed two nights in Aschaffenburg. Upon arriving at our hotel, we could hear "Rocky Top" being played. Following the music as we walked across a bridge on the Main River, we learned we were at a volk festival. The games, rides, food, and music were similar to what you would find at a carnival in our hometown in Indiana. A John Denver cover band was a favorite among the locals in the beer tent. We saw little evidence that this small town was a victim of war seventy years ago. Many people we talked with could not recall that their city played a part in World War II. A castle along the Main River was the headquarters for the Nazi army. Major Lambert commanded his soldiers to fight to the death. His surrender came only after about ten days of American pressure. The castle has since been restored and is a museum that includes paintings dating as far back as the late 1500s.—Mark and Krista Kirchgassner]

March 28–The advance continued unopposed throughout the morning as the three rifle battalions made long shuttles toward the towns of Aschaffenburg and Schweinheim, reportedly cleared several days before by Third Army forces. Third and Second Battalions crossed the Main River on the planked railroad bridge, then in attacking Schweinheim and Aschaffenburg respectively, encountered heavy sniper and machine-gun fire. In Regimental Reserve, First Battalion was ordered to cross the river at 1530 hours and was committed in attack on the north flank of Third Battalion. Moving forward, Company C, in the lead, came under heavy sniper fire and upon regimental order, held up its advance. The battalion tied in with Second and Third Battalions and established its position for the night.

Information gathered from civilian and patrol reports indicated that the unexpected resistance had been hastily planned and that the main defenders were a few hundred untrained young Germans who were under the command of a captain. Under the threat that the towns would be blown up, the civilians had taken in their white f lags, it was reported, and Germans in some force occupied reinforced barracks where officer candidates had been trained. Houses had been converted into pillboxes, and with limited artillery, mortars, and anti-tank guns to support them, the Germans were pledged to defend their positions to the utmost.

That afternoon, regimental headquarters personnel were notified of the location of a German warehouse in which were stored thousands of cases of cognac, Benedictine, champagne, and other liquors. In some of the most successful requisitioning in which the regiment ever had engaged, a group of officers and enlisted men at dusk ventured ahead of the lines and returned with thirty to forty cases of the precious liquids. For two days following, truckloads of liquor, virtually impossible to obtain in Paris, London, or the cities in the United States, were hauled to the forward troops. One battalion issued twenty-six cases of cognac to each company.

Also located was a German motor pool in which sat eighteen one-and-a-half-ton Ford trucks, none of which showed having been driven more than twenty kilometers. The trucks lacked tires and batteries, but with GI ingenuity, regimental personnel towed them out of the pool under the cover of darkness and by the following night had them equipped and running.

Company C-Pvt. Allen H. Brooks, S/Sgt. Ray or Roy L. Burke, PFC George W. Evans, Pvt. Stanley W. Grudzien, PFC Richard E. Hart, Pvt. J. C. Hoff, Pvt. David C. Holmes, PFC Timothy F. Kelly, Sgt. Arnulfo a. Rios, S/Sgt. Raymond J. Sniffen, PFC Daniel Stern and PFC William L. Ware are WIA.

March 29-In a drizzling rain, Third Battalion, with Company L and Company I abreast, jumped off in attack upon Schweinheim, meeting heavy concentrations of small-arms and mortar fire before it reached the edge of the town. Pressing forward, elements of both companies had moved into the streets by 0830 hours, meeting stubbornly resisting Germans, who, assisted by civilians, engaged them in house-to- house fighting. Company C was committed on the Third Battalion left flank but also met desperate resistance and was able to make only limited gains. While all the artillery available was poured into the towns, the battalions established positions for the night and prepared to renew their assaults the following morning. Heavy-caliber artillery and mortar fire fell upon the troops during the hours of darkness.

Shortly after midnight, the enemy, in strength of approximately fifty men, attacked Company K, falling back only after a heavy firefight. The Germans, in strength of sixty to seventy-five men, again launched an assault upon the company at 0320 hours, inflicting and suffering serious losses before retiring under heavy fire two hours later. At approximately the same time, Company L received an attack by an estimated 170 Germans, who, abetted by an enemy patrol that worked to the rear of the company, placed the unit in serious difficulty until the approach of daylight when fire of all types forced the opposing forces into withdrawal.

Company C-PFC Floyd Bonner is KIA. Pvt. Earl R. Brutcher, T/5 Clarence L. Chilcutt, 2nd Lt. Carl H. Glendening, 1st Lt. Robert B. Hopfan, and PFC Donald M. Vee are WIA. PFC Edward A. Terepka is injured.

March 30–At 0745 hours in the murky morning, Third Battalion began attacking through the streets of Schweinheim, meeting intense resistance in house-to-house fighting. Company L, in a morning of intense action, made slow progress. Then at 1125 hours, Company K reported engaging an estimated three hundred enemy who were situated on a hill to its rear. In an assault upon the German positions, the company forced the stubborn forces to disperse, half of the enemy troops moving toward Company L, which took them under fire and routed them once more, capturing thirty enemy soldiers. Resistance immediately decreased, and by nightfall Company I and Company L had reached the last row of houses in the town. The main obstacle remaining was the group of heavily fortified barracks on the eastern edge of Schweinheim.

In the Second Battalion sector, Company G and Company E made limited progress in streets fighting in Aschaffenburg, meeting heavy sniper and mortar fire. At 1830 hours elements of the Sixty-Fourth Fighter Wing f lew a bombing and strafing mission over the city, blasting the castle, known to be an enemy command post, and machine-gunning the German positions that lay along the east side of the Main River. Limited f lak fire met the aerial attack.

Company C-PFC Stanley S. Norton and Sgt. Vernon E. Pederson are KIA. Cpl. Joseph Cottone is WIA. Pvt. Samuel L. Weiner is injured.

March 31–While friendly aircraft, taking advantage of a sudden change in weather, pummeled both Schweinheim and Aschaffenburg, the 157th Infantry renewed its attacks upon the two towns. Troops fighting in Aschaffenburg still were unable to make gains, but the heaviest fighting occurred in Schweinheim.

Every house was a defensive position, and Germans gave ground room by room, frequently sneaking back to snipe at the advancing troops from the rear. While American artillery leveled buildings ahead of the hard-pressed infantrymen, hundreds of rounds of German mortar fire impeded the advance. From 1,200 to 1,500 rounds alone fell in the northeastern and eastern parts of the town, and at one time two hundred rounds fell on the Third Battalion position during a fifteen-minute interval. By nightfall, however, the companies, having suffered heavy losses, had cleared all but the northernmost houses and still under an intense volume of small- arms and mortar fire, established their positions for the night.

During the afternoon Capt. Anse Speairs, the regimental adjutant, dropped a mimeographed ultimatum from a Piper Cub into Aschaffenburg. The document read as follows:

To the Commandant of the City of Aschaffenburg, Aschaffenburg A/M:

Your situation is hopeless. Our superiority in men and material is overpowering.

You are offered herewith the opportunity, by accepting unconditional surrenders, to save the lives and property of countless civilians. The conditions of the Geneva Convention are assured to you and to your garrison.

The following is requested immediately upon receipt of this message.

1. The raising of the white f lag on the engineer barracks.
2. The sending of a delegation under a white f lag which will be authorized to negotiate for the conclusion of the capitulation of Aschaffenburg.

Should you refuse to accept these conditions, we shall be forced to level Aschaffenburg.

The fate of Aschaffenburg is in your hands.

The commander of the American troops and his staff awaited results.

[Grandma Dorie received the following letter dated April 4, 1945:

Mrs. Dora Kirchgassner
Yorkville, Indiana

Dear Madam:

Your son, S/Sgt. Robert L. Kirchgassner, was admitted to this hospital this date. His condition is not serious.

Mail may addressed as follows:

Convalescent Reconditioning Service
Wakeman General and Convalescent Hospital
Camp Atterbury, Indiana
Very truly yours,
David A. Baker
1st Lt, MAC
Personal Affairs Officer]

April 1945–Grayish, bespectacled Major Von Lambert, commander of the German garrison defending Aschaffenburg and Schweinheim, was a soldier's soldier, a firm believer in the principles of Nazism, and one of the most noteworthy adversaries the 157th Infantry Regiment ever encountered. Acting under the direct orders of the National Socialist Party, the major was determined first that Aschaffenburg and Schweinheim would not fall; second, that if the towns were forced into surrender, the defeat would be a glorious one, to be viewed with pride by the entire fatherland. Characteristically he issued the dictum:

> "Soldiers, men of the Volkssturm, comrades! The fortress of Aschaffenburg will be defended to the last man. As long as the enemy gives us time, we will prepare to employ our troops to our best possible advantage. This means: 1. Fight. 2. Erect dugouts. 3. And barriers. 4. Get supplies. 5. Win. As of today, everyone is to give his last. I order that none will rest more than three hours out of twenty- four. I forbid any sitting around and loafing. Our belief is that it is our mission to give the cursed enemy the greatest resistance and to send as many as possible to the devil."

To further instill the nationalistic spirit in the populace, Kreisleiter Wohlgemuth **[Relatively high ranking Nazi political leader.—Hugh F. Foster III]** also issued a written proclamation:

> "My dear brothers. For several days I have asked you to leave the city as there exists the danger that it will be the focal point of our nation's battle. Due to the latest developments, there is no doubt that this has now become a reality. We expect a fight for life or death. This afternoon and evening will be the last opportunity for women, children, the sick, and the very old to leave the city. Those who do not leave cannot say they had not been warned in time. The women and men who remain must be prepared to give their lives for their children. Whoever is in the city tomorrow morning belongs to a battle group which will know no selfishness, but which will

know only unlimited hatred against this cursed enemy of ours. They will only know complete sacrifice for the Fuhrer and for our nation. Day and night we will work. We will commit all our power to do the enemy the greatest damage because we know Germany will live if we are prepared to die."

April 1–The 157th Infantry Regiment continued its assault on the fanatically defended city of Aschaffenburg and neighboring Hailbach. The First Battalion, driving toward Hailbach, encountered some resistance, the bulk of which was small-arms fire. By nightfall, the town had been cleared. Aschaffenburg itself was attacked from the southwest by the Second Battalion. There the American troops met bitter resistance. Throughout the day the air corps pilots f lying speedy fighter-bombers circled overhead and supported the infantry's attack with bombing and strafing missions. An M12 self-propelled gun **[A M12 was an armored, tracked artillery piece in 155mm caliber.—Hugh F. Foster III]** was brought into action to place direct fire upon enemy strong points. Progress was slow as the fighting moved from house to house. Company F was relieved by the Forty-Fifth Division Reconnaissance Troop and sent Schweinheim. Company K led the attack when it jumped off in the morning at 0600 hours. Crossing the two hundred yards of f lat field before reaching the barracks made it a haven for German snipers. Many casualties were suffered before the first American soldier set foot in the buildings. They were stubbornly defended, and it was necessary to clear them room by room. Several hundred POWs were taken during the day's action. The 179th Infantry Regiment attacked on the right and forcing enemy artillery to withdraw.

Company C-2nd Lt. Abe Barnett is WIA.

April 2–The First Battalion of the 157th Infantry Regiment continued to attack to the north. It succeeded in cutting the Aschaffenburg-Laufach Road. Company B then moved to the southwest to the town of Goldbach, clearing small pockets of resistance, while Company A, after moving northeast and reporting friendly troops in the town of Hosbach, backtracked to the southwest to join Company B in Goldbach. Large groups of enemy personnel were observed at that time as they attempted to escape Aschaffenburg. By this time the only route of withdrawal was through woods north of the city itself. Companies A and B engaged the fleeing Germans, and a small-arms battle raged toward the close of the day.

The Second Battalion continued with its mission of clearing Aschaffenburg. The enemy was determined to make any advance costly and defended the city street by street, house by house. After many buildings were demolished by direct fire from the M12 self-propelled gun, they defended cellar to cellar. By nightfall the companies reached the center of town. Third Battalion skirted the eastern edge and cleared small pockets of resistance. Company K advanced through Aschaffenburg on the eastern end of town and met very little resistance. Company L moved along the southern edge of the Aschaffenburg railroad until it made contact with Company K. Company I left its position on a nearby hill and occupied the streets cleared by the other companies. Approximately a thousand enemy soldiers had been captured that day. Enemy artillery and mortars were practically nonexistent.

By 1300 hours Second Battalion had moved to an assembly area in Goldbach. The Third Battalion continued its attack until word reached it later in the day of the surrender of the German forces. Second Battalion received a message during the early morning hours that the German garrison in the city wished to surrender. At about 0900 hours, an American soldier who had been a POW walked into battalion lines bearing Major Von Lambert's offer to surrender. First Lt. Fritz Schnaittacher and 2nd Lt. Fred Kaufman, both regimental officers, accompanied the soldier back to Nazi headquarters. They then accompanied Von Lambert as he toured segments of the city that were still holding out and called upon the troops to lay down their arms. He had done what he had killed others for suggesting; he had surrendered.

Evidence of Major Von Lambert's fanaticism was revealed in a note that had been sent him by a Luftwaffe captain. The contents of the note mentioned the fact that as a Luftwaffe officer he had no reason for being in town.

Enraged, Von Lambert ordered that the captain be executed immediately. Further evidence was noted in the body of a German lieutenant who had been hung. It was revealed later that this officer had neglected to attend a meeting called by Major Von Lambert for the purpose of outlining a defense for the city. The lieutenant had been wounded and considered himself a convalescent, but the major thought otherwise. He was hung and his body lay in the street for all to see.

During the battle of Aschaffenburg, the enemy had lost 3,200 men, 1,500 of whom were either KIA or WIA.

> [The regiment found itself involved in close-quarter fighting against bitterly resisting SS troops in the city; all three battalions were committed to the attack. The fierce fighting, including a pitched battle for the town castle, went on until the city fell on the April 3, 1945.—Hugh F. Foster III]

Bombed city of Aschaffenburg
SC Photo

Johannisburg castle at Aschaffenburg, Germany
April 1945

Castle at Aschaffenburg
45th Infantry Division WWII Reenactors

Aschaffenburg, June 2013

April 4–The entire regiment was placed in Division Reserve. During the day, the regimental command post moved from Hosbach to Phaffenhofen. The First Battalion moved from Goldbach to Oberndorf. The Second Battalion moved from Hosbach to the vicinity of Florsbach. Company E occupied Wiessen and Company G, Lettgenbrunn. Company G also placed a roadblock to the northeast of town. During the evening hours, the battalion sent patrols to contact the Third Battalion positions. Company F of the 114th Infantry Regiment contacted Company G roadblock at 1700 hours. At 2300 hours a patrol from Company G reported that it had contacted Company F of the 114th Infantry. The Third Battalion moved from Goldbach to the vicinity of Bourjois. During the odd hours, it sent patrols to the Second Battalion position.

April 5-Dawned cold and raining. The 157th Infantry continued in reserve, and the First Battalion remained in Oberndorf. The 1277th Engineer Regiment reported contact with the enemy, and one platoon of B Company was sent with tanks to go to its aid. They made no contact, however, and returned to the assembly area that day. The Second Battalion moved from Florsbach to the vicinity of Hutton. The Third Battalion moved from Burjos to the vicinity of Eichenried. Both the Second and Third Battalion operated local patrols that night. The regimental command post moved from Phaffenhofen to Gundheim.

April 6 found the 157th Infantry Regiment still following behind the 179th and 180th Infantry Regiments. Each of the battalions moved forward, the First moving from Oberndorf to Dietershausen, the Second from Hutton to Buchenburg, and the Third from Eichenried to Luter. The First and Third Battalions maintained physical contact with one another by means of patrols. The regimental command post moved forward to Schmalnau.

Company C-PFC Thomas C. Hendrix DOW received on March 28, 1945.

Jared, Mark and Krista at a Volk Fest

American soldiers marching out of Aschaffenburg
SC Photo-T/5 Jerry Rutberg

April 7–The battalions again moved forward. The First moved to Mosbach, the Second moved to Buchenburg, and the Third moved to the top of a mountain where there were barracks. A German glider school had formerly occupied the site. The regimental command post moved to Gersfeld.

April 8–The entire regiment remained in position. Col. Walter P. O'Brien left the regiment on detached service and was replaced by Lt. Col. Laurence C. Brown, who had been CO of 2nd Battalion. Lt. Col. Ralph M. Krieger left command of First Battalion to become regimental executive officer. Maj. Charles R. Edwards became commanding officer of the First Battalion.

April 9–The three battalions moved forward once again. The First moved to Kl Eibstadt. The Second moved to Gr Eibstadt area. The Third moved to Gr Bardorf. The regiment opened its command post at Saal.

April 10–11–The entire regiment remained in position. Maintenance of vehicles, cleaning of equipment, and personal hygiene were stressed during this period. The entire regiment was afforded the opportunity to shower and receive a change of clothing. Enemy stragglers continued to be rounded up, and during these two days an undetermined number of POWs were accounted for.

* * *

[Jared's Blog:
June 17, 2013—5:30 AM--Today we got up early and took the train to Aschaffenburg. This small town in western Germany sits on the Main River. The city is the site of the 157th's last major battle. Major Lambert of the German army and three hundred of his troops were able to hold off the 157th for ten days here.

Since it is a Monday, the town museum is closed. We will use today to recoup as Mark has an abscessed tooth, I'm having an allergic reaction to curry, and the ladies are worn out. This is also our first stay in a hotel, so we are going to enjoy the amenities and explore the city after it cools down a little outside. We will do our research tomorrow.

We all took naps and enjoyed the weather on our patio in the middle of small-town Germany. We happened to be here during the local festival. There were some pretty impressive carnival rides. By far our favorite attraction, though, was a country music band made up entirely of German citizens. The crowd had a different line dance for every song. I've never seen anything like it. We stayed until the band finished and then stuck around to talk to the musicians. They gave Rita a free CD. The band was called *Flaggstaff*, yes with two *g*'s. What a great night in Germany! Back to work tomorrow– The Allies were closing in on Aschaffenburg, and the Germans were ready to put up one final battle. The Germans were commanded at Aschaffenburg by the very strict Major Lambert. He had sent a notice to his men that no one was to surrender and that they were to fight to the bitter end. They were to sleep only three hours a day. Prior to the Americans arriving, the Germans had blown up every bridge into the city over the Main River except one railroad bridge. The Americans were able to secure this bridge, which proved critical.

Prior to the battle in Aschaffenburg and its twin city, General Patton had sent a group of men to bypass the town and enter enemy territory to liberate a POW camp that held his son-in-law and several officers from the 157th. The plan turned out to be a bust as the men were unable to complete the mission without many casualties.

[The POW camp was located at Hammelburg, Germany. The entire force was lost, except for a couple of survivors, who made it back to American lines. Patton's son-in-law, was seriously wounded in the attempt to free him and nearly lost his life!—Hugh F. Foster III]

The battle in Aschaffenburg was slow and brutal. In the history of the 157th says that you could watch a platoon enter a house, listen to fighting for twenty minutes, and then watch the platoon leave with Germans and casualties. The Americans were forced to fight door to door, using many hand grenades and bazookas to blast into homes along the way. Casualties were high. Some three thousand Germans and two hundred Americans were lost. German snipers were embedded throughout the city in bomb-ridden buildings and piles of rubble.

After slow fighting, the Forty-Fifth was able to encircle and take the city in the final major battle for the 157th. After being surrounded, the Germans surrendered. The war was over not much longer after that.

The heavily bombed town has been rebuilt and its people have moved on. Unlike Berlin and Munich, there is little evidence that a fierce battle occurred here. Talking with residents, we did not gain much information.

We toured a castle built in the days of the Holy Roman Empire. The German army had claimed it, but we could not learn if Major Lambert had directed his battle from here from the residents. The only other landmark we could find was the Main River, which the Americans had to cross.

Our trip now moves to Epinal on June 19, where Sgt. Robert Kirchgassner was seriously wounded and much of his platoon was taken prisoner. Our attempts to reach France have been frustrating to say the least. We keep missing our connecting trains because they are always delayed. On the train platform, an old German man said, "What's the difference between a broken clock and the trains? A broken clock is on time at least twice a day." It has also been brutally hot, and we can't find air conditioning or a fan anywhere. We are crossing our fingers in making it to France.—Jared Leiker]

April 12-The 157th Infantry was once again ready to return to the line. The First Battalion loaded on DUKW amphibious vehicles and at evening was awaiting orders to move on. The Second Battalion moved to an assembly area just south of Lauf. The Third Battalion crossed the Main River and was placed in position to the east and southeast of Lauf to protect the division's left flank. Once again the men of the 157th Infantry Regiment were ready for battle.

The 157th Regiment met little or no resistance as it moved to attack on the morning of April 13. The First Battalion moved from Kraisdorf, pausing several times during the day to await further orders, clear roadblocks, and pick up enemy stragglers. It arrived at Starkenschwin where it stayed for the night. The Second Battalion met very little resistance as it cleared town after town in its surge forward. The Third Battalion moved forward with K Company leading. Enemy personnel were spotted in Scheslitz but were dispersed by artillery fire. A number of towns were cleared before the battalion set up for the night. The Third Battalion of the 179th Infantry Regiment was attached to the 157th Infantry at 0800 and proceeded to join in the attack. The battalion cleared a number of villages and towns before setting up for the night. At least twenty towns were cleared during the day's activity.

[President Roosevelt passed away. Prisoners were permitted to fall out on a hill for a devotional.—Richard Adams]

April 14–The 157th Infantry Regiment continued to attack to the south toward Nurnberg. The First Battalion launched a twin-pronged attack and was able to secure two bridges intact over the Wiesen River. Several times during the day in an attempt at delaying the speedy advance, the enemy launched countermeasures, but each time the enemy resistance was broken. The Second Battalion cleared a number of towns and then moved by motor to an assembly area to the rear of the First Battalion's right column. The Third Battalion cleared several towns and moved by motor to an assembly area behind the First Battalion's left column. Enemy patrols were unusually active throughout the night.

April 15–The drive toward the city of Nurnberg continued. The First Battalion continued to spearhead the 157th Infantry's advance. The main effort of this twin-pronged drive was exerted on the right column, which was the side on which Nurnberg lay. The right column encountered a roadblock consisting of a Mark V tank, and many enemy personnel. It was quickly reduced and the advance continued. The left column encountered a battery of four 88mm guns and their crews. The opposition was quickly cleared and the advance continued. Numerous prisoners of war were accounted for. The Second and Third Battalions followed the attacking columns closely, ready to go to their aid should the need arise. A total of 787 enemy soldiers were taken in the day's action.

April 16–The 157th Infantry Regiment continued its attack to the south. The plan called for the regiment to skirt the eastern part of the city and then cut back to the west and enter the city from the southeast. The Second Battalion led the attack, passing through the First Battalion's positions during the early morning hours. The surprise of the advance resulted in the capture of two four-gun batteries of 88mm and their crews. The First Battalion launched an attack later in the day and after reaching its objective was ordered to assemble in the vicinity of Diepersdorf. The Third Battalion launched an attack toward Feucht. Its path was blocked by enemy tanks, 88mm guns, and many personnel. At the close of the period, it had made substantial gains before stopping for the night. Enemy artillery was unusually active, interdicting the towns of Fischbach and Lauf throughout the day.

The First Battalion passed through the Second Battalion roadblock early on the morning of the seventeenth and began its attack toward the city of Nurnberg. Resistance was spotty, but as the companies advanced they received small-arms and automatic weapons fire. Sniper fire harassed the troops as they prepared to dig in for the night. The Third Battalion began its attack toward Feucht early in the morning, and by 0900 the town was cleared. The troops continued westward, clearing several smaller villages on the road to Nurnberg. At 1600 the battalion was relieved by the First Battalion, 179th Infantry Regiment, and launched an attack to close the gap on the First Battalion's right flank. The Second Battalion moved forward behind the other two battalions and set up roadblocks.

Nurnberg was the capital of Nazism in Germany. Here many of the edicts proclaiming the members of the Jewish religion to be non-Aryans and unfit for a part in the future glory of the Reich originated. It was here in the huge Nurnberg stadium that many of the Nazi festivals and pageants were held. It also was here that the Eighth Air Force chose to bomb in 1943, and as a result the city's railroads and other installations of vital military value were totally destroyed. Mile after mile of the city was huge piles of rubble.

Company C-PFC James A. Johnson and PFC C. J. Johnston are WIA and DOW on the same day. S/Sgt. William M. Grant is KIA. Pvt. Carl E. Link and PFC Ralph A. Martin are WIA. S/Sgt. Chester J. Stevens is injured.

April 18--The First and Third Battalions attacked the city from the southeast. The progress made by the two battalions was slow but steady. Heavy machine-gun and sniper fire was encountered to the front. Occasional artillery rounds harassed the troops. It was necessary to advance house by house while moving forward.

A picture of things to come was revealed when a captured German revealed the plan for the defense of the city. "The German plan," he said, "was to withdraw to the railroad running east-west through the city and make a stand. When this line of defense breaks, they were to withdraw to the old part of the city." By nightfall, as troops of the Second Battalion occupied a position on the left flank of the First Battalion, the line had moved 1,500 yards into Nurnberg itself. A total of 1,045 enemy soldiers were taken.

Company C-Cpl. Edward G. Wilkin is KIA. PFC Joseph A. Major and PFC Howard A. Thomas are WIA.

April 19–The 157th Infantry Regiment continued with its mission to clear the southern portion of Nurnberg. The First Battalion met very stiff resistance. Baker Company led the attack through a railroad underpass and was met on the north side by heavy machine-gun and sniper fire. The enemy also used bazooka and faustpatronen in their defense of the northern side of the railroad. Charlie

Company attempted to cross the railroad embankment but met the same type of resistance. Baker Company passed through the Second Battalion's sector and launched an attack through the warehouse district. Able Company followed to offer close support. The German defenders offered stiff resistance and progress was slow. Charlie Company broke contact at the embankment and followed the other companies through the warehouse district. By nightfall the First Battalion had reached the highway connecting Feucht and the main part of the city.

The Second Battalion met very stiff resistance. After three hours of house-to-house fighting against the same opposition that had held the First Battalion in check, E and F Companies were able to gain but a hundred yards. The battalion moved to the southeast along the Ludwig Canal while elements of the 179th Infantry Regiment relieved it at its former positions. The troops succeeded in cutting the Furth-Nurnberg highway at another point and pushed on to reach their objective. The Third Battalion met sporadic resistance as it advanced that day. All companies of the battalion reached their objectives and were slowly squeezed out by advancing troops of the 180th Infantry Regiment. By nightfall the sector of town had been cleared except for a small party of the old city. Contact with the Seventh Infantry on the northern flank had also been established.

Company C-2nd Lt. Leonard G. Zankel is WIA.

April 20–The 157th Infantry Regiment continued to clear small pockets of resistance throughout the day. The First Battalion's Able Company (phonetic identifications for companies) encountered heavy rifle fire in its attempt to clear the Rosenau woods. However, by aggressively attacking the woods, the company routed the enemy and a large number of enemy soldiers were taken. Charlie Company contacted the Seventh Infantry and outposted the south side of the Pognite River line. The battalion maintained motorized patrols in its sector until the close of the period. The Second Battalion moved forward until it contacted King Company and then returned to an assembly area. The Third Battalion's King Company advanced until it contacted elements of the Second Battalion whereupon it returned to an assembly area. Love Company was given the mission of clearing the marshalling yards and warehouses south of Rothenburger Street. Though some small-arms and machine-gun fire was met, the yards and warehouses were cleared by 1210. The battalion also started patrols in its own sector. Throughout the day, all the battalions reported picking up stragglers. By nightfall all organized resistance in the regimental sector and ceased.

Company C-PFC Robert D. Gorman is WIA.

April 21–Action was limited to skirmishes with groups of German soldiers attempting to infiltrate to the south. The First Battalion maintained motor patrols throughout the period, and it was one of these that engaged an enemy group in a firefight. The resistance was short-lived and some POWs were taken. Toward the close of the period, the battalion moved to Katzwang. The Third Battalion picked up enemy troops attempting to infiltrate after engaging them in a short firefight. The Second Battalion moved to an assembly area with the exception of Company K which participated in Seventh Army ceremonies. The Second Battalion patrolled its sector hourly with no contacts reported. It moved to the vicinity of Worseldorf as the period came to a close.

Company C-T/5 James V. Crane is WIA.

April 22–During the fighting in and around Nurnberg, German troops had ample time to destroy bridges, build roadblocks, and in general plant numerous obstacles in the way of any troop movement to the south. As a result, when the 157th Infantry Regiment resumed its attack to the south, the main difficulty encountered was these prepared obstacles. The Third Battalion mounted on tanks and at this time launched a twin-pronged assault to the south. Company K on the left flank met a column of horse-drawn and motorized vehicles. These were brought under fire and many casualties were inf licted. Company I led the right flank column. The Second and First Battalions remained in reserve and followed behind the attacking Third Battalion. Thirty towns were cleared during the day's activity, and though the roads were poor, the progress was very satisfactory.

April 23–Advancing troops of the 157th Infantry's Third Battalion found their road strewn with huge mud holes, roadblocks, and dead ends. The twin-pronged armored column crossed the Altmuhl River, though every bridge in the assigned areas had been blown. By nightfall the battalion had crossed the river and seized the high ground to the south. The First and Second Battalions continued in reserve and after crossing the Altmuhl River took positions on the high ground to the south.

April 24–The Third Battalion of the 157th Infantry Regiment continued its attack southward. After an early morning delay due to tanks being unable to cross a bridge, the columns moved on. Item Company led the right column's attack. So quick and surprising were these armored thrusts that a German artillery and tank convoy was forced to stand and fight in Monheim. After a battle that lasted for nearly six hours, the town was cleared. Love Company pushed through Item and secured Warehing. The First and Second Battalions remained in reserve and closely followed the Third.

That night Col. Walter P. O'Brien returned to his post as commanding officer of the regiment.

April 25–The 157th Infantry Regiment opened the day by continuing its attack southward. At the opening of the period, the First and Second Battalions passed through both columns of the Third. At 0800 the Third Battalion resumed its offensive to the south and in turn passed through the First and Second. Love Company cleared Blasnau and Gansheim. A bridge crossing a stream just south of Gansheim was blown when the infantry was but two hundred yards from it. The column forded the stream and continued forward. King Company pushed forward and cleared several small towns and woods. In the late afternoon it had reached Rohrbach whereupon the Second Battalion pushed through again. The First Battalion pushed through Love Company.

The plan was for the two battalions to seize the north side of the river and cross in assault boats. They were then to continue forward and establish a bridgehead. However, the river was anything but the beautiful blue Danube. A swift current made crossing the river extremely dangerous, and it was decided to wait until the next day. By the close of the period, the regiment had seized and controlled the northern bank of the Danube in its sector.

April 26–The First and Second Battalions crossed the Danube. Prior to the crossings, some casualties were caused by artillery, mortar, machine-gun, and small-arms fire. Apparently the enemy was determined to make the crossing a costly one. Engineers began working on a bridge at 2030 after elements of the two battalions had seized the far shore. Enemy artillery occasionally harassed the working engineers. The battalions reached their objectives by dusk and held their positions for the night. The Third Battalion remained in an assembly area during the entire period.

Company C-Pvt. Joseph Marshall and T/Sgt. Debro L. Newman are WIA.

April 27–Contact with the enemy was extremely light as troops of the 157th Infantry Regiment continued southward. In the early hours of this period, the First Battalion received a small counterattack. It was easily repelled. The First and Second Battalions continued to attack toward the bridgehead line and successfully cleared several towns. The Third Battalion, meanwhile, had crossed the Danube and had assembled with elements of the 191st Tank Battalion. By 1800 they were ready and the Third once again moved forward. By the close of the period, the Third Battalion had cleared numerous towns and had reached the bridgehead line in the towns of Walda, Schron, and Pottmes.

April 28–The Third Battalion continued its twin-pronged armored attack toward Munchen. Resistance was spotty throughout the day although two enemy columns were spotted and mauled during the resulting fights. During the morning hours, blown bridges slowed the attack, but it continued with excellent results. The First and Second Battalions continued to follow behind the two columns.

April 29–The Third Battalion launched a triple-pronged armored attack toward Munchen. Love Company occupied and cleared the town of Prittlbach, approximately two miles from the large town of Dachau. Advancing toward a canal that ran east-west through Dachau, the doughboys discovered that all bridges crossing this canal in their sector had been blown. A check via radio revealed that a similar condition existed in the entire battalion sector.

The situation looked anything but good. A German woman cycling northward on the road was stopped and questioned by the American troops. She revealed that she had just come from Munchen and had crossed a bridge in the town of Dachau itself. Love Company swung quickly into action, mounted the tanks, and raced for Dachau.

German soldiers scattered to the four winds as the armored column tore into the town, spitting lead from its gun to all sides. This unorthodox approach caused much confusion among the enemy personnel. The lead tank had reached a point just twenty yards from the bridge when the structure blew up, raining debris upon all those riding the tank.

The company commander, 1st Lt. L.R. Stewart, and the first sergeant, Robert Wilson, made a personal reconnaissance of the canal in town and found a nearby footbridge intact. They radioed the message to the rear and were ordered to protect the bridge at all costs. The men took their posts and waited.

The concentration camp at Dachau was the most infamous of all the German horror camps. Originally created to purge those members of the Reich who spoke against National Socialism, it became a place to house and exterminate many Poles, French, Russians, Czechs, Greeks, Italians, and Serbs. Throughout Germany, the name Dachau struck horror into the hearts of the people.

On April 29, 1945, Third Battalion liberated the concentration camp, and at the close of the day regimental units were near the outskirts of Munich.—Hugh F. Foster III.]

[June 9, 2013--The travel to Munich was difficult. Germany had floods not seen for a hundred years. Trains could not travel because of the f looding. Instead of riding in a sleeper car, we had to take a Greyhound bus overnight. Arriving in the early hours of the morning, we decided to visit Dachau. Words cannot describe Dachau. I will say that the Germans did not hide their past with the Nazis and the Holocaust. The displays and information were overwhelming. I had a sick feeling in my stomach the entire day at Dachau. Being a history teacher, I think I can understand why things happen, but I cannot understand Dachau.—Mark Kirchgassner]

Dachau June 2013

Tattered clothes of prisoners killed
SC Photo-T/4 Sidney Blau

As the Thunderbird infantrymen made their way into the camp, evidence of Nazi handiwork stared them in the face. Boxcars on a railroad siding contained human beings, each starved to thinness, each starved to death. They had been waiting on the siding until they could be removed on to the crematorium to be burned to ashes. Even from this stench of death, the advancing infantrymen had pulled several who were still alive. They were nothing more than skin and bones.

Here they saw reason enough for their long and bitter struggle against Nazism. The bodies were unidentifiable. They could have been Americans.

Some turned their heads, white-faced and sick. Others with horrible fascination looked at the pile of dead. All clutched their guns a bit tighter, squared their jaws, and walked forward with a grimmer purpose in mind. As one infantryman said, "I've been in the army for thirty-nine months. I've been overseas in combat for twenty-three. I'd gladly go through it all again if I knew that things like this would be stopped."

Advancing into camp, the leading elements of the company were met by three prisoners. They were walking skeletons.

Enraged and shocked by this display of wanton brutality, the Americans swept into camp. SS troopers and prison guards fleeing the Americans were shot and killed. Some prisoners while attempting to break out of their enclosure were electrocuted by the electrically charged barbed- wire fence. Others more fortunate succeeded in making their escape. They turned on their guards and beat them with sticks and their fists. The jailers were kicked, gouged, and beaten by the avenging inmates as if with every blow they were being repaid.

A Pole volunteered to point out several of the more "notable" sights in the camp. The first was the dog-pen enclosure. "The guards used dogs to help them track down anybody that might have succeeded in escaping," said the Pole. The dogs had their own kitchen and received better food than the prisoners. "The SS troopers would stand a prisoner against the wall, nude, and tap at his testicles with a stick," continued the Pole. "The huge dogs would snap and rip the organs from the body." He led the way to the adjacent crematorium.

"Here, about 100 to 150 men were put to death each day," he said. "They were stripped of their clothing and taken to a room which closely resembled a shower room."

What looked like shower heads were evenly spaced on the ceiling, and the floor gently sloped as if to provide proper drainage. The only ominous feature was that the room lacked windows.

He led them way to the gravel pits behind the building, pointing to huge piles of discarded clothing as he passed them. "Live men once wore these," he said. Reaching the pits, he told of how men had been forced to kneel in the pits to be shot. He pointed to an embankment at the foot of which was a ditch covered by a wooden grating.

"The men were forced to kneel like this," he continued as he knelt to demonstrate the position, "and then be shot. Their blood drained into the ditch."

Brown stains were everywhere.

A Russian, thin and emaciated from his starvation diet, told of the food the prisoners were given. "One loaf of bread for eight men each day," he told. "For dinner one liter of water. For supper some tea. Twice a week they were treated to a bowl of soup. Hundreds died from starvation daily."

A former prisoner, clutching a piece of white bread to his bosom, was mobbed by the other prisoners as they sought a piece. His clothing was torn from his body; the bread lay upon the ground in crumbs.

The prison camp itself was barbed-wired and electrically charged. To touch this meant certain death. Just inside the fence was a huge ditch; just outside, a fast-running stream, its far side lined with pillboxes. The main gate bore the inscription "Albeit Macht Frei," "Work makes free."

Within the camp was another enclosure. In here were the quarantine cases, those with typhus and tuberculosis. In here were the walking dead.

Those confined at Dachau were so overcome at the appearance of the Americans that some sang songs of their homeland; others danced and others wept tears of joy, others whose spirits had so been broken by the long years of imprisonment stood petrified and stone-faced as the Americans went about the job of cleaning house. When the camp was cleared, it was turned over to the Allied military government.

The First and Second Battalions pushed through the Third Battalion and continued the attack toward Munchen. Resistance was scattered and light. The troops made excellent gains to the city limits of Munchen before stopping for the night.

April 30–The First Battalion of the 157th Infantry Regiment resumed the attack toward the center of town. It met little resistance and captured a concentration camp with eight thousand prisoners. Able Company was left to guard the camp until relieved by King Company. The other two companies pressed forward and contacted elements of the Forty-Second Division. As the period drew to a close, they had crossed a river and were in Munchen proper. The Second Battalion moved forward. Scattered resistance was encountered and some pockets had to be cleared, but by late afternoon the battalion was moving in Munich with little or no opposition. The Third Battalion had its Item and Love Companies remain in position guarding the Dachau concentration camp until relieved by corps troops. At that time the companies moved to the southeastern edge of Dachau and remained there. King Company relieved Able Company at the other concentration camp.

Company C-PFC John M. Idol Jr. is WIA.

[April 30, 1945, was the last day of combat for the regiment.—Hugh Foster III]

* * *

[Jared's Blog:
June 9, 2013--Our journey to Munich has tested us. First, we had to wait around all day in Venice. You might think that wouldn't be an issue, but Venice wasn't our kind of town. Finally, we went to catch our train and discovered that it had changed stations. So we had to sprint to catch a train at a different station. We jumped on that train and didn't have tickets. We reached the Mestre station with two minutes to board our train to Munich. We checked the board for the departure platform and couldn't find our train. We ran to customer service to ask. I watched our departure time of 8:57 come and go on my Timex and my heart sank. We found out the train was canceled because of heavy rain along the way in Germany. Cancellations weren't posted on the board. Very convenient, huh? We were unsure what to do and were barely able to communicate with the ticket agent. He told us to see the bus people. At 8:59, we walked into the bus office, which was closing at 9:00. The plan didn't go quite as expected, but we are making the five-hundred-kilometer trip to Munich by bus.

Funny moment: I had to use Rita's deodorant, body spray, and face cleanser on the bus since our bags are stowed underneath. So, Sarah Leiker, if you are attracted to the smell of Dry Idea and cucumber-melon body spray, you are in luck. St. Rita is the saint for the impossible. She was working today for us! We made it to Munich! The only bad part is that we got in at 4 a.m. and can't check into our hostel until 2 p.m. Nothing like sausage and kraut for breakfast at 6 a.m.! We are off to the former concentration camp in Dachau for a 9 a.m. tour. The Forty-Fifth was one of the first Allied Divisions to enter the camp.

* * *

Dachau was a Nazi concentration camp just outside of Munich. It was designed to house six thousand prisoners but held up to thirty thousand. The facility was also a major base for the Nazi SS. Everything at the facility has been bulldozed except the perimeter of the concentration camp, the barracks foundations, two barracks, a maintenance building, a jail, and a crematorium. As the war progressed, not only Jews but homosexuals, opponents of Hitler's regime, citizens of rival countries, and many other people the Nazi party considered of lesser value were taken prisoner.

Upon arrival, prisoners were stripped of their identities and belongings. Prisoners were forced to work long hours of heavy labor and were fed only four hundred calories per day. Every day prisoners would have to stand at perfect attention for up to several hours no matter the weather. Often those too weak would collapse, resulting in punishment. Prisoners were tortured and beaten. With overcrowding, many were killed and incinerated. According to Nazi records, the camp processed almost 289,000 people. Executions were well into the tens of thousands, though records of the killings weren't always kept. At the time of liberation, Dachau housed more than thirty-one thousand people. The Thunderbirds succeeded again!

Due to their graphic and terrible nature, I left out many pictures and stories from the camp. The Nazis showed a complete disregard for humanity, and what happened at Dachau is completely unimaginable. The images are the worst things I have ever seen.

We had dinner at the world-famous Hof brahaus tonight. We sat with a German man because every table was full. It was a neat experience, but I thought the dinner tasted just like the one my wife and I had on our first date in Newport, Kentucky. We learned that much of the original hall was destroyed in World War II bombings. The rebuilt place is thriving.

Tonight before bed, we met a world-renowned landscape artist from Uganda named Paulo Akiiki. You can check him out at pauloakiiki.com

The Austrian and German country sides offered some spectacular views today. There must be something about this place: Kirch just bought f lowers to grow. Yes, you read that right.

We took it easy at night because tomorrow we will have a long day in Munich. It rained all night.

* * *

We learned a lot and not very much yesterday about Munich and World War II. I know that doesn't make much sense, but bear with me. During World War II about 60 to 70 percent of Munich was destroyed.

After liberating the Dachau concentration camp, the Forty-Fifth moved on with several other divisions to liberate Munich. At this point the Allies were moving through Europe with so much force that it was only a matter of time before the war was won. The Germans were so depleted that they put up little resistance as the Allies marched into Munich.

June 12, 2013--We took a bus tour of Munich, visiting several landmarks. We saw a castle and historical and government buildings and spent time walking around the park that hosted the 1972 Olympics. The X Games will be in Munich at the end of the month. It was pretty cool to watch all the ramps and other facilities being built.

In the afternoon, we did laundry and explored the city. Munich is a safe city, so in the evening we explored it to see how the Germans live. We met several English-speaking citizens and learned a lot about their culture. Munich provides a lane just for bicycles between the road and the sidewalk, so there are lots of cyclists. They have a saying in Munich that goes "Ding ding dead." If you walk in that lane, cyclists will give you a ding with their bike bells, but they won't stop. They will hit you. We got dinged a couple times out of our ignorance, but never got hit.

After exploring the city more and becoming better educated, I see that our original tour was clearly inadequate. We were able to learn World War II history later in the day by hanging out with local citizens for the evening. Germany is a beautiful place, and I look forward to learning more about the country, the people, and the culture.—Jared Leiker]

May 1945–The month of May saw the end of hostilities in the European Theater, but for the men of the 157th Infantry there was nothing dramatic about it. They captured central Munich with little difficulty and on May 1, 1945, established a command post in Hitler's famous Munich beer hall, mainly for publicity purposes. Billeted in the residential districts where bombing had done little damage, they began polishing their shoes, taking close-order drill, cleaning their weapons, and standing reveille and retreat as befitted soldiers serving in occupational status. Motorized patrols roamed the streets at night, ordering civilians into their homes after curfew hours and stopping minor riots caused frequently by released Allied POWs who had just cause for celebration.

German prisoners
SC Photo-T/4 A. B. Musser

Krista, Jared and Mark in Munich

The official announcement declaring hostilities at an end came on May 9, 1945, but the 157th Infantry took it as a matter of course. The Hitler dynasty had collapsed, but overshadowing the good news was the constant threat that the regiment, with the Forty-Fifth Division, might suddenly be sent to the Pacific Theater. Few cherished the thought of going into battle again, this time against the Japanese, but all were prepared come what may. As always, they assumed the attitude "If ya gotta go, ya gotta go" and determined to enjoy a life in peace as much as possible. A group of four-year men was sent home, probably to be discharged from the army, and according to plan, others soon were to go. But the vast majority of men comprising the 157th Infantry were relatively new to the service and with reason took a cryptic view of the future.

May 6-Company C-Pvt. Virgil S. Key-KIA.

May 10–May 31–The 157th Infantry Regiment improved its installations and expanded its recreational program. Taking over the former Jungend Stadium on Dante Strasse in Munich, special services made excellent use of the structure. Several baseball diamonds were laid out on the field, and the cinder track was restored to its pre-war condition. In the evenings, outdoor movies were shown. The rooms in the interior of the stadium were used to house the regimental photo shop, hot showers were available to the men of the organization during the daytime, and a fully equipped gymnasium was at the disposal of the more athletic members of the outfit.

A former German military installation in the heart of the Bavarian capital was taken over and turned into a provisional training center. Christened "West Point II," the school taught such basic training subjects as close-order drill, bayonet drill, assembly and disassembly of the M-1 rifle, nomenclature of the Browning Automatic Rifle, military courtesy, and discipline. Courses in military government and military law were also included in the curriculum. This was to help the former combatants of the organization make a painless readjustment to garrison life and to train new noncoms so that they would be able to instruct the men under their command. Gradually, the men began to realize that the war in Europe had actually ended and everything possible was being done to make their set-up as comfortable as possible.

However, a close watch was maintained on newspapers reporting the events in the Pacific. The combat-hardened doughboys, now laboring under a spit-and-polish routine, assumed a policy of watchful waiting. For what, they did not know.

[May 29, 1945-I was liberated from Stalag 12 A. The Australian tanks arrived and our guards disappeared. I weighed 157 pounds when I returned to the front line in December 1944 and weighed 115 pounds when liberated in May. I did not have a shower during that time until I arrived at a hospital in England sometime around the first of June. As a POW, besides minimal food, I experienced no heat in the winter, two men had to share a small bed and sleep in the fetal position and lice infestation around the neck and waist. -Richard Adams]

Richard Adams

[War: It is an experience that you only live through one time. If you are lucky enough."—Richard Adams]

[The plan to invade France from the North and South worked and on May 8, 1945 the war in Europe was over.—John Kirchgassner

[In its 667 days overseas, the regiment was in battle for about 470 days. During this time soldiers of the regiment were awarded three Medals of Honor, twenty Distinguished Service Crosses, 376 Silver Stars, 1,054 Bronze Stars, and 1,694 Purple Hearts.—Hugh F. Foster III]

* * *

Other blog entries from our journey:

[Jared's Blog:

June 9, 2013--After resting in Rome, it was time for the Forty-Fifth to get ready to make the final push to take down the Germans and save humanity. The plan was to return to sea and come ashore in France. They would land at St. Maxime and push east. Anticipating another fierce battle on the beach, the Forty-Fifth would need to prepare. The division moved back south to train at Naples, Anzio, and Salerno, Italy. Returning to these sites, which had been hell for them, must have been emotional, but they had to learn from their struggles in these places and be ready to fight again.

Now:

June 8, 2013--We are off to Venice, Italy, for a quick stop. We had to get up pretty early, but the Italian countryside offers some lovely sights for my tired eyes. This high-speed train is the way to travel. It's not quite a Tiger bus, but it's pretty darn nice.

We made it safely to Venice. It's a pretty neat city from what we have seen in the walk from the train station to the hostel. We were particularly struck by an ambulance boat that went storming down a canal.

Venice is definitely a tourist town. After the novelty of the canals wears off, you're left with tons of shops, many of the high-end variety. The streets are extremely difficult to navigate. We've often been wandering aimlessly, but this is also an enjoyable way to see the city. I'm glad we came to Venice, but it's a tourist trap. I'll be ready to leave for Munich tomorrow. I didn't know that the Germans used Venice for their naval operations. Originally I didn't think Venice played a major role in World War II, but I was wrong. I was naive to think the city was immune to the largest war.

We have today free in Venice. We stayed up late last night listening to music on the canal, playing cards, and talking to other travelers. We slept in a bit, then had a typical European breakfast on the back patio. Church this morning, and then stroll the streets until our train leaves for Munich tonight.

While we were out getting lost, we randomly stumbled across a small plaque on a random wall. The plaque was a dedication to remember the innocent civilians who lost their lives. About the time we were trying to figure out what the plaque said, a local citizen came up and started talking to us. In our discussion he said that his mom worked on the docks for the Germans. He grew up only a few blocks from there. During the war the English bombed the harbor. Their bombs weren't very accurate and several of them landed in a local borough killing 50-60 Venetians.

The local docks today are used to host the massive cruise liners that come in. That brings us to our other interesting event if the day. Mark stumbled across a protest going on. Later in the day, we went back and observed the protesters. They were protesting against cruise liners parking directly at the island. The massive ships move so much water that they are eroding some of the island. The protest started in a local circle and moved to boats. It was really neat.

Finally and most importantly...Happy Birthday to my beautiful niece, Kerrigan. Sorry I missed your birthday bash, and am not able to talk to you on your special day. Hope you had a great day, and I Love You.

Flash back to Anzio for a quick story. During the storming of Anzio, Robert Kirchgassner shared a foxhole for quite some time with S/Sgt. Max L. Johnson. Max would write poems for Robert to send back to Indiana to his sweetheart, Anna Jo (Rita's mom, who still lives in Indiana. Note: Anna Jo, passed away December 19, 2013).

Bob's Best Girl

Bob showed me a pictured of his best girl.
You can tell it just by looking that she's really a pearl.
It's gals like her at home
That make everything worthwhile.
You can have the girls you pin up, with their glamour and their fame, But
with guys like us there's one thing that will always be the same.
Now when the fighting's heavy and the shells begin to fly, You
just keep right on going; you're out to do or die.
You know what kept you going along with all the rest.
It wasn't thoughts of being killed that kept your mind awhirl.
It was just the thoughts of the picture, The one like Bob's best girl.
—S/Sgt. Max L. Johnson
Anzio, 1944

June 19, 2013--We made it to France! Strasbourg, to be exact. We got stranded here for the night. We were forced to grab a hotel and get a train out tomorrow at 6:29 to Nancy and then to Epinal. This is definitely an adventure.

Now:

June 25, 2013--Trying to wrap up this journey of a lifetime is nearly impossible, so will just call this the final travel blog entry.

This journey has allowed us to learn so much about the Thunderbirds. Visiting the places where they fought has been a pleasure and a learning experience. Now when we read reports or books about World War II, we find it much easier to understand and to imagine where these men were and what they saw. The people we met along the way were friendly and helpful. The tour guides, local citizens, site experts, and historians, particularly Lise, were invaluable. We cannot thank them enough for spending time with us. The Forty-Fifth Yahoo group, Dave Kerr, and many others gave us support along the way and taught us a great deal.

Besides those involved specifically with the Forty-Fifth Division, many other people have helped make this trip the experience it was. My wife Sarah has always supported my crazy adventures and ideas. All of our families have helped out while we were gone, sharing our enthusiasm for chasing this dream. The Lawrenceburg Community School Corporation and our local media supported who promoted our journey and shared in the excitement. The Lawrenceburg High School football staff picked up the slack while Kirch and I were gone for an entire month of workouts. Most important, the Lilly Foundation provided a Teacher Creativity grant to make all this possible. This inspiring program gives teachers opportunities they would otherwise never have.

The Thunderbirds are a special group of heroes, ordinary Americans willing to take on the world's greatest challenge and to make the ultimate sacrifice for something greater than themselves. I don't know if there will ever be another generation of men willing to battle the way they did. Any attempt to summarize what I learned about them or to describe who they truly are would do them an injustice. All I know is that they are heroes.

I want to leave you with a picture of a monument that we saw in Berlin. The monument shows a mother holding a soldier on a battlefield. It does not mention the soldier's country, but that's not its purpose. The monument is supposed to show how terribly sad war is for all people and for all nations.

Never forgotten: Richard Badgett and Roscoe Prince.—Jared Leiker]

To read Jared's blog and view his photos, go to the following site: http://blog.travelpod.com/travel-blog/jcleiker3/1/tpod.html

Epilogue

[ON OCTOBER 27, 1944, AT 1500 hours, Robert Kirchgassner received multiple penetrating wounds in the left and right anterior of his chest and left scapular area and lacerating wounds to the right lobe of the liver. Both of his lungs were lacerated, his ribs were severely fractured, and his diaphragm perforated, with lacerating wounds on the left lower lobe. All this was the result of enemy shell action near a small town near Jeanmenil, France.

Dad received emergency treatment at the Eleventh Field Hospital. Thanks to John Schweisthal's quick action, he arrived at the hospital at 1830 hours. His condition was critical, with a blood pressure reading of 0/0, according to the hospital report. Surgery was done on the right chest to remove foreign bodies, and the wound was enlarged to suture two perforations of the right diaphragm. (Dad told me that the doctors did not expect him to live and sewed his chest together with only seventeen stitches.) Medical reports show that Dad almost passed away the first night. The drainage tube in his chest fell out, and he was drowning in his own blood. Blood had to be constantly sucked out, and he was placed in a head-down position.

At 1900 hours he was given four units of plasma. His blood pressure was 110/40. At 1920 hours, he was given a unit of blood, and by 1930 hours his blood pressure was

120/55. The only medications available to him were sulfa and penicillin. (Dad had served one year, eight months, and sixteen days in the European Theater of Operations before his injuries left him unable to return to his company.) For two days he had hemoptysis.

On November 6, 1944, Dad was transferred to the Ninety Third Evacuation Hospital and on November 11 to the forty-sixth general hospital in France where the left anterior chest wound was closed and his right chest aspirated. (At this hospital Dad was presented with the Bronze Star that had been awarded to him in September of 1944.) The other wounds were healing slowly. After a stop at the 217th General Hospital, Dad was sent to the 91st General Hospital on December 18, 1944, where he remained until January 12, 1945. At this hospital a large metallic foreign body was removed from his right axilla. All wounds healed without infection. Dad's writings and primary records lead me to believe he was transferred between Paris and London for medical treatment. Dad departed for the United States by boat after being released from the 318th Station Hospital in France(where he was placed for rehabilitation and limited duty) on February 14, 1945, and arrived in this country on February 23. He boarded a train for Denver, Colorado, via Camp Edwards, Massachusetts, and arrived on February 26. After rehabilitation at Fitzsimons General Hospital in Denver, he arrived at Wakeman Convalescent Hospital, Camp Atterbury, Indiana, on April 4, 1945. Dad's only medical complaint at that time was a constant dull pain in the left anterior chest wall. He said it hurt worse when the weather changed. His medical report said, "Well developed, well-nourished white male soldier not acutely ill. Seventy one inches and weighed 170 pounds. (Ten more pounds than when he had enlisted.) Uses alcohol moderately and uses pack of cigarettes per week. No drugs or history of familial diseases. Had measles and mumps as a child and malaria in Sicily in August of 1943 with no recurrence." Dad was officially honorably discharged from the army on July 5, 1945.

Dad after the war.

Floyd Hornbach, Murriel Weber and Dad.

Grandma Dorie and Mom planned to travel by train to Camp Attebury to visit dad. Heavy rains made the trip impossible. (Thunderbird weather.)

Dad returned to his beloved farm in Yorkville, Indiana, in July of 1945, almost nine months after he was critically wounded in battle. While he was away serving his country, Grandma Dorie went to daily Mass at St. Martin Church and lit a blessed candle in for his safe return. After learning about the wounds he suffered in battle, everyone thought his journey back to health was nothing short of miraculous. My brother-in-law, Floyd Trossman, said Dad must have had a strong will to live. I believe that God answered my grandmother's prayers and sent her son back to her.

Dad, Esther Klein Detzel and Harry Nordmeyer.

Not long after he returned to Yorkville, Dad proposed to his girlfriend, Anna Josephine Hoffmeier, oldest child of Joe and Bess Hoffmeier, also residents of Yorkville. Before they married, Dad went to the probate court in Cincinnati, Ohio, to have his name legally changed to Kirchgassner. The court record reads, "It is, therefore, by the Court ordered and decreed that the name of the Petitioner be and it is hereby changed from Robert Lee Nordmeyer to Robert Lee Kirchgassner as prayed for on the 21st of August, 1945."

Mom and Dad were married at St. Martin Church at 7:30 a.m. on September 1, 1945. Mom said she woke up to a rainy morning, but after putting a statue of the Blessed Mother outside, the rain dissipated. A reception followed at the Kirchgassner family farm with a short honeymoon to North Vernon, Indiana. Though Dad had almost given his life for his country, some invitees did not attend the wedding because of the circumstances of his birth.

Mom and Dad on their wedding day
Witnesses: Francis Hoffmeier, L. Miller and Jean Bonomini.

Mom and Dad resided at the Kirchgasssner farm until Dad finished building our home on Burtzelbach Road. We grew up on twenty acres of property connected to the Kirchgassner farm. A lane across the field was our highway to the house owned by Grandma Dorie and Grandpa Mike. We celebrated all the holidays there and at Grandpa Joe and Grandma Bessie's place. We were the only grandchildren on the Kirchgassner side, and we were treated as such. Throughout childhood, we were taught the same principles by Grandma Dorie and my Dad: to love our Catholic faith (St. Martin Parish), our family, and Yorkville, Indiana, in that order.

Our life centered on those three things when we were kids, and we shared these ideals with our extended family. Grandma Dorie would take us to Mass whenever she could, bring us back to her house, and tell us stories of the past that mesmerized us. The *Rose Parade* on New Year's Day and the series *Wagon Train* were must-sees when we were with her. On Sundays, if we were not milking the cows or at Sunday benediction, she would teach us to play cards. What a delight it would be to see her again in her farm dress, standing in the barnyard, surrounded by her chickens, and calling for Grandpa Mike to come for supper.

Mom, Grandma Mary Nordmeyer. (1st Row)
Grandpa Mike, Aunt Theresa Detzel and Grandma Dorie. (2nd Row)

Though Dad was classified more than 80 percent disabled from wounds suffered in the war, he never once complained. Roman "Butch" Fuchs, a friend of Uncle Red's, said that when Dad came home in 1945, he could put a fist in one of the wounds. Dad and Butch worked together building fence for Wilbur Hornbach. Butch remembers, when dad took off his shirt, his back looked like someone threw acid on it as it was burnt that badly. Dad underwent an exam at the VA in 1947 and would not return there until forty years later when he sought medical treatment.

Uncle Red and Butch Fuchs

Dad worked twenty-five-plus years as a laborer at the Yorkville feedmill to support his family. Cornelius Widolff, who had served with the US Marine Corps at Iwo Jima, was his employer. Farmers would bring their grain to the mill for Dad to grind, and he would put the ground feed in sacks. Every day he would come home on his lunch break to read the *Cincinnati Enquirer.*

Cornelius Widolff "Dutch" and his wife Rita "Mickey

But after World War II, society changed even in Yorkville. Uncle Robert Hoffmeier once told me that of all the men and women who left Yorkville to serve, only two worked as full-time farmers upon their return. With farming on the decline, Dad left the feedmill and went to work for the Dearborn County Highway Department in the early 1970s. The department was the only other place my father worked until his retirement.

Girlfriends at the feedmill.

Six children were born to Mom and Dad: Essie (January, 20, 1947), Dan (March 9, 1948), Mary (May 11, 1949), John (October 13, 1950), Rita (March 15, 1953), and Mark (April 23, 1958). When we were quite young, Dad taught us how to fish and hunt; he always said that we needed to know these skills. How proud he was to be an American—just as the Romans valued their citizenship in ancient times. I always think of him fighting on some of the same land where Julius Caesar battled for Rome two millennia ago. Caesar had his standard-bearers, but my father had the American flag. As Toby Keith sings in "Courtesy of the Red, White and Blue," "My daddy served in the army ... but he flew a flag in our yard till the day he died. He wanted my mother, my brother, my sister and me to grow up happy in the land of the free." That was my dad! The flag always flew at the Kirchgassner farm.

Our family was a top priority in Dad's life. The larger the family grew, the happier he was. Christmas Eve was always set aside for a family gathering. In his later years, Dad would sit in his rocking chair by the wood stove, waiting for everyone to arrive. He was eager to hold the infant grandchildren. And that is where he stayed the entire evening, rocking and feeding the babies while enjoying the clamor of our family.

Dad and Daniel

Essie, Dad, and Kim

Zak, Mark, Dad and Brooks

Dad and Abby

When it came to sports, basketball was always his favorite—he would never let his sons play football. All three sons played varsity basketball and played in a regional game. Dad taught them the fundamentals from the time they were small. (Grandma Dorie did not even want the boys to play basketball. She thought they would get hurt.) When the next generation of Kirchgassners went on to play football, Dad kept up with the games but worried about the potential for injury. However, Notre Dame Football was a must-see for him every season thanks to his son Mark. (And I wonder if it had anything to do with his chaplain during WWII who was from Notre Dame.) Dad also loved Indiana University basketball. Sorry, Paul Trossman, with the tie, Purdue University came in second. Coach Bobby Knight was a big favorite.

As children, we were part of a working family on a farm. Chores were a way of life. There were no Saturday morning cartoons or movies for the Kirchgassner kids. We never saw the endings of many black-and-white Tarzan movies because we were sent outside to work. Every summer we grew vegetables, raised beef and poultry, and picked blackberries on the edge of the woods. We canned or froze vegetables, meats, and fruits so that we would have food for a family of eight throughout the winter. During the summer there was work to be done every day.

I dreaded two things about preparing food for the winter: getting chicken entrails on me or getting smacked in the back of the head with a mud clod while digging potatoes on Labor Day weekend. John and Mark had wicked right arms. I cannot forget to mention Friday nights. After a long workweek, we were treated to a glass of pop, a delicacy that we always eagerly anticipated. I took my pop warm, without ice, since I figured I could get more of it. (I still do to this day.) Plus we could watch *Rawhide*, our favorite show, with Clint Eastwood as Rowdy Yates. If Mom made us pray the rosary before the TV was turned on, my brother Dan would always choose to lead, watching the clock out of the corner of his eye. He made sure we did not miss one minute of the episode.

The only movie of note that I saw with my Dad was *Patton*. George Patton was his favorite general in World War II. Dad also enjoyed watching the TV series *Combat*, though he pointed out that on the show, the soldiers knew they would be back next week. During the war, they couldn't be sure of the next minute. He also liked watching the Billy Graham crusades.

Dad especially enjoyed nature. He loved to plant a garden, reap the harvest and pick the first tomato of the season. To him there was nothing prettier than the night sky, a rainbow, a sunset, or the North Star. He took many pictures of rainbows, and he would gather us kids wherever we were when he spotted one. When I was vacationing with the Robert Schaeff ler/Karen Geis families on a beach in South Carolina in July of 2014, I brought this manuscript to work on during my stay. I planned to stay inside and write while everyone was enjoying the surf and the sun. But then came Hurricane Arthur and all became housebound. The hurricane skirted us, and after the storm, there was a double rainbow over the ocean. I could only believe that Dad was encouraging me to continue my work.

Robert Schaeff ler/Karen Geis family and friends

Another Kirchgassner trait is a love of photography, which comes not only from Dad but from Grandma Dorie. But if Dad, like his mother, hated a photo he would literally cut himself out of the photo, especially if someone took the picture before he was ready. (Notice Grandpa Mike was cut out of the wedding photo. Guess it was not a good photo op for him.) Dad would also hide behind someone if he was not feeling photogenic. Today we do not cut ourselves out of pictures. The delete button serves that same purpose. Ask Barbara Rennekamp and Rachel Mersmann how many times they stand behind someone when their photos are being taken or have grabbed the camera from Megan Swales to hit "delete." I am the same way when looking at photos of myself.

One photo that didn't get deleted:
Nat and I

I could not find any photos from our first family vacation, which was to Parma, Ohio, to visit the Schweisthals in the 1960s. Dan could not go because he was working at the Monarch Grill, owned by Jerry and Foxie Martini (Jerry is Aunt Ruthie's husband), but the rest of us packed up the station wagon and headed north. It was my first time traveling outside the Cincinnati area. My parents instructed me to be on my best behavior, which was sometimes a challenge. I think I did okay. In Cincinnati, I saw a pop vending machine and city lights for the first time. The lights seemed magical, as if lit by Disney's Tinkerbell. This preteen was captivated by those lights, since the night lights in the country came only from the moon and lightning bugs.

Aunt Ruthie and Uncle Jerry on their
wedding day with Aunt Jean and Uncle Ed.

The Schweisthals in turn came to Yorkville during many summers, but no one discussed the war when the kids were around. We doubt it was ever mentioned except to catch up on old friends. The only fact about their service together that we knew as kids was that John had saved my dad's life in World War II. We never knew until recently that something had happened to John on the same day. The records show that he was also admitted to the field hospital and did not return to action.

John and Katherine Schweisthal

The bond between my father and John was unbreakable due to the amount of time they had spent together and their shared experiences in battle throughout Italy and France. The only address that Dad would have given John in France in 1944 was: Robert Kirchgassner, Yorkville, Indiana. Yet without all the communication technology that we have today, the families were always in touch. I will always wonder how they made the transition back to their former lives after the war.

Bob and John years after the war

And in the twenty-first century, seventy years later, the Kirchgassners and the Schweisthals were together again in the summer of 2014. We met at Widolff's where Dad worked most of his life and where his son Dan works now in his semi-retirement. The third generation of Kirchgassner met Katherine Schweisthal, John's wife. Funny how life circles back around.

Katherine and the next generations of the Kirchgassners. June 2014

Katherine, Brandon and Dan

Dad never liked attention drawn to himself and didn't want his children to do wrong. My father always said he did not want to give anyone something negative to say about the family. Some of the scars from his birth remained with him throughout his life, and he was proud of and loved the Kirchgassner name. He did not want anything or anyone to taint it.

When he was not with the family, Dad could relax in the company of John Schweisthal, fishing with Charlie Wells, or playing cards after his retirement with Charlie Wells, Dutch Widolff, Charlie Widolff, Dan Bertotti, Mark Widolff and Charlie White.

Dad also enjoyed the company of Mom's siblings and their spouses (Edward and his wife Jean, Jean and her husband Ted, Robert and his wife Joan, William and his wife Lou, and Ruth and her husband Jerry) and their families. The gatherings on summer weekends with the Hoffmeier family on Grandpa Joe and Grandma Bessie's farm were packed with extended members of the Hayes family. Hayes was Grandma Bessie's maiden name. Riding horses, jumping from the loft into the haystack, and fishing were among the festivities available for the grandchildren. We never knew what the word "bored" meant.

Joseph & Bess Hoffmeier Family-
Ruth, Anna Jo, Jean, Joan, Red, Bill, Ed,
Grandma Bessie and Grandpa Jo

Dad and Uncle Ed

For me, however, the highlight of those summer days was when darkness approached and we played "ghost in the graveyard." The yard was a perfect fit for the game. The area had huge trees with long, droopy branches, a fenced-in border, and f lower beds lining a sloping terrain that led to fruit trees growing on the right side of the house. The landscape gave us many places to hide in the shadowy dusk. I don't know how many times Nancy Hoffmeier Davis, Gary Bonomini, or I got clotheslined bolting out of those shadows. We would race as fast as we could to "home base" on the left side of the house, and invariably one of us would run into Grandma Bessie's clothesline. The metal line strung across the yard caught us at neck level, and the pain was so intense upon impact that we would drop to our knees. We were certain that we had broken our windpipes and would never speak again. However, the pain was never great enough for us to quit playing or to tell an adult. We were just a little more cautious the next time.

Nancy, Rita and Regina

Gary

Mary John, Julie and Dave. (1st Row)
Susie, Bill, Joe and Pat. (2nd Row)

Hayes cousins at the farm
Essie and Dan in front

Uncle Bill and Aunt Lou on their wedding day

But life continues and changes. The Kirchgassner children grew up and after high school went to college. Essie graduated from Good Samaritan School of Nursing and the other five siblings graduated from Marian College. Three of the children had weddings in a six-month period. The grandchildren arrived and the family continued to grow. Life settled into a familiar pattern. My siblings and I were not prepared when Dad was diagnosed with cancer soon after the start of 1993. (He had diabetes and suffered a stroke when he was in his sixties, but managed the diabetes and recovered from the stroke.) I had never thought about my dad's mortality—or the possibility of life without him. We spent many days in tears, knowing what lay ahead for my dad. The doctor had given him no more than a year to live.

On March 15, 1993, my fortieth birthday, Dad had his first chemotherapy treatment. He told me that he had been in a hospital forty years ago and might as well be in one again that day. His prognosis was never good, and the fragments of shrapnel still scattered throughout his body did not help. It did not take long for the cancer to spread.

Dad was in his beloved Yorkville for the last time on a Saturday in November of 1993. I stood in the barnyard as the ambulance departed, taking a left on Leatherwood Road and transporting him to the Veterans hospital in Cincinnati where he would finish out his life. The day was dismal and gray. Dan, the eldest son, was by his side and watched as our patriarch was secured in the ambulance to start his final journey home.

I took one sweeping, 360-degree look at the house and the farm as the ambulance faded from my sight. Memories came f looding in, beginning with the move to the Kirchgassner home on Leatherwood Road in the spring of 1970 after the passing of Grandma Dorie. Grandpa Mike had passed earlier, before dawn in his sleep on Easter Sunday, April 10, 1966. Mark and I stayed home from school and helped Dad move furniture using a hay wagon from Burtzelbach Road to Leatherwood Road. Our new neighbors were Willard and Florence Aust, Charles and Bernice Wells, Lawrence and Marilyn Joerger and their children welcomed us to our new residence.

Deb Wells Amburgey. (1st Row)
Angie Aust White, Jane Aust Hiltz and Rita

Angie Aust White, Jim Schweisthal, Mark and Tammy Hornbach Cunningham. (1st Row) John Schwiesthal. (2nd Row)

Even though Essie and Dan never lived there, they still think of it as their family home. Mark and John had shot baskets at a hoop attached to the red barn with the name Kirchgassner under the tin roof. I walked over to the barn door where Mary Jo had backed over the lawn mower with the family car. We knew that Dad would not be thrilled to see the smashed mower. We had left the mower and the car and had walked to our house on Burtzelbach within minutes. The old red shed was my next stop. He always maintained that we, like him, might have to defend our country someday. These memories stood out as reminders of days that would never be again.

Lastly, I made my way over to the edge of the lane that was our path in all kinds of weather to Grandma's house. The lane was wet, muddy, and overgrown with brown grass; it would soon be in the icy grips of winter. The paths of the Kirchgassner grandchildren were no more. The memories of Grandma playing her favorite song, "There Is No Place Like Home," on the piano seemed to float softly in the gray mist enveloping the farm and closing in on her favorite view of St. Martin Church. The memory of that day when I said good-bye to my Dad and to the life we shared is frozen in time for me.

Dad never regained consciousness after that day. The night before I had brought him a fried chicken carryout dinner from the Old Brick Tavern, owned by Bob and Dot James. He thoroughly enjoyed the meal. My daughter Abigail and I spent the night, and in the morning, Dad had fallen out of bed and was not conscious. Floyd and Mary came to help me get him back into the bed. Cancer had done its damage and its effects were escalating. Mom never left Dad's side at the VA hospital, and my brothers and sisters took turns visiting him. Mom's brothers and sisters and their children, the extended Hoffmeier family, greatly supported the Kirchgassners throughout Dad's illness.

On January 1, 1994, when I took my daughter Abby to see him, I let Dad know that she was by his side. Though he did not open his eyes or say a word, he squeezed Abby's hand as if to tell her good-bye. His time was obviously near. Dad had fought the good fight but could do more. A heavy snow and cold weather had moved in on January 4 when God called him. The same pattern had developed around the time of his birth in 1917. Mary, Dan, and I never got to say good-bye as the snow hindered us on our journey. Floyd was driving us to the hospital, and we got no further than the Indiana-Ohio state line when the call came for us to turn back. Dad was gone.

On the day of his funeral, the temperature felt like twenty degrees below zero. Conditions were miserable, with snow on the ground and icy roads. When my family gathered for the Mass of the Resurrection at St. Martin's Church, we could not believe that there was a rainbow in the sky. I know it was Dad saying, "Farewell until we meet again."

The church was packed to capacity, and John Schweisthal, accompanied by his wife Katherine, came to say good-bye to his brother in arms. As my brother John, who delivered the eulogy, said, "Dad did not have any blood siblings, but he counted John Schweisthal as one." How true that was. Dad was proud of his service as a Thunderbird, and John closed with a quote from Crazy Horse, a Native American chief, who would shout as he went into battle, "Hoka hey," or "It is a good day to die." As my brother John left the podium, he was greeted by our brother Mark. Legion Post 452 provided military escort to the cemetery for the burial rites.

Requiescat in pace, Dad. The ancient Romans believed that those found worthy would spend eternity in the Elysian Fields, a glorious meadow. But your faith in Jesus Christ has gained you eternity in heaven. I know that you are enjoying the kingdom, but you are greatly missed by all of us. As my brother Mark said, "What I would give to have another go with you." Since your passing, another granddaughter has joined the Kirchgassner family—Kari Kirchgassner, daughter of Mark and Anne. Kari is studying photography in college, and I know that you would be delighted with her choice of profession.

Paul and Kari

Paul, Matt, Tony.
Last Christmas Eve at the farm with dad.

Kirchgassner grandchildren circa 1992-93

You would also be pleased to know that your eldest five great-grandchildren are in college,—Emily, Jacob, and Kathryn Rennekamp along with Christopher Kirchgassner and Z. Alex Noble, Dan and Judy's grandchildren. Their aspirations are varied, some medical, maybe business, but they are knowledgeable in general history and geography thanks to Mark (King#46.)

Your granddaughter Abby (daughter of John Grathwohl and me) joined the United States Army in June of 2012 in your honor. She married Michael Weber in February of 2013 at Fort Knox, Kentucky. Michael is the son of Joe and Connie Weber from Yorkville, Indiana. Michael is also the grandson of Cletus and Coletta Weber.

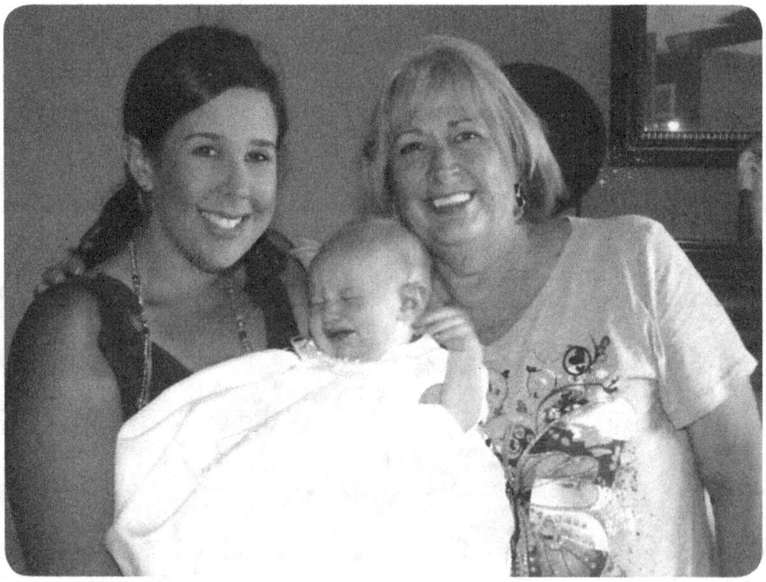

Abby, Kate Swales and Rita.
Day before Abby leaves for basic training

Col. Michael Hauser and his wife Rhonda hosted Abby and Michael's wedding. Colonel Hauser is the grandson of Effie Hauser, who worked with you at the Dearborn County Highway Department for many years. This is another example of how life continues to circle around with connections from your life to mine to Abby's.

Abby and Michael Weber's wedding.
John Grathwohl
Colonel Michael Hauser and Rita Kirchgassner

Cletus Weber and Dad

Great grandsons at Ft. Knox
Andrew Rennekamp, Sam Kirchgassner, Noah Mersmann and Jack Seaver (1st Row)
Hayden Trossman and Joe Kirchgassner (2nd Row)

Abby has promised that she will let the next generation know that the Kirchgassners are here today because God placed John Schweisthal in your life. For the Kirchgassner family, John's act of heroism will not fade with the passage of time.

Good-bye, Dad. By now I probably have embarrassed you and the family enough with my memories and musings. So I will close by saying thank you with all my heart for the ultimate legacy a father can give his children. I know of none better. I would never trade the love of St. Martin Parish, our family, and Yorkville, Indiana. Your faith in Christ has blessed the family greatly.

P.S. As I put the final touches on this manuscript during the early part of March of 2015, there is a winter storm warning for the Cincinnati area. Amount of snowfall and low temperatures are predicted to break the record. I cannot ignore the similarity of the weather when you were born, during your service, at your death and now at the retelling of your life. (Thunderbird weather.)

I learned so many things along way and want to note a couple: The people of France, in gratitude to the USA, sent a Merci Train after the war which consisted of forty-nine box cars filled with gifts. The box car for Indiana is on display in Fort Wayne, Indiana. In the near future, I plan to make a visit.

Also, there is a website, **www.echodelta.net/mbs/eng-overview.php** that will be useful in the future. Using the translator and the 6 digit coordinate numbers one can determine latitude and longitude of the places Company C served. So, Michael and Mark Kirchgassner, are you ready to use your geography skills for the second edition of *Semper Anticus*?—Rita Kirchgassner]

June 2015-

June 24, 2015-I did a radio interview on WSCH 99.3 with Bubba Bo discussing my book.

June 27, 2015-I hosted a party with family and friends to celebrate the first printing of Semper Anticus with proceeds going to the Anna Jo Kirchgassner Memorial Fund. The night before, we were getting the venue ready and a storm moved in over Yorkville, Indiana. As the storm passed there was a double rainbow. Just could not help believe that Dad was there with us.

Over two hundred people were at the celebration and I was so grateful to all who came and joined the festivities. I do feel compelled however to talk about one person who was at the event. Terry Miller, (son of Bud and Margie Miller,) a lifetime member of Yorkville. The reason I mention Terry is that he was going through a different situation a stark contrast to mine. He was fighting stage 4 cancer with no hope of remission and I am sharing my life work with family and friends. Not only did he attend but he help prepare food and clean up afterwards. I will always be in awe of his presence and his self-less act of kindness shown that day.

Since his passing in November of 2015, he is greatly missed by his wife Pam, two children Matt and Mallory in addition to extended family and friends.

Terry Miller and Rita Klump

September 2015-Lise Pommois came to Lawrenceburg High School to speak with the students about her research on World War II.

December 2015-My brother Mark and Jim Schweisthal and families met in Arizona.

Jessica Moore, Cody House, Anne and Kari Kirchgassner (1st Row)
Brooks and Mark Kirchgassner and Jim Schweisthal (2nd Row)

Also, some extended family gathered at the Barn Winery for a book signing and a painting class.

Joelee Ritzi, Peggy Lyness, Melody Gutzwiller, Rhonda Trabel,
Cheryl Lieland and Rita Klump (1st Row)
Lisa Nobbe, Rita Kirchgassner and Skip Henlein (2nd Row)

Jared and Sarah Leiker welcomed Owen Leiker on December 9.
Mark and Krista Kirchgassner welcomed Thomas Kirchgassner on December 16.

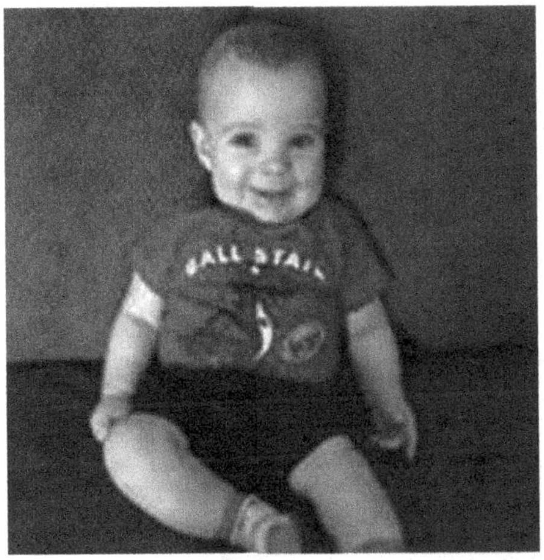

Owen Leiker

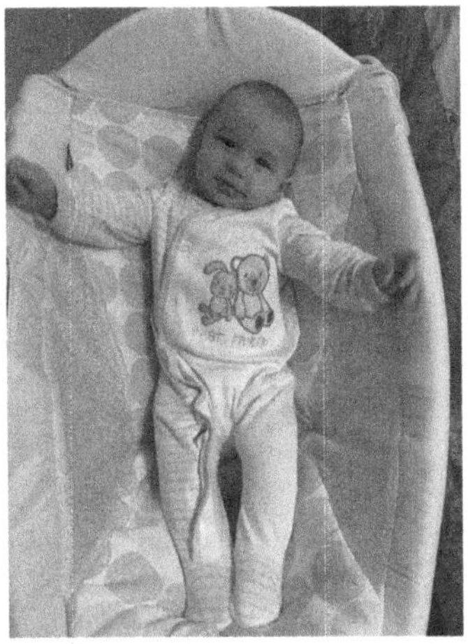

Tommy Kirchgassner

May 2016

Megan and Travis Swales welcomed Caroline Emma Swales on May 6, 2016—youngest Kirchgassner as of this printing.

Caroline

John Schweisthal

John Schweisthal was born on July 28, 1923, in Cleveland, Ohio. He had four siblings, one of whom, Adelbert, would die at seven. He had two older sisters, Bernadette and Rita, and one younger sister, Mary Ann. John and his family would live through the Great Depression that started with the stock market crash in October of 1929 and would last into the 1930s.

Katherine and John's sister Mary Ann (1st Row)
John, Kathy and Jim (2nd Row)

Kathy, Katherine and Jim

His father was a hardware store owner in Cleveland and his mom was a seamstress. John attended Our Lady of Good Counsel Catholic School during his elementary school years and would go on to Rhodes Junior High and to West Technical High School where he received his diploma.

When he was nineteen, the world was turned completely upside down for John and for millions of other young men. On March 11, 1943, John was drafted into the army. The United States was fully engaged in war with the Axis powers—Germany, Japan, and Italy.

John would witness an incredible loss of life—including many of his fellow soldiers. He would be shot multiple times during his engagements in Naples-Foggia, Rome, the Rhineland, and southern France. John served with the Army's 157th Infantry Regiment, Forty-Fifth Division. He would receive numerous military awards including the Purple Heart, four Bronze Stars (Campaign), the Good Conduct Ribbon, the Theater Ribbon, and the Oak Leaf Cluster.

In October of 1944, John's section chief, Robert Kirchgassner, was critically injured during a battle in northern France. John is credited with saving Robert's life through his swift actions. He removed Robert from the battle zone, placed him in a Jeep, and rushed him to a field hospital. Robert would be treated for nine months before returning home to the United States. Robert and John would become lifelong friends. John was discharged from the military on October 24, 1945.

At twenty-two, John returned to the United States like millions of other veterans to start his postwar life. He married the love of his life, Katherine Bednar, and built a home with the help of his brothers-in-law in Parma Heights, Ohio. Katherine and John returned to Europe during the early years of their marriage to visit the sites of some of the horrific battles John had fought.

John and Katherine

Katherine and John had three children—John, Cathy, and James. Each year the family traveled to Yorkville, Indiana, to visit Robert Kirchgassner and his family. The children enjoyed the time they spent on the sprawling farm with the children of Robert and Anna Jo Kirchgassner. Robert and Anna Jo raised six children on the farm.

John was a skilled machinist and worked for the Eaton Corporation in Cleveland. He also was a self-taught financial investor and analyzed the markets every day. His wife Katherine worked at General Motors for more than three decades before her retirement. John and Katherine took their children on many vacations including several trips to sunny Florida. All three of their children earned college degrees.

John loved to decorate the house during the holidays and put everyone in the holiday spirit with his efforts. He also maintained his yard in immaculate fashion with beautiful f lowers and a seasonal garden.

Katherine, Austin, Maribeth (John's niece), Jim, Jeannie, and Bernie (John's sister)

Austin, Katherine, Christy and Jim

John was a dedicated member of Holy Family Catholic Church in Parma, Ohio. He was the head usher for the 8:30 a.m. Mass every Sunday and spent forty years in service to his church. He volunteered at church carnivals, belonged to the Holy Name Society, and headed the senior citizen hospitality program.

In their retirement years. John and Katherine traveled extensively and visited their son James in Arizona and their daughter Cathy in Piqua, Ohio. John entertained numerous guests at parties at his home on Ann Arbor Drive in Parma Heights. He had a vast knowledge of model trains and built a showcase room for them in the basement of his home.

John and Katherine were married fifty-two years at the time of his passing. John left this world peacefully in his sleep at his home on June 30, 1997. He is now reunited with his fellow soldiers, his family members, and his friends who preceded him in death. He made an impact on this earth that few men will have the opportunity and the motivation to achieve.—Jim Schweisthal

Roscoe Prince

Roscoe was born on February 23, 1914, in Buckhannon, West Virginia. His parents, Thaddeus Osburn Prince and Antres Fay (Beverage) Prince, were married on September 21, 1908.

Roscoe married Roberta Pearl Peters on December 22, 1941.

Roscoe enlisted in the army on June 6, 1941. Dad and he served together from Pine Camp in 1943 until his death on December 2, 1943. Three miles north of Pozzilli, Italy, shell fragments fatally struck Roscoe on the head, the right side, the right hip, and both legs. He was interred in a temporary American military cemetery in R. Fratelli, Italy (eighteen miles southeast of Cassino, Italy), at 1300 hours on December 5, 1943, in plot B, row two, grave nineteen. His effects were three pencils, one fountain pen, a knife, a lead holder, an address book, papers, four photos, a Social Security card, and $1.01. On his right side is Pvt. Leonard Santibanez, Company D of the Second Chemical Battalion. On his left is Cpl. I. A. Schwirtlich, Company C of Battery 997 Field Artillery.

On May 5, 1948, Corporal Prince's remains were prepared to be sent to the Naples port morgue for his final interment in Nettuno, Italy, under the care of the American Battle Monuments Commission. A letter dated December 16, 1948, was sent to his widow, Roberta P. Prince Allen, who had remarried, informing her of move and noting that customary military funeral services were conducted.

Roscoe Prince

Roscoe's home in West Virginia

Richard Badgett

In 2011, Richard Adams and I attempted to contact any living relatives of Richard Badgett. From our research, we concluded that he was the only sibling to reach adulthood. He was born in Washington County, Kentucky, on December 30, 1923. He attended school through ninth grade and worked as a farmhand. He enlisted in the army on March 3, 1943, and joined Company C in Anzio, Italy, in February of 1944. He listed his father, Richard Matthew Badgett Sr., and his brother, James Thomas Badgett, of Springfield, Kentucky, as his next of kin.

Army records list his date of death as October 28, 1944. PFC Richard Badgett Jr. was buried in a temporary grave near Epinal, France, at 1031 hours on October 31, 1944. He suffered a gunshot wound to the left chest. On his right was buried Kraemer, L.V.T., rank and organization unknown, serial number 37073134. On his left side was Pvt. Isaac Cooper, Company G of the 157th Infantry.

The effects found with Badgett and shipped to the family on June 22, 1945, were a certificate of the Roman Catholic Church, two fountain pens, a badly damaged Bible, a wallet, a rosary, a crucifix, a religious card, a watch with the second hand damaged, seven photos, one souvenir coin, and four souvenir notes.

His body was permanently interred at plot A, row forty-four, grave twenty-one in Epinal, France, under the care and supervision of the American Battle Monuments Commission. A letter from the army was sent to Richard Badgett Sr. on February 2, 1949.

Richard Badgett

Richard Adams

Richard was born on September 7, 1924, and was the son of Charles C. and Mamie Still Adams. He graduated from Felton High School in Felton, Delaware, in 1942.

He served in the army and joined Company C in Anzio, Italy, in April of 1944. He received two Purple Hearts and the Bronze Star. He was captured and became a POW in January of 1945 and was not liberated until May of that year. Richard told me that he did not have a change of clothes or a shower during that time.

His brother Loran C. Adams, a medic, was KIA on June 2, 1944, just before the fall of Rome.

After being discharged from the army, Richard returned to Felton. He married Rose in 1946 and had three children, Richard Jr., Cathy, and Keith. He worked for Felton Hardware, was an insurance salesman for MetLife, and held many other positions.

His favorite pastime was playing golf with his friend Tom, and he was a fan of the Philadelphia Eagles and Phillies.

Essie and Tedd Adams, along with Rita and Abby, traveled to Felton in June of 2011 to record Richard's experience in the army during World War II. Richard's memories of the war helped Rita to fill in gaps in her father's service record.

Richard passed away on October 10, 2012, at Bayhealth/Kent General Hospital in Dover, Delaware.

Essie (1st Row)
Cathy, Rose, Dick and Rita (2nd Row)

Thomas Briggs

We came across PFC Thomas Briggs when we were in Bru, France, with Lise Pommois during our trip in the summer of 2013. Jared spotted a plaque at a crossroads in the town, so Lise parked the car for us to investigate. The plaque said that Briggs (born June 28, 1925) had disappeared while on guard duty at 1500 hours on October 12, 1944. He was on combat patrol and became separated from the other soldiers when they ran into a strong German position and was not seen again. Briggs was listed as MIA.

Bru, France

Leopald and Marie Briggs, his parents, lived at 736 Riverside Drive, New York, New York. They were in contact with the War Department for several years for details about their son's last day and the possible whereabouts of his body. In a letter dated April 26, 1951, Col. James B. Clearwater wrote:

> The American Graves Registration Service conducted extensive investigations in the vicinity of Bru in an attempt to recover and identify the remains of your son. The information you furnished to this Office, which you had obtained from personnel in that area, was used during the course of the investigation. The former Mayor of Bru, Mr. Mangin, was interrogated concerning his knowledge of this case. He was unable to furnish additional information even though he organized several search parties in your behalf.
>
> Attempts were made to locate men in your son's organization. These men likewise were contacted but all attempts to secure definite information concerning disposition of your son's remains were unsuccessful. (Lt. Phillip Gellar of 1207 W. 6th Street, Little Rock, Arkansas, wrote in a letter: "I was there at the time that the boy disappeared and I am pretty certain that he was captured as he ran right into enemy lines in his excitement and we never saw him again. I am certain that one of them was named Smith. The turnover was frequent and we never got to know each other.")
>
> Investigators came up with five men with the name of "Smith" who witnesses thought were with PFC when he went missing. One Smith, Walter of St. Albans, New York, wrote a letter on October 25, 1950. He recalled, "That a German in a farmhouse, on the upper floor, shot PFC Briggs and he went down." Walter took cover and saw the Germans come out of the house and drag him in. Not known if he was alive. Another Smith, John J., wrote on November 9, 1950, that the PFC received machine-gun fire.
>
> All unknowns recovered from the general area in which your son was reported as missing in action were examined by an accredited anthropologist utilizing advanced

> scientific and technical procedures. This examination disclosed that none of these remains could be associated with your son.

I found it heartbreaking to read about the parents' pain as they sought to find their son and to give him a proper burial. They even wrote to President Truman asking for his assistance, but there is no documentation in Briggs's file that his body was ever located. Nor did the German army state that he was a POW.

The Briggs family immigrated to the United States in 1939 and was from Austria. Thomas Briggs became a naturalized citizen on October 30, 1943, at Fort McClellan, Alabama. His older brother, S/Sgt. Harry Briggs, served in the signal corps in Japan.

Robert Rodenbaugh

I began corresponding with Robert about the same time I did with Richard Adams in 2010. Private Rodenbaugh joined Company C in December of 1944, two months after my dad was wounded. He never met my dad until the reunions in the late 1980s.

His path in the army was different from my father's. Robert joined the Pennsylvania National Guard when he was eighteen. In 1939, he was in New York for training when he heard that Hitler had invaded Poland. He was discharged from the National Guard since he was married and went to work in a defense plant. Later he was drafted, and due to a delay for a dental appointment, he was sent to the European Theater and did not go with the men he had trained with stateside. Robert became a POW in January 1945, a month after joining Company C. He attempted to escape two times but was recaptured. On the third attempt he was successful and walked at night until he came to a village in Germany. The villagers, leaving the area, told him that American troops were a day away. (Robert told me never to believe what I saw in the movies about being a POW. The portrayals were mild compared with what he endured. One of his assignments was burying the dead.)

After six weeks in the hospital recuperating, Robert was given a forty-nine-day leave. Upon his return home, he discovered that his wife was with child by another man. Robert was reassigned to Oklahoma and later divorced his wife and received custody of his two children.

My last contact with him came when he was still living in the St. Louis area with his current wife, Katherine. Robert said he still got emotional when he was thanked for his service during World War II.

George White, Dad, Ralph Krieger, Jose Pagilla, Anse Speairs,
J. C. Hogg and Donald Arvin (1st Row)
John Schweisthal, Bob Wiley, Isaac
Caudle, Howard Shultis, Eugene Drenon, Robert Rodenbaugh (2nd Row)

Servicemen and women from St. Martin parish, Yorkville, Indiana, who served during World War II: (A plaque hangs in the back of St. Martin Church.)

Edward Aust (WIA), Willard Aust, Herbert Aust (KIA), Hurbert Buscher, Daniel Buschur, Joseph Buschur, Norbert Fuchs, Joseph Hartman, Edward Hoffmeier, Victor Hoffmeier (KIA), Floyd Hornbach, Joseph Hornbach (died on his way home from the Pacific), George Hornbach (WIA), Robert Kirchgassner (WIA), Urban Kuebel, Ralph Kuebel, Irvin Miller, Maurice Miller, John Miller, Raymond Miller, Thomas Nead, Harry Nordmeyer, Lester Nordmeyer, John Schantz, Ralph Schantz, Sylvester Scheibel (WIA), Louis Steinmetz, John Schott, Cletus Weber, Murrell Weber, Norbert Wiedeman, Paul Wiedeman, Anthony Westerkam, Robert Westerkam, Cornelius Widolff (WIA), Eugene Widolff, Rose Marie Widolff, Edward Winter, and Francis Winter.

"I would like to dedicate this space to my wife of forty years. We were married September 1, 1945. With her letters and prayers, she kept me going when my spirits were low during the war. I love her and am forever grateful."—Robert L. Kirchgassner, forty years after the war.

[In World War I, may men were accepted into the service from this area. Father Sonderman stated that one out of 25 people were in the service. St. Martin had one out ten members in St. Martin Parish in the service. This includes children even babies as full time members. The Parish outshone any Parish in the State and probably in the United States.

In World War II, Father Sonderman reported that 75% of the eligible men were accepted into the service. Three veterans died as a result of the war. At least five were injured and stall have scars to show for it. Our community is proud of this record.—Floyd Hornbach]

Kirchgassner family circa 1963
Mark (1st Row), Rita (2nd Row)
Mary, Essie and John (3rd Row)
Dan, Dad and Mom (4th Row)

Essie, Susie Adams Everly, Tedd Adams, and Abby Weber

Shaun holding Emory, Kim holding Avery Simpson

Dan and Judy

Andrew, Kathryn and Barbara (1st Row)
Jacob, Eric and Emily Rennekamp (2nd Row)

Samuel and Elizabeth (1st Row)
Robyn, Joseph and Daniel Kirchgassner (2nd Row)

Michael, Christopher and Natalie Kirchgassner

Mark and Krista Kirchgassner

Alex Noble, Owen and Noah (1st Row)
Rachel and Jeff Mersmann (2nd Row)

Scarlett and Grace (1st Row)
Zak and Denise Kirchgassner (2nd Row)

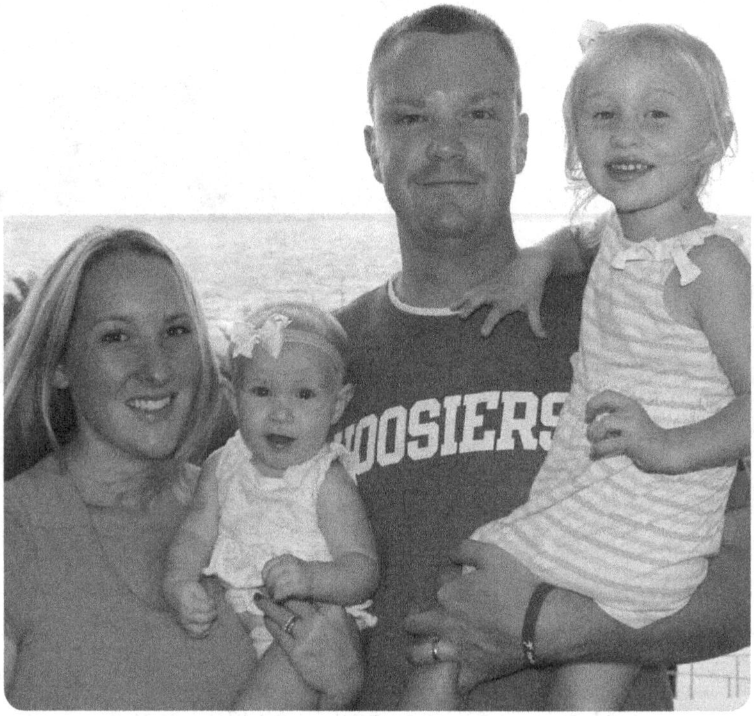

Megan, Courtney, Travis and Kate Swales

Christine and David Eppert
Tony Trossman and David
Floyd, Mary Trossman and David
Harper, Dedra, Paul and Hayden Trossman
Abraham and Charlotte (1st Row)
Matt and Marcie (2nd Row)
Isaac and Ella (3rd Row)

"Jonah Trossman"

Patricia, Carmen and John

Sarah and Robert Kirchgassner

Chris and Pepper Wright

Laura, John and Preston Wright

John Grathwohl, Michael and Abby Weber and Rita Kirchgassner

Mark, Anne, Kari and Brooks Kirchgassner

Appendix

Military Biography: LTC Hugh F. Foster III, USA (Ret.)

I WAS BORN INTO AN ARMY family at the US Army Hospital, West Point, NY, on 3 March 1947. My father, a signal officer, was an instructor at the Academy at the time. He is a USMA graduate, Class of 1941. His wartime assignments include service in North Africa, Italy and Sicily in WWII; in Vietnam, he commanded the 1st Signal Brigade. He retired in 1976 as a major general with more than 36 years of service to our great country. My mother was an Army nurse during WWII. With this as a background, I was pretty much destined to be a professional soldier.

In September 1966 I enlisted in the Army (enlistment option: Infantry) in San Diego, CA. After basic and advanced Infantry training I remained at Ft. Ord, CA as a bayonet instructor and assistant drill instructor in a basic training company. After a few months I was selected to attend Infantry Officer Candidate School and duly reported to Ft. Benning, GA. Upon graduation from OCS in October 1967 I received orders assigning me to 5th Battalion, 12th Infantry at Ft. Lewis, WA.

My arrival at Ft. Lewis coincided with the activation of the battalion. I was assigned to C Company as the 3rd Platoon Leader. We trained at Ft. Lewis for about five months and then deployed to Vietnam, where the battalion joined the 199th Infantry Brigade (Separate) (Light). I remained with C Company for a year in combat as platoon leader and executive officer. In September 1968 I must have annoyed some enemy troops, for they mortared and shot me; I received what we called "Chicken Gumbo," being hit almost simultaneously with mortar fragments and machine-gun fire. The wounds were slight -- fragments in my face, hands, and arms and a machine-gun bullet through the meaty part of the inside of my right upper thigh ("Very close to some rather important parts!") I was flash-blinded for about four hours.

Upon return from Vietnam in April 1969, I was assigned to the Advanced Individual Training Committee Group at Ft. Dix, NJ. There I operated the Survival, Escape and Evasion Range and taught patrolling and booby-traps for several months before taking command of a basic training company. After seven month of this, I volunteered to return to Vietnam.

I spent most of my second tour in Vietnam as an infantry company commander (B Company, 1st Battalion, 5th Cavalry) in the First Cavalry Division. I managed not to get shot this time. I commanded the company for seven months, from August 1970 until it was inactivated in March 1971, whereupon I was assigned as a staff officer at Headquarters, US Army Vietnam. One of my many jobs in the Operations and Training Division was to serve as the War Dog Officer for US Forces in Vietnam. I returned to the States in July 1971 escorting a C-141 airplane loaded with about 200 war dogs!

Back in the States, I attended the Infantry Officer Advance Course (1971-72), at Ft. Benning, GA. At this time I began to experience severe troubles with my back, which would ultimately lead to retirement. Following the Advance Course, I was selected for the Degree Completion Program, and attended the University of Southern Mississippi, in Hattiesburg, graduating with a BS in History (Honors) in the summer of 1974.

Then, it was off to Berlin, Germany to command Headquarters Company, 4th Battalion, 6th Infantry, Berlin Brigade. I commanded the company for 18 months, then was the battalion's S-4 (Supply Officer) for 18 months (1974-77).

I returned to Ft. Dix, NJ, to work as an Infantry advisor to the NJ National Guard and the Army Reserve -- interesting, but frustrating. At this point, my back problems became more and more severe, resulting in increasingly restrictive physical profiles. While I retained my infantry branch affiliation, this was the last job I had involving field work.

In the summer of 1980 I was assigned to Ft. Lee, VA, to lend combat arms guidance to the creation of doctrine for the Combat Service Support (logistics) branches. I spent three years at the Quartermaster School and two years at the Logistics Center.

My last job in the Army was as The Inspector General of the US Army Depot System Command, a world-wide command headquartered at Letterkenny Army Depot, Chambersburg, PA. This was a fine job and the general officers for whom I worked directly restored much of my confidence in the Army's leaders. I enjoyed the job thoroughly, but my physical condition degraded to the point that I was given a P-4 profile which limited my physical activity to walking slowly for short distances. I decided to retire voluntarily, and I did so in May 1990, having served almost 25 years.

I married while in college in Mississippi. While I am now divorced, I have a fine son, who remained with me after the divorce. In the summer of 1999 he graduated from West Point and was commissioned a 2nd Lieutenant of Infantry. Today, he is a major and in addition to being a qualified Army parachutist and Ranger, he has accepted his fate as a Foster, by being the third generation 'first son' to be wounded in action, having taken an AK-47 bullet to his left wrist in Iraq. He has completed overseas tours in the Sinai, Afghanistan, Iraq and Germany and is presently again serving in Afghanistan.

I am fully retired. I am an avid collector of US and German WWII militaria. Much of my time is spent in helping veterans and families of veterans seeking to document wartime service. If I had known retirement would be this much fun, I'd have retired when I made PFC!.

AWARDS AND DECORATIONS:

Combat Infantry Badge
Legion of Merit
Bronze Star Medal with V-device and 3 oak leaf clusters
Purple Heart Medal
Meritorious Service Medal with 2 oak leaf clusters
Army Commendation Medal with V-device and 3 oak leaf clusters
Air Medal with oak leaf cluster
Army Achievement Medal
Good Conduct Medal
Vietnam Honor Medal, 1st Class
Vietnam Campaign Medal
Vietnam Service Medal with 6 campaign stars
Army of Occupation Service Medal with Germany clasp
National Defense Service Ribbon
Army Reserve Service Medal with bronze hourglass device

The following is a list of the men who served in the 157th Infantry, Company C. Research was completed by LTC HUGH F. Foster III, USA (Ret.).

1.	**Abbott, Alden L.** 20838340 PCM-F (Boulder, CO)	CPL	F, C	F Co Boulder, CO, as PVT per Induction Roster, 16Sep40; F Co per Pine Camp menu MOS duty 653 ASGD fr Co F 28Sep43; evac sk 30Nov43 per MR 04Dec43; already evac sk TFRD to DofP, DFR per MR 14Dec43; RTD fm DofP 01Apr44 (per MR 11Apr44); MIA 28May44, DFR 01Jun44; change from MIA to **KIA** 28May44 (07Jun44) ; buried in Sicily-Rome Cemetery No discovered GO for CIB or GCM	**KIA 28May44**
2.	Abraham, Fred 42074553	PVT	C	MOS 745 ASGD fm 3rd Repl Bn 24Jan45 (per MR 26Jan45) CIB 01Mar45 (10/45); GCM (32/45)	
3.	Acton, John W. 35597854	CPL	C	MOS 653 ASGD fm 71st Reinf Bn 20Apr45 (per MR 24Apr45) CIB 01May45 (15/45); GCM (32/45)	
4.	Adamek, Robert A. 37559438	PFC	C	MOS 745 ASGD fm 71st Reinf Bn 20Apr45 (per MR 24Apr45) CIB 01May45 (15/45); GCM (32/45)	
5.	Adams, Benjamin S. 20846284 PCM-H	SGT	H, C	H Co per Pine Camp menu **(Unknown date of assignment)** Evac sk 03Nov43 (per MR 06Nov43); already evac sk, DFR per MR 26Nov43 CIB FM 01Jan44 (14/44)	

6.	**Adams, James R. (B.) 38510302**	PVT	C	MOS 590 ASGD & jnd fm 2nd Repl Det 24Feb44 per MR 9 & 10Mar44; pmtd to PFC 01May44; MIA 08May & DFR (per MR 20May44); **KIA** 08May44 (MR 10Jul44) (buried in USA) (not on ABMC register) No discovered GO for CIB or GCM	**KIA 08May44**
7.	Adams, John (NMI) 33668046	PVT	C	MOS 745 Deployed w/the company. Evac sk 15Nov43 (per MR 18Nov43); already evac sk TFRD to DofP, DFR per MR 18Dec43; RTD fm DofP 05Jul44; evac sk 08Jul44; RTD fm sk 10Jul44; TFRD to 7th Repl Depot 14Jul44 CIB DP (07/44)	
8.	**Adams,** Richard F. (E.) 32958105	PVT-PFC	C	MOS 745 asgd fm 2nd Repl Dep 23Apr44 (per MR 29Apr44); pmtd to PFC 01Jul44 (MR 02Jul44); **WIA** not hosp 26Sep44 (per MR 17Oct44); evac **WIA**, TFRD to DofP 25Nov44 (per MR 28Nov44); REASG fm 3rd Repl Bn 28Dec44; MIA 21Jan45 MOS 607 (per MR 23Jan45) **(POW 20JAN45)** Mstr POW reg gives unit type as Division Artillery, rpt date of 21JAN45, Stalag 11B Fallingbostel, Prussia (Work Camps) 53-09, repatriated. CIB 01May44 (06/44 CC); GCM as PVT F. (08/44);	WIA 26Sep44 WIA 25Nov44 POW 20Jan45
9.	**Affley, Frank W. PCM-I O-422200 (Denver, CO)**	**CAPT**	RHQ, I, C	SSG in RHQ, Denver, CO, per Induction Roster, 16Sep40; XO I Co as 2LT per PCCM42; Deployed w/the company. **KIA** 10Nov43 per MR 16Nov43 (buried in USA) (not on ABMC register) No discovered GO for CIB	**KIA 10Nov43**
10.	Agathangelon, Andrew 32784926	PFC	C	GCM (32/45)	
11.	**Akin**, William J. 34817302	PVT-PFC	C	MOS 745 ASGD 05Jun44 (09Jun44); evac sk, TFRD to DofP 06Nov44; REASG fm 71st Repl Dep 01Dec44; evac sk 06Dec44; RTD fm sk 15Dec44; **WIA** not hosp 18Dec44 (per MR 31Dec44); promoted to PFC 25Dec44 (per MR 26Dec44); Evac sk, TFRD to DofP 14Jan45 (per MR 14Jan45) CIB 01Sep44 (13/44); GCM (08/44)	WIA 18Dec44
12.	Albero (Possibly Albers), John J. 31405718	PVT	C	MOS 745 asgd fm 2nd Repl Dep 23Apr44 (per MR 29Apr44); atchd to 45 Cav Rcn Trp 19May44 (per MR 21May44); already SD w/45th Cav Rcn Trp, evac sk (per MR 05Aug44); already evac sk TFRD to DofP/DFR 07Aug44 (11Aug44); RTD fm 2nd Repl Dep 27Oct44 (per MR 30Oct44); corr to MR 29Oct44, s/b RTD fm 2nd Repl Dep 27Oct44 then TFRD to 45th Cav Rcn Trp on 29Oct44 (30Oct44); TFRD to 45th Cav Rcn Trp 29Oct44	
13.	Aldrich, John O. or D. 32213454	PVT	C, RHQ	**(Unknown date of assignment, not on Pine Came menu)** TFRD to RHQ 07Aug43 CIB (01/44 - 01Jan44 per CC as member of RHQ)	

14.	**Allee, Joseph D. PCM-K 38005177**	**1SG**	K, C	**SSG in K Co per Pine Camp menu;** ASGD fr Co K per MR 05Dec43; evac sk 02May44 (MR 07May44); RTD 05May44 (MR 11May44); MIA 28May44, DFR; to **KIA** 28May44 (MR 17Jul44) (Per Speairs, Allee was hit directly by a German mortar shell.) (buried in USA)(not on ABMC register) **Distinguished Service Cross** **CIB (01/44 - 01Jan44 per CC); GCM (02/44)**	**KIA 28May44**
15.	Allen, Garland E. 34893586	PVT	C	MOS 745 ASGD 29May44 (09Jun44); evac sk, TFRD to DofP 09Sep44 CIB FM 01Sep44 (14/44)	
16.	**Allen**, James C. 34816869	PVT	C	MOS 745 ASGD 29May44 (09Jun44); evac **WIA**, TFRD to DofP 23Sep44 CIB FM 01Sep44 (14/44)	WIA 23Sep44
17.	Alton, Bruno R. O-2017329	2LT	C	ASGD fm 71st Reinf Bn 27May45 (per MR 29May45) No discovered GO for CIB	
18.	Anderson, Charles S. 33837423 PCM-A	PFC	A, C	A Co per Pine Camp menu CIB as PFC in A Co 01Mar45 (9/45); GCM as PFC in C Co. (35/45)	
19.	Anderson, Emil (NMI) 36227113	PVT-PFC-PVT	G, C, G	ASGD fr Co G 28Sep43; pmtd PFC 14Jan44 per MR 15Jan44; Tfr in grade of PVT to G Co per MR 05Mar44 CIB (01/44 - 01Jan44 per CC); GCM SGT (17/44) – both in G Co	
20.	Anderson, John L. 37592458	PVT-PFC	C	MOS 745 ASGD fm 2nd Repl Dep 11Nov44 (per MR 13Nov44); promoted to PFC 25Dec44 (per MR 26Dec44); evac sk 28Dec44; already evac sk, TFRD to DofP 29Dec44 CIB 01Dec44 (01/45)	
21.	Anderson, Julius R. 16033252	PFC	C	**(Unknown date of assignment, not on Pine Camp menu)** TFR in grade to E Co per MR 05Mar44 No discovered GO for CIB or GCM	
22.	**Anderson,** Leslie A. 20837131 PCM-C	PVT	C	Deployed w/the company; **WIA** on beach 10Jul43 CIB FM as C Co PVT 01Jan44 (14/44)	WIA 10Jul43
23.	Anderson, Walden B. 36975354	PVT	C	MOS 745 ASGD fm 2nd Repl Dep 11Nov44 (per MR 13Nov44); evac sk, TFRD to DofP 06Dec44; RTD fm 71st Reinf Bn 30Apr45 (per MR 01May45); Evac NBI (SIW GSW L hand), TFRD to DofP 27May45 (per MR 27May45) GCM (32/45); no discovered GO for CIB	
24.	Andrechick, Ernest L. 32776859 PCM-C	PVT	C	(Deployed w/the company, is on the Pine Camp menu) MIA 13Dec43, DFR per MR 25Dec43 **(POW 13Sep43)** Mstr POW reg gives rpt date of 13 1k 43, 100th Div area!!, Stalag 2B Hammerstein, West Prussia, repatriated CIB FM 01Jan44 (14/44)	POW 13Sep43

25.	Anello, Neil S. 32839991	PVT	C	MOS 745 ASGD fm 7th Repl Dep 25Sep43; attached to 45th Div Mule Train 16Dec43; already special duty to 45th Div Mule Train, evac sk 16Dec43 per MR 27Dec43; RTD fm sk 02Jan44 per MR 06Jan44; evac sk (exhaustion) 09Feb44; already evac sick, trf to DofP and DFR per MR 06Mar44; RTD fm DofP 18Jun44 (19Jun44); TFRD to 2nd Repl Dep but not dptd 19Jul44; s/b ATCHD & jnd (MR 23Jul44) CIB PFD (07/44); GCM (08/44)	
26.	**Angelastro**, Philip V. 32787964	PVT-PFC	C	MOS 745 ASGD (03Aug43); evac sk 04Aug43 (per MR 06Aug43); RTD fr hosp 09Aug43 (per MR 10Aug43); evac **WIA** 12Nov43 per MR 15Nov43; already evac **WIA** TFRD to DofP, DFR per MR 15Dec43; RTD fm DofP 11Jan44 per MR 14Jan44; Pmtd to PFC 04Mar44 per MR 12Mar44; evac **WIA** (pen W R chest, L lumbar region, R leg shell frag) 27May44; already evac **WIA**, TFRD to DofP/DFR 02Jun44 (per MR 14Jun44); RTD from DofP 27Jun44 (per MR 28Jun44); erron rptd as AWOL 0630 03Jul44 s/b evac sk 03Jul44; RTD fm sk 19Jul44 (MR 20Jul44); evac sk, tfr to DofP 04Sep44; RTD 22Sep44; **WIA,** tfr to DofP 23Sep44; REASG fm 2nd Repl Dep 18Oct44; evac **WIA**, TFRD to DofP 27Oct44 CIB (01/44 - 01Jan44 per CC)	WIA 12Nov43 WIA 27May44 WIA 23Sep44 WIA 27Oct44
27.	Anglemyer, Leon N. 35549776	PVT-PFC	C	MOS 745 (sometimes shown as 607) asgd & jnd fm 2nd Repl Dep 24 Feb44 per MR 10Mar44; pmtd to PFC 01May44; evac sk 13May44 (MR 20May44); already evac sk, TFRD to DofP and DFR 02Jun44 (per MR 11Jun44); RTD fm DofP 01Jul44 (MR 02Jul44); MIA 21Jan45 (per MR 23Jan45) **(POW 20JAN45)** Mstr POW reg gives rpt date of 21Jan45, parent unit as Division Artillery, Stalag 11B Fallingbostel Prussia, repatriated CIB PFD (07/44)	POW 20Jan45
28.	Angley, Patrick A. 20223712	PVT	C	MOS 745 ASGD 05Jun44 (per MR 09Jun44); evac sk 09Jul44; RTD 11Jul44 (MR 11Jul44); evac sk, TFRD to DofP 08Oct44 CIB FM 01Sep44 (14/44)	
29.	**Annetts**, Winthrop E. 20110319	PVT	C	MOS 746 ASGD & jnd fm 2nd Repl Dep 26Feb44 per MR 08Mar44; evac **WIA** (Pen w. right chest & l. shoulder, Shell frag) 03Apr44; tfrd to DofP 15Apr44 & DFR (per MR 06May44); RTD fm DofP 21Jul44; TFRD to 1HQ 28Jul44 CIB PFD (07/44)	WIA 03Apr44

30.	**Anthony,** Donald R. 33171406	SGT-SSG-TSG	C	MOS 653 ASGD fm 2nd Repl Dep 01Jun44 (per MR 11Jun44); promoted to SSG MOS 653 07Oct44; evac sk 08Nov44; RTD fm sk 23Nov44; evac sk, TFRD to DofP 12Dec44; REASG fm 3rd REpl Bn 11Jan45 (per MR 11Jan45); EVAC **WIA** 14Jan45 (per MR 14Jan45); RTD fm sk 18Jan45 (per MR 18Jan45); PMTD to TSG, MOS 651 04Feb45 (per MR 04Feb45); Evac INJ 18Mar45 (per MR 18Mar45); RTD fm INJ 19Mar45 (per MR 19Mar45) GCM (08/44); CIB S/SGT 01Sep44 (13/44)	WIA 14Jan45 INJ 18Mar45
31.	**Aragon, Gilbert (NMI)** 38006551	**CPL-SGT**	C	(Deployed w/the company, is on the Pine Camp menu) Pmtd to SGT, MOS 652 (04Aug43); **KIA** 14Sep43 (per MR 18Sep43) (buried in USA) (not on ABMC register) KIA as SGT C Co by shrapnel per master 157 casualty list No discovered GO for CIB or GCM	**KIA 14Sep43**
32.	Archambeau, John H. 31060846 PCM-C	PVT	C	**(**Deployed w/the company, is on the Pine Camp menu) MIA 13Sep43 DFR (per MR 24Sep43) **(POW 23Feb43 – probably a typo for 13Sep43)** Mstr POW reg gives rpt date of 23NOV43, Stalag 2B Hammerstein, West Prussia, repatriated --CONFLICT OF REPORTED DATES! CIB FM 01Jan44 (14/44)	POW 13Sep43
33.	**Arvin**, Donald C. 36695292	PVT-CPL	C	MOS 745 ASGD 29May44 (09Jun44); evac **WIA**, TFRD to DofP 23Sep44; REASGD fm 2nd Repl Dep 09Dec44; promoted to CPL MOS 653 24Dec44; evac sk 28Dec44; Already evac sk, TFRD to DofP 01Jan45 (per MR 01Jan45); REASG fm 3rd Repl Bn 11Jan45 (per MR 11Jan45); MIA 21Jan45 (per MR 23Jan45) **(POW 20JAN45)** Mstr POW reg gives rpt date of 21Jan45, parent unit as Division Artillery, Stalag 12A to 9B Limburg An Der Lahn Hessen-Nassau, Prussia, repatriated CIB FM 01Sep44 (14/44)	WIA 23Sep44 POW 20Jan45
34.	Asbury, Edgar H. PCM-C	PVT	C	Pine Camp menu No discovered GO for CIB or GCM	
35.	**Ashe,** Clyde D. 34893187	PVT	C	MOS 745 ASGD 29May44 (09Jun44); **WIA** not hosp 24Sep44 (per MR 17Oct44); evac **WIA**, TFRD to DofP 30Sep44; REASGD fm 2nd Repl Dep 13Oct44; evac sk, TFRD to DofP 22Oct44 No discovered GO for CIB or GCM	WIA 24Sep44 WIA 30Sep44
36.	Ashmore, Thomas J. 35003161	PVT	C	MOS 060 ASGD fm 2nd Repl Det 04Jun44 (19Jun44); evac sk 12Jun44 (MR 20Jun44); already evac sk, to DofP/DFR 19Jun44 (26Jun44) No discovered GO for CIB or GCM	

37.	**Auldridge,** Burnice N. 38454963	PVT-PFC-CPL	C	MOS 745/607/653 ASGD & jnd fm 2nd Repl Dep 24 Feb44 per MR 10Mar44; PFC evac **WIA** (BC Lw scalp shell frag) 31May44; RTD fm **WIA** 15Jun44 (16Jun44); **(Missing entry of evac)**; TFRD to DofP 01Aug44; REASG but not jd fm 7th Repl Dep 17Aug44; Joined 16Sep44; promoted to CPL MOS 653 24Dec44; CPL MOS 607 MIA 21Jan45 (per MR 23Jan45) **(POW 20JAN45)** Stalag 12A to 9B Limburg an der Lahn Hessen-Nassau, Prussia -- repatriated CIB PFD (07/44)	WIA 31May44 POW 20Jan45
38.	Aultman, Paul B. 34914747	PVT	C	MOS 745 ASGD fm 3rd Repl Bn 24Jan45 (per MR 26Jan45); Evac sk 30Jan45 (per MR 30Jan45); already Evac sk, TFRD to DofP 02Feb45 (per MR 02Feb45); RTD 04May45 (per MR 04May45) CIB 01Mar45 (10/45)	
39.	Babel, George J. 36691031	PVT	C	MOS 745 ASGD 29May44 (09Jun44); evac sk 26Nov44 (per MR 28Nov44); RTD fm sk 30Nov44 (per MR 02Dec44); evac sk, TFRD to DofP 04Dec44; REASG fm 3rd Repl Bn 20Dec44; evac sk 23Dec44; already evac sk, TFRD to DofP 24Dec44; REASG fm 3rd Repl Bn 07Jan45 (per MR 07Jan45); Evac sk, TFRD to DofP 15Jan45 (per MR 15Jan45); REASG fm 3rd Repl Bn 25Jan45 (per MR 25Jan45); Evac INJ 18Mar45 (per MR 18Mar45); RTD fm INJ 19Mar45 (per MR 19Mar45) CIB 01Sep44 (13/44)	
40.	**Badgett, Richard M. Jr. 35698261**	**PVT**	C	MOS 745 ASGD & jnd fm 2nd Repl Dep 24 Feb44 per MR 10Mar44; pmtd to PFC 01May44; MIA 28Oct44 (30Oct44); to **KIA** 28Oct44 (per MR 08Nov44) (buried in Epinal Cemetery) CIB (04/44); 01Apr44 per CC	**KIA 28Oct44**
41.	Baer, George 32810449	PFC	C	GCM (32/45)	
42.	Baer, Rupert A. 36478615	PFC	B, C, 1HQ	ASGD fm Co B 06Dec44 (per MR 08Dec44); TFRD to 1HQ 02Feb45 (per MR 02Feb45) CIB PFD (07/44); GCM as PFC (08/44)	
43.	**Bakay**, Stanley 20220364	PVT	B, C	MOS 745 ASGD fm Co B 21Dec44 (per MR 21Dec44); Evac **WIA**, TFRD to DofP 14Jan45 (per MR 14Jan45); REASG but DS to 71st Reinf Bn 09Apr45 (per MR 11Apr45); Relieved of DS to 71st Reinf Bn 11Apr45 (per MR 11Apr45); AWOL 0630 02May45 (per MR 04May45); fm AWOL to Regt'l Stockade 23May45 (per MR 24May45); RTD fm Regt'l Stockade 31May45 (per MR 31May45) CIB 01Oct44 (13/44)	WIA 14Jan45
44.	**Baker**, Ross L. 37226641	CPL	C	ASGD fr Co G 28Sep43; evac **WIA** 12Nov43 per MR 15Nov43; already evac **WIA** TFRD to DofP, DFR per MR 12Dec43CIB FM 01Jan44 (14/44)	WIA 12Dec43

45.	**Baker**, Ryan D. 36453946	PVT- PFC-PVT	C, L	MOS 745 **(Unknown date of assignment; not on Pine Camp menu)** evac sk 15Dec43 per MR 21Dec43; already evac sk, TFRD to DofP, DFR per MR 16Jan44; RTD fm sk 15Mar44 per MR 20Mar44; **WIA** not hosp (pen w chin & neck shell frag) 16Apr44 (per MR 22Apr44); pmtd to PFC 01May44; MIA 25May44 (MR 27May44) CORR: AWOL 25May44 (MR 30May44); AWOL to confinement Fifth Army Stockade 31May44; RTD fm confinement, went AWOL 1200 04Jun44 (MR 08Jun44); already AWOL, reduced to PVT 05Jun44 (MR 08Jun44); RTD from AWOL 1200 12Jun44 (13Jun44); to Regimental Stockade 25Jun44 (28Jun44); RTD fm Regtl Stockade 10Jul44 (MR 12Jul44); TFR to Co L 12Jul44 CIB (03/44); 01Jan44 per CC; CIB PVT in L FM 01Jan44 (14/44)	WIA 16Apr44
46.	**Baker**, Solomon 42015422	PVT	C	MOS 745 ASGD 09Sep44 (per MR 16Sep44); **WIA** not hosp 07Sep44 (per MR 20Sep44); evac **WIA**, TFRD to DofP 23Sep44; **(missing entry of return to duty)** evac sk 06Nov44; RTD fm sk 13Nov44; MIA 30Nov44 (per MR 06Dec44); MIA 30Nov44 changed to AWOL 2259 30Nov44 per MR 09Dec44; RTD fm AWOL, TFRD to Co A 09Dec44 CIB 01Oct44 (13/44); GCM (16/44)	WIA 25Sep44
47.	**Baldassari,** William (NMI) 32268408	PFC	C	**(Unknown date of assignment; not on Pine Camp menu) SWIA** 11Jul43 (per MR 19Jul43), TFR to DofP N. Africa and DFR CIB FM 01Jan44 (14/44)	WIA 11Jul43
48.	**Baldridge,** Robert J. 35792007	PVT-PFC	C	MOS 745 ASGD fm 7th Repl Dep 25Sep43; evac **WIA** 12Nov43 per MR 15Nov43; already evac **WIA** TFRD to DofP, DFR per MR 15Dec43; RTD fm DofP 19Dec43 per MR 24Dec43; pmtd PFC 14Jan44 per MR 15Jan44; evac **WIA** (pen w r neck shell frag) 18Feb44; RTD 28Feb44; TFRD to 7th Repl Dep for trans-ship to USA 16Jul44 CIB FM 01Jan44 (14/44) CIB (03/44); 01Jan44 per CC; GCM (08/44)	WIA 12Nov43 WIA 18Feb44
49.	Baldwin, Ralph R., Jr. (Delta, CO)	PVT	C	Induction roster, 16Sep40 No discovered GO for CIB or GCM	
50.	Balwierz, Stanley	PVT	C	MOS 238 ASGD fm 1HQ 24Jun44 (assignment rescinded per MR 28Jun44) **NOT ASSIGNED**	
51.	Banar, Robert T. 35601919	PVT	C	MOS 745 ASGD (03Aug43); MIA 13Sep43 DFR (per MR 24Sep43) **(POW 13Sep43)** Mstr POW reg gives rpt date of 13Sep43, Stalag 2B Hammerstein, West Prussia, repatriated CIB FM 01Jan44 (14/44)	POW 13Sep43

52.	**Barefoot**, Jesse R. 38565036	PVT-PFC	C	MOS 745 ASGD 29May44 (09Jun44); **WIA** not evac 22Aug44; promoted to PFC 20Nov44 (per MR 27Nov44); evac sk 16Dec44; already evac sk, TFRD to DofP 17Dec44 CIB 01Sep44 (13/44); GCM PFC as Jesse (16/44)	WIA 22Aug44
53.	**Barkley**, James W. 34210725	PVT-PFC	C	MOS 745 (Deployed w/the company, is on Pine Camp menu.) Pmtd PFC 01Jul43 (Fm MR 20Jul43); promoted to PFC **(again?)** 03Nov43 per MR 05Nov43; evac **WIA** 12Nov43 per MR 15Nov43; already evac **WIA** TFRD to DofP, DFR per MR 15Dec43; RTD fm DofP 16Jan44 per MR 20Jan44; transferred in grade to E Co per MR 05Mar44 No discovered GO for CIB or GCM	WIA 12Nov43
54.	Barnes, Donald M. 36650452	PVT-PFC	C	MOS 745/607 ASGD & jnd fm 2nd Repl Dep 24 Feb44 per MR 10Mar44; promoted to PFC 05Aug44 (per MR 05Aug44); **(Missing entry of evacuation or departure);** REASG w/MOS of 607 fm 2nd Repl Dep 24Nov44 (per MR 27Nov44); evac sk, TFRD to DofP 25Nov44 (per MR 28Nov44) CIB PFD (07/44); GCM (08/44)	
55.	**Barnett,** Abe O-1014099	2LT	B, D, C	ASGD fm Co D 01Apr45 (per MR 01Apr45); Evac **WIA** 01Apr45 (per MR 1Apr45); Already evac **WIA**, TFRD to DofP 02Apr45 (per MR 02Apr45) CIB 01Jan45 (15/45) in B Co (No! not on that GO in B Co)	WIA 01Apr45
56.	Barron, George A. PCM-C	PVT	C	On Pine Camp menu No discovered GO for CIB or GCM	
57.	**Barth, Carl (NMI)** **38006009**	**T-5**	MD		**KIA 31May44**
58.	**Bartley, Robert J.** **35305422**	**PFC**	C	MOS 745 ASGD 09Sep44 (per MR 16Sep44); **WIA** not hosp 24Sep44 (per MR 17Oct44); evac S**WIA**, TFRD to DofP 31Oct44; DOW 02Nov44 (per MR 08Nov44) (buried in Epinal Cemetery) CIB 01Oct44 (13/44) PH w/OLC	WIA 24Sep44 WIA 31Oct44 **DOW 02Nov44**
59.	Bassi, Guido P. PCM-C	**PVT**	C	On Pine Camp menu No discovered GO for CIB or GCM	
60.	Batchelor, Hiram (NMI) 34571743	PVT	C	MOS 745 ASGD 05Jun44 (MR 09Jun44); evac sk 14Jun44 (16Jun44); RTD fm sk 27Jun44 (28Jun44); evac sk 15Jul44 (MR 16Jul44); already evac sk, TFRD to 2nd Rep Dep, not dptd 19Jul44; s/b ATCHD & jnd (MR 23Jul44) No discovered GO for CIB or GCM	
61.	Battaglia, John J. PCM-C 32216838	CPL	C, A	(Deployed w/the company, is on the Pine Camp menu) TFRD to Co A (04Aug43) CIB CPL in A Co FM 01Jan44 (14/44)	
62.	Baumgardner, Jackson J. 38631569	PVT-PFC	C	MOS 745 ASGD fm 3rd Repl Bn 24Jan45 (per MR 26Jan45); PMTD to PFC 06Mar45 (per MR 06Mar45); Evac sk, TFRD to DofP 11Apr45 (per MR 11Apr45) CIB 01Mar45 (10/45)	

63.	**Baynes,** George A. PCM-C 32109144	PVT-PFC	C	(Deployed w/the company, is on Pine Camp menu as CPL) Pmtd PFC 01Jul43 (Fm MR 20Jul43), **WIA** 14Jul43; already evac **WIA**, DFR (01Aug43) CIB as PFC in C Co FM 01Jan44 (14/44)	WIA 14Jul43
64.	**Bean**, Ivan L. 38006732	T/4-SSG	C	MOS 060 (Deployed w/the company, is on Pine Camp menu) **(Missing entry of evacuation);** RTD fm sk 29Oct43 per MR 01Nov43; **WIA** not hosp 16Jan45 (pen wnd forehead) (per MR 19Jan45); evac sick, 56 Evac Hosp 31Jan44; RTD 22Feb44; **(Missing entry of evacuation);** evac sk 18Oct44; RTD fm hosp 21Oct44; Evac sk 06Feb45 (per MR 06Feb45); Already evac sk, TFRD to DofP 07Feb45 (per MR 07Feb45); REASGD 22Feb45 (per MR 22Feb45); PMTD to SSG, MOS 824 04May45 (per MR 04May45); Evac sk 20May45 (per MR 20May45); RTD fm sk 20May45 (per MR 22May45); TFRD to Ft. Sam Houston, TX, for separation 28May45 (per MR 28May45) CIB at T-4 in C Co (04/44); 01Jan44 per CC; GCM (16/44)	WIA 16Jan45
65.	Beattie, Edward 31447668	PVT	C	MOS 745 ASGD 09Sep44 (per MR 16Sep44); MIA 31Oct44 (per MR 06Nov44) – corr to AWOL 2359 31Oct44 (per MR 22Nov44); corrected again to AWOL 2359 31Oct44 (per MR 24Feb45); Fm AWOL to confinement at unk loc 10Nov44 (per MR 22Nov44); AWOL to confinement Gray, France, 10Nov44 (per MR 24Feb45); Fm confin at Gray, France, to Regt'l Stockade 21Nov44 (per MR 22Nov44); REASG fm 71st Repl Dep 04Dec44 (per MR 05Dec44); evac sk 16Dec44; RTD fm sk 20Dec44; evac sk 26Dec44; already evac sk, TFRD to DofP 28Dec44; RTD fm Regt'l Stockade 17Jan45 (per MR 17Jan45); AWOL 2359 17Jan45 (per MR 19Jan45); Corr to MIA 31Oct44; S/B AWOL 2359 31Oct44 (per MR 24Feb45); AWOL to confinement Gray, France, 10Nov44 (per MR 24Feb45); Confinement Gray, France, to Regt'l Stockade 21Nov44 (per MR 24Feb45); **AWOL AGAIN?????;** AWOL to confinement Dijon, France 17Feb45 (per MR 24Feb45); Confinement Dijon, France, to Regt'l Stockade 20Feb45 (per MR 24Feb45); RTD fm Regt'l Stockade 12Mar45 (per MR 12Mar45); AWOL 0600 14Mar45 (per MR 14Mar45); fm AWOL to Regt'l Stockade 25May45 (per MR 25May45) CIB 01Oct44 (13/44 - w/drawn eff 17Jan45 32/45)	

66.	**Beck,** Eugene 36578064	PFC-CPL	C	MOS 745 ASGD fm 71st Repl Bn 09Dec44; evac sk, TFRD to DofP 31Dec44; REASG fm 2nd Reinf Dep 05Mar45 (per MR 05Mar45); Evac **WIA**, TFRD to DofP 18Mar45 (per MR 18Mar45); REASG fm 71st Reinf Bn, and placed on DS with 71st Reinf Bn 25Mar45 (per MR 03Apr45); Pmtd to CPL 04May45 (per MR 04May45) CIB 01Jan45 (01/45)	WIA 18Mar45
67.	Belanger, Louis H. 31447864	PVT	C	MOS 745 (or 521) ASGD 09Sep44 (per MR 16Sep44); Change to MR of 16Sep44, middle initial given then as J s/b H. (01Oct44); evac sk 19Oct44; already evac sk, TFRD to DofP 21Oct44; REASG fm 2nd Repl Dep 08Jan45 (per MR 08Jan45); Evac sk 09Jan45 (per MR 09Jan45); Already evac sk, TFRD to DofP 16Jan45 (per MR 16Jan45) CIB FM 01Oct44 (14/44)	
68.	Bellanca, Lewis 33837897	PFC	C	No mention in Morning Reports GCM (32/45)	
69.	**Belo**, John C. 32972801	PVT	C	MOS 745 ASGD & jnd fm 2nd Repl Dep 24 Feb44 per MR 10Mar44; evac **WIA** (Lacerating Wound, nose shell blast) 29May44; RTD fm **WIA** 25Jun44 (28Jun44); evac sk 17Jul44; already evac sk, TFRD to 2nd Rep Dep, not dptd 19Jul44; s/b ATCHD & jnd (MR 23Jul44); RTD fm sk 22Jul44 (MR24Jul44); evac sk, TFRD to DofP 03Aug44 CIB PFD (07/44)	WIA 29May44
70.	Bennett, Charlie E. PCM-C O-1287651	1LT	C, A	2LT Platoon Leader in C Co per Pine Camp menu CIB (01/44 - 01Jan44 per CC) as CO of A Co	
71.	**Benoit**, Bernard F. 20106627	TSG	C	MOS 651 ASGD fm B Co 26Jun44 (27Jun44); evac **WIA** 24Sep44; REASG fm 3rd Repl Bn 28Dec44; Evac sk 21Mar45 (per MR 21Mar45); RTD fm sk 23Mar45 (per MR 23Mar45); Evac sk, TFRD to DofP 24Apr45 (per MR 24Apr45); REASGD fm 71st Reinf Bn 11May45 (per MR 11May45) GCM (08/44); CIB S/SGT FM 01Sep44 (14/44)	WIA 24Sep44
72.	**Benson, Eugene L.** **PCM-C** **37163949**	**PVT-PFC**	C	(Deployed w/the company, is on the Pine Camp menu) Pmtd PFC 10Aug43; evac **WIA** 12Sep43 (per MR 20Sep43); RTD fm DofP 12Nov43 per MR 17Nov43; **KIA** 15Dec43 (per MR 20Dec43) (buried in USA) (not on ABMC register) KIA by shrapnel No discovered GO for CIB or GCM	WIA 12Sep43 **KIA 15Dec43**
73.	Berg, John H. 32867415	PVT	C	MOS 745 **(Unknown date of assignment, not on Pine Camp menu)** Evac sk 18Nov43 per MR 12Dec43; already evac sk TFRD to DofP 26Feb44, DFR per MR 19Dec43; RTD fm DofP 19Jan43 per MR 21Jan44; evac sk 19Jan44 per MR 22Jan44 CIB FM 01Jan44 (14/44)	
74.	Berk, Eugene 36578064	SSG	C	Not in Morning Reports GCM (32/45)	

75.	Berry, Newell E. Jr. 35632195	PVT	C	MOS 745 ASGD fm 7th Repl Dep 25Sep43; evac sk 17Nov43 (per MR 21Nov43); RTD fm sk 27Nov43 per MR 29Nov43; MIA 15Dec43, DFR per MR 25Dec43 **(POW 15Dec43);** Mstr POW reg gives rpt date of "05 1K 43", Stalag 7A, repatriated CIB FM 01Jan44 (14/44)	POW 15Dec43
76.	**Best,** Charles M. 18156919	PVT-PFC	B, C	MOS 745 ASGD fm Co B 06Dec44; promoted to PFC 25Dec44 (per MR 26Dec44); Evac **WIA**, TFRD to DofP 14Jan45 (per MR 14Jan45); REASG fm 71st Reinf Bn 26May45 (per MR 26May45) CIB 01Oct44 (13/44); GCM in C Co (32/45)	WIA 14Jan45
77.	Bevins, Lawrence F. 31254321	PVT	C	MOS 745 ASGD fm 7th Repl Dep 25Sep43; evac sk 11Dec43 per MR 14Dec43; already evac sk TFRD to DofP, DFR per MR 25Dec43 CIB FM 01Jan44 (14/44)	
78.	**Bianco**, Vito J. 42052151	PFC	C	MOS 745 ASGD 09Sep44 (per MR 16Sep44); evac **WIA** 24Sep44; REASG mf 2nd Repl Dep 05Dec44; MIA 21Jan45 (per MR 23Jan45) **(POW 20JAN45);** Mstr POW reg gives rpt date of 03Mar45, Stalag 11B, repatriated -- actual date of capture was 20Jan45 at Reipertswiller CIB FM 01Oct44 (14/44)	POW 20Jan45
79.	**Bibb,** Douglas A. 33627507	PVT-PFC	C	MOS 745/590 ASGD fm 7th Repl Dep 25Sep43; pmtd to PFC 01Dec43; evac sk 01Jan44 per MR 04Jan44; already evac sk TFRD to DofP, DFR per MR 25Jan44; MOS 590 RTD fm DofP 02Mar44 per MR 10Mar44; **WIA** not hosp 10Jun44; evac sk, TFRD to DofP 17Dec44 CIB (03/44); 01Jan44 per CC; CIB (04/44); 01Jan44 per CC; GCM (08/44)	WIA 10Jun44
80.	Biddle, Howard G. 33763788	PVT-PFC	C	MOS 745 ASGD & jnd fm 2nd Repl Dep 24 Feb44 per MR 10Mar44; pmtd PFC 01May44; evac sk 11May44 (MR 15May44); to DofP/DFR 19May44 (MR 27May44) CIB FM 01Mar44 (14/44)	
81.	Bietta (or Biette), Frank H. 32851422	PVT-PFC	C	MOS 745 ASGD & jnd fm 2nd Repl Dep 24 Feb44 per MR 10Mar44; pmtd to PFC 01May44; evac sk, TFRD to DofP 25Nov44 (per MR 28Nov44); REASG fm 71st Repl Dep 04Dec44 (per MR 05Dec44); evac sk 16Dec44; RTD fm sk 20Dec44; evac sk 26Dec44; already evac sk, TFRD to DofP 28Dec44 CIB (04/44); 01Apr44 per CC	
82.	Bilinski, Joseph (NMI) 33182353 PCM-C	PVT	C	(Deployed w/the company, is on the Pine Came menu) MIA 13Sep43 DFR (per MR 24Sep43) **(POW 13Sep43);** Mstr POW reg gives rpt date of 13Sep44, Stalag 2B, repatriated CIB FM 01Jan44 (14/44)	POW 13Sep43
83.	Bill, Falker (or Felker) 20829682 PCM-A	PFC	A, 1HQ, C	PFC in A Co per Pine Camp menu; ASGD fm 1HQ 20Oct44; TFRD to Co A 03Nov44 No discovered GO for CIB or GCM	

84.	Black, Victor S. 35758897	PVT	C	MOS 745 ASGD & jnd fm 2nd Repl Dep 24 Feb44 per MR 10Mar44; evac sk 07May44 (MR 11May44); tfrd to DofP/DFR 13May44 (MR 23May44) CIB FM 01Mar44 (14/44)	
85.	Blackwell, William P. O-1031535	1LT	C	Not in Morning Reports CIB FM 01Oct44 (14/44)	
86.	Blair, Hanzel (NMI) 35426202	PVT	C	MOS 745 ASGD fr 158th FA Bn 31Aug43 (per MR 01Sep43); evac sk (FUO) 15Feb44; RTD fm sk 09May44 (per MR 17May44); Evac sk 03Jun44; already evac sk TFRD to DofP/DFR 13Jun44 (20Jun44) CIB Former Pers 01Jan44 (10/44 CC)	
87.	**Blaise,** Stanley C. 32942388	PVT-PFC	C	MOS 745 ASGD & jnd fm 2nd Repl Dep 24 Feb44 per MR 10Mar44; promoted to PFC 05Aug44 (per MR 05Aug44); evac **WIA** 24Sep44; REASG fm 2nd Repl Dep 17Oct44; evac sk,TFRD to DofP 28Oct44 CIB PFD (07/44)	WIA 24Sep44
88.	**Blalock,** Cleveland (NMI) 34447909	CPL- SSG	C	MOS 653 ASGD fr 2 Repl Dep 04Jun44 (14Jun44); promoted to SGT (per MR 05Aug44); evac **WIA**, TFRD to DofP 19Aug44; REASGD fm 2nd Repl Dep 10Oct44; promoted to SSG 24Nov44; MIA 21Jan45 (per MR 23Jan45) **(POW 20JAN45);** Mstr POW reg gives rpt date of 21Jan45, parent unit as Divisional Artillery, Stalag 12A - 9B, repatriated CIB 01Sep44 (13/44)	WIA 19Aug44 POW 20Jan45
89.	Blanchette, Leo J. 31063076	PVT-PFC-CPL	C	MOS 745/653 (Deployed w/the company, is on the Pine Camp menu) Pmtd PFC 01Jul43 (Fm MR 20Jul43); pmtd to CPL per MR 02Dec43; evac sk 01Jan44 per MR 04Jan44; already evac sk TFRD to DofP, DFR per MR 21Jan44; RTD DofP 09May44 (MR 17May44); evac sk LD 09May44 (MR19May44); already evac sk, TFRD to DofP and DFR 06Jun44 (15Jun44) CIB FM as CPL C Co 01Jan44 (14/44)	
90.	Blea, Manuel PCM-C	PVT	C	On Pine Camp menu	
91.	Blizzard, Edward A. 35644223	PFC-CPL	C	MOS 745/653 ASGD fm 2nd Repl Dep 23Apr44 (per MR 29Apr44); MOS 653 CPL promoted to CPL 24Dec44; MIA 21Jan45 (per MR 23Jan45) **(POW 20JAN45);** Mstr POW reg gives rpt date of 21Jan45, parent unit as Divisional Artillery, Stalag 12A - 9B, repatriated CIB 01May44 (06/44 CC); GCM (08/44)	POW 20Jan45
92.	**Bloomfield,** Robert J. 38416982	PFC	C	MOS 745 ASGD fm 2nd Repl Dep 24Feb44 per MR 09Mar44 & MR 10Mar44; evac **WIA** (BC perf GSW L arm) 31May44; already evac **WIA** TFRD to DofP and DFR 03Jun44 (14Jun44) CIB DP (07/44)	WIA 03Jun44

93.	**Blumengold**, Irving (NMI) 32992386	PVT	C	MOS 745 ASGD & jnd fm 2nd Repl Dep 24 Feb44 per MR 10Mar44; evac **SWIA** (Pen w both arms, hand, face –frag) 08Apr44 (MR 12Apr44); RTD fm **WIA** 05May44 (per MR 12May44); TFRD to 2nd Rep Dep, not dptd 19Jul44; s/b ATCHD & jnd (MR 23Jul44); already attached fm 2nd Repl Det reld fm atchment (per MR 05Aug44) CIB PFD (07/44)	WIA 08Apr44
94.	Bocha, Stanley P. 32919580	PVT	C	MOS 745 **(Unknown date of assignment, not on Pine Camp menu) (Missing entries of assignment and evacuation);** REASG fm hosp 25Sep44 (per MR 27Sep44) No discovered GO for CIB or GCM	
95.	Bodziak, Charles (NMI) 32248293	PFC	C	ASGD FM Co L 28Sep43; **(Missing entry of evacuated sick);** RTD fm sk 29Oct43 per MR 01Nov43; MIA 10Nov43, per MR 27Nov43; RTD fm MIA 23Nov43 per MR 28Nov43; Evac sk 05Dec43 per MR 14Dec43; already evac, TFRD to DofP, DFR per MR 06Jan44 CIB FM 01Jan44 (14/44)	
96.	Boesel, Jacob W. PCM-3 O-1284638 3HQ/C/RHQ/C/RHQ	1LT	C	On Pine Camp menu as 1LT in 3HQ; **(Unknown date of assignment**) (Co XO) TFRD to RHQ 01Sep43; ASGD fr RHQ as Commanding Officer per MR 23Nov43; Tfrd to RHQ 01Mar44 (per MR 09May44) CIB as 1LT in C Co (01/44 - 01Jan44 per CC)	
97.	**Boggs,** John E. 33627440	PVT- SGT	C	ASGD fm Co A 14Jan44 per MR 15Jan44; **(Missing promotion to PFC & CPL);** promoted to SGT (per MR 05Aug44); evac **WIA**, TFRD to DofP 30Sep44 CIB (01/44 – 01Jan44 per CC)GCM (08/44)	WIA 30Sep44
98.	Bolduc, Joseph P. 11047996	PVT	C	(Deployed w/the company, is on the Pine Camp menu) MIA 13Sep43 DFR (per MR 24Sep43) **(POW 13Sep43);** Mstr POW reg gives rpt date of 13Sep43, Stalag 2B, repatriated CIB MIA (05/44); 01Jan44 per CC	POW 13Sep43
99.	**Bombard,** Alfred R. 32850445	PVT- SSG	C	MOS 745/653 ASGD fm 7th Repl Dep 25Sep43; evac **WIA** 16Dec43 per MR 19Dec43; already evac **WIA** TFRD to DofP, DFR per MR 19Jan44; RTD fm DofP 02Mar44 per MR 10Mar44; pmtd to CPL 10Apr44 (per MR 11Apr44); pmtd to SGT **(Missing date of promotion);** pmtd SSG MOS 653 24May44; evac **WIA**, TFRD to DofP 23Sep44 CIB (03/44); 01Jan44 per CC	WIA 16Dec43 WIA 23Sep44
100.	**Bombard, Ronald J. 32226494**	**PVT**	C	ASGD fr Co I 28Sep43; **(Missing promotion to PFC) KIA** 10Nov43 per MR 17Nov43; KIA by shrapnel per master 157 casualty list (buried in Sicily-Rome Cemetery) No discovered GO for CIB or GCM	**KIA 10Nov43**

101.	Bonds, Charlie W. 34825733	PVT	C	MOS 745 ASGD (per MR 09Jun44) 29May44; evac sk, TFRD to DofP 22Oct44; REASG fm 71st Repl Dep 01Dec44; evac INJ 03Dec44; already evac, TFRD to DofP 04Dec44 CIB FM 01Sep44 (14/44)	
102.	**Bonner, Floyd** 18091041	**PVT-PFC**	C	MOS 745 ASGD fm 3rd Repl Bn 20Dec44 (per MR 21Dec44); PMTD to PFC 06Mar45 (per MR 06Mar45); MIA 29Mar45 (per MR 02Apr45); to **KIA** 29Mar45 (per MR 05Apr45) (buried in Lorraine Cemetery); KIA Aschaffenburg CIB 01Jan45 (01/45)	**KIA 29Mar45**
103.	**Bonner**, Lloyd 38662238	PVT	C	MOS 745 ASGD fm 3rd Repl Bn 20Dec44 (per MR 21Dec44); Evac sk, TFRD to DofP 03Jan45 (per MR 03Jan45); RTD fm 3rd Repl Bn 13Feb45 (per MR 13Feb45); Evac **WIA**, TFRD to DofP 18Mar45 (per MR 18Mar45); RTD fm 71st Reinf Bn 30Apr45 (per MR 01May45); Evac sk 01May45 (per MR 01May45); already evac sk, TFRD to DofP 02May45 (per MR 02May45) CIB 01Jan45 (01/45)	WIA 18Mar45
104.	**Booker, Medford C.** **35052589**	**PVT**	C	**(Unknown date of assignment, is not on Pine Camp menu) (Missing assignment info and evacuation info)** RTD fm sk 29Oct43 per MR 01Nov43; **KIA** 11Nov43 (per MR 17Nov43) (buried in USA) (Not on ABMC register) KIA by shrapnel No discovered GO for CIB or GCM	**KIA 11Nov43**
105.	**Bosse,** Joseph (NMI) 42022740	PVT	C	MOS 745 ASGD 30May44 (per MR 09Jun44); evac sk 30Jul44 (02Aug44); already evac sk TFRD to DofP/DFR 31Jul44 (05Aug44); REASG but not jd fm 7th Repl Dep 17Aug44; joined 19Sep44; **WIA** not hosp 25Sep44 (per MR 17Oct44); RTD fm 3rd Repl Bn 12Jan45 (per MR 12Jan45); Evac INJ, TFRD to DofP 14Jan45 (per MR 14Jan45); REASGD fm 71st Reinf Bn 19Mar45 (per MR 19Mar45); Evac sk, TFRD to DofP 20Mar45 (per MR 20Mar45) CIB FM 01Sep44 (14/44)	WIA 25Sep44
106.	Bouffard, Oscar J. 34792324	PVT-PFC	C	MOS 745 ASGD 09Sep44 (per MR 16Sep44); promoted to PFC 25Dec44 (per MR 26Dec44); Evac sk,TFRD to DofP 14Jan45 (per MR 14Jan45); RTD fm 2nd Rein Dep 27Feb45 (per MR 27Feb45); Evac sk 15Mar45 (per MR 15Mar45); Already Evac, TFRD to DofP 20Mar45 (per MR 20Mar45) CIB 01Oct44 (13/44); GCM (32/45)	

107.	**Boughton**, Clyde A. 37343090	PVT-CPL	C	MOS 745/653 ASGD & jnd fm 2nd Repl Dep 24 Feb44 per MR 10Mar44; Evac sk (FUO) 02May44 (per MR 07May44); RTD fm sk 14May44) (per MR 18May44); evac sk 09Jul44; RTD fm sk 11Jul44; evac **WIA**, TFRD to DofP 23Sep44; 745 REASG fm 3rd Repl Bn 18Dec44 (per MR 19Dec44); MOS 653 CPL promoted to CPL MOS 653 24Dec44; Evac sk 01Feb45 (per MR 01Feb45); RTD fm sk 08Feb45 (per MR 08Feb45); Evac **WIA**, TFRD to DofP 19Mar45 (per MR 19Mar45) CIB PFD (07/44); CIB FM 01Mar44 (14/44); GCM CPL (08/454)	WIA 23Sep44 WIA 19Mar45
108.	Bouton, Harold S. 36651674	PVT-PFC	C	MOS 745 ASGD fm Div HQ Co 23Oct44 (per MR 25Oct44); Special Duty with Div HQ 23Oct44 (per MR 02Nov44); Pmtd to PFC 01Feb45 (per MR 01Feb45); Already abs DS to Div HQ Co, TFRD to Div HQ Co 12Feb45 (per MR 12Feb45) No discovered GO for CIB or GCM	
109.	Bowerman, Leroy PCM-C	PVT	C	On Pine Camp menu No discovered GO for CIB or GCM	
110.	Brackett, Harold W. 11065087	PVT	C	MOS 745 ASGD 05Jun44 (09Jun44); evac sk 15Aug44 (18Aug44); RTD 18Aug44; evac sk 19Aug44; already evac TFRD to DofP 20Aug44; RTD fm hosp 26Aug44; evac sk, TFRD to DofP 24Oct44 CIB FM 01Sep44 (14/44)	
111.	**Branim,** William (NMI) 34722361	PVT	C	MOS 745 ASGD fm 7th Repl Dep 25Sep43; evac **WIA** 12Nov43 per MR 16Nov43; already evac **WIA** TFRD to DofP, DFR per MR 15Dec43 CIB FM 01Jan44 (14/44)	WIA 12Nov43
112.	Brannon, Timothy C. 33233901	SSG	C	MOS 653 ASGD fm 2nd Repl Dep 11Nov44 (per MR 13Nov44) No discovered GO for CIB or GCM	
113.	Braswell, Clarence A. 6287161	PVT	G, C	ASGD fr Co G. 14Jan44 per MR 15Jan44; AWOL 0700 26Jan44; apprehended 1200 26Jan44; RTD 1400 26Jan44; AWOL 0700 26Feb44; Confinement by military authorities 07Apr44; RTD fm confinement 1200 11Apr44 (per MR 19May44); Evac sk (NB perf W L foot SIW) 07May44 LOD NO (per MR 19May44); SHOULD BE: Evac SIW (NB perf W L foot self infl) 07May44 LOD NO; RTD fm DofP 12Jun44 (13Jun44); evac sk 13Jun44; already evac, Tfrd to DofP/DFR 03Jun44 CIB PVT FM C Co 01Jan44 (14/44)	

114.	**Bregante,** Attilio D. 39394294	PFC	C	MOS 653 ASGD fm 2nd Repl Dep 24Feb44 per MR 09Mar44 & MR 10Mar44; evac **WIA**, TFRD to DofP 23Sep44; REASG fm 2nd Repl Dep 27Oct44; evac sk 22Nov44; RTD fm hosp 30Nov44; evac sk, TFRD to DofP 06Dec44; REASG fm 3rd Repl Bn 26Dec44; MIA 21Jan45 (per MR 23Jan45) **(POW 20JAN45)** CIB (04/44); 01Apr44 per CC	WIA 23Sep44 POW 20Jan45
115.	Brenner, Leo PCM-C	PVT	C	On Pine Camp menu No discovered GO for CIB or GCM	
116.	Brewer, Cecil G. PCM-RHQ 18103664	PVT-PFC	RHQ,C	On RHQ Pine Camp menu; **(Unknown date of assignment)** Pmtd PFC 10Aug43; evac sk 10Aug43 (per MR 11Aug43); RTD fm sk 05Sep43 (per MR 07Sep43); evac **LIA** 29Nov43 per MR 03Dec43; already evac **LIA** TFRD to DofP, DFR per MR 31Dec43 CIB FM as PFC in C Co 01Jan44 (14/44)	LIA 29Nov43
117.	Breyer, Teunis 42058593	PVT-PFC	C	MOS 605 ASGD & joined fm 2nd Repl Dep 04Nov44 (per MR 09Nov44); already evac sk, TFRD to DofP 15Nov44 – corr in MR 16Nov44 to evac sk, TFRD to DofP; REASGD fm 2nd Repl Dep 09Dec44; promoted to PFC 25Dec44 (per MR 26Dec44); Evac sk, TFRD to DofP 16Jan45 (per MR 16Jan45) CIB 01Dec44 (01/45)	
118.	**Briggs, Thomas M. 42033979**	**PVT-PFC**	C	MOS 745 asgd fm 2nd Repl Dep 23Apr44 (per MR 29Apr44); pmtd to PFC 01Jul44 (MR 02Jul44); evac sk 21Jul44 (MR 22Jul44); already sk evac TFRD to DofP/DFR 21Jul44 (26Jul44); RASGD fm DofP 06Aug44; evac **WIA**, TFRD to DofP 23Sep44; REASG fm 2nd Repl Dep 07Oct44; **KIA** 12Oct44 (per MR 15Oct44) MIA per master 157 casualty list; FOD13Oct45 per Div casualty list; MIA12OCT44 per Adj Notebook; ABMC 13Oct45, Commemorated at Epinal Cemetery BSM, PH w/OLC (ABMC date of 1945 is a Finding of Death one year and a day after MIA); Still MIA; commemorated at Epinal Cemetery BSM, PH w/OLC CIB 01May44 (06/44 CC)	WIA 23Sep44 **MIA 12Oct44**
119.	**Brockhoff,** Paul C. O-1032375	2LT	2HQ, C	ATCHD & Jd fm 2nd Repl Dep 24Jul44 (27Jul44); evac sk, TFRD to DofP 23Aug44; RTD fm hosp 26Aug44; evac **WIA**, TFRD to DofP 28Oct44; already TFRD to DofP promoted to 1LT 27Oct44 (per MR 29Oct44); REASG fm 3rd Repl Bn 23Jan45 (per MR 24Jan45); Evac sk, TFRD to DofP 24Jan45 (per MR 24Jan45) CIB 01Sep44 (11/44); CIB 01Sep44 (13/44)	WIA 28Oct44

120.	**Brooks,** Allen H. 31409016	PVT	C	MOS 504 ASGD 09Sep44 (per MR 16Sep44); evac **WIA** 24Sep44; RTD fm 3rd Repl Bn 13Feb45 (per MR 13Feb45); Evac **WIA** 28Mar45 (per MR 28Mar45); Already evac **WIA**, TFRD to DofP 30Mar45 (per MR 30Mar45); CIB FM 01Oct44 (14/44); GCM (08/45)	WIA 24Se[44 WIA 28Mar45
121.	**Brooks, James C. PCM-C 34212565**	PVT	C	(Deployed w/the company, is on the Pine Camp menu) MIA 13Sep43 DFR (per MR 24Sep43) **(Though he did not return to the company, he was not a POW, nor is he still MIA, nor is he buried in an American Military Cemetery overseas. It is possible that he was KIA and returned home for burial, or that he was WIA and evacuated without the knowledge of the company, or that he evaded capture and returned to US custody other than via the company.)** CIB FM as PVT in C Co 01Jan44 (14/44)	**MIA 13Sep43**
122.	**Broome**, William R. Jr. 14116404	PVT-PFC	C	MOS 745 ASGD & jnd fm 2nd Repl Dep 24 Feb44 per MR 10Mar44; pmtd to PFC 01May44; evac **WIA** 27May44; already evac **WIA** TFRD to DofP and DFR 13Jun44) (20Jun44) CIB FM 01Mar44 (14/44)	WIA 27May44
123.	Brossett, Joseph C. PCM-C 38173253	PFC	C	(Deployed w/the company, is on Pine Camp menu) Evac sk 01Jun44; already evac sk TFRD to DofP and DFR 05Jun44 (15Jun44) CIB as PFC in C Co (01/44 - 01Jan44 per CC); GCM (02/44)	
124.	Brouillard, Lyle L. 39463416	CPL	C	MOS 745 ASGD 09Sep44 (per MR 16Sep44); evac sk, TFRD to DofP 17Dec44 CIB 01Oct44 (13/44)	
125.	Brown, Bernard 31024088	PFC	C	GCM (32/45)	
126.	Brown, George R. 36479304	SGT-SSG	C	MOS 653 ASGD fm 71st Repl Bn 09Dec44; promoted to SSG 24Dec44; evac sk, TFRD to DofP 29Dec44 CIB 01Jan45 (01/45)	
127.	**Brown,** Hugh M. 36110613	SGT-SSG	C	MOS 653 ASGD fr 2 Repl Dep 04Jun44 (14Jun44); promoted to SSG MOS 653 07Oct44; evac **WIA**, TFRD to DofP 05Dec44; RTD 05May45 (per MR 06May45) GCM (08/44); CIB S/SGT 01Sep44 (13/44)	WIA 05Dec44
128.	Brown, Hymie L. 32714303	PVT	C	MOS 745 ASGD 03Aug43 (03Aug43); MIA 13Sep43 DFR (per MR 24Sep43) **(POW 13Sep43);** Mstr POW reg gived rpt date of 13Sep44 w/o unit ID, Stalag 2B, repatriated CIB FM 01Jan44 (14/44)	POW 13Sep43
129.	Broyles, Herbert Jr. PCM-C	PVT	C	On Pine Camp menu No discovered GO for CIB or GCM	
130.	Bruce, Russell J. 33547072	SSG	C	MOS 652 ASGD fm 44th Inf Div 25Jan45 (per MR 01Feb45) No discovered GO for CIB or GCM	

131.	Brumbelow, Elmer (NMI) 34441930	PVT	C	MOS 745 ASGD 03Aug43 (03Aug43); MIA 13Sep43 DFR (per MR 24Sep43) **(POW 13Sep43);** Mstr POW reg gives rpt date of 13Sep44 as member of 100th ID, Stalag 2B, repatriated CIB FM 01Jan44 (14/44)	POW 13Sep43
132.	Bruno, Raymond 33850689	PVT-PFC	C	MOS 745 ASGD fm 3rd Repl Bn 24Jan45 (per MR 26Jan45); PMTD to PFC 06Mar45 (per MR 06Mar45); Evac INJ, TFRD to DofP 18Mar45 (per MR 18Mar45) CIB 01Mar45 (10/45)	
133.	Bruno, Samuel J. 35547072	SSG-TSG	C	MOS 652 **(Unknown date of assignment)** PMTD to TSG, MOS 651 09May45 (per MR 09May45); TDY to **USA** 04Mar45 (per MR 04Mar45); RTD fm TDY to **UK** 26Mar45 (per MR 27Mar45) GCM (8/45)	
134.	**Brutcher**, Earl R. 42093230	PVT	C	MOS 605 ASGD and joined fm 2nd Repl Dep 04Nov44 (per MR 09Nov44); evac sk, TFRD to DofP 10Dec44; REASGD fm 2nd Rein Dep 25Feb45 (per MR 25Feb45); evac **WIA** 29Mar45 (per MR 29Mar45); already evac **WIA**, TFRD to DofP 30Mar45 (per MR 30Mar45) CIB 01Mar45 (9/45)	WIA 29Mar45
135.	Brutting, William A. PCM-C 12042411	PFC	C, 2HQ	PFC in C Co per Pine Camp meun CIB FM as PVT in 2HQ (05/44); 01Jan44 per CC	
136.	Bruyere, Charles PCM-C 32212699	PVT	C	(Deployed w/the company, is on the Pine Camp menu) MIA 16Sep43 DFR (per MR 24Sep43) **(POW 16Sep43);** Mstr POW reg gives rpt date of 16Sep43, Stalag 2B, repatriated CIB FM as PVT in C Co 01Jan44 (14/44)	POW 16Sep43
137.	**Bryant**, James C. 36740552	PVT-PFC-CPL-SGT	C	MOS 745 ASGD & jnd fm 2nd Repl Dep 24 Feb44 per MR 10Mar44; pmtd to PFC 01May44; **(Missing entry for evacuation);** RTD fm sk 19Jul44 (MR 20Jul44); evac sk 26Jul44; already evac sk, TFRD to DofP/DFR 29Jul44 (per 05Aug44); RTD fm hosp 10Sep44 (per MR 11Sep44); **WIA** not hosp 25Sep44 (per MR 17Oct44); evac sk, TFRD to DofP 08Nov44; REASG fm 3rd Repl Bn10Dec44 (per MR 11Dec44); evac sk, TFRD to DofP 18Dec44; REASG fm 3rd Repl Bn 23Jan45 (per MR 23Jan45); PMTD to CPL, MOS 653 04Feb45 (per MR 04Feb45); PMTD to SGT 09Mar45 (per MR 09Mar45); Evac sk 04Apr45 (per MR 04Apr45); Already evac sk, TFRD to DofP 05Apr45 (per MR 05Apr45) CIB (03/44 - 01Apr44 per CC); GCM CPL (08/45)	WIA 25Sep44

138.	**Bryant**, Tom (NMI) 38133697	PVT-PFC-PVT	C	MOS 521 ASGD fm 2nd Repl Dep per MR 11Dec43; evac sk 25Dec43 per MR 28Dec43; already evac sk TFRD to DofP, DFR per MR 21Jan44; RTD fm sk 28Feb44 per MR 05Mar44; Pmtd to PFC 04Mar44 per MR 12Mar44; **WIA** not hosp (ow r knee, lw r hand shell frag) 13Apr44 (per MR 20Apr44); AWOL04Jun44 (08Jun44); RTD fm AWOL 09Jun44 (10Jun44); reduced to PVT 11Jun44 (13Jun44); to Regimental Stockade (30Jun44); RTD fm Regtl Stockade 05Jul44; TFRD to 2nd Repl Dep but not departed 19Jul44; s/b ATCHD & jnd (MR 23Jul44); AWOL 0300 24Jul44; RTD fm AWOL 1130 25Jul44 (27Jul44); already attached fm 2nd Repl Det reld fm atchment (per MR 05Aug44) CIB FM 01Jan44 (14/44)	WIA 13Apr44
139.	Bucholz, Earl R. 36587332	PVT	C	MOS 745 ASGD fm 7th Repl Dep 25Sep43 No discovered GO for CIB or GCM	
140.	Bucknam, Charles F. ???7645	PVT	C	**(Unknown date of assignment, not on Pine Camp menu)** TFRD to Regimental Band per MR 23Nov43 No discovered GO for CIB or GCM	
141.	**Buell**, Austin E. 0-1311603	2LT	C	ASGD (05Aug43); evac sk 16Aug43 (per MR 26Aug43); RTD 26Aug43; **WIA** evac 12Sep43 (per MR 18Sep43) CIB FM 01Jan44 (14/44)	WIA 12Sep43
142.	**Buhrman, Roy C. 33500050**	**PVT**	C	MOS 745 ASGD 03Aug43; MIA 16Aug43 (per MR 21Aug43) (DFR per MR 07Sep43) **(believed drowned in landing accident. STILL MIA);** commemorated at Sicily-Rome Cemetery -- no PH CIB FM 01Jan44 (14/44)	**MIA 16Aug43**
143.	Burgess, Glen K. 39336271	PVT-PFC-CPL	C	MOS 745 ASGD fm 2nd Repl Dep 24Feb44 per MR 05Mar44; pmtd to PFC 01Jul44 (MR 02Jul44); **(Missing entry of AWOL);** fm AWOL 0600 (per MR 05Aug44) to confinement/arrest 06Aug44 (16Aug44); RTD fm arrest 01Sep44; promoted to CPL 24Dec44; MOS 655 MIA 21Jan45 (per MR 23Jan45) **(POW 20JAN45);** Mstr POW reg gives rpt date of 21Jan45, parent unit as Divisioni Artillery, Stalag 12A - 9B, repatriated CIB PFD (07/44); GCM as PVT (08/44); GCM (16/44);	POW 20Jan45
144.	**Burke,** Ray L. or Roy 37603253	SSG	C	MOS 653 ASGD fm 44th Inf Div 25Jan45 (per MR 01Feb45); Evac **WIA** 28Mar45 (per MR 28Mar45); already evac **WIA**, TFRD to DofP 30Mar45 (per MR 30Mar45) CIB 01Mar45 (10/45); GCM (8/45)	WIA 28Mar45

145.	**Burkey**, Albert R. 33940929	PVT	C	MOS 745 ASGD fm 3rd Repl Bn 11Dec44 (per MR 12Dec44); evac sk, TFRD to DofP 15Dec44; REASG fm 3rd Repl Dep 08Jan45 (per MR 08Jan45); Evac **WIA**, TFRD to DofP 14Jan45 (per MR 14Jan45) CIB 01Jan45 (01/45)	WIA 14Jan45
146.	Burkhardt, John S. PCM-C	PFC	C	On Pine Camp menu No discovered GO for CIB or GCM	
147.	Burns, Dave (Delta, CO)	PVT	C	Induction Roster, Delta, CO, 16Sep40	
148.	Burt, Elmer W., Jr. 39834282	PFC	C	GCM (32/45)	
149.	Busbee, James E. or Buzbee NOT ASSIGNED	PVT	C	MOS 677 ASGD fm RHQ 24Jun44 (assignment rescinded per MR 28Jun44) **NOT ASSIGNED**	
150.	**Butts**, Ronald A. 32745427	PVT-PFC-T-5	C	MOS 745 ASGD 03Aug43; evac sk 04Sep43 (per MR 06Sep43); RTD frm sk 23Sep43 (per MR 29Sep43); evac **WIA** 12Nov43 per MR 15Nov43; already evac **WIA** TFRD to DofP, DFR per MR 15Dec43; RTD fm DofP (**WIA**) 27Dec43 per MR 31Dec43; Pmtd to PFC 04Mar44 per MR 12Mar44; MOS 511 Pmtd to T-5 (28Jun44) CIB (01/44 - 01Jan44 per CC); GCM as PFC (08/44)	WIA 12Nov43
151.	**Cady**, Harold J. (M.) 36458319	PVT-PFC	C	MOS 745 ASGD & jnd fm 2nd Repl Dep 24 Feb44 per MR 10Mar44; pmtd to PFC 01May44; evac **WIA** 24Sep44; REASG but not joined fm 2nd Repl Dep 04Oct44; joined 05Oct44; TFRD to Med Det 29Oct44 CIB PFD (07/44)	WIA 24Sep44
152.	**Cahoon**, Calvin L. 33533241	PVT-PFC	C	MOS 745 ASGD fm 7th Repl Dep 25Sep43; evac **LIA** 21Dec43 (s/b 17th per MR 27Dec43); RTD fm INJ 02Jan44 (per MR 06Jan44; Pmtd to PFC 04Mar44 per MR 12Mar44; evac **WIA** (pen W L shoulder shell frag) 29May44; already evac **WIA** TFRD toDofP and DFR 03Jun44 (20Jun44); REASG but not jd fm 7th Repl Dep 17Aug44; joined 16Sep44 CIB 01Oct44 (13/44); CIB FM 01Jan44 (14/44)	LIA 21Dec43 WIA 03Jun44
153.	Cain, Edward R. PCM-A O-1311868	2LT-1LT	A, C, F	2LT 3rd Platoon Leader, A Co per Pine Camp menu **(Unknown date of assignment)** TFRD to Co F 04Aug43 CIB 1LT 01Sep44 (13/44); CIB FM 01Jan44 (14/44)	
154.	**Caldwell,** Adrian B. **O-1305159**	2LT-1LT	C	**(Unknown date of assignment, not on Pine Camp menu) SWIA** 14Jul43; RTD fr 7th Repl Dep 12Sep43 (per MR 14Sep43); evac sk 05Oct43; RTD fm sk 28Oct43; evac sk 29Oct43 per MR 01Nov43; RTD fm sk 11Nov43 (per MR 14Nov43); evac sk 30Nov43 (per MR 07Dec43); RTD fm sk 02Jan44 per MR 06Jan44; Pmtd to 1LT 04Jan44 per MR 15Jan44; reld fr asgn & duty and asgd to Pers Center #1 05Apr44 per MR 06Apr44 No discovered GO for CIB or GCM	WIA 14Jul43

155.	**Caldwell**, Tom R. 34770264	PVT-PFC	C	MOS 745 ASGD fm 3rd Repl Bn 11Dec44 (per MR 12Dec44); evac sk, TFRD to DofP 15Dec44; REASG fm 3rd Repl Bn 31Dec44; Evac sk, TFRD to DofP 04Jan45 (per MR 04Jan45); REASG fm 71st Reinf Bn 27May45 (per MR 27May45); PMTD to PFC 06Mar45 (per MR 06Mar45); Evac **WIA**, TFRD to DofP 18Mar45 (per MR 18Mar45) CIB 01Jan45 (01/45); GCM (8/45)	WIA 18Mar45
156.	Calhoun, Charles V. 36696187	SGT-SSG	C	MOS 653/652 ASGD fm 36th Inf Div 26Jan45 (per MR 01Feb45); evac sk 26Feb45 (per MR 26Feb45); RTD fm evac sk 03Mar45 (per MR 03Mar45); Pmtd to SSG, change in MOS to 652 14Apr45 (per MR 14Apr45) GCM (8/45)	
157.	**Callahan**, Michael (NMI) 32240581	PFC	C	Deployed w/the company, is in the Pine Camp menu) Pmtd PFC 10Aug43; Evac **WIA** 13Sep43 (per MR 20Sep43); RTD fr DofP 05Dec43 per MR 12Dec43; attached to 45th Div Mule Train 16Dec43; already Special Duty to 45th Inf Div Mule Train (Prov), evac sk 07Mar44 per MR 12Mar44; already evac sk, tfrd to DofP and DFR 10Mar44 per MR 04Apr44 CIB as PFC in C Co FM 01Jan44 (14/44)	WIA 13Sep43
158.	Calvary, Frank L. 35077313	PVT	C	MOS 745 ASGD & jnd fm 2nd Repl Dep 24 Feb44 per MR 10Mar44; evac sk 17Apr44 (per MR 22Apr44); tfrd to DofP, DFR (per MR 08May44); already evac sk, tfrd to DofP and DFR on 27Apr44 CIB FM 01Mar44 (14/44)	
159.	Camomile, Emery R. 39026019	SGT	C	MOS 653 ASGD but DS to 3rd Reinf Bn 08May45 (per MR 14May45); relieved of DS to 3rd Reinf Bn 13May45 (per MR 14May45) GCM (32/45)	
160.	**Campana,** Thomas A. 35606286	PVT-PFC	C	**(Unknown date of assignment, not on Pine Camp menu)** Evac sk 09Dec43 per MR 14Dec43; already evac sk TFRD to DofP, DFR per MR 31Dec43; RTD from DofP 03Jun44; evac sk 14Jun44 (16Jun44); RTD fm sk (29Jun44); AWOL 0545 17Jul44 (MR 20Jul44); RTD fm AWOL 0600 29Jul44; **WIA** not hosp 05Nov44 (per MR 09Nov44); promoted to PFC 07Oct44; evac sk,TFRD to DofP 28Oct44; **(Missing RTD entry);** evac sk, TFRD to DofP 15Nov44 CIB 01Jan44 (11/44)	WIA 05Nov44
161.	Campbell, John L. 38400135	PVT	C	MOS 745 ASGD fm 7th Repl Dep 25Sep43; evac sk 14Dec43 per MR 24Dec43; already evac sk, TFRD to DofP, DFR per MR 15Jan44 CIB FM 01Jan44 (14/44)	
162.	Campbell, Kenneth (Delta, CO)	CPL	C	Induction Roster, Delta, CO, 16Sep40	

163.	Cannady, Jack T. 38388578	PVT-PFC	C	MOS 504 ASGD fm 2nd Repl Dep per MR 11Dec43; Pmtd to PFC 04Mar44 per MR 12Mar44; evac sk 03Jun44; already evac sk TFRD to DofP and DFR 09Jun44 (17Jun44) CIB FM 01Jan44 (14/44)	
164.	Canter, Roy A. 34609285	PVT-PFC	C	MOS 745/604 ASGD fm 7th Repl Dep 25Sep43; evac sk 16Nov43 per MR 22Nov43; RTD fm sk 29Nov43 (per MR 02Dec43); evac sk (abdominal pains) 25Apr44 (per MR 28Apr44); already evac sk, tfrd to DofP and DFR 01May44 (per MR 19May44); RTD fm DofP (10Jun44); Pmtd to PFC 04Mar44 per MR 12Mar44; evac sk, TFRD to DofP 03Sep44; REASG fm hosp 16Sep44; evac sk 30Sep44; already evac sk, TFRD to DofP 01Oct44; RTD fm sk 29Nov43 per MR 02Dec43; evac **LIA** 15Dec43 per MR 19Dec43; REASG fm 3rd Repl Bn 18Dec44 (per MR 19Dec44); **(Missing entry of evacuation);** already evac sk, TFRD to DofP, DFR per MR 16Jan44; RTD fm DofP 19Jan44 per MR 21Jan44; MIA 21Jan45 (per MR 23Jan45) **(POW 20JAN45)** CIB (01/44 - 01Jan44 per CC); CIB PFD (07/44); GCM as PFC PFD (08/44)	POW 20Jan45
165.	Capuano, Albert C. PCM-C	PVT	C	On Pine Camp menu	
166.	Caputo, Fred D. 42011002	PVT	C	MOS 745 ASGD 29May44 (09Jun44); evac sk 18Jun44 (19Jun44); already evac sk TFRD to 2d Repl Dep & reclassified limited assignment 18Jul44 No discovered GO for CIB or GCM	
167.	Cardameni, Joseph J. 36194321	PVT	C	MOS 504 ASGD fm Co E 22Oct44 (per MR 25Oct44); MIA 26Oct44 (per MR 28Oct44); PVT corr: from MIA 26Oct44 to AWOL 2359 26Oct44, to Regt'l Stockade 27Oct44 (per MR 30Oct44); RTD fm Regt'l Stockade01Dec44; evac sk 03Dec44; already evac, TFRD to DofP 04Dec44 No discovered GO for CIB or GCM	
168.	**Carnathan, Robert C. 34625098**	**PVT**	C	**(Unknown date of assignment, not on Pine Camp menu)** MIA 15Dec43, DFR (per MR 25Dec43), to **KIA** 15Dec43 (per MR 28Oct44) (buried in Mt. Gilead Cemetery, Union County, MS) POW 15Dec43; **murdered by Germans** No discovered GO for CIB or GCM	**KIA 13Apr44**
169.	Carr, Eldred E. (Delta, CO)	PVT	C	Induction roster, Delta, CO, 16Sep40	
170.	**Carr,** Henry E. 36583139	PFC	C	ASGD from L Co; evac sk 13Apr44 (MR 20Apr44); RTD 16Apr44 (per MR 20Apr44); evac sk 03Jun44; RTD fm sk 17Jun44 (19Jun44); evac **WIA**, TFRD to DofP 25Nov44 (per MR 28Nov44); REASG fm 3rd Repl Bn 23Dec44; **(Missing entry of evac)**; already evac sk, TFRD to DofP 28Dec44; CIB PFD (07/44)	WIA 25Nov44

171.	**Carrick,** Clyde H. (Garrick) 34594022	PVT- SSG	C	MOS 745 ASGD fm 2nd Repl Dep 24Feb44 per MR 05Mar44; promoted to PFC (per MR 05Aug44); promoted to CPL MOS 653 07Oct44; promoted to SSG MOS 542 24Dec44; Evac **WIA**, TFRD to DofP 14Jan45 (per MR 14Jan45); REASGD fm 2nd Rein Dep 25Feb45 (per MR 25Feb45); Evac INJ 18Mar45 (per MR 18Mar45); Already Evac, TFRD to DofP 20Mar45 (per MR 20Mar45) CIB PFD (07/44); GCM (02/44); GCM (08/44)	WIA 14Jan45
172.	**Carter**, Charles (NMI) 35653298	PVT-PFC-PVT-PFC-SGT	C	MOS 745 ASGD & jnd fm 2nd Repl Dep 24 Feb44 per MR 10Mar44; pmtd to PFC 01May44; AWOL 0630 03Jul44 (MR 04Jul44); RTD 2300 03Jul44 (MR 04Jul44); reduced to PVT 04Jul44; promoted to PFC (per MR 05Aug44); evac **WIA** 24Sep44; REASG fm 2nd Repl Dep 17Oct44; evac sk 24Oct44; already evac sk, TFRD to DofP 26Oct44; REASG fm 2nd Repl Dep 11Nov44; MOS 653 promoted to SGT 24Nov44; MIA 21Jan45 (per MR 23Jan45) **(POW 20JAN45)** CIB (04/44); 01Apr44 per CC; GCM as PVT (08/44)	WIA 24Sep44 POW 20Jan45
173.	**Castro,** Victor V. 38160168	T-5	C	MOS 653/745 ASGD fm 24th Repl Dep 26Jan45 (per MR 30Jan45); Evac **WIA**, TFRD to DofP 18Mar45 (per MR 18Mar45) CIB 01Mar45 (10/45)	WIA 18Mar45
174.	Caswell, Lloyd H. 31471434	PFC	C	No mention in Morning Reports GCM (32/45)	
175.	Caudle, Isaac F. 38510768	PVT-PFC	C	MOS 745 ASGD & jnd fm 2nd Repl Dep 24 Feb44 per MR 10Mar44; pmtd to PFC 01Jul44 (MR 02Jul44; MIA 21Jan45 (per MR 23Jan45) **(POW 20JAN45);** Mstr POW reg gives rpt date of 21Jan45, Stalag 11B, repatriated CIB PFD (07/44)	POW 20Jan45
176.	Cervone, Peter M. 32217098	PVT	C, CN	**(Unknown date of assignment, not on Pine Camp menu)** TFRD to Cannon Co. 13Aug43 (name blurred, verified by GOs of CN Co) CIB 01Jan44 (06/44 CC); GCM PVT (16/44)	
177.	Chadderton, Harold J. 35112491	PFC	C	GCM (32/45)	
178.	Chapman, Archibald H. 33535520	PVT-PFC	C, G	MOS 745 ASGD fm 7th Repl Dep 25Sep43; evac sk 22Dec43 per MR 27Dec43; RTD fm sk 02Jan44 per MR 06Jan44; pmtd PFC 14Jan44 per MR 15Jan44; evac sick (appendicitis) to 93 Evac Hosp 02Feb44; RTD 15Feb44; Tfr in grade to G Co per MR 05Mar44 CIB PFD in G Co (07/44)	
179.	**Chapman, Howard 35839226**	**PVT-PFC**	C	MOS 745 ASGD fm 3rd Repl Bn 11Dec44 (per MR 12Dec44); Pmtd to PFC 07Jan45 (per MR 08Jan45); MIA 21Jan45 (per MR 23Jan45) (**KIA** O/A 20JAN45) (buried in USA); MIA 21JAN45; not on 157 list; not on ABMC reg CIB 01Jan45 (01/45);	**KIA 20Jan45**

180.	**Chavez**, John B. PCM-C 38006140	PVT-PFC	C	(Deployed w/the company, is on the Pine Camp menu) Pmtd to PFC 01Dec43; evac **WIA** 12Dec43 (per MR 15Dec43); RTD fm **WIA** 04Jan44 per MR 07Jan44; **WIA** (perf w r side mandible shell frag) 22Feb44; tfrd in grade to Pers Center #1 05Apr44 per MR 06Apr44 CIB DP as PFC in C Co (07/44)	WIA 12Dec43 WIA 22Feb44
181.	**Chavez**, Juan A. PCM-C 38005269	PFC	C	(Deployed w/the company, is on Pine Camp menu) **(Missing entry of WIA evac)**; Already evac **WIA**, trfd to DofP and DFR 01Mar44 per MR 15Mar44 CIB as PVT in C Co DP (07/44)	WIA
182.	**Chilcutt**, Clarence L. 33007665	T-5	C	MOS 745 ASGD fm 24th Repl Dep 26Jan45 (per MR 30Jan45); evac **WIA** 29Mar45 (per MR 29Mar45); Already evac **WIA**, TFRD to DofP 30Mar45 (per MR 30Mar45) CIB 01Mar45 (10/45)	WIA 29Mar45
183.	Chorba, John A. PCM-C 32207036	PFC	C	MOS 675 (Deployed w/the company, is on the Pine Camp menu) Evac sk 26Dec43 per MR 28Dec43; already evac sk TFRD to DofP, DFR (erron entry per MR 30Jan44); **(Missing entry of evacuation);** Tfr to DofP and DFR 12Feb44; RTD from DofP 20May44 (per MR 21May44); evac sk 28Jul44 (MR 29Jul44); TFRD to 2nd Repl Dep but not departed 19Jul44; s/b ATCHD & jnd (MR 23Jul44); already evac sk, relieved fm atchment fr 2nd Repl Det (per MR 05Aug44) CIB as PFC in C Co (04/44); 01Jan44 per CC; GCM (08/44)	
184.	Ciesinski, Adam J. 32302535	PVT	C	CIB FM 01Jan44 (14/44)	
185.	**Clements,** John R. 38338061	SSG-TSG	C	SSG-1SG-PVT-TSG MOS 651/585 ASGD fm 2nd Repl Dep 11Jan44 per MR 13Jan44; evac **WIA** (pen w r cheek & thigh shell frag) 17Feb44; RTD 27Feb44; RTD fm **WIA** 27Feb44 per MR 03Mar44; evac sk (colitis spastic cause unknown) 28Mar44 fm MR 05Apr44; RTD fm sk 20Apr44 (per MR 24Apr44); promoted to TSG (per MR 05Aug44); evac sk 01Sep44; already evac sk, TFRD to DofP 02Sep44; RTD fm hosp 06Sep44; promoted to 1SG MOS 585 07Oct44; reduced to PVT, promoted to TSG, TFRD to Co D 02Dec44 CIB (03/44); 01Feb44 per CC; GCM (02/44)	WIA 17Feb44

186.	Coatney, Lester A. 20838090 INDUCTION IN 2HQ	SSG	2HQ, C	PVT in 2HQ per Induction Roster,16Sep40; MOS 070 **(Unknown date of assignment, not on Pine Camp menu)** Deployed w/the battalion; on Pine Camp menu as SSG in 2HQ; Evac sk 17Aug43 (per MR 21Aug43); RTD fm sk 22Aug43 (per MR 23Aug43); evac sk 18Dec43 per MR 21Dec43; already evac sk TFRD to DofP, DFR per MR 19Jan44; **(Missing entry of RTD and another evacuation)** already evac sk, tfr to DofP & DFR 26Feb44 CIB DP (07/44) as SSG in C Co	
187.	Cobb, Delbert C. PCM-1 20847270	SGT	1HQ, C	SGT in 1HQ per Pine Camp meun; CIB SGT in 1HQ (01/44 - 01Jan44 per CC); GCM (02/44); CIB DP (07/44); CIB PVT in C Co 01Jan45 (01/45)	
188.	**Cobb**, Thomas L. 34096505	SGT-SSG	C	MOS 812 ASGD 15Sep44; **WIA** not hosp 05Dec44 (per MR 10Dec44); promoted to SSG 24Dec44; MIA 21Jan45 (per MR 23Jan45 **(POW 20JAN45)** CIB 01Oct44 (13/44)	WIA 05Dec44 POW 20Jan45
189.	Cohen, Jack J. 36541532	PFC	C	GCM (32/45)	
190.	Cole, Clarence H.	PVT	RHQ, C	MOS 677 ASGD fm RHQ 24Jun44 (assignment rescinded per MR 28Jun44) **NOT ASSIGNED** CIB Present Pers in RHQ 01Jan44 (10/44 CC)	
191.	Cole, Glenn M. (Delta, CO)	PVT	C	Induction Roster, 16Sep40	
192.	**Coleman**, Donald A. PCM-C 11048023	PVT-PFC	C	(Deployed w/the company, is on the Pine Camp menu as PVT) Evac **WIA** (pen w r foot bomb frag) 17Feb44; already evac **WIA** tfrd to DofP and DFR 15Mar44 per MR 04Apr44 CIB DP as PFC in C Co (07/44)	WIA 17Feb44
193.	**Collins,** Otis (NMI) 37610788	PVT-PFC	C	ASGD fm Co B 14Jan44 per MR 15Jan44; pmtd to PFC 01May44; **WIA** not hosp 24Mar45 (pen w L knee) (per MR 25May45); Evac sk 12Apr45 (per MR 12Apr45); Already evac sk, TFRD to DofP 14Apr45 (per MR 14Apr45); REASG but DS to 71st Reinf Bn 01May45 (per MR 03May45; Relieved of DS to 71st Reinf Bn 03May45 (per MR 03May45) CIB (04/44); 01Jan44 per CC; GCM (16/44)	
194.	Colvin, Charles B. 0-1315559	2LT	H, C, D	**(Unknown date of assignment, not on Pine Camp menu)** TFRD to Co D per MR 05Dec43 CIB 01Jan44 (11/44); CIB 01Jan44 (13/44) – both in H Company	
195.	**Connell**, Edwin R. 31003325	PVT	C	MOS 745 ASGD 28Sep43 (per MR 30Sep43); evac **WIA** (Punct W R shoulder shell frag) 30May44**;** already evac sk, DFR per MR 17Nov43 CIB FM 01Jan44 (14/44)	WIA 30May44
196.	Connor, James W. 36680070	PVT	C	MOS 745 ASGD fm 2nd Repl Dep 24Feb44 per MR 05Mar44; evac sk (exhaustion) 11Apr44 (per MR 18Apr44); already evac sk tfrd to 7th Repl Depot 02May44 (per MR 13May44) CIB FM 01Mar44 (14/44)	

197.	**Connor**, Karl R. (Conner) (or Merle, or Marl) **33763756**	PVT-PFC	C	MOS 745 ASGD & jnd fm 2nd Repl Dep 24 Feb44 per MR 10Mar44; pmtd to PFC 01May44; RTD fm **WIA** (23Jun44); **(Missing entry for RTD);** TFRD on rotation to USA 09Oct44 CIB 01Mar44 (11/44)	WIA 23Jun44
198.	Conrad, Windel G. 39687123	PVT	I, C	MOS 745 ASGD fm 2nd Repl Dep 08Aug44 (31Aug44); evac sk, TFRD to DofP 25Sep44; REASG fm 71st Repl Dep 01Dec44; duty to Regt'l Stockade 02Dec44 (per MR 10Dec44); correction to MR 09Dec44 of evac sk, TFRD to DofP – s/b duty to Regt'l Stockade 02Dec44; evac sk from stockade, TFRD to DofP 09Dec44 (per 10Dec44) CIB (01/44); 01Mar44 per CC; CIB FM 01Mar44 (14/44)	
199.	Conti, Peter L. 0-1331607	2LT	A, C	**(Unknown date of assignment)(Missing date of evac)**; RTD 09May45 (per MR 09May45) CIB 01Apr45 (15/45) Bronze Star	
200.	Coogins, Ervin W. (Goggins) 31471645	PFC	C	GCM (32/45)	
201.	Cook, Donald W. 32585651	T-5	C	MOS 745 ASGD fm 24th Repl Dep 26Jan45 (per MR 30Jan45); evac sk, TFRD to DofP 26Feb45 (per MR 26Feb45) CIB 01Mar45 (10/45)	
202.	Cooke, Elton F. PCM-G	PVT	G, RHQ, C	MOS 677 ASGD fm RHQ 24Jun44 (assignment rescinded per MR 28Jun44) **NOT ASSIGNED** PVT in G Co per Pine Camp menu; CIB as PVT in RHQ 01Jan44 (03/44 CC)	
203.	Cope, Sy C. 7010010	SGT	C	MOS 653 ASGD 15Sep44; evac sk 07Dec44; RTD fm sk 10Dec44; Evac sk 03Jan45 (per MR 04Jan45); Already evac sk, TFRD to DofP 04Jan45 (per MR 04Jan45); REASG fm 3rd Repl Bn 26Jan45 (per MR 26Jan45); evac sk 22Oct44; already evac sk, TFRD to DofP 23Oct44; REASG fm 2nd Repl Dep 21Nov44 (per MR 22Nov44) CIB FM 01Oct44 (14/44)	
204.	Corbin, Lon H. 37536830	CPL	C	MOS 653 ASGD and joined fm 2nd Repl Dep 04Nov44 (per MR 09Nov44); evac sk, TFRD to DofP 08Dec44 CIB 01Mar45 (9/45)	
205.	Corsaro, Frank (NMI) C32204846 PCM-C	T-5/ PFC	C	(Deployed w/the company, is on the Pine Camp menu as PVT) Evac sk 14Aug43 (per MR 16Aug43); RTD fm sk 24Aug43; MIA 13Sep43 DFR (per MR 24Sep43) **(POW 13Sep43)** CIB MIA as T-5 in C Co (05/44); 01Jan44 per CC; Mstr POW reg gives rpt date of 13Sep43, Stalag 18A, repatriated	POW 13Sep43

206.	**Cottone,** Joseph 32698487	CPL	C	MOS 653 ASGD fm 24th Repl Dep 26Jan45 (per MR 30Jan45); evac **WIA** 29Mar45 (per MR 29Mar45); Already evac **WIA**, TFRD to DofP 30Mar45 (per MR 30Mar45); REASG 29May45 (per MR 30May45) CIB 01Mar45 (10/45); GCM (8/45)	WIA 30Mar45
207.	Couturier, Edmund J. 31068241 PCM-C	PVT	C	(Deployed w/the company, is on the Pine Camp menu as PVT) Evac sk 23Aug43 (per MR 24Aug43); RTD fm SK 31Aug43 (per MR 01Sep43) **NO ENTRY OF MIA??** CIB FM as PVT in C Co 01Jan44 (14/44); Mstr POW reg gives rpt date of 13Sep44, Stalag 2B, repatriated	POW 13Sep43
208.	Cowles, Coy 35810486	PVT-PFC	C	MOS 745 ASGD fm 3rd Repl Bn 11Dec44 (per MR 12Dec44); Pmtd to PFC 07Jan45 (per MR 08Jan45); MIA 21Jan45 (per MR 23Jan45) **(POW 20JAN45)** CIB 01Jan45 (01/45); Mstr POW reg gives rpt date of 21Jan45, parent unit as Divisional Artillery, Stalag 11B, repatriated	POW 20Jan45
209.	Craig, Samuel E. PCM-C	PFC	C	C Co per Pine Camp menu **DID NOT DEPLOY**	
210.	CRAIG, Vachel H. 35906296	PVT	C	GCM (35/45)	
211.	**Craig**, Wilbur H. 36918832	SGT	C	**(Unknown date of assignment, not on Pine Camp menu)** Evac **WIA** 12Dec43 per MR 19Dec43; already evac **WIA** TFRD to DofP, DFR per MR 13Jan44; RTD fm DofP 13Feb; evac **LIA** (pen w r thumb, self-inflicted) 19Feb44; already evac **WIA**, trfd to DofP and DFR 03Mar44 per MR 15Mar44 CIB FM 01Jan44 (14/44)	WIA 12Dec43 LIA 19Feb44
212.	**Crain,** Oris H. 35841231	PVT-PFC	C	MOS 745/603 ASGD fm 3rd Repl Bn 11Dec44 (per MR 12Dec44); Pmtd to PFC 07Jan45 (per MR 08Jan45); Evac INJ, TFRD to DofP 15Jan45 (per MR 15Jan45); REASG fm 2nd Reinf Dep 11Mar45 (per MR 11Mar45); Evac **WIA**, TFRD to DofP 18Mar45 (per MR 18Mar45) CIB 01Jan45 (01/45)	WIA 18Mar45
213.	Crane, James V. 33165767	T-5	C	MOS 745 ASGD fm 24th Repl Dep 26Jan45 (per MR 30Jan45); Evac sk 06Mar45 (per MR 06Mar45); already evac sk, TFRD to DofP 08Mar45 (per MR 08Mar45); RTD fm 71st Reinf Bn 24Mar45 (per MR 26Mar45); Evac **WIA** 21Apr45 (per MR 21Apr45); already evac **WIA**, TFRD to DofP 22Apr45 (per MR 22Apr45) CIB 01Mar45 (10/45); GCM (8/45)	WIA 21Apr45
214.	Crawley, William E. (Delta, CO)	SGT	C	Induction Roster, 16Sep40	

215.	Crispo, Leo H. PCM-C 31068184	PFC	C	(Deployed w/the company, is on the Pine Camp menu as PFC) Evac sk 03Aug43 (per MR 04Aug43); RTD fm sk 05Aug43 (per MR 06Aug43) **NO MIA REPORT???** CIB MIA as PFC in C Co (05/44); 01Jan44 per CC; Mstr POW reg gives rpt date of 13Sep43, Stalag 2B, repatriated	POW 13Sep43
216.	**Criss**, Lawrence (NMI) 38006156 PCM-C	PFC- SSG	C	(Deployed w/the company, is on the Pine Camp menu as PFC) Promoted to CPL 05Nov43 per MR 05Nov43; pmtd to SGT per MR 02Dec43; evac sk 14Jan44 per MR 17Jan44; pmtd SSG per MR 28Jan44; RTD fm sk 04Feb44, evac sk (FUO) 08Feb44; evac **WIA** (pen W L arm & shoulder, L upper eyelid shell frag) 30May44; already evac **WIA** TFRD to DofP and DFR 06Jun44 (17Jun44) CIB as SSG in C Co (01/44 - 01Jan44 per CC); GCM (02/44)	WIA 30May44
217.	Critchfield, Albert L. 38156089	CPL	C	MOS 653 ASGD fm 24th Repl Dep 26Jan45 (per MR 30Jan45); Evac sk, TFRD to DofP 18Mar45 (per MR 18Mar45) CIB 01Mar45 (10/45)	
218.	Cromer, Elmo F. PCM-H 20838694 (Ft. Collins, CO)	1SG	H, C	CPL in H Co per Induction Roster, 16Spe40; (Deployed w/H Company as 1SG) MIA 13Sep43 DFR (per MR 24Sep43) **(POW 13Sep43);** Mstr POW reg gives rpt date as13Sep43, rank as 1SG, Stalag Luft 3, repatriated CIB FM as SGT in C Co 01Jan44 (14/44)	POW 13Sep43
219.	Cross, Lewis M. 33454739	PVT-PFC	C	MOS 745 ASGD 13Aug43; promoted PFC 01Jan44 per MR 05Jan44; Evac sk 17Jan45 (per MR 17Jan45); already evac sk, TFRD to DofP 18Jan45 (per MR 18Jan45); evac sk (FUO) 08Feb44; RTD fm sk 15Feb44; evac sk (I. Pleurisy Ac fibricus 2. Sprain lumbar region acc) 31Mar44 per MR 08Apr44; already evac sk, tfrd to DofP and DFR 05May44 (per MR 14May44); RTD fm DofP (10Jun44); evac sk 05Jul44; RTD fm sk 11Jul44 (MR 13Jul44); **(Missing entry for evacuation sick);** already evac sk on Ship Acadia TFRD to DofP/DFR 17Aug44; REASG fm 2nd Repl Dep 21Nov44 (per MR 22Nov44) CIB (01/44 - 01Jan44 per CC); CIB PFD (07/44); GCM (08/44)	
220.	Crowe, Henry D. PCM-C 33360431	PVT-PFC	C	(Deployed w/the company, is on the Pine Camp menu as PVT) Pmtd PFC 01Jul43 (Fm MR 20Jul43); evac sk 12Sep43 (per MR 20Sep43) CIB FM as PFC in C Co 01Jan44 (14/44)	
221.	Crucitti, Martin (NMI) SN NA PCM-F	PVT	F, RHQ, C	CPL in F Co per Pine Camp menu; MOS 677 ASGD fm RHQ 24Jun44 (assignment rescinded per MR 28Jun44) **NOT ASSIGNED** CIB as PVT in RHQ 01Jan44 (03/44 CC)	

222.	CRUIKSHANK, Chester G. PCM-3 (Delta, CO)	1LT, MAJ	C, 3HQ	1LT CO of C Co per Induction Roster, 16Sep40; MAJ XO of 3/157 per Pine Camp Menu No discovery of CIB GO	
223.	Cruz, Michael A. PCM-C	PVT	C, L	PVT in C Co per Pine Camp menu CIB DP as PVT in L Co (07/44)	
224.	Culp, George K. Jr. (Walsh, CO) 20838153	PVT-PFC-CPL-SGT-PVT	E, B, C, G	PVT in E Co per Induction Roster, 16Sep40; NOT ON ANY PCM; MOS 653 ASGD fm Co B 14Jan44 per MR 15Jan44; **(Missing entry for evac sk);** RTD fm sk 02Mar44 per MR 10Mar44; Pmtd to PFC 04Mar44 per MR 12Mar44; **(Missing entry for evac sk);** RTD fm sk 04Feb44; evac sk (gonorrhea) 08Feb44; **pmtd to Cpl UNK DATE;** evac sk 14May44 (MR 19May44); erron rptd RTD fm sk 21May44 on MR 24May44; RTD fm sk 21May44 (fm MR 24May44); erron entry (per MR 30May44); s/b fm sk to AWOL 30May44; pmtd to SGT MOS 653 24May44; AWOL to confinement Fifth Army Stockade 31May44; from 5th Army confine to 45th Div Stkd (02Jun44); AWOL from 45th Div Stkd 0700 04Jun44; Red to PVT 06Jun44 while AWOL; RTD fm AWOL 0700 12Jun44 (19Jun44); RTD fm Regtl Stockade 10Jul44 (MR 12Jul44); TFR to Co G 12Jul44 CIB as PVT in G Co 01Jan44 (11/44); CIB CPL (03/44 -- 01Feb44 per CC)	
225.	Curry, James 35906300	PFC	C	GCM (35/45)	
226.	**Curtis**, Maurice (NMI) 34732958	PFC	C	MOS 607 ASGD fm 2nd Repl Bn 18Dec43 per MR 22Dec43; **WIA** (Perf W R thigh, perf W finger) 10Feb44; TFRD to DofP & DFR 15Feb44; already evac **WIA** tfrd to DofP, DFR 15Feb44; RTD fm DofP 29Mar44 per MR 08Apr44; evac sk (FUO) 07Jun44; RTD fm sk 11Jun44 (13Jun44); evac sk, TFRD to DofP 03Sep44; REASG not joined fm 2nd Repl Dep 29Sep44 (per MR 30Sep44); joined 04Oct44; evac sk, TFRD to DofP 02Nov44 CIB PFD (07/44)	WIA 10Feb44
227.	Czarnecki, Stanley J. 32217079 PCM-C	PVT	C, AT, RHQ	(Deployed w/the company, is on the Pine Camp menu as PVT) Sk evac 24Jul43 (per MR 25Jul43); RTD fm hosp 01Aug43 (per MR 02Aug43); TFRD to RHQ 28Aug43 CIB as PFC in AT Co FM 01Jan44 (14/44)	
228.	Czechel, Stanley (NMI) 31386019	PVT	C	MOS 745 ASGD fm E Co (27Jun44); TFRD to 2nd Repl Dep but not dptd 19Jul44; s/b ATCHD & jnd (MR 23Jul44); AWOL 0530 29Jul44 (31Jul44); RTD fm AWOL 0645 31Jul44; evac sk 03Aug44; ASGD fm 2nd Repl Dep 19Oct44; MIA 08Nov44 (per MR 10Nov44) **(POW 08Nov44)** CIB 01Sep44 (13/44); Mstr POW reg gives rpt date of 08Nov44, Stalag 7A, repatriated	POW 08Nov44

229.	**Czerpak, Anthony E. 31062744 PCM-C**	**PFC**	C	Deployed w/the company, is on the Pine Camp menu as PVT) **KIA** 12Nov43 (per MR 17Nov43) (buried in USA); KIA as PFC in C Co per master 157 casualty list; not on ABMC reg No discovered GO for CIB or GCM	**KIA 12Nov43**
230.	**Dalessandro, Nicholas (NMI) 32762797**	**PVT**	C	MOS 745 ASGD 03Aug43; erron rptd evac sk 07Aug43 (per MR 12Aug43); MIA 16Aug43 (per MR 21Aug43) (DFR per MR 07Sep43) **(Drowned in Sicily landings; still MIA)** commemorated at Sicily-Rome Cemetery no awards CIB FM 01Jan44 (14/44); NOT on Div casualty list; ABMC 16Aug43, still MIA No discovered GO for CIB or GCM	**MIA 16Aug43**
231.	**Dalton**, Edward (NMI) 13094522	SSG	C	MOS 651 ASGD fr 2 Repl Dep 04Jun44 (14Jun44); **WIA** not hosp 28Oct44; evac **WIA**, TFRD to DofP 31Oct44 CIB 01Sep44 (13/44)	WIA 28Oct44 WIA 31Oct44
232.	**Daschke,** Vincent J. 36577939	PVT	C	MOS 745 ASGD fm 7th Repl Dep 25Sep43; evac **WIA** 15Oct43 (per MR 18Oct43); already evac **WIA**, DFR per MR 23Nov43; RTD fm DofP 24Dec43 (per MR 27Dec43); evac sk 02Jan44 (per MR 05Jan44); already sk abs, tfr to 2nd Repl Dep (per MR 14Feb44) CIB FM (05/44); 01Jan44 per CC	WIA 23Nov43
233.	Davenport, Ward B. PCM-C SN NA	PFC	C	C Co per Pine Camp menu	
234.	Davidson, Douglas R. SN NA	PFC	1HQ, C	MOS 521 ASGD fm 1HQ 24Jun44 (assignment rescinded MR 28Jun44) **NOT ASSIGNED** CIB (04/44); 01Jan44 per CC	
235.	Davis, George M. O-1312751	1LT	C, B	ASGD fm 1HQ 20Aug44 (per MR 20Sep44); TFRD to Co B 27Sep44 CIB (03/44); eff 01Jun44 per CC	
236.	Davis, John C. 37684834	PVT-PFC	C	MOS 745 ASGD fm 2nd Repl Dep 11Nov44 (per MR 13Nov44); evac sk, TFRD to DofP 04Dec44; Evac Inj, TFRD to DofP 14Jan45 (per MR 14Jan45); RTD fm 71st Reinf Bn 24Mar45 (per MR 26Mar45); Evac sk 26Mar45 (per MR 26Mar45); REASG fm 71st Reinf Bn 28May45 (per MR 28May45) CIB 01Dec44 (01/45); GCM as PFC (32/45)	
237.	Davis, Kenneth D. 31253532	PVT	C	MOS 745 ASGD (03Aug43); MIA 13Sep43 DFR (per MR 24Sep43) **(POW 13Sep43)** CIB FM 01Jan44 (14/44); Mstr POW reg gives rpt date of 13Sep43 as member of 116TH Infantry, 100th ID (116th was not a component of the 100ID), Stalag Luft 1, repatriated	POW 13Sep43
238.	Davis, Russell A. 32894059	PVT	C	ASGD fm HHC 1st Bn 25Apr44; evac sk 03Jun44; already evac sk TFRD to DofP/DFR 10Jun44 (17Jun44) CIB FM 01Jan44 (14/44)	

239.	Davy, Victor R. 20546023	TSG	C	MOS 651 ASGD fm 71st Repl Bn 09Dec44; MIA 21Jan45 (per MR 23Jan45) **(POW 20JAN45)** CIB 01Jan45 (01/45)	POW 20Jan45
240.	**Dean,** John W. PCM-C 31068189	PFC	C	Deployed w/the company, is on the Pine Camp menu as PFC; Seriously wounded on beach 10Jul43, TFR to DofP N. Africa and DFR CIB FM as PFC in C Co 01Jan44 (14/44)	WIA 10Jul43
241.	DeAngelis, Armando F. SN NA PCM-C	PVT	C	C Co per Pine Camp menu	
242.	Dearden, Robert J. 37471775	CPL-SGT	C	MOS 653 ASGD and joined fm 2nd Repl Dep 04Nov44 (per MR 09Nov44); promoted to SGT 24Dec44; MIA 21Jan45 (per MR 23Jan45) **(POW 20JAN45)** MIA21JAN45 per ANB; Mstr POW reg gives rpt date of 21Jan45, parent unit as Divisional Artillery, Stalag 12A to 9B, repatriated CIB 01Dec44 (01/45)	POW 20Jan45
243.	**Dearduff, James W. 6565837**	**TSG**	C	MOS 604 ASGD fm 2nd Repl Dep 29Sep4; evac INJ, TFRD to DofP 27Dec44; REASG fm 3rd Repl Bn 09Feb45 (per MR 09Feb45); MIA 18Mar45 (per MR 20Mar45) changed to **KIA** 18Mar45 (per MR 26Mar45); MIA/KIA18MAR45 per ANB -- NOT ON OTHER LISTS; not on ABMC register; nothing on web CIB 01Oct44 (13/44); GCM DEARDUFF (08/45);	**KIA 18Mar45**
244.	**Decker**, Leonard F. 33565612	PVT	C	**(Unknown date of assignment, not on Pine Camp menu)** Evac **LIA** 01Dec43 per MR 06Dec43; already evac **LIA** TFRD to DofP, DFR per MR 12Dec43; **(Missing entry of RTD)** evac sk 25Apr44; RTD fm DofP 01Apr44 (per MR 11Apr44); RTD fm sk 15May44 (per MR 19May44); evac **WIA** 23May44 (MR 24May44); to DofP/DFR 30May44 (MR 11Jun44); REASG fm 2nd Repl Dep 05Dec44; evac sk, TFRD to DofP 12Dec44 CIB FM 01Jan44 (14/44)	LIA 01Dec43 WIA 23May44
245.	Degilio, Nicholas (NMI) SN NA	PVT	RHQ, C	MOS 677 ASGD fm RHQ 24Jun44 (assignment rescinded per MR 28Jun44) **NOT ASSIGNED** CIB Present Pers 01Jan44 (10/44 CC)	
246.	DeLasso, Henry P. 42010620	PVT	C	MOS 745 ASGD fm 2nd Repl Dep 23Apr44 (per MR 29Apr44); evac sk 02Jun44; RTD fm sk 07Jun44; AWOL 0700 13Jun44 (16Jun44); erron rptd AWOL 13Jun44, s/b evac sk 13Jun44 (19Jun44); TFRD to DofP/DFR 27Jun44 (MR 23Jul44); REASG fm 2nd Repl Dep 30Sep44; under arrest 15Oct44; RTD fm arrest; TFRD to Co I 31Oct44 CIB 01May44 (06/44 CC)	

247.	**DeLeon**, Catarino A. 39857084	PVT	C, G	MOS 745 ASGD fm 7th Repl Dep 25Sep43; evac sk 18Nov43 (per MR 22Nov43); RTD fm sk 29Nov43 (per MR 02Dec43); evac **WIA** 15Dec43 per MR 23Dec43; already evac **WIA** TFRD to DofP, DFR per MR 16Jan44; RTD from **WIA** 03Feb44; Tfr in grade to G Co per MR 05Mar44 CIB FM 01Jan44 (14/44) in G Co	WIA 03Feb44
248.	Dell Isola, Eugene J. 31069562	T-5	C, 1HQ	MOS 014 ASGD & jd fm 2nd Repl Dep 29Feb44 per MR 14Mar44; Tfrd to 1HQ 22May44 CIB PFD (07/44)	
249.	**DeLong**, Beattie M. O-1328241	2LT	C	ASGD fm 3rd Repl Bn 24Jan45 (per MR 12Feb45); Evac **WIA**, TFRD to DofP 18Mar45 (per MR 18Mar45) CIB 01Mar45 (09/45)	WIA 18Mar45
250.	**Dennehy**, Richard R. PCM-C 31068257	PVT-PFC	C	(Deployed w/the company, is on the Pine Camp menu as PVT) Promoted to PFC 03Nov43 (per MR 05Nov43); evac **WIA** 13Nov43 per MR 16Nov43; already evac **WIA** TFRD to DofP, DFR per MR 14Dec43 CIB FM as PFC in C Co 01Jan44 (14/44)	WIA 13Nov43
251.	**Denton,** Cecil P. 38323654	PVT	C	**(Unknown date of assignment, not on Pine Cap menu)** Evac **WIA** 15Sep43 (per MR 20Sep43) CIB FM 01Jan44 (14/44)	WIA 15Sep43
252.	**Deppen**, Robert M. 33516186	PVT-PFC	C	MOS 745 ASGD fm 2nd Repl Dep 23Apr44 (per MR 29Apr44); evac sk 09Jul44; RTD fm sk 15Jul44; promoted to PFC (per MR 05Aug44); evac sk, TFRD to DofP 23Sep44; REASG fm 2nd Repl Dep 20Oct44; Evac **WIA**, TFRD to DofP 16Jan45 (per MR 16Jan45); RTD fm 2nd Reinforcement Dep 20Feb45 (per MR 21Feb45); TDY to UK 13Mar45 (per MR 13Mar45); RTD fm TDY to UK 05Apr45 (per MR 05Apr45); Evac **LIA** 26Apr45 (per MR 26Apr45); Already evac sk, TFRD to DofP 27Apr45 (per MR 27Apr45); REASG fm 71st Reinf Bn 14May45 (per MR 15May45) CIB 01May44 (06/44 CC)	WIA 16Jan45 LIA 26Apr45
253.	Des Ermia, Robert G. 20837698 (Delta, CO) PCM-C	SGT-1SG	C	SGT in C Co per Induction Roster, 16Sep40; 1SG in C Co per Pine Camp menu CIB FM as 1SG of A Co 01Jan44 (14/44)	
254.	DeTillio, Joseph C. PCM-C 31068054	PVT-PFC	C	(Deployed w/the company, is on the Pine Camp menu as PVT) Evac sk 18Aug43 (per MR 04Sep44); RTD fm evac sk 31Aug43 (per MR 04Sep43); Evac sk 30Oct43 per MR 02Nov43; already evac sk, DFR 01Dec43; RTD fr DofP 08Dec43 per MR 12Dec43; **(Missing entry of evac);** REASG fm 3rd Repl Bn 28Dec44; evac sk 21Jul44; already evac sk TFRD to DofP/DFR 01Aug44 (per MR 05Aug44); **(Missing entry of RTD);** TFRD to 516th MP Bn 23Jan45 (per MR 23Jan45) CIB as PFC in C Co DETILLO (03/44); 01Jan44 per CC; GCM (02/44)	

255.	Detonancourt, Omer E. 31061127 PCM-C	PVT	C	(Deployed w/the company, is on the Pine Camp menu as PVT) Evac SK 14Jul43 (per MR 17Jul43); already evac sk, DFR (01Aug43) CIB FM as PVT in C Co 01Jan44 (14/44)	
256.	DeVacarri, Michale J. PCM-C	PVT	C	C Co per Pine Camp menu	
257.	Dewitt, Arthur D. O-1062485	2LT	C	ASGD fm 3rd Repl Bn 12Dec44 (per MR 14Dec44); MIA 21Jan45 (per MR 23Jan45) **(POW 20JAN45)** MIA21JAN45 per ANB; Prob 2nd Plt Ldr; Mstr POW reg gives rpt date of 21Jan45, parent unit as Divisional Artillery, Oflag 13B, repatriated CIB 01Jan45 (01/45)	POW 20Jan45
258.	DeWitt, Paul (NMI) O-414587	1LT	C	ATCHD fm 2nd Repl Dep for training 09Mar44 per MR 03Apr44; evac sk 17Jun44 (per MR 19Jun44); already evac sk, ASGD to DofP/DFR 30Jun44 CIB FM 01Apr44 (14/44)	
259.	DiBruno, Pasquale W. 33467225roach	PVT	C	MOS 745 ASGD fm 7th Repl Dep 25Sep43; evac sk 08Dec43 per MR 14Dec43; already evac sk TFRD to DofP, DFR per MR 08Jan44 CIB FM (05/44); 01Jan44 per CC	
260.	Diehl, James H. 32817273	PVT	C	**(Unknown date of assignment, not on Pine Camp menu)** MIA 15Dec43, DFR per MR 25Dec43 **(POW 15Dec43);** Mstr POW reg gives rpt date of "15 1K 1943" w/o unit ID, Stalag 7A, repatriated CIB FM 01Jan44 (14/44);	POW 15Dec43
261.	DiMartino, Joseph F. 420431?0	PVT	C	MOS 745 ASGD but DS to 3rd Reinf Bn 08May45 (per MR 14May45); relieved of DS to 3rd Reinf Bn 13May45 (per MR 14May45) No discovery of CIB or GCM GOs	
262.	Dimino, Lawrence J. (Dinina) 42016069	PFC	C	MOS 745 ASGD but DS to 3rd Reinf Bn 08May45 (per MR 14May45); relieved of DS to 3rd Reinf Bn 13May45 (per MR 14May45) GCM (32/45)	
263.	Dini, Aido (NMI) PCM-C 32219213	PVT	C, B	(Deployed w/the company, is on the Pine Camp menu as PVT) Evac sk 01Aug43 (per MR 04Aug43); already sk evac, TFRD to Co B (04Aug43) CIB FM as PVT in B Co 01Jan44 (14/44)	
264.	DiNino, James 32787802	PVT	C	MOS 745 ASGD fr 158th FA Bn 31Aug43 (per MR 01Sep43); MIA 13Sep43 DFR (per MR 24Sep43) **(POW 13Sep43);** Mstr POW reg gives rpt date of 13Sep43 w/o middle initial, w/o unit ID, Stalag 2B, repatriated CIB FM 01Jan44 (14/44)	POW 13Sep43
265.	**DiTomaso,** Philip T. PCM-C 32219299	PVT	C	(Deployed w/the company, is on the Pine Camp menu as PVT) **WIA** 29Jul43; already **WIA** evac, DFR CIB FM as PVT in C Co 01Jan44 (14/44)	WIA 29Jul43

266.	DiVaccaro, Michael J. 32219321 PCM-C	PVT-PFC	C	(Deployed w/the company, is on the Pine Camp menu) pmtd PFC 10Aug43; Evac sk 27Sep43 (per MR 03Oct43); RTD 03Sep44; evac sk (FUO) 27May44; RTD fm sk (23Jun44); evac sk, TFRD to DofP 28Aug44; **(Missing entry of RTD);** evac sk, TFRD to DofP 21Nov44 CIB (01/44 - 01Jan44 per CC); GCM 2/44)	
267.	Dixon, Jack C. O-1315151	2LT	C, RHQ	**(Unknown date of assignment, not on the Pine Camp menu)** TFRD to RHQ 26Aug43 S-2 CIB (3/44 - 01Jan44 per CC)	
268.	**Doby**, Charlie H. 34603375	PVT	C	ASGD fm Co B 14Jan44 per MR 15Jan44; evac **WIA** (Pen w r leg shell frag) 15Feb44; already evac LWA ftrd to DofP and DFR 15Mar44 per MR 04Apr44; RTD fm DofP 27Jun44 (28Jun44); evac sk 28Jun44 (29Jun44); already evac sk TFD to DofP/DFR 30Jul44; REASGD fm 2nd Repl Dep 09Dec44; evac sk, TFRD to DofP 12Dec44 CIB PFD (07/44); CIB FM 01Jan44 (14/44)	WIA 15Feb44
269.	Dochod, Edward J. 36195747	PFC-PVT-PFC	C, 1HQ	(Unknown date of assignment, not on Pine Camp menu as PFC) Evac sk 03Aug43 (per MR 04Aug43); already evac sk, DFR 07Sep43; **(Missing entry of RTD);** evac sk 01Dec43 (per MR 14Dec43); RTD fm sk 20Dec43 per MR 24Dec43; Reduced to PVT 01Apr44 per MR 06Apr44; pmtd to PFC 01Jul44 (MR 02Jul44); TFRD to 1HQ 15Sep44 CIB as PFC in C Co (01/44 - 01Jan44 per CC); GCM in 1HQ (16/44)	
270.	Dolan, Eugene W. (Delta, CO)	PVT	C	Induction Roster, 16Sep40	
271.	Domanski, Stanley J. 36457543	PFC	C	MOS 604 ASGD & joined 07Feb44; evac sk 01Aug44; already evac skTFRD to DofP 09Aug44; RTD 12Aug44 (13Aug44); evac sk 28Oct44; already evac sk, TFRD to DofP 29Oct44; REASG fm 2nd Repl Dep 02Nov44 (per MR 08Nov44); under arrest 03Nov44 (per MR 08Nov44); RTD fm arrest 21Nov44 CIB PFD (07/44); GCM (02/44)	
272.	**Dombrowski**, Ladislaus S. 36652238	PFC	C	MOS 746 or 604 ASGD & joined 07Feb44; LWA not-hosp (LW R hand shell frag) 10May44 (per MR 16May44); evac sk 06Jul44; already evac sk TFRD to DofP/DFR 18Jul44 (MR 23Jul44); REASD fm 7th Repl Dep 22Sep44; **WIA** not hosp 22Oct44 (per MR 23Oct44); evac sk 06Nov44; RTD fm sk 08Nov44; evac sk, TFRD to DofP 12Dec44; REASG fm 2nd Repl Dep 14Dec44 (per MR 24Dec44); MIA 21Jan45 (per MR 23Jan45) **(POW 20JAN45);** Mstr POW reg gives rpt date of 21Jan45, as "DOMBROWSKI, L S", parent unit as divisional artillery, Stalag 11B, repatriated CIB (04/44); 01Mar44 per CC; CIB DP (07/44); GCM (16/44)	WIA 22Oct44 POW 20Jan45

273.	Dominguez, Pedro M. 39268391	PVT	C	**(Unknown date of assignment, not on Pine Camp menu)** Evac sk 03Aug43 (per MR 04Aug43); RTD fm sk 05Spe43 (per MR 07Sep43); MIA 13Sep43 DFR (per MR 24Sep43) **(POW 13Sep43);** Mstr POW reg gives rpt date of 13Sep43, Stalag 2B, repatriated CIB FM 01Jan44 (14/44)	POW 13Sep43
274.	Domitrovich, Peter P. 38072486	PFC	C	MOS 745 ASGD but DS to 3rd Reinf Bn 08May45 (per MR 14May45); relieved of DS to 3rd Reinf Bn 13May45 (per MR 14May45) No discovered CIB or GCM GOs	
275.	Dondella, Angelo A. 33504725	PFC	C	CIB PFD (07/44)	
276.	Donnelly, Clifford W. 37675269	T-5	C	GCM (32/45)	
277.	Donovan, Vincent P. 31415343	PFC	C	MOS 745 ASGD but DS to 3rd Reinf Bn 08May45 (per MR 14May45); relieved of DS to 3rd Reinf Bn 13May45 (per MR 14May45) GCM (32/45)	
278.	**Dougherty**, Dan P. 17144035	SSG	C	MOS 653 or 652 ASGD fm 44th Inf Div 25Jan45 (per MR 01Feb45); Evac **WIA** 18Mar45 (per MR 18Mar45); Already Evac, TFRD to DofP 20Mar45 (per MR 20Mar45); 652 REASG fm 71st Reinf Bn, and placed on DS with 71st Reinf Bn 28Mar45 (per MR 03Apr45); REASG fm 71st Reinf Bn 02Apr45 (per MR 03Apr45) CIB from 44ID; GCM (8/45)	WIA 18Mar45
279.	Douglas, James 6828115	SGT	C	MOS 653 ASGD fm 24th Repl Dep 26Jan45 (per MR 30Jan45); evac sk 26Feb45 (per MR 26Feb45); Already evac sk, TFRD to DofP 01Mar45 (per MR 01Mar45); REASG but DS to 71st Reinf Bn 05Apr45 (per MR 11Apr45); Relieved of DS to 71st Reinf Bn 11Apr45 (per MR 11Apr45); Evac sk 02May45 (per MR 02May45); Already evac sk, TFRD to DofP 03May45 (per MR 03May45) CIB 01Mar45 (10/45)	
280.	**Dowds, Robert S. PCM-C** 38005245	**PVT**	C	(Deployed w/the company, is on the Pine Camp menu as PVT) MIA 16Aug43 (per MR 21Aug43) (DFR per MR 07Sep43) **(believed drowned in 2nd Sicily landings. Still MIA)** KIA as PVT in C Co 16Aug45 per Div & 157 casualty list -- believed drowned; ABMC 16Aug43, still MIA BSM no PH CIB MIA (05/44); 01Jan44 per CC	**MIA 16Aug43**
281.	Doyle, Norris S. PCM-C 38018500	PFC-SGT-SSG	C	(Deployed w/the company, is on the Pine Camp menu as PFC) Pmtd to SSG per MR 02Dec43; evac sk 15Dec43 per MR 21Dec43; already evac sk TFRD to DofP, DFR per MR 16Jan44; **(Missing entry of RTD & evac);** already evac sk TFRD to DofP & DFR 21Feb44 CIB DP as SSG in C Co (07/44)	

282.	Dralle, Robert B. O-1825526	2LT	C	ASGD fm 3rd Repl Bn 12Dec44 (per MR 14Dec44); MIA 21Jan45 (per MR 23Jan45) **(POW 20JAN45**); 1st Plt Ldr; Mstr POW reg gives rpt date of 21Jan45 as "DRALLE O1825526"; Stalag 12Ato 9B, repatriated CIB 01Jan45 (01/45);	POW 20Jan45
283.	Drazen, Milton (NMI) 31068202 PCM-C	CPL	C	(Deployed w/the company, is on the Pine Camp menu as PFC) MIA 13Sep43 DFR (per MR 24Sep43) **(POW 13Sep43);** Mstr POW reg gives rpt date of 13Sep43, Stalag 3B, repatriated CIB MIA as CPL in C Co (05/44); 01Jan44 per CC	POW 13Sep43
284.	**Drennen**, Eugene (NMI) 38006224 PCM-C	PFC	C	(Deployed w/the company, is on the Pine Camp menu as PFC) MIA 13Sep43 DFR (per MR 24Sep43); (to **WIA** per MR 30Oct43) actually, POW 13Sep43; Mstr POW reg gives rptdate of 13Sep43, Stalag 2B, repatriated **NO CORRECTION TO MIA?????** CIB MIA as PFC in C Co (05/44); 01Jan44 per CC;	WIA 13Sep43 POW 13Sep43
285.	DuBois, Herbert G. O-1328131	2LT	C	ASGD fm 3rd Repl Bn 24Jan45 (per MR 24Jan45); TFRD to SHAEF Civil Affairs Div 12Feb45 (per MR 12Feb45) No discovered CIB GOs	
286.	**Dudics**, George (NMI) 33263456 PCM-L	CPL	L, I, C	Deployed w/the regiment; is on Pine Camp menu as PVT in L Co; ASGD fr Co I 28Sep43; evac **WIA** 12Nov43 (per MR 16Nov43); already evac **WIA** TFRD to DofP, DFR per MR 06Dec43 CIB FM as CPL in C Co 01Jan44 (14/44); CIB 01Jan44 (40/45)	WIA 12Nov43
287.	**Duff, Earl (NMI) PCM-C** 38006398	**PVT- SSG**	C	MOS 745 (Deployed w/the company, is on the Pine Camp menu as PVT) **SWIA** 11Jul43 (per MR 19Jul43); already evac **SWIA**, DFR 01Aug43; REASG fm DofP 18Oct43 per MR 01Nov43; promoted to PFC 03Nov43 (per MR 05Nov43); promoted to CPL 04Jan44 per MR 05Jan44; pmtd SGT per MR 25Jan44; pmtd SSG per MR 28Jan44; evac **WIA** (FW head shell frag) 22Feb44; **DOW** 27Feb44 per MR 05Mar44 (buried in USA) DOW as SSG in C Co 27Dec44 per Div & 157 casualty list; not on ABMC reg; nothing on web No discovered GO for CIB or GCM	SWIA 11Jul43 WIA 22Feb44 **DOW27Feb44**
288.	**Duff,** Paul F. 33582226	PVT	C	MOS 745 ASGD 06Aug43; evac **WIA** 14Sep43 (per MR 18Sep43); PVT erroneously reported RTD fm **WIA** 18Oct43 per MR 11Nov43; already evac **WIA**, DFR per MR 12Nov43 CIB FM 01Jan44 (14/44)	WIA 18Oct43
289.	Duggan, Michael J. 31066561 PCM-C	PVT	C	(Deplolyed w/the company, is on the Pine Camp menu) MIA 13Sep43 DFR (per MR 24Sep43) **(POW 13Sep43);** Mstr POW regis gives no date of capture or reporting, Freising Hospital (Stalag 7A), repatriated CIB MIA (05/44); 01Jan44 per CC; MIA13SEP43 per ANB	POW 13Sep43

290.	Dulmovits, Frank (NMI) 32218434 PCM-C	PVT- SGT	C	(Deployed w/the company, is on the Pine Camp menu as PVT) Pmtd PFC 10Aug43; evac sk 26Dec43 (per MR 28Dec43); RTD fm sk 13Jan44 per MR 18Jan44; pmtd to CPL 10Apr 44 (per MR 11Apr44); pmtd to SGT **(unknown date);** TFRD to Pers Center #6 for rotation to USA (10Jun44) CIB as PFC in C Co (01/44 - 01Jan44 per CC); GCM as SGT in C Co (02/44)	
291.	**Dumont**, Anthonoy L. 31069237	PVT-PFC	C	**(Unknown date of assignment, not on Pine Camp menu)** Evac **WIA** (pen w. scalp shell frag) 27Feb44 per MR 03Mar44; already evac **WIA** trfd to DofP and DFR 05Mar44 (per MR 22Mar44); RTD from DofP 28Apr44 (per MR 06May44); promoted to PFC 20Nov44 (per MR 27Nov44); TFRD to 516th MP Bn 23Jan45 (per MR 23Jan45) CIB (03/44); 01Jun44 per CC; GCM as PVT (08/44)	WIA 27Feb44
292.	Dussault, Clinton 42106462	PVT-PFC	C	MOS 745 ASGD fm 3rd Repl Bn 24Jan45 (per MR 26Jan45) PMTD to PFC 06Mar45 (per MR 06Mar45); Evac sk 14Apr45 (per MR 14Apr45); Already evac sk, TFRD to DofP 14Apr45 (per MR 14Apr45); REASG fm 71st Reinf Bn 28May45 (per MR 28May45) CIB 01Mar45 (10/45); GCM (32/45)	
293.	**Easton, Frank T. 38400690**	**SSG**	C	MOS 653 ASGD fm 44th Inf Div 25Jan45 (per MR 01Feb45); **KIA** 05Feb45 (per MR 06Feb45) (buried in USA) Listed on the War Memorial of Gavin County, OK No discovered GO for CIB or GCM	**KIA 05Feb45**
294.	Edmunds, Bert V. O-1030467	1LT	B, C, E, 1HQ	ASGD fm Co B 29Mar45 as CO (per MR 08Apr45); TFRD to 1HQ 17May45 (per MR 17May45) CIB FM 01Sep44 (14/44)	
295.	**Edwards, John C.** 38287159	**PVT**	C	**(Unknown date of assignment, not on Pine Camp menu)** MIA 16Aug43 (per MR 21Aug43) (DFR per MR 07Sep43) (**KIA** per MR 26May44) KIA15Aug43 per Div casualty list; ABMC 16Aug43, still MIA, most likely killed in landing craft accident; commemorated at Sicily-Rome Cemetery BSM no PH CIB FM 01Jan44 (14/44)	**MIA 16Aug43**
296.	Eikenbary, Albert R. O-403717 (Brush, CO) PCM-C	1LT-CPT	L, C	SGT in L Co per Induction Roster, 16Sep40; 1LT XO of C Co per Pine Camp menu CIB as CPT (01/44 - 01Jan44 per CC)	
297.	Eirmann, Ernest G. 42083573	PFC	C	GCM (32/45)	
298.	Eisner, Harry 42175490	PVT	C, 1HQ	MOS 745 ASGD fm 3rd Repl Bn 24Jan45 (per MR 26Jan45); PMTD to PFC 06Mar45 (per MR 06Mar45); Evac sk 09Feb45 (per MR 09Feb45); RTD fm sk 12Feb45 (per MR 12Feb45) CIB 01Mar45 (10/45); GCM as PFC in 1HQ (33/45)	

299.	**Eledge**, Norman L. 38413036	T-5	C	MOS 745 or 653 ASGD fm 24th Repl Dep 26Jan45 (per MR 30Jan45); Evac **WIA**, TFRD to DofP 19Mar45 (per MR 19Mar45) CIB 01Mar45 (10/45); GCM (8/45)	WIA 19Mar45
300.	Emanuel, Sam 34969730	PVT-PFC	C	MOS 745 ASGD fm 3rd Repl Bn 11Dec44 (per MR 12Dec44); Pmtd to PFC 07Jan45 (per MR 08Jan45); MIA 21Jan45 (per MR 23Jan45) **(POW 20JAN45)**); Mstr POW reg gives rpt date as 21Jan45, parent unit as divisional artillery, Stalag 11B, repatriated CIB 01Jan45 (01/45	POW 20Jan45
301.	Emig, Raymond M. 19135891	PVT	C	**(Unknown date of assignment, not on Pine Camp menu)** Evac sk 22Nov43 per MR 24Nov43; already evac sk TFRD to DofP, DFR per MR 23Dec43 CIB FM 01Jan44 (14/44)	
302.	Emrick, Stephen E., Jr.	PFC	C	MOS 345 ASGD fm SV Co 24Jun44 (assignment rescinded per MR 28Jun44) **NOT ASSIGNED**	
303.	Engasser, Charles A., Jr. 42106718	PVT-PFC	C	MOS 745 ASGD fm 3rd Repl Bn 24Jan45 (per MR 26Jan45); PMTD to PFC 06Mar45 (per MR 06Mar45); Evac sk 02Apr45 (per MR 02Apr45); Already evac sk, TFRD to DofP 03Apr45 (per MR 03Apr45); RTD fm 3rd Reinf Bn 05May45 (per MR 05May45) CIB 01Mar45 (10/45); GCM as PFC (32/45)	
304.	English, Alfred B. PCM-C 31065196	T-5	C	(Deployed w/the company, is on Pine Camp menu) MIA 13Sep43 DFR (per MR 24Sep43) **(POW 13Sep43)** MIA13SEP43 per ANB; Mstr POW reg gives rpt date of 13Sep44, Stalag 3B, repatrited CIB MIA as T-5 in C Co (05/44); 01Jan44 per CC	POW13Sep43
305.	Enneman, Eugene E. O-304445	1LT	C	ASGD fm 3rd Repl Bn 13Feb45 (per MR 14Feb45) No discovered GO for CIB or GCM	
306.	Enzyk, John M. 32260555	PVT	C	MOS 745 ASGD fm 2nd Repl Dep 20Jan45 (per MR 31Jan45) No discovered GO for CIB or GCM	
307.	**Eoviero**, Frank J. 32867664	PVT	C	**(Unknown date of assignment, not on Pine Camp menu)** Evac **WIA** 10Nov43 per MR 13Nov43; already evac **WIA** TFRD to DofP, DFR per MR 12Dec43 CIB FM 01Jan44 (14/44)	WIA 10Nov43
308.	Equsquiza, Joe N. PCM-C (Equsquizu) 39545726	PVT-PFC	C	(Deployed w/the company, is on the Pine Camp menu) Pmtd to Pfc 04Mar44 per MR 12Mar44; evac sk 02Jun44; RTD fm sk 11Jun44 (13Jun44); evac sk 27Jun44 (29Jun44); RTD fm sk 03Jul44; evac sk 17Jul44; already evac sk, TFRD to DofP/ DFR 19Jul44 (22Jul44) CIB 01Jan44 (03/44); as ESQUSQUIZU per CC; CIB FM 01Jan44 (14/44)	

309.	Ervin, Bill E. (Delta, CO) PCM-I	PVT	C, I	PVT in C Co per Induction Roster, 16Sep40; PVT in I Co per Pine Camp menu	
310.	Esquibel, Benjamin I. PCM-C	CPL	C	C Co per Pine Camp menu	
311.	Evans, Charles L. 34364541	PVT	C	MOS 745 ASGD but DS to 3rd Reinf Bn 08May45 (per MR 14May45); 745 relieved of DS to 3rd Reinf Bn 13May45 (per MR 14May45) GCM (32/45)	
312.	**Evans,** George W. 42083741	PVT	C	MOS 745 ASGD fm 3rd Repl Bn 24Jan45 (per MR 26Jan45); Evac sk 01Mar45 (per MR 01Mar45); RTD fm sk 07Mar45 (per MR 07Mar45); Evac **SWIA**, TFRD to DofP 28Mar45 (per MR 28Mar45) CIB 01Mar45 (10/45)	WIA 28Mar45
313.	Evans, James W. 37735035	PVT	C	GCM (32/45)	
314.	Ewell, Joseph R. 33891628	PFC	C	GCM (32/45)	
315.	Ewing, Benjamin E., Jr. 34787918	SSG-TSG	C	MOS 653/651 ASGD fm 103rd Inf Div 26Jan45 (per MR 01Feb45); Pmtd to TSG, change in MOS to 651 14Apr45 (per MR 14Apr45); TDY to UK 25May45 (per MR 26May45) GCM (08/45)	
316.	Faiola, Emelio E. 31290923	PVT	C	**(Unknown date of assignment, not on Pine Camp menu)** Evac sk 15Nov43 per MR 17Nov43; already evac sk TFRD to DofP, DFR per MR 06Dec43 CIB FM 01Jan44 (14/44)	
317.	Fanon (spelling?), Robert W SN NA	PFC	C	MOS 745 31390778 ASGD but DS to 3rd Reinf Bn 08May45 (per MR 14May45); relieved of DS to 3rd Reinf Bn 13May45 (per MR 14May45) No discovered GO for CIB or GCM	
318.	Farmer, Claude L. PCM-G **32213875**	PFC	G, C	PVT in G Co per Pine Camp menu; 2nd Squad, 1st Platoon, G Co **(Unknown date of assignment to C Co)** Evac sick (frostbite both feet) to 56th Evac Hosp (MR 08Jan44) per MR 19Nov43 CIB as PFC in G Co (04/44); 01Jan44 per CC; CIB as PVT eff 01May44 (18/44); GCM (08/44)	
319.	Farrell, Brady O. 37639117	PVT	C	MOS 745 **(Unknown date of assignment)** Already evac sk, TFRD to DofP 05Mar45 (per MR 05Mar45) No discovered GO for CIB or GCM	
320.	Fedak, Michael A., Sr. 33833508	PVT	F, C	MOS 745 ASGD 30May44 (per MR 09Jun44); evac sk 01Jul44 (MR 02Jul44); RTD fm sk 02Jul44 (MR 03Jul44); TFRD to 2nd Repl Dep but not dptd 19Jul44; s/b ATCHD & jnd (MR 23Jul44); already attached fm 2nd Repl Det reld fm atchment (per MR 05Aug44) CIB 01Sep44 (11/44)	

321.	**Federico, Manuel M.** 20837528 PCM-1	**PVT-PFC**	1HQ, C	On Pine Camp menu in 1HQ; Pmtd PFC 10Aug43; MIA 16Aug43 (per MR 21Aug43); (DFR per MR 07Sep43) **(believed drowned in 2nd Sicily landings, Still MIA)**; commemorated at Sicily-Rome Cemetery BSM, no PH CIB FM as PFC in C Co 01Jan44 (14/44)	**MIA 16Aug43**
322.	**Feinberg**, William V. 15104662	PVT	C, G	MOS 745 ASGD fm 2nd Repl Dep per MR 11Dec43; evac **WIA** 12Dec43 per MR 16Dec43; already evac **WIA** TFRD to DofP, DFR per MR 07Jan44; RTD fm DofP 26Feb44 per MR 03Mar44; Tfr in grade to G Co per MR 05Mar44 CIB PFD (07/44); GCM (08/44); CIB 01Jan44 (11/44) (not on GO 07/44 in C or G)	WIA 12Dec43
323.	Felt, LeVant (NMI) 39086903 PCM-C	PVT	C, RHQ, AT	(Deployed w/the company, is on the Pine Camp menu) Sk evac 25Jul43; RTD fm sk 22Aug43 (per MR 25Aug43); TFRD to RHQ 28Aug43 CIB as PFC in AT Co (01/44 – 01Jan44 per CC)	
324.	Fenna, Robert W. 31390778	PFC	C	GCM (32/45)	
325.	Fenner, Alfred H. 36994006	PFC	C	GCM (32/45)	
326.	Ferrandino, Joseph D. 32745892	PVT	C, G	MOS 745 ASGD 03Aug43 (name blurred on MR, but confirmed w/GO register); Tfr in grade to G Co per MR 05Mar44 CIB (01/44 - 01Jan44 per CC); GCM in G Co as PVT (08/44) (Not on GO 01/44 in C or G)	
327.	Ferrell, Brady O. 37639117	PVT	C	MOS 745 ASGD fm 2nd Repl Dep 11Nov44 (per MR 13Nov44); evac sk 22Nov44; RTD fm hosp 29Nov44; evac sk 05Dec44; already evac sk, TFRD to DofP 08Dec44; REASG fm 2nd Repl Dep 13Dec44 (per MR 14Dec44); evac **LIA**, TFRD to DofP 14Dec44; RTD fm 2nd Reinforcement Dep 20Feb45 (per MR 21Feb45) CIB 01Mar45 (9/45)	LIA 14Dec44
328.	Fianos, William J. 33856858	PFC	C	GCM (32/45)	
329.	Ficco, Daniel A. PCM-C 38006201	CPL-SGT-SSG	C	MOS 652/821 (Deployed w/the company, is on the Pine Camp menu as CPL) Pmtd SGT MOS 652 04Aug43; pmtd to SSG per MR 02Dec43; evac sk (01Jul44); RTD fm sk 09Jul44; evac sk 28Nov44; RTD fm sk 01Dec44; MIA 17Jan45 w/Duty MOS 821 (per MR 19Jan45) **(POW 16JAN45)**); Mstr POW reg gives rpt date of 16Jan45, no camp info, repatriated was supply sgt when POW CIB as SSG in C Co (01/44 - 01Jan44 per CC); GCM (02/44	POW 16Jan45

330.	**Ficuciello,** Angelo L. 12051068	CPL	C	MOS 603 (Deployed w/the company, is on the Pine Camp menu as PFC) Evac sk 30Sep43 (per MR 03Oct43); **(Missing entry of RTD);** evac INJ (self-inflicted) 16Dec43 (per MR 19Dec43); already evac **WIA** TFRD to DofP, DFR per MR 19Jan44; **(Missing entry of RTD);** evac **WIA** 04Feb44 LWA; already evac **WIA**, ZI'd & DFR 12Jul44 CIB DP as CPL in C Co (07/44)	INJ 16Dec43 WIA 19Jan44
331.	Fidanza, Vincent S. PCM-3 32205026	PFC	C	PFC in 3HQ per Pine Camp menu; MOS 745 TFR fr HQ Co, 3rd Bn 16Aug43 – erroneous entry per MR 28Agu43 CIB as SGT in 3HQ (04/44); 01Jan44 as PFC per CC **NOT ASSIGNED**	
332.	Fie, Herman N. 34935303	PFC	C	GCM (32/45)	
333.	Finley, James W. 36993348	PFC	C	GCM (32/45)	
334.	Finneran, Thomas J. PCM-C	2LT	C	Platoon Leader C Co per Pine Camp menu	
335.	Fiondella, Agelo A. 31312686	PVT-PFC	C	MOS 745 ASGD 03Aug43; evac sk 26Sep43 (per MR 30Sep43); (Missing entry of RTD); evac INJ 12Nov43 per MR 15Nov43; already evac **LIA** TFRD to DofP, DFR per MR 15Dec43; RTD fm DofP 13Jan44 per MR 18Jan44; Evac sk (Trench foot bilat) 02Mar44 per MR 13Mar44; already evac sk, Tfrd to DofP and DFR 14Mar44 per MR 05Apr44; RTD fm DofP 23May44; evac sk 21Jun44 (MR 22Jun44); already evac sk to DofP/ DFR 26Jun44 (30Jun44); REASG fm 2nd Repl Dep 21Nov44 (per MR 22Nov44); PVT promoted to PFC 25Dec44 (per MR 26Dec44); MIA 21Jan45 (per MR 23Jan45) **(POW 20JAN45)** CIB FM 01Jan44 (14/44)	POW 20Jan45
336.	Fisher, Byron J. PCM-I SN NA (Delta, CO)	2LT-CPT	C, I	2LT in C Co per Induction Roster, 16Sep40; CPT CO I Co per Pine Camp menu No discovered GO for CIB	
337.	**Fisher,** John A. Jr. 33763756	PVT-PFC	C	MOS 603 ASGD fm 2nd Repl Bn 18Dec43 per MR 22Dec43; evac sk (exhaustion) 17Feb44; already evac sk, Tfrd to DofP and DFR 09Mar44 per MR 27Mar44; RTD from 2nd Repl Dep 02Jun44; promoted to PFC (per MR 05Aug44); evac **WIA** 24Sep44; REASG fm 2nd Repl Dep 09Oct44; evac sk, TFRD to DofP 26Oct44; REASGD fm 2nd Repl Dep 19Nov44; evac sk 01Dec44; already evac sk, TFRD to DofP 03Dec44 CIB 01Jan44 (11/44)	WIA 24Sep44
338.	Flocken, Robert L. 33504725	PVT	C	MOS 745 ASGD fm 2nd Repl Dep per MR 11Dec43; evac sk 20Jan44 per MR 22Jan44; already evac sk, tfr to DofP & DFR 26Feb44 CIB FM 01Jan44 (14/44)	

339.	Floyd, John E. O-401430	1LT	C	TFRD fm Co A 10Jun44 (11Jun44); evac sk 16Jun44; RTD fm sk 25Jun44 (28Jun44); change in duties from XO to CO 13Oct44; Co Commander MIA 21Jan45 (per MR 23Jan45) **(POW 20JAN45);** Mstr POW reg gives rpt date of 21Jan45, parent unit as divisional artillery, Oflag 13B, repatriated CIB (01/44 - 01Jan44 per CC);	POW 20Jan45
340.	Flum, Joseph 32991572	PFC	C	GCM (32/45)	
341.	Foley, George 42142370	PVT-PFC	C	MOS 745 ASGD fm 3rd Repl Bn 24Jan45 (per MR 26Jan45); PMTD to PFC 06Mar45 (per MR 06Mar45); Evac sk, TFRD to DofP 26Apr45 (per MR 26Apr45) CIB 01Mar45 (10/45); GCM as PFC (32/45)	
342.	**Forbes**, Alexander J. O-1310362	2LT	C	ASGD fm B Co per MR 10Mar44; evac **WIA** 23May44; RTD fm **WIA** (23Jun44); TFRD to 2nd Rep Dep, not dptd 21Jul44; s/b atchd & jnd 21Jul44 (MR 24Jul44); 2LT promoted to 1LT, DOR 27Jul44 (per 01Aug44); already attached fm 2nd Repl Det reld fm atchment (per MR 05Aug44) CIB (01/44 - 01Jan44 per CC)	WIA 23May44
343.	**Foreman**, Alvie E. 39579379	PVT- PFC-CPL	C	MOS 745 ASGD fm 2nd Repl Dep 02Nov44 (per MR 13Nov44); evac **WIA**, TFRD to DofP 05Dec44; REASG fm 3rd Repl Bn 17Jan45 (per MR 17Jan45); PMTD to PFC 06Mar45 (per MR 06Mar45); PMTD to CPL, MOS 542 20May45 (per MR 20May45); TDY to UK 17May45 (per MR 20May45) CIB 01Mar45 (9/45); GCM as CPL (32/45)	WIA 05Dec44
344.	Fortson, Willis B. 34833921	PVT	C	MOS 605 ASGD and joined fm 2nd Repl Dep 04Nov44 (per MR 09Nov44); evac sk 28Nov44; RTD fm sk 11Dec44; evac **LIA**, TFRD to DofP 18Dec44; RTD fm 3rd Repl Bn 12Jan45 (per MR 12Jan45); Evac sk, TFRD to DofP 15Jan45 (per MR 15Jan45) No discovered GO for CIB or GCM	LIA 18Dec44
345.	**Foss, Norman C. 36446132**	**PVT- PFC-CPL- SGT-SSG**	C	MOS 745/652 ASGD 03Aug43; promoted to PFC 03Nov43 per MR 05Nov43; evac sk 22Nov43 per MR 30Nov43; pmtd to CPL per MR 23Nov43; RTD fm sk 07Dec43 per MR 12Dec43; evac sk 26Dec43 per MR 28Dec43; RTD fm sk 13Jan44 per MR 18Jan44; pmtd SGT per MR 25Jan44; pmtd to SSG per MR 10Mar44; evac **WIA** (pen W R wrist R elbow L Lumbar region back shell frag) 30May44; already evac **WIA** TFRD to DofP and DFR 02Jun44 (15Jun44); RTD fm DofP 27Jul44; fm MIA 19Aug44 to **KIA** 19Aug44 (22Aug44) (buried in Rhone Cemetery); KIA19Aug44 per Div & 157 casualty list; MIA/KIA19AUG44 per ANB; ABMC 19Aug44 as SSG, PH w/2OLC CIB (01/44 - 01Jan44 per CC	WIA 30May44 **KIA 19Aug44**

346.	Fountain, Curtis L. 34980509	PVT	C	MOS 745 ASGD fm 2nd Repl Dep 02Nov44 (per MR 13Nov44); AWOL 2359 05Dec44 (per MR 18Jan45); evac SIW, TFRD to DofP 07Dec44(per MR 18Jan45); CORRECTION: Rpt of 07Dec44 of evac SIW, s/b AWOL 2359 05Dec44, Evac SIW 07Jan45 (per MR 18Jan45) No discovered GO for CIB or GCM	
347.	Franz, Albert J. 33940892	PVT	C	MOS 745 ASGD fm 3rd Repl Bn 11Dec44 (per MR 12Dec44); evac sk, TFRD to DofP 21Dec44 CIB 01Jan45 (01/45)	
348.	**Fraser,** William J. 12148689	PVT	C	**(Unknown date of assignment, not on Pine Camp menu)(Missing entry of evac)** Already evac sk, DFR 27Aug43 CIB FM 01Jan44 (14/44**)**	
349.	Frazier, Jimmie B. PCM-C 38019051	PVT	C	Deployed w/the company; PVT in C Co per Pine Camp menu CIB FM as PVT in C Co 01Jan44 (14/44)	
350.	Free, Grady E. 34839138	PFC	C	GCM (32/45)	
351.	Freeman, John L. 38323605	PVT	C	**(Unknown date of assignment, not on Pine Camp menu)** MIA 13Sep43 DFR (per MR 24Sep43) **(POW 13Sep43)**; Mstr POW reg gives rpt date of 13Sep43, Stalag 2B, repatriated CIB FM 01Jan44 (14/44)	POW 13Sep43
352.	Freetor, William F. 36928985	PVT	C	MOS 745 ASGD fm 3rd Repl Bn 20Dec44 (per MR 21Dec44) No discovered GO for CIB or GCM	
353.	Frell, Henry T. 35159070	PFC	C	ASGD fm 1HQ 20Oct44 No discovered GO for CIB or GCM	
354.	Freshour, Russell W. 37695487	PVT	C	MOS 745 ASGD fm 2nd Repl Dep 02Nov44 (per MR 13Nov44); AWOL 2359 10Dec44 (per MR 10Jan45); Already AWOL to Confinement Toules 18Dec44 (per MR 10Jan45); promoted to PFC 25Dec44 (per MR 26Dec44); Erron rptd pmtd to PFC 25Dec44; name removed fr list (per MR 10Jan45); Duty to Regt'l Stockade 27Dec44 (29Dec44); actually, from Toules confinement to Regt'l Stockade (not from duty) (per MR 10Jan45); Entry of 29Dec44 showing Regt'l Stockade fm duty on 27Dec44, s/b AWOL 2359 10Dec44, Confinement Toules 18Dec44, Regt'l Stockade 27Dec44 (per MR 10Jan45); Erron rptd pmtd to PFC 25Dec44; name removed fr list (per MR 10Jan45); RTD fm Regt'l Stockade 17Jan45 (per MR 17Jan45); AWOL 2359 17Jan45 (per MR 19Jan45); RTD fm AWOL 1830 22Jan45 (per MR 26Jan45) CIB 01Dec44 (01/45); GCM as PVT(!) (32/45)	

355.	**Fritsch,** Marvin M. 37637072	PVT-PFC	C	MOS 745 ASGD fm 3rd Repl Bn 24Jan45 (per MR 26Jan45); PMTD to PFC 06Mar45 (per MR 06Mar45); Evac **WIA**, TFRD to DofP 18Mar45 (per MR 18Mar45); REASG fm 71st Reinf Bn 16Apr45 (per MR 16Apr45) CIB 01Mar45 (10/45); GCM as PFC (32/45)	WIA 18Mar45
356.	Frizzell, Cecil R. 35904641	PVT-PFC	C, SV	MOS 745 ASGD fm 3rd Repl Bn 24Jan45 (per MR 26Jan45); Evac sk, TFRD to DofP 28Jan45 (per MR 28Jan45); RTD fm 3rd Reinforcement Bn 16Feb45 (per MR 16Feb45); Corr of "Frizzel" in MR 06Apr45 to "Frizzell" (per MR 13Apr45); PMTD to PFC 06Mar45 (per MR 06Mar45) (second L in last name added per MR 13Apr45) CIB 01Mar45 (10/45); GCM as PFC in SV (32/45)	
357.	**Fry, William E.** 35623758	**SSG**	A, C	MOS 653 ASGD fm Co A 06Dec44; **WIA** not hosp 10Dec44; evac sk 24Dec44; RTD fm sk 31Dec44; MIA 21Jan45 (per MR 23Jan45) (**KIA** 0/A 20JAN45) Sill MIA, commemorated at Luxembourg Cemetery BSM w/OLC, PH CIB (01/44 - 01Jan44 per CC)	WIA 10Dec44 MIA 20Jan45
358.	Fuller, Chester D. 34834886	PVT-PFC	C	MOS 605 ASGD and joined fm 2nd Repl Dep 04Nov44 (per MR 09Nov44); Pmtd to PFC 07Jan45 (per MR 08Jan45); MIA 21Jan45 (per MR 23Jan45) **(POW 20JAN45)** CIB 01Dec44 (01/45)	POW 20Jan45
359.	Gabriel, James M. 33922515	PVT-PFC	C	MOS 745 ASGD fm 3rd Repl Bn 24Jan45 (per MR 26Jan45); PMTD to PFC 06Mar45 (per MR 06Mar45) CIB 01Mar45 (10/45); GCM as PFC (32/45)	
360.	Gaff, William M. 42122463	PVT-PFC	C	MOS 745 ASGD fm 3rd Repl Bn 24Jan45 (per MR 26Jan45); PMTD to PFC 06Mar45 (per MR 06Mar45) GCM (32/45)	
361.	Garcia, Paul L. 38359079	PVT	C	**(Unknown date of assignment, not on Pine Camp roster)** Evac sk 04Sep43 (per MR 05Sep43); RTD fm sk 07Sep43 (per MR 10Sep43); MIA 13Sep43 DFR (per MR 24Sep43 **(POW 05Oct43) (Discrepancy could be time in evasion before capture, or merely late reporting by the Germans);** Mstr POW reg gives rpt date of 21Jan45, Stalag 2B, repatriated POW date was 13Sep43 CIB FM 01Jan44 (14/44)	POW 13Sep43
362.	Garcia, Ramon V. 39545743	PVT-PFC	C	**(Unknown date of assignment, not on Pine Camp menu)** Pmtd to PFC 04Mar44 per MR 12Mar44; evac sk 11Apr44 (per MR 18Apr44); already evac sk, tfrd to DofP and DFR 08May44 (per MR 15May44) CIB FM 01Jan44 (14/44)	

363.	**Garcia, Theodore (NMI)** 38323487	**PVT-PFC**	C	**(Unknown date of assignment, not on Pine Camp menu)** Pmtd PFC (unknown date); MIA 16Sep43 DFR (per MR 24Sep43) (**KIA** 17Sep43 per MR 07Oct43) (buried in Sicily-Rome Cemetery) **(Disparity in dates: MR gives KIA 17Sep43; adjutant's notebook gives 13Sep43; ABMC gives 17Sep43 – most likely is 17Sep43)** KIA 17Sep43 per Div & 157 casualty list; MIA/KIA 13SEP43 per ANB; ABMC 17Sep43, Sicily-Rome Cemetery PH No discovered GO for CIB or GCM	**KIA 17Sep43**
364.	Garofaro, Andrew PCM-C SA NA	**PVT**	C	On Pine Camp menu No discovered GO for CIB or GCM	
365.	Garrett, James H. 37643853	PVT-PFC	C	MOS 745 ASGD fm 3rd Repl Bn 24Jan45 (per MR 26Jan45); PMTD to PFC 06Mar45 (per MR 06Mar45); Evac NBI (GSW pen L leg while on guard duty) 31May45 (per MR 31May45) CIB 01Mar45 (10/45)	
366.	Gassman, Morris (NMI) 32658300	PVT	C, G	MOS 761 ASGD fm 2nd Repl Bn 14Jan44 per MR 18Jan44; Tfr in grade to G Co per MR 05Mar44 CIB FM 01Feb44 (14/44)	
367.	Gates, George D. (Cates) 37602765	PVT	C	MOS 745 ASGD fm 7th Repl Dep 25Sep43; Evac **LIA** (GSW l thumb, self-inflicted) 22Feb44 No discovered GO for CIB or GCM	LIA 22Feb44
368.	Gatlin, James E. Jr. 38631563	PVT-PFC	C	MOS 745 ASGD fm 3rd Repl Bn 24Jan45 (per MR 26Jan45); PMTD to PFC 06Mar45 (per MR 06Mar45); Evac INJ, TFRD to DofP 30Mar45 (per MR 30Mar45); RTD fm 71st Reinf Bn 21May45 (per MR 21May45 CIB 01Mar45 (10/45); GCM as PFC (32/45)	
369.	Gay, Charles A. 34838224	PFC	C	GCM (32/45)	
370.	Geger, Paul F. 6886253	SGT	C	MOS 653 ASGD fm 36th Inf Div 26Jan45 (per MR 01Feb45); TFRD to Co I 02Feb45 (per MR 09Feb45) No discovered GO for CIB or GCM	
371.	Gehring, William A. PCM-C 20837700 (Delta, CO)	SSG	C, G	SGT in C Co per Induction Roster, 16Sep40; SSG in C Co per Pine Camp menu CIB as SSG in G Co (01/44 - 01Jan44 per CC); PSG 1st Platoon G Co	
372.	**Geller**, Phillip F. O-1293237	1LT	C	ASGD 27Sep44 (per MR 30Sep44); evac **WIA**, TFRD to DofP 05Nov44; REASG fm 3rd Repl Bn 17Dec44 (per MR 18Dec44); MIA 21Jan45 (per MR 23Jan45) **(POW 20JAN45)** 3rd Plt Ldr; Mstr POW reg gives rpt date of 21Jan45, parent unit as divisional artillery, Oflag 13B, repatriated; MIA21JAN45 per ANB CIB eff 01Oct44 (13/44)	WIA 05Nov44 POW 20Jan45

373.	Geller, Walter R. 32207806	PFC	H, C, E	**(Unknown date of assignment, on Pine Camp menu as PVT in H Co)** TFR in grade to E Co per MR 05Mar44 CIB FM as PFC in E Co 01Jan44 (14/44)	
374.	Geonetta, John F. PCM-C 38006133	PFC	C	(Deployed w/the company, is on Pine Camp menu) Duty 345 MIA 17Jan45 (per MR 19Jan45) **(POW 16JAN45);** Mstr POW reg gives rpt date of 17Jan45, Stalag 12A to 9B, repatriated armorer when POW CIB as PFC in C Co (04/44); 01Jan44 per CC; GCM as F. (08/44)	POW 16Jan45
375.	George, Frank A. Jr. 33615845	PFC	C	GCM (32/43)	
376.	Geuse, Veldane J. 34385331	PVT	C	**(Unknown date of assignment, not on Pine Camp menu)** TFRD to RHQ 07Aug43 PER MR 07Aug43 No discovered GO for CIB or GCM	
377.	Gibson, Edwin C. O-1326026	2LT	C	**(Unknown date of assignment)** REASG fm 71st Reinf Bn, and placed on DS with 71st Reinf Bn 29Mar45 (per MR 04Apr45); REASG fm 71st Reinf Bn 02Apr45 (per MR 03Apr45); TFRD to 1HQ 01May45 (per MR 03May45) CIB 01Mar45 (9/45)	
378.	Gillespie, William E. 6950366	PVT	F, C	MOS 745 ASGD fm Co F 25Jul44; evac sk 27Jul44; already evac sk, TFRD to DofP/DFR 25Jul44 (05Aug44); RTD fm hosp 25Aug44; AWOL 1200 28Aug44 (16Sep44); AWOL for 30 days, DFR 28Sep44 CIB (01/44 - 01Jan44 per CC)	
379.	**Glavaz, Richard D. 36035442 PCM-C**	**PFC**	C	(Deployed w/the company, is on Pine Camp menu as PFC) Sk evac 22Jul43 (Per MR 23Jul43); RTD fm sk 02Aug43 (per MR 05Aug43); rptd on 24Sep43 as MIA 13Sep43, DFR (**KIA** 13Sep43, buried in Sicily-Rome Cemetery) No discovered GO for CIB or GCM	**KIA 13Sep43**
380.	Glavin, Felix P. 37643846	PVT-PFC	C	MOS 745 ASGD fm 3rd Repl Bn 24Jan45 (per MR 26Jan45); PMTD to PFC 06Mar45 (per MR 06Mar45) CIB 01Mar45 (10/45); GCM as PFC (32/45)	
381.	Glawe, Donald E. 36005609	PVT-PFC	C	MOS 745 ASGD fm 3rd Repl Bn 24Jan45 (per MR 26Jan45); PMTD to PFC 06Mar45 (per MR 06Mar45) CIB 01Mar45 (10/45); GCM as PFC (32/45)	
382.	**Glendening,** Carl H., Jr. O-1331605	2LT	C	ASGD fm 71st Reinf Bn 19Mar45 (per MR 20Mar45); Evac **WIA**, TFRD to DofP 29Mar45 (per MR 29Mar45) No discovered GO for CIB	WIA 29Mar45
383.	Goolsby, Loyd L. 38631792	PVT-PFC	C	MOS 745 ASGD fm 3rd Repl Bn 24Jan45 (per MR 26Jan45); PMTD to PFC 06Mar45 (per MR 06Mar45) CIB 01Mar45 (10/45); GCM as PFC (32/45)	

384.	**Gorecki, Leonard A. 33024942**	**PVT**	C	**(Unknown date of assignment, not on Pine Camp menu)** Evac sk 08Aug43 (per MR 09Aug43); RTD fm sk 13Aug43 (per MR 14Aug43); MIA 16Aug43 (per MR 21Aug43) (DFR per MR 07Sep43) **(believed drowned in landing accident in 2nd Sicily landing. Still MIA)** commemorated at Sicily-Rome Cemetery BSM, no PH CIB MIA as PVT in C Co (05/44) 01Jan44 per CC	**MIA 16Aug43**
385.	**Gorman,** Robert D. 36740560	PVT-PFC	C	MOS 745 ASGD fm 3rd Repl Bn 24Jan45 (per MR 26Jan45); PMTD to PFC 06Mar45 (per MR 06Mar45); Evac **WIA** 20Apr45 (per MR 20Apr45); Already evac **WIA**, TFRD to DofP 21Apr45 (per MR 21Apr45) CIB 01Mar45 (10/45); GCM as PFC (32/45)	WIA 20Apr45
386.	Gould, William F. 20837713 (Delta, CO)	T-4	C, RHQ	PFC in C Co per Induction Roster, 16Sep40; NOT ON and Pine Camp menu CIB at T-4 in RHQ (07/44)	
387.	**Gover, Grant 20825085**	SGT	C	ASGD fm 24th Repl Dep 19Sep44; Fm MIA 01Nov44 to **KIA** 01Nov44 (buried in OK, USA) No discovered GO for CIB or GCM	**KIA 01Nov44**
388.	**Grabus**, Raymond L. 38005816 PCM-C	PVT	C	(Deployed w/the company, is on the Pine Camp menu) Evac **WIA** 14Sep43 (per MR 18Sep43); RTD fr DofP 27Dec43 (per MR 20Jan44); evac sk 28Dec43 (per MR 21Jan44); already evac sk TFRD to DofP, DFR (erron entry per MR 30Jan44); already sk abs tfrd to DofP & DFR **(Unknown date)** No discovered GO for CIB or GCM	WIA 14Sep43

389.	**Grace**, William H. 33393905	PVT-PFC-PVT-PFC-PVT-CPL-SGT-SSG-TSG	C	**(Unknown date of assignment, not on Pine Camp menu)** Evac sk 26Aug43 (per MR 28Aug43); **(Missing date of RTD)** Special Duty to 45th Inf Div Mule Pack Train (prov) 14Nov43 (per MR 30Nov43); already special duty with 45th Div Mule Train evac sk 18Dec43 per MR 27Dec43; RTD fm sk 01Jan44 per MR 06Jan44; evac sk LOD no on 06Feb44 RTD LOD NO 21Feb44; Pmtd to Pfc 04Mar44 per MR 12Mar44; Reduced to PVT 01Jun44 (per MR 07Jun44);pmtd to PFC (01Jul44); evac sk 21Jul44; reduced to PVT while evac sk 01Aug44; already evac sk TFRD to DofP 16Aug44; REASG fm 2nd Repl Dep 25Sep44; evac **WIA**, TFRD to DofP 29Oct44; REASGD fm 2nd Repl Dep 19Nov44; MOS 653 promoted to CPL 24Nov44; **WIA** not hosp 18Dec44 (per MR 31Dec44); promoted to SGT 24Dec44; **(Missing promotion to SSG)**; SSG TD to UK 15Feb45 (per MR 17Feb45); RTD fm TDY to UK 24Feb45 (per MR 11Mar45); PMTD to TSG, MOS 651 24Feb45 (per MR 24Feb45); RTD fm TDY to UK 11Mar45 (per MR 11Mar45); TDY to Ft. Dix, NJ, dptd 22Mar45 (per MR 23Mar45); TDY to US, DFR 21May45 (per MR 21May45) CIB (04/44); 01Jan44 per CC; CIB PFD (07/44)	WIA 29Oct44 WIA 18Dec44
390.	Graham, Rex C. 33410623	PVT	C, D	MOS 745 ASGD 20Aug43; TFRD to Co D 25Sep43 (per MR 28Sep43) CIB (01/44 - 01Jan44 per CC); GCM (02/44)	
391.	**Granger, Stanley P. 33624854**	**PFC-CPL-SGT**	C	MOS 603/653 ASGD fm 2nd Repl Bn 18Dec43 per MR 22Dec43; pmtd to CPL 10Apr 44 (per MR 11Apr44); MOS 653 pmtd SGT 24May44; evac **WIA** 31May44 (MR 07Jun44); **DOW** 08Jun44 (MR 08Jun44) (buried in USA) CIB (01/44 - 01Jan44 per CC)	WIA 31May44 **DOW 08Jun44**
392.	Grant, Thomas P., Jr. 18232031	PVT	C, 1HQ	MOS 745 ASGD and joined fm 2nd Repl Dep 04Nov44 (per MR 09Nov44); evac sk 14Nov44; already evac sk, TFRD to DofP 15Nov44; REASG mf 2nd Repl Dep 05Dec44; TFRD to 1HQ 06Dec44 CIB 01Dec44 (01/45); GCM as PFC (26/45)	
393.	**Grant, William M. 32243147**	**CPL-SSG**	C	MOS 653 ASGD fm 44th Inf Div 25Jan45 (per MR 01Feb45); Pmd to SSG MOS 652 24Jan45 (per MR 24Jan45); 653 MIA 16Apr45 (per MR 19Apr45); to **KIA** 16Apr45 (per MR 27Apr45) (buried in USA) No discovered GO for CIB; GCM (8/45)	**KIA 16Apr45**
394.	**Gray, Donald R. 35094156**	**PFC**	C	MOS 745 ASGD and joined fm 2nd Repl Dep 02Nov44 (per MR 09Nov44); MIA 05Dec44 (07Dec44) – to **KIA** (per MR 13Dec44) (buried in USA) No discovered GO for CIB or GCM	**KIA 13Dec44**
395.	Gray, Orvill H. (Delta, CO)	PFC	C	AWOL per Induction Roster, 16Sep40; no indication he ever rejoined the unit.	

396.	**Green, Charles C. (IO) (or Charlie) 34574404**	**PFC**	C	MOS 729 ASGD fm 2nd Repl Dep 29Sep44; MIA 27Oct44 (30Oct44) – to **KIA** 27Oct44 (per MR 08Nov44) (buried in USA) CIB 01Sep44 (13/44)	**KIA 27 Oct44**
397.	Green, Ivan I. 36958674	PVT	C	MOS 745 ASGD fm 2nd Repl Dep 11Nov44 (per MR 13Nov44); evac sk, TFRD to DofP 07Dec44 No discovered GO for CIB or GCM	
398.	**Green**, Robert D. 36470640	PVT	C	MOS 745 ASGD fm 3rd Repl Bn 24Jan45 (per MR 26Jan45); Evac S**WIA**, TFRD to DofP 19Mar45 (per MR 19Mar45); REASG 29May45 (per MR 30May45) CIB 01Mar45 (10/45); GCM (32/45)	WIA 19Mar45
399.	Green, Virgil H. (or E.) 37247915	PVT- SGT	C	ASGD fr Co G 28Sep43; promoted PFC 01Jan44 per MR 05Jan44; pmtd CPL 25Jan44 per MR 26Jan44; pmtd SGT per MR 28Jan44; evac sk 14Jul44 (MR 15Jul44) – Not Line of Duty (MR 30Jul44); RTD fm sk 19Jul44 (MR 20Jul44); RTD fm Not Line of Duty 14-18Jul44 inclusive (30Jul44); reduced to PVT MOS 745 04Aug44; evac sk 08Aug44, TFRD to DofP 08Aug44 (09Aug44); REASD fm 7th Repl Dep 24Sep44; **(Missing entry for promotion to PFC)**; promoted to CPL MOS 653 07Oct44; **WIA** not hosp 09Nov44 (per MR 11Nov44); MOS 653 promoted to SGT 24Nov44; evac sk, TFRD to DofP 25Nov44 (per MR 28Nov44) CIB (01/44 - 01Jan44 per CC); GCM as E. (08/44)	WIA 09Nov44
400.	Gregg, Lester L. 37205076	CPL	C	MOS 653 ASGD fm 103rd Inf Div 26Jan45 (per MR 01Feb45); Evac sk 29Jan45, TFRD to DofP (per MR 02Feb45) No discovered GO for CIB or GCM	
401.	Greylock, Joseph Jr. 33940750	PVT	C	MOS 745 ASGD fm 3rd Repl Bn 11Dec44 (per MR 12Dec44); evac sk, TFRD to DofP 24Dec44 CIB 01Jan45 (01/45)	
402.	Griebel, Ralph J. 37362857	PVT	C	MOS 745 ASGD and joined fm 2nd Repl Dep 04Nov44 (per MR 09Nov44); evac sk 07Dec44; RTD fm sk 19Dec44; MIA 21Jan45 (per MR 23Jan45) **(POW 20JAN45);** Mstr POW reg gives rpt date of 21Jan45, no camp info, repatriated CIB 01Dec44 (01/45)	POW 20Jan45
403.	Grifhorst, Howard R., Sr. 36470567	PVT-PFC	C	MOS 745 ASGD fm 3rd Repl Bn 24Jan45 (per MR 26Jan45); PMTD to PFC 06Mar45 (per MR 06Mar45) CIB 01Mar45 (10/45); GCM as PFC (32/45)	
404.	**Groh, Robert W. 33892241**	**PVT**	C	MOS 745 Asgd fm 2nd Repl Det 26Feb44 per MR 25Mar44; **KIA** 27Feb44 (per MR 06Apr44); change in date of **KIA** to 29Feb44 (per MR 19Apr44) **(KIA the day after assignment)** (buried in USA) No discovered GO for CIB or GCM	**KIA 27Feb44**
405.	Grubb, Edmund E. (Delta, CO)	PFC	C	Induction Roster, 16Sep40	

406.	**Grudzien**, Stanley W. 31412042	PVT	C	MOS 745 ASGD fm 3rd Repl Bn 24Jan45 (per MR 26Jan45); Evac sk, TFRD to DofP 24Feb45 (per MR 24Feb45); REASG fm 2nd Reinf Dep 11Mar45 (per MR 11Mar45); Evac **WIA** 28Mar45 (per MR 28Mar45); already evac **WIA**, TFRD to DofP 29Mar45 (per MR 29Mar45) CIB 01Mar45 (10/45)	WIA 28Mar45
407.	Grundon, Kenneth L. 32505331	PVT-PFC	C	**(Unknown date of assignment, not on Pine Camp menu)** pmtd PFC 01Jul43 (Fm MR 20Jul43); MIA 13Sep43 DFR (per MR 24Sep43) **(POW 13Sep43);** Mstr POW reg gives rpt date of 13Sep43 w/o unit ID, Stalag 2B, repatriated CIB MIA (05/44); 01Jan44 per CC	POW 13Sep43
408.	Gueli, Michael R. 31305363	PVT	C	(Unknown date of assignment, not on Pine Camp menu) Evac WIA 09Dec43 per MR 13Dec43; RTD fm WIA 11Dec43 per MR 14Dec43; MIA 15Dec43, DFR per MR 25Dec43 Was among five men from C Co (GuelI, Morris, Tourtilotte, Koziol, McCoy) captured 15Dec43 near Venafro, who escaped from a POW train as it was being bombed in northern Italy on 28Jan44 and who made it back to Allied lines, but did not return to the unit CIB FM 01Jan44 (14/44)	WIA 09Dec43 POW 15Dec43
409.	Guellich, Walter A. 32207668	PVT	H, C	**(Unknown date of assignment, on Pine Camp menu as PVT in H Co)** Evac sk 26Nov43 per MR 29Nov43; already evac sk, TFRD to DofP, DFR per MR 26Dec43; RTD fm DofP 27Feb44 per MR 05Mar44; evac sk (NYD Manifested by painful arches) 18Apr44 (per MR 22Apr44); RTD fm sk 15May44 (MR 19May44); evac sk LD 16May44 (MR 20May44); RTD fm sk 02Jun44; erron rptd TFRD to 2nd Repl Dep 19Jul44 – order rescinded (MR 24Jul44); TFRD to 2nd Repl Dep but not departed 19Jul44; s/b ATCHD & jnd (MR 23Jul44) – order rescinded (MR 24Jul44); TFRD to 7th Repl Dep 21Jul44, reclassified limited assignment (MR 24Jul44) CIB FM as PVT in C Co 01Jan44 (14/44)	
410.	**Gunning**, Thomas A. 37639362	PVT	C	MOS 745 ASGD fm 2nd Repl Dep 11Nov44 (per MR 13Nov44); evac **WIA**, TFRD to DofP 05Dec44; REASGD fm 3rd Repl Bn 11Feb45 (per MR 11Feb45); Evac sk, TFRD to DofP 24Feb45 (per MR 24Feb45) CIB 01Dec44 (34/45)	WIA 05Dec44
411.	Guthrie, Theodore C. 38005326 PCM-C	PFC	C, B	(Deployed w/the company, is on the Pine Camp menu) TFRD to Co B (04Aug43) PFC in C Co per PCCM42; CIB FM as PFC in B Co 01Jan44 (14/44)	

412.	**Hagenbuch**, Willoughby G. 33490089	PVT	C	MOS 745 ASGD (03Aug43); evac sk 26Sep43 (per MR 30Sep43); **(Missing entry of RTD)**; evac **LIA** 30Nov43 per MR 03Dec43; RTD fm **LIA** 25Dec43) per MR 29Dec43; evac sick (fracture) 27Jan44, DFR 05Feb44; RTD fm DofP 03Apr44 (per MR 12Apr44); evac sk 18Jun44 (MR 19Jun44); RTD fm sk 29Jun44 (30Jun44); pmtd to PFC 01Jul44 (MR 02Jul44); evac sk 26Jul44; RTD fm sk 03Aug44; evac sk, TFRD to DofP/DFR 10Aug44 (15Aug44); REASG not joined fm 2nd Repl Dep 25Sep44; joined 26Sep44 (per MR 27Sep44); evac **WIA** 20Oct44 CIB PFD (07/44); GCM (08/44)	WIA 20Oct44
413.	**Hager, Howard 35203781**	**PFC**	C	MOS 746 ASGD fm 3rd Repl Bn 10Dec44; MIA 11Dec44 (per MR 14Dec44); MIA 11Dec44 (14Dec44) – to **KIA** (per MR 24Dec44) (buried in USA) No discovered GO for CIB or GCM	**KIA 11Dec44**
414.	Hall, Desmond C. 35771707	PVT-PFC	C	MOS 745 ASGD 30May44 (per MR 09Jun44); promoted to PFC 07Oct44; evac sk, TFRD to DofP 12Dec44 CIB 01Sep44 (13/44)	
415.	Hall, Woodrow 36030724	PVT-PFC	C	MOS 745 ASGD and joined fm 2nd Repl Dep 04Nov44 (per MR 09Nov44); evac sk, TFRD to DofP 05Dec44; REASG fm 2nd Repl Dep 13Dec44 (per MR 15Dec44); promoted to PFC 25Dec44 (per MR 26Dec44); Evac INJ 01Jan45 (per MR 01Jan45); Already evac sk, TFRD to DofP 02Jan45 (per MR 02Jan45); REASG fm 3rd Repl Bn 04Feb45 (per MR 04Feb45); Evac INJ 18Mar45 (per MR 18Mar45); Already Evac INJ, TFRD to DofP 19Mar45 (per MR 19Mar45); RTD 08May45 (per MR 08May45) CIB 01Dec44 (01/45)	
416.	**Hallgren,** Richard C. 37741112		C	PVT MOS 745 ASGD and joined fm 2nd Repl Dep 04Nov44 (per MR 09Nov44); evac **WIA**, TFRD to DofP 05Dec44 CIB 01Dec44 (15/45); 2nd CIB as PFC (40/45)	WIA 05Dec44
417.	Halterbrand, James R.	PVT	C	**(Unknown date of assignment)** TFRD to 1HQ 27May45 (per MR 27May45) No discovered GO for CIB or GCM	
418.	**Hamblin,** Leo E. PCM-C 20837706 (Delta, CO)	CPL-SGT	C	CPL in C Co per Induction Roster, 16Sep40; (Deployed w/the company, is on the Pine Camp menu as SGT) Evac sk 14Aug43 (per MR 16Aug43); RTD fm sk 12Sep43 (per MR 14Sep43); evac **WIA** 11Nov43 per MR 13Nov43; already evac **WIA** TFRD to DofP, DFR per MR 15Dec43 CIB DP as SGT in C Co (07/44)	WIA 11Nov43
419.	**Hancock, Devon W. 35243928**	**PVT**	C	MOS 745 ASGD fm 2nd Repl Dep 11Nov44 (per MR 13Nov44); **KIA** 15Jan45 (per MR 17Jan45) (buried in USA) CIB 01Dec44 (01/45)	**KIA 15Jan45**

420.	Handy, Edwin R. 39622663	PVT	C	MOS 745 ASGD fm 2nd Repl Dep 11Nov44 (per MR 13Nov44); evac sk, TFRD to DofP 08Dec44; already evac sk, TFRD to DofP 24Dec44 No discovered GO for CIB or GCM	
421.	**Haney, Louis R. 36771286**	**PVT**	C	MOS 603 ASGD fr 2nd Repl Dep 04Jun44 (11Jun44); TFRD to 2nd Repl Dep but not departed 19Jul44; s/b ATCHD & jnd (MR 23Jul44); evac sk 20Jul44 (28Jul44); already evac sk TFRD to DofP/ DFR 22Jul44 (28Jul44); REASG but not jd fm 7th Repl Dep 17Aug44; joind 17Sep44; MIA 04Nov44 (per MR 06Nov44) – to **KIA** 04Nov44 (per MR 12Nov44) (buried in USA) CIB 01Oct44 1344)	**KIA 04Nov44**
422.	Hanisko, Frank V. 35525305	PVT	C, G	MOS 761 ASGD fm 2nd Repl Dep 11Jan44 per MR 13Jan44; Tfr in grade to G Co per MR 05Mar44 CIB FM 01Feb44 (14/44)	
423.	Hankiewicz, Frank 36948269	PFC	C	GCM (32/45)	
424.	Hankins, Harold W. PCM-I (Cp. Perry, OH)	SGT	C, I	SGT in C Co per Induction Roster, 16Sep40; CPL in I Co per Pine Camp menu No discovered GO for CIB or GCM	
425.	**Hanlin, Roy H., Jr. 35079514**	**PVT**	C	MOS 745 ASGD fm 2nd Repl Dep 11Nov44 (per MR 13Nov44); MIA 04Dec44 (per MR 06Dec44); Fm MIA 04Dec44 to **KIA** 04Dec44 (per MR 13Dec44) (buried in Lorraine Military Cemetery) No discovered GO for CIB or GCM	**KIA 04Dec44**
426.	Hann, Aaron C. 6553050	CPL-SGT-SSG	C	MOS 539 **(Unknown date of assignment, not on Pine Camp menu)** RTD fm 2nd Repl Dep 11Jan44 per MR 13Jan44; pmtd SGT per MR 25Jan44; pmtd SSG per MR 28Jan44; evac sk, TFRD to DofP 19Aug44; RTD 22Aug33 (23Aug44); evac sk, TFRD to DofP 08Dec44 CIB (01/44); 01Feb44 per CC; GCM (02/44)	
427.	**Hanna, Robert F., Jr. (Hannah) 20837705 (Delta, CO) PCM-C**	**SGT**	C	CPL in C Co per Induction Roster, 16Sep40; (Deployed w/the company, is on the Pine Camp menu as SGT) **KIA** 28Jul43 (per MR 01Aug43) (buried in USA) KIA as SGT in C Co per Div casualty list as HANNAH; as HANNA per 157 list; not on ABMC reg as Hannah or Hanna No discovered GO for CIB or GCM	**KIA 28Jul43**
428.	Hanscom, Bradford A. 31471644	PFC	C	GCM (32/45)	
429.	Hansen, John PCM-C SA NA	PVT	C	On Pine Camp menu Do discovered GO for CIB or GCM	
430.	Hanson, Karlson E., Jr. (or Hansen)	PVT	C	MOS745 ASGD and joined fm 2nd Repl Dep 04Nov44 (per MR 09Nov44); evac sk, TFRD to DofP 03Dec44 (per MR 05Dec44) CIB 01Dec44 (40/45)	

431.	Harbour, Raymond T. 34980196	PVT-PFC-CPL	C	MOS 745 ASGD fm 2nd Repl Dep 02Nov44 (per MR 13Nov44); promoted to PFC 25Dec44 (per MR 26Dec44); evac sk, TFRD to DofP 30Dec44; REASG fm 71st Reinf Bn 02Apr45 (per MR 03Apr45); Pmtd to CPL 04May45 (per MR 04May45); Evac sk 19May45 (per MR 19May45); RTD fm sk 21May45 (per MR 21May45) CIB 01Dec44 (01/45); GCM as PVT(!) (32/45)	
432.	Hardin, Arthur E. 15362389	PFC	C	GCM (32/54)	
433.	Hargrove, George M. L. 34358795 PCM-C	PVT-CPL-SGT	C, I	(Deployed w/the company, is on the Pine Camp menu as PVT) Evac sk 03Aug43 (per MR 04Aug43); already evac sk, DFR 07Sep43; MIA16FEB44 per ANB; KIA16Feb44 as SGT per Div casualty list; KIA in I Co per 157 list; not on ABMC reg **(most likely KIA in I Company)** CIB FM in C Co 01Jan44 (14/44); CIB FM in I Co 01Feb44 (14/44);	(KIA16Feb44 in I Co)
434.	Harman, Harry E. (or R.) 38006178	PFC-T-5-T-4	C	MOS 060 (Deployed w/the company, is on the Pine Camp menu as PFC) Evac sk, TFRD to DofP 22Nov44; REASG fm 3rd Repl Bn 23Dec44; PMTD to T-4 20May45 (per MR 20May45) CIB as T-5 in C Co (01/44 - 01Jan44 per CC); GCM (02/44)	
435.	Harman, Joseph L. 35017339	SSG	C	**(Unknown date of assignment, not on Pine Camp menu)** TFRD to RHQ 25Sep43 (per MR 28Sep43) No discovered GO for CIB or GCM	
436.	Harper, Francis E. R. 35095146	PVT-PFC	C	**(Unknown date of assignment, not on Pine Camp menu))** Pmtd PFC 14Jan44 per MR 15Jan44; evac sk (abdominal pain) 19May44 (MR 21May44); RTD fm sk 24May44; evac sk 24Sep44; RTD fm sk 26Sep44; TFRD to 1HQ 02Oct44 CIB (01/44 - 01Jan44 per CC); GCM (08/44)	
437.	Harper, I. J. 36972272	PVT	C	MOS 745 ASGD fm 2nd Repl Dep 11Nov44 (per MR 13Nov44); evac sk, TFRD to DofP 14Dec44; REASGD fm 3rd Repl Bn 11Feb45 (per MR 11Feb45); Evac sk, TFRD to DofP 01Mar45 (per MR 01Mar45) CIB 01Mar45 (9/45)	
438.	Harrell, Leo C. 38524863	PVT-PFC	C	MOS 745 ASGD fm 2nd Repl Dep 11Nov44 (per MR 13Nov44); evac INJ LOD, TFRD to DofP 22Nov44; **(Missing entry of RTD)**; evac sk 05Mar45 (per MR 05Mar45); RTD fm sk 06Mar45 (per MR 06Mar45); PMTD to PFC 06Mar45 (per MR 06Mar45); **(Missing entry of evac)**; Already Evac INJ, TFRD to DofP 19Mar45 (per MR 19Mar45); RTD fm 2nd Reinforcement Dep 20Feb45 (per MR 20Feb45) CIB 01Dec44 (01/45)	

439.	**Hart**, Richard E. 42106904	PVT-PFC	C	MOS 745 ASGD fm 3rd Repl Bn 24Jan45 (per MR 26Jan45); PMTD to PFC 06Mar45 (per MR 06Mar45); **WIA** not hosp (perf R thumb, elbow) 28Mar45 (per MR 30Mar45); Evac sk 02Feb45 (per MR 02Feb45); RTD fm sk 09Feb45 (per MR 09Feb45) CIB 01Mar45 (10/45); GCM as PFC (32/45)	WIA 28Mar45
440.	**Hartung,** Willis A. 37592323	PVT	C	MOS 745 ASGD fm 2nd Repl Dep 11Nov44 (per MR 13Nov44); evac **WIA**, TFRD to DofP 15Dec44; RTD fm 2nd Reinforcement Dep 20Feb45 (per MR 20Feb45); Evac sk 04Apr45 (per MR 04Apr45); Already evac sk, TFRD to DofP 05Apr45 (per MR 05Apr45) CIB 01Mar45 (9/45)	WIA 15Dec44
441.	**Harvey,** Nelson L. 36590387	PVT	C, AT	MOS 610 ASGD fm 2nd Repl Dep per MR 11Dec43; evac **WIA** 15Dec43 per MR 17Dec43; already evac **WIA** TFRD to DofP, DFR per MR 16Jan44; RTD fr DofP 16Jan44 per MR 20Jan44; TFRD to AT Co 20Jan44 per MR 21Jan44; Mstr POW reg gives rpt date of 23Feb44 as Air Corps!, Stalag 7A, repatriated (POW in AT Company) CIB FM 01Jan44 (14/44)	WIA 15Dec43 (POW 23Feb44)
442.	**Hatchett**, Jack L. 39418138	PVT-SSG	C	MOS 745/653 ASGD fm 2nd Repl Dep 23Apr44 (per MR 29Apr44); pmtd to PFC 01Jul44 (MR 02Jul44); promoted to CPL (per MR 05Aug44); evac **WIA** 24Sep44; REASG fm hosp 03Oct44; promoted to SGT MOS 653 07Oct44; evac **WIA**, TFRD to DofP 07Nov44; REASG fm 71st Repl Dep 04Dec44 (per MR 05Dec44); promoted to SSG 24Dec44; MIA 21Jan45 (per MR 23Jan45) **(POW 20JAN45);** Mstr POW reg gives rpt date of 21Jan45 as SSG, parental unit as divisional artillery, no camp info, repatriated CIB 01May44 (06/44 CC); GCM SGT (16/44)	WIA 24Sep44 WIA 07Nov44 POW 20Jan45
443.	Hauser, William R. 34892107	PVT-PFC	C	MOS 745/675 ASGD fm 2nd Repl Dep 23Apr44 (per MR 29Apr44); promoted to PFC (per MR 05Aug44; MIA 21Jan45 (per MR 23Jan45) **(POW 20JAN45);** Mstr POW reg gives rpt date of 21Jan45 as PFC, parental unit as divisional artillery, Stalag 11B, repatriated CIB 01May44 (06/44 CC)	POW 20Jan45
444.	Hawley, Roy J. 39472892	PVT	C	MOS 745 ASGD fm 2nd Repl Dep 11Nov44 (per MR 13Nov44); evac INJ 04Dec44; already evac sk, TFRD to DofP 05Dec44**;** REASG fm 3rd REpl Bn 23Jan45 (per MR 23Jan45); Evac INJ, TFRD to DofP 04Feb45 (per MR 04Feb45) No Discovered GO for CIB or GCM	

445.	**Hayford,** Donald L. 31398818	PVT-PFC	C	MOS 745 ASGD fm 2nd Repl Dep 23Apr44 (per MR 29Apr44); promoted to PFC (per MR 05Aug44); evac sk 17Aug44; RTD fm sk 18Aug44; evac **WIA** 24Sep44; REASG but not joined fm 2nd Repl Dep per MR 05Oct44; joined 07Oct44; evac **WIA** 03Dec44; already evac, TFRD to DofP 04Dec44 CIB 01May44 (06/44 CC); CIB as PFD (07/44)	WIA 24Sep44 WIA 03Dec44
446.	Hayner, Edward J. 42083676	PVT-PFC	C	MOS 745 ASGD fm 3rd Repl Bn 24Jan45 (per MR 26Jan45); PMTD to PFC 06Mar45 (per MR 06Mar45); Evac sk 06Mar45 (per MR 06Mar45); TFRD to DofP 17Mar45 (per MR 17Mar45); REASG fm 71st Reinf Bn 16Apr45 (per MR 16Apr45) CIB 01Mar45 (10/45); GCM as PFC (32/45)	
447.	**Heath**, Robert A. 31268887	PVT	C	MOS 504 ASGD fm 2nd Repl Bn 18Dec43 per MR 22Dec43; evac sk 26Dec43 per MR 28Dec43; already evac sk TFRD to DofP, DFR 28Jan44 (erron entry per MR 30Jan44); Tfr to DofP and DFR 12Feb44; RTD fm DofP 06Mar44 per MR 10Mar44; evac **WIA** 08Apr44 (MR 12Apr44); tfrd to DofP, DFR 17Apr44 (MR 09May44) CIB FM 01Jan44 (14/44)	WIA 08Apr44
448.	Hebb, Kenneth E. 35932849	PVT	C, G	MOS 745 ASGD 30May44 (per MR 09Jun44); TFRD to 2nd Repl Dep but not departed 19Jul44; s/b ATCHD & jnd (MR 23Jul44); already attached fm 2nd Repl Det reld fm atchment (per MR 05Aug44) CIB 01Sep44 (11/44)	
449.	Hedrick, Cleave E. 33883460	PVT	C	MOS 745 ASGD and joined fm 2nd Repl Dep 02Nov44 (per MR 09Nov44); evac sk, TFRD to DofP 21Nov44 No discovered GO for CIB or GCM	
450.	Heikes, Floyd F., Jr. 33872975	PFC	C	GCM (32/45)	
451.	Helms, William Jr. 37643850	PVT- CPL	C	MOS 745/652 ASGD fm 3rd Repl Bn 24Jan45 (per MR 26Jan45); PMTD to PFC 06Mar45 (per MR 06Mar45); PMTD to CPL MOS 652 09May45 (per MR 09May45) CIB 01Mar45 (10/45); GCM as CPL (32/45)	
452.	Helterbrand, James R. 35087410	PVT	C, 1HQ	MOS 745 ASGD fm 3rd Repl Bn 11Dec44 (per MR 12Dec44); evac sk, TFRD to DofP 29Dec44; REASD fm 2nd Reinf Dep 08Mar45 (per MR 08Mar45); Evac sk 15Mar45 (per MR 15Mar45); TFRD to DofP 18Mar45 (per MR 18Mar45); REASG but DS to 71st Reinf Bn 03Apr45 (per MR 11Apr45); Relieved of DS to 71st Reinf Bn 11Apr45 (per MR 11Apr45) CIB 01Jan45 (01/45); GCM in 1HQ (26/45)	
453.	**Henderson**, Thomas C. 14117414	PVT-PFC	C	MOS 675 ASGD fm 2nd Repl Bn 18Dec43 per MR 22Dec43; Pmtd to PFC 04Mar44 per MR 12Mar44; evac **WIA** 24Sep44; REASG fm 71st Repl Dep 08Dec44 CIB PFD (07/44); GCM (08/44)	WIA 24Sep44

454.	**Hendrix, Thomas C. 37643732**	**PVT-PFC**	C	MOS 745 ASGD fm 3rd Repl Bn 24Jan45 (per MR 26Jan45); PMTD to PFC 06Mar45 (per MR 06Mar45); Evac S**WIA**, TFRD to DofP 28Mar45 (per MR 28Mar45); **DOW** 06Apr45 (per MR 09Apr45) (buried in USA) CIB 01Mar45 (10/45)	WIA 28Mar45 **DOW 06Apr45**
455.	Henneman, Eugene E. O-304445	1LT	C, 1HQ	**(Unknown date of assignment)** TFRD to 1st Bn HQ 04Apr45 (per MR 08Apr45) CIB 01Mar45 (15/45)	
456.	Henry, Hammon R. 34980770	PVT	C	MOS 745 ASGD fm 2nd Repl Dep 11Nov44 (per MR 13Nov44); evac sk, TFRD to DofP 06Dec44 CIB 01Dec44 (34/45)	
457.	**Henry, Wilford L. PCM-C 37087411**	**PVT-CPL**	C	(Deployed w/the company, is on Pine Camp menu as PVT) **KIA** 28Jul43 (Per MR 01Aug43) (buried in Sicily-Rome Cemetery); KIA as CPL in C Co 27Jul43 per Div casualty list; KIA 28Jul43 per 157 list; ABMC 28Jul43, Sicily-Rome Cemetery PH No discovered GO for CIB or GCM	**KIA 28Jul43**
458.	Herburger, Martin J. 38006165 PCM-C	CPL-SGT	C	(Deployed w/the company, is on the Pine Camp menu as CPL) MIA 13Sep43 DFR (per MR 24Sep43) **(POW 13Sep43);** Mstr POW reg gives rpt date of 13Sep43 as SSG, Stalag 3B, repatriated CIB MIA as SGT in C Co (05/44); 01Jan44 per CC	POW 13Sep43
459.	Herd, Leck R. SN NA (Delta, CO)	PFC	C	Induction Roster 16Sep40	
460.	**Herring**, Woodson (NMI) JR. 20837348 (Craig, CO)	PFC-PVT	A, C	PFC in A Co per Induction Roster, 16Sep40; ASGD fm Co A 14Jan44 per MR 15Jan44; red to PVT 08Jan44 per MR 16Jan44; **WIA** (pen wound right orbital region shell frag) 07Feb44; already evac **WIA**, trfd to DofP and DFR 03Mar44 per MR 15Mar44 CIB FM as PVT in C Co 01Jan44 (14/44)	WIA 07Feb44
461.	**Hicks**, George A. 38071888	T-4	C	MOS 745 ASGD fm 2nd Repl Dep 20Jan45 (per MR 31Jan45); Evac **WIA** 18Mar45 (per MR 18Mar45); Already Evac **WIA**, TFRD to DofP 19Mar45 (per MR 19Mar45) CIB 01Mar45 (10/45)	WIA 18Mar45
462.	Hicks, Herman M. 34285586	PVT	L, 3HQ, C	MOS 745 PVT in L Co per Pine Camp menu; ASGD fr 3HQ 21Aug43; AWOL 0330 02Sep43 (per MR 04Sep43); RTD fm AWOL 1415 04Sep43 (per MR 05Sep43); evac sk 17Nov43 (per MR 21Nov43); already evac sk TFRD to DofP, DFR per MR 18Dec43 CIB FM as PVT in 3HQ (05/44); 01Jan44 per CC; CIB FM as PVT in C Co 01Jan44 (14/44)	

463.	**Higgins,** George D. 34593320	PVT-PFC	C	MOS 504 **(Unknown date of assignment, not on Pine Camp menu)** RTD fm 2nd Repl Dep 11Jan44 per MR 13Jan44; Pmtd to PFC 04Mar44 per MR 12Mar44; evac **WIA** (BC pen GSW scalp) 31May44; already evac **WIA** to DofP/ DFR 06Jun44 (15Jun44); RTD fm DofP 27Jun44 (28Jun44); evac **WIA**, TFRD to DofP 23Sep44 CIB (01/44 - 01Jan44 per CC); CIB PFC FM 01Feb44 (14/44)	WIA 23Sep44
464.	Hildreth, George E., Jr. 31065203 PCM-C	PVT	C	(Deployed w/the company, is on the Pine Camp menu) Sk evac 16Jul43 (Fm MR 20Jul43); RTD fm sk 25Jul43 (per MR 31Jul43), evac sk 30Jul43 (per MR 04Aug43); already evac sk TFRD to RHQ (07Aug43) No discovered GO for CIB or GCM	
465.	Hill, Albert 34868227	PVT	C, E	MOS 745 ASGD fm 3rd Repl Bn 24Jan45 (per MR 26Jan45) CIB 01Mar45 (9/45); 2nd CIB, as PVT in C Co (10/45); GCM as PFC in E Co (26/45)	
466.	Hill, Clell 36610602	SGT	C	MOS 653 ASGD fm 24th Repl Dep 15Sep44 (per MR 24Nov44); evac sk 15Sep44 (24Nov44), TFRD to DofP 10Oct44 (per MR 24Nov44); already evac sk, TFRD to DofP 10Oct44 (per MR 24Nov44); REASG fm 2nd Repl Dep 26Dec44; TFRD to Co I 27Dec44 (MIA28Dec44 per ANB; Mstr POW reg gives rpt date of 28DEC44, Stalag 5A, repatriated) CIB 01Jan45 (01/45)	(POW 28Dec44 in I Co)
467.	Hill, Clifford 33935139	PVT-PFC	C	**(Unknown date of assignment)** PMTD to PFC 06Mar45 (per MR 06Mar45) CIB 01Mar45 (15/45); GCM (32/45)	
468.	Hill, Henry H. PCM-C 38022502	PFC	C, SV	(Deployed w/the company, is on the Pine Camp menu) TFRD to Co A 04Aug43 – erroneous entry per MR 07Aug43; TFRD to SV Co. 07Aug43 No discovered GO for CIB or GCM	
469.	Hillard, Roy L. 38696225	PVT	C	MOS 745 ASGD fm 3rd Repl Bn 24Jan45 (per MR 26Jan45); Evac sk 12Feb45 (per MR 12Feb45); Already Evac sk, TFRD to DofP 17Feb45 (per MR 17Feb45); REASGD fm 2nd Reinf Dep 12Mar45 (per MR 12Mar45); Evac sk 19Mar45 (per MR 19Mar45); Already evac sk, TFRD to DofP 22Mar45 (per MR 22Mar45); RTD 04May45 (per MR 04May45) CIB 01Mar45 (10/45)	
470.	Hillhouse, Kenneth C. SN NA PCM-C	PFC	C	On Pine Camp menu	
471.	**Hirschman**, Charles Sr. 34352149	PVT	C	MOS 745/504 ASGD fm 3rd Repl Bn 24Jan45 (per MR 26Jan45); Evac sk 02Feb45 (per MR 02Feb45); RTD fm sk 06Feb45 (per MR 06Feb45); Evac **WIA**, TFRD to DofP 19Mar45 (per MR 19Mar45); RTD 06May45 (per MR 06May45) CIB 01Mar45 (10/45); GCM as PFC (32/45)	WIA 19Mar45

472.	**Hodges**, Rudolph T. 34870936	PVT-PFC	C	MOS 745 ASGD 30May44 (per MR 09Jun44); pmtd to PFC 01Jul44 (MR 02Jul44); evac sk, TFRD to DofP 26Aug44; RTD 26Aug44; **WIA** not hosp 26Sep44 (per MR 17Oct44); evac **WIA** 03Nov44; RTD 07Nov44; evac sk, TFRD to DofP 08Nov44 CIB 01Sep44 (13/44)	WIA 25Sep44
473.	**Hoff**, J. C. 38631748	PVT	C, RHQ	MOS 745 ASGD fm 3rd Repl Bn 24Jan45 (per MR 26Jan45); Evac **WIA** 28Mar45 (per MR 28Mar45); Already evac **WIA**, TFRD to DofP 29Mar45 (per MR 29Mar45); REASG fm 71st Reinf Bn 26May45 (per MR 26May45) CIB 01Mar45 (10/45); GCM as PFC in RHQ (32/45)	WIA 28Mar45
474.	**Hoffman,** Israel A. 31051520	PVT	C	MOS 745 ASGD 30May44 (per MR 09Jun44); TFRD to 2nd Repl Dep but not departed 19Jul44; s/b ATCHD & jnd (MR 23Jul44) – erron entry already evac sk per MR 05Aug44; evac sk 27Jul44; already evac sk; TFRD to DofP/DFR 28Jul44 (05Aug44); REASG but not jd fm 7th Repl Dep 17Aug44; Rptd as TFRD to 2nd Repl Dep 19Jul44 – erron entry, not TFRD, already evac sk; TFRD to DofP/DFR 28Jul44 (per 05Aug44); joined from 7th Repl Dep 22Sep44; **WIA** not hosp 25Sep44 (per MR 17Oct44); evac sk, TFRD to DofP 24Oct44 CIB FM 01Sep44 (14/44)	WIA 25Sep44
475.	Holbrook, Fredrick D. 37675746	PVT-PFC	C	MOS 745 ASGD & jnd fm 2nd Repl Dep 24 Feb44 per MR 10Mar44; pmtd to PFC 01Jul44 (MR 02Jul44); Evac sk 13Apr44 (per MR 20Apr44); RTD fm sk 16Apr44 (per MR 20Apr44); evac sk, TFRD to DofP 09Sep44; REASGD 17Sep44; evac sk 24Sep44; already evac sk, TFRD to DofP 25Sep44 CIB PFD (07/44)	
476.	Holder, Tillman (NMI) 34129565 PCM-C	PVT-PFC	C, E	(Deployed w/the company, is on the Pine Camp menu as PVT) Promoted to PFC 03Nov43 per MR 05Nov43; tfr in grade to E Co per MR 05Mar44 CIB as PFC in E Co 01Jan44 (06/44 CC)	
477.	**Holmes,** David C. 34937415	PVT	C	MOS 745 ASGD fm 3rd Repl Bn 24Jan45 (per MR 26Jan45); Evac sk 01Feb45 (per MR 01Feb45); RTD fm sk 12Feb45 (per MR 12Feb45; Evac sk 13Feb45 (per MR 13Feb45); RTD fm sk 19Feb45 (per MR 19Feb45); Evac **WIA** 28Mar45 (per MR 28Mar45); Already evac **WIA**, TFRD to DofP 29Mar45 (per MR 29Mar45); RTD fm 71st Reinf Bn 17May45 (per MR 17May45) CIB 01Mar45 (10/45); GCM as PFC (32/45)	WIA 28Mar45
478.	Holzmiller, James R. (or Holsmiller) 36843509	PVT	C	MOS 745 ASGD fm 3rd Repl Bn 24Jan45 (per MR 26Jan45); Evac sk, TFRD to DofP 28Jan45 (per MR 28Jan45); REASG fm 3rd Repl Bn 09Feb45 (per MR 09Feb45); **LIA** not hosp (contusion, heel L, Severe) 29Mar45 (per MR 02Apr45) CIB 01Mar45 (10/45); GCM (32/45)	

479.	**Hoover,** R. (I.O.) H. 38430683	PVT-PFC-CPL-SGT	C	MOS 504 ASGD & jnd fm 2nd Repl Dep 26Feb44 per MR 08Mar44; promoted to PFC (per MR 05Aug44); evac **WIA**, TFRD to DofP 23Sep44; **(Missing entry of RTD)**; Evac sk 09Mar45 (per MR 09Mar45); RTD fm sk 17Mar45 (per MR 17Mar45); PMTD to CPL, change in MOS to 653 24Mar45 (per MR 26Mar45); RTD fm 2nd Rein Dep 27Feb45 (per MR 27Feb45); PMTD to SGT, MOS 652 09May45 (per MR 09May45); TDY to UK 23May45 (per MR 23May45) CIB PFD (07/44); GCM as R. B. (08/44)	WIA 23Sep44
480.	**Hopfan,** Robert B. O-1312843	1LT	C, RHQ	ASGD fm 3rd Repl Bn 13Feb45 (per MR 14Feb45); evac **WIA**, TFRD to DofP 29Mar45 (per MR 29Mar45); REASG fm 71st Reinf Bn w/duty as Ass't Pers Off?? 28May45 (per MR 28May45) Asst Pers Officer, per sig block GO 23/45; WIA Aschaffenburg CIB 01Mar45 (15/45) --	WIA 29Mar45
481.	**Horn,** Frederick E. 32772318	PVT	C	MOS 745 ASGD fm 7th Repl Dep 25Sep43; **(Missing entry of evac);** RTD fm sk 30Oct43 per MR 03Nov43; evac **WIA** 12Nov43 per MR 15Nov43already evac **WIA** TFRD to DofP, DFR per MR 12Dec43 CIB FM 01Jan44 (14/44)	WIA 12Nov43
482.	House, William D. PCM-C	CPL	C	On Pine Camp menu	
483.	**Howard**, James C. 33446142	PFC	C	MOS 014 **(Unknown date of assignment, not on Pine Camp menu) (Missing entry of WIA evac)**; already evac **WIA** TFRD to DofP, DFR per MR 06Dec43; ASGD fm 2nd Repl Dep per MR 11Dec43; evac sk 11Dec43 per MR 23Dec43; RTD fm sk 19Jan44 per MR 21Jan44; evac sk 21Jan44 per MR 23Jan44; RTD fm sk 22Dec43 per MR 25Dec43; evac sk 22Dec43 (per MR 08Jan44); RTD fm sk 25May44; Evac **WIA** (Concussion shell blast) 28May44; already evac **WIA** TFRD to DofP and DFR 21Jun44 (28Jun44) CIB FM 01Jan44 (14/44)	WIA 06Dec43 WIA 28May44
484.	**Howard**, Walter N. 34592201	PVT	C, AT	MOS 745 ASGD 09Sep44 (per MR 16Sep44); **WIA** not hosp 20Oct44 (per MR 21Oct44); evac sk, TFRD to DofP 23Oct44; REASGD fm 2nd Repl Dep 19Nov44; evac sk, TFRD to DofP 25Nov44 (per MR 28Nov44); REASG fm 71st Repl Dep 04Dec44 (per MR 05Dec44); evac sk 06Dec44; RTD fm sk 11Dec44; TFRD to AT Co 26Dec44 CIB FM 01Oct44 (14/44);p CIB PFC in AT Co 01Oct44 (07/45); GCM (08/45)	WIA 20Oct44
485.	Howell, George R. 34979583	PVT	C	MOS 745 ASGD fm 3rd Repl Bn 11Dec44 (per MR 12Dec44); Duty to SIW, TFRD to DofP 30Dec44 CIB 01Jan45 (01/45)	

486.	Hubbard, Francis L. 39322856	PFC	A, C	MOS 745/607 ASGD fm Co A 06Dec44; evac SIW, TFRD to DofP 12Dec44; REASG fm 3rd Repl Bn 21Dec44; MIA 21Jan45 (per MR 23Jan45) **(POW 20JAN45);** Mstr POW reg gives rpt date of 21Jan45, parent unit as division artillery, Stalag 11B, repatriated CIB 01Oct44 (13/44)	POW 20Jan45
487.	Hubble, John 36729929	PFC-SGT	C, F	MOS 745 ASGD fm 36th Inf Div 26Jan45 (per MR 01Feb45) (name changed from "Hubbie" in MR 04Feb45); TFRD to Co F 02Feb45 (per MR 04Feb45) GCM (30/45)	
488.	**Huckabay, Robert M. 20837717 PCM-C**	**SGT**	C	(Deployed w/the company, is on the Pine Camp menu as SGT) **WIA** 29Jul43 (**KIA**, per MR 04Aug43) (buried in Sicily-Rome Cemetery) KIA as SGT in C Co 29Jul43 per Div & 157 casualty list; ABMC 29Jul43, Sicily-Rome Cemetery PH No discovered GO for CIB or GCM	**KIA 29Jul43**
489.	**Huddleston,** Jennings 38697207	PVT	C	MOS 745 ASGD and joined fm 2nd Repl Dep 02Nov44 (per MR 09Nov44); **WIA** not hosp 07Dec44 (per MR 10Dec44); Promoted to PFC 25Dec44 (per MR 26Dec44); Evac **SWIA**, TFRD to DofP 05Jan45 (per MR 05Jan45) CIB 01Dec44 (01/45)	WIA 05Jan45
490.	Hudkins, Earnest J. 35761011	PVT	C	MOS 745 ASGD 05Jun44 (09Jun44) probably from G Co; AWOL 0700 08Jun44 (13Jun44); fm AWOL to Regtl Stockade 1830 06Jul44 (MR 07Jul44); RTD fm Confinement 10Jul44; TFRD to 2nd Repl Dep but not dptd 19Jul44; s/b ATCHD & jnd (MR 23Jul44); already attached fm 2nd Repl Det reld fm atchment (per MR 05Aug44) CIB FM 01Sep44 (14/44) **(No Former Members on this GO!)**	
491.	Hudnall, Glynn D. 38673844	PVT-PFC	C	MOS 745 ASGD and joined fm 2nd Repl Dep 02Nov44 (per MR 09Nov44); evac sk 04Dec44; RTD fm sk 08Dec44; promoted to PFC 25Dec44 (per MR 26Dec44); Evac sk 01Jan45 (per MR 01Jan45); Already evac sk, TFRD to DofP 02Jan45 (per MR 02Jan45); REASG fm 3rd Repl Bn 07Feb45 (per MR 07Feb45); Evac sk 13Feb45 (per MR 13Feb45); RTD fm sk 16Feb45 (per MR 16Feb45); **(Missing entry of evac sk)** Already evac sk, TFRD to DofP 05Mar45 (per MR 05Mar45) CIB 01Dec44 (01/45)	

492.	Huffman, Will E. 35726559	PVT-PFC	C	MOS 504 ASGD & jnd fm 2nd Repl Dep 26Feb44 per MR 08Mar44; evac sk 05Apr44 (per MR 14Apr44); RTD fm sk 13Apr44 (per MR 18Apr44; pmtd to PFC 01May44; evac sk (ankle problems) 31May44; RTD fm sk 11Jun44 (13Jun44); evac sk 20Aug44; already evac sk TFRD to DofP 20Aug44 (22Aug44); REASG fm hosp 15Sep44; evac sk, TFRD to DofP 28Sep44; REASGD but not joined fm 2nd Repl Dep 13Oct44; joined 13Oct44; MIA 21Jan45 (per MR 23Jan45) **(POW 20JAN45);** Mstr POW reg gives rpt date of 21Jan45, parent unit as division artillery, no camp info, repatriated CIB PFD (07/44)	POW 20Jan45
493.	Hughes, Donald N. 38006191	SSG	C	MOS 653 (Deployed w/the company, is on the Pine Camp menu as SGT) INJ (concussion) not hosp 17Jan45 (per MR 19Jan45); Evac sk 24Jan45 (per MR 25Jan45); RTD fm sk 30Jan45 (per MR 30Jan45); Evac sk, TFRD to DofP 20Mar45 (per MR 20Mar45); MOS 824 REASG fm 71st Reinf Bn, and placed on DS with 71st Reinf Bn 31Mar45 (per MR 03Apr45); REASG fm 71st Reinf Bn 02Apr45 (per MR 03Apr45); TDY to Ft. Devens, Mass. 26Apr45 (per MR 26Apr45); TDY to US, 21May45 (per MR 21May45) CIB as SSG in C Co (01/44 - 01Jan44 per CC); GCM (02/44)	
494.	**Hughes**, James D. 35630277	PVT-PFC	C	**(Unknown date of assignment, not on Pine Camp menu))** Evac **SWIA** 12Nov43 per MR 15Nov43; RTD fm DofP 27Feb44 per MR 05Mar44; pmtd to PFC 01May44; evac **WIA** 31May44 (per MR 06Jun44); already evac **WIA** to DofP/DFR 11Jun44 (17Jun44) CIB Former Pers 01Jan44 (10/44 CC)	WIA 12Nov43 WIA 31May44
495.	Hulse, Walter R. 32827558	PVT-PFC	C	MOS 746 asgd & joined 07Feb44; pmtd PFC 01May44; evac sk 02May44 (MR 07May44); to DofP/DFR 07May44 (MR 14May44) CIB FM 01Mar44 (14/44)	
496.	**Humenik,** John G. 33439594	PVT- SGT	C	MOS 745 ASGD fm 7th Repl Dep 25Sep43; promoted PFC 01Jan44 per MR 05Jan44; pmtd to CPL 18Jan44 per MR 19Jan44; evac sk (jaundice) 26Feb44 per MR 04Mar44; already evac sk, tfrd to DofP & DFR 22Mar44; pmtd SGT per MR 25Jan44; RTD fm DofP 28May44; evac **WIA**, TFRD to DofP 07Nov44 CIB (01/44 - 01Jan44 per CC); CIB (04/44); GCM (08/44)	WIA 07Nov44
497.	Humphreys, Edward J., Jr. 33890169	PVT-PFC	C	MOS 745 ASGD fm 3rd Repl Bn 11Dec44 (per MR 12Dec44); Pmtd to PFC 07Jan45 (per MR 08Jan45); MIA 21Jan45 (per MR 23Jan45) **(POW 20JAN45);** Mstr POW reg gives rpt date of 21Jan45, Stalag 12A to 9B, repatriated CIB 01Jan45 (01/45)	POW 20Jan45

498.	Hunter, Lawrence E. 34731128	PVT-PFC	C	MOS 745 ASGD fm 2nd Repl Bn 18Dec43 per MR 22Dec43; evac sk 26Dec43 per MR 28Dec43; RTD fm sk 14Feb44; pmtd to PFC 01Jul44 (MR 02Jul44); evac sk, TFRD to DofP 05Dec44; already evac sk TFRD to DofP, DFR per MR 21Jan44 CIB (04/44); 01Jan44 per CC; CIB as PFD (07/44); GCM PFC (16/44)	
499.	**Hurt**, Oliver I. 38631214	PVT-PFC	C	MOS 745 ASGD fm 3rd Repl Bn 24Jan45 (per MR 26Jan45); PMTD to PFC 06Mar45 (per MR 06Mar45); Evac **WIA**, TFRD to DofP 20Mar45 (per MR 20Mar45); REASG fm 71st Reinf Bn 26May45 (per MR 26May45) CIB 01Mar45 (10/45); GCM as PFC (32/45)	WIA 20Mar45
500.	**Hurtado**, Teton (NMI) 37087382 PCM-C	PVT-PFC	C	(Deployed w/the company, is on the Pine Camp menu as PVT) Promoted PFC 25Aug43; evac **WIA** 07Dec43 (per MR 13Dec43); already evac **WIA** TFRD to DofP, DFR per MR 31Dec43; Reasgd & jnd from DofP 01Mar44 per MRs 9 & 10Mar44; evac **WIA** (BC CG R Knee acc) 03Mar44 per MR 09Mar44; **(Missing entry of RTD)**; evac **LIA** (cg R Knee acc) 03Mar44 per MR 10Mar44; RTD fm **WIA** 24Apr44 (per MR 30Apr44; TFRD on rotation to US 08Sep44 CIB as PFC in C Co (03/44) HURTALCO; 01Jan44 HURTADTO per CC; GCM HURTADO (08/44) HURTADO is correct	WIA 13Dec43 WIA 03Mar44 WIA 24Apr44
501.	**Hussey**, John J. O-1322554	1LT	C	ASGD fm 2nd Repl Dep 11Nov44 (per MR 13Nov44); evac **WIA**, TFRD to DofP 05Dec44 CIB 01Dec44 (15/45)	WIA 05Dec44
502.	Hussey, Robert L. (Delta, CO)	PVT	C	Induction roster 16Sep40	
503.	**Hutson**, Elton E. 38673856	PVT-PFC	C	MOS 745 ASGD fm 2nd Repl Dep 11Nov44 (per MR 13Nov44); promoted to PFC 25Dec44 (per MR 26Dec44); Evac S**WIA**, TFRD to DofP 14Jan45 (per MR 14Jan45) CIB 01Dec44 (01/45)	WIA 14Jan45
504.	**Idol**, John M., Jr. 34868182	PVT-PFC	C, 1HQ	MOS 745 ASGD fm 3rd Repl Bn 24Jan45 (per MR 26Jan45); **(Missing entry of evac sk)**; RTD fm sk 07Feb45 (per MR 07Feb45); Already evac sk, TFRD to DofP 01Mar45 (per MR 01May45); **(Missing entry of RTD)** PMTD to PFC 06Mar45 (per MR 06Mar45); **WIA** 30Apr45 (per MR 30Apr45) **CIB 01Mar45 (10/45); GCM as PFC in 1HQ (33/45)**	WIA 30Apr45

505.	**Iron Hawk,** Claude A. 37249605	PVT	C	MOS 605 (Deployed w/the company, is on the Pine Camp menu as PVT) **WIA** evac 12Sep43 (per MR 18Sep43); RTD fr DofP 04Dec43 per MR 08Dec43; evac sk 19Dec43 (per MR 01Jan44); RTD fm sk 04Jan44 per MR 07Jan44; evac sk 13Jan44 per MR 16Jan44; RTD fm sk 18Feb44; evac **WIA** (pen w l arm, r wrist, thumb & index finger shell frag) 20Feb44; TFRD to DofP and DFR 27Feb44; already evac **WIA**, trfd to DofP and DFR 27Feb44 per MR 14Mar44 CIB DP (07/44)	WIA 12Sep43 WIA 20Feb44
506.	Ivins, Ralph D. 39148952	PVT-PFC	C	MOS 745 ASGD fm 3rd Repl Bn 24Jan45 (per MR 26Jan45); PMTD to PFC 06Mar45 (per MR 06Mar45) CIB 01Mar45 (10/45); GCM (32/45)	
507.	Izzo, Michael A. Jr. 31291815	PVT	F, C	MOS 745 ASGD 21Aug44 (22Aug44) probably from F Co; evac sk, TFRD to DopP 20Nov44; REASG fm 2nd Repl Dep 26Nov44 (per MR 28Nov44); TFRD to 10th Repl Dep for ship to USA 23Jan45 (per MR 23Jan45) CIB PFD (07/44)	
508.	Izzyk, John N. 32260555	PVT	C, A	**(Unknown date of assignment)** Evac sk 31Jan45, TFRD to Co A (per MR 02Feb45) No discovered GO for CIB or GCM	
509.	**Jackson, Hugo W. 38005261 PCM-C**	**CPL**	C	(Deployed w/the company, is on the Pine Camp menu as PFC) MIA 16Aug43 (per MR 21Aug43) (DFR per MR 07Sep43) **(believed drowned on N. coast of Sicily. Still MIA. Commemorated at Sicily-Rome Cemetery) BSM -- no PH** **CIB FM as CPL in C Co 01Jan44 (14/44)**	**MIA 16Aug43**
510.	Jackson, Warren M. SN NA (Delta, CO)	**CPL**	C	Induction Roster 16Sep40	
511.	Jaimes, Perfecto (NMI) 38001023	PFC-PVT-PFC	C	MOS 746 (Deployed w/the company, is on the Pine Camp menu as PFC) Reduced to PVT 10Aug43; pmtd PFC 01Jul43 (Fm MR 20Jul43); pmtd **(again?)** to PFC 01Dec43; MIA 14Dec43, DFR (per MR 25Dec43)(s/b evac sk 14Dec43 per MR 27Dec43); already evac sk, TFRD to DofP, DFR per MR 15Jan44 CIB FM as PFC in C Co (05/44); 01Jan44 per CC; CIB DP (07/44)	
512.	**James**, Bernard 38584551	PVT	C	MOS 745 ASGD fm 3rd Repl Bn 24Jan45 (per MR 26Jan45); Evac sk 27Jan45 (per MR 01Feb45); RTD fm 3rd Repl Bn 13Feb45 (per MR 13Feb45); PMTD to PFC 06Mar45 (per MR 06Mar45); Evac **WIA**, TFRD to DofP 18Mar45 (per MR 18Mar45); RTD fm 71st Reinf Bn 17May45 (per MR 17May45) CIB 01Mar45 (10/45); GCM as PFC (32/45)	WIA 18Mar45

513.	Jarvis, Ervin C. 34729037	PVT	C	MOS 745 ASGD fm 2nd Repl Bn 18Dec43 per MR 22Dec43; evac sk 04Jan44 per MR 06Jan44; already evac sk, trfd to 2nd Repl Dep 23Feb44 per MR 15Mar44 CIB FM 01Jan44 (14/44)	
514.	Jaynes, Claude 38684614	PVT	C	MOS 745 ASGD and joined fm 2nd Repl Dep 02Nov44 (per MR 09Nov44); MIA 21Jan45 (per MR 23Jan45) **(POW 20JAN45);** Mstr POW reg gives rpt date of 21Jan45, parent unit as division artillery, no camp info, repatriated CIB 01Dec44 (01/45)	POW 20Jan45
515.	Jeffcoat, Charley E. 34129648mitrow PCM-C	PFC-PVT-PFC	C	(Deployed w/the company, is on the Pine Camp menu as PFC) Evac sk 25Sep43 (per MR 29Sep43); already evac sk TFRD to DofP, DFR per MR 18Dec43; RTD fm sk 29Oct43 per MR 01Nov43; evac sk 17Nov43 per MR 21Nov43; already evac sk, TFRD to DofP 02Dec44; RTD fm DofP 20Dec43 (per MR 26Dec43); Pmtd to PFC 04Mar44 per MR 12Mar44 CIB PFC in C Co per PCCM42; CIB as PVT in C Co (01/44 - 01Jan44 per CC); GCM as PFC (08/44)	
516.	Jefford, Robert S. 33052064	TSG	C	MOS 651 ASGD fm 24th Repl Dep 05Dec44 (per MR 08Dec44); Evac sk 05Jan45 (per MR 05Jan45); Already evac sk, TFRD to DofP 06Jan45 (per MR 06Jan45) CIB 01Jan45 (01/45)	
517.	**Jenkins,** George W. (or M.) **O-541167**	2LT	C	ASGD fm 3rd Repl Bn 21Dec44 (per MR 25Dec44); Evac **WIA**, TFRD to DofP 14Jan45 (per MR 14Jan45) No discovered GO for CIB	WIA 14Jan45
518.	Jensen, Frode W. 36989099	PVT	C	MOS 745 ASGD fm 3rd Repl Bn 24Jan45 (per MR 26Jan45); Evac sk 26Apr45 (per MR 26Apr45); Already evac sk, TFRD to DofP 27Apr45 (per MR 27Apr45); RTD fm 71st Reinf Bn 17May45 (per MR 17May45) CIB 01Mar45 (10/45); GCM (32/45)	
519.	Jividen, Thurman H. 37010190 PCM-C	PFC-CPL-T-5	C	(Deployed w/the company, is on the Pine Camp menu as PFC) Promoted to CPL per MR 05Nov43; evac sk as T-5 19Apr44 (per MR 25Apr44); already evac sk, tfrd to 7th Repl Depot 09May44 (per MR 17May44) CIB as T-5 in C Co (01/44 - 01Jan44 per CC)	
520.	Johnson, Edgar W. 34129700 PCM-C	PVT	C	(Deployed w/the company, is on the Pine Camp menu as PVT) MIA 13Sep43 DFR (per MR 24Sep43) **(POW 13Sep43);** Mstr POW reg gives rpt date of 13Sep43, Stalag 2B, repatriated CIB FM as PVT in C Co 01Jan44 (14/44)	POW 13Sep43
521.	Johnson, Harold G. 42145778	PVT-PFC	C	MOS 745 ASGD fm 3rd Repl Bn 24Jan45 (per MR 26Jan45); PMTD to PFC 06Mar45 (per MR 06Mar45); Evac sk, TFRD to DofP 07May45 (per MR 07May45); RTD 09May45 (per MR 09May45) CIB 01Mar45 (10/45)	

522.	Johnson, Horace C. 34624427	PVT	C	CIB 01Jan44 (14/44)	
523.	Johnson, James A. 38570053	PVT	C	MOS 745 **(Unknown date of assignment)** MIA 15Dec43, DFR (per MR 25Dec43) (actually AWOL per MR 12Jan44); erron rptd on 25Dec43 as MIA 15Dec43 s/b AWOL 15Dec43 per MR 12Jan44; AWOL to confinement Naples, pending trial 08Jan44 per MR 12Jan44; from conf to present, under arrest, awaiting trial 17Jan44 (per MR 24Jan44, s/b in conf, awaiting trial) per MR 20Jan44; moved from 5th Army Stockade to hospital (psychoneurosis) 22Mar44 (per MR 17Apr44); already evac sk tfrd to Pers Ctr 6, 7th Repl Dep 17May44 (MR 18May44); ASGD fm 3rd Repl Bn 24Jan45 (per MR 26Jan45); Evac sk 25Jan45 (per MR 27Jan45)	
524.	**Johnson, James A. 38570053**	**PVT-PFC**	C	MOS 745 **(Unknown date of assignment, not on Pine Camp menu) (Missing entry for evac sk)**; RTD fm sk 04Feb45 (per MR 04Feb45); PMTD to PFC 06Mar45 (per MR 06Mar45); **(Missing entry for evac)**; already evac **SWIA** 16Apr45, **DOW** 16Apr45 (per MR 19Apr45) (buried in the USA); DOW16Apr45 per Div & 157 casualty list; not on ABMC reg CIB 01Mar45 (10/45)	WIA 16Apr45 **DOW 16Apr45**
525.	**Johnson, James H. 36661113**	**PVT**	C	MOS 745 ASGD fm 2nd Repl Bn 18Dec43 per MR 22Dec43; MIA 31May44, DFR (06Jun44); MIA to **KIA** 31May44 (06Jun44) (buried in Sicily-Rome Cemetery); KIA03May44 per Div casualty list; KIA31MAY44 per 157 list; MIA/KIA31MAY44 as JAMES W. per ANB; ABMC 31May44, Sicily-Rome Cemetery PH No discovered GO for CIB or GCM	**KIA 31May44**
526.	Johnson, Lyle C. (ston?) 39336607	PVT	C	MOS 745 ASGD fm 2nd Repl Dep 24Feb44 per MR 05Mar44; Evac sick NYD (per MR 02May44); already evac sk, tfrd to DofP and DFR 01May44 (per MR 19May44); MOS 745 RTD fm DofP 21Jul44; evac sk 26Jul44 (27Jul44); already evac sk reclassified limited assignment 28Jul44 CIB PFD (07/44) (as Johnston)	
527.	Johnson, Max L. PCM-C 38006223	SSG-TSG	C	(Deployed w/the company, is on the Pine Camp menu as SGT) Evac sk 29Nov43 (per MR 04Dec43); RTD fm sk 24Dec43 per MR 27Dec43; evac sk 31Dec43 (per MR 05Jan44); RTD fm sk 24Feb44 per MR 03Mar44; pmtd to TSG per MR 10Mar44; evac sk 10Jun44; already evac sk TFRD to DofP and DFR 14Jun44 (20Jun44) CIB as TSG in C Co (01/44 - 01Jan44 per CC); GCM (02/44)	

528.	Johnson, Samuel C. 20837718	PVT	C	MOS 745 ASGD fm 3rd Repl Bn 24Jan45 (per MR 26Jan45); Evac sk 09Feb45, TFRD to DofP (per MR 09Feb45); REASG 10Apr45 (per MR 13Apr45) CIB 01Mar45 (10/45); GCM (32/45)	
529.	Johnson, William J. 33740031	PVT	C	MOS 745 ASGD fm 2nd Repl Bn 18Dec43 per MR 22Dec43; Tfr in grade to G Co per MR 05Mar44 No discovered GO for CIB or GCM	
530.	**Johnston, C. J.** 38631749	**PVT-PFC**	C	MOS 745 ASGD fm 3rd Repl Bn 24Jan45 (per MR 26Jan45); PMTD to PFC 06Mar45 (per MR 06Mar45); Evac **SWIA**, TFRD to DofP 16Apr45 (per MR 16Apr45); **DOW** 16Apr45 per MR 19Apr45) (buried in USA) CIB 01Mar45 (10/45)	WIA 16Apr45 **DOW 16Apr45**
531.	Joiner, Bennie L. 34089025	SGT-SSG	C	MOS 653 ASGD fm 36th Inf Div 26Jan45 (per MR 01Feb45); Evac sk 03Feb45 (per MR 03Feb45); RTD fm sk 15 Feb45 (per MR 15Feb45); PMTD to SSG 09Mar45 (per MR 09Mar45); Evac INJ 18Mar45 (per MR 18Mar45); already Evac INJ, TFRD to DofP 19Mar45 (per MR 19Mar45) No discovered GO for CIB or GCM	
532.	Jones, Carl E. 42095401	PVT	C	MOS 745 ASGD fm 3rd Repl Bn 24Jan45 (per MR 26Jan45); Evac sk, TFRD to DofP 02Feb45 (per MR 02Feb45); REASG fm 2nd Reinf Dep 02Mar45 (per MR 02Mar45) CIB 01Mar45 (10/45); GCM as PFC (32/45)	
533.	Jones, Frederick SN NA (Delta, CO)	PVT	C	Induction Roster 16Sep40	
534.	**Jones**, Henry W. O-514007	2LT	C	ATCHD fm 25 Repl Det (25Jun44); ASGD fr 2nd Repl Dep 05Jun44 (07Jun44); Reld of atch and ASGD 29Sep44 **????**; promoted to 1LT 27Oct44 (per MR 29Oct44); evac **WIA**, TFRD to DofP 09Dec44; RTD fm 3rd Repl Bn 17Jan45 (per MR 17Jan45); Reld of duties of Executive Officer, assumes command 21Jan45 (per MR 30Jan45); Evac **WIA**, TFRD to DofP 18Mar45 (per MR 18Mar45) WIA, lost leg per Speairs CIB eff 01Sep44 (13/44)	WIA 18Mar45
535.	Jones, James H. PCM-C 20837731 (Delta, CO)	SSG	C	On Induction Roster 16Sep40 as PVT (Deployed w/the company, is on the Pine Camp menu as SSG) MIA 13Sep43 DFR (per MR 24Sep43) **(POW 13Sep43)**; Mstr POW reg gives rpt date of 13Sep43, Stalag 3B, repatriated CIB MIA as SSG in C Co (05/44); 01Jan44 per CC	POW 13Sep43
536.	Jones, James L. 34937461	PVT	C	MOS 745 ASGD fm 3rd Repl Bn 24Jan45 (per MR 26Jan45); Evac sk 31Jan45 (per MR 31Jan45); Already Evac sk, TFRD to DofP 13Feb45 (per MR 13Feb45) No discovered GO for CIB or GCM	

537.	**Jones, Johnnie B.** **38631152**	**PVT**	C	MOS 745 ASGD fm 3rd Repl Bn 24Jan45 (per MR 26Jan45); Evac sk 31Jan45 (per MR 31Jan45); RTD fm sk 08Feb45 (per MR 08Feb45)**;** Evac **SWIA**, TFRD to DofP 18Mar45 (per MR 18Mar45); **DOW** 19Mar45 (buried in USA); DOW19Mar45 per Div & 157 casualty list; not on ABMC reg CIB 01Mar45 (10/45)	WIA 18Mar45 **DOW 19Mar45**
538.	Jones, Olen D. 38697760 Kia?????	PVT	C	MOS 745 ASGD and joined fm 2nd Repl Dep 02Nov44 (per MR 09Nov44); evac sk, TFRD to DofP 04Dec44; REASG fm 3rd Repl Bn 15Jan45 (per MR 15Jan45); MIA 21Jan45 (per MR 23Jan45) **(POW 20JAN45);** MIA21Jan45 per MR 23Jan45; MIA21Jan45 per ANB -- NOT on Mstr POW register; not on ABMC reg No discovered GO for CIB or GCM	POW 20Jan45
539.	**Jones,** Robert C. PCM-C 38018895	T-5- T-4	C	(Deployed w/the company, is on the Pine Camp menu as PFC) Evac sk 25Sep43 (per MR 03Oct43); **(Missing entry for RTD)**; **WIA** 14Jan45 not hosp (pen wnd right thumb) (per MR 27Jan45); PMTD to T-4 09May45 (per MR 09May45); TFRD 28May45 to Camp Chaffee, AR, for separation (per MR 28May45) CIB PFD as T-5 in C Co (07/44); GCM (02/44)	WIA 14Jan45
540.	**Jones, Russell W.** **35101872**	**PFC-CPL-SGT-SSG**	C	MOS 653 (Deployed w/the company, is on the Pine Camp menu as PFC) Pmtd CPL (04Aug43); **WIA** evac 12Sep43 (per MR 18Sep43); RTD fm DofP 24Apr44 (per MR 30Apr44); promoted to SGT (per MR 05Aug44); evac **WIA**, TFRD to DofP 23Sep44; REASG not joined 26Sep44; joined 26Sep44 (per MR 27Sep44); promoted to SSG MOS 653 07Oct44; evac **WIA**, TFRD to DofP 20Oct44; **DOW** 20Oct44 per MR 25Oct44 (buried in USA); DOW26Oct44 as SSG per Div casualty list; KIA20OCT44 per 157 list; not on ABMC reg CIB as CPL in C Co (03/44); 01Jan44 per CC; GCM (08/44)	WIA 12Sep43 WIA 23Sep43 WIA 20Oct44 **DOW 20Oct44**
541.	Jones, Wilber C. 32838852	PVT-PFC	C, E	MOS 745 ASGD fm 7th Repl Dep 25Sep43; pmtd to PFC 01Dec43; evac sk 05Dec43 per MR 13Dec43; already evac sk TFRD to DofP, DFR per MR 14Dec43; RTD fm DofP (16Jun44); TFRD to 2nd Repl Dep but not departed 19Jul44; s/b ATCHD & jnd (MR 23Jul44); already attached fm 2nd Repl Det reld fm atchment (per MR 05Aug44) CIB PFD in C Co (07/44); GCM in E Co (17/44)	
542.	Joplin, Charles H. O-2017862	2LT	C	ASGD fm 71st Reinf Bn 27May45 (per MR 29May45) No discovered GO for CIB or GCM	

543.	Jordan, Carl W. 38696257	PVT	C	MOS 745 ASGD and joined fm 2nd Repl Dep 02Nov44 (per MR 09Nov44); evac sk, TFRD to DofP 15Dec44; RTD 19May45 (per MR 19May45); Evac sk 23May45 (per MR 23May45); RTD fm sk 26May45 (per MR 26May45) GCM (32/45)	
544.	**Jordan,** Harold R. 38546092	PVT-PFC	C	MOS 745 ASGD and joined fm 2nd Repl Dep 02Nov44 (per MR 09Nov44); evac sk, TFRD to DofP 06Dec44; RTD fm 2nd Reinforcement Dep 20Feb45 (per MR 20Feb45); PMTD to PFC 06Mar45 (per MR 06Mar45); Evac **WIA**, TFRD to DofP 18Mar45 (per MR 18Mar45) CIB 01Mar45 (09/45)	WIA 18Mar45
545.	Jordan, Robert J. 31376765	PVT-PFC	C	MOS 745 ASGD fm 3rd Repl Bn 24Jan45 (per MR 26Jan45); PMTD to PFC 06Mar45 (per MR 06Mar45) CIB 01Mar45 (10/45); GCM as PFC (32/45)	
546.	**Jordan,** Wallace L. 33539703	PVT	C, D	MOS 745 ASGD 20Aug43; **WIA** evac 12Sep43 (per MR 18Sep43); TFRD to Co D 25Sep43 (per MR 28Sep43) CIB (04/44); 01Jan44 per CC; GCM (02/44)	WIA 12Sep43
547.	**Jose, Anthony (NMI) 38003878 PCM-C**	**PVT-PFC**	C	(Deployed w/the company, is on the Pine Camp menu as PVT) Promoted to PFC 03Nov43 per MR 05Nov43; **KIA** 15Dec43 (per MR 20Dec43) (buried in the USA); KIA as PFC in C Co 15DEC43 per Div & 157 casualty list; not on ABMC reg No discovered GO for CIB or GCM	**KIA 15Dec43**
548.	**Jozefowicz,** Roman C. 35017319 PCM-C	CPL	C	(Deployed w/the company, is on the Pine Camp menu as PFC) Evac **WIA** 12Nov43 per MR 15Nov43; already evac **WIA** TFRD to DofP, DFR per MR 06Dec43 CIB FM as CPL in C Co 01Jan44 (14/44)	WIA 12Nov43
549.	Jucoff, Robert N. 35841232	PVT-PFC	C	MOS 745 ASGD fm 3rd Repl Bn 11Dec44 (per MR 12Dec44); Pmtd to PFC 07Jan45 (per MR 08Jan45); MIA 21Jan45 (per MR 23Jan45) **(POW 20JAN45);** Stalag 11B Fallingbostel Prussia (Work Camps) 53-09; liberated CIB 01Jan45 (01/45)	POW 20Jan45
550.	Jungemann, Milton L. 37565569	PVT	C, G	MOS 745 ASGD fm 2nd Repl Bn 14Jan44 per MR 18Jan44; Tfr in grade to G Co per MR 05Mar44 CIB FM 01Feb44 (14/44)	
551.	Jusseaume, Joseph J. M. 31428567	PFC-PVT	C, 1HQ	ASGD fm 1HQ 20Oct44 ; TFRD to 1HQ as PVT 02Feb45 (per MR 02Feb45) CIB in C Co 01Oct44 (13/44); GCM PFC in 1HQ (26/45)	

552.	**Kacarab (or Karacab)**, Michael Jr. 35841164	PVT	C	MOS 745 ASGD fm 3rd Repl Bn 11Dec44 (per MR 12Dec44); evac **WIA**, TFRD to DofP 14Dec44; RTD fm 3rd Repl Bn 30Jan45 (per MR 30Jan45); Evac sk 24Feb45 (per MR 24Feb45; RTD fm evac sk 03Mar45 (per MR 03Mar45); **WIA** not hosp 29Mar45 (per MR 02Apr45); Evac sk 09May45 (per MR 09May45); Already evac sk, TFRD to DofP 10May45 (per MR 10May45) CIB 01Jan45 (01/45)	WIA 14Dec44 WIA 29Mar45
553.	Kadlubowski, Chester (NMI) 31065124	PVT	C	**(Unknown date of assignment, not on Pine Camp menu)** MIA 13Sep43 DFR (per MR 24Sep43) **(POW 13Sep43);** Mstr POW reg gives rpt date of 13Sep43, Stalag 2B, repatriated CIB FM 01Jan44 (14/44)	POW 13Sep43
554.	Kalski, Chester PCM-C SN NA	PVT	C	On Pine Camp menu	
555.	Kane, James T. 33702222	PVT-PFC	C	MOS 745 ASGD fm 2nd Repl Dep 23Apr44 (per MR 29Apr44); promoted to PFC (per MR 05Aug44); evac sk, TFRD to DofP 27Aug44; RTD fm hosp 16Sep44; evac sk 19Sep44; already evac sk, TFRD to DofP 20Sep44; RTD fm 3rd Repl Bn 31Jan45 (per MR 31Jan45); Evac sk 12Feb45 (per MR 12Feb45); RTD fm sk 16Feb45 (per MR 16Feb45) CIB 01May44 (06/44 CC); GCM PFC (08/45)	
556.	**Kantola**, Lawrence E. 36215594	PFC	C	**(Unknown date of assignment, not on Pine Camp menu)** Evac **WIA** 10Nov43 per MR 13Nov43; already evac sk, DFR per MR 26Nov43 CIB FM 01Jan44 (14/44)	WIA 10Nov43
557.	**Kapica, Leonard L.36570516**	**PFC**	C	MOS 504 **(Unknown date of assignment) (Missing evac entry)** RTD fm 2nd Repl Dep 11Jan44 per MR 13Jan44; MIA 28May44, DFR 01Jun44; change fm MIA 28May44 to **KIA** 28May44 (29Jun44) (buried in USA); KIA28May44 per Div & 157 casualty list; MIA/KIA28MAY44 per ANBl not on ABMC reg No discovered GO for CIB or GCM	**KIA 28May44**
558.	Karobonik, Alec (NMI) 39708557 Kia??????	PVT	C	MOS 745 ASGD 05Jun44 (09Jun44); evac sk 27Jun44 (28Jun44); RTD fm sk (30Jun44); TFRD to 2nd Repl Dep but not dptd 19Jul44; s/b ATCHD & jnd (MR 23Jul44); 745 already attached fm 2nd Repl Det reld fm atchment (per MR 05Aug44); ASGD fm 2nd Repl Dep 08Aug44 (31Aug44); evac sk, TFRD to DofP 08Nov44; REASG fm 3rd Repl Bn10Dec44 (per MR 11Dec44); evac sk, TFRD to DofP 13Dec44; REASG fm 3rd REpl Bn 11Jan45 (per MR 11Jan45); MIA 21Jan45 (per MR 23Jan45) **(POW 20JAN45);** MIA21Jan45 per MR 23Jan45 -- NOT on Mstr POW register by name or by SN; not on ABMC reg CIB 01Sep44 (13/44)	POW 20Jan45

559.	Katan, Robert T. 32506484	PVT	C	**(Unknown date of assignment, not on Pine Camp menu)** MIA 13Sep43 DFR (per MR 24Sep43) **(POW 13Sep43)** Mstr POW reg gives rpt date of 13Sep43 w/o unit ID, Stalag 2B, repatriated CIB FM 01Jan44 (14/44)	POW 13Sep43
560.	Kayner, Edward 42083676	PFC	C	**(Unknown date of assignment)** Evac sk 11Mar45 (per MR 11Mar45) No discovered GO for CIB or GCM	
561.	Keil, Joseph C. PCM-C SN NA	PVT	C	On Pine Camp menu	
562.	**Kellner,** Miles A. 36448926	PFC	C	MOS 745 ASGD 09Sep44 (per MR 16Sep44); joined 15Sep44 (per MR 16Sep44); evac **SWIA**, TFRD to DofP 18Oct44 CIB FM 01Oct44 (14/44)	WIA 18Oct44
563.	**Kelly,** Timothy F. 42106915	PVT-PFC	C	MOS 745 ASGD fm 3rd Repl Bn 24Jan45 (per MR 26Jan45); PMTD to PFC 06Mar45 (per MR 06Mar45); Evac **WIA** 28Mar45 (per MR 28Mar45); Already evac sk, TFRD to DofP 30Mar45 (per MR 30Mar45) CIB 01Mar45 (10/45)	WIA 28Mar45
564.	**Kemper**, Edward N. O-1296537	2LT	C, 1HQ, C	ASGD fr 29th Repl Bn 14Nov43 per MR 23Nov43; evac **WIA** 22Dec43 per MR 25Dec43; already evac **WIA**, DFR per MR 25Jan44; RTD fm **WIA** 25Feb44, Tfrd to 1HQ 25Feb44; Tfrd to 1HQ 25Feb44; ASGD fm 1HQ, assumed duties as CO 28May45 (per MR 28May45) CIB (01/44 - 01Jan44 per CC)	WIA 22Dec43
565.	Kennedy, Michael J. 32226814	PVT	C	**(Unknown date of assignment, not on Pine Camp menu)** MIA 13Sep43 DFR (per MR 24Sep43) **(POW 13Sep43)** Mstr POW reg gives rpt date of 13Sep43, Stalag 2B, repatriated CIB FM 01Jan44 (14/44)	POW 13Sep43
566.	**Kerttu**, Carl W. 39602759	PVT-PFC	C	MOS 603 (Deployed w/the company, is on the Pine Camp menu as PVT) Promoted to PFC 03Nov43 (per MR 05Nov43); Special Duty to 45th Inf Div Mule Pack Train (prov) 14Nov43 (per MR 30Nov43); RTD fm SD w/Div Mule Train 01Jan44 per MR 06Jan44; evac **WIA** (pen W R side neck, R shoulder shell frag) 15Feb44; already evac **WIA**, tfrd to DofP and DFR 18Mar44 per MR 28Mar44; RTD fm DofP 24Apr44 (per MR 30Apr44); Pfc evac sk (05May44 (MR 13May44); RTD 07May44 (MR 13May44); evac sk 19May44 (MR 21May44); already evac sk, TFRD to DofP/DFR 29May44 (MR 11Jun44); already evac sk, TFRD to DofP and DFR 29May44 (12Jun44) CIB FM as PFC in C Co 01Jan44 (14/44)	WIA 15Feb44

567.	**Key, Virgil S. 37750793 last digit poss 8**	**PVT**	C	MOS 745 ASGD fm 71st Reinf Bn 20Apr45 (per MR 24Apr45); Evac **WIA**, TFRD to DofP 25Apr45 (per MR 25Apr45) CIB 01May45 (15/45); ASGD 20APR45 per MR; WIA 25APR45 per MR; DOW06MAY45 per MR; DOW06MAY45 per 157 list; ABMC 06May45, Cambridge Cemetery PH No discovered CO for CIB or GCM	WIA 25Apr45 **DOW06May45**
568.	Kiewiet, George Jr. (NMI) (Kiewiest?) 16086521	PVT-PFC	C	MOS 745 **(Unknown date of assignment, not on Pine Camp menu)** Promoted to PFC 03Nov43 per MR 05Nov43; evac sk 03Nov44; already evac sk, TFRD to DofP 04Nov44; **(Missing entry for RTD)**; AWOL 0700 31May44 (per MR 08Jun44); **(Missing entry of RTD from AWOL)**; evac sk 15Jul44; **(Missing entry of RTD)** ; evac sk 19Jul44 (MR 21Jul44); **(Missing entry of RTD)**; evac sk 06Aug44, TFRD to DofP/DFR 06Aug44 (10Aug44); REASG but not jd fm 7th Repl Dep 17Aug44 No discovered GO for CIB or GCM	
569.	Kilcrease, John M. 38695231	PVT	C	MOS 745 ASGD and joined fm 2nd Repl Dep 02Nov44 (per MR 09Nov44); evac sk, TFRD to DofP 15Dec44; REASG fm 3rd Repl Bn 31Dec44; MIA 21Jan45 (per MR 23Jan45) **(POW 20JAN45)** Mstr POW reg gives rpt date of 21Jan45, parent unit as division artillery, no camp info, repatriated CIB 01Dec44 (40/45)	POW 20Jan45
570.	Killingbeck, Glenn R. 42122526	PVT-PFC	C	MOS 745 ASGD fm 3rd Repl Bn 24Jan45 (per MR 26Jan45); PMTD to PFC 06Mar45 (per MR 06Mar45); Evac sk 10May45 (per MR 10May45); RTD fm sk 13May45 (per MR 13May45) CIB 01Mar45 (10/45); GCM as PFC (32/45)	
571.	Killingbeck, James E. 39477665	PVT-PFC	C	**(Unknown date of assignment)** PMTD to PFC 06Mar45 (per MR 06Mar45) CIB 01Mar45 (10/45); GCM as PFC (32/45)	
572.	Kimbrell, William B. 38695980	PVT	C	MOS 745 ASGD and joined fm 2nd Repl Dep 02Nov44 (per MR 09Nov44); evac sk, TFRD to DofP 04Dec44; RTD fm 71st Reinf Bn 20Apr45 (per MR 21Apr45) CIB 01Dec44 (15/45); GCM (32/45)	
573.	**Kinkead**, Ralph E. 37695378	PVT-PFC	C	MOS 745 ASGD and joined fm 2nd Repl Dep 02Nov44 (per MR 09Nov44); promoted to PFC 25Dec44 (per MR 26Dec44); Evac **WIA**, TFRD to DofP 14Jan45 (per MR 14Jan45); REASG fm 3rd Repl Bn 04Feb45 (per MR 04Feb45); Evac **WIA** 18Mar45 (per MR 18Mar45); Already Evac **WIA**, TFRD to DofP 19Mar45; RTD fm 71st Reinf Bn 24Mar45 (per MR 26Mar45) CIB 01Dec44 (01/45)	WIA 14Jan45 WIA 18Mar45

574.	Kip, Herbert W. 12203372	PFC	C	MOS 745 ASGD fm 71st Reinf Bn 20Apr45 (per MR 24Apr45); TDY w/HQ 45ID 23May45 (Per MR 29May45) CIB 01May45 (15/45); GCM (32/45)	
575.	**Kirchgassner**, Robert L. 35101920	SGT-SSG	C	MOS 653 (Deployed w/the company as CPL, is on Pine Camp menu) Evac sk 18Aug43 (MR 31Aug43); RTD fm sk 05Sep43 (per MR 06Sep43); evac sk 13Dec43 per MR 16Dec43; already evac sk TFRD to DofP, DFR per MR 14Jan44; RTD fm DofP 19Jan44 per MR 21Jan44; pmtd to SSG per MR 25Jan44; sk evac (Furuncle back of neck) 03Feb44; RTD fm sk 13Feb44; evac sk 20Jul44; RTD fm sk 22Jul44 (MR 23Jul44); evac **SWIA**, TFRD to DofP 27Oct44 CIB as SSG in C Co (01/44 - 01Jan44 per CC); GCM (02/44)	WIA 27Oct44
576.	Kirth, John J. 39101107	CPL	C, 1HQ	MOS 653 ASGD fm 71st Reinf Bn 20Apr45 (per MR 24Apr45) CIB 01May45 (15/45); GCM in 1HQ (33/45)	
577.	**Kishbach, Edwin R. 33465255**	**PVT**	C	MOS 745 ASGD fm 2nd Repl Det 26Feb44 per MR 25Mar44; **KIA** 29Feb44 per MR 01May44 (buried in USA); KIA29Feb44 per Div & 157 casualty list; KISBACH per 157 list; MIA/KIA29FEB44 as KISBACH per ANB; not on ABMC reg No discovered GO for CIB or GCM	**KIA 29Feb44**
578.	Kissell, Nathan N. 36057116	PVT	C	MOS 745 ASGD 20Aug43; MIA 13Sep43 DFR (per MR 24Sep43) **(POW 13Sep43);** Mstr POW reg gives rpt date of 13Sep43 w/o unit ID as 100th ID area, Stalag 2B, repatriated CIB FM 01Jan44 (14/44)	POW 13Sep43
579.	Klingensmith, Joseph N. 33703060	PVT-PFC	C	MOS 745/607 ASGD 30May44 (per MR 09Jun44); promoted to PFC 07Oct44; evac sk 03Nov44; RTD fm sk 11Nov44; evac sk 02Dec44; RTD fm sk 07Dec44; evac sk 08Dec44; already evac sk, TFRD to DofP 13Dec44; RTD fm 3rd Repl Bn 12Jan45 (per MR 12Jan45); MIA 23Mar45 (per MR 29Mar45); corr to evac NBI 23Mar45 (per MR 06Apr45); Correction of MR 29Mar45 of MIA 23Mar45; s/b Evac NBI 23Mar45 (contusion & abrasion mild rt thigh lt knee & chest) (per MR 06Apr45); Already evac NBI, TFRD to DofP 01Apr45 (per MR 06Apr45); REASG but DS to 71st Reinf Bn 12Apr45 (per MR 19Apr45); Relieved of DS to 71st Reinf Bn 19Apr45 (per MR 19Apr45; ANB: MIA23MAR45 = EBC CIB 01Sep44 (13/44); GCM (16/44)	
580.	Klopwyk, Arie PCM-C SN NA	PFC	C	On Pine Camp menu	

581.	Klymn, William J. 32803417	PVT-PFC	C	MOS 745 ASGD fm 2nd Repl Dep per MR 11Dec43; attached to 45th Div Mule Train 12Dec43 (per MR 13Dec43); RTD fm SD w/Div Mule Train 02Jan44 per MR 06Jan44; evac sick (jaundice) 02Feb44; already evac sk, tfr to DofP and DFR per MR 03Mar44; RTD fm DofP 09Apr44 (per MR 17Apr44); TFRD to 2nd Repl Dep but not departed 19Jul44; s/b ATCHD & jnd (MR 23Jul44); already attached fm 2nd Repl Det reld fm atchment (per MR 05Aug44); ASGD fm 2nd Repl Dep 08Aug44 (31Aug44); promoted to PFC 07Oct44; MIA 08Nov44 (per MR 10Nov44) **(POW 08Nov44);** Mstr POW reg gives rpt date of 08Nov44, no camp info, repatriated CIB PFD (07/44); GCM (08/44)	POW 08Nov44
582.	Kobak, Chester A. 36587376	PVT	C	MOS 745 ASGD fm 7th Repl Dep 25Sep43; evac sk 03Jan44 per MR 06Jan44; already evac sk TFRD to DofP, DFR per MR 22Jan44; RTD fm DofP 15May44 (per MR 21May44); MIA 25May44 (MR 27May44) (corrected not MIA MR 01Jun44); TFRD to 2nd Repl Dep but not departed 19Jul44; s/b ATCHD & jnd (MR 23Jul44); already attached fm 2nd Repl Det reld fm atchment (per MR 05Aug44) CIB PFD (07/44)	
583.	Koch, James R., Jr. 33703039	PVT	C	MOS 745/653/607 ASGD 30May44 (per MR 09Jun44); evac sk, TFRD to DofP 12Sep44; REASG fm 2nd Repl Dep 25Sep44; **(Missing entry of RTD)**; REASD fm hosp 04Oct44; evac sk, TFRD to DofP 19Oct44 CIB FM 01Sep44 (14/44)	
584.	Koehler, Jack W. PCM-C SN NA	PFC	C	On Pine Camp menu	
585.	**Koenig, Harld C. 37639146**	**PVT**	C	MOS 745 ASGD fm 2nd Repl Dep 11Nov44 (per MR 13Nov44); evac **WIA**, TFRD to DofP 25Nov44 (per MR 28Nov44) – **DOW** 01Dec44 (23Dec44) (buried in USA); DOW01Dec44 per Div & 157 casualty list; not on ABMC reg No discovered GO for CIB or GCM	WIA 25Nov44 **DOW 01Dec44**
586.	**Kontros**, John F. 33699095	**PVT**	C	MOS 745 Asgd fm 2nd Repl Det 26Feb44 per MR 25Mar44; Evac **WIA** (shell frag w abdomen) 29Feb44; already evac **WIA**, tfrd to DofP and DFR 20Mar44 (per MR 19Apr44) CIB FM 01Mar44 (14/44)	WIA 29Feb44

587.	Kopina (or Kopins), Albert J. 35414821	PVT-PFC	C	MOS 745 ASGD 28Sep43 (per MR 30Sep43); promoted to PFC 03Nov43 (per MR 05Nov43); evac sk 18Dec43 (per MR 27Dec43); sk – erroneously tfrd to DofP and DFR 18Jan44; already evac sk TFRD to DofP, DFR per MR 19Jan44; RTD fm sk 17Feb44 01Mar44; sk evac (exhaustion) 21Feb44 per MR 02Mar44; already evac sk, tfrd to 7 Repl. Dep for tvl to USA 10May44 (MR 24May44) CIB FM 01Jan44 (14/44)	
588.	Kos, Albert W. PCM-C 32209204	PVT	C, D	On Pine Camp menu as PVT in C Co CIB DP as PVT in D Co (07/44)	
589.	**Koss,** Raymond W. 32773606	PFC-CPL-SGT-SSG	C	MOS 745/653 ASGD fm 2nd Repl Dep per MR 11Dec43; sk 04Jan44 per MR 14Jan44; already evac sick, DFR 05Feb44, RTD fm DofP 26Feb44; RTD fm DofP 26Feb44 per MR 03Mar44; pmtd to Cpl **(unknown date)**; **(Missing date of WIA)**; already evac **WIA** TFRD to DofP/DFR 09Jul44 (25Jul44); **(Missing entry for RTD)**; evac sk, TFRD to DofP 01Oct44; REASG fm 2nd Repl Dep 22Oct44; promoted to SGT 24Nov44; evac **WIA**, TFRD to DofP 25Nov44 (per MR 28Nov44); **(Missing entry for RTD)**; evac **WIA** 03Dec44; already evac sk, TFRD to DofP 05Dec44; REASG but DS to 71st Reinf Bn 03Apr45 (per MR 11Apr45); Relieved of DS to 71st Reinf Bn 11Apr45 (per MR 11Apr45); Pmtd to SSG 04May45 (per MR 04May45) CIB 01Jan44 (13/44); GCM SGT (16/44)	WIA unk WIA 03Dec44 WIA 24Nov44
590.	**Kotai, John F. 35067309**	**PVT**	C	MOS 745 ASGD fm 2nd Repl Dep 23Apr44 (per MR 29Apr44); TFRD to 2nd Repl Dep but not departed 19Jul44; s/b ATCHD & jnd (MR 23Jul44); already attached fm 2nd Repl Det reld fm atchment (per MR 05Aug44); KIA25SEP44 per 157 & ANB -- NOT ON DIV LIST; ABMC 25Sep44, Epinal Cemetery PH CIB 01May44 (06/44 CC)	**KIA 25Sep44**
591.	Kotsch, Harry G. 33024241	PFC	C	**(Unknown date of assignment, not on Pine Camp menu)** MIA 13Sep43 DFR (per MR 24Sep43) **(POW 13Sep43);** Mstr POW reg gives rpt date of 13Sep43, Stalag 2B, repatriated CIB MIA (05/44); 01Jan44 per CC	POW 13Sep43
592.	**Kowalski**, Edward J. 33697732	PVT	C	MOS 745 ASGD fm 2nd Repl Det 26Feb44 per MR 25Mar44; evac **SWIA** (FCC r tibia, r 1st Metacarpal, Mult pen wnds L leg, thigh, arm) 27Feb44; tfrd to DofP 05Mar44, DFR per MR 07Apr44 CIB FM 01Mar44 (14/44)	WIA 05Mar44

593.	Koziol, Joseph E. 31288013	PVT	C	(Unknown date of assignment, not on Pine Camp menu) MIA 15Dec43, DFR per MR 25Dec43 Was among five men from C Co (Guell, Morris, Tourtilotte, Koziol, McCoy) captured 15Dec43 near Venafro, who escaped from a POW train as it was being bombed in northern Italy on 28Jan44 and who made it back to Allied lines, but did not return to the unit CIB FM 01Jan44 (14/44)	POW 15Dec43 ESCAPED
594.	Kramer, Alfred 38674376	PVT	C	MOS 745607 ASGD and joined fm 2nd Repl Dep 02Nov44 (per MR 09Nov44); evac sk 22Nov44; RTD fm hosp 28Nov44; 745 evac sk, TFRD to DofP 06Dec44; REASG fm 3rd Repl Bn 23Dec44; MIA 21Jan45 (per MR 23Jan45) **(POW 20JAN45);** Mstr POW reg gives rpt date of 21Jan45, parent unit as division artillery, no camp info, repatriated CIB 01Dec44 (01/45)	POW 20Jan45
595.	Kramer, Ben 37592888	PVT	C	MOS 745 ASGD and joined fm 2nd Repl Dep 02Nov44 (per MR 09Nov44); evac sk 11Nov44; RTD fm sk 12Nov44; evac sk 26Nov44 (per MR 28Nov44); RTD fm sk 29Nov44 (per MR 01Dec44); evac sk 30Nov44 (per MR 01Dec44); already evac sk, TFRD to DofP 01Dec44 No discovered GO for CIB or GCM (Kramer, Benjamin was on Pine Camp menu in E Co, but no GO for him, either)	
596.	Kratz, Sylvester J. 32107163	1SG	C	MOS 585 ASGD fm 71st Repl Bn 09Dec44 CIB 01Jan45 (01/45); GCM (8/45)	
597.	**Krawczel,** Peter F. 33621220	PVT-PFC	C	**(Unknown date of assignment, not on Pine Camp menu)** Promoted PFC 01Jan44 per MR 05Jan44; evac **WIA** (pen w r shoulder shell frag) 19Feb44; TFRD to DofP & DFR 25Feb44 per MR 14Mar44 CIB FM 01Jan44 (14/44)	WIA 25Feb44
598.	Kreutzjans, Richard H. SN NA PCM-C	SGT	C	On Pine Camp menu	
599.	Kubik, Alexander A. PCM-C 33147615	CPL	C, A	PVT in C Co per Pine Camp menu; TFRD to Co A (04Aug43) CIB FM as CPL in A Co 01Jan44 (14/44)	
600.	Kuhl, John F. 32852969	PVT-PFC	C, G	MOS 745 ASGD fm 2nd Repl Bn 18Dec43 per MR 22Dec43; pmtd PFC 14Jan44 per MR 15Jan44; Tfr in grade to G Co per MR 05Mar44 CIB Former Pers 01Jan44 (10/44 CC)	
601.	Kuhlman, Herbert H. 37249291 PCM-C	PVT	C, H	PVT in C Co per Pine Camp menu CIB PFD as PFC in H Co (07/44)	
602.	Kunze, Dale A. 37599200	PVT-PFC	C, 1HQ	MOS 745 ASGD fm 3rd Repl Bn 24Jan45 (per MR 26Jan45); PMTD to PFC 06Mar45 (per MR 06Mar45); TFRD to 1HQ as PFC 27May45 (per MR 27May45) CIB 01Mar45 (10/45); GCM as PFC in 1HQ (26/45)	

603.	**Kustra**, Rudolph (NMI) 31007181	SGT	C	MOS 813 ASGD fm 2nd Repl Dep 24Feb44 per MR 05Mar44; evac sk (SIW gunshot R foot) 12Mar44 – Battle Casualty, per MR MR 24Mar44; evac **WIA** tfrd to DofP and DFR 17Mar44 per MR 04Apr44 CIB FM 01Mar44 (14/44)	WIA 17Mar44
604.	Kuszyna, John J. 33813807	PVT-PFC-CPL	C	MOS 745 ASGD fm 3rd Repl Bn 24Jan45 (per MR 26Jan45) PMTD to PFC 06Mar45 (per MR 06Mar45); Pmtd to CPL 04May45 (per MR 04May45) CIB 01Mar45 (10/45); GCM as SGT (32/45)	
605.	Kuzina, Frank (NMI) 32212522 PCM-C	PFC	C	On Pine Camp menu as PVT) MIA 16Sep43 DFR (per MR 24Sep43) **(POW 21Feb44) (discrepancy in date of MIA vs date of reported POW could be time spent in evasion or just late reporting by the Germans);** Mstr POW reg gives rpt date of 21Feb44 w/o unit ID; shown as captured in Germany, which makes the date impossible, Stalag 2B, repatriated POW date was 16Sep43 CIB MIA as PFC in C Co (05/44); 01Jan44 per CC	POW 16Sep43
606.	La Salle, Frank A. 31041023 PCM-C	PFC	C	(Deployed w/the company, is on the Pine Camp menu) sk evac 22Jun43, TFR to DofP N. Africa and DFR CIB FM 01Jan44 (14/44)	
607.	**Laible,** William H. 36051055	PVT	M, C	**(Unknown date of assignment, on the Pine Camp menu as CPL in M Co)** Evac **WIA** 12Nov43 per MR 15Nov43; already evac **WIA** TFRD to DofP, DFR per MR 15Dec43; NOT POW CIB FM as PVT in C Co 01Jan44 (14/44)	WIA 12Nov43
608.	Lambro, William G. 16156952	PFC	C	MOS 521 ASGD fm 1HQ 24Jun44 (assignment rescinded per MR 28Jun44); actually assigned to 1HQ CIB PFD (07/44); GCM as PFC (08/44)	
609.	**Lampasso, Conio (Conie) J. 32869877**	PVT-PFC-PVT	C	**(Unknown date of assignment, not on Pine Camp menu)** Promoted PFC 01Jan44 per MR 05Jan44; reduced to Pvt 05Apr44 (per MR 12Apr44); evac **SWIA** (BC pen W R abdo shell frag) 23May44 (per MR 24May44); already evac **WIA**, TFRD to DofP and DFR; DOW23Jun44 per Div & 157 casualty list; not on ABMC reg (buried in USA) CIB (01/44 - 01Jan44 per CC)	WIA 23May44 **DOW 23Jun44**
610.	Landholt, Howard C. 37603318	PFC	C	MOS 745 ASGD fm 44th Inf Div 25Jan45 (per MR 01Feb45); TDY w/HQ 45ID 23May45 (Per MR 29May45) CIB 01Mar45 (10/45)	
611.	Lang, Jack T. PCM 38006161	PVT	RHQ, C, 1HQ	MOS 775 duty MOS 745 PVT in RHQ per Pine Camp menu; ASGD fr RHQ 31Aug43; MIA 13Sep43 DFR (per MR 24Sep43); RTD 09Oct43 per MR 10Oct43; **Missing TFR to 1HQ??** CIB as PFC (03/44 - 01Jan44 per CC); GCM as PVT in 1HQ (02/44); CIB PFC PFD (07/44)	

612.	Langner, Charley W. SN NA PCM-C	PFC	C	On Pine Camp menu	
613.	**Lantt**, Frank W. 32880193	PVT	C	**(Unknown date of assignment, not on Pine Camp menu)** Evac **WIA** 12Nov43 per MR 15Nov43; already evac **WIA**, TFRD to DofP, DFR per MR 06Dec43 CIB FM 01Jan44 (14/44)	WIA 12Nov43
614.	Larocco, Ted L. 39023001	PFC	C	MOS 745 ASGD (per MR 09Jun44) 29May44; evac sk, TFRD to DofP 07Dec44; Already evac sk, TFRD to DofP 05Mar45 (per MR 05Mar45); REASG fm 3rd Repl Bn 07Jan45 (per MR 07Jan45); Evac sk, TFRD to DofP 14Jan45 (per MR 14Jan45); REASG fm 3rd Repl Bn 04Feb45 (per MR 04Feb45) GCM (08/44); CIB 01Sep44 (13/44)	
615.	**Lata**, Stanley J. 36483238	PVT-PFC	C	MOS 745 ASGD fm 2nd Repl Bn 18Dec43 per MR 22Dec43; evac sk 26Dec43 per MR 28Dec43; already evac sk, TFRD to DofP, DFR per MR 15Jan44; RTD fm DofP 17Mar44 per MR 21Mar44; pmtd to PFC 01May44; evac **WIA** (pen W L chest shell frag) 29May44; already evac **WIA** TFRD to DofP and DFR 04Jun44 (15Jun44); REASG but not jd fm 7th Repl Dep 17Aug44; joined 28Oct44; evac sk, TFRD to DofP 04Nov44 CIB 01Jan44 (13/44)	WIA 29May44
616.	Latta, John E., Jr. PCM-2 20837732 (Delta, CO)	PVT	C, 2HQ, F	PVT in C Co per Induction Roster, 16Sep40; PVT in 2HQ per PCCM42; CIB as PVT in F Co (04/44); 01Jan44 per CC	
617.	Lattig, Robert B. (Lottig) 33251404	CPL	C	MOS 653 ASGD fm 71st Reinf Bn 20Apr45 (per MR 24Apr45) CIB 01May45 (15/45); GCM (32/45)	
618.	Lauro, Peter 31249563	PFC	C	MOS 745 ASGD and joined fm 2nd Repl Dep 02Nov44 (per MR 09Nov44); evac sk 28Nov44; already evac sk, TFRD to DofP 29Nov44; REASG fm 3rd Repl Bn 23Dec44; already evac sk, TFRD to DofP 27Dec44; REASD fm 3rd Repl Bn 11Jan45 (per MR 11Jan45); Evac sk, TFRD to DofP 14Jan45 (per MR 14Jan45); RTD fm sk 15Jan45 (per MR 15Jan45); AWOL 2359 15Jan45 (per MR 27Jan45); AWOL to Regt'l Stockade 22Feb45 (per MR 24Feb45); RTD fm Regt'l Stockade 24Feb45 (per MR 24Feb45); PFC evac sk 26Feb45 (per MR 26Feb45); Already evac sk, TFRD to DofP 04Mar45 (per MR 04ZMar45) CIB 01Dec44 (01/45)	
619.	**Law**, Rollin F. 38697595	PVT	C	MOS 745 ASGD and joined fm 2nd Repl Dep 02Nov44 (per MR 09Nov44); evac **WIA**, TFRD to DofP 25Nov44 (per MR 28Nov44); REASG fm 3rd Repl Bn 28Jan45 (per MR 28Jan45); **(Missing entry of evac)**; already Evac sk, TFRD to DofP 13Feb45 (per MR 13Feb45) CIB 01Mar45 (9/45)	WIA 25Nov44

620.	**Lawson, Clifford M. 32909785**	**PVT**	C	**(Unknown date of assignment, not on Pine Camp menu) KIA** 13Nov43 (per MR 24Nov43) (date changed to 11Nov43 by MR 02Dec43); erron rptd on 24Nov43 as **KIA** 13Nov43, s/b **KIA** 11Nov43 per MR 02Dec43 (buried in USA); KIA11Nov43 per Div & 157 casualty list -- SHRAPNEL; not on ABMC reg No discovered GO for CIB or GCM	**KIA 11Nov43**
621.	Lay, Francis G. 38005380 PCM-C PFC-CPL-SGT-PVT-PFC	PFC- PFC	C	(Deployed w/the company, is on the Pine Camp menu) Evac sk 26Sep43 (per MR 30Sep43); **(Missing entry of RTD)**; pmtd to CPL 18Jan44 per MR 19Jan44; pmtd SGT per MR 25Jan44; reduced to PVT, promoted to PFC, Tfrd to Pers Center per MR 27Mar44 PFC in C Co per PCCM42; CIB DP as PFC in C Co (07/44)	
622.	**Laymon,** Dencil A. (Laymon) 35841258	PVT- SSG	C	MOS 745/653/651/652 ASGD fm 3rd Repl Bn 11Dec44 (per MR 12Dec44); evac **WIA** 25Dec44; already evac, TFRD to DofP 26Dec44; 745 REASG fm 3rd Repl Bn 26Jan45 (per MR 26Jan45); PMTD to PFC 06Mar45 (per MR 06Mar45); PMTD to CPL, change in MOS to 653 24Mar45 (per MR 26Mar45); Pmtd to SGT, MOS 651 24Apr45 (per MR 25Apr45); PMTD to SSG, MOS 652 20May45 (per MR 20May45) CIB 01Jan45 (01/45); GCM as S/SGT (32/45)	WIA 25Dec44
623.	Ledoux, Gerard A. 31464167	PVT	C	MOS 745 ASGD and joined fm 2nd Repl Dep 02Nov44 (per MR 09Nov44); evac sk, TFRD to DofP 06Dec44 CIB 01Dec44 (34/45)	
624.	**Leek,** Orville E. 35033394	T-4	C	MOS 653/060 (Deployed w/the company, is on the Pine Camp menu as CPL) Evac sk 03Aug43 (per MR 04Aug43); RTD fm SK 04Aug43 (per MR 05Aug43); evac **WIA** 13Jun44; already evac TFR to DofP 16Aug44; REASG but not jd fm 7th Repl Dep 17Aug44; joined 15Sep44 (per MR 16Sep44); **WIA** not hosp 10Oct44 (per MR 22Nov44); Evac sk 09Jan45 (per MR 09Jan45); Already evac sk, TFRD to DofP 10Jan45 (per MR 10Jan45); REASG 19Jan45 (per MR 19Jan45); Evac sk 27Jan45 (per MR 27Jan45); RTD fm sk 06Feb45 (per MR 06Feb45); Evac sk, TFRD to DofP 24Apr45 (per MR 24Apr45); RTD 05May45 (per MR 06May45) CIB as T-4 in C Co (04/44); 01Jan44 per CC; GCM (02/44)	WIA 13Jun44 WIA 10Oct44
625.	Leger, Daniel J. 31062548	PVT	F, C	**(Unknown date of assignment, on Pine Camp menu as PVT in F Co)** MIA 13Sep43 DFR (per MR 24Sep43) **(POW 13Sep43);** Mstr POW reg gives rpt date of 13Sep43, Stalag 7A, repatriated CIB FM as PVT in C Co 01Jan44 (14/44)	POW 13Sep43

626.	Leiva, Edward W. 20836346	PVT	C	MOS 345 ASGD 08May45 but DS to 3337 QM Truck Co (per MR 12May45); relieved of DS to 3337 QM Truck Co 11May45 (per MR 12May45); MOS 345 TFRD to SV Co 12May45 (per MR 12May45) No discovered GO for CIB or GCM	
627.	Leonard, Gerald H. 32213863 PCM-3	PVT	3HQ, B, C	PVT in 3HQ per Pine Camp menu; ASGD fr Co B 11Dec45 per MR 12Dec43; evac sk 15Dec43 per MR 21Dec43; RTD fm sk 01Jan44 per MR 06Jan44; evac sk 06Jan44 per MR 08Jan44; already evac sick, trf to DofP and DFR per MR 06Mar44; RTD from Sk 07Feb44; evac sk (exhaustion 10Feb44) CIB FM as PVT in C Co 01Jan44 (14/44)	
628.	Lepore, John J. Jr. 32869212	PVT-PFC	C	MOS 745 **(Unknown date of assignment, not on Pine Camp menu)** Evac **LIA** 17 Dec43 per MR 19Dec43; already evac INJ TFRD to DofP, DFR per MR 19Jan44**;** RTD fm DofP 12Apr44 (per MR 18Apr44); promoted to PFC 07Oct44**;** **WIA** not hosp 11Oct44 (per MR 18Oct44); evac sk 07Nov44; already evac sk, TFRD to DofP 13Nov44; REASG fm 3rd Repl Bn 20Dec44; evac sk, TFRD to DofP 21Dec44; REASG fm 3rd Repl Bn 07Jan45 (per MR 07Jan45); MIA 21Jan45 (per MR 23Jan45) **(POW 20JAN45)** ; Mstr POW reg gives rpt date of 03Mar45 w/o unit ID, Stalag 11B, repatriated -- actual capture on 20Jan45 at Reipertswiller! CIB PFD as PVT in C Co (07/44); GCM (08/44)	WIA 11Oct44 POW 20Jan45
629.	LePresto, Leo P. 36699762	PVT	C	MOS 603 ASGD fr 2nd Repl Dep 04Jun44 (11Jun44) No discovered GO for CIB or GCM	
630.	Lerch, Edward C. 33890177	PVT-PFC	C	MOS 745 ASGD fm 3rd Repl Bn 11Dec44 (per MR 12Dec44); Evac sk, TFRD to DofP 03Jan45 (per MR 03Jan45); **(Missing entry of RTD)**; PMTD to PFC 06Mar45 (per MR 06Mar45) CIB 01Jan45 (01/45); GCM as PFC (32/45)	
631.	Lessard, Lionel 6130477	PVT	C	MOS 745 ASGD and joined fm 2nd Repl Dep 02Nov44 (per MR 09Nov44); MIA 05Dec44 (per MR 08Dec44) – erron entry (per MR 24Dec44); Evac sk, TFRD to DofP 06Jan45 (per MR 06Jan45) CIB 01Dec44 (01/45)	
632.	Lewis, Irving A. 42033687	PVT	C	MOS 745 ASGD fm 2nd Repl Dep 23Apr44 (per MR 29Apr44); **(Missing entry of evac)**; RTD fm sk 07Jul44; TFRD to 2nd Repl Dep but not departed 19Jul44; s/b ATCHD & jnd (MR 23Jul44); evac sk 28Jul44 (29Jul44); already evac sk, relieved fm atchment fr 2nd Repl Det (per MR 05Aug44) CIB 01May44 (06/44 CC)	

633.	**Lewis**, James M. 33885098	PVT-PFC	C	MOS 745 ASGD and joined fm 2nd Repl Dep 02Nov44 (per MR 09Nov44); evac sk 04Dec44; RTD fm sk 09Dec44; promoted to PFC 25Dec44 (per MR 26Dec44); 745 Evac **WIA**, TFRD to DofP 14Jan45 (per MR 14Jan45); REASG fm 3rd Repl Bn 20Jan45 (per MR 20Jan45); Evac sk, TFRD to DofP 28Jan45 (per MR 28Jan45) CIB 01Dec44 (01/45)	WIA 14Jan45
634.	Leyva, Roberto R. 20844876 PCM-C	PVT-PFC	C	(Deployed w/the company, is on the Pine Camp menu as PVT) Pmtd PFC 10Aug43; Evac sk 13Sep43 (per MR 23Sep43) CIB FM as PFC in C Co 01Jan44 (14/44)	
635.	Libonati, Vincent J. 32880913	PFC	1HQ, C	**(Unknown date of assignment, not on Pine Camp menu)** Evac sk 15Nov43 per MR 18Nov43; RTD fm sk 29Nov43 (per MR 02Dec43; AWOL 1600 30Nov43 (per MR 15Dec43); Fm AWOL to confinement in Naples, pending trial 05Jan44 per MR 07Jan44; from confinement to present, under arrest, awaiting trial 17Jan44 per MR 20Jan44; Present arrest to absent confinement 5th Army Stockade 23Jan44 per MR 25Jan44; fm confinement in 5th Army stockade to under arrest in unit 17Mar44, to RTD 18Mar44 (per MR 22Mar44); evac sk (scabies) 17May44 (per MR 20May44); RTD fm sk (10Jun44; TFRD to 1HQ (24Jul44) CIB (07/44); CIB PFD (07/44); GCM PFC (26/45)	
636.	**Lineberry**, Warren C. 33656632	PVT-PFC	C	MOS 745 ASGD fm 2nd Repl Dep 29Apr44 (per MR 06May44); pmtd to PFC 01Jul44 (MR 02Jul44); evac **WIA** 24Sep44; REASG fm 3rd Repl Bn 31Jan45 (per MR 31Jan45); Evac **WIA**, TFRD to DofP 18Mar45 (per MR 18Mar45); asgd fm 2nd Repl Dep 29Apr44 CIB 01Jun44 (06/44 CC)	WIA 24Sep44
637.	**Link**, Carl E. 33885099	PVT	C	MOS 745 ASGD and joined fm 2nd Repl Dep 02Nov44 (per MR 09Nov44); evac sk, TFRD to DofP 06Dec44; REASG fm 3rd Repl Bn 19Jan45 (per MR 19Jan45); AWOL 2359 03Feb45 (per MR 05Feb45); AWOL to Regt'l Stockade 04 Feb45 (per MR 09Feb45); erron entry per MR 12Feb45; AWOL to confinement Saverne, France 05 Feb45 (per MR 12Feb45); Confinement to Regt'l Stockade 06Feb45 (per MR 12Feb45); RTD fm Regt'l Stockade 06 & 09Feb45 (per MR 09Feb45); RTD fm Regt'l Stockade 08 Feb45 (per MR 12Feb45; RTD fm Regt'l Stockade 12Feb45 (per MR 12Feb45), erron entry per MR 12Feb45); Evac INJ 18Mar45 (per MR 18Mar45); Already Evac INJ, TFRD to DofP 19Mar45 (per MR 19Mar45); REASG 10Apr45 (per MR 13Apr45); Evac **WIA**, TFRD to DofP 16Apr45 (per MR 16Apr45); RTD 08May45 (per MR 08May45) CIB 01Mar45 (9/45)	WIA 16Apr45

638.	Linville, Donald C. 37248631	CPL	C	MOS 745/653 ASGD and joined fm 2nd Repl Dep 04Nov44 (per MR 09Nov44); evac INJ, TFRD to DofP 04Dec44; REASG fm 2nd Repl Dep 08Jan45 (per MR 08Jan45); Evac sk, TFRD to DofP 10Jan45 (per MR 10Jan45); REASGD fm 2nd Rein Dep 25Feb45 (per MR 25Feb45); AWOL 0600 14Mar45 (per MR 14Mar45); Fm AWOL to Regt'l Stockade 09May45 (per MR 09May45); RTD fm Regt'l Stockade 18May45 (per MR 18May45) CIB 01Mar45 (09/45)	
639.	**Lipps, Ralph E. 35800537**	**PVT-PFC**	C	MOS 745 ASGD fm 2nd Repl Bn 18Dec43 per MR 22Dec43; evac sk 08Jan44 per MR 10Jan44; RTD from Sk 07Feb44 pmtd to PFC 01May44; MIA 31May44 (per MR 08Jun44); to **KIA** 31May44 (per MR 25Apr45) (buried in Sicily-Rome Cemetery); KIA31May44 per Div & 157 casualty list; MIA/ KIA31MAY44 per ANB; ABMC 31May44, PH CIB FM 01Jan44 (14/44)	**KIA 31May44**
640.	Lischetti, James C. 32647466	PVT	C	MOS 504 ASGD and joined fm 24th Repl DEp 15Sep44 (per MR 23Sep44); evac sk 08Nov44; RTD fm sk 10Nov44; MIA 30Nov44 (per MR 06Dec44); fm MIA 30Nov44 to AWOL 2259 30Nov44 (per MR 09Dec44); RTD fm AWOL, TFRD to Co A 09Dec44 CIB 01Oct44 (13/44)	
641.	Littler, Robert D. 42146416	PVT	C	MOS 745 ASGD fm 71st Reinf Bn 20Apr45 (per MR 24Apr45) CIB 01May45 (15/45); GCM as PFC (32/45)	
642.	Loisel, Robert W. 36422969	SGT	C	MOS 653 ASGD fm 44th Inf Div 25Jan45 (per MR 01Feb45); Evac INJ 17Mar45 (per MR 17Mar45); Already Evac sk, TFRD to DofP 18Mar45 (per MR 18Mar45) No discovered GO for CIB or GCM	
643.	Lonczak, Adam T. 31006938	PVT	C	MOS 745 PVT in K Co per Pine Camp menu; ASGD fr Co F 28Sep43; AWOL 0001 19Feb44; AWOL to sk (exhaustion) 14Mar44 per MR 20Mar44; already evac sk, tfrd to DofP & DFR 24Mar44 CIB FM as PVT in C Co 01Jan44 (14/44)	
644.	Lopez, Magdaleno (NMI) 36479619	PVT	C	MOS 745 ASGD fm 7th Repl Dep 25Sep43; evac sk 17Dec43 per MR 27Dec43; already evac sk TFRD to DofP, DFR per MR 31Dec43 CIB FM 01Jan44 (14/44)	
645.	Lopresti, Salvatore (NMI) 42036610	PVT	C, A	MOS 745 ASGD 30May44 (per MR 09Jun44); TFRD to 2nd Rep Dep, not dptd 19Jul44; s/b ATCHD & jnd (MR 23Jul44); already attached fm 2nd Repl Det reld fm atchment (per MR 05Aug44) CIB 01Sep44 (13/44)	

646.	LoPresto, Leo F. 36699762	PVT-PFC	C	MOS 603 **(Unknown date of assignment)** evac sk 21Jul44; already evac sk, TFRD to DofP/DFR 26Jul44 (02Aug44); REASG fm 2nd Repl Dep 28Oct44; evac sk, TFRD to DofP 13Nov44; REASG fm 3rd Repl Bn10Dec44 (per MR 11Dec44); promoted to PFC 25Dec44 (per MR 26Dec44); evac INJ, TFRD to dofP 28Dec44 CIB 01Sep44 (01/45)	
647.	Lorenz, Anthony W. 12045708	PVT	C	MOS 014 ASGD & jd fm 2nd Repl Dep 29Feb44 per MR 14Mar44; TFRD to 1HQ 03Aug44 CIB PFD (07/44)	
648.	Loria, Harry R. 32921803	PVT	C	MOS 603 ASGD and jnd fr 2nd Repl Dep 24Feb44 per MR 07Mar44; evac inj (concussion from shell burst) 23May44 (per MR 24May44); already evac **LIA**, TFRD to DofP 16Aug44; REASG but not jd fm 7th Repl Dep 17Aug44 – erron entry MR 03Nov44; joined 22Sep44 (27Oct44) – erron entry MR 03Nov44; REASG but not joined 17Aug44, joined 22Sep44, evac sk, TFRD to DofP 27Oct44 – s/b REASG but not joined 01Oct44, AWOL 2359 01Oct (per MR 03Nov44); RTD 2359 26Oct44 (per MR 03Nov44); evac sk, TFRD to DofP 27Oct44; SWIA 23May44 in Anzio breakout, per note from father in Thunderbird News, 01Apr47 CIB 01Mar44 (11/44)	INJ 23May44
649.	**Love**, Efird E. 34609109	PVT-PFC	C	MOS 745 ASGD fm 7th Repl Dep 25Sep43; promoted PFC 01Jan44 per MR 05Jan44; evac **WIA** 31May44 (06Jun44); already evac **WIA** to DofP/DFR 05Jun44 (18Jun44) CIB (01/44 - 01Jan44 per CC)	WIA 31May44
650.	**Lower**, William G. 15341636	PVT	C	MOS 745 ASGD 30May44 (per MR 09Jun44); already attached fm 2nd Repl Det reld fm atchment (per MR 05Aug44); REASG fm 2nd Repl Dep 21Aug44; evac **WIA**, TFRD to DofP 23Sep44; REASG fm 71st Repl Bn 04Dec44 (per MR 05Dec44); evac sk, TFRD to DofP 07Dec44; already evac sk, TFRD to DofP 29Dec44; ASGD fm 3rd Repl Bn 31Jan45 (per MR 31Jan45); Evac sk 01Feb45 (per MR 01Feb45); RTD fm sk 08Feb45 (per MR 08Feb45); Evac sk 10Feb45, TFRD to DofP (per MR 10Feb45); REASG fm 2nd Reinf Dep 02Mar45 (per MR 02Mar45); Evac sk16Mar45 (per MR 16Mar45); Already Evac, TFRD to DofP 21Mar45 (per MR 21Mar45); REASG 10Apr45 (per MR 13Apr45); TFRD to 2nd Repl Dep but not departed 19Jul44; s/b ATCHD & jnd (MR 23Jul44); evac sk 27Jul44; RTD fm sk 31Jul44 (02Aug44); REASG but not joined fm 2nd Repl Dep 04Oct44; joined 07Oct44; evac sk,TFRD to DofP 28Oct44 CIB 01Sep44 (13/44); CIB FM 01Jun44 (14/44)	WIA 23Sep44

651.	Lozowski, Harry J. 36661810	PVT-PFC	C	MOS 745 ASGD fm 2nd Repl Bn 18Dec43 per MR 22Dec43; evac sk 04Jan44 per MR 07Jan44; already sk abs tfrd to DofP & DFR **(Unknown date);** RTD fm DofP 12Apr44 (per MR 18Apr44); promoted to PFC (per MR 05Aug44); evac sk, TFRD to DofP 08Nov44 CIB 01Jan44 (11/44); CIB 01Jan44 (13/44)	
652.	Lucke, Laurence H. PCM-C 20837733 (Delta, CO)	SGT	C	(PVT in C Co per Induction Roster 16Sep40; Deployed w/the company, is on the Pine Camp menu as SGT) Evac sk 20Aug43 (per MR 23Aug43); RTD frm evac sk 03Sep43 (per MR 04Sep43); MIA 13Sep43 DFR (per MR 24Sep43) **(POW 13Sep43);** Mstr POW reg gives rpt date of 13Sep43, Stalag 3B, repatriated CIB FM as SGT in C Co 01Jan44 (14/44)	POW 13Sep43
653.	**Lusk,** Wesley L. 35554974	PFC	C	MOS 745 ASGD fm 2nd Repl Dep per MR 11Dec43; evac **SWIA** 14Dec43 (per MR 16Dec43); already evac **WIA** TFRD to DofP, DFR per MR 15Jan44; **Missing RTD action**; already evac sk, trfd to DofP and DFR per MR 17Mar44 CIB FM 01Jan44 (14/44)	WIA 14Dec43
654.	Lynch, Howard (NMI) 32869892	PVT	C	MOS 745 **(Unknown date of assignment, not on Pine Camp menu)** Evac sk 22Dec43 per MR 28Dec43; already evac sk TFRD to DofP, DFR per MR 23Jan44; already sk abs, tfr to 2nd Repl Dep **(Unknown date)** CIB FM 01Jan44 (14/44) -- listed elsewhere as POW, not on Mstr POW reg.	
655.	Mabry, Charlie J. 33655479	PVT	C	MOS 745 ASGD & jnd fm 2nd Repl Dep 24 Feb44 per MR 10Mar44; evac sk 09Jul44; already evac sk TFRD to DofP/DFR 26Jul44 (02Aug44) CIB PFD (07/44)	
656.	**Macauley,** Floyd B. (MacC) 35124564	PVT-PFC	C	MOS ASGD fm RHQ 06May44; Promoted to PFC 20Nov44 (per MR 27Nov44); evac INJ 25Dec44; already evac sk, TFRD to DofP 26Dec44 CIB 01Jan44 (11/44)	Inj 25Dec44
657.	**MacDonald,** Ronald M. (H.) 31201863	PVT	C	MOS 745 ASGD fr Co I 28Sep43; **(Missing entry of WIA)**; already evac **WIA**, DFR per MR 17Nov43 CIB FM 01Jan44 (14/44)	**WIA unk**
658.	MacDougall, Robert E. 31136461	PFC	C	ASGD fm 71st Reinf Bn 20Apr45 (per MR 24Apr45) CIB 01May45 (15/45); GCM (32/45)	
659.	**MacFarland,** Harold E. 31296053	PFC	A, 1HQ, C	**(Earlier in A Co, per CIB orders)** ASGD fm 1HQ 20Oct44; Evac **SWIA**, TFRD to DofP 10Dec44 CIB (01/44 - 01Jan44 per CC); GCM as PFC (08/44)	WIA 10Dec44
660.	Magliano, John A. (Magliana) 32437642	PVT	C	MOS 745 ASGD fm 71st Reinf Bn 20Apr45 (per MR 24Apr45) CIB 01May45 (15/45) GCM as PFC Magliana (32/45)	

661.	Maglietti, Frank 39473971	PVT	C	MOS 745 ASGD fm 2nd Repl Dep 11Nov44 (per MR 13Nov44); evac sk, TFRD to DofP 06Dec44; REASG fm 3rd Repl Bn NOT joined 10Jan45, to AWOL 2359 10Jan45 (per MR 19Jan45), to Confinement Vesoul, France 16Jan45 (per MR 19Jan45), to Regt'l Stockade 18Jan45 (per MR 19Jan45); RTD fm Regt'l Stockade 19Jan45 (per MR 21Jan45); Evac sk, TFRD to DofP 02Feb45 (per MR 02Feb45) No discovered GO for CIB or GCM	
662.	**Major**, Joseph A. 39588870	PVT-PFC	C	MOS 745 **(Unknown date of assignment)** Evac INJ, TFRD to DofP 15Jan45 (per MR 15Jan45); RTD fm 2nd Reinforcement Dep 20Feb45 (per MR 20Feb45); PMTD to PFC 06Mar45 (per MR 06Mar45); Evac **WIA**, TFRD to DofP 18Apr45 (per MR 18Apr45); REASG fm 71st Reinf Bn 26May45 (per MR 26May45) CIB 01Jan45 (01/45); GCM as PFC (32/45)	INJ 15Jan45 WIA 18Apr45
663.	Manella, Frank (NMI) 36661999	PVT	C	MOS 590 ASGD fm 2nd Repl Bn 18Dec43 per MR 22Dec43; Tfr in grade to G Co per MR 05Mar44	
664.	Maneri, Charles T. PCM-C (Mameri, Carl T.) 32197873	PVT	C	On Pine Camp menu as Mameri, Carl T.) Evac sk 14Aug43 (per MR 16Aug43); RTD fm evac sk 29Aug43 (per MR 30Aug43); MIA 13Sep43 DFR (per MR 24Sep43) **(POW 13Sep43);** Mstr POW reg gives rpt date of 13Sep43, Stalag 2B, repatriated CIB MIA (05/44); 01Jan44 per CC	POW 13Sep43
665.	Manger, Harold 33500343	PFC	C	MOS 745 **(Unknown date of assignment)** Evac sk, TFRD to DofP 29Mar45 (per MR 29Mar45) No discovered GO for CIB or GCM	
666.	Maniscalco, Anthony (NMI) 33140750	PVT	3 H Q , RHQ, C	**(Unknown date of assignment, on Pine Camp menu as PVT in 3HQ)** MIA 13Sep43 DFR (per MR 24Sep43) RTD 09Oct43 per MR 10Oct43 **(Apparently, he survived the actions on 13Sep43 and made his way back to the company by 09Oct43. He might have been evading capture, he might have escaped capture, or he might have been injured/ wounded and evacuated and returned to C Company through the replacement system. It is surprising that nothing else is heard from him throughout the war.)** CIB as PFC in RHQ (01/44 - 01Jan44 per CC)	
667.	**Manny, Ramon (Ray) (NMI) 36660052**	**PVT-PFC**	C	MOS 603 ASGD fm 2nd Repl Bn 18Dec43 per MR 22Dec43; Pmtd to PFC 04Mar44 per MR 12Mar44; MIA 28May44, DFR 01Jun44; change from MIA to **KIA** 28May44 (07Jun44) (buried in Sicily-Rome Cemetery) PH CIB (01/44 - 01Jan44 per CC)	**KIA 28May44**

668.	Manosh, Bernard E. 31464274	PVT	C	MOS 745 ASGD fm 3rd Repl Bn 11Dec44 (per MR 12Dec44); evac sk, TFRD to DofP 14Dec44 CIB 01Jan45 (01/45)	
669.	Marburger, Otto C. R. 38568699	PFC	C	MOS 745 ASGD fm 2nd Repl Dep 11Nov44 (per MR 13Nov44); evac sk, TFRD to DofP 05Dec44 No discovered GO for CIB or GCM	
670.	**Marcus**, Morris M. 36660648	PVT	C	MOS 603 ASGD fm HHC 1st Bn **(Unknown date)**; evac **WIA** 03Jun44; RTD fm **WIA** 27Jun44 (28Jun44); evac **WIA**, TFRD to DofP 28Sep44 **(Unknown date)**; TFRD to 2nd Repl Dep but not departed 19Jul44; s/b ATCHD & jnd (MR 23Jul44); already attached fm 2nd Repl Det reld fm atchment (per MR 05Aug44); ASGD fm 2nd Repl Dep 08Aug44 (31Aug44); REASG fm 3rd Repl Bn 28Dec44; Evac sk, TFRD to DofP 03Jan45 (per MR 03Jan45) CIB PFD (07/44)	WIA 03Jun44
671.	Marmottin, George (Marmatten) 18171699	SGT	C	MOS 653 attached fm 3rd Reinf Bn 04May45 (per MR 07May45); relieved from attached status, to ASGD 07May45 (per MR 07May45) GCM (32/45)	
672.	Marsek, Theodore J. 32182394	PFC	C	MOS 745 ASGD fm 71st Reinf Bn 20Apr45 (per MR 24Apr45) CIB 01May45 (15/45); GCM (32/45)	
673.	Marsh, John B. 36877401	PVT	C	MOS 745 ASGD fm 2nd Repl Dep 11Nov44 (per MR 13Nov44); evac sk, TFRD to DofP 06Dec44; REASG fm 3rd Repl Bn 04Feb45 (per MR 04Feb45); Evac sk 11Feb45 (per MR 11Feb45; Already evac sk, TFRD to DofP 14Feb45 (per MR 14Feb45); **(Missing entry of RTD)**; Evac sk16Mar45 (per MR 16Mar45); Already evac sk, TFRD to DofP 17Mar45 (per MR 17Mar45); REASG fm 2nd Reinf Dep 02Mar45 (per MR 02Mar45); RTD 08May45 (per MR 08May45); Evac sk 18May45 (per MR 18May45); RTD fm sk18May45 (per MR 22May45) CIB 01Mar45 (10/45)	
674.	**Marsh,** Lloyd E. 20837718 (Delta, CO)	SSG-TSG	C	MOS 542 PFC in C Co per Induction Roster 16Sep40; Deployed w/the company, is on the Pine Camp menu as SGT) Evac sk 30Sep43 (per MR 03Oct43; already evac sk, TFRD to DofP and DFR per MR 04Nov43; RTD fm DofP 05Dec43 per MR 12Dec43; pmtd to TSG per MR 25Jan44; **WIA** (not hosp) (shell frag R knee) 15Mar44 per MR 22Mar44; Tfrd to Pers Ctr 6 for tvl to US 19May44 (MR 20May44) CIB as TSG in C Co (01/44 - 01Jan44 per CC); GCM (02/44)	WIA 15Mar44
675.	**Marshall**, Josephogl 42117361	PVT	C	MOS 745 ASGD fm 71st Reinf Bn 20Apr45 (per MR 24Apr45); Evac **WIA**, TFRD to DofP 26Apr45 (per MR 26Apr45); RTD 05May45 (per MR 06May45) CIB 01May45 (15/45); GCM (32/45)	WIA 26Apr45

676.	Martin, Charles F. 33889997	PVT-PFC	C	MOS 745/761 ASGD fm 3rd Repl Bn 11Dec44 (per MR 12Dec44); Pmtd to PFC 07Jan45 (per MR 08Jan45); MIA 21Jan45 (per MR 23Jan45) **(POW 20JAN45);** Mstr POW reg gives rpt date of 21Jan45, parent unit as division artillery, no camp info, repatriated CIB 01Jan45 (01/45)	POW 20Jan45
677.	Martin, Gordon G. 32930916	PVT	C	MOS 745 ASGD fm 2nd Repl Dep per MR 11Dec43; evac sk 03Jan44 per MR 06Jan44; Tfr to DofP and DFR 12Feb44 CIB FM 01Jan44 (14/44)	
678.	**Martin, Paul T.** **32942553**	**PVT**	C	MOS 745 ASGD 29May44 (09Jun44); promoted to PFC (per MR 05Aug44); fm MIA 19Aug44 to **KIA** 19Aug44 (22Aug44) (buried in Rhone Cemetery) PH KIA18Aug44 per Div & 157 list; MIA/KIA19AUG44 per ANB; ABMC 19Aug44 No discovered GO for CIB or GCM	**KIA 19Aug44**
679.	Martin, Ralph A. 37745011	PVT-PFC	C	MOS 745 ASGD fm 3rd Repl Bn 24Jan45 (per MR 26Jan45); PMTD to PFC 06Mar45 (per MR 06Mar45); Evac **WIA** 16Apr45 (per MR 16Apr45); Already evac **WIA**, TFRD to DofP 18Apr45 (per MR 18Apr45) CIB 01Mar45 (10/45)	WIA 16Apr45
680.	Martin, William J. 32264922	T-4	C	MOS 745 ASGD fm 71st Reinf Bn 20Apr45 (per MR 24Apr45) CIB 01May45(15/45)GCM (32/45)	
681.	Martinez, Ben D. 20837708 (Delta, CO)	TSG	C, 1HQ, A, I	MOS 651 PFC in C Co per Induction Roster, 16Sep40; SSG in C Co per Pine Camp menu; ASGD fm 1HQ 20Oct44; TFRD to Co A 06Dec44 CIB FM as TSG in I Co 01Jan44 (14/44)	
682.	Martino, Joseph F. 42043150	PFC	C	GCM (32/45)	
683.	Masloski, Frank J. 13054740	PFC	C	MOS 677 ASGD fm 2nd Repl Dep 29Sep44; evac sk, TFRD to DofP 13Nov44; REASG fm 71st Repl Dep 01Dec44; evac sk 06Dec44; already evac sk, TFRD to DofP 08Dec44; REASG fm 3rd Repl Dep 08Jan45 (per MR 08Jan45); Evac sk, TFRD to DofP 15Jan45 (per MR 15Jan45) CIB 01Oct44 (13/44)	
684.	**Masucci,** Vincent D. 32771468	PVT	C	MOS 745 **(Unknown date of assignment, not on Pine Camp menu)** Evac **WIA** 12Nov43 per MR 15Nov43; already evac **WIA** TFRD to DofP, DFR per MR 15Dec43; RTD fm DofP (**WIA**) 27Dec43 per MR 31Dec43; evac sk 27Dec43 (per MR 01Jan44); already evac sk TFRD to DofP, DFR (erron entry per MR 30Jan44); already evac sk, tfr to 2nd Repl Depot 02Mar44 CIB FM 01Jan44 (14/44)	WIA 12Nov43

685.	**Matlavage,** Alexander A. 33623930	PVT-PFC	C	MOS 521 ASGD fm 2nd Repl Bn 18Dec43 per MR 22Dec43; pmtd PFC 14Jan44 per MR 15Jan44; **WIA** evac (LW L elbow) 12Feb44, DFR 09Mar44; already evac **WIA**, tfr to DofP and DFR per MR 9 & 10Mar44 CIB FM 01Jan44 (14/44)	WIA 10Mar44
686.	**Mayo**, Herbert J. 11061676	CPL-SGT	C	MOS 653 (Deployed w/the company, is on the Pine Camp menu as PFC) Pmtd to SGT per MR 02Dec43; evac **WIA** (BC pen W L arm shell frag) 31May44; already evac **WIA** to DofP/ DFR 03Jun44 (14Jun44); RTD fm DofP 27Jun44 (28Jun44); evac sk, TFRD to DofP 25Nov44 (per MR 28Nov44) CIB as SGT in C Co (01/44 - 01Jan44 per CC); GCM (02/44)	WIA 31May44
687.	**McAnelly**, Ernest W. 36773372	PFC	C	MOS 745 ASGD fm 2nd Repl Dep 11Nov44 (per MR 13Nov44); evac **WIA**, TFRD to DofP 15Dec44 No discovered GO for CIB or GCM	WIA 15Dec44
688.	**McBride, Robert C. Jr. 34609282**	**PVT**	C	MOS 745 ASGD fm 7th Repl Dep 25Sep43; MIA 13Nov43 per MR 27Nov43; DFR (**KIA** 10Nov43 per MR 01Dec43); erron rptd 27Nov43 as MIA 13Nov43 and DFR, s/b **KIA** 10Nov43 per MR 01Dec43 (buried in USA); KIA10Nov43 per div casualty list; DOW10NOV43 per 157 list; MIA/ KIA13NOV43 per ANB; not on ABMC reg No discovered GO for CIB or GCM	**KIA 10Nov43**
689.	**McCarthy**, Frank J. 32883021	PVT	C	MOS 010/745 ASGD fm 2nd Repl Bn 18Dec43 (per MR 22Dec43); evac sk 03Jan44 per MR 06Jan44; already evac sk TFRD to DofP, DFR per MR 22Jan44; RTD fm DofP 18Apr44 (per MR 22Apr44); evac sk 13May44 (MR 17May44); evac sk 13May44 (MR 24May44) **(evac sk twice?)**; RTD 14May44 (MR 24May44); to DofP/DFR 24May44 (MR 30May44); RTD fm DofP (10Jun44); reduced to PVT (01Jul44); evac **WIA** 16Aug44 (17Aug44); already evac **WIA** on Ship Acadia TFRD to DofP/ DFR 17Aug44 **(Undated entry of already sk abs)** CIB PFD (07/44)	WIA 16Aug44
690.	**McChesney, Robert B. 36590174**	**PVT**	C	MOS 745 ASGD fm 7th Repl Dep 25Sep43; **KIA** 24Nov43 per MR 28Nov43 (buried in USA); KIA24Nov43 per div & 157 casualty list; not on ABMC reg No discovered GO for CIB or GCM	**KIA 24Nov43**
691.	McClain, Lomax (NMI) SN NA	PVT	1HQ, C	MOS 641 ASGD fm 1HQ 24Jun44 (assignment rescinded per MR 28Jun44) **NOT ASSIGNED** CIB 01Sep44 (11/44); GCM (16/44)	

692.	McClain, Walter E. 33889993	PVT-PFC	C	MOS 745 ASGD fm 3rd Repl Bn 11Dec44 (per MR 12Dec44); Pmtd to PFC 07Jan45 (per MR 08Jan45); MIA 21Jan45 (per MR 23Jan45) **(POW 20JAN45);** Mstr POW reg gives rpt date of 21Jan45, parent unit as division artillery, no camp info, repatriated CIB 01Jan45 (01/45)	POW 20Jan45
693.	McClenon, Olin S. 42120866	PVT	C	MOS 605 ASGD fm 2nd Repl Dep 11Nov44 (per MR 13Nov44); evac sk, TFRD to DofP 10Dec44; RTD fm 2nd Rein Dep 27Feb45 (per MR 27Feb45) CIB 01Dec44 (15/45); GCM as PFC (32/45)	
694.	**McClung, William S. 13111505**	**PVT**	C	**(Unknown date of assignment, not on Pine Camp menu)** MIA 16Aug43 (per MR 21Aug43) (DFR per MR 07Sep43) **(believed drowned in landing accident, commemorated in Sicily-Rome Cemetery) Still MIA BSM no PH** CIB MIA (05/44); 01Jan44 per CC	**MIA 16Aug43**
695.	McCool, Kenneth R. 34828965	PVT-PFC	C	MOS 745 ASGD fm 3rd Repl Bn 24Jan45 (per MR 26Jan45); PMTD to PFC 06Mar45 (per MR 06Mar45) CIB 01Mar45 (10/45)	
696.	**McCoy, Chester G. 38005394 PCM-G**	**PVT**	G, C	(Deployed w/the regiment, is on G Company Pine Camp menu as PFC) ASGD fr Co G 28Sep43; pmtd to PFC 01Dec43; MIA 15Dec43, DFR per MR 25Dec43 Was among five men from C Co (Guell, Morris, Tourtilotte, Koziol, McCoy) captured 15Dec43 near Venafro, who escaped from a POW train as it was being bombed in northern Italy on 28Jan44 and who made it back to Allied lines, but did not return to the unit CIB FM as PFC in C Co 01Jan44 (14/44)	POW 15Dec43 ESCAPED
697.	**McCraney**, Silas T. 35841268	PVT-PFC	C	MOS 745 ASGD fm 3rd Repl Bn 11Dec44 (per MR 12Dec44); Pmtd to PFC 07Jan45 (per MR 08Jan45); Evac **WIA**, TFRD to DofP 14Jan45 (per MR 14Jan45) CIB 01Jan45 (01/45)	WIA 14Jan45
698.	**McCue**, Harold J. 37481343	PVT	C	MOS 745 asgd & jnd fm 2nd Repl Dep 24 Feb44 per MR 10Mar44; evac **WIA** 01Apr44 per MR 07Apr44;tfrd to DofP, DFR 14Apr44 (per MR 25Apr44); RTD fm DofP 20May44 (per MR 21May44); evac sk 01Jun44 (16Jun44); RTD fm sk 13Jun44 (16Jun44); evac sk 17Jul44 (MR 24Jul44); erron rptd TFRD to 2nd Repl Dep19Jul44 – order rescinded (MR 24Jul44); TFRD to 2nd Repl Dep but not departed 19Jul44; s/b ATCHD & jnd (MR 23Jul44); already evac sk, TFRD to 7th Repl Dep 21Jul44, reclassified limited assignment (MR 24Jul44) CIB FM 01Mar44 (14/44)	WIA 01Apr44
699.	McCurry, Robert M. O-1822162	1LT	C	ASGD fm 2nd Repl Dep 11Nov44 (per MR 13Nov44); evac **WIA**, TFRD to DofP 05Dec44 No discovered GO for CIB or GCM	WIA 05Dec44

700.	**McGibney,** Bradford W. 33890215	PVT-PFC	C	MOS 745 ASGD fm 3rd Repl Bn 11Dec44 (per MR 12Dec44); PVT Pmtd to PFC 07Jan45 (per MR 08Jan45); Evac **WIA**, TFRD to DofP 14Jan45 (per MR 14Jan45) CIB 01Jan45 (01/45)	WIA 14Jan45
701.	**McGinniss**, Francis E. 42039537	PVT-PFC	C	MOS 745 ASGD 29May44 (09Jun44); pmtd to PFC 01Jul44 (MR 02Jul44); evac **WIA**, TFRD to DofP 19Aug44; REASG fm 2nd Repl Dep 18Oct44; evac sk 08Nov44; already evac sk, TFRD to DofP 09Nov44; **(Missing entry of RTD)**; evac sk, TFRD to DofP 21Dec44; REASG fm 3rd Repl Bn 31Dec44; Evac sk, TFRD to DofP 02Jan45 (per MR 02Jan45) CIB 01Sep44 (13/44)	WIA 19Aug44
702.	McGovern, John F. O-1327966	2LT	C	ASGD fm 71st Reinf Bn 08May45 as A&P Platoon Off??? (per MR 09May45) No discovered GO for CIB or GCM	
703.	McGuire, Thomas L. 39336593	PVT	C	MOS 745 ASGD & jnd fm 2nd Repl Dep 24 Feb44 per MR 10Mar44; evac **WIA** 01Jun44; already evac **WIA** to DofP/DFR 06Jun44 (15Jun44) CIB DP (07/44)	WIA 01Jun44
704.	McInerney, William P. 31190929	PVT	C	**(Unknown date of assignment, not on Pine Camp menu)** sk evac 22Jul43 (Per MR 23Jul43); RTD fom sk evac 23Jul43 (per MR 24Jul43); MIA 13Sep43 DFR (per MR 24Sep43) **(POW 13Sep43);** Mstr POW reg gives rpt date of 13Sep43, Stalag 2B, repatriated CIB MIA (05/44); 01Jan44 per CC	POW 13Sep43
705.	McIntyre, Alan G. O-1323338	2LT	C, E	ASGD & jnd 07Mar44 per MR 13Mar44; tfrd to Co E (per MR 01May44); (KIA28May44 per div & 157 cas list; ABMC 28May44, Sicily-Rome Cemetery SS, PH)	(KIA 28May44 in E Co)
706.	**McIntyre,** Howard R. 33780064	PVT-PFC-CPL	C	MOS 504/653 **(Unknown date of assignment)** RTD fm 2nd Repl Dep 11Jan44 per MR 13Jan44; Evac **WIA** 23May44 (MR 24May44); to DofP/DFR 30May44 **(MR 11 or 12Jun44);** RTD fm DofP 15Jun44 (16Jun44); pmtd to PFC 01Jul44 (MR 02Jul44); evac sk, TFRD to DofP 27Aug44; REASG fm hosp 22Sep44; promoted to CPL 24Dec44; MIA 21Jan45 (per MR 23Jan45) **(POW 20JAN45);** MIA21JAN45 per ANB; Mstr POW reg gives rpt date of 21Jan45, parent unit as division artillery, no camp info, repatriated CIB PFD (07/44); GCM (16/44)	WIA 23May44 POW 20Jan45
707.	**McKay,** Thomas H. 35498849	CPL-SGT-SSG	C	MOS 653 ASGD fr 2 Repl Dep 04Jun44 (14Jun44); evac **WIA**, TFRD to DofP 06Nov44; RTD fm 2nd Rein Dep 27Feb45 (per MR 27Feb45); **WIA** not hosp 18Mar45 (pen w R hand) (per MR 06May45); PMTD to SGT, 24Mar45 (per MR 26Mar45); PMTD to SSG, MOS 652 09May45 (per MR 09May45) CIB 01Sep44 (13/44)	WIA 06Nov44 WIA 18Mar45

708.	McLean, Robin S. 34706501	PVT	K, E, C	MOS 745 ASGD fm Co E 31Oct44; AWOL 2359 31Oct44 (09Nov44); PVT AWOL 2359 31Oct44 (per MR 09Nov44); fm AWOL to Regt'l Stockade 07Nov44 (per MR 09Nov44); Fm Regt'l Stockade to evac sk, TFRD to DofP 23Nov44 CIB PFD (07/44)	
709.	McMahon, James J. 32891201	PVT	C, G	MOS 603 ASGD fm 2nd Repl Bn 18Dec43 per MR 22Dec43; tfr in grade to G Co per MR 05Mar44; Mstr POW reg gives rpt date of 02Oct44, Stalag 2B, repatriated CIB 01Jan44 (11/44)	(POW in G Co 20Oct44)
710.	**Meekins**, LeRoy S. 33555592	PVT	C	MOS 745 ASGD 20Aug43; evac **WIA** 12Sep43 (per MR 20Sep43) CIB FM 01Jan44 (14/44)	WIA 12Sep43
711.	Meigs, William R. O-1465294	2LT	C	ASGD fm 2nd Repl Dep 23Dec43 per MR 25Dec43; promoted to 1LT 31Mar44 per MR 08Apr44; change in duties from platoon commander to XO 13Oct44; MIA 21Jan45 (per MR 23Jan45) **(POW 20JAN45);** Mstr POW reg gives rpt date of 21Jan45, parent unit as division artillery, no camp info, repatriated CIB (01/44 - 01Jan44 per CC)	POW 20Jan45
712.	Melton, Harvey J. D. 38344692	PFC	C	GCM (32/45)	
713.	Melville, James (NMI) 33396270	PVT	C	**(Unknown date of assignment, not on Pine Camp menu)** Tfr in grade to G Co per MR 05Mar44 No discovered GO for CIB or GCM	
714.	**Mendel, Lawrence E. 35048497**	**PVT**	C	MOS 055 ASGD fm 2nd Repl Dep per MR 11Dec43; evac **WIA** (pen W L side L thigh, upper 3 R leg & FCC lower 3 tibia & fibula shell frag 14Feb44; **DOW** 15Feb44 (buried in Sicily-Rome Cemetery); DOW15Feb44 per div & 157 cas list; ABMC 15Feb44, PH No discovered GO for CIB or GCM	WIA 14Feb44 **DOW 15Feb44**
715.	**Menefee,** Elmer E. 35765276	PVT	C	MOS 745 ASGD & jnd fm 2nd Repl Dep 24 Feb44 per MR 10Mar44; evac sk 08June (10Jun44); RTD fm sk 10Jun44; Evac **WIA**, TFRD to DofP 05Jan45 (per MR 05Jan45) CIB PFD (07/44)	WIA 05Jan45
716.	**Merchant**, Clifford E. 32212343	PFC	C	MOS 745 ASGD & jnd fm 2nd Repl Det 24Feb44 per MR 9 & 10Mar44; evac **WIA** (perf w/r heel shell frag) 05Apr44 per MR 10Apr44; already evac **WIA**, tfrd to DofP and DFR 03May44 (per MR 15May44) CIB FM 01Mar44 (14/44)	WIA 05Apr44
717.	Meringolo, Joseph J. 20110103	PVT	C	MOS 745 ASGD & jnd fm 2nd Repl Dep 26Feb44 per MR 08Mar44; evac sk (cellulitis l. wrist) 28Mar44 per MR 08Apr44; RTD 01Apr44 (MR 15Apr44); evac sk (MR 02May44); tfrd to DofP, DFR 30Apr44 (MR 19May44) No discovered GO for CIB or GCM	

718.	**Merly,** Anton (NMI) 30336599	PVT-PFC	C	MOS 745 ASGD & jnd fm 2nd Repl Dep 24 Feb44 per MR 10Mar44; pmtd to PFC 01May44; evac **WIA** 24Sep44; REASGD but not joined fm 2nd Repl Dep 13Oct44; joined 13Oct44; evac sk 03Dec44; already evac, TFRD to DofP 04Dec44 CIB (04/44); 01Apr44 per CC; GCM (08/44)	WIA 24Sep44
719.	**Messick, Richard (NMI) 33731803**	**PVT**	C	MOS 745 ASGD & jnd fm 2nd Repl Dep 24 Feb44 per MR 10Mar44; MIA 26May44 (per MR 27May44); to **KIA** 26May44 (18Aug44) (buried in Florence Military Cemetery); KIA26May44 per div & 157 cas list; MIA/KIA26MAY44 per ANB; ABMC 26May44, PH No discovered GO for CIB or GCM	**KIA 26May44**
720.	**Messineo, Stephen M. O-1300199**	**2LT**	C	**(Unknown date of assignment, not on Pine Camp menu)** evac **WIA** 12Dec43 per MR 16Dec43; RTD fm **WIA** 01Jan44 per MR 06Jan44; **KIA** 18Feb44 per MR 08Mar44 (buried in USA); KIA18Feb44 per div & 157 cas list -- SHRAPNEL; not on ABMC reg No discovered GO for CIB or GCM	WIA 12Dec43 **KIA 18Feb44**
721.	Messmer, Lawrence F. 35867559	PVT	C	MOS 745 ASGD fm 2nd Repl Bn 14Jan44 per MR 18Jan44; evac sk (trenchfoot bilateral) 24Feb44 per MR 02Mar44; already evac sk, trfd to DofP and DFR 01Mar44 per MR 15Mar44; attached fm 3rd Reinf Bn 04May45 (per MR 07May45); relieved from attached status, to ASGD 05May45 (per MR 07May45) CIB FM 01Feb44 (14/44)	
722.	Mesmier, Robert (Messmier) 33556396	PFC	C	GCM (32/45)	
723.	Metcalfe, Johnnie J. 6351244	TSG	C	MOS 651 ASGD fm 103rd Inf Div 26Jan45 (per MR 01Feb45); Evac INJ 18Mar45 (per MR 18Mar45); Already Evac INJ, TFRD to DofP 19Mar45 (per MR 19Mar45); CIB 01Mar45 (9/45); GCM (8/45)	
724.	**Metz**, Robert M. 33427734	PVT	C	MOS 745 ASGD 20Aug43; erron rptd on 18Nov43 as TFRD to DofP and DFR, should be RTD fm sk 18Nov43 per MR 19Nov43; evac **SWIA** 14Dec43 per MR 16Dec43; erroneously tfrd to DofP and DFR 14Jan44; already evac **WIA** tfrd to DofP/ DFR 15Apr44(per MR 09May44; RTD 30May44 (MR 09Jun44) CIB FM 01Jan44 (14/44)	WIA 14Dec43

725.	**Metz,** William E. 35916356	PVT-PFC	C	MOS 745 ASGD 30May44 (09Jun44); evac sk, TFRD to DofP 09Sep44; REASG fm hosp 23Sep44; promoted to PFC 07Oct44; evac **WIA**, TFRD to DofP 06Nov44; REASGD fm 2nd Repl Dep 19Nov44; Evac **WIA**, TFRD to DofP 14Jan45 (per MR 14Jan45); REASG but DS to 71st Reinf Bn 07Apr45 (per MR 11Apr45); Relieved of DS to 71st Reinf Bn 11Apr45 (per MR 11Apr45) CIB 01Sep44 (13/44)	WIA 06Nov44 WIA 14Jan45
726.	**Meyers, Norman H. 36586292**	**PVT- PFC**	C	MOS 745 ASGD fm 2nd Repl Bn 18Dec43 per MR 22Dec43; pmtd to PFC 01May44; MIA 31 May44 (per MR 06Jun44); change from MIA to **KIA** 28May44 (07Jun44) (buried in USA); KIA31Jul44 per div cas list; KIA31MAY44 per 157 list; MIA/KIA31MAY44 per ANB; not on ABMC reg No discovered GO for CIB or GCM	**KIA 28May44**
727.	Michaelis, Erwin F. 35345090	CPL	C	MOS 521 ASGD 15Aug43 (per MR 16Aug43); MIA 13Sep43 DFR (per MR 24Sep43) **(POW 13Sep43);** MIA13SEP43 per ANB; on master POW register as Philippine Scout in 100ID area!!!!, Stalag 3B, repatriated CIB FM 01Jan44 (14/44)	POW 13Sep43
728.	Michelek, Stephen J. (Michalek) 32227167	PFC	I, C	ASGD fr Co I 28Sep43; MIA 15Dec43, DFR per MR 25Dec43 **(POW 15Dec43);** MIA15DEC43 per ANB; Mstr POW reg gives rpt date of "15 1K 43", Oflag 64 or 21B, repatriated CIB FM 01Jan44 (14/44)	POW 15Dec43
729.	Michalak, Lynn W. 37231551	PVT	C	MOS 745 attached fm 3rd Reinf Bn 04May45 (per MR 07May45); relieved from attached status, to ASGD 05May45 (per MR 07May45) No discovered GO for CIB or GCM	
730.	Michalowski, Stanley E., Jr. SN NA PCM-C	PVT	C	On Pine Camp menu	
731.	Michewicz, Charles F. 33618914	PFC	C	MOS 746 ASGD & jnd fm 2nd Repl Det 24Feb44 per MR 9 & 10Mar44; evac sk (16Jun44); already evac sk to DofP/DFR 25Jun44 (30Jun44) CIB (04/44); 01Mar44 per CC; CIB DP (07/44)	
732.	Mickel, Mitchell (NMI) 15316168	PVT-PFC	C	MOS 745 **(Unknown date of assignment, not on Pine Camp menu)** RTD fm 2nd Repl Dep 11Jan44 (date is not clear) (per MR 13Jan44); pmtd to PFC 01May44; evac sk 31May44 (per MR 20Jun44); TFRD to DofP and DFR 03Jun44 (20Jun44) CIB DP (07/44)	
733.	Miears, Raymond T. 39288965	PVT	C	MOS 745 attached fm 3rd Reinf Bn 04May45 (per MR 07May45); 745 relieved from attached status, to ASGD 05May45 (per MR 07May45) No discovered GO for CIB or GCM	

734.	**Miles,** Theodore E. 33461676	PFC-PVT-CPL-SGT	C	MOS 745/653 ASGD fm 2nd Repl Dep 24Feb44 per MR 05Mar44; evac **WIA** (pen W R leg shell frag) 30May44; RTD fm **WIA** 25Jun44 (27Jun44) RTD; AWOL 0630 03Jul44; RTD fm AWOL 2300 03Jul44 (MR 04Jul44); reduced to PVT 04Jul44; promoted to CPL MOS 653 07Oct44; evac **WIA**, TFRD to DofP 11Oct44; REASG fm 3rd Repl Bn 20Dec44; promoted to SGT 24Dec44; evac sk 30Dec44; already evac sk, TFRD to DofP 31Dec44; Sk Not LD fr 30Dec44 – 09Jan45 inclusive (per MR 15Jan45); RTD fm Sk Not LD 09Jan45 (per MR 15Jan45); PMTD to SSG 09Mar45 (per MR 09Mar45); Evac Sk Not LD (per MR 15Jan45); REASG fm 3rd Repl Bn 14Jan45 (per MR 14Jan45); Evac sk 18Mar45 (per MR 18Mar45); Already Evac, TFRD to DofP 20Mar45 (per MR 20Mar45) CIB PFD (07/44); GCM (08/44)	WIA 30May44 WIA 11Oct44
735.	Milewski, John S. 31129686	PVT	C	MOS 745 attached fm 3rd Reinf Bn 04May45 (per MR 07May45); 745 relieved from attached status, to ASGD 05May45 (per MR 07May45) No discovered GO for CIB or GCM	
736.	**Miller**, Alfred C. 33565451	PVT-PFC-CPL	C	MOS 745/653 ASGD fm 7th Repl Dep 25Sep43; pmtd to PFC 01Dec43; evac sk 27Dec43 (per MR 01Jan44); RTD fm sk 21Jan44 per MR 23Jan44; **WIA** not hosp (LW 3rd middle finger – shell frag) 05Apr44 (per MR 14Apr44); evac sk 15Jul44; **(Missing entry of RTD)**; evac sk 20Jul44 (MR 21Jul44); already evac sk, TFRD to DofP/DFR 30Jul44 (per MR 05Aug44); **(evac sk 30Jul44 (31Jul44)??;** REASG fm hosp 15Sep44; evac **WIA**, TFRD to DofP 05Nov44; REASG fm 3rd Repl Bn 12Dec44; promoted to CPL MOS 653 24Dec44; Evac sk 09Jan45 (per MR 09Jan45); RTD fm sk 15Jan45 (per MR 15Jan45) CIB (01/44 - 01Jan44 per CC)	WIA 05Apr44 WIA 05Nov44
737.	**Miller**, Hyman (NMI) 33000443	SGT	C	MOS 652 **(Unknown date of assignment, not on Pine Camp menu)** RTD fm 2nd Repl Dep 11Jan44 per MR 13Jan44; evac **WIA** (perf w r buttock, perf w r foot shell frag) 19Feb44; TFRD to DofP and DFR 27Feb44 per MR 14Mar44; RTD fm DofP 13Jul44; **WIA** not hosp 26Sep44 (per MR 17Oct44); evac sk 21Dec44; RTD fm 3rd Repl Bn 30Jan45 (per MR 30Jan45); Evac sk 01Feb45 (per MR 01Feb45); Already Evac sk, TFRD to DofP 02Feb45 (per MR 02Feb45) CIB PFD (07/44); GCM (16/44)	WIA 19Feb44 WIA 26Sep44

738.	**Miller,** Jack S. 38006157	SGT-TSG	C	MOS 653/651 Deployed w/the company, is on Pine Camp menu as CPL) Evac sk 26Sep43 (per MR 02Oct43); already evac sk, DFR per MR 23Nov43; RTD fm sk 06Jan44 per MR 11Jan44; pmtd to TSG per MR 25Jan44; evac **WIA** (pen w l thigh shell frag) 22Feb44; RTD fr **WIA** 27Mar44 per MR 03Apr44; evac **WIA** (pen wound chin, L arm shell frag) 28Mar44 fm MR 05Apr44; tfrd to DofP, DFR 06Apr44 (MR 24Apr44); RTD fm DofP 02May44 (per MR 07May44); TFRD on rotation to USA 01Aug44 CIB as TSG in C Co (01/44 - 01Jan44 per CC); CIB (03/44); GCM (02/44)	WIA 22Feb44 WIA 28Mar44
739.	**Miller**, Robert A. 35218727	PVT-PFC	C	MOS 745 ASGD fm 2nd Repl Bn 18Dec43 per MR 22Dec43; pmtd to PFC 01Jul44 (MR 02Jul44); evac **WIA**, TFRD to DofP 30Sep44; REASG fm 2nd Repl Dep 25Oct44; **(Missing entry of evac)**; REASGD fm 2nd Repl Dep 19Nov44; evac sk, TFRD to DofP 14Dec44 **(Miller, Robert A. Pvt WIA, not hosp (pen w. r. thumb shell frag – unknown date)** CIB PFD (07/44); GCM (16/44)	WIA 30Sep44
740.	Miller, T. A., Jr. 18176079	PVT	C	MOS 745 attached fm 3rd Reinf Bn 04May45 (per MR 07May45); relieved from attached status, to ASGD 05May45 (per MR 07May45) No discovered GO for CIB or GCM	
741.	**Miller,** Wesley V. 38005327	CPL-SSG	C	MOS 652 (Deployed w/the company, is on the Pine Camp menu as PFC) evac sk 16Aug43 (per MR 02Sep43); RTD fm evac sk19Aug43 (per MR 02Sep43); **(Missing entry for WIA)**; already evac **WIA**, DFR per MR 17Nov43; RTD fm DofP 05Dec43 per MR 12Dec43; pmtd to SSG per MR 25Jan44; evac **WIA** (Pen w back shell frag) 15Feb44; trfd to DofP and DFR 27Feb44 per MR 14Mar44; RTD fr DofP 27Mar44; evac sk (old wound) 19Apr44 (MR 25Apr44); already evac sk, tfrd to DofP and DFR 19May44 (per MR 27May44) CIB FM as SSG in C Co 01Jan44 (14/44)	**WIA unk** WIA 15Feb44
742.	**Miller**, Wilbur M. 37663539	PVT	C	MOS 745 **(Unknown date of assignment, not on Pine Camp menu)** RTD fm 2nd Re Dep 11Jan44 (date unclear) (per MR 13Jan44); evac sk (exhaustion) 17Feb44; **(Missing entry of RTD & WIA)**; already evac **WIA**, trfd to DofP and DFR 03Mar44 per MR 15Mar44 CIB FM 01Feb44 (14/44)	WIA unk

743.	**Milliman, Harold L.** 36460415	**PVT-PFC**	C	MOS 745 ASGD fm 2nd Repl Bn 18Dec43 per MR 22Dec43; evac 08Jan44 per MR 10Jan44; RTD fm sk 04Feb44; Pmtd to PFC 04Mar44 per MR 12Mar44; PFC evac sk 25Jul44 (26Jul44); RTD fm sk (26Jul44) -- erron entry per MR 06Aug44; already evac sk TFRD to DofP/DRR 01Aug44 (per 08Aug44); REASGD fm DofP 10Aug44 (18Aug44); evac **LIA** to Ship Acadia, TFRD to DofP 18Aug44; erron rptd as RTD fm sk 26Jul44, actually still sk evac (06Aug44); REASG fm hosp 15Sep44; **(Missing entry of DOW)** correction to MR entry 20Oct44 of **DOW**; s/b evac **SWIA**, **DOW** 20Oct44 (per MR 28Oct44) (buried in Epinal Cemetery); DOW20Oct44 per div & 157 cas list CIB (01/44 - 01Jan44 per CC)	WIA 20Oct44 **DOW 20Oct44**
744.	**Mills, Lucian (NMI)** **35772729**	**PVT-PFC**	C	MOS 746 asgd fm 2nd Repl Dep 29Apr44 (per MR 06May44); MIA 30May44, DFR 01Jun44; erroneously rptd MIA 30May44, should be evac sk 30May44 (14Jun44); RTD fm sk 02Jun44 (14Jun44); pmtd to PFC 01Jul44 (MR 02Jul44); evac sk 12 Jul44; already evac sk TFRD to DofP/DFR 01Aug44 (per 05Aug44); REASG fm hosp 15Sep44; MIA 23Sep44 (25Sep44) – to **KIA** 23Sep44 (per MR 12Nov44) (buried in USA); KIA23SEP44 per Div, 157 & ANB; not on ABMC reg CIB 01Apr44 (06/44 CC)	**KIA 23Sep44**
745.	Mills, William G. PCM-C 20837734 (Olathe, CO)	PVT-TSG	C, AT	PVT in C Co per Induction Roster, 16Sep40; SGT in C Co per Pine Camp menu CIB as TSG in AT Co 01Jan44 (03/44 CC)	
746.	**Millspaugh**, Henry J. 11112195	PVT- TSG	C	MOS 745 ASGD fm 2nd Repl Dep per MR 11Dec43; promoted PFC 01Jan44 per MR 05Jan44; pmtd to CPL 10Apr 44 (per MR 11Apr44); **(Missing entry for promotion to SGT)** Duty MOS 652 pmtd to SSG 11Jul44; MOS 661 promoted to TSG 24Nov44evac **WIA**, TFRD to DofP 25Nov44 (per MR 28Nov44); REASG fm 3rd Repl Bn 14Jan45 (per MR 14Jan45) CIB (01/44 - 01Jan44 per CC); GCM S/SGT (16/44)	WIA 25Nov44
747.	Millwood, Haskel T. 20406301	PVT	C	MOS 745 ASGD fm 2nd Repl Dep per MR 11Dec43; MIA 15Dec43, DFR (per MR 25Dec43) **(POW 15Dec43);** MIA15DEC43 per ANB; Mstr POW reg gives rpt date of "15 1K 43" w/o unit ID, Stalag 7A, repatriated CIB FM 01Jan44 (14/44)	POW 15Dec43
748.	**Milstead, James W.** **33890107**	**PVT**	C	MOS 745 ASGD fm 3rd Repl Bn 11Dec44 (per MR 12Dec44); MIA 18Dec44 (per MR 24Dec44) **(KIA 18Dec44 in Bundenthal, Germany)** (buried in USA); KIA18Dec44 per div cas list -- NOT ON 157 LIST; MIA/KIA18DEC44 in Bundenthal per ANB; not on ABMC reg CIB 01Jan45 (01/45)	

749. **Minahan**, Victor I., Jr. O-449501	2LT-1LT	C	ASGD fm 2nd Repl Dep 29Dec43 (per MR 05Jan44); **WIA** not hosp (LW hand, 4th finger, gunshot) 04Apr44 (per MR 14Apr44); Evac sk 12May44 (MR16May44); LOD no, RTD 16May44 (MR 20May44); evac sk 20Jun44 (22Jun44); RTD fm sk 28Jun44 (29Jun44); evac sk 29Jun44 (30Jun44); 2LT RTD fm sk 10Jul44; (atchd fm 2nd Repl Dep) Promoted to 1LT 17Jul44 (MR 24Jul44); MR of 21Jul44 stating 'not dptd' s/b atchd & jnd (MR 24Jul44); 2LT TFRD to 2nd Rep Dep, not dptd 21Jul44; s/b atchd & jnd 21Jul44 (MR 24Jul44); already attached fm 2nd Repl Det reld fm atchment (per MR 05Aug44) CIB (01/44 - 01Jan44 per CC)	WIA 04Apr44
750. Mindock, William E. 36675963	CPL	C	MOS 653 ASGD fm 36th Inf Div 26Jan45 (per MR 01Feb45); Evac INJ 18Mar45 (per MR 18Mar45); Already Evac, TFRD to DofP 20Mar45 (per MR 20Mar45) GCM (8/45)	
751. Minear, Frank R. (Delta, CO)	PVT	C	Induction Roster 16Sep40	
752. Minear, Merle T. 20837719 (Delta, CO)	PVT	C, I, 1HQ, C	MOS 744, duty MOS 745 PFC in C Co per Induction Roster, 16Sep40; PFC in I Co per Pine Came menu; ASGD fr 1HQ 31Aug43; MIA 13Sep43 DFR (per MR 24Sep43) **(POW 13Sep43);** Mstr POW reg gives rpt date of 13Sep43, Stalag 3B, repatriated CIB FM as PVT in C Co 01Jan44 (14/44)	POW 13Sep43
753. **Miranda, Anthony J. 32212435 PCM-C**	**PVT**	C	(Deployed w/the company, is on the Pine Camp menu as PVT) **KIA** 14Jul43 (buried in USA); KIA as PVT in C Co 14Jul43 per div & 157 cas list -- SHRAPNEL; not on ABMC reg **FIRST KIA OF THE COMPANY** No discovered GO for CIB or GCM	**KIA 13Jul43**
754. Miser, Donald B. 16039537	PVT	C, B	MOS 745 **(Unknown date of assignment, not on Pine Camp menu)** already attached fm 2nd Repl Det reld fm atchment (per MR 05Aug44); Evac sk 14Aug43 (per MR 16Aug43); already evac sk, DFR 10Sep43; Rtd fm DofP 23Mar44 per MR 08Apr44; evac sk 27Mar44; to DofP/DFR 09Apr44 (MR 24Apr44); RTD 23Mar44; evac sk (cioatrios Lympha-dentis inguinal region bilat) 27Mar44 per MR 08Apr44; RTD fm DofP 20May44 (MR 21May44); evac sk 21May44; RTD fm sk 25Jun44 (27Jun44); TFRD to 2nd Repl Dep but not departed 19Jul44; s/b ATCHD & jnd (MR 23Jul44); AWOL 0530 29Jul44 (31Jul44); RTD fm AWOL 0645 31Jul44 CIB FM 01Jan44 (14/44 in E Co**)**	
755. Miske, Harold F. 36284718	PFC	C	GCM (32/45)	

756.	**Mitchell**, Robert D. 35697952	PFC	C	**(Unknonw date of assignment, not on Pine Camp menu)** Evac **WIA** 01Jun44 (06Jun44); already evac TFRD to DofP/DFR 30Jun44 (30Jul44); RTD fm 2nd Repl Dep 11Jan44 (date is not clear) (per MR 13Jan44) CIB PFD (07/44)	WIA 01Jun44
757.	Mitchell, Warren E. 16156631	PVT	C	MOS 745 attached fm 3rd Reinf Bn 04May45 (per MR 07May45); relieved from attached status, to ASGD 05May45 (per MR 07May45) No discovered GO for CIB or GCM	
758.	**Mitchell**, William O. (C.) 35235419	PVT	C	MOS 745 ASGD 30May44 (09Jun44); evac sk 13Jun44; RTD fm sk (23Jun44); evac **WIA**, TFRD to DofP 23Sep44; REASG fm 2nd Repl Dep 09Oct44; evac sk, TFRD to DofP 07Dec44 CIB 01Sep44 (9/45)	WIA 23Sep44
759.	**MItrowski,** Frank (NMI) 32812648 PCM-C	PVT-PFC	C	(Deployed w/the company, is on the Pine Camp menu as PVT) evac sk 03Aug44; already sk evac TFRD to DofP 04Aug44; RTD (23Jun44); **SWIA** 14Jul43; already evac **SWIA**, DFR (01Aug43); **(Missing entry of RTD)** evac **WIA** 30Nov43 per MR 03Dec43; RTD fm hosp 15Dec43 per MR 19Dec43; Pmtd to PFC 04Mar44 per MR 12Mar44; evac sk 05May44 (MR 13May44); RTD 07May44 (MR 13May44); evac **WIA** 31May44; **(Missing entry of RTD)** evac sk 17Jul44; RTD fm sk 22Jul44; **(Missing entry of evac)** RTD fm 7th Repl Dep 21Sep44; evac **WIA**, TFRD to DofP 31Oct44 CIB as PVT in C Co (01/44 - 01Jan44 per CC); GCM (08/44)	WIA14Jul43 WIA 30Nov43 WIA 31May44 WIA 31Oct44
760.	Mobley, Vernon 14028448	PVT	C	MOS 745 attached fm 3rd Reinf Bn 04May45 (per MR 07May45); relieved from attached status, to ASGD 05May45 (per MR 07May45) No discovered GO for CIB or GCM	
761.	**Moffitt,** Wallace Jr. 33583636	PFC-CPL-SGT	C	MOS 653/746 **(Unknown date of assignment, not on Pine Camp menu)** Evac sk 13Aug44 (per MR 17Sep44); already evac sk, TFRD to DofP 27Aug44 (per MR 17Sep44); RTD fm 2nd Repl Dep 11Jan44 per MR 13Jan44; pmtd to Cpl **(Unknown date)**; evac **WIA** 04Jun44; RTD fm **WIA** (23Jun44); promoted to SGT (per MR 05Aug44); evac sk 13Aug44 (17Sep44); already evac sk, TFRD to DofP 27Aug44 (17Sep44); REASG fm 2nd Repl Dep 25Sep44; evac sk, TFRD to DofP 30Oct44 CIB (01/44); 01Feb44 per CC	WIA 04Jun44

762.	**Mondora**, Dominick (NMI) 32655658	PVT-PFC	C	MOS 745 **(Unknown date of assignment, not on Pine Camp menu) (Missing entry of evac)** RTD fm 2nd Re Dep 11Jan44 (date unclear) (per MR 13Jan44); Pmtd to PFC 04Mar44 per MR 12Mar44; evac **WIA** (battle casualty, Lacerating Wound scalp shell frag) 29Mar44 per MR 03Apr44; RTD fm **WIA** 20May44 (MR 21May44); evac **WIA** 23May44 (MR 24May44); already evac **WIA** to DofP/DFR 31May44 (MR 11 or 12Jun44) CIB FM 01Feb44 (14/44)	WIA 29Mar44 WIA 23May44
763.	Mongioi, Sebastiano (NMI) 32916810	PVT	C, G	MOS 745 ASGD fm 2nd Repl Bn 18Dec43 per MR 22Dec43; evac sk 11Jan44 per MR 14Jan44; RTD fm sk 21Feb44; Tfr in grade to G Co per MR 05Mar44; POW in G Co -- Mstr POW reg gives rpt date of 02Oct44, parent unit as division artillery, Stalag 9C, repatriated CIB (04/44); 01Jan44 per CC	(POW 02Oct44 in G Co)
764.	**Monteith,** Robert S. 32923036	PVT	C	MOS 745 ASGD 29May44 (09Jun44); evac sk 28Jun44 (29Jun44); RTD fm sk (02Jul44); evac **WIA**, TFRD to DofP 20Aug44; REASG fm 2nd Repl Dep 28Oct44; evac sk, TFRD to DofP 14Nov44 GCM (08/44); CIB FM 01Sep44 (14/44)	WIA 20Aug44
765.	Montgomery, Henry P.	2LT	C	ASGD 14Nov43 fm 29 Repl Bn – erron entry per MR 23Nov43 **NOT ASSIGNED** CIB (01/44 - 01Jan44 per CC)	
766.	**Moody, Clarence E. 36590875**	**PVT**	C	MOS 745 ASGD fm 2nd Repl Dep per MR 11Dec43; MIA 15Dec43, DFR (per MR 25Dec43), to **KIA** per MR 28Oct44 (**KIA 13Apr44 – murdered by Germans after evading capture)** No discovered GO for CIB or GCM	MIA15Dec43 **KIA 13Apr44**
767.	**Moore,** Daniel J. 31390513	PVT-PFC	C	MOS 745 ASGD fm 2nd Repl Dep 23Apr44 (per MR 29Apr44); **WIA** not hosp 01Oct44 (per MR 18Oct44); promoted to PFC 07Oct44; evac sk, TFRD to DofP 23Oct44; REASGD fm 2nd Repl Dep 19Nov44; AWOL 2359 21Nov44; fm AWOL 2359 23Nov44 (per MR 27Nov44); evac INJ 03Dec44; already evac, TFRD to DofP 04Dec44 CIB PFD (07/44)	WIA 01Oct44
768.	Moore, Derwood C. SN NA	2LT	C	ASGD fm 2nd Repl Dep 01Feb45 (per MR 02Feb45); erron entry per MR 20Feb45 – **NOT ASSIGNED** he was assigned to B Co.	

769.	**Moore**, James (NMI) 34768552	PVT-PFC	C	MOS 745 ASGD fm 2nd Repl Bn 18Dec43 per MR 22Dec43; evac sk 26Dec43 per MR 28Dec43; already evac sk, TFRD to DofP, DFR per MR 13Jan44; RTD fm DofP 26Feb44 per MR 03Mar44; evac sk (trench foot bilat) 02Mar44 per MR 07Mar44; RTD fm sk 05May44 (MR 12May44); evac **WIA** 31May44; RTD fm **WIA** 25Jun44 (27Jun44); promoted to PFC (per MR 05Aug44); evac sk, TFRD to DofP 06Sep44; REASG fm hosp 25Sep44; evac **WIA** 20Oct44; RTD fm 3rd Repl Bn 13Feb45 (per MR 13Feb45); Evac **WIA**, TFRD to DofP 18Mar45 (per MR 18Mar45) CIB PFD (07/44); GCM PFC (08/45)	WIA 31May44 WIA 20Oct44 WIA 18Mar45
770.	Moore, Laverne (NMI) 38006554 PCM-C		C	PFC **(Unknown date of assignment, on Pine Camp menu as PFC)** MIA 13Sep43 DFR (per MR 24Sep43) **(POW 13Sep43);** Mstr POW reg gives rpt date of 13Sep43, Stalag 2B, repatriated CIB MIA as PFC in C Co (05/44); 01Jan44 per CC	POW 13Sep43
771.	Moquin, Walter E. 31253528	PVT	C	MOS 745 attached fm 3rd Reinf Bn 04May45 (per MR 07May45); relieved from attached status, to ASGD 05May45 (per MR 07May45) No discovered GO for CIB or GCM	
772.	Moretz, Kennedy Y. 34935057	PFC	C	GCM (32/45)	
773.	Morgan, Calvin L. 38088976	PVT	C	MOS 745 attached fm 3rd Reinf Bn 04May45 (per MR 07May45); relieved from attached status, to ASGD 05May45 (per MR 07May45) No discovered GO for CIB or GCM	
774.	**Morgenrath, Louis A. O-1311534**	**2LT**	A, C	ASGD 14Nov43 fr 29 Repl Bn – erron entry per MR 23Nov43; ASGD from Co A per MR 02Dec43; MIA 15Dec43, DFR per MR 25Dec43 (buried in Ardennes Cemetery) **(There is a discrepancy in the dates of death given: the unit indicates he was MIA on 15Dec44, but the American Battle Monuments Commission gives his date of death as 07Jan45, as he died in German captivity according to the Master POW Register.;** on master POW register as 116Inf, 100th ID!; KIA07JAN45 per 157 list; MIA/KIA16DEC43 per ANB; ABMC 07Jan45, Ardennes Cemetery no awards given Died as POW CIB FM eff 01Jan44 (14/44)	MIA/WIA 15Dec44 **DOW 07Jan45**
775.	**Morin, Hubert A. 31150334**	**PVT**	C	ASGD fr Co B 25Sep43 (per MR 28Sep43); evac sk 30Sep43 (per MR 03Oct43; RTD fm sk 08Oct43 per MR 01Nov43; evac **WIA** 13Nov43 per MR 16Nov43; RTD fm **WIA** 07Dec43 per MR 12Dec43; **KIA** 15Dec43 per MR 19Dec43 (buried in USA); KIA 15Dec43 per div & 157 cas list -- SHRAPNEL; not on ABMC reg No discovered GO for CIB or GCM	WIA 13Nov43 **KIA 15 Dec43**

776.	**Morris**, Buckner S. 15316225	PVT-CPL-SGT	C	MOS 745/653 **(Unknown date of assignment, not on Pine Camp menu)** RTD fm 2nd Repl Dep 11Jan44 (date is not clear) per MR 13Jan44; Pmtd to PFC 04Mar44 per MR 12Mar44; **(Missing evac WIA)** RTD fm **WIA** (23Jun44); **WIA** not hosp 06Oct44 (per MR 18Oct44); **WIA** not hosp 30Oct44 (05Nov44); promoted to CPL 24Nov44; promoted to SGT 24Dec44; Evac sk, TFRD to DofP 14Jan45 (per MR 14Jan45); already evac sk, TFRD to DofP 03Feb45 (per MR 03Feb45) CIB 01Feb44 (11/44); CIB 01Feb44 (13/44); GCM (16/44)	WIA unk WIA 06Oct44 WIA 30Oct44
777.	Morris, Duard L. PCM-A 20837736 (Delta, CO)	CPL	C, A	PFC in C Co per Induction Roster, 16Sep40; PVT in A Co per PCCM42; CIB FM as CPL in A Co 01Jan44 (14/44)	
778.	Morris, Harry F. 35715543	SSG	C	MOS 653 **(Unknown date of assignment)** MIA 21Jan45 (per MR 23Jan45) **(POW 20JAN45);** Mstr POW reg gives rpt date of 21Jan45, parent unit as division artillery, no camp info, repatriated CIB 01Jan45 (01/45)	POW 20Jan45
779.	**Morris, Richard A. 20838320 PCM-E (Boulder, CO)**	**SSG**	C	PFC in F Co per Induction Roster, 16Sep40; SSG in E Co per PCCM42; ASGD fr Co E 28Sep43; MIA 15Dec43, DFR per MR **25Dec43** Was among five men from C Co (Guell, Morris, Tourtilotte, Koziol, McCoy) captured 15Dec43 near Venafro, who escaped from a POW train as it was being bombed in northern Italy on 28Jan44 and who made it back to Allied lines, but did not return to the unit CIB MIA as SSG in C Co (05/44); 01Jan44 per CC	POW15Dec43 ESCAPED
780.	**Morris, Roy J. 38424615**	**PVT- -SSG**	C	MOS 745/653 ASGD fm 7th Repl Dep 25Sep43; pmtd to PFC 01Dec43; pmtd to CPL **(unknown date)**; pmtd SGT MOS 653 24May44; evac **WIA** (pen W R elbow shell frag) 29May44; **(Missing entry for RTD)**; pmtd to SSG (01Jul44); evac sk, TFRD to DofP 04Sep44; REASG fm hosp 03Oct44; MIA 06Nov44 (per MR 09Nov44) – to **KIA** 06Nov44 (per MR 12Nov44) (buried in Epinal Cemetery); KIA06Nov44 per div & 157 cas list; MIA/KIA06NOV44 per ANB; ABMC 06Nov44 as SSG, PH CIB (01/44 - 01Jan44 per CC); GCM as CPL (02/44)	WIA 29May44 **KIA 06Nov44**

781.	Moscato, Joseph V. 31337861	PVT-PFC	C	MOS 745 Adjutant's Notebook P.1M = MIA13JUL43 (RTD21JUL43); ASGD fm 2nd Repl Dep 24Feb44 per MR 05Mar44; evac sk (FUO) 27Jun44 (28Jun44); RTD fm sk 05Jul44; promoted to PFC 07Oct44; evac sk 05Dec44; RTD fm sk 08Dec44; MIA 21Jan45 (per MR 23Jan45) **(POW 20JAN45)**; Mstr POW reg gives rpt date of 21Jan45 as PFC, parent unit as division artillery, no camp info, repatriated CIB PFD (07/44); GCM PFC (16/44);	POW 20Jan45
782.	Mosher, Franklin C. 42123656	PFC	C	GCM (32/45)	
783.	Moss, Harry (NMI) PCM-F 32219191	PVT	F, 2HQ, C, E	MOS 745 PVT in F Co per Pine Camp menu; ASGD fm 2HQ 22Sep43; KIA as PVT in E Co 10Nov43 per div & 157 cas list; not on ABMC reg No discovered GO for CIB or GCM	(KIA 10Nov43 in E Co)
784.	**Mucha,** Stephen (NMI) 11064954	PVT-PFC	C	MOS 675 (Deployed w/the company; is on Pine Camp menu as PVT) promoted to PFC 03Nov43 per MR 05Nov43; evac **WIA** 22Dec43 per MR 25Dec43; erroneously tfrd to DofP and DFR 22Jan44; already evac **WIA** TFRD to DofP, DFR per MR 23Jan44; RTD fm hosp 12Apr44 (per MR 18Apr44); MIA 25May44 (MR 27May44) (evac sk MR 28May44); CORR: rptd MIA 25May44 on MR 27May44; s/b evac sk 25May44; RTD fm sk 02Jun44; evac sk 17Jul44; already evac sk, TFRD to 2nd Rep Dep, not dptd 19Jul44; s/b ATCHD & jnd (MR 23Jul44) – order rescinded (MR 24Jul44); already evac sk TFRD to 7th Repl Dep 21Jul44, reclassified limited assignment (MR 24Jul44) CIB as PFC in C Co (01/44 - 01Jan44 per CC)	WIA 22Dec43
785.	**Mueller, John F.** **32334142**	**PFC**	C	**(Unknown date of assignment, not on Pine Camp menu)** MIA 16Aug43 (per MR 21Aug43) (DFR per MR 07Sep43) **(believed drowned in landing accident in 2ND Sicily landing; still MIA; commemorated at Sicily-Rome Cemetery)**; KIA16Aug43 as PFC per div & 157 cas list; ABMC 16Aug43, still MIA, commemorated at Sicily-Rome Cemetery BSM; blvd drowned in landing craft acc't -- no PH CIB MIA (05/44); 01Jan44 per CC	**MIA 16Aug43**

786.	**Mundt,** Frederick J. 20838376	PVT-PFC	C	MOS 745 (Deployed w/the company, is on the Pine Camp menu as PFC) Evac sk 02Nov43 per MR 04Nov43; promoted to PFC 03Nov43 (per MR 05Nov43); already evac sk TFRD to DofP, DFR per MR 06Dec43; RTD fm DofP 07Dec43 (per MR 12Dec43); evac sk 21Jan44 per MR 23Jan44; RTD fm sk 15Feb44; evac sk 07Jul44; RTD fm sk 15Jul44; evac sk 30Jul44 (02Aug44); already evac sk,TFRD to DofP/DFR 31Jul44 (05Aug44); REASG fm DofP 06Aug44; **WIA** not hosp 26Sep44 (per MR 17Oct44); evac sk, TFRD to DofP 08Nov44; REASG fm 2nd Repl Dep 14Nov44; evac **WIA** 03Dec44; already evac, TFRD to DofP 04Dec44; REASG fm 3rd Repl Bn 15Jan45 (per MR 15Jan45); TDY to UK 26Feb45 (per MR 26Feb45); RTD fm TDY to UK 19Mar45 (per MR 21Mar45) CIB as P:FC in C Co (01/44 - 01Jan44 per CC)	WIA 26Sep44 WIA 03Dec44
787.	Munsell, Dale M. 15098312	PFC- SSG	C	MOS 745/653/651 **(Unknown date of assignment)** Promoted to CPL 24Nov44; promoted to SGT 24Dec44; **(Missing entry of evac)**; RTD fm 2nd Repl Dep 11Jan44 (date is not clear) per MR 13Jan44; Evac sk 16Jan45 (per MR 16Jan45); RTD fm sk 18Jan45 (per MR 18Jan45); PMTD to SSG, MOS 651 **(Unknown date)**; Evac sk 15Mar45 (per MR 15Mar45); RTD fm sk 17Mar45 (per MR 17Mar45); Evac sk 23Mar45 (per MR 23Mar45); already evac sk, TFRD to DofP 24Mar45 (per MR 24Mar45) CIB (04/44); 01Feb44 per CC; GCM (08/44)	
788.	Murphy, David M. 34939678	PVT	C	GCM (35/45)	
789.	Murphy, Leonard D. 34801737	PVT	C	MOS 745 ASGD fm 2nd Repl Dep per MR 11Dec43; evac sk 14Dec43 (per MR 17Dec43); RTD fm sk 15Dec43 (per MR 19Dec43); evac 16Dec43 per MR 05Jan44; already evac sk TFRD to DofP, DFR per MR 19Jan44; already evac sk, TRFD to DofP 16Aug44 CIB FM 01Jan44 (14/44)	
790.	Murray, James C. 20954743	TSG	C	MOS 651 attached fm 3rd Reinf Bn 04May45 (per MR 07May45); relieved from attached status, to ASGD 05May45 (per MR 07May45) GCM (32/45)	
791.	Muse, Howard L. 35873362	PVT-PFC	C	MOS 745 ASGD fm 2nd Repl Dep 24Feb44 per MR 05Mar44; pmtd to PFC 01May44; evac sk 27Jun44 (29Jun44); RTD fm sk (02Jul44); evac sk, TFRD to DofP 23Sep44; REASGD but not joined fm 2nd Repl Dep 13Oct44; joined 13Oct44; evac sk, TFRD to DofP 16Oct44 CIB (04/44 - 01Apr44 per CC); GCM (02/44); CIB FM 01Mar44 (14/44)	

792.	**Mutchler**, William J. 13020870	PVT-PFC-CPL-SGT	C	MOS 745/653 **(Unknown date of assignment, not on Pine Camp menu)** Dvac sk 01Sep43; RTD 04Sep43 (per MR 06Sep43); promoted PFC 01Jan44 per MR 05Jan44; AWOL 0700 31May44 (per MR 08Jun44); **(Missing RTD from AWOL entry)**; evac **WIA**, TFRD to DofP 23Sep44; REASG but not joined fm 2nd Repl Dep 04Oct44; joined 07Oct44; promoted to CPL MOS 653 07Oct44; promoted to SGT 24Nov44; evac sk 03Dec44; already evac, TFRD to DofP 04Dec44 CIB (01/44 - 01Jan44 per CC)	WIA 23Sep44
793.	Mycawka, William (NMI) 33182327 PCM-C	PVT	C	Deployed w/the company; is on Pine Camp menu as PVT; MIA 13Sep43 DFR (per MR 24Sep43) **(POW 13Sep43)**; Mstr POW reg gives rpt date of 13Sep43, Stalag 2B, repatriated CIB FM as PVT in C Co 01Jan44 (14/44)	POW 13Sep43
794.	Nadeau, Joseph A. PCM-C SN NA	PVT	C	On Pine Camp menu	
795.	**Nagel,** Walter A. 22212501	PVT- SSG	C	MOS 652 (Deployed w/the company, is on the Pine Camp menu) Pmtd to PFC 01Dec43; evac **WIA** 15Dec43 per MR 25Dec43; RTD fm **WIA** 21Dec43 per MR 26Dec43; evac sk (pleurisy fibrinbus sc); pmtd to CPL per MR 11Mar44; already evac sk, promoted to SGT per MR 20Mar44; already evac sk tfrd to DofP & DFR 22Mar44 (per MR 18Apr44) already evac sk to DofP/DFR 22Mar44; RTD 23Apr44 (MR 30Apr44); pmtd SSG 24May44; evac sk 03Dec44; already evac, TFRD to DofP 04Dec44 CIB (01/44 - 01Jan44 per CC); GCM as S/SGT (08/44)	WIA 15Dec43
796.	**Narozny**, Henry P. 36743810	PVT	C	MOS 745 ASGD fm 2nd Repl Dep per MR 11Dec43; evac **INJ** 14Dec43 per MR 21Dec43; already evac **INJ** TFRD to DofP, DFR per MR 15Jan44 CIB FM 01Jan44 (14/44)	INJ 14Dec43
797.	**Nash, Robert C.** 33563425	**PFC-CPL**	C	MOS 607/653 ASGD and jnd fr 2nd Repl Dep 24Feb44 per MR 07Mar44; evac sk (Nephrelitissis) 26Feb44 per MR 03Mar44; already evac sk tfrd to DofP and DFR 11 Mar44 per MR 05Apr44; evac **WIA** (BC pen W L leg shell frag) 31May44; already evac **WIA** TFRD to DofP and DFR 06Jun44 (15Jun44); RTD fm DofP 21Jul44; Promoted to CPL 26Dec44; MIA 21Jan45 (per MR 23Jan45) **(DIED AS POW)** (buried in Lorraine Cemetery); MIA21JAN45 per 157 list; ABMC DOW02MAR45 -- NOT ON DIV LIST; MIA21JAN45 per ANB; died as POW per master POW register -- no camp given; ABMC 02Mar45, PH CIB PFD (07/44)	WIA 06Jun44 POW 20Jan45 **DOW as POW 02Mar45**

798.	Natino, Erme R. 32541280	PFC	C	MOS 745 attached fm 3rd Reinf Bn 04May45 (per MR 07May45); relieved from attached status, to ASGD 05May45 (per MR 07May45) GCM (32/45)	
799.	**Nayback**, Wilford H. 36457018	PVT-PFC	C	MOS 604 ASGD fm 2nd Repl Dep per MR 11Dec43; pmtd PFC 14Jan44 per MR 15Jan44; evac sk unknown date in Jan44 per MR 17Jan44; RTD fm sk 04Feb44; evac sk 31Jul44; RTD fm sk 01Aug44; evac **WIA** 14Sep44; already evac **WIA**, TFRD to DofP 15Sep44; REASG fm 3rd Repl Bn 06Feb45 (per MR 06Feb45); Evac sk, TFRD to DofP 10Mar45 (per MR 10Mar45) CIB (04/44 - 01Jan44 per CC); GCM (08/45)	WIA 14Sep44
800.	**Nebelecky,** John NNMI) (Neblecky) 32212679 PCM-C	PVT	C	(Deployed w/the company, is on the Pine Camp menu as PVT Neblecky) **WIA** on beach 10Jul43; **(Missing entry for RTD)**; RTD fm sk 04Aug43 (per MR 25Aug43); **(Missing entry for evac sk)**; already evac sk, DFR per MR 23Nov43; RTD fm DofP 28Nov43 (per MR 02Dec43); RTD fm DofP 28Nov43 per MR 02Dec43; evac **SWIA** 15Dec43 per MR 19Dec43; already evac **WIA** TFRD to DofP, DFR per MR 16Jan44 CIB as PVT in C Co as NEBELECKY FM 01Jan44 (14/44)	WIA 10Jul43 WIA 15Dec43
801.	Neff, Edgar (NMI) 35659719	PVT	C	MOS **754 (Unknown date of assignment, not on Pine Camp menu**) RTD fm 2nd Repl Dep 11Jan44 (date is not clear) per MR 13Jan44; Evac sk (Nephrelitissis) 26Feb44; already evac sk tfrd to DofP and DFR 11 Mar44; MOS 745 RTD fm DofP 13Jul44; evac sk 27Aug44 (28Sep44); NLD 27Aug44-12Sep44, inclusive (per MR 28Sep44); RTD 25Sep44 (per MR 28Sep44); evac sk, TFRD to DofP 24Oct44; REASG fm 2nd Repl Dep 25Oct44 (per MR 31Oct44); evac sk 31Oct44; already evac sk, TFRD to DofP 03Nov44 CIB 01Feb44 (11/44)	
802.	Neitz, Ray E. PCM-B 38005251	CPL-PVT- CPL-SGT	C	**(Deployed w/the battalion; is on Pine Camp menu as CPL in B Co)** Reduced fm CPL to PVT 11Aug43; Evac sk 21Sep43 (per MR 23Sep43); **(Missing entry for RTD & promotion to PFC)**; promoted to CPL 04Jan44 per MR 05Jan44; pmtd SGT per MR 25Jan44; evac **LIA** (sprain in ankle) 29May44; **(Missing entry for RTD)(Missing entry for evac WIA)**; RTD fm **WIA** 27Jun44 (28Jun44); evac sk 26Jul44 (27Jul44); already evac sk reclassified limited assignment 28Jul44 CIB as SGT in C Co (01/44 - 01Jan44 per CC); GCM (02/44)	WIA unk

803.	**Nestor, Charlie C. Jr.** **34722848**	**PVT**	C	**already absent in confinement, tfrd to NATOUSA Disciplinary Training Center, North Africa, per General Court Martial Order #8, HQ 45th Inf Div dated 28Mar44 per MR 10Apr44** **No discovered GO for CIB or GCM (probably deserted prior to Sicily landings)**	
804.	Newhouse, Leonard A. 34990676	PVT- CPL	C	MOS 745 ASGD fm 3rd Repl Bn 24Jan45 (per MR 26Jan45); PMTD to PFC 06Mar45 (per MR 06Mar45); PMTD to CPL, MOS 652 20May45 (per MR 20May45) CIB 01Mar45 (10/45)	
805.	**Newman**, Debro L. 34516376	SSG-TSG	C	MOS 653 ASGD fm 103rd Inf Div 26Jan45 (per MR 01Feb45); Pmtd to TSG, change in MOS to 651 14Apr45 (per MR 14Apr45); **WIA** not hosp 26Apr45 (pen w R leg) (per MR 05May45); **WIA** not hosp 26Apr45 (pen w R leg) (per MR 05May45) GCM (8/45)	WIA 26Apr45
806.	**Newton,** Cephus G. 34805172	PVT-PFC	C	MOS 504 **(Unknown date of assignment, not on Pine Camp menu) (Missing entry for evac)**; RTD fm 2nd Repl Dep 11Jan44 per MR 13Jan44; Pmtd to PFC 04Mar44 per MR 12Mar44; pmtd to Cpl **(Unknown date)**; **WIA** 31May44 (06Jun44); already evac **WIA** TFRD to DofP/DFR 30Jun44 (30Jul44); already evac **WIA** TFRD to DofP/DFR 30Jun44 (30Jul44) CIB FM 01Feb44 (14/44)	WIA 31May44
807.	Newton, Charles G., Jr. 34722848	PVT	C	**(Unknown date of assignment, not on Pine Camp menu)** AWOL (per MR 14Jan44) per MR 13Dec43; MIA 15Dec43, DFR (erron per MR 14Jan44 s/b AWOL 13Dec43) per MR 25Dec43; RTD fm AWOL 2000 10Jan44 per MR 14Jan44; duty to confinement 5th Army Stockade 23Jan44 per MR 25Jan44; fm confinement in 5th Army stockade to under arrest in unit 17Mar44, to RTD 18Mar44 (per MR 22Mar44); duty to confinement 22Mar44 (per MR 29Mar44) **(then what?????)** No discovered GO for CIB or GCM	
808.	**Newton**, James M. O-1311271	2LT	C	ASGD fr 29th Repl Dep 28Sep43 (per MR 30Sep43); evac **WIA** 11Nov43 per MR 13Nov43; already evac **WIA**, DFR per MR 23Nov43; RTD fm hosp 11Aug44; TFRD to Co B 25Aug44 (20Sep44) CIB Present Pers eff 01Jan44 (10/44 CC)	WIA 11Nov43
809.	Newton, Robert Jr. 44013050	PFC	C	GCM (32/45)	

810.	Nice, Carl J. 31301883	PVT	C, G	MOS 521 **(Unknown date of assignment, not on Pine Camp menu) (Missing evac entry)**; RTD fm 2nd Repl Dep 11Jan44 (date is not clear) per MR 13Jan44; Tfr in grade to G Co per MR 05Mar44); KIA11NOV43 per 157 list; MIA/ KIA25SEP44 per ANB -- NOT ON DIV LIST; not on ABMC reg CIB PFD (07/44); GCM as J. (08/44)	(KIA 25Sep44 in G Co)
811.	Nichols, Clarence E., Jr. SN NA (Delta, CO)	PVT	C	Induction Roster 16Sep40	
812.	**Nickell,** Holly P. 39160583	SSG	C	MOS 653 ASGD fm 2nd Repl Dep 01Jun44 (11Jun44); evac sk 14Jun44 (19Jun44); RTD fm sk 17Jun44 (19Jun44); evac **WIA** 24Sep44; REASG fm 2nd Repl Dep 22Oct44; **WIA** not hosp 07Nov44 (per MR 20Nov44); evac sk, TFRD to DofP 28Nov44; REASG fm 71st Repl Dep 08Dec44; MIA 21Jan45 (per MR 23Jan45) **(POW 20JAN45)** GCM (08/44); CIB 01Sep44 (13/44); CIB 01Jul44 (40/45)	WIA 24Sep44 WIA 07Nov44 POW 20Jan45
813.	**Nickell, Walker H. (Walter) 35642843**	**PVT-PFC**	C	MOS 504 **(Unknown date of assignment, not on Pine Camp menu) (Missing evac entry)**; RTD fm 2nd Repl Dep 11Jan44 per MR 13Jan44; Pmtd to PFC 01May44; Evac **WIA**, TFRD to DofP 23Sep44; REASG fm hosp 02Oct44; MIA 04Dec44 (per MR 06Dec44); Fm MIA 04Dec44 to **KIA** 04Dec44 (per MR 13Dec44) (buried in USA); KIA04Dec44 as Walker per div cas list; MIA/KIA04DEC44 as WALTER per ANB; not on ABMC reg CIB (04/44); 01Feb44 per CC; GCM as Walker (08/44);	WIA 23Sep44 **KIA 04Dec44**
814.	**Nickels/Nickles, Edwin H. 33555690**	**PVT**	C	MOS 745 ASGD fm Co A 14Jan44 per MR 15Jan44; evac sk 17Jan44 per MR 21Jan44; already evac sk, tfr to DofP & DFR 24Feb44; RTD fm DofP 08Apr44 (per MR 17Apr44); MIA 25May44 (MR 27May44); corrected to MIA 30 May & DFR MR 01Jun44); erron rptd on 27May44 as MIA 25May44; s/b MIA 30May44, DFR (01Jun44); change from MIA to **KIA** 28May44 (07Jun44) as NICKLES (buried in USA); MIA25MAY44 as NICKELS per ANB; KIA30May44 per div & 157 casualty list; MIA/KIA30MAY44 per ANB; not on ABMC reg as Nickles or as Nickels No discovered GO for CIB or GCM	KIA 28May44

815.	**Noack,** August J. 32919053	PVT-PFC	C	MOS 745 **(Unknown date of assignment, not on Pine Camp menu) (Missing entry for evac)**; RTD fm 2nd Repl Dep 11Jan44 (date is not clear) per MR 13Jan44; Pmtd to PFC 04Mar44 per MR 12Mar44; evac sk LD 13May44 (MR 17May44); RTD 25May44 (MR 27May44); evac sk 28May44 (MR 10Jun44); RTD (10Jun44); evac sk 22Jul44 (MR 23Jul44); RTD fm sk 24Jul44; evac **WIA** 24Sep44; 745 REASG fm 2nd Repl Dep 18Oct44; evac sk, TFRD to DofP 25Oct44 CIB (01/44 - 01Feb44 per CC); GCM PFC (08/44); CIB FM PFC 01Feb44 (14/44)	WIA 24Sep44
816.	Noles, Grover 34947502	PVT	C	MOS 745 ASGD fm 3rd Repl Bn 24Jan45 (per MR 26Jan45); Evac sk, TFRD to DofP 01Mar45 (per MR 01Mar45) CIB 01Mar45 (10/45)	
817.	**Norton,** Daniel H. 33886459	PVT	C	MOS 745 ASGD fm 2nd Repl Dep 04Nov44 (per MR 13Nov44); evac **WIA**, TFRD to DofP 05Dec44 CIB 01Dec44 (15/45)	WIA 05Dec44
818.	**Norton, Stanley S. 35815356**	**PVT-PFC**	C	MOS 745 ASGD fm 3rd Repl Bn 24Jan45 (per MR 26Jan45); PMTD to PFC 06Mar45 (per MR 06Mar45); **KIA** 30Mar45 (per MR 2Apr45) (also per MR 05Apr45) (buried in USA); KIA30Mar45 per Div, 157 & ANB; not on ABMC reg CIB 01Mar45 (10/45)	**KIA 30Mar45**
819.	Noyes, Leonard C. 31363879	PVT-PFC	C	ASGD fm Co B 14Jan44 per MR 15Jan44; evac sk 24Sep44; already evac sk TFRD to DofP 25Sep44; **(Missing entry of RTD)**; Pmtd to Pfc 04Mar44 per MR 12Mar44 CIB (01/44 - 01Jan44 per CC)	
820.	**Oates,** George D. 37602765	PVT	C	**(Unknown date of assignment, not on Pine Camp menu)(Missing entry for WIA)** Already evac **WIA**, trfd to DofP and DFR 28Feb44 per MR 14Mar44 No discovered GO for CIB or GCM	WIA unk date
821.	O'Brien, John E. PCM-C 32204749	PVT	C	(Deployed w/the company, is on the Pine Camp menu as PVT) Evac sk 07Sep43 (per MR 11Nov43) CIB Former Pers as PVT in C Co 01Jan44 (10/44 CC); CIB FM 01Jan44 (14/44)	
822.	**Oeschger, Vincent C. 37670945**	PVT	C	MOS 745 **(Unknown date of assignment, not on Pine Camp menu)(Missing entry for evac)**; RTD fm 2nd Repl Dep 11Jan44 (date is not clear) per MR 13Jan44; Pmtd to Pfc 04Mar44 per MR 12Mar44; MIA 27May44 (per MR 31May44) (to **KIA** per MR 22 or 23Jun44) (buried in USA) CIB 01/44	**KIA 27May44**
823.	Oglesby. Jack B. (Olglesby) 34937414	PFC	C	MOS 745 ASGD fm 3rd Repl Bn 24Jan45 (per MR 26Jan45); **(Missing entry for evac)**; Already evac sk (NBI stepped on glass), TFRD to DofP 24Mar45 (per MR 24Mar45) CIB 01Mar45 (10/45); GCM (32/45)	

824.	Oiler, Trilby H. (Tribby) 35225142	PVT-PFC	C	MOS 745 MOS 745 ASGD fm 2nd Repl Dep 24Feb44 per MR 05Mar44; pmtd to PFC 01May44; evac sk 09Jul44 (MR 11Jul44); RTD fm sk 15Jul44; reduced to PVT 04Aug44; promoted to PFC 04Sep44; evac sk 03Nov44; RTD fm sk 06Nov44; evac sk 07Nov44; RTD fm sk 10Nov44; **(Missing entry for evac)**; already evac sk, TFRD to DopP 20Nov44; REASG fm 2nd Repl Dep 26Nov44 (per MR 28Nov44) CIB (04/44); 01Apr44 per CC; GCM (02/44)	
825.	O'Keefe, William L. 33702397	PVT-PFC	C	MOS 745 ASGD 30May44 (per MR 09Jun44); promoted to PFC 07Oct44; evac sk 28Nov44; already evac sk, TFRD to DofP 29Nov44; REASG fm 3rd Repl Bn 15Jan45 (per MR 15Jan45); 745 MIA 21Jan45 (per MR 23Jan45) **(POW 20JAN45)**; Mstr POW reg gives rpt date of 21Jan45 as "OKEEFE", parent unit as division artillery, Stalag 12A to 9B, repatriated CIB 01Sep44 (13/44)	POW 20Jan45
826.	Olerta, Peter C. PCM-C SN NA	PVT	C	On Pine Camp menu	
827.	**Olinger**, Harvard E. 13061012 PCM-C	PVT-PFC	C	(Deplolyed w/the company, is on the Pine Camp menu as PVT) Pmtd PFC 10Aug43; evac **SWIA** 26Sep43 (per MR 30Sep43); already evac **SWIA**, TFRD to DofP and DFR per MR 04Nov43 CIB FM as PFC in C Co 01Jan44 (14/44)	WIA 26Sep43
828.	Oliver, Patrick (NMI) 33110415	PFC	C	(Deployed w/the company, is on the Pine Camp menu) Evac sk (exhaustion) 20Feb44; already evac sk tfrd to 7th Repl Dep 08Apr44 (per MR 18Apr44) CIB DP as PFC in C Co (07/44)	
829.	**O'Neill,** Constantine L. 20836804 PCM-C (Denver, CO)	PVT-PFC-CPL	RHQ, C	PVT in RHQ per Induction Roster, 16Sep40; Deployed w/the company, is on Pine Camp menu as PFC) Pmtd to CPL (04Aug43); **SWIA** 12Jul43 (Per MR 20Jul43), RTD fm **SWIA** 17Jul43; MIA 13Sep43 DFR (per MR 24Sep43) **(POW 13Sep43);** Mstr POW reg gives rpt date as 13Sep43 as "ONEILL", Stalag 3B, repatriated CIB MIA as PFC in C Co (05/44); 01Jan44 per CC	WIA 12Jul43 POW 13Sep43
830.	**Ondrik**, Andrew M. 34734845	PVT-PFC	C	MOS 745 ASGD 29May44 (09Jun44); pmtd to PFC 01Jul44 (MR 02Jul44); erron rptd 29Sep44 as reduced to PVT, s/b pmtd to PFC (per MR 18Oct44); evac sk, TFRD to DofP 11Sep44; REASG fm hosp 26Sep44 (per MR 27Sep44); evac **WIA**, TFRD to DofP 06Nov44 CIB 01Sep44 (13/44)	WIA 06Nov44
831.	**Oswald, Byron J. 35545747**	**PVT-PFC**	C	MOS 745 ASGD 20Aug43; promoted to PFC 03Nov43 per MR 05Nov43; **KIA** 24Nov43 per MR 28Nov43 (buried in USA); KIA24Nov43 per div & 157 cas list; not on ABMC reg No discovered GO for CIB or GCM	**KIA 24Nov43**

832.	**Otter,** William J. 33726435	PVT	C	MOS 745 ASGD fm 2nd Repl Bn 14Jan44 per MR 18Jan44; **WIA** (pen wound anterior tibia shell frag) 07Feb44; TFRD to DofP & DFR 28Feb44; already evac **WIA**, trfd to DofP and DFR 28Feb44 per MR 15Mar44; RTD fm DofP (23Jun44); evac sk 06Jul44; already evac sk TFRD to DofP/DFR 08Jul44 CIB FM 01Feb44 (14/44)	WIA 07Feb44
833.	**Ousey,** Alvin E. O-1285283	1LT	C	**(Unknown date of assignment) (Missing entry of evac)**; REASG fm 3rd Repl Bn 25Jan45 (per MR 25Jan45); Assumes duties of executive officer 30Jan45 (per MR 30Jan45); entry of 30Jan45 of assuming duties of XO is erroneous (per MR 07Mar45); **WIA** not hosp 18Mar45 (pen w R hand) (per MR 15May45); Evac sk, TFRD to DofP 25Mar45 (per MR 25Mar45); REASG fm 71st Reinf Bn 13May45 (per MR 15May45); TFRD to Co D 17May45 (per MR 17May45) CIB eff 01Sep44 (13/44)	WIA 18Mar45
834.	Owen, Edward E. O-2006071	2LT	A, C, A	ASGD fm Co A as XO 01Apr45 (per MR 01Apr45); TFRD to Co A 03Apr45 (per MR 08Apr45) CIB 01Feb45 (28/45)	
835.	Owens, Obie G. 34981602	PVT	C	MOS 745 ASGD and joined fm 2nd Repl Dep 04Nov44 (per MR 09Nov44); evac sk 04Dec44; already evac sk, TFRD to DofP 05Dec44; RTD fm 2nd Repl Dep 08Jan45 (per MR 08Jan45); Evac sk 08Jan45 (per MR 08Jan45); Evac sk NOT LD 08Jan45 (per MR 23Jan45); fm Evac sk NOT LD to 3rd Repl Bn (per MR 23Jan45); REASG fm 3rd Repl Bn 23Jan45 (per MR 23Jan45); AWOL 2359 23Jan45 (per MR 01Feb45); RTD fm AWOL 1500 26Jan45 (per MR 01Feb45); Evac sk 02Feb45 (per MR 02Feb45); Already Evac sk, TFRD to DofP 05Feb45 (per MR 05Feb45); RTD fm 71st Reinf Bn 16Mar45 (per MR 16Mar45); Evac INJ 30Mar45 (per MR 30Mar45); Already evac INJ, TFRD to DofP 31Mar45 (per MR 31Mar45); RTD 05May45 (per MR 06May45) No discovered GO for CIB of GCM	
836.	Pack, James F. (or E.) 35767817	PVT	C, G	MOS 745 ASGD fm 2nd Repl Bn 14Jan44 per MR 18Jan44; Tfr in grade to G Co per MR 05Mar44 CIB FM 01Feb44 (14/44)	

837.	**Padilla**, Jose (NMI) 38005554	CPL-SGT-SSG	C	MOS 652 ASGD fr Co E 28Sep43; CPL pmtd to SGT per MR 02Dec43; evac **WIA** 14Dec43 per MR 17Dec43; RTD fm **WIA** 19Dec43 (per MR 23Dec43); pmtd SSG per MR 28Jan44; **WIA** (pen W L arm & forearm, LW dorsum, R hand shell frag 07Feb44; TFRD to DofP & DFR 23Feb44; already evac **WIA**, trfd to DofP and DFR 23Feb44 (change in hosp ID, MR 20May44) per MR 14Mar44; RTD fm DofP 11 Jun44 (13Jun44); evac sk 10Jul44; RTD fm sk 19Jul44 (MR 20Jul44); evac sk 30Jul44; already evac sk, TFRD to DofP/DFR 30Jul44 (05Aug44); REASG fm hosp 15Sep44; evac **WIA**, TFRD to DofP 28Oct44 CIB PFD (07/44); GCM (08/44)	WIA 14Dec43 WIA 07Feb44 WIA 23Feb44 WIA 28Oct44
838.	**Palkendo**, Andrew G. 33831087	PVT-PFC	C	MOS 745 ASGD 29May44 (09Jun44); PVT **WIA** (Pen wnd L foot – Germany) not hosp 18Dec44 per MR 03Jan45); Pmtd to PFC 07Jan45 (per MR 08Jan45); Duty 177 Evac **WIA**, TFRD to DofP 17Jan45 (per MR 17Jan45) CIB 01Sep44 (13/44); GCM (16/44)	WIA 18Dec44 WIA 17Jan45
839.	**Pallozzi,** Guiodo G. 32851432	PFC-CPL	C	MOS 746/653 ASGD & joined 07Feb44; evac **WIA** (BC Pen W L buttock shell frag) 31May44; already evac **WIA** TFRD to DofP/DFR 27Jun44 (MR 23Jul44); REASG but not jd fm 7th Repl Dep 17Aug44; joined 24Sep44; evac **WIA**, TFRD to DofP 31Oct44; REASG fm 2nd Repl Dep 22Nov44; evac sk, TFRD to DofP 26Nov44 (per MR 28Nov44); REASG fm 71st Repl Dep 08Dec44; promoted to CPL MOS 653 24Dec44; MIA 21Jan45 (per MR 23Jan45) **(POW 20JAN45);** Mstr POW reg gives rpt date of 21Jan45, parent unit as division artillery, Stalag 12A to 9B, repatriated CIB DP (07/44)	WIA 31May44 WIA 31Oct44 POW 20Jan45
840.	Palumbo, Ambrose J. 35066146	PVT	C	MOS 745 ASGD fm 2nd Repl Bn 14Jan44 per MR 18Jan44; Evac sk (nausea & abdominal pain) **(Unknown date)**; already evac sk TFRD to DofP/DFR 27Jun44 (MR 23Jul44) CIB FM 01Feb44 (14/44)	
841.	**Pape,** Frederick D. 33351809	PVT-PFC	C	MOS 803 (Deployed w/the company, is on the Pine Camp menu as PVT) Pmtd PFC 10Aug43; evac **WIA** 16Dec43 (per MR 27Dec43)(earlier entry of MIA 14Dec43 per MR 25Dec43 is erroneous); already evac **WIA** TFRD to DofP, DFR per MR 19Jan44; **(Missing entry of RTD)**; already evac sk **(Unknown date)(Missing entry of evac WIA)**; already evac **WIA** TFRD to 2677 HQ Co 13Jul44 CIB DP as PFC in C Co (07/44)	WIA 16Dec43 **WIA unk**

842.	Papst, Stanley J. PCM-C 33110654	PFC	C	(Deployed w/the company, is on Pine Camp menu as PFC) MIA 13Sep43 DFR (per MR 24Sep43) **(POW 13Sep43);** MIA13SEP43 per ANB; Mstr POW reg gives rpt date of 13Sep43, Stalag 3B, repatriated CIB MIA as PFC in C Co (05/44); 01Jan44 per CC;	POW 13Sep43
843.	Parrone, Alfred N. 32776539	**PVT**	C	**(Unknown date of assignment)** Tfr in grade to G Co per MR 05Mar44 No discovered GO for CIB or GCM	
844.	**Pass**, John E. 34689494	PVT	C	MOS 745 ASGD fm 2nd Repl Bn 14Jan44 per MR 18Jan44; evac **WIA** (LW scalp shell frag) 18Feb44; TFRD to DofP & DFR 27Feb44; already evac **WIA**, trfd to DofP and DFR 27Feb44 per MR 15Mar44 CIB FM 01Feb44 (14/44)	WIA 18Feb44
845.	**Patterson,** Jack H. (R.) 36904865	PVT	C	MOS 745/504/604 ASGD fm 3rd Repl Bn 24Jan45 (per MR 26Jan45); Evac **WIA**, TFRD to DofP 19Mar45 (per MR 19Mar45); RTD fm 71st Reinf Bn 17May45 (per MR 17May45) CIB 01Mar45 (10/45); GCM as PFC (32/45)	WIA 19Mar45
846.	Patterson, William W. 35221625	PVT-PFC	C	MOS **745** ASGD fm 2nd Repl Bn 14Jan44 per MR 18Jan44; evac sk (trenchfoot bilateral) 24Feb44 per MR 02Mar44**;** already evac sk tfrd to DofP & DFR 10Apr44 (per MR 24Apr44); RTD fm DofP 26May44; evac sk, TFRD to DofP 03Sep44; AWOL 0630 03Jul44; changed to evac sk 03Jul44 (MR 04Jul44); RTD fm sk 06Jul44; REASG not joined from 2nd Repl Dep 24Sep44; joined 26Sep44 (per MR 27Sep44); promoted to PFC 07Oct44; evac sk, TFRD to DofP 03Nov44 CIB PFD (07/44)	
847.	Paulsen, Howard L. 37566653	PVT	C, G	MOS 745 ASGD fm 2nd Repl Bn 14Jan44 per MR 18Jan44; Tfr in grade to G Co per MR 05Mar44 No discovered GO for CIB or GCM	
848.	Pavelich, Nick (NMI) 35573860	PFC	C	MOS 745/607 ASGD fr 2 Repl Dep 29May44 (per MR 14Jun44); MIA 21Jan45 (per MR 23Jan45) **(POW 20JAN45);** Mstr POW reg gives rpt date of 21Jan45, parent unit as division artillery, Stalag 11B, repatriated GCM (08/44); CIB 01Sep44 (13/44)	POW 20Jan45
849.	**Pawlik, Joseph W. 36587098**	**PVT-PFC**	C	MOS 745 ASGD fm 7th Repl Dep 25Sep43; **KIA** 15Dec43 (per MR 20Dec43) (buried in Sicily-Rome Cemetery); KIA15Dec43 per div & 157 cas list; ABMC 15Dec43, PH No discovered GO for CIB or GCM	**KIA 15Dec43**
850.	**Payton**, Forest (NMI) 35711238	PVT-PFC	C	MOS 531/521 **(Unknown date of assignment) (Missing entry for evac)**; RTD fm 2nd Repl Dep 11Jan44 per MR 13Jan44; Pmtd to PFC 04Mar44 per MR 12Mar44; Evac sk, TFRD to DofP 27Sep44; REASG fm hosp 01Oct44; evac **SWIA**, TFRD to DofP 27Oct44 CIB PFD (07/44); GCM (08/44); CIB FM 01Feb44 (14/44)	WIA 27Oct44

851.	**Peck, Ray A. PCM-C 20837738 (Delta, CO)**	**SGT**	C	PVT in C Co per Induction Roster, 16Sep40; Deployed w/the company, is on the Pine Camp menu as SGT) MIA 16Aug43 (per MR 21Aug43) (DFR per MR 07Sep43) **(believed drowned in landing accident, still MIA; commemorated in Sicily-Rome Cemetery);** BSM no PH CIB MIA as SGT in C Co (05/44); 01Jan44 per CC	**MIA 16Aug43**
852.	**Pederson, Vernon E. 36251738**	**SGT**	C	MOS 653 ASGD fm 63rd Inf Div 26Jan45 (per MR 01Feb45); From MIA 30Mar45 (per MR 02Apr45) to **KIA** 30Mar45 (per MR 05Apr45) (buried in Lorraine Cemetery); KIA30Mar45 per Div, 157 & ANB; ABMC 30Mar45, PH CIB 01Mar45 (10/45); GCM (8/45)	**KIA 30Mar45**
853.	Pedery, Steve E. (Pedfry) 35065889	PVT	C, G	MOS 745 ASGD fm 2nd Repl Bn 14Jan44 per MR 18Jan44; Tfr in grade to G Co per MR 05Mar44 as PEDERY CIB FM 01Feb44 (14/44)	
854.	**Pellegrino, Joseph C. 32217253 PCM-C**	**PVT**	C	(Deployed w/the company, is on the Pine Camp menu) Sk evac 17Jul43, RTD fm sk evac 18Jul43 (per MR 24Jul43); MIA 13Sep43 DFR (per MR 24Sep43) (per MR 12Oct43, **KIA** 14Sep43) (buried in USA); KIA14Sep43 per div cas list; KIA13SEP43 per 157 list; MIA/KIA13SEP43 per ANB; not on ABMC reg No discovered GO for CIB or GCM	**KIA 14Sep43**
855.	**Peluso, Louis (NMI) O-1302873**	**2LT**	C	**(Unknown date of assignment, not on Pine Camp menu) KIA** 12Sep43 (per MR 18Sep43) (buried in Sicily-Rome Cemetery); KIA12Sep43 per div & 157 cas list -- GUNSHOT; ABMC 12Sep43, PH No discovered GO for CIB	**KIA 12Sep43**
856.	**Pena,** Rudesino F. 32904857	PVT- CPL	C	MOS 745/653 ASGD fm 2nd Repl Bn 14Jan44 per MR 18Jan44; pmtd to PFC 01May44; promoted to CPL (per MR 05Aug44); evac **WIA** 24Sep44; REASG fm 2nd Repl Dep 09Nov44 (per MR 10Nov44); promoted to SGT 24Nov44; evac sk, TFRD to DofP 25Nov44 (per MR 28Nov44) CIB (01/44); 01Feb44 per CC	WIA 24Sep44
857.	Penney, James S., Jr. O-1332526	2LT	C	ASGD, but placed on DS with 71st Reinf Bn 01Apr45 (per MR 08Apr45); Released fm DS with 71st Reinf Bn 02Apr45 (per MR 08Apr45); Assumed Command 17May45 (per MR 17May45); Relieved as CO 28May45 (per MR 28May45) CIB 01May45 (15/45)	
858.	Penny, Raymond L. 35803150	PVT	C, G	MOS 745 ASGD fm 2nd Repl Bn 14Jan44 per MR 18Jan44; Tfr in grade to G Co per MR 05Mar44 CIB PFD (07/44)	
859.	Pereira, Francisco A. O-1332527	2LT	C	ASGD, but placed on DS with 71st Reinf Bn 01Apr45 (per MR 08Apr45); Released fm DS with 71st Reinf Bn 02Apr45 (per MR 08Apr45) No discovered GO for CIB	

860.	Perino, Bruno D. 38778877	PVT	F, C	MOS 745 ASGD fm Co F 22Feb45 (per MR 27Feb45); AWOL 0600 15Mar45 (per MR 17Mar45); RTD fm AWOL 1000 20Mar45 (per MR 23Mar45) CIB 01Oct44 (13/44)	
861.	Perrone, Alfred N. 32776539	PVT	B, C	ASGD fm Co B 14Jan44 per MR 15Jan44 CIB (04/44); 01Jan44 per CC; 1st Squad, 1st Platoon, G (C?) Co	
862.	Persichetti, Joseph L. 33693227	PVT	C, G	MOS 745 ASGD fm 2nd Repl Bn 14Jan44 per MR 18Jan44; Tfr in grade to G Co per MR 05Mar44 CIB PFD (07/44); 3rd Squad, 1st Platoon, G Co	
863.	Peterhausen, Bearington (NMI) 35174827	PVT	C, G	MOS 745 ASGD fm 2nd Repl Bn 18Dec43 (per MR 22Dec43); Tfr in grade to G Co per MR 05Mar44 No discovered GO for CIB or GCM	
864.	Peterson, Biss (NMI) 34608644	PVT-PFC	C	MOS 745/675 ASGD fm 7th Repl Dep 25Sep43; evac sk 17Nov43 per MR 21Nov43; already evac sk TFRD to DofP, DFR per MR 18Dec43; RTD fm DofP 01Jan44 per MR 06Jan44; evac sk (Pharyngitis) 09Feb44; RTD 15Feb44; Pmtd to PFC 04Mar44 per MR 12Mar44; evac sk 30May44; RTD fm sk 08Jun44; evac **WIA** 24Sep44; REASG & joined fm hosp 30Sep44; MIA 21Jan45 (per MR 23Jan45) **(POW 20JAN45);** Mstr POW reg gives rpt date of 21Jan45 as PFC, parent unit as division artillery, Stalad 11B, repatriated CIB (01/44 - 01Jan44 per CC); GCM as PFC (08/44)	WIA 24Sep44 POW 20Jan45
865.	Peterson, Grant E. (Delta, CO)	PFC	C	Induction Roster, 16Sep40	
866.	Petrovich, Theodore J. 32927024	PVT	C, G	MOS 745 ASGD fm 2nd Repl Bn 14Jan44 per MR 18Jan44; Tfr in grade to G Co per MR 05Mar44 CIB FM 01Feb44 (14/44)	
867.	Phelps, Roland A. SN NA (Delta, CO)	PVT	C	Induction Roster, 16Sep40	
868.	Phelps, Russell R. 35093024	PVT	C, G	MOS 745 ASGD fm 2nd Repl Bn 14Jan44 per MR 18Jan44; evac sk 20Jan44 per MR 22Jan44; RTD fm sk 04Feb44; Tfr in grade to G Co per MR 05Mar44; KIA20Mar45 per Div, 157 & ANB; not on ABMC reg CIB PFD (07/44); GCM (08/45);	(KIA 20Mar45 in G Co)

869.	**Phillips,** Fred S. 35093024	PVT-PFC-CPL-SGT	C	MOS 745/653 ASGD fm 2nd Repl Bn 18Dec43 per MR 22Dec43; evac sk 04Jan44 per MR 06Jan44; already evac sk TFRD to DofP, DFR per MR 22Jan44; RTD fm DofP 17Mar44 per MR 21Mar44; evac **WIA** 31May44 (BC SFW lac R small toe mild) (per MR 11Jun44); RTD fm **WIA** 11Jun44; pmtd to PFC 01Jul44 (MR 02Jul44); evac sk 17Jul44; already evac sk, TFRD to 2nd Rep Dep, not dptd 19Jul44; s/b ATCHD & jnd (MR 23Jul44); RTD fm sk 22Jul44 (MR 24Jul44); evac **WIA**, TFRD to DofP 23Sep44; REASG but not joined fm 2nd Repl Dep 04Oct44; joined 05Oct44 already evac sk **(Unknown date);** Promoted to CPL 24Nov44; evac sk, TFRD to DofP 05Dec44; REASG but DS to 71st Reinf Bn 03Apr45 (per MR 11Apr45); Relieved of DS to 71st Reinf Bn 11Apr45 (per MR 11Apr45); Pmtd to SGT 04May45 (per MR 04May45 CIB PFD (07/44); GCM CPL (16/44)	WIA 31May44 WIA 23Sep44
870.	**Phillips,** Holice W. 34939929	PVT-PFC	C	MOS 745 ASGD fm 3rd Repl Bn 24Jan45 (per MR 26Jan45); PMTD to PFC 06Mar45 (per MR 06Mar45); Evac **WIA**, TFRD to DofP 18Mar45 (per MR 18Mar45); REASG but DS to 71st Reinf Bn 04Apr45 (per MR 11Apr45); Relieved of DS to 71st Reinf Bn 11Apr45 (per MR 11Apr45) CIB 01Mar45 (10/45); GCM as PFC "Halice" (32/45)	WIA 18Mar45
871.	Phillips, James L. 33776745	PVT-PFC	C	MOS 745 ASGD fm 2nd Repl Dep 24Feb44 per MR 05Mar44; pmtd to PFC 01May44; evac sk 14Jun44 (16Jun44); already evac sk, TRFD to DofP 16Aug44; REASG but not jd fm 7th Repl Dep 17Aug44; joined 24Sep44; evac sk, TFRD to DofP 05Oct44; REASG fm 2nd Repl Dep 11Nov44; evac sk, TFRD to DofP 19Nov44 CIB (04/44); 01Apr44 per CC; CIB PFD (07/44)	
872.	**Phillips,** John B. 34706078	PVT-PFC	C	MOS 745 ASGD 13Aug43; evac sk 28Sep43 (per MR 02Oct43); already evac sk, TFRD to DofP and DFR per MR 04Nov43; erroneously rptd on 04Nov43 as DFR should be RTD per MR 05Nov43; evac sk 05Nov43 per MR 07Nov43; already evac sk TFRD to DofP, DFR per MR 15Dec43; RTD fm DofP 08Apr44 (MR 17Apr44); evac sk 09Apr44 (MR 20Apr44); RTD 13Apr44 (MR 20Apr44); evac sk 15Apr44 (MR 20Apr44); RTD 20Apr44 (per MR 24Apr44); LWA not-hosp 14May44 (MR 19May44); evac sk 23May44 (MR 27May44); RTD 29May44; **(Missing entry of evac sk)**; already attached fm 2nd Repl Det reld fm atchment (per MR 05Aug44); ASGD fm 2nd Repl Dep 08Aug44 (31Aug44); evac sk, TFRD to DofP 03Nov44; **(Missing entry of RTD)**; **WIA** not hosp 10Oct44 (per MR 18Oct44) CIB PFD (07/44); GCM as PVT (08/44)	WIA 18Oct44

873.	Pickering, Frank A. 20110054	PVT	C, RHQ	MOS 345 ASGD & jnd fm 2nd Repl Dep 24 Feb44 per MR 10Mar44; evac sk (FUO) 30May44; RTD fm sk 08Jun44; TFRD to RHQ 23Jul44 CIB (04/44 - 01Mar44 per CC); CIB PFD (07/44); GCM PFC in RHQ (08/45)	
874.	Pickrell, Robert W. 19132814	CPL	C	MOS 653 ASGD fr 2 Repl Dep 04Jun44 (14Jun44); evac sk 31Aug44; already evac sk, TFRD to DofP 01Sep44 CIB FM 01Sep44 (14/44); CIB 01Jul44 (34/45)	
875.	**Pieczynaki,** Bernard D. 32212532	PFC-CPL	C	MOS 745/653 (Deployed w/the company, is on the Pine Camp menu as PFC) Sk evac 18ul43 (Per MR 20Jul43), RTD fm sk 19Jul43 (per MR 25Aug43); **WIA** evac 12Sep43 (per MR 18Sep43); **(Missing entry of RTD)**; evac sk 24Nov43 (non-battle GSW to big toe) (per MR 29Nov43); already evac TFD to DofP, DFR per MR 14Dec43; RTD fm DofP 01Apr44 (per MR 11Apr44); pmtd to CPL **(Unknown date)**; Evac **WIA** 08May44 (MR 10May44); to DofP/DFR 14May44 (MR 23 May44); RTD fm DofP 15Jun44 (16Jun44); evac sk, TFRD to DofP 30Aug44; REASG fm hosp 15Sep44 (per MR 16Sep44); evac **WIA**, TFRD to DofP 25Sep44; REASG but not joined fm 2nd Repl Dep 04Oct44; joined 07Oct44; evac sk, TFRD to DopP 20Nov44 CIB as CPL in C Co (03/44); 01Jan44 per CC; CIB PFD (07/44); GCM (08/44)	WIA 12Sep43 WIA 08May44 WIA 25Sep44
876.	**Pierce, Clarence E. 17010733**	**PVT-PFC**	C	MOS 652 ASGD fr 2nd Repl Dep 04Jun44 (11Jun44); pmtd to PFC 01Jul44 (MR 02Jul44); MIA 13Dec44 (per MR 14Dec44); Fm MIA 13Dec44 to **KIA** 13Dec44 (per MR 21Dec44) (buried in USA); KIA13Dec44 per div & 157 list; MIA/KIA13DEC44 per ANB; not on ABMC reg CIB 01Sep44 (13/44)	**KIA 13Dec44**
877.	Pilius, William O. 11064953 PCM-C	PVT-PFC	C	(Deployed w/the company, is on the Pine Camp menu as PVT) Sk evac 25Jul43, RTD fm sk 29Jul43; MIA 13Sep43 DFR (per MR 24Sep43) **(POW 13Sep43);** Mstr POW reg gives rpt date of 13Sep43, Stalag 2B, repatriated CIB FM 01Jan44 (14/44)	POW 13Sep43
878.	Podell, Charles PCM-C SN NA	PVT	C	On Pine Camp menu	
879.	**Pollock,** Sidney (NMI) 33593131	PVT-PFC-CPL	C	MOS 745 ASGD fm 7th Repl Dep 25Sep43; **(Missing entry of evac WIA)**; already evac **WIA**, DFR per MR 23Nov43; RTD fm DofP 17Mar44 per MR 21Mar44; pmtd to PFC 01May44; evac **WIA** 31May44; RTD from **WIA** 02Jun44; promoted to CPL MOS 653 07Oct44; evac sk, TFRD to DofP 21Oct44 CIB (03/44); 01Jan44 per CC; GCM (08/44)	**WIA unk** WIA 31May44

880.	Popuch, Leonard S. 36809920	SGT-SSG	C	MOS 653 ASGD fm 44th Inf Div 25Jan45 (per MR 01Feb45); PMTD to SSG 09Mar45 (per MR 09Mar45); TDY to UK 23May45 (per MR 23May45) GCM (32/45)	
881.	Posluszny, Anthony 36667922	PFC	C	MOS 745 ASGD fm 71st Repl Bn 09Dec44; MIA 21Jan45 (per MR 23Jan45) **(POW 20JAN45);** Mstr POW reg gives rpt date as 21Jan45 as PFC, parent unit as division artillery, Stalag 11B, repatriated CIB 01Jan45 (01/45)	POW 20Jan45
882.	Powell, Brabson A. 38390843	PVT-PFC	C	MOS 745 ASGD fm 2nd Repl Bn 14Jan44 per MR 18Jan44; evac sk (FUO) 15Feb44; RTD fm sk 02Mar44 per MR 10Mar44; pmtd to PFC 01Jul44 (MR 02Jul44); evac sk, TFRD to DofP 05Dec44 CIB PFD (07/44)	
883.	Prell, Henry 35159070	PFC	C, 1HQ	**(Unknown date of assignment)** TFRD to 1HQ 02Feb45 (per MR 02Feb45); DOI21Mar45 per div & 157 list; ABMC 21Mar45, Lorraine Cemetery PH CIB (GO 4/44); 01Feb44 per Corrected copy;	(DOI 21Mar45 in 1HQ)
884.	Presor, William J. 12148689	PFC	C	**(Unknown date of assignment, not on Pine Camp menu)** Sk evac 25Jul43 No discovered GO for CIB or GCM	
885.	Preston, William H. PCM-C	CPL	C	On Pine Camp menu	
886.	**Prince, Roscoe (NMI) 35206974 PCM-C**	**CPL**	C	(Deployed w/the company, is on the Pine Camp menu as PFC) **KIA** 02Dec43 per MR 10Dec43 (buried in Sicily-Rome Cemetery); KIA as CPL in C Co 02Dec43 per div & 157 list -- SHRAPNEL; ABMC 02Dec43, PH No discovered GO for CIB or GCM	**KIA 02Dec43**
887.	Privette, George C. 34669741	PVT-PFC	C	ASGD fm Co A 14Jan44 per MR 15Jan44; Pmtd to PFC 01May44; evac sk, TFRD to DofP 27Sep44; REASG fm 2nd Repl Dep 18Oct44; evac sk, TFRD to DofP 25Nov44 (per MR 28Nov44) CIB (01/44 - 01Jan44 per CC)	
888.	**Proctor**, William F. 35928985	PVT	C	**(Unknown date of assignment)** Evac **WIA**, TFRD to DofP 15Jan45 (per MR 15Jan45) No discovered GO for CIB or GCM	WIA 15Jan45
889.	Profazren, George (NMI) 33141272 PCM-K (Profozich)	PVT	K, C, RHQ	PVT in K Co per Pine Camp memu AS Profozich **(Unknown date of assignment)** TFRD to RHQ 07Aug43 CIB as PVT in RHQ 01Jan44 (03/44 CC); GCM (08/45)	
890.	Propulipac, Michael W. SN NA PCM-C	SGT-PVT	C, L	(Deployed w/the company, is on Pine Camp menu) TFRD in grade of PVT to Co L per MR 17Nov43; KIA07Dec43 per div& 157 list; not on ABMC reg No discovered GO for CIB or GCM **NOT ON MR 17NOV 43**	(KIA 07Dec43 in L Co)

891.	Pruitt, Charles D. 13121085	SGT	C	MOS 653 ASGD fm 70th Inf Div 26Jan45 (per MR 01Feb45) CIB 01Mar45 (10/45); GCM (8/45)	
892.	**Pullman**, Frank T. 33612701	PVT-PFC	C	MOS 745 ASGD 05Jun44 (09Jun44); PVT evac sk 15Jul44 (MR 16Jul44); already evac sk, TFRD to 2nd Rep Dep, not dptd 19Jul44; s/b ATCHD & jnd (MR 23Jul44); already evac sk, relieved fm atchment fr 2nd Repl Det (per MR 05Aug44); MOS 745 ASGD fm 2nd Repl Dep 10Oct44; promoted to PFC 20Nov44 (per MR 27Nov44); evac **WIA**, TFRD to DofP 03Dec44 CIB 01Sep44 (13/44)	WIA 03Dec44
893.	**Quinn, Thomas J. 31065219 PCM-C**	**PVT**	C	(Deployed w/the company, is on Pine Camp menu as PVT) died of unknown fever 16Jul43 (per MR 18Jul43) (buried in Sicily-Rome Cemetery) DIED OF DISEASE 16JUL43 -- NOT ON DIV LIST CIB FM as PVT in C Co 01Jan44 (14/44)	**Died 18Jul43**
894.	Rabe, Irving L. 42131045	PVT	C, D	MOS 745 ASGD fm 3rd Repl Bn 20Dec44 (per MR 21Dec44); Evac sk, TFRD to DofP 03Jan45 (per MR 03Jan45); REASG fm 3rd Repl Bn 04Feb45 (per MR 04Feb45); TFRD to Co D 06Feb45 (per MR 06Feb45) CIB 01Jan45 (01/45); GCM as PFC in D Co (26/45)	
895.	Race, Jefferson D. 35124550	CPL	C	MOS 653/668 (Deployed w/the company, is on the Pine Camp menu as PFC) Evac sk 13Dec43 (per MR 16Dec43); REASG 17Dec44; evac INJ 27Dec44; RTD fm sk 27Dec43 (per MR 31Dec43); Evac sk 30Nov44; already evac sk, TFRD to DofP 01Dec44; REASGD fm 71st Reinf Bn 19Mar45 (per MR 19Mar45); Evac sk 15 Feb45 (per MR 15Feb45); Already Evac sk, TFRD to DofP 17Feb45 (per MR 17Feb45); RTD fm sk 02Jan45 (per MR 02Jan45) CIB as CPL in C Co (04/44); 01Jan44 per CC; GCM (02/44)	
896.	Rayborn, Stanley H., Sr. SN NA	PVT	C	MOS 745 ATCHD fm 71st Reinf Bn 17May45 (per MR 18May45); Change from ATCH to ASGD 18May45 (per MR 18May45) No discovered GO for CIB or GCM	
897.	**Reames**, James R. 36668593	PVT	C	MOS 745 ASGD fm 2nd Repl Bn 14Jan44 per MR 18Jan44; **WIA** 10Feb44, not hosp, perf GSW and FCC 3rd & 4th fingers left hand; evac sk (defective vision bilateral) 22Feb44; RTD 27Feb44 per MR 03Mar44; evac **WIA** (BC pen W L wrist & R buttock, perf W R let frag 31May44; already evac **WIA** TFRD to DofP/DFR 28Jun44 (MR 23Jul44); RTD fm DofP 04Aug44; evac sk, TFRD to DofP 04Aug44; REASG fm 3rd Repl Bn 28Dec44; evac sk, TFRD to DofP 29Dec44 CIB FM 01Feb44 (14/44)	WIA 10Feb44 WIA 31May44

898.	Rebovich, John (NMI) 13048742	SGT-PVT	C	MOS 653, duty MOS 745 SGT in K Co per PCCM42; ASGD fr Co K 23Aug43 as PVT; MIA 13Sep43 DFR (per MR 24Sep43 **(POW 13Sep43);** Mstr POW reg gives rpt date of 13Sep43, Stalag 2B, repatriated CIB FM as PVT in C Co 01Jan44 (14/44) POW 13/9/43	POW 13Sep43)
899.	Reed, Earl K. 37840765	PVT	C	MOS 745 ASGD fm 3rd Repl Bn 20Dec44 (per MR 21Dec44); MIA 21Jan45 (per MR 23Jan45) **(POW 20JAN45);** MIA21JAN45 per ANB; NOT ON MSTR POW REGISTER; POW20JAN45 PER MR; not on ABMC reg CIB 01Jan45 (01/45)	POW 20Jan45
900.	Reed, Eugene PCM-C 38005315	PFC	C, SV	On Pine Camp menu CIB 01Apr45 (28/45) in SV	
901.	Reeves, Paul W. PCM-1 (Washington, CO)	2LT-MAJ	C, 1HQ	2LT in C Co per Induction Roster, 16Sep40; MAJ XO of 1/157 per Pine Camp menu CIB as MAJ regimental officer (01/44 - 01Jan44 per CC)	
902.	Renfrow, Louis A. PCM-C 20837740 (Delta, CO)	PFC	C	(Original member from Denver, CO, as PVT; is on Pine Camp menu as PFC) MIA 13Sep43 DFR (per MR 24Sep43) (POW 13Sep43); Mstr POW reg gives rpt date of 13Sep43, Stalag 2B, repatriated CIB MIA as PFC in C Co (05/44); 01Jan44 per CC	POW 13Sep43
903.	Renfrow, Melvern (Delta, CO)	PVT	C	Induction Roster, 16Sep40	
904.	Renzo, Albert A. (Rengo) 33923221	PVT	C	ATCHD fm 71st Reinf Bn 17May45 (per MR 18May45); Change from ATCH to ASGD 18May45 (per MR 18May45) GCM (32/45)	
905.	Rias, Arnulfo A. 18199488	SGT	C	GCM (32/45)	
906.	Ricard, Raoul E. 31469490	PVT-PFC	C	MOS 745 ASGD fm 3rd Repl Bn 20Dec44 (per MR 21Dec44); evac sk 20Dec44 (30Dec44); name corrected fm "Richard" to "Ricard" (per MR 30Dec44); Already evac sk, TFRD to DofP 02Jan45 (per MR 02Jan45); REASG fm 3rd Repl Bn 17Jan45 (per MR 17Jan45); PMTD to PFC 06Mar45 (per MR 06Mar45); Evac sk 14Apr45 (per MR 14Apr45); RTD fm sk 22Apr45 (per MR 22Apr45) CIB 01Jan45 (01/45); GCM as PFC (32/45)	
907.	Riccardo, George J. 32204938 PCM-C	PVT	C	(Deployed w/the company, is on the Pine Camp menu as PVT) Pmtd PFC 01Jul43 (Fm MR 20Jul43), sk evac 18Jul43 (Per MR 20Jul43); RTD fm sk 23 or 28Jul43 (per MR 25Aug43); MIA 13Sep43 DFR (per MR 24Sep43) **(POW 13Sep43);** Mstr POW reg gives rpt date of 13Sep43 as PVT, Stalag 2B, repatriated CIB MIA as PFC in C Co (05/44); 01Jan44 per CC	POW 13Sep43

908.	Richardson, Thomas L. 34760025	PVT-PFC	C	MOS 745 ASGD 13Aug43; pmtd PFC 01May44; erroneously rptd MIA 25May44 on MR 27May44 – duty (06Jun44); evac sk 15Aug44 (18Aug44); RTD 18Aug44; evac sk, TFRD to DofP 20Nov44 CIB (01/44 - 01Jan44 per CC); GCM as PFC (08/44)	
909.	Richert, Jack A. 36769322	PVT	C	MOS 745 ASGD fm 2nd Repl Dep 04Jun44 (15Jun44); AWOL 0700 08Jun44 (18Jun44); RTD fm AWOL 0700 12Jun44 (18Jun44); evac sk 01Aug44 (per 02Aug44); already evac sk TFRD to DofP/DFR 01Aug44 (per 06Aug44); REASG fm 3rd Repl Bn 28Jan45 (per MR 28Jan45); **(Missing entry of evac in Feb)**; Already Evac sk, TFRD to DofP 13Feb45 (per MR 13Feb45); REASG fm 2nd Reinf Dep 02Mar45 (per MR 02Mar45); TFRD to 1HQ 27May45 (per MR 27May45) CIB 01Mar45 (10/45)	
910.	Richter, Lawrence 36228770	CPL-SGT	C	MOS 653 ASGD fm 70th Inf Div 26Jan45 (per MR 01Feb45); Pmtd to SGT 14Apr45 (per MR 14Apr45); Evac sk 24Apr45 (per MR 24Apr45); Already evac sk, TFRD to DofP 25Apr45 (per MR 25Apr45) GCM (8/45)	
911.	Ridley, James L.	PVT-PFC	C, G	MOS 745 ASGD fm 7th Repl Dep 25Sep43; promoted PFC 01Jan44 per MR 05Jan44; Tfr in grade to G Co per MR 05Mar44; KIA31MAY44 per div & 157 list; MIA/KIA31MAY44 per ANB; not on ABMC reg No discovered GO for CIB or GCM	(KIA 31MAY44 in G Co)
912.	**Riley, Clarence (NMI) Jr. 20837754 PCM-C (Delta, CO)**	PVT-PFC	C	Induction Roster, 16Sep40 as PVT; PFC in C Co per Pine Camp menu; MIA 16Aug43 (per MR 21Aug43) (DFR per MR 07Sep43) **(believed drowned in landing accident. Still MIA. Commemorated in Sicily-Rome Cemetery);** death 16AUG43 per div list; KIA16AUG43 per 157 list -- BELIEVED DROWNED; ABMC 16Aug43, sill MIA, BSM -- no PH CIB MIA as PFC in C Co (05/44); 01Jan44 per CC	**MIA 16Aug43**
913.	Riley, David L. 38712101	PVT	C, 1HQ	MOS 745 ASGD fm 3rd Repl Bn 24Jan45 (per MR 26Jan45); Evac sk, TFRD to DofP 24Feb45 (per MR 24Feb45); **(Missing entry of RTD)**; Evac INJ, TFRD to DofP 16Mar45 (per MR 16Mar45);REASG fm 71st Reinf Bn, and placed on DS with 71st Reinf Bn 30Mar45 (per MR 03Apr45); REASG fm 71st Reinf Bn, and placed on DS with 71st Reinf Bn 30Mar45 (per MR 03Apr45) CIB 01Mar45 (10/45); GCM as PFC in 1HQ (33/45)	
914.	Ring, Wilfred L. 36765644	PVT-PFC	C	MOS 745 ASGD fm 2nd Repl Dep 24Feb44 per MR 05Mar44; pmtd to PFC 01Jul44 (MR 02Jul44); TFRD to 1HQ 15Sep44 CIB PFD 07/44	

915.	**Rios**, Arnulfo A. 18199488	SGT	C	MOS 653 ASGD fm 103rd Inf Div 26Jan45 (per MR 01Feb45); Evac **WIA** 28Mar45 (per MR 28Mar45); Already evac **WIA**, TFRD to DofP 30Mar45 (per MR 30Mar45); REASG fm 71st Reinf Bn 11Apr45 (per MR 11Apr45) No discovered GO for CIB or GCM	WIA 28Mar45
916.	Ritzel, Frank Jr. 33779205	PFC	C	MOS 745 ASGD fm 36th Inf Div 26Jan45 (per MR 01Feb45); AWOL 2359 30Jan45 (per MR 03Feb45); AWOL to Confinement 09Feb45 (per MR 10Feb45); RTD fm Confinement 10Feb45 (per MR 10Feb45) No discovered GO for CIB or GCM	
917.	Rizzotti, John R. PCM-G 32193420	PFC	G, C	**(Unknown date of assignment, is on Pine Camp menu as PFC in G Co)** Evac sk 12Sep43 (per MR 20Sep43) CIB FM as PFC in C Co 01Jan44 (14/44)	
918.	Roach, Cletus W. PCM-C 38006200	SGT	C	(Deployed w/the company, is on the Pine Camp menu as CPL) Evac sk 30Aug43 (per MR 31Aug43); RTD fm evac sk 03Sep43; MIA 13Sep43 DFR (per MR 24Sep43) **(POW 13Sep43);** Mstr POW reg gives rpt date of 13Sep43, Stalag Luft 3, repatriated CIB MIA as SGT in C Co (05/44); 01Jan44 per CC; CIB FM 01Jan44 (14/44);	POW 13Sep43
919.	Roach, Emery 34839681	PFC	C	GCM (32/45)	
920.	Roberts, Elwood (NMI) 6666802	1SG	C, B	**(Unknown date of assignment)** Erron rptd evac sk 02Oct, s/b TFRD to Co B 01Oct44 (per MR 03Oct44) CIB (04/44); 01Mar44 per CC	
921.	Roberts, Jim PCM-F 20837742 (Delta, CO)	PVT	C, F	PVT in C Co per Induction Roster, 16Sep40; PVT in F Co per Pine Camp menu CIB as PVT in F Co (01/44 - 01Jan44 per CC)	
922.	Roberts, Melford 38698253	PVT	C	MOS 745 ASGD fm 3rd Repl Bn 20Dec44 (per MR 21Dec44); Evac sk, TFRD to DofP 11Jan45 (per MR 11Jan45) CIB 01Jan45 (01/45)	
923.	**Robinson,** Dewey (NMI) 35680744	PVT	C	MOS 745 ASGD fm 7th Repl Dep 25Sep43; evac **WIA** 15Nov43 per MR 17Nov43; already evac **WIA** TFRD to DofP, DFR per MR 18Dec43 CIB FM 01Jan44 (14/44)	WIA 15Nov43
924.	**Robinson, George H.** 34760111	**PVT**	C	MOS 745 ASGD 13Aug43; MIA 13Sep43, DFR (per MR 09Nov43) (**KIA**, per adjutant's notebook. (Buried in USA); KIA10OCT43 per 157 list; MIA/KIA13SEP43 per ANB -- NOT ON DIV LIST; not on ABMC reg No discovered GO for CIB or GCM	**KIA 13Sep43**
925.	Robley, Donald L. SN NA	PVT	C	MOS 745 ATCHD fm 71st Reinf Bn 17May45 (per MR 18May45); Change from ATCH to ASGD 18May45 (per MR 18May45) No discovered GO for CIB or GCM	

926.	Rodda, Paul M. SN NA	PVT	C	MOS 745 ATCHD fm 71st Reinf Bn 17May45 (per MR 18May45); Change from ATCH to ASGD 18May45 (per MR 18May45) No discovered GO for CIB or GCM	
927.	Rodenbaugh, Robert C. 33941474	PVT	C	MOS 745 ASGD fm 3rd Repl Bn 20Dec44 (per MR 21Dec44); MIA 21Jan45 (per MR 23Jan45) **(POW 20JAN45);** Mstr POW reg gives no unit ID and no rpt date, Stalag 12 to 9B, repatriated CIB 01Jan45 (01/45)	POW 20Jan45
928.	**Rodriguez**, Antonio 39588742	PVT	C	MOS 745 ASGD fm 3rd Repl Bn 20Dec44 (per MR 21Dec44); Evac **WIA**, TFRD to DofP 14Jan45 (per MR 14Jan45) CIB 01Jan45 (01/45)	WIA 15Jan45
929.	Rogers, Ralph E. 35815084	PVT	C	MOS 745 ATCHD fm 71st Reinf Bn 17May45 (per MR 18May45); Change from ATCH to ASGD 18May45 (per MR 18May45) GCM (32/45)	
930.	Rogo, Jacob J. 42039132	PVT	C, B	MOS 745 ASGD 29May44 (per MR 09Jun44); TFRD to 2nd Repl Dep but not departed 19Jul44; s/b ATCHD & jnd (MR 23Jul44); already attached fm 2nd Repl Det reld fm atchment (per MR 05Aug44) CIB 01Sep44 (13/44)	
931.	Rolves, Wilbert V. 36482701	PVT	C	MOS 603 ASGD fm 2nd Repl Dep per MR 11Dec43; MIA 15Dec43, DFR per MR 25Dec43 **(POW 15Dec43);** MIA15DEC43 per ANB; Mstr POW reg gives rpt date of "15 1K 43" w/o unit ID, Stalag 13D, repatriated CIB FM 01Jan44 (14/44)	POW 15Dec43
932.	Romero, Jose R. 38006149	CPL-SGT	C	MOS 056/405 On Pine Camp menu as CPL in C Co; Evac sk 18Apr44 (per MR 19Apr44); RTD fm sk 17May44; PMTD to SGT, MOS 405 15May45 (per MR 15May45) GCM as CPL in C Co (02/44); CIB SGT in C Co 01Jan45 (22/45)	
933.	Romero, Pedro 39588746	PVT	C	MOS 745 ASGD fm 3rd Repl Bn 20Dec44 (per MR 21Dec44); MIA 21Jan45 (per MR 23Jan45) **(POW 20JAN45);** pow 21/1/45 per MR; Mstr POW reg gives rpt date of 03Mar45 w/o unit ID, Stalag 11B, repatriated CIB 01Jan45 (01/45)	POW 20Jan45
934.	**Rose, Floyd G. 33888645**	**PVT-PFC**	C	MOS 745 ASGD fm 3rd Repl Bn 24Jan45 (per MR 26Jan45); PMTD to PFC 06Mar45 (per MR 06Mar45); Evac **SWIA**, TFRD to DofP 18Mar45 (per MR 18Mar45) No discovered GO for CIB or GCM	WIA 18Mar45
935.	Rose, Gerald L. (Delta, CO)	CPL	C	Induction Roster 16Sep40	

936.	Rosenmeyer, Robert F. 171?1393	PVT	C, E	MOS 504 **(Unknown date of assignment, not on Pine Camp menu)** RTD fm 2nd Repl Dep 11Jan44 per MR 13Jan44; tfr in grade to E Co per MR 05Mar44 No discovered GO for CIB or GCM	
937.	Ross, Floyd G. 33888645	PVT	C	CIB 01Mar45 (10/45)	
938.	**Roth, Harold L. 36104675**	**PFC**	C	MOS 745 ASGD 29May44 (09Jun44); evac sk 30Aug44; 675 RTD fm hosp 04Sep44 (per MR 05Sep44); evac sk, TFRD to DofP 04Sep44; reduced to PVT; erron entry per MR 18Oct44; erron rptd 29Sep44 as reduced to PVT, s/b PFC (per MR 18Oct44); MIA 13Dec44 (per MR 14Dec44); Fm MIA 13Dec44 to **KIA** 13Dec44 (per MR 21Dec44) (buried in USA); KIA13Dec44 per div& 157 list; MIA/KIA13DEC44 per ANB; not on ABMC CIB 01Sep44 (13/44)	**KIA 13Dec44**
939.	Rowe, Francis B. 33526045	PVT	C	MOS 745 ASGD 05Jun44 (09Jun44); TFRD to 2nd Repl Dep but not departed 19Jul44; s/b ATCHD & jnd (MR 23Jul44); already attached fm 2nd Repl Det reld fm atchment (per MR 05Aug44) GCM (08/44)	
940.	Rowlett, Louis C. 35696824	PVT	C	MOS 745 ASGD fm Co G 12Jul44; evac sk 24Jul44 (25Jul44); already evac sk, TRFD to DofP 16Aug44 – erron entry per MR 25Sep44, s/b RTD 16Aug44 (25Sep44) CIB PFD (07/44)	
941.	Ruble, Robert F. SN NA	PVT	C	MOS 745 ATCHD fm 71st Reinf Bn 17May45 (per MR 18May45); Change from ATCH to ASGD 18May45 (per MR 18May45) No discovered GO for CIB or GCM	
942.	Ruch, Paul J. (Delta, CO)	PFC	C	Induction Roster 16Sep40	
943.	Russell, Charles L., Jr. 34950821	PVT	C, 1HQ	MOS 745 ASGD fm 3rd Repl Bn 20Dec44 (per MR 21Dec44); evac sk, TFRD to DofP 04Jan45 (per MR 04Jan45); REASGD fm 2nd Rein Dep 25Feb45 (per MR 25Feb45) CIB 01Jan45 (01/45); GCM as PFC in 1HQ (33/45)	
944.	Russell, George W. 11047999	PVT	C	**(Unknown date of assignment, not on Pine Camp menu)** Evac injured (accidental GSW) 15Sep43 (per MR 20Sep43) CIB FM 01Jan44 (14/44)	
945.	**Sabel**, Sidney J. SGT 38086320	SGT	C	MOS 653 ASGD fm 44th Inf Div 25Jan45 (per MR 01Feb45); Evac sk 28Jan45, TFRD to DofP (per MR 02Feb45); RTD fm 3rd Reinforcement Bn 16Feb45 (per MR 16Feb45); Evac **WIA**, TFRD to DofP 18Mar45 (per MR 18Mar45) No discovered GO for CIB or GCM	WIA 18Mar45

946.	Saettel, Paul (NMI) O-1302892	2LT	K, C	ASGD fr Co K 20Aug43; TFRD out of the division (per MR 02Sep43) – erroneous entry, per MR 09Sep43); TFRD to 7th Repl Dep 26Sep43 (per MR 28Sep43) No discovered GO for CIB or GCM	
947.	Saiz, Antonio P. PCM-C SN NA	PVT	C	On Pine Camp menu	
948.	**Sallas**, Eustaquio (NMI) 38352511	PVT-PFC	C	MOS 745 ASGD fm 2nd Repl Dep 24Feb44 per MR 05Mar44; evac sk 23Jun44 (26Jun44); RTD fm sk 25Jul44, pmtd PFC 04Aug44 (per MR 05Aug44); evac **WIA** 20Oct44; REASG fm 2nd Repl Dep 11Nov44; evac sk, TFRD to DofP 10Dec44 CIB (04/44); 01Apr44 per CC	WIA 20Oct44
949.	Salazar, Joe (NMI) 37343403	PVT	C	**(Unknown date of assignment, not on Pine Camp menu)** Evac sk 08Dec43 per MR 14Dec43; RTD fm sk 20Dec43 per MR 26Dec43; AWOL 1200 27Dec43 per MR 31Dec43; Fm AWOL to Confinement in Naples, pending trial 05Jan44 per MR 07Jan44; from confinement to present, under arrest, awaiting trial 17Jan44 per MR 20Jan44; Present arrest to absent confinement 5th Army Stockade 23Jan44 per MR 25Jan44; fm confinement in 5th Army stockade to under arrest in unit 17Mar44, to RTD 18Mar44 per MR 22Mar44; duty to confinement 22Mar44 per MR 29Mar44; already absent in confinement, tfrd to NATOUSA Disciplinary Training Center, North Africa, per General Court Martial Order #7, HQ 45th Inf Div dated 28Mar45 per MR 10Apr44. No discovered GO for CIB or GCM	
950.	**Sampier,** Clarence J. 36987082	PVT	C	MOS 745 ASGD fm 3rd Repl Bn 20Dec44 (per MR 21Dec44); Evac **WIA**, TFRD to DofP 16Jan45 (per MR 16Jan45) CIB 01Jan45 (01/45)	WIA 16Jan45
951.	Santacroce, John A. 31327932	PVT	I, C	MOS 745/604 ASGD 21Aug44 (22Aug44) (probably from I Co); MIA 21Jan45 (per MR 23Jan45) **(POW 20JAN45);** Mstr POW reg tives rpt date of 03Mar45, Stalag 11B, repatriated -- was captured on/before 20Jan45 at Reipertswiller as a member of C Co CIB PFD (07/44)	POW 20Jan45
952.	**Santerre,** William E. 32944249	PVT-PFC	C	MOS 745 ASGD 30May44 (per MR 09Jun44); evac sk, TFRD to DofP 24Aug44; RTD fm hosp 04Sep44 (per MR 05Sep44); promoted to PFC 07Oct44; evac **WIA**, TFRD to DofP 25Nov44 (per MR 28Nov44); REASG fm 3rd Repl Bn 28Dec44; Evac **WIA**, TFRD to DofP 17Jan45 (per MR 17Jan45) CIB 01Sep44 (13/44)	WIA 25Nov44 WIA 17Jan45

953.	**Sarisky**, John C. 35172958	PVT	C	MOS 745 ASGD fm 2nd Repl Bn 14Jan44 per MR 18Jan44; evac **LIA** (BC sprain L ankle) 11May44 (per MR 16May44); RTD fm INJ 25Jun44 (27Jun44); evac **WIA**, TFRD to DofP 19Aug44 CIB PFD (07/44)	WIA 19Aug44
954.	Sartori, John A. 35846279	PFC	C	GCM (35/45)	
955.	**Sauls**, John R. **38455021**	PFC	C	MOS 746/607 ASGD & joined 07Feb44; evac **WIA** (BC LW R Shell frag) 31May44; RTD fm **WIA** 15Jun44 (16Jun44); evac sk, TFRD to DofP 04Dec44; REASG fm 3rd Repl Bn 21Dec44; MIA 21Jan45 (per MR 23Jan45) **(POW 20JAN45);** Mstr POW reg gives rpt date of 21Jan45, Stalag 12F, repatriated CIB PFD (07/44)	WIA 31May44 POW 20Jan45
956.	**Sayhouse, Harold R. 38005542 PCM-L**	**CPL-SGT**	L, C	CPL in L Co per Pine Camp menu; ASGD fr Co L 28Sep43; evac sk 30Sep43 (per MR 03Oct43); Promoted to SGT per MR 05Nov43; **KIA** 15Dec43 per MR 19Dec43 (buried in Sicily-Rome Cemetery); KIA as SGT in C Co 15Dec43 per div & 157 list -- GUNSHOT; ABMC 15Dec43, BSM, PH No discovered GO for CIB or GCM	**KIA 15Dec43**
957.	**Scaletta,** Peter B. 36831880	PVT-PFC-CPL	C	MOS 745 ASGD 29May44 (per MR 09Jun44); pmtd to PFC 01Jul44 (MR 02Jul44); **WIA** not hosp 06Nov44 (per MR 20Nov44); evac sk, TFRD to DofP 08Nov44; REASGD fm 2nd Repl Dep 19Nov44; evac sk, TFRD to DofP 28Dec44; 745 RTD fm 2nd Reinforcement Dep 20Feb45 (per MR 20Feb45); PMTD to CPL, MOS 652 09May45 (per MR 09May45) CIB 01Sep44 (13/44); GCM (08/45)	WIA 06Nov44
958.	Scally, Philip W. 33689271	PVT-PFC	C	MOS 745 ASGD fm 2nd Repl Bn 14Jan44 per MR 18Jan44; evac sk13Apr44 (MR 20Apr44); RTD fm sk 16Apr44 (per MR 20Apr44); promoted to PFC (per MR 05Aug44); evac sk 23Sep44; RTD 25Sep44; evac sk, TFRD to DofP 29Sep44; REASG fm 2nd Repl Dep 07Oct44; evac sk 03Nov44; already evac sk, TFRD to DofP 06Nov44 CIB (04/44); 01Feb44 per CC	
959.	Scarboro, Mose O. 34964887	PVT	C	MOS 745 ASGD fm 3rd Repl Bn 20Dec44 (per MR 21Dec44); MIA 21Jan45 (per MR 23Jan45) **(POW 20JAN45);** Mstr POW reg gives rpt date of 21Jan45, Stalag 11B, repatriated CIB 01Jan45 (01/45)	POW 20Jan45
960.	**Schade**, Ferdinand J. 32853454	PVT- SSG	C	MOS 745 ASGD fm 7th Repl Dep 25Sep43; promoted PFC 01Jan44 per MR 05Jan44; pmtd to CPL 10Apr 44 (per MR 11Apr44); pmtd to SGT **(unknown date)**; pmtd to SSG (01Jul44); evac **WIA** 19Aug44; already evac **WIA**, TFRD to DofP 20Aug44 CIB (01/44 - 01Jan44 per CC); GCM as S/SGT (08/44)	WIA 19Aug44

961.	**Schaff, Adam** 37595473	**PVT**	C	MOS 745 ASGD fm 3rd Repl Bn 20Dec44 (per MR 21Dec44); MIA 21Jan45 (per MR 23Jan45) (**KIA** 20Jan45) (buried in Lorraine Cemetery); KIA21Jan45 per div & 157 list; MIA/KIA21JAN45 per ANB; ABMC 21Jan45, 1st Sqd, 1st Plt, KIA in breakout attempt 20Jan45 at Reipertswiller PH CIB 01Jan45 (01/45);	**KIA 20Jan45**
962.	**Schauman, Ignatius (NMI) 36685530**	**PVT-PFC**	C	MOS 745 ASGD 29May44 (09Jun44); promoted to PFC 07Oct44; MIA 06Nov44 (per MR 09Nov44) – to **KIA** 06Nov44 (per MR 12Nov44) (buried in Epinal Cemetery); KIA06Nov44 per div & 157 list; MIA/KIA06NOV44 per ANB; ABMC 06Nov44, Epinal Cemetery PH CIB 01Sep44 (13/44)	**KIA 06Nov44**
963.	Schecter, Ben (NMI) O-1299121	2LT	C, B	ASGD fm 2nd Repl Dep 29Dec43 (per MR 05Jan44); tfrd to B Co per MR 10Mar44 CIB (01/44 - 01Jan44 per CC)	
964.	**Schemansky**, Edward A. 36577945	PVT-PFC	C	**(Unknown date of assignment, not on Pine Camp menu)** Evac sk 26Dec43 per MR 28Dec43; already evac sk, TFRD to DofP, DFR per MR 15Jan44; RTD fm DofP 25May44; **WIA** not hosp 23Sep44 (per MR 27Oct44); promoted to PFC 07Oct44; evac sk 17Oct44; RTD fm Med Bn 23Oct44; evac sk 04Nov44; RTD fm sk 10Nov44; evac sk, TFRD to DofP 21Nov44 CIB PFD (07/44); GCM (08/44)	WIA 23Sep44
965.	Scherer, John F. 33835819	PVT-PFC	C	MOS 745 ASGD fm 3rd Repl Bn 20Dec44 (per MR 21Dec44); evac sk 23Dec44; RTD fm sk 27Dec44; PMTD to PFC 06Mar45 (per MR 06Mar45); AWOL 2359 03Feb45 (per MR 05Feb45); AWOL to Regt'l Stockade 04Feb45 (per MR 09Feb45); RTD fm Regt'l Stockade 09Feb45 (per MR 09Feb45) CIB 01Jan45 (01/45)	
966.	Schiavone, Salvatore 32864783	CPL	C	MOS 653 attached fm 3rd Reinf Bn 04May45 (per MR 07May45); rlvd fm attached status, to ASGD 07May45 (per MR 07May45) GCM (32/45)	
967.	Schiff, William 32898296	PVT	C, A	MOS 745 ASGD fm 36th ID 26Jan45 (per MR 01Feb45) per MR 07Feb45 rank is PVT; CORR to MR 01Feb45 and 02Feb45 (of ASGD fm 36ID on 26Jan45, and TFRD to A Co 02Feb45) to change rank from PFC to PVT (per MR 07Feb45) GCM (26/45)	
968.	**Schill,** Thomas A. 33682332	PVT	C	MOS 745 ASGD fm 2nd Repl Dep 24Feb44 per MR 05Mar44; **LWA** not-hosp 10May44 (MR 16May44); MIA 20May44 (MR 01Jun44) -- erroneous, per MR 06Jun44); evac **WIA** 28May44 (MR 06Jun44); RTD fm **WIA** 06Jun44; evac sk 28Jun44 (29Jun44); RTD fm sk 04Jul44; evac sk 27Sep44; already evac sk, TFRD to DofP 28Sep44 CIB PFD (07/44)	WIA 10May44 WIA 28May44

969.	Schilling, Wallace R., Jr. 32207645 PCM-C	PFC	C, AT	PVT in C Co per Pine Camp menu CIB as PFC in AT Co 01Jan44 (03/44 CC)	
970.	**Schimp**, Robert H. 33682426	PFC-CPL-SGT-SSG	C	MOS 745 ASGD fm 2nd Repl Dep 24Feb44 per MR 05Mar44; Evac sk 14May44 (MR 19May44); RTD 22May44 (MR 23May44); Pmtd to PFC 01Jul44 (MR 02Jul44); Evac **WIA** 17Aug44, evac to Ship Acadia TFRD to DofP/DFR 17Aug44; REASG fm 2nd Repl Dep 18Oct44; evac **WIA**, TFRD to DofP 27Oct44; REASG fm 2nd Repl Dep 11Nov44; evac sk, TFRD to DofP 26Nov44 (per MR 28Nov44); REASG fm 71st Repl Dep 04Dec44 (per MR 05Dec44); evac sk 07Dec44; already evac sk, TFRD to DofP 08Dec44; REASG fm 3rd Repl Bn 11Jan45 (per MR 11Jan45); Evac sk 13Jan45 (per MR 13Jan45); RTD fm sk 18Jan45 (per MR 18Jan45); PMTD to CPL, MOS 653 04Feb45 (per MR 04Feb45); PMTD to SGT, 24Mar45 (per MR 26Mar45); Pmtd to SSG 04May45 (per MR 04May45) CIB (04/44 - 01Mar44 per CC); CIB PFD (07/44); GCM CPL (08/45)	WIA 17Aug44
971.	Schoenewolf, Edward 38631070	PVT	C	MOS 745 ASGD fm 3rd Repl Bn 24Jan45 (per MR 26Jan45); Evac sk 10Feb45 (per MR 10Feb45); Already Evac sk, TFRD to DofP 11Feb45 (per MR 11Feb45) CIB 01Mar45 (10/45)	
972.	Schoening, Fredrich A. 35708281	PVT	C	MOS 745 ASGD 29May44 (09Jun44); evac sk, TFRD to DofP 27Sep44; REASG fm 2nd Repl Dep 08Oct44; evac sk, TFRD to DofP 28Oct44 CIB Fredrich 01Sep44 (13/44); CIB FM Frederich 01Sep44 (14/44)	
973.	**Schreibeck,** William J. 33620179	PVT	C	MOS 745 ASGD fm 7th Repl Dep 25Sep43; evac **WIA ??Nov43** per MR 16Nov43; already evac **WIA** TFRD to DofP, DFR per MR 18Dec43 CIB FM 01Jan44 (14/44)	**WIA ??Nov43**
974.	Schreiner, William 38076157	CPL	C	MOS 653 attached fm 3rd Reinf Bn 04May45 (per MR 07May45); relieved from attached status, to ASGD 07May45 (per MR 07May45) GCM (32/45)	
975.	**Schuler**, James P. 32952455	PVT	C	MOS 745 745 Already attached fm 2nd Repl Det reld fm atchment (per MR 05Aug44); ASGD 21Aug44 (22Aug44); ASGD 05Jun44 (09Jun44); TFRD to 2nd Repl Dep but not departed 19Jul44; s/b ATCHD & jnd (MR 23Jul44); evac **SWIA,** TFRD to DofP 01Nov44 CIB 01Sep44 (13/44)	WIA 01Nov44

976.	**Schulte**, Charles F., Jr. 15362278	PVT	C	MOS 745 ASGD fm 2nd Repl Dep 24Feb44 per MR 05Mar44; evac **WIA** 01Apr44 MR 07Apr44 ; to DofP/DFR 25Apr44 (MR 19May44); **(Missing entry for RTD)**; evac **WIA** 29May44; already evac **WIA** TFRD to DofP and DFR 05Jun44 (15Jun44) CIB FM 01Mar44 (14/44)	WIA 01Apr44 WIA 29May44
977.	Schultz, Starling D. 39342342	PVT-PFC	C, 1HQ	MOS 745 ASGD fm 2nd Repl Dep 29Sep44; evac sk, TFRD to DofP 06Nov44; REASG fm 3rd Repl Bn 17Jan45 (per MR 17Jan45); PMTD to PFC 06Mar45 (per MR 06Mar45); Evac sk, TFRD to DofP 18Apr45 (per MR 18Apr45); REASG fm 71st Reinf Bn 14May45 (per MR 15May45) CIB in C Co 01Oct44 (13/44); GCM PFC in 1HQ (33/45)	
978.	**Schweisthal**, John J. 35051605	PVT-PFC	C	MOS 603 **(Unknown date of assignment, not on Pine Camp menu)** promoted PFC 01Jan44 per MR 05Jan44; **WIA** not hosp 17Feb44; evac **WIA** 16Aug44 (17Aug44); already evac **WIA** on Ship Acadia TFRD to DofP/DFR 17Aug44; REASG not joined fm 2nd Repl Dep 25Sep44; joined 29Sep44; evac sk 27Oct44; TFRD to DofP 28Oct44 CIB (01/44 - 01Jan44 per CC); GCM (08/44)	WIA 17Feb44 WIA 16Aug44
979.	Scott, Harold N. 35052955	PVT-PFC	C	MOS 603/504 ASGD fm 2nd Repl Dep per MR 11Dec43; Pmtd to Pfc 04Mar44 per MR 12Mar44; evac sk 12Jun44 (13Jun44); RTD fm sk (23Jun44); evac sk 09Jul44; RTD fm sk 15Jul44; evac sk, TFRD to DofP 09Sep44; REASG fm 2nd Repl Dep 18Oct44; AWOL 2359 19Oct44 (per MR 21Oct44); fm AWOL to under arrest 2359 22Oct44; RTD fm arrest 31Oct44; TFRD to Co K 31Oct44 CIB (01/44 - 01Jan44 per CC); GCM as PFC (08/44)	
980.	**Scott**, Leland E. **38444253**	PVT- SSG	C	MOS 616/652 **(Unknown date of assignment, not on Pine Camp menu)** Pmtd PFC 10Aug43; **(Missing entry of evac)**; RTD 26Aug43; promoted to PFC 03Nov43 (per MR 05Nov43); pmtd to CPL per MR 02Dec43; pmtd SGT per MR 25Jan44; **WIA** not hosp 15Feb44; evac sk 03Jun44; RTD fm sk 14Jun44 (16Jun44); pmtd to SSG 04Jul44; evac sk, TFRD to DofP/DFR 10Aug44 (15Aug44); RTD fm hosp 10Sep44 (per MR 11Sep44); evac **WIA**, TFRD to DofP 03Nov44 CIB (01/44 - 01Jan44 per CC); GCM (02/44)	WIA 15Feb44 WIA03Nov44
981.	**Scott, Virgil O. 37516951**	**PVT**	C	**(Unknown date of assignment, not on Pine Camp menu) KIA** 12Nov43 per MR 17Nov43 (buried in Sicily-Rome Cemetery); KIA12Nov43 per div & 157 list; ABMC 12Nov43, PH No discovered GO for CIB or GCM	**KIA 12Nov43**

982.	Scout, Leland E. PCM-C 12055084	PFC	C	(Deployed w/the company, is on the Pine Camp menu as PVT) MIA 13Sep43 DFR (per MR 24Sep43) **(POW 13Sep43)**; Mstr POW reg gives rpt date of 13Sep43 as PVT, Stalag 2B, repatriated CIB MIA as PFC in C Co (05/44); 01Jan44 per CC	POW 13Sep43
983.	**Seaman,** Michael 33613886	PVT-PFC	C, 1HQ	MOS 745 ASGD fm 2nd Repl Dep 29Sep44; evac sk, TFRD to DofP 04Nov44; REASGD fm 2nd Repl Dep 19Nov44; promoted to PFC 20Nov44 (per MR 27Nov44); evac sk 07Dec44; already evac sk, TFRD to DofP 08Dec44; REASG fm 3rd Repl Bn 18Dec44 (per MR 19Dec44); Evac **WIA**, TFRD to DofP 14Jan45 (per MR 14Jan45); REASGD fm 2nd Rein Dep 25Feb45 (per MR 25Feb45); Evac sk 23Mar45 (per MR 23Mar45); Already evac sk, TFRD to DofP 24Mar45 (per MR 24Mar45); REASG fm 71st Reinf Bn 16Apr45 (per MR 16Apr45); TFRD to 1HQ 27May45 (per MR 27May45) CIB 01Oct44 (13/44); GCM PFC in 1HQ (26/45)	WIA 14Jan45
984.	Seay, Raleigh F. SN NA	1LT	C	ASGD fm Co D 05Apr45 (per MR 05Apr45); erron entry per MR 08Apr45; entry of 05Apr45 of ASGD is erron; officer not assigned. **NOT ASSIGNED**	
985.	Secorski, Frank L. 36856743	PVT	A, C	MOS 745 ASGD 21Aug44 (22Aug44) probably from A Co; evac sk, TFRD to DofP 09Sep44; REASGD fm 2nd Repl Dep 09Dec44; evac sk 16Dec44; correction of MR 18Dec44 RTD fm sk – erron entry (per MR 31Dec44); Duty to Regt'l Stockade 21Dec44 (22Dec44) – erron entry (per MR 31Dec44); RTD fm sk 18Dec44 – correction: s/b AWOL 2359 (per MR 31Dec44); Fm AWOL to Regt'l Stockade 23Dec44 (per MR 31Dec44); evac sk fm stockade 25Dec44; already evac sk, TFRD to DofP 26Dec44; REASG fm 3rd Repl Bn 07Jan45 (per MR 07Jan45); Regt'l Stockade 07Jan45 (per MR 07Jan45); RTD fm Regt'l Stockade 17Jan45 (per MR 17Jan45); AWOL 2359 17Jan45 (per MR 19Jan45); **(Missing entry for RTD fm AWOL)**; evac sk 07Feb45 (per MR 07Feb45); RTD fm sk 13Feb45 (per MR 13Feb45); Evac sk 14Feb45 (per MR 14Feb45); RTD fm sk 19Feb45 (per MR 19Feb45); Evac sk 17Mar45 (per MR 17Mar45); TFRD to DofP 18Mar45 (per MR 18Mar45) CIB PFD in A Co (07/44); CIB FM in C Co 01Feb44 (14/44)	
986.	Sedelsky, Samuel G. SN NA	PVT	C	ATCHD fm 71st Reinf Bn 17May45 (per MR 18May45); Change from ATCH to ASGD 18May45 (per MR 18May45) No discovered GO for CIB or GCM	

987.	**Seeman,** William F. 33431694	PFC	C	MOS 746 ASGD & joined 07Feb44; evac **WIA** 23May44 (per MR 26May44); RTD fm **WIA** 11Jun44 (13Jun44); **WIA** not hosp 08Oct44 (per MR 18Oct44); evac **WIA**, TFRD to DofP 28Oct44; REASG fm 2nd Repl Dep 11Nov44; evac sk, TFRD to DofP 25Nov44 (per MR 28Nov44) CIB (01/44); 01Mar44 per CC; GCM (08/44)	WIA 23May44 WIA 28Oct44
988.	Segay, Joseph W. 31041164	PFC	A, C	MOS 745 ASGD 21Aug44 (22Aug44) (probably from A Co); evac sk, TFRD to DofP 24Oct44; REASG fm 71st Repl Dep 01Dec44; evac sk 04Dec44; already evac sk, TFRD to DofP 05Dec44 CIB (01/44 - 01Jan44 per CC); CIB PFC Joe W. (06/44 CC); CIB PFC FM in C Co 01Jan44 (14/44)	
989.	**Seidle**r, Victor C. 36478922	PVT-PFC	C	MOS 745 ASGD fm 7th Repl Dep 25Sep43; pmtd to PFC 01Dec43; evac S**WIA** 14Dec43 (per 17Dec43); RTD fm **WIA** 11Jan44 per MR 14Jan44; evac sk (old wound lumbar region) 07Feb44; RTD fr sk 27Mar44 03Apr44 per MR 25Mar44; evac sk 04Apr44 (MR 12Apr44); RTD 08Apr44 (MR 12Apr44); evac sk LD (Psychoneurosis anxiety state chronic) 21May44; already evac, Tfrd to DofP and DFR 03Jun44 CIB FM 01Jan44 (14/44)	WIA 14Dec43
990.	Selvage, George W. 34975733	PVT-PFC	C	MOS 745 ASGD fm 3rd Repl Bn 24Jan45 (per MR 26Jan45); 745 PMTD to PFC 06Mar45 (per MR 06Mar45); Evac INJ 18Mar45 (per MR 18Mar45); Already Evac INJ, TFRD to DofP 19Mar45 (per MR 19Mar45) CIB 01Mar45 (10/45)	
991.	**Senape, Alfred L. 33611373**	**PVT**	C	MOS 745 ASGD 29May44 (09Jun44); evac **WIA** 31Oct44, DOW 31Oct44 (buried in USA); DOW31Oct44 per div & 157 list; not on ABMC reh CIB 01Sep44 (13/44)	WIA 31Oct44 **DOW 31Oct44**
992.	Setterbo, Melton E. 36458451	PVT	C	MOS 745 ASGD fm 7th Repl Dep 25Sep43; **(Missing entry of evac)**; already evac sk TFRD to DofP, DFR per MR 08Jan44; RTD fm DofP 13Feb44; evac sk (exhaustion) 20Feb44; already evac sk TFRD to DofP and DFR 08June (20Jun44) CIB FM 01Jan44 (14/44)	
993.	Shafer, Okey O., Jr. 35758432	PVT-PFC	C	MOS 604/745 ASGD 21Aug44 (22Aug44); promoted to PFC 20Nov44 (per MR 27Nov44); evac **LIA**, TFRD to DofP 03Dec44; REASG 17Dec44; MIA 21Jan45 (per MR 23Jan45) **(POW 20JAN45);** Mstr POW reg gives rpt date of 21Jan45 as PFC, parent unit as division artillery, Stalag 11B, repatriated CIB 01Sep44 (13/44)	POW 20Jan45

994.	Shaffer, Rollo W. PCM-C 38006206	PFC	C	(Deployed w/the company, is on the Pine Camp menu as PVT) Pmtd PFC 10Aug43; MIA 13Sep43 DFR (per MR 24Sep43) **(POW 13Sep43);** Mstr POW reg givee rpt date of 13Sep43, Stalag 2B, repatriated CIB MIA as PFC in C Co (05/44); 01Jan44 per CC POW 13/9/43	POW 13Sep43
995.	Shane, Jesse P. 39616661	PVT	A, C	MOS 745 ASGD fm 2nd Repl Dep 20Jan45 (per MR 31Jan45); ANB: MIA20APR45 = DUTY CIB 01Mar45 (9/45) **–IN A CO**	
996.	Shanno, Joseph A. 36611375	PVT-PFC	C	MOS 745/607 ASGD 29May44 (09Jun44); promoted to PFC 07Oct44; evac sk, TFRD to DofP 17Nov44; REASG fm 3rd Repl Bn 26Dec44; MIA 21Jan45 (per MR 23Jan45) **(POW 20JAN45);** CIB 01Sep44 (13/44)	POW 20Jan45
997.	Shannon, Carl E. 35757774	PVT-PFC	C	**(Unknown date of assignment, not on Pine Camp menu)** Pmtd to PFC 01Dec43; evac sk 09Dec43 per MR 14Dec43; already evac sk, TFRD to DofP, DFR per MR 11Jan44 CIB DP (07/44)	
998.	Shannon, Timothy C. 33233901	SSG	C	**(Unknown date of assignment)** Evac sk 04Dec44; already evac sk, TFRD to DofP 06Dec44 No discovered GO for CIB or GCM	
999.	**Sherr,** William H. 35916259	PVT	C	MOS 745 ASGD 30May44 (09Jun44); evac **WIA**, TFRD to DofP 23Sep44; REASGD fm 2nd Repl Dep 10Oct44; evac **WIA** 05Nov44; already evac sk, TFRD to DofP 10Nov44; REASG fm 3rd Repl Bn 23Dec44; evac sk, TFRD to DofP 23Dec44 CIB 01Sep44 (13/44)	WIA 23Sep44
1000.	Shoelen, James E. 34936161	PVT-PFC	C	MOS 745 ASGD fm 3rd Repl Bn 24Jan45 (per MR 26Jan45); PMTD to PFC 06Mar45 (per MR 06Mar45); 18Mar45 (per MR 18Mar45); Already Evac INJ, TFRD to DofP 19Mar45 (per MR 19Mar45) CIB 01Mar45 (10/45)	
1001.	Sholtz, Sidney (NMI) 33454666	PVT-CPL	C	MOS 405/607 ASGD fm 2nd Repl Dep per MR 11Dec43; Pmtd to PFC 26Dec44 (per MR 03Jan45); PMTD to CPL 15May45 (per MR 15May45) GCM (16/44); CIB CPL 01Apr45 (28/45)	
1002.	**Shue,** Douglas E. 33735221	PVT	C	MOS 604 ASGD 21Aug44 (22Aug44); rank corrected to PFC (MR 13Sep44); erron rptd on 22Aug44 as ASGD fm 2nd Repl Dep 21Aug44 as PVT, s/b PFC per MR 13Sep44; evac **WIA** 24Sep44; RTD fm 3rd Repl Bn 30Jan45 (per MR 30Jan45); Evac sk, TFRD to DofP 05Feb45 (per MR 05Feb45) CIB FM 01Sep44 (14/44)	WIA 24Sep44
1003.	Shultis, Howard M. 12057041 PCM-C	PVT-CPL	C	(Deployed w/the company, is on the Pine Camp menu as PVT) Evac sk 17Nov43 per MR 21Nov43; already evac sk TFRD to DofP, DFR per MR 18Dec43 CIB as CPL in C Co 01Jan44 (9/44 CC)	

1004.	Shultz, Ivan A. 33876137	PVT	C	MOS 745 ASGD fm 3rd Repl Bn 24Jan45 (per MR 26Jan45); Evac sk, TFRD to DofP 20Feb45 (per MR 20Feb45) CIB 01Mar45 (10/45)	
1005.	Shurbutt, James G. O-1323074	1LT	B, C, D	ASGD fm Co B 25Jan45 (per MR 25Jan45); assumed duties of XO 30Jan45 (per MR 07Mar45); Reld as XO, assumes cmd 18Mar45 [poss 15Mar45] (per MR 22Mar45); evac sk, TFRD to DofP 29Mar45 (per MR 29Mar45); Already evac sk, TFRD to DofP 31Mar45 (per MR 31Mar45); RTD 15May45 (per MR 16May45); TFRD to Co D 17May45 (per MR 17May45 CIB 01Dec44 (01/45)	
1006.	**Shutack**, Joseph R. 33575779	PVT	C	MOS 745 ASGD fm 2nd Repl Dep 24Feb44 per MR 05Mar44; evac **WIA** 01Jun44; already evac **WIA** to DofP/DFR 06Jun44 (15Jun44); REASG fm DofP 06Aug44; evac **WIA**, TFRD to DofP 23Sep44; REASG but not joined fm 2nd Repl Dep 04Oct44; joined 05Oct44; evac sk, TFRD to DofP 30Oct44 CIB DP (07/44)	WIA 01Jun44 WIA 23Sep44
1007.	Siegrist, John 42126919	PVT	C	MOS 745 ASGD fm 3rd Repl Bn 20Dec44 (per MR 21Dec44); MIA 21Jan45 (per MR 23Jan45) **(POW 20JAN45);** Mstr POW reg gives rpt date of 03Mar45 w/o unit ID, Stalag 11B, repatriated -- captured on or before 20Jan45 near Reipertswiller CIB 01Jan45 (01/45)	POW 20Jan45
1008.	Simmons, Eugene B., Jr. 38026471	PFC	C	MOS 745 ASGD fm 36th Inf Div 26Jan45 (per MR 07Feb45); TFRD to 2nd Reinf Dep for shipment to Ft. Sam Houston, TX 14May45 (per MR 14May45) No discovered GO for CIB or GCM	
1009.	**Simmons,** Richard A. 20837702 (Delta, CO) (Simons) PCM-C	SGT-SSG	C	MOS 651 CPL in C Co per Induction Roster, 16Sep40; Deployed w/the company, is on the Pine Camp menu); **SWIA** 14Jul43; already evac **SWIA**, DFR (01Aug43); RTD fr DofP 14Dec43 (per MR 15Dec43); pmtd to SSG per MR 10Mar44; already attached fm 2nd Repl Det reld fm atchment (per MR 05Aug44); ASGD fm 2nd Repl Dep 31Aug44; TFRD to 2nd Repl Dep but not dptd 19Jul44; s/b ATCHD & jnd (MR 23Jul44); evac sk, TFRD to DofP 23Sep44 CIB as SGT in C Co (01/44 - 01Jan44 per CC); GCM as S/SGT (08/44)	WIA 14Jul43
1010.	**Simon,** Horace B., Jr. 13130311	PVT-PFC	C	MOS 745 ASGD 15Aug43 (per MR 16Aug43); pmtd PFC 14Jan44 per MR 15Jan44; evac **WIA** (pen w r elbow & thigh bomb frag) 17Feb44; TFRD to DofP & DFR 27Feb44; already evac **WIA**, trfd to DofP and DFR 27Feb44 per MR 14Mar44 CIB DP (07/44)	WIA 17Feb44

1011.	Simonian, Paranas R. 31389508	PVT	C	MOS 745 ASGD fm 2nd Repl Dep 24Feb44 per MR 05Mar44; evac sk 10Apr44 (MR 18Apr44); RTD fm sk 15Apr44 (per MR 20Apr44); MIA 20May44, DFR (MR 01Jun44); erron rptd MIA 29May44, s/b evac sk 31May44 (11Jun44); already evac sk, TFRD to DofP/DFR 09Jun44 (per MR 05Aug44) CIB FM 01Mar44 (14/44)	
1012.	**Singleton, William G. 31065317 PCM**	**PFC**	C	MOS 302/duty MOS 745 (Deployed w/the company, is on the Pine Camp menu as PFC) **WIA** 14Jul43; already evac **WIA**, DFR (01Aug43); RTD fm 7th Repl Dep 12Sep43 (per MR 14Sep43); **KIA** 15Dec43 (per MR 20Dec43) (buried in USA); KIA as PFC in C Co 15Dec43 per div & 157 list -- GUNSHOT; not on ABMC reg No discovered GO for CIB or GCM	WIA 14Jul43 **KIA 15Dec43**
1013.	Skiff, William J. 38005446 PCM	PVT-SGT	I, C, K, RHQ	MOS 745 PFC in I Co per Pine Camp menu; ASGD 21Aug44 (22Aug44) probably from I Co; TFRD to RHQ 06Oct44 (per MR 16Oct44) CIB as SGT in I Co (01/44 - 01Jan44 per CC); CIB PFD PVT K Co (07/44); GCM PVT K Co (08/44)	
1014.	**Skowronek,** Michael A. 31380786	PVT	C	MOS 745 ASGD 21Aug44 (22Aug44); evac **WIA**, TFRD to DofP 27Oct44; REASG fm 71st Repl Dep 01Dec44; evac **INJ** 03Dec44; already evac, TFRD to DofP 04Dec44 CIB FM 01May44 (14/44); GCM (16/44)	WIA 27Oct44 INJ 03Dec44
1015.	**Slade**, Thomas J. Jr. PCM O-1283507	1LT	1HQ, C	**(Unknown date of assignment, is on 1st Bn HQ Co Pine Camp menu)** REASGD & jnd fm hospital 02Mar44 per MR 10Mar44; evac **WIA** 23May44; already evac **WIA** TFRD to DofP and DFR 05Jun44 (08Jun44) CIB as 1LT in C Co (01/44 - 01Jan44 per CC)	WIA 23May44
1016.	**Slover**, Lloyd L. 36649115	SGT-SSG	C	MOS 653/651 ASGD fm 44th Inf Div 25Jan45 (per MR 01Feb45); PMTD to SSG MOS 651 09Mar45 (per MR 09Mar45); Evac **WIA** 18Mar45 (per MR 18Mar45); Already Evac **WIA**, TFRD to DofP 19Mar45 (per MR 19Mar45) No discovered GO for CIB or GCM	WIA 18Mar45
1017.	Smelley, Alvin H. 34801744	PVT	C	MOS 745 ASGD 21Aug44 (22Aug44); evac sk 24Sep44; RTD sm sk 26Sep44; evac sk, TFRD to DofP 05Oct44 CIB PFD in I Co (07/44); CIB FM in C Co 01Jan44 (14/44)	
1018.	Smith, J. D. W. 18126549	PVT	RHQ, C	MOS 745 ASGD fr RHQ 14Apr45 (per MR 14Apr45); Evac sk, TFRD to DofP 14Apr45 (per MR 14Apr45) No discovered GO for CIB or GCM	

1019.	Smith, J. W. (IO) 34731876	PVT-PFC-CPL	C	MOS 745/603/653 ASGD fm 2nd Repl Bn 18Dec43 per MR 22Dec43; evac sk 05Jan44 per MR 08Jan44; already evac sk TFRD to DofP, DFR per MR 25Jan44; RTD fm sk 14Feb44; promoted to PFC (per MR 05Aug44); evac sk, TFRD to DofP 03Sep44; REASG fm hosp 15Sep44; evac sk 24Sep44 (per MR 25Sep44); RTD fm sk 25Sep44; promoted to CPL MOS 653 07Oct44; evac sk, TFRD to DofP 04Nov44 CIB PFD (07/44)	
1020.	**Smith,** John J. 33797170	PVT	C	MOS 745 ASGD 05Jun44 (09Jun44); evac **WIA**, TFRD to DofP 07Nov44 CIB 01Sep44 (13/44)	WIA 07Nov44
1021.	**Smith, Kenneth L. R.** 33556684	**PVT-PFC**	C	MOS 745 ASGD 05Jun44 (09Jun44); promoted to PFC (per MR 05Aug44); MIA 09Dec44 (per MR 11Dec44); Fm MIA 09Dec44 to **KIA** 09Dec44 (per MR 21Dec44); (buried in USA); KIA09DEC44 as PFC per div & 157 list; MIA/KIA09DEC44 per ANB; not on ABMC reg GCM (08/44); CIB PFC 01Sep44 (13/44)	**KIA 09Dec44**
1022.	Smith, Leonard W. 33890831	PVT	C	MOS 745 ASGD fm 3rd Repl Bn 20Dec44 (per MR 21Dec44); MIA 21Jan45 (per MR 23Jan45) **(POW 20JAN45);** Mstr POW reg gives rpt date of 21Jan45, parent unit as division artillery, Stalag 11B, repatriated CIB 01Jan45 (01/45)	POW 20Jan45
1023.	Smith, Thomas I., Jr. 37750111	PFC	C	GCM (35/45)	
1024.	Smith, Walter W. 32869404	PVT	I, C	MOS 745 ASGD 21Aug44 (22Aug44) probably from I Co; evac sk, TFRD to DofP 03Nov44 CIB (04/44 - 01Jan44 per CC)	
1025.	Smith, William L. 34890380 PVT-PFC-PVT-PFC	PVT-PFC-	C	MOS 745 ASGD 30May44 (09Jun44); promoted to PFC 07Oct44; Reduced to PVT 18May45 (per MR 18May45); PMTD to PFC 21May45 (per MR 23May45) CIB 01Sep44 (13/44); GCM (08/.45)	
1026.	**Sniffen,** Raymond J. 6668327	SSG	C	MOS 653 ASGD fm 70th Inf Div 26Jan45 (per MR 01Feb45); Evac **WIA** 28Mar45 (per MR 28Mar45)**;** Already evac **WIA**, TFRD to DofP 29Mar45 (per MR 29Mar45); REASG but DS to 71st Reinf Bn 07May45 (per MR 08May45); relieved of DS to 71st Reinf Bn 08May45 (per MR 08May45) CIB 01Mar45 (10/45); GCM (8/45)	WIA 28Mar45
1027.	Socha, Stanley P. 32919580	PVT	C, CN	MOS 531 ASGD 21Aug44 (22Aug44); evac sk, TFRD to DofP 11Sep44; **Missing entry for RTD)**; TFRD to Cannon Co 23Oct44 CIB (07/44); GCM (16/44)	
1028.	**Socher**, Raymond J. 33689235	PVT	C	MOS 745 ASGD 21Aug44 (22Aug44); evac **SWIA**, TFRD to DofP 23Sep44 CIB FM 01Mar44 (14/44)	WIA 23Sep44

1029.	**Sojak, Andrew J., Jr.** **33131218 PCM-C**	**PFC**	C	(Depoloyed w/the company, is on the Pine Camp menu as PFC) **(Missing entry of evac)**; RTD fm hosp 01Aug43 (per MR 02Aug43); evac for unknown reasons, but specified as LOD 23Jul43 (per MR 25Jul43); KIA as PFC in C Co 07Oct43 per div & 157 list; ABMC 07Oct43, Sicily-Rome Cemetery PH	**KIA 07Oct43**
1030.	Solis, Ovidio (NMI) 38458778	PVT	C, G	MOS 745 ASGD fm 2nd Repl Bn 14Jan44 per MR 18Jan44; tfr in grade to G Co per MR 05Mar44 CIB FM 01Feb44 (14/44)	
1031.	**Sorensen**, Walter B. 32598265	PVT-PFC-CPL	C	MOS 745/653 ASGD fm 2nd Repl Bn 14Jan44 per MR 18Jan44; evac sk 15Jan44 per MR 21Jan44; RTD from Sk 07Feb44; evac sk (NYD Manifested by pain in arches) 18Apr44 (per MR 22Apr44); RTD fm sk 15May44 (MR 19May44); evac sk LD 16May44 (MR 20May44); RTD fm sk 02Jun44; evac sk 17Jul44 (MR 20Jul44); RTD fm sk 22Jul44; promoted to PFC (per MR 05Aug44); **WIA** not hosp 30Oct44 (per MR 05Nov44); MOS 653 promoted to CPL 24Nov44; evac **WIA**, TFRD to DofP 25Nov44 (per MR 28Nov44 CIB PFD (07/44); GCM PFC (16/44)	WIA 30Oct44 WIA 25Nov44
1032.	Souffard, Oscar J. SN NA	PFC	C	MOS 745 **(Unknown date of assignment) (Missing entry of evac)**; RTD fm 71st Reinf Bn 17May45 (per MR 17May45) No discovered GO for CIB or GCM	
1033.	Spahn, Frederick J., Jr. 32869481	PVT	C	MOS 745 ASGD 21Aug44 (22Aug44); MIA 22Sep44 (25Sep44); changed to evac sk 22Sep44 (per MR 30Sep44); RTD fm sk 28Sep44 (per MR 30Sep44); evac sk, TFRD to DofP 07Nov44; REASG fm 3rd Repl Bn 20Dec44; Evac sk, TFRD to DofP 11Jan45 (per MR 11Jan45); RTD fm 71st Reinf Bn 21Apr45 (per MR 21Apr45) CIB 01Mar44 (11/44)	
1034.	**Speairs,** Anse H. PCM-C O-428346	1LT-CPT	C, L, 1HQ, RHQ	(Deployed w/the battalion, is on the C Company Pine Camp menu as 1st Platoon Leader) Asgd & jd from HQ 1st Bn 14Jul43; evac **WIA** 11Nov43 per MR 13Nov43; already evac **WIA**, DFR per MR 21Dec43; RTD fm **WIA** unknown date in Jan44 per MR 21Jan44; asgd to HHC 1st Bn 21Jan44 per MR 22Jan44; ASGD fr 1HQ 01Mar44 as CO (per MR 09May44); **WIA** not hosp 10Jun44; pmtd to Capt DOR 27Jun44; evac sk, TFRD to DofP 20Aug44; RTD fm sk 22Aug44 (23Aug44); TFRD to RHQ 13Oct44; Regt Adj Capt per sig on GO 14/45 Multiple WIA CIB as 1LT in C Co (01/44 - 01Jan44 per CC)	WIA 11Nov43 WIA 10Jun44
1035.	Spence, George H. 35206742	PFC	C	MOS 745 ASGD fm Div HQ Co 23Oct44 (per MR 25Oct44); Special Duty with Div HQ 23Oct44 (per MR 02Nov44); Already abs DS to Div HQ Co, TFRD to Div HQ Co 15Feb45 (per MR 15Feb45) No discovered GO for CIB or GCM	

1036.	**Spicer**, Charles H., Jr. 32959322	PVT	C	MOS 745 ASGD 21Aug44 (22Aug44); evac **WIA**, TFRD to DofP 23Sep44; REASGD fm 2nd Repl Dep 10Oct44; evac, TFRD to DofP 27Oct44 – erron entry MR 03Nov44; REASG fm 2nd Repl Dep 11Nov44; evac sk, TFRD to DopP 20Nov44 CIB FM 01Sep44 (14/44)	WIA 23Sep44
1037.	**Sponder, Henry J. 36316849**	**PVT**	C	MOS 745 ASGD fm 2nd Repl Dep 24Feb44 per MR 05Mar44; MIA 26May44 (per MR 27May44); Fm MIA 26May44 to **KIA** 26May44 (buried in USA); KIA26May44 per div & 157 list; MIA/KIA26MAY44 in C Co per ANB; not on ABMC reg No discovered GO for CIB or GCM	**KIA 26May44**
1038.	**Stafford, John M. 33887601**	**PVT**	C	MOS 745 ASGD fm 3rd Repl Bn 20Dec44 (per MR 21Dec44); MIA 21Jan45 (per MR 23Jan45) (**KIA O/A 20JAN45**) (buried in USA); MIA21JAN45 per ANB; KIA21Jan45 per div list -- NOT ON DIV LIST; not on ABMC reg CIB 01Jan45 (01/45)	**KIA 20Jan45**
1039.	**Staley**, Victor F. 20310730	PFC-CPL-SGT-SSG	I, C	MOS 745 ASGD fr Co I 28Sep43; evac INJ 13Nov43 per MR 16Nov43; RTD fm **LIA** 07Dec43 (per MR 12Dec43); evac **LIA** 15Dec43 (per MR 19Dec43); already evac **WIA** TFRD to DofP, DFR per MR 31Dec43; RTD fr DofP 17Jan44 per MR 20Jan44; Pmtd to Cpl per MR 11Mar44; promoted to Sgt per MR 20Mar44; pmtd to SSG 10Apr44 (per MR 11Apr44); evac **WIA** (pen W Rbuttock, Pen W & FC L elbow shell frag) 29May44; already evac **WIA** TFRD to DofP and DFR 14Jun44 (20Jun44) CIB (01/44 - 01Jan44 per CC); GCM as S/SGT (02/44)	INJ 13Nov43 INJ 15Dec43 WIA 29May44
1040.	Standlea (or Standles), Carl (NMI) 37353333	PVT-PFC	C	MOS 504 **(Unknown date of assignment) (Missing entry of evac)**; RTD fm 2nd Repl Dep 11Jan44 per MR 13Jan44; Pmtd to PFC 04Mar44 per MR 12Mar44; evac **SIW** non-battle GSW perf W Left hand 29Mar44 per MR 03Apr44; to DofP & DFR 13Apr44 (per MR 25Apr44) CIB FM 01Feb44 (14/44)	
1041.	Stanlewicz, Walter P. 31387830	PVT	C	MOS 745/604 ASGD 30May44 (per MR 09Jun44); AWOL 2359 21Nov44; RTD fm AWOL 2359 23Nov44 (per MR 27Nov44); AWOL 2359 13Dec44 (per MR 22Dec44); fm AWOL 2359 13Dec44 to confinement unknown 15Dec44; Reg't Stockade 17Dec44; RTD 18Dec44 (per MR 22Dec44); MIA 21Jan45 (per MR 23Jan45) **(POW 20JAN45);** Mstr POW reg gives rpt date of 21Jan45, parent unit as division artillery, Stalag 11B, repatriated CIB 01Sep44 (13/44)	POW 20Jan45

1042.	**Steele**, Quienton (NMI) 34079742	PVT-PFC-CPL-SGT	C	MOS 653 **(Unknown date of assignment, not on Pine Camp menu)** Promoted PFC 01Jan44 per MR 05Jan44; evac sk 03Jan43 per MR 06Jan44; already evac sk TFRD to DofP, DFR per MR 22Jan44; RTD fm DofP 12Apr44 (per MR 18Apr44); promoted to CPL (per MR 05Aug44); evac sk, TFRD to DofP 01Oct44; REASG fm 2nd Repl Dep 18Oct44; **WIA** not hosp 30Oct44 (05Nov44); promoted to SGT 24Nov44; evac **SWIA**, TFRD to DofP 03Dec44 CIB (03/44); 01Jan44 per CC; CIB (04/44); 01Jan44 per CC; GCM (08/44)	WIA 30Oct44 WIA 03Dec44
1043.	**Stengel**, George J. 35124181	CPL	C	MOS 821/653 ASGD fm 2nd Repl Dep per MR 11Dec43; **(Missing entry of evac)**; RTD fm sk 20Jan44 per MR 22Jan44; evac sk (hepatitis) 28Feb44 per MR 06Mar44; already evac sk, tfr to DofP & DFR per MR 05Mar44; RTD from DofP 20Mar44 per MR 02Apr44; evac **WIA** (BC pen W L thigh shell frag) **(Unknown date)**; already evac **WIA** TFRD to DofP and DFR 02Jun44 (14Jun44); REASG but not jd fm 7th Repl Dep 17Aug44; joined 25Sep44; evac sk, TFRD to DofP 26Sep44 GC (02/44); CIB FM 01Jan44 (14/44)	WIA 02Jun44
1044.	**Stephens, James O. 20810764**	**PVT**	C	MOS 604 ASGD 21Aug44 (22Aug44) probably from I Co; evac **WIA**, TFRD to DofP 23Sep44; REASGD fm 2nd Repl Dep 10Oct44; MIA 03Nov44 (05Nov44) – to **KIA** 03Nov44 (per MR 08Nov44) (buried in USA); KIA03Nov44 per div list; KIA03NOV44 in C Co per 157 list; MIA/KIA03NOV44 per ANB; not on ABMC reg CIB PFD (07/44)	WIA 23Sep44 **KIA 03Nov44**
1045.	**Stern**, Daniel 32822123	PFC	C	MOS 745 ASGD fm 3rd Repl Bn 20Dec44 (per MR 21Dec44) – s/b PFC (22Dec44); Evac sk 03Jan45 (per MR 03Jan45); Already evac sk, TFRD to DofP 04Jan45 (per MR 04Jan45); RTD fm 3rd Repl Bn 31Jan45 (per MR 31Jan45); Evac **WIA** 28Mar45 (per MR 28Mar45); Already evac **WIA**, TFRD to DofP 29Mar45 (per MR 29Mar45) CIB 01Jan45 (01/45); GCM (8/45)	WIA 28Mar45
1046.	Stevens, Chester J. 33028105	SSG	C	MOS 653 ASGD but placed on DS to 71st Reinf Bn 28Mar45 (per MR 10Apr45); Relieved of DS to 71st Reinf Bn 04Apr45 (per MR 10Apr45); Evac **NBI** (fell off moving truck) 16Apr45 (per MR 16Apr45); Already evac **NBI,** TFRD to DofP 17Apr45 (per MR 17Apr45); RTD 04May45 (per MR 04May45) CIB 01Apr45 (28/45); GCM (32/45)	INJ 16Apr45

1047.	Stewart, James L. 34354355	PVT-PFC	C	ASGD fr Co L 28Sep43; evac sk 29Nov43 per MR 04Dec43; already evac sk TFRD to DofP, DFR per MR 31Dec43; 745 RTD fm DofP 01Jan44 per MR 06Jan44; evac sk 01Jan44 per MR 07Jan44; evac sk (exhaustion) 20Feb44; RTD 27Feb44 per MR 03Mar44; evac sk (hepatitis) 28Feb44; RTD fm sk 18Apr44 (per MR 21Apr44); evac 07May44, reported on MR 17May44; pmtd PFC 01May44; evac sk **SIW** 07May44 (MR 17May44); LD no (MR 20May44); already evac, TFRD to DofP/DFR 11Jul44 CIB (01/44 - 01Jan44 per CC)	
1048.	Stibley, Bernard C. 20839351	PFC	L, 3HQ, C, 2HQ	MOS 014, duty MOS 345 PVT in L Co per Induction Roster, 16Sep40; PFC in 3HQ per Pine Camp menu; ASGD fm 2HQ 22Sep43; TFRD to 2HQ 30Sep43 CIB FM as CPL in 3HQ (05/44); 01Jan44 per CC	
1049.	Stinnette, James W. 33089651	PVT	A, C, 1HQ	MOS 521 PFC in A Co per Pine Camp menu; ASGD fm Co A 25Jan44 per MR 26Jan44; evac sk 29Jul44 (30Jul44); RTD fm sk 03Aug44 – erron entry per MR 05Aug44; already evac sk TFRD to DofP/DFR 03Aug44; REASG but not jd fm 7th Repl Dep 17Aug44; joined 26Sep44 (per MR 03Oct44); evac sk, TFRD to DofP 03Oct44; REASG fm 2nd Repl Dep 07Oct44; TFRD to 1HQ 04Nov44 CIB as PVT in C Co 01Jan44 (11/44); GCM PFC in 1HQ (26/45)	
1050.	Stocker, Ernest L. 36986887	PVT-PFC	C	MOS 745 ASGD fm 3rd Repl Bn 20Dec44 (per MR 21Dec44); evac sk, TFRD to DofP 30Dec44; RTD fm 3rd Reinforcement Bn 15Feb45 (per MR 15Feb45); PMTD to PFC 06Mar45 (per MR 06Mar45) CIB 01Jan45 (01/45)	
1051.	Stocklose, August 36964605	SGT	C	MOS 653 ASGD fm 36th Inf Div 26Jan45 (per MR 01Feb45); Evac sk 28Apr45 (per MR 28Apr45); Already evac sk, TFRD to DofP 29Apr45 (per MR 29Apr45) GCM (8/45)	
1052.	**Stogel**, Syd 32160961	1SG	C	MOS 585 ASGD 15Sep44; evac **WIA**, TFRD to DofP 30Sep44 CIB FM 01Oct44 (14/44)	WIA 30Sep44
1053.	**Stone**, Richard M. O-1302166	2LT-1LT	C	**(Unknown date of assignment, not on Pine Camp menu)** Promoted 1LT 08Sep43 (per MR 30Sep43); evac **WIA** 22Dec43 per MR 25Dec43; already evac **WIA**, DFR per MR 12Jan44; RTD fm 1HQ 27May44; TFRD to 7th Repl Dep for trans-ship to USA 16Jul44 CIB (01/44 - 01Jan44 per CC) 4th PL	WIA 23Dec43

1054.	Stover, Clyde 20822532	PVT	C	**(Unknown date of assignment, not on Pine Camp menu)** MIA 13Sep43 DFR (per MR 24Sep43) **(POW 13Sep43);** MIA13SEP43 per ANB; Mstr POW reg gives rpt date of 13Sep44, Stalag 2B, repatriated CIB FM 01Jan44 (14/44)	POW 20Jan45
1055.	Straub, Lester R. 37561039	T-4	C	MOS 745 ASGD fm 71st Repl Bn 09Dec44; evac sk, TFRD to DofP 28Dec44; REASG fm 3rd REpl Bn 11Jan45 (per MR 11Jan45); MIA 21Jan45 (per MR 23Jan45) **(POW 20JAN45);** Mstr POW reg gives rpt date of 21Jan45 as T-4, parent unit as division artillery, no camp info, repatriated CIB 01Jan45 (01/45)	POW 20Jan45
1056.	Stuck, Robert D., Jr. (Delta, CO)	PVT	C	Induction Roster, 16Sep40	
1057.	**Sucher, Robert R.** **PCM-I** 20838355 (Boulder, CO)	**PFC**	F, I, C	(Original National Guard Member from Boulder, CO, with earlier service in F and I Companies; on Pine Camp menu in I Co) ASGD fr Co I 28Sep43; evac **WIA** 13Nov43 per MR 16Nov43; **DOW** 28Nov43 per MR 13Dec43 (07Dec43 entry of evac **WIA** TFRD to DofP & DFR is erroneous) (buried in USA); DOW as PFC in C Co 28Nov43 per div & 157 list; not on ABMC reg No discovered GO for CIB or GCM	WIA 13Nov43 **DOW 28Nov43**
1058.	Susylo (or Suzylo), Andrew 33837768	PVT-PFC	C	MOS 745 ASGD fm 3rd Repl Bn 24Jan45 (per MR 26Jan45); PMTD to PFC 06Mar45 (per MR 06Mar45); Evac sk 20Mar45 (per MR 20Mar45); RTD 22Mar45 (per MR 22Mar45); Evac sk 30May45 (per MR 30May45); Already evac sk, further evac 31May45 (per MR 31May45) CIB 01Mar45 (10/45); GCM as PFC in 1HQ (33/45)	
1059.	Sutter, Winston PCM-C 33089661	PFC	C	(Deployed w/the company, is on Pine Camp menu as PFC) MIA 13Sep43 DFR (per MR 24Sep43) **(POW 13Sep43);** Mstr POW reg gives rpt date of 13Sep44, Stalag 3B, repatriated CIB MIA as PFC in C Co (05/44); 01Jan44 per CC	POW 20Jan45
1060.	Sutton, James E. PCM-E 20837744 (Delta, CO)	CPL	C, E	PVT in C Co per Induction Roster, 16Sep40; CPL in E Co per Pine Camp menu; CIB FM as CPL in E Co 01Jan44 (14/44)	
1061.	Sutton, William F. 14189310	SSG	C	MOS 653 ASGD fm 63rd Inf Div 26Jan45 (per MR 01Feb45) No discovered GO for CIB or GCM	
1062.	Swartz, Raymond W. 35546586	SGT-SSG	C	MOS 653/652 ASGD fm 44th Inf Div 25Jan45 (per MR 01Feb45); PMTD to SSG, MOS 652 09May45 (per MR 09May45); Evac sk 29May45 (per MR 29May45) CIB 01Mar45 (10/45); GCM as S/SGT (32/45)	

1063.	Sweeney, Joe J. 37710011	PVT-PFC	C	MOS 745 ASGD fm 3rd Repl Bn 24Jan45 (per MR 26Jan45); PMTD to PFC 06Mar45 (per MR 06Mar45); Evac sk 21Mar45 (per MR 21Mar45); Already evac sk TFRD to DofP 22Mar45 (per MR 22Mar45) CIB 01Mar45 (10/45)	
1064.	Sweic, Thaddeus PCM-C SN NA	PFC	C	On Pine Camp menu	
1065.	**Sykora,** Fred P. 7030077	CPL	C	MOS 653 ASGD fm 103rd Inf Div 27Jan45 (per MR 01Feb45); Evac **WIA** 18Mar45 (per MR 18Mar45); Already Evac **WIA**, TFRD to DofP 19Mar45 (per MR 19Mar45); REASG but DS to 71st Reinf Bn 07May45 (per MR 08May45); relieved of DS to 71st Reinf Bn 08May45 (per MR 08May45) GCM (8/45)	WIA 18Mar45
1066.	**Sylvester**, Lee A. 16063725 PCM-C	CPL-SGT	C	(Deployed w/the company, is on the Pine Camp menu as PVT) Pmtd to SGT per MR 02Dec43; evac sk 13Dec43 (per MR 16Dec43); RTD fm sk 27Dec43 (per MR 31Dec43); evac 30Dec43 (per MR 05Jan43); RTD fm sk 17Jan44 per MR 20Jan44; evac **WIA** (FC rside mandible shell concussion) 20Feb44; RTD 24Feb44; evac sk Neuritis r side face & head) 29Feb44; RTD fm **WIA** 24Feb44 per MR 03Mar44; evac sk (Neuritis r side face & head) 29Feb44 per MR 06Mar44; RTD fm sk 17Mar44 per MR 22Mar44; evac sk 11Apr44 (MR 18Apr44); to DofP and DFR 23Apr44 (per MR 08May44); Already evac sk ftrd to DofP and DFR 23Apr44 CIB as SGT in C Co (01/44 - 01Jan44 per CC)	WIA 20Feb44
1067.	**Taksony**, Alexander (NMI) 36599045	PVT-PFC	C, 1HQ	MOS 603 ASGD fm 2nd Repl Bn 18Dec43 per MR 22Dec43; pmtd PFC 14Jan44 per MR 15Jan44; evac **WIA** (pen w l thigh, leg & foot, r ankle & foot & both buttocks) 24Feb44 per MR 02Mar44; already evac **WIA** trfd to DofP and DFR 07Mar44 per MR 22Mar44; RTD fm DofP 28Apr44 (per MR 06May44); evac sk 03Jun44; RTD fm sk 11Jun44 (13Jun44); TFRD to 1HQ 28Jul44 CIB 01Jan44 (11/44); GCM (16/44)	WIA 24Feb44
1068.	Talarico, Vincent A. 33500480	PVT	C, G	MOS 745 ASGD 21Aug44 (22Aug44); AWOL 2359 05Oct44 (per MR 06Oct44); RTD fm AWOL 2359 07Oct44; under arrest 15Oct44; RTD fm arrest; TFRD to Co G 31Oct44 No discovered GO for CIB or GCM	
1069.	Talbot, Arthur A. SN NA	SSG	C	MOS 653 attached fm 3rd Reinf Bn 04May45 (per MR 07May45); 653 relieved from attached status, to ASGD 07May45 (per MR 07May45) No discovered GO for CIB or GCM	

1070.	**Tapley**, Raymond B. 38510733	PVT	C	MOS 745 ASGD fm 2nd Repl Dep 24Feb44 per MR 05Mar44; evac **SWIA** 08Apr44 (MR 12Apr44); to DofP/DFR 19Apr44 (MR 09May44) CIB FM 01Mar44 (14/44)	WIA 08Apr44
1071.	Taudte, James H. 33728955	PVT	C	MOS 745 ASGD fm 2nd Repl Dep 24Feb44 per MR 05Mar44; evac sk (Myocarditis chr obsn for) [observation for chronic Myocarditis) 15Mar44 per MR 19Mar44; already evac sk, tfrd to DofP & DFR 22Mar44 (per MR 18Apr44) CIB FM 01Mar44 (14/44)	
1072.	**Taylor**, John W. 33151885	PVT-PFC-PVT-CPL-SGT	C	MOS 745/653 ASGD fm 2nd Repl Dep 24Feb44 per MR 05Mar44; pmtd to PFC 01May44; evac sk 18Jun44 (21Jun44); RTD fm sk 01Jul44 (MR 02Jul44); reduced to PVT 10Jul44; promoted to PFC 10Aug44; promoted to CPL MOS 653 07Oct44; evac **WIA**, TFRD to DofP 07Nov44; RTD fm 2nd Rein Dep 27Feb45 (per MR 27Feb45); Evac INJ, TFRD to DofP 18Mar45 (per MR 18Mar45); 653 REASG but DS to 71st Reinf Bn 03Apr45 (per MR 11Apr45); Relieved of DS to 71st Reinf Bn 11Apr45 (per MR 11Apr45); Pmtd to SGT 04May45 (per MR 04May45) CIB (04/44); 01Apr44 per CC	WIA 07Nov44
1073.	Taylor, Omer D. SN NA	PVT	C	**(Unknown date of assignment, not on Pine Camp menu)** Duty to confinement 14Jul43 – rape charge; awaiting court martial; Dishonorable Discharge per General Court Martial 26Aug43 No discovered GO for CIB or GCM	
1074.	**Taylor, Ortha (or Ortha or Othra) F. 19076343**	**SGT**	C	MOS 653 ASGD fm 63rd Inf Div 26Jan45 (per MR 01Feb45); **(Missing entry of evac)**; RTD fm sk 16Feb45; Evac **WIA,** TFRD to DofP 19Mar45 (per MR 19Mar45); **DOW** 25Mar45 (per MR 01Apr45) (buried in Lorraine Cemetery); DOW25Mar45 per div & 157 list; ABMC 25Mar45, PH No discovered GO for CIB or GCM	WIA 19Mar45 **DOW 25Mar45**
1075.	Taylor, Ralph C. 35635660	PVT	C, G	ASGD fm Co A 14Jan44 per MR 15Jan44; Tfr in grade to G Co per MR 05Mar44 CIB 01Jan44 (03/44 CC); 2nd Squad, 1st Platoon, G Co	
1076.	**Tencza, Sylvester A. 36661195**	**PVT**	C	MOS 605 ASGD fm 2nd Repl Dep per MR 11Dec43; **KIA** 13Dec43 per MR 19Dec43 (buried in USA); KIA13Dec43 per div & 157 list; not on ABMC No discovered GO for CIB or GCM	**KIA 13Dec43**
1077.	Tenute, Norman E. **36732791**	PVT-PFC	C	MOS 745 ASGD 05Jun44 (09Jun44); promoted to PFC 20Nov44 (per MR 27Nov44); evac sk 01Dec44; already evac sk, TFRD to DofP 02Dec44; REASG fm 3rd Repl Bn 15Jan45 (per MR 15Jan45); MIA 21Jan45 (per MR 23Jan45) **(POW 20JAN45);** Mstr POW reg gives rpt date of 21Jan45 as PFC, parent unit as division artillery, Stalag 11B, repatriated CIB 01Sep44 (13/44)	POW 20Jan45

1078.	Terepka, Edward A. 42106269	PVT-PFC	C	MOS 745 ASGD fm 3rd Repl Bn 24Jan45 (per MR 26Jan45); PMTD to PFC 06Mar45 (per MR 06Mar45); Evac **INJ**, TFRD to DofP 29Mar45 (per MR 29Mar45); REASG but DS to 71st Reinf Bn 07May45 (per MR 08May45); relieved of DS to 71st Reinf Bn 08May45 (per MR 08May45) GCM (32/45)	INJ 29Mar45
1079.	**Terry,** Dean W. (or N.) 20844379 PCM-C	PVT	C	(Deployed w/the company, is on Pine Camp menu as PVT Terry N.) **WIA** 29Jul43 CIB FM as PVT W. in C Co 01Jan44 (14/44)	WIA 29Jul43
1080.	Terry, Glenn PCM-L O-	2LT	L, C	Commissioned from the ranks in L Co; CPL in L Co per Pine Camp menu CIB as SSG in L Co (01/44 - 01Jan44 per CC); GCM (08/44)	
1081.	Thiel, Michael A. PCM-I 35017335	PFC	I, C	PFC in I Co per Pine Camp menu; ASGD fr Co I 28Sep43; **(Missing entry of evac)**; already evac **WIA**, DFR per MR 23Nov43 CIB FM as PFC in C Co 01Jan44 (14/44)	WIA 23Nov43
1082.	Tholl, Arthur A. 37599059	PVT	C	MOS 745 ASGD fm 3rd Repl Bn 24Jan45 (per MR 26Jan45) CIB 01Mar45 (10/45); GCM as PFC (32/45)	
1083.	Thomann, George M. 35844810	PVT	C	MOS 745 ASGD fm 3rd Repl Bn 24Jan45 (per MR 26Jan45); Evac sk, TFRD to DofP 02Feb45 (per MR 02Feb45); RTD fm 71st Reinf Bn 24Mar45 (per MR 26Mar45) CIB 01Mar45 (10/45)	
1084.	**Thomas**, Howard A. 37734379	PVT-PFC	C	MOS 745 ASGD fm 3rd Repl Bn 24Jan45 (per MR 26Jan45); PMTD to PFC 06Mar45 (per MR 06Mar45); Evac **WIA**, TFRD to DofP 18Apr45 (per MR 18Apr45); RTD 04May45 (per MR 04May45) CIB 01Mar45 (10/45)	WIA 18Apr45
1085.	**Thomas, Woodrow W. 35637523**	**PVT**	C	**(Unknown date of assignment, not on Pine Camp menu)** Evac sk 15Nov43 per MR 17Nov43; RTD fm sk 29Nov43 (31Jul44); already evac sk TFRD to DofP, DFR per MR 18Dec43; MIA 15Dec43, DFR (31Jul44), to **KIA** per MR 28Oct44; erron rptd DFR 18Dec43, s/b RTD fm sk 29Nov43; MIA 15Dec43, DFR (31Jul44) **(Murdered by Germans 13Apr44. Buried in Sicily-Rome Cemetery);** KIA per ABMC; MIA 15Dec44, executed by Germans 13Apr44; KIA13APR44 per div cas & 157 list; MIA/KIA15DEC44 per ANB; KIA13APR44 per ABMC; ABMC 13Apr44, PH w/OLC No discovered GO for CIB or GCM	**KIA 13Apr44**
1086.	Thomason, Albert L. (Delta, CO)	PVT	C	Induction Roster, 16Sep40	
1087.	Thompson, Howard M. (Delta, CO)	PVT	C	Induction Roster, 16Sep40	

1088.	Thompson, Robert E. (Delta, CO)	PVT	C	Induction Roster, 16Sep40	
1089.	Thorhauer, Robert H. 33698097	PVT-PFC-CPL	C	MOS 745/653 AsSGD fm 2nd Repl Dep 24Feb44 per MR 05Mar44; evac sk 27Jun44 (29Jun44); pmtd to PFC 01Jul44 (MR 02Jul44); erron rptd on 01Jul44 as evac sk, s/b RTD fm sk (MR 10Jul44); 653 PMTD to CPL 15Jan45 (per MR 15Jan45); MIA 21Jan45 (per MR 23Jan45) **(POW 20JAN45);** Mstr POW reg gives rpt date of 21Jan45 as CPL, parent unit as division artillery, Stalag 11B, repatriated CIB PFD (07/44)	POW 20Jan45
1090.	Thormann, George H. 35844810	PFC	C	GCM (32/45)	
1091.	Thurston, Russell J. 20303068	PFC	C	**(Unknown date of assignment, not on Pine Camp menu)** Sk evac 24Jul43 (per MR 26Jul43); RTD fm hosp 01Aug43 (per MR 02Aug43); evac sk 23Aug43 (per MR 24Jul43); RTD fm sk 07Sep43 (per MR 18Sep43); MIA 13Sep43 DFR (per MR 24Sep43) **(POW 13Sep43);** Mstr POW reg gives rpt date of 13Sep43, Stalag 2B, repatriated CIB FM 01Jan44 (14/44)	POW 13Sep43
1092.	Tiberio, James A. 35027381	PFC	C	MOS 745/521 ASGD fm Div HQ Co 23Oct44 (per MR 25Oct44); Special Duty with Div HQ 23Oct44 (per MR 02Nov44); Already abs DS to Div HQ Co, TFRD to Div HQ Co 15Feb45 (per MR 15Feb45) No discovered GO for CIB or GCM	
1093.	**Tillman**, George V. 32488999	PVT-PFC	C	MOS 745 ASGD 20Aug43; promoted PFC 01Jan44 per MR 05Jan44; **WIA** 31May44 (06Jun44); already evac **WIA** to DofP/DFR 02Jun44 (18Jun44); RASGD fm DofP (29Jun44); evac **WIA** 16Aug44 (19Aug44); already evac **WIA** TFRD to DofP/DFR 18Aug44 (19Aug44); REASGD fm 2nd Repl Dep 10Oct44; evac **WIA**, TFRD to DofP 05Nov44; Evac sk 01Feb45 (per MR 01Feb45); Already Evac sk, TFRD to DofP 02Feb45 (per MR 02Feb45); REASG fm 3rd Repl Bn 25Jan45 (per MR 25Jan45) CIB (01/44 - 01Jan44 per CC); GCM (08/44)	WIA 31May44 WIA 16Aug44 WIA 05Nov44
1094.	**Timmons,** Byron E. 34278971 PCM-C	PVT- SGT	C	(Deployed w/the company, is on Pine Camp menu as PVT) Promoted PFC 25Aug43; evac **WIA** 12Nov43 (per MR 15Nov43); already evac **WIA** TFRD to DofP, DFR per MR 06Dec43; RTD fm DofP 06Mar44 per MR 10Mar44; pmtd to CPL 10Apr 44 (per MR 11Apr44); pmtd to SGT; evac sk, TFRD to DofP 23Sep44 CIB as SGT in C Co (03/44); 01Jan44 per CC; GCM (02/44)	WIA 06Dec43
1095.	Tooker, Harry L. PCM-C	PVT	C	On Pine Camp menu	

1096.	Toratti, Arthur W. 37599967	PVT	C	MOS 745 ASGD fm 3rd Repl Bn 24Jan45 (per MR 26Jan45) CIB 01Mar45 (10/45); GCM (32/45)	
1097.	Tourtilotte, John H. 31000334	PVT-PFC	C	MOS 745 ASGD 28Sep43 (per MR 30Sep43); promoted to PFC 03Nov43 (per MR 05Nov43); MIA 15Dec43, DFR (per MR 25Dec43) Was among five men from C Co (Gueil, Morris, Tourtilotte, Koziol, McCoy) captured 15Dec43 near Venafro, who escaped from a POW train as it was being bombed in northern Italy on 28Jan44 and who made it back to Allied lines, but did not return to the unit CIB MIA (05/44); 01Jan44 per CC	POW 15Dec43 ESCAPED
1098.	**Trainor**, James B. (Trainer) 11027904	CPL-SGT-SSG-TSG	L, C	MOS 651 On Pine Camp menu as CPL in L Co; ASGD fr Co L 28Sep43; promoted to SGT per MR 05Nov43; pmtd to SSG 18Jan44 per MR 19Jan44; pmtd to TSG per MR 25Jan44; evac **LIA** (FC wrist r) 14Feb44; RTD 16Feb44; LWA not-hosp 09May44 (MR 17May44); evac **WIA** 31May44; RTD fm **WIA** 13Jul44]; evac sk 15Jul44; RTD 19Jul44 (MR 21Jul44); 651 evac **WIA**, TFRD to DofP 23Sep44; evac sk, TFRD to DofP 30Sep44; REASG but not joined fm 2nd Repl Dep 28Sep44; joined 29Sep44; **(Missing entry of evac)**; REASG fm hosp 05Oct44; 651 evac **WIA**, TFRD to DofP 07Nov44; REASGD fm 2nd Repl Dep 19Nov44; evac sk, TFRD to DofP 22Nov44 CIB (01/44 - 01Jan44 per CC); GCM (16/44)	INJ 14Feb44 WIA 31May44 WIA 23Sep44 WIA 07Nov44
1099.	Trainor, William F. 31345568	PVT	C, G	MOS 745 ASGD fm 2nd Repl Bn 14Jan44 per MR 18Jan44; Tfr in grade to G Co per MR 05Mar44 CIB 01Feb44 (06/44 CC); 3rd Squad, 1st Platoon, G Co	
1100.	Treder, Myron M. 37598976	PVT	C	MOS 745 ASGD fm 3rd Repl Bn 24Jan45 (per MR 26Jan45); Evac sk, TFRD to DofP 02Feb45 (per MR 02Feb45); REASG fm 2nd Reinf Dep 11Mar45 (per MR 11Mar45) CIB 01Mar45 (10/45); GCM as PFC (32/45)	
1101.	Trujillo, Ignacio (NMI) 38005342 PCM-C	PFC	C	(Deployed w/the company, is on the Pine Camp menu) evac 31Dec43 per MR 05Jan44; RTD fm sk 11Jan44 per MR 14Jan44; evac sk (arthritis ankle) 21Mar44 per MR 25Mar44; already evac sk, tfrd to DofP & DFR 31Mar44 (per MR 14Apr44) PFC in C Co per PCCM42; CIB DP as PFC in C Co (07/44)	
1102.	**Trygestad,** Harvey O. 37599218	PVT-PFC	C	MOS 745 ASGD fm 3rd Repl Bn 24Jan45 (per MR 26Jan45); PMTD to PFC 06Mar45 (per MR 06Mar45); Evac **WIA**, TFRD to DofP 29Mar45 (per MR 29Mar45); REASG 29May45 (per MR 30May45) CIB 01Mar45 (10/45); GCM (32/45)	WIA 29Mar45

1103.	Trytten, Ervin S. 37599017	PVT-PFC	C	MOS 745 ASGD fm 3rd Repl Bn 24Jan45 (per MR 26Jan45); PMTD to PFC 06Mar45 (per MR 06Mar45) CIB 01Mar45 (10/45); GCM as PFC (32/45)	
1104.	Tuck, Jack S. 38506222	PVT-PFC-CPL	C	MOS 745/405 ASGD fm 2nd Repl Bn 14Jan44 per MR 18Jan44; Pmtd to PFC 04Mar44 per MR 12Mar44; promoted to CPL 17Sep44; Evac sk 05Apr45 (per MR 05Apr45); RTD fm sk 08Apr45 (per MR 08Apr45); Evac sk 29Apr45 (per MR 29Apr45); Already evac sk, TFRD to DofP 30Apr45 (per MR 30Apr45) CIB (01/44 - 01Feb44 per CC); GCM CPL (08/45)	
1105.	Tucker, Jesse V. (or U. 37217136	PVT	C, RHQ	**(Unknown date of assignment, not on the Pine Camp menu)** TFRD to RHQ 07Aug43 CIB (07/44)	
1106.	Tucker, Lawrence K. PCM-C O-1287439	1LT	A, C, D	Platoon Leader in C Co per Pine Camp menu; ASGD fr Co A per MR 05Dec43; evac sk 24Jan44 per MR 27Jan44; RTD fm sk evac 13Feb44; Reld fm asgn as CO, tfr to D Co 28Feb44 CIB as 1LT (01/44 - 01Jan44 per CC) (WIA 12 Sep43 & 13Sep44)	
1107.	Tucker, Nathen (NMI) 34544169	PVT	C	**(Unknown date of assignment, not on Pine Camp menu)** MIA 11Nov43 (per MR 27Nov43 – 01 EM MIA) **(POW 17May44) (Discrepancy: in date of MIA and date of stated capture could be result of evasion or just late reporting by the Germans);** MIA11NOV43 per ANB; Mstr POW reg gives rpt date of 17May44 w/o unit ID, Stalag 2B, repatriated POW date is 11Nov43 CIB FM 01Jan44 (14/44)	POW 11Nov43
1108.	Tudico, Louis E. 35837077	PVT-PFC	C	MOS 745 ASGD fm 71st Repl Bn 09Dec44; promoted to PFC 25Dec44 (per MR 26Dec44); MIA 21Jan45 (per MR 23Jan45) **(POW 20JAN45);** Mstr POW reg gives rpt date of 21Jan45, parent unit as division artillery, Stalag 11B, repatriated CIB 01Jan45 (01/45)	POW 20Jan45
1109.	Tudisco, Joseph J. 32002310	SSG	C	MOS 653 ASGD fm 44th Inf Div 25Jan45 (per MR 01Feb45) GCM (8/45)	
1110.	Tunney, John S. 32862411	PFC	1 H Q , C, 1HQ	MOS 745 ASGD fm 1HQ 20Oct44; evac sk 13Nov44; already evac sk, TFRD to DofP 14Nov44; REASG fm 71st Repl Dep 01Dec44; evac sk, TFRD to DofP 02Dec44; REASG 17Dec44; TFRD to 1HQ 02Feb45 (per MR 02Feb45) CIB in 1HQ PFD (07/44); GCM PFC in C Co (16/44)	
1111.	Tutt, Charles E. 38687496	PVT	C	MOS 745 ASGD fm 71st Repl Bn 09Dec44; evac **LIA**, TFRD to DofP 24Dec44 CIB 01Jan45 (01/45)	INJ 24Dec44

1112.	Twohey, James J. 31289327	PVT	C	MOS 745 ASGD fr 158th FA Bn 31Aug43 (per MR 01Sep43); MIA 13Sep43 DFR (per MR 24Sep43) **(POW 13Sep43);** Mstr POW reg gives rpt date of 13Sep43 as 116th IN, Stalag 2B, repatriated CIB FM 01Jan44 (14/44)	POW 13Sep43
1113.	Tyler, Glenn R. (Delta, CO)	CPL	C	Induction Roster, 16Sep40	
1114.	Tyler, Stephen A. PCM-M 20837748 (Delta, CO)	T-4	C, M, AT	Induction Roster 16Sep40 as PVT in C Co; SGT in M Co per Pine Camp menu CIB FM as T-4 in AT Co 01Jan44 (12/44)	
1115.	Tyrrell, Sidney J. 37675295	PVT	C	MOS 745 ASGD fm 2nd Repl Dep 24Feb44 per MR 05Mar44; evac sk, **INJ** (right lower eyelid abrasion cornea) 28Mar44 fm MR 05Apr44; RTD fm hosp 04Apr44 (per MR 12Apr44); evac sk 01Jun44; already evac sk to DofP/DFR 07Jun44 (15Jun44) CIB FM 01Mar44 (14/44)	INJ 28Mar44
1116.	Tyson, George N., Jr. 33939401	PVT	C	MOS 745 ASGD fm 3rd Repl Bn 24Jan45 (per MR 26Jan45); Evac sk 10Feb45 (per MR 10Feb45); Already Evac sk, TFRD to DofP 11Feb45 (per MR 11Feb45); REASGD fm 2nd Rein Dep 25Feb45 (per MR 25Feb45); Evac INJ 17Mar45 (per MR 17Mar45); 745 REASG 10Apr45 (per MR 13Apr45); Evac sk 24Apr45 (per MR 24Apr45); Already evac sk, TFRD to DofP 25Apr45 (per MR 25Apr45) CIB 01Mar45 (10/45)	
1117.	Valdez, Michael A. (Valdes) 42134906	PVT	C	MOS 745 ASGD fm 71st Repl Bn 09Dec44; evac sk, TFRD to DofP 17Dec44 CIB 01Jan45 (01/45)	
1118.	**Valdez, Paul H. (or R. per Pine Camp menu)** **38006151**	**PFC-CPL**	C	MOS 745 (Deployed w/the company as PFC R. in Pine Camp menu); evac sk 28Sep43 (per MR 02Oct43); RTD fr DofP 12Nov43 per MR 17Nov43; pmtd to **CPL** per MR 02Dec43; MIA 15Dec43, DFR (per MR 25Dec43), to **KIA** per MR 28Oct44 **(Murdered by Germans 13Apr44. Buried in USA);** MIA15DEC43 per ANB; MURDERED by Germans 13Apr44; KIA13Apr44 per div cas list -- NOT ON 157 LIST; not on ABMC reg CIB MIA as CPL H. in C Co (05/44); 01Jan44 per CC	**KIA 13Apr44**
1119.	Van Rosson, Peter C. 32963676	PVT-PFC	C	MOS 605 ASGD and jnd fr 2nd Repl Dep 24Feb44 per MR 07Mar44; pmtd to PFC 01May44; evac sk 26Jun44) (27Jun44); RTD fm sk 11Jul44; evac sk 03Aug44 (per 04Aug44); already evac sk TFRD to DofP/DFR 03Aug44 GCM (08/44); CIB FM 01Mar44 (14/44)	

1120. Van Syckle, Richard P. O-1283519 PCM-L	1LT	L, RHQ, C	1LT platoon leader in L Co per Pine Camp menu; ASGD fr RHQ 01Sep43; MIA 13Sep43 DFR (per MR 24Sep43) **(POW 13Sep43);** Mstr POW reg gives rpt date of 13Sep43, Stalag Luft 1, repatriated CIB FM as 1LT regimental officer eff 01Jan44 (14/44)	POW 13Sep43
1121. Van Uden, Herman H. 37597354	PVT	C	GCM (32/45)	
1122. Vargas, Manuell G. PCM-C 38005260	PFC	C, CN	PFC in C Co per Pine Camp menu CIB as PVT in CN Co (07/44)	
1123. **Vee,** Donald M. 37599018	PVT-PFC	C	MOS 745 37699018 PVT MOS 745 ASGD fm 3rd Repl Bn 24Jan45 (per MR 26Jan45); PMTD to PFC 06Mar45 (per MR 06Mar45); evac **WIA** 29Mar45 (per MR 29Mar45); Already evac **WIA**, TFRD to DofP 30Mar45 (per MR 30Mar45) CIB 01Mar45 (10/45)	WIA 29Mar45
1124. Vigil, Juan L. 38581376	PVT-PFC	C	MOS 746 ASGD fm 3rd Repl Bn 10Dec44; promoted to PFC 25Dec44 (per MR 26Dec44); MIA 21Jan45 (per MR 23Jan45) **(POW 20JAN45);** Mstr POW reg gives rpt date of 21Jan45, parent unit as division artillery, Stalag 11B, repatriated CIB 01Jan45 (01/45)	POW 20Jan45
1125. Vigliante, Alfred J. 32209021	PFC-CPL	C	MOS 056 (Deployed w/the company, is on the Pine Camp menu as PFC Vigliante) Evac sk 06Aug43 (per MR 07Aug43); evac sk 06Aug43 (per MR 09Aug43) – double entry; erron rptd evac sk on MR 09Aug43 – already rptd MR 07Aug43 (17Aug43); RTD fr hosp 08Aug43 (per MR 10Aug43); pmtd CPL MOS 056 24May44; **INJ** 21Jan45 not hosp (concussion) (per MR 27Jan45); TD to Ft. Dix, NJ 25Feb45 (per MR 25Feb45); TDY to US, DFR 21May45 (per MR 21May45) CIB as PFC Vigliente in C Co (01/44 - 01Jan44 per CC); GCM as T/5 VIGLIANTE (08/44)	INJ 21Jan45
1126. Villareal, John (NMI) 38433902	PVT	C, C	MOS 745 ASGD fm 2nd Repl Bn 14Jan44 per MR 18Jan44; Tfr in grade to G Co per MR 05Mar44 KIA02Jun44 per div & 157 list; MIA/KIA02JUN44 per ANB; not on ABMC as Villareal or as Villereal No discovered GO for CIB or GCM	(KIA 02Jun44 in G Co)
1127. Vilonna, Anthjony B. (R.) 32863310	PVT	C, G	MOS 745 ASGD fm 2nd Repl Bn 14Jan44 per MR 18Jan44; Tfr in grade to G Co per MR 05Mar44 CIB (04/44); 01Feb44 per CC	

1128.	Vincent, Lloyd L. 38006131	PFC-T-5	C	MOS 745 (Deployed w/the company, is on the Pine Camp menu as PFC) Evac sk 11Jan45 (per MR 11Jan45); Already evac sk, TFRD to DofP 17Jan45 (per MR 17Jan45); RTD fm 2nd Reinforcement Dep 20Feb45 (per MR 20Feb45); evac sk 05Mar45 (per MR 05Mar45); **(Missing entry of RTD)**; Evac sk 11Mar45 (per MR 11Mar45); PMTD to T-5, MOS 060 09May45 (per MR 09May45); TFRD to 2nd Reinf Dep for shipment to Ft. Logan, CO 14May45 (per MR 14May45) CIB PFD as PFC in C Co (07/44); GCM as L. (08/44)	
1129.	**Vlaming**, James 39588923	PVT	C	MOS 746 ASGD fm 3rd Repl Bn 10Dec44; promoted to PFC 25Dec44 (per MR 26Dec44); Evac **WIA**, TFRD to DofP 05Jan45 (per MR 05Jan45); RTD fm 2nd Rein Dep 27Feb45 (per MR 27Feb45); Evac **WIA**, TFRD to DofP 18Mar45 (per MR 18Mar45) CIB 01Jan45 (01/45)	WIA 05Jan45 WIA 18Mar45
1130.	**Vogel, Fred L. PCM-C** 39602800	**CPL**	C	(Deployed w/the company, is on the Pine Camp menu as PFC) **KIA** 12Sep43 (per MR 18Sep43) (buried in Sicily-Rome Cemetery); KIA as CPL in C Co 12Sep43 per div & 157 list -- GUNSHOT; ABMC 12Sep43, PH No discovered GO for CIB or GCM	**KIA 12Sep43**
1131.	Vosburgh, Burt V. 39588765	PVT	C	MOS 746 ASGD fm 3rd Repl Bn 10Dec44; evac sk 16Dec44; already evac sk, TFRD to DofP 20Dec44; REASG fm 3rd Repl Bn 09Feb45 (per MR 09Feb45); Evac sk 24Feb45 (per MR 24Feb45); Already evac sk, TFRD to DofP 26Feb45 (per MR 26Feb45); RTD fm 71st Reinf Bn 06May45 (per MR 06May45) CIB 01Jan45 (01/45); GCM as PFC (32/45)	
1132.	**Vounatso**, John (NMI) 31345493	PVT-PFC	C	MOS 745 ASGD fm 2nd Repl Bn 14Jan44 per MR 18Jan44; Pmtd to PFC 04Mar44 per MR 12Mar44; evac sk non-battle **INJ** FB R thumb obsn for) 14Mar44 per MR 18Mar44; RTD fm sk 10May44 (per MR 17May44); **WIA** 01Jun44 (06Jun44); already evac TFRD to DofP and DFR 08Jun44 (17Jun44); RTD fm DofP 21Jul44; evac sk, TFRD to DofP 03Aug44; REASG fm 2nd Repl Dep 31Oct44; evac sk 28Nov44; already evac sk, TFRD to DofP 29Nov44; REASG not joined fm 71st Repl Bn 08Dec44 (per MR 01Jan45); AWOL 2359 08Dec44 en route to REASG fm 71st Repl Bn (per MR 01Jan45); fm AWOL to Regt'l Stockade 01Jan45 (per MR 01Jan45); RTD fm Regt'l Stockade 11Jan45 (per MR 11Jan45); Evac sk 13Jan45 (per MR 13Jan45); RTD fm sk 15Jan45 (per MR 15Jan45); AWOL 2359 **(Incomplete entry)** CIB PFD (07/44 - w/drn PVT eff 15Jan45 10/45)	INJ 14Mar44 WIA 01Jun44

1133.	**Vroman, Carl J. PCM-F 32854998**	**PFC**	C	(Deployed as PVT in F Company **Unknown date of assignment**) erron rptd on 12Dec43 as **KIA** 08Dec43, S/B **KIA** 07Dec43 per MR 16Dec43 (buried in USA); KIA07Dec43 per div & 157 list; not on ABMC reg No discovered GO for CIB or GCM	**KIA 07Dec43**
1134.	**Wachter, Frank J. 31342553**	**PVT**	C	MOS 743 ASGD fm 2nd Repl Dep per MR 11Dec43; evac **WIA** 15Dec43 per MR 17Dec44; already evac **WIA** TFRD to DofP, DFR per MR 16Jan44; RTD fm DofP 28Mar44 per MR 08Apr44; evac **WIA** (BC pen W L shoulder shell frag) 31May44; already evac **WIA** TFRD to DofP/DFR 30Jun44 (30Jul44); RTD fm DofP 04Aug44; fm MIA 19Aug44 to **KIA** 19Aug44 (22Aug44) (buried in Rhone Cemetery); KIA19Aug44 per div & 157 list; MIA/KIA19AUG44 per ANB; ABMC 19Aug44, PH w/OLC No discovered GO for CIB or GCM	WIA 15Dec43 WIA 31May44 **KIA 19Aug44**
1135.	Wade, Joseph C. 34764081	PVT	C	MOS 137 ASGD fm 2nd Repl Dep per MR 11Dec43; evac sk 27Dec43 (per MR 01Jan44); already sk abs tfrd to DofP & DFR **(incomplete entry)**; RTD fm DofP (10Jun44); promoted to PFC (per MR 05Aug44); evac sk 14Sep44; already evac sk, TFRD to DofP 23Sep44; RTD fm sk 17Sep44; evac sk 27Dec43 per MR 01Jan44; already evac sk TFRD to DofP, DFR (erron entry per MR 30Jan44 CIB PFD (07/44); GCM (08/44)	
1136.	Wadley, William D. 34934493	PVT-PFC	C, 1HQ	MOS 745 ASGD fm 3rd Repl Bn 24Jan45 (per MR 26Jan45); PMTD to PFC 06Mar45 (per MR 06Mar45); TFRD to HQ 1st Bn 08Apr45 (per MR 08Apr45) CIB 01Mar45 (10/45); GCM as PFC in 1HQ (26/45)	
1137.	**Waefler, Arnold B. 20837561 PCM-B (Greeley, CO)**	**SGT-PVT-PFC**	B, C	(Original member of National Guard, inducted in Company B as PVT; on Pine Camp menu as SGT in B Co; ASGD fr Co B 25Sep43 as PVT (per MR 28Sep43); Promoted to PFC 03Nov43 per MR 05Nov43; **KIA** 10Nov43 per MR 17Nov43 (buried in Sicily-Rome Cemetery); KIA as PFC in C Co 10Nov43 per div & 157 list -- SHRAPNEL; ABMC 10Nov43, PH No discovered GO for CIB or GCM	**KIA 10Nov43**
1138.	Wagner, Paul E. 33720050	PVT	C	MOS 125 ASGD fm 2nd Repl Dep per MR 11Dec43; MIA 15Dec43, DFR per MR 25Dec43 **(POW 16Dec43)**; Mstr POW reg gives rpt date of "16 1K 43" w/o unit ID, in 100th Div area, Stalag 2B, repatriated No discovered GO for CIB or GCM	POW 16Dec43

1139.	**Wahl**, Charlie P. PCM 20837609	SGT-SSG-1SG	B, C, B	**(Unknown date of assignment. Is on Pine Camp menu as SGT in Company B; On Pine Camp menu as SSG in B Co) (Unknown date of WIA)** already evac **WIA**, DFR per MR 11Nov43; RTD fm DofP 24Dec43 (per MR 26Dec43); TFRD in grade to Co B per MR 27Dec43 CIB in B Co (01/44 - 01Jan44 per CC); GCM (02/44) (earlier 1SG of C Co, per MR 18Oct43)	**WIA unk**
1140.	**Walker,** Oress M. 39588277	PVT-PFC	C	MOS 745 ASGD fm 71st Repl Bn 09Dec44; promoted to PFC 25Dec44 (per MR 26Dec44); Evac sk, TFRD to DofP 03Jan45 (per MR 03Jan45); REASGD fm 2nd Rein Dep 25Feb45 (per MR 25Feb45); Evac **WIA**, TFRD to DofP 19Mar45 (per MR 19Mar45) CIB 01Jan45 (01/45)	WIA 19Mar45
1141.	Walker, William H. PVT-PFC-CPL-PVT-PFC 38687654	PVT-PFC	C, 1HQ	MOS 745/653 ASGD fm 71st Repl Bn 09Dec44; promoted to PFC 25Dec44 (per MR 26Dec44); evac sk, TFRD to DofP 28Dec44; ASGD fm 3rd Reinforcement Bn 15Feb45 (per MR 15Feb45); Pmtd to CPL, change in MOS to 653 14Apr45 (per MR 14Apr45); Reduced to PVT, MOS 745 18May45 (per MR 18May45); PMTD to PFC 21May45 (per MR 23May45) CIB 01Jan45 (01/45); GCM (8/45); 2nd GCM in 1HQ (33/45)	
1142.	Walton, Harvey J. D. 38344592	PFC	C	MOS 745 attached fm 3rd Reinf Bn 04May45 (per MR 07May45); relieved from attached status, to ASGD 05May45 (per MR 07May45) No discovered GO for CIB or GCM	
1143.	**Wardrop**, Earl D. 33615972	PVT-PFC	C	MOS 745 ASGD fm 3rd Repl Bn 24Jan45 (per MR 26Jan45); PMTD to PFC 06Mar45 (per MR 06Mar45); Evac **WIA**, TFRD to DofP 18Mar45 (per MR 18Mar45); RTD fm 71st Reinf Bn 21May45 (per MR 21May45) CIB 01Mar45 (10/45); GCM as PFC (32/45)	WIA 18Mar45
1144.	**Ware,** William L. 39592076	PVT-PFC	C	MOS 745 ASGD fm 3rd Repl Bn 24Jan45 (per MR 26Jan45); PMTD to PFC 06Mar45 (per MR 06Mar45); Evac **WIA**, TFRD to DofP 18Mar45 (per MR 18Mar45) CIB 01Mar45 (10/45)	WIA 18Mar45
1145.	**Warner**, Charles R. 39599448	PVT-PFC	C	MOS 745 ASGD fm 3rd Repl Bn 24Jan45 (per MR 26Jan45); PMTD to PFC 06Mar45 (per MR 06Mar45); Evac **WIA** 28Mar45 (per MR 28Mar45); Already evac sk, TFRD to DofP 29Mar45 (per MR 29Mar45) CIB 01Mar45 (10/45)	WIA 28Mar45

1146.	Warner, Deloss L. 20837205 PCM-G	PVT	C	MOS 745 PVT in RHQ (AT platoon) per Induction Roster, 16Sep40; PFC in G Co per Pine Camp menu; ASGD fr Co G 28Sep43; **(MISSING ENTRY OF TFR TO G CO);** KIA as PVT in G Co 07Oct43 per div & 157 list No discovered GO for CIB or GCM (Cannon City, CO) on KIA list of Freemont County, CO	(KIA 07Oct43 in G Co)
1147.	**Warnock, Frank E.** 35237158	**PVT-PFC**	C	MOS 745 ASGD fm 3rd Repl Bn 24Jan45 (per MR 26Jan45); PMTD to PFC 06Mar45 (per MR 06Mar45); **KIA** 18Mar45 (per MR20ar45) (buried in Lorraine Cemetery);); KIA18Mar45 as PFC per div & 157 list; ABMC 18Mar45, PH CIB 01Mar45 (10/45)	**KIA 18Mar45**
1148.	Wasdin, Lyndon SGT-SSG-PVT-PFC	**SGT-PFC**	C	MOS 653 ASGD fm 103rd Inf Div 26Jan45 (per MR 01Feb45); PMTD to SSG 09Mar45 (per MR 09Mar45); Reduced to PVT, MOS 745 18May45 (per MR 18May45); PMTD to PFC 21May45 (per MR 23May45) GCM (8/45)	
1149.	Watkins, Donald L. 35413950	PFC-CPL	C	MOS 745/653 ASGD fm 36th Inf Div 26Jan45 (per MR 01Feb45); AWOL 2359 30Jan45 (per MR 03Feb45); AWOL to Confinement 09Feb45 (per MR 10Feb45); RTD fm Confinement 10Feb45 (per MR 10Feb45); Pmtd to CPL, change in MOS to 653 14Apr45 (per MR 14Apr45) No discovered GO for CIB or GCM	
1150.	Watkins, James E., Jr. **38472652**	PFC	C	MOS 745 ASGD fm 71st Repl Bn 09Dec44; evac sk, TFRD to DofP 12Dec44 CIB 01Jan45 (01/45)	
1151.	Watson, Robert D. 12055335	PVT	2HQ, C	MOS 503, duty MOS 745 CPL in 2HQ per Pine Camp menu; ASGD fm 2HQ 22Sep43; evac sk 28Sep43 (per MR 02Oct43); already evac sk, TFRD to DofP and DFR per MR 04Nov43 CIB FM as PVT in C Co 01Jan44 (14/44)	
1152.	Watts, Sam B. 38679634	PVT	C	MOS 745 ASGD fm 3rd Repl Bn 24Jan45 (per MR 26Jan45); Evac sk, TFRD to DofP 25Jan45 (per MR 27Jan45) CIB 01Mar45 (10/45)	
1153.	**Waugh, Donald L.** O-1303236	**2LT-1LT**	C	**(Unknown date of assignment, not on Pine Camp menu)** Evac sk per MR 04Jan44; RTD fm sk 27Jan44 per MR 31Jan44; evac sk (sprain old lumbar back, slipped on rock) 22Feb44; already evac sk, promoted to 1LT, DOR 08Mar44 per MR 21Mar44; RTD fr sk 27Mar44 03Apr44 per MR 25Mar44; evac sk 02Jun44 (MR 03Jun44); RTD fm sk 25Jun44 (27Jun44); fm MIA 19Aug44 to **KIA** 19Aug44 (22Aug44) (buried in Rhone Cemetery) (**Silver Star**); KIA19Aug44 per div & 157 list; MIA/KIA19AUG44 per ANB; ABMC 19Aug44, SS, PH CIB (01/44 - 01Jan44 per CC)	**KIA 19Aug44**

1154.	Waugh, Marion 38687904	PVT	C	MOS 745 ASGD fm 71st Repl Bn 09Dec44; evac sk, TFRD to DofP 16Dec44; REASG fm 3rd Repl Bn 28Dec44; MIA 21Jan45 (per MR 23Jan45) **(POW 20JAN45);** Mstr POW reg gives rpt date of 03Mar45 w/o unit ID, Stalag 11B, repatriated -- was captured 20Jan45 or earlier at Reipertswiller CIB 01Jan45 (01/45)	POW 20Jan45
1155.	Weams, Charles T. (Delta, CO)	PVT	C	Induction Roster 16Sep40	
1156.	Weams, Howard L. (Delta, CO)	PFC	C	Induction Roster 16Sep40	
1157.	Weasner, Donald E. 35172245	PVT	F, C	**(Unknown date of assignment, is on Pine Camp menus as PVT in F Company)** Evac sk 11Aug43; RTD fm sk 05Sep43 (per MR 07Sep43); evac sk 11Sep43 (per MR 20Sep43) CIB FM as PVT in C Co 01Jan44 (14/44)	
1158.	**Wehner,** Raymond L. 35683715	PFC	C, 1HQ	MOS 504 ASGD fm 2nd Repl Dep per MR 11Dec43; evac **WIA** (BC Punc W L hip shell frag) 30May44; RTD fm **WIA** 27Jun44 (28Jun44); TFRD to 1HQ 26Sep44 (per MR14Oct44) CIB in C Co (01/44 - 01Jan44 per CC); GCM in 1HQ (16/44)	WIA 30May44
1159.	**Weicht, Earl T.** **33759707**	**PVT**	C	MOS 653 **(Unknown date of assignment)** **(Missing entry of evac)** RTD fm 2nd Repl Dep 11Jan44 per MR 13Jan44; evac sk 23Jan44 per MR 27Jan44; **(Missing entry of RTD)**; **(Missing entry of WIA)**; already evac **WIA**, trfd to DofP and DFR 24Feb44 per MR 14Mar44; RTD fr DofP 27Mar44 per MR 03Apr44; **KIA** 12May44 (per MR 19May44) (buried in USA); KIA12May44 per div & 157 list; not on ABMC reg No discovered GO for CIB or GCM	**WIA unk** **KIA 12May44**
1160.	Weidner, Clarence T. 33950357	PVT	C	MOS 745 ASGD fm 3rd Repl Bn 24Jan45 (per MR 26Jan45); Evac sk, TFRD to DofP 01Feb45 (per MR 01Feb45) CIB 01Mar45 (10/45)	
1161.	Weiner, Samuel L. 31644234	PVT	C	MOS 745 ASGD fm 3rd Repl Bn 24Jan45 (per MR 26Jan45); Evac **INJ,** TFRD to DofP 30Mar45 (per MR 30Mar45) CIB 01Mar45 (10/45)	INJ 30Mar45
1162.	Weinino, Jack M. 37568540	PVT	1HQ, C	MOS 745 ASGD fm 1HQ 10Jun44 (11Jun44) No discovered GO for CIB or GCM	
1163.	Weinkam, Charles S. 33556280	PVT	C, 1HQ	MOS 745 ASGD fm 2nd Repl Bn 14Jan44 per MR 18Jan44; tfrd to HHC, 1st Bn 02May44 CIB PFD (07/44); GCM PFC (25/45)	

1164.	**Weinstein**, Saul (NMI) 31382117	PVT	C	MOS 745 ASGD fm 2nd Repl Dep 23Apr44 (per MR 29Apr44); evac **WIA** (BC perf W thigh shell frag) 31May44; already evac **WIA** TFRD to DofP and DFR 06Jun44 (15Jun44); **(Missing entry of RTD)**; evac sk 26Jul44 (27Jul44); RTD fm DofP 13Jul44; evac sk 04Aug44; already evac sk TFRD to DofP/DFR 04Aug44 (08Aug44); 745 REASD not joined fm 7th Repl Dep; joined 23Sep44**;** evac sk, TFRD to DofP 03Oct44 CIB PFD (07/44)	WIA 31May44
1165.	**Weis,** William P. 33141489	CPL-SSG	I, C, G	MOS 653 ASGD fr Co I 28Sep43; evac **WIA** 12Nov43 per MR 12Nov43; already evac **WIA** TFRD to DofP, DFR per MR 15Dec43; RTD fm DofP 01Jan44 per MR 06Jan44; pmtd to SGT 18Jan44 per MR 19Jan44; pmtd to SSG per MR 25Jan44 (probably later transferred to G Co) CIB (01/44); 01Jan44 as WEIS per CC	WIA 12Nov43
1166.	**Welch,** R. L. 38677700	PVT	C	MOS 745 ASGD fm 71st Repl Bn 09Dec44; evac **WIA**, TFRD to DofP 14Dec44; Reasg fm 2nd Repl Dep 01Jan45 (per MR 03Jan45); Evac **WIA**, TFRD to DofP 14Jan45 (per MR 14Jan45) CIB 01Jan45 (01/45)	WIA 14Dec44 WIA 14Jan45
1167.	**Wenger**, Harold (NMI) 33500343	PVT-PFC	C	MOS 745 ASGD 05Jun44 (09Jun44); promoted to PFC 20Nov44 (per MR 27Nov44); evac **WIA** 14Jan45 (per MR 14Jan45); RTD 19Jan45 (per MR 19Jan45) CIB 01Sep44 (13/44); GCM PFC (08/45)	WIA 14Jan45
1168.	**Wensley**, Herbert D. 31374857	PVT	C	MOS 745 ASGD fm 2nd Repl Dep 23Apr44 (per MR 29Apr44); **WIA** 01Jun44 (06Jun44); already evac **WIA** to DofP/DFR 06Jun44 (18Jun44) CIB FM 01May44 (14/44)	WIA 01Jun44
1169.	West, Leeman C. 35700059	PVT	C, G	MOS 745 ASGD fm 2nd Repl Dep per MR 11Dec43; evac sk 25Dec43 per MR 27Dec43; erron TFRD to DofP, DFR on 28Jan44 per MR 30Jan44; RTD fm Sk 21Feb44; Tfr in grade to G Co per MR 05Mar44; (KIA25SEP44 per 157 & ANB -- NOT ON DIV LIST; not on ABMC reg) CIB 01Jan44 (06/44 CC)	(KIA 25Sep44 in G Co)
1170.	West, Nelson K. 14049646	PVT	C	MOS 603 ASGD fm 2nd Repl Bn 18Dec43 per MR 22Dec43; evac sk 03Jan44 per MR 06Jan44; already evac sk, tfrd to 2nd Repl Dep CIB FM 01Jan44 (14/44)	
1171.	**Weston, John S.** 34935727	**PVT-PFC**	C	MOS 745 ASGD fm 3rd Repl Bn 24Jan45 (per MR 26Jan45); PMTD to PFC 06Mar45 (per MR 06Mar45); MIA 18Mar45 (per MR 20Mar45) to **KIA** 18Mar45 (per MR 26Mar45) (buried in Lorraine Cemetery); KIA18Mar45 as PFC per Div, 157 & ANB; ABMC 18Mar45, PH CIB 01Mar45 (10/45)	**KIA 18Mar45**

1172.	Whalley, James J. PCM-C 33073817	PFC	C	(Deployed w/the company, is on the Pine Camp menu) Sk evac 22Jul43 (Per MR 23Jul43); RTD fm sk 02Aug43 (per Mr 05Aug43); MIA 13Sep43, DFR (per MR 09Nov43) **(POW 13Sep43);** Mstr POW reg gives rpt date of 13Sep43, Stalag 2B, repatriated CIB FM 01Jan44 (14/44)	POW 13Sep43
1173.	Wheeler, Frank W. 38293438	PVT	C, G	**(Unknown date of assignment, not on Pine Camp menu)** Special Duty 11Nov43 to 45th Inf Div Mule Pack Train (Prov) (MR 26Dec43); (POW 26/9/44 in G Co) CIB DP (07/44) in G Co	(POW 26Sep44 in G Co)
1174.	**Whisenhunt,** Doyle W. 6862085	PVT-PFC	C	MOS 745 ASGD fm 71st Repl Bn 09Dec44; promoted to PFC 25Dec44 (per MR 26Dec44); evac sk, TFRD to DofP 28Dec44; RTD fm 2nd Reinforcement Dep 20Feb45 (per MR 20Feb45); Evac **WIA**, TFRD to DofP 20Mar45 (per MR 20Mar45) CIB 01Jan45 (01/45)	WIA 20Mar45
1175.	White, Burley L. 34138561	PVT	C	MOS 504 ASGD fm 2nd Repl Dep 23Apr44 (per MR 29Apr44); evac sk 25Jul44 (26Jul44) – Not Line of Duty (MR 30Jul44); RTD fm sk 29Jul44; RTD fm Not Line of Duty 25-27Jul44 (30Jul44); TFRD to DofP 01Aug44; RTD fm hosp 21Aug44 (sk NLD 01-07Aug44) (22Aug44); evac sk, TFRD to DofP 24Oct44 CIB FM 01May44 (14/44)	
1176.	**White**, George S. 33701223	PVT-PFC	C	MOS 745/746 ASGD 29May44 (09Jun44); evac sk 13Jul44; already evac sk TFRD to dofP/DFR 26Jul44 (02Aug44); REASG not joined fm 2nd Repl Dep 25Sep44; joined 29Sep44; **WIA** not hosp 22Oct44 (per MR 23Oct44); evac **WIA**, TFRD to DofP 04Nov44; REASGD fm 2nd Repl Dep 19Nov44; promoted to PFC 20Nov44 (per MR 27Nov44); evac sk 27Dec44; Already evac sk, TFRD to DofP 01Jan45 (per MR 01Jan45); REASG fm 3rd Repl Bn 29Jan45 (per MR 29Jan45); Evac **WIA** 18Mar45 (per MR 18Mar45); Already Evac **WIA**, TFRD to DofP 19Mar45 (per MR 19Mar45) CIB 01Sep44 (13/44); GCM PFC (16/44)	WIA 22Oct44 WIA 04Nov44 WIA 18Mar45
1177.	White, Pete 38677695	PVT-PFC	C	MOS 745 ASGD fm 71st Repl Bn 09Dec44; promoted to PFC 25Dec44 (per MR 26Dec44); evac sk, TFRD to DofP 28Dec44 CIB 01Jan45 (01/45)	
1178.	White, Robert J. 32922290	PVT	C, E	MOS 504 **(Unknown date of assignment, not on Pine Camp menu)** RTD fm 2nd Repl Dep 11Jan44 per MR 13Jan44; tfr in grade to E Co per MR 05Mar44 (DOW 03Jun44 per div & 157 list; not on ABMC reg) No discovered GO for CIB or GCM	(DOW 05Mar44 in E Co)

1179.	Whitfield, Leroy (NMI) SN NA	PVT	C	erroneously rptd 09Nov43 as ASGD fm Co F – did not join per MR 30Nov43 **NOT ASSIGNED** No discovered GO for CIB or GCM	
1180.	**Whitworth,** Roger B. 34634586	CPL- SSG	C	MOS 653 **(Unknown date of assignment, not on Pine Camp menu)** RTD fm 2nd Repl Dep 11Jan44 per MR 13Jan44; pmtd SGT per MR 25Jan44; pmtd SSG per MR 28Jan44; evac **WIA** (GSW left ankle 09Feb44) CIB FM 01Feb44 (14/44)	WIA 09Feb44
1181.	Whorley, Everett C. PCM-C	PFC	C	On Pine Camp menu	
1182.	Wicker, James M. PCM-C	PVT	C	On Pine Camp menu	
1183.	Widmier, Hugh E. 38006557 PCM-C	SGT	C	(Deployed w/the company, is on Pine Camp menu as SGT) MIA 13Sep43 DFR (per MR 24Sep43) **(POW 13Sep43);** Mstr POW reg gives rpt date of 13Sep43, Stalag 3B, repatriated CIB MIA as SGT in C Co (05/44); 01Jan44 per CC	POW 13Sep43
1184.	**Wild, Henry J. 33693413**	**PVT-PFC-CPL**	C	MOS 745/653 ASGD fm 2nd Repl Bn 14Jan44 per MR 18Jan44; pmtd to PFC 01May44; evac **WIA** 28May44; RTD fm **WIA** (16Jun44); evac **WIA**, TFRD to DofP 27Oct44; REASGD fm 2nd Repl Dep 19Nov44; promoted to CPL MOS 653 24Nov44; MIA 03Dec44 (per MR 06Dec44); Fm MIA 03Dec44 to **KIA** 03Dec44 (per MR 13Dec44) (buried in USA); KIA w/o date per div list; KIA03DEC44 per 157 list; MIA/KIA03DEC44 per ANB; not on ABMC reg CIB PFD (07/44)	WIA 28May44 WIA 27Oct44 **KIA 03Dec44**
1185.	Wiley, Louis J. 35556990	PVT	C, G	MOS 745 ASGD fm 2nd Repl Bn 14Jan44 per MR 18Jan44; Tfr in grade to G Co per MR 05Mar44 CIB (01/44); 01Feb44 per CC; 3rd Squad, 1st Platoon, G Co	
1186.	**Wiley,** Robert F. O-463325	2LT	C	ASGD 24Sep43 (per MR 28Sep43); evac **WIA** 13Nov43 per MR 16Nov43; already evac **WIA**, DFR per MR 23Nov43 CIB FM eff 01Jan44 (14/44)	WIA 13Nov43
1187.	Wilkens, Warren C. 12057993 PCM-C	PFC-CPL-SGT	C	(Deployed w/the company, is on the Pine Camp menu as PVT) Pmtd to CPL per MR 02Dec43; evac sk 01Jan44 per MR 04Jan44; promoted to SGT 04Jan44 per MR 05Jan44; already evac sk TFRD to DofP, DFR per MR 20Jan44; **(Missing entry of RTD) (Missing entry of evac sk)**; already evac sk, trfd to 2nd Repl Dep per MR 17Mar44 CIB FM as SGT in C Co (05/44); 01Jan44 per CC; CIB DP (07/44)	

1188. **Wilkin, Edward G.** **31416626**	**PVT-CPL**	C	MOS 745/653 ASGD fm 71st Repl Bn 09Dec44; promoted to PFC 25Dec44 (per MR 26Dec44); Evac sk, TFRD to DofP 07Jan45 (per MR 07Jan45); REASG fm 3rd Repl Bn 17Jan45 (per MR 17Jan45); PMTD to CPL, change in MOS to 653 24Mar45 (per MR 26Mar45); **KIA** 18Apr45 (per MR 21Apr45)**;** KIA18Apr45 as CPL per Div list; as CPL WILKINS in 157 list; not on ABMC reg as Wilkin or as Wilkins CIB 01Jan45 (01/45); GCM (8/45)	**KIA 18Apr45**
1189. Wilkins, James D. 33813162	PFC	C	GCM (32/45)	
1190. Williams, Charley (NMI) 38018912	PVT-PFC-CPL	C	MOS 653 (Deployed w/the company, is on the Pine Camp menu AS pvt) Promoted to PFC 03Nov43 per MR 05Nov43; pmtd to CPL 18Jan44 per MR 19Jan44; evac sk (burns 1st degree eyes and face, accident) 03Feb44; already evac sk, tfrd to DofP, DFR 04Mar44 per MR 05Apr44; RTD 08Apr44 (MR 17Apr44); TFRD on rotation to USA 01Aug44 GCM as CPL in C Co (02/44); CIB (03/44 - 01Jan44 per CC)	
1191. Williams, Cletis (NMI) 36446910	PVT-CPL	C	MOS 745/653 ASGD fm Co A 01Aug44; sk NLD 23 – 29Aug44 (25Nov44); evac sk, TFRFD to DofP 22Aug44; REASG not joined fm 2nd Repl Dep 25Sep44; joined 20Sep44 (per MR 25Nov44); **(Missing entry for promotion to PFC)**; promoted to CPL 24Dec44; MIA 21Jan45 (per MR 23Jan45) **(POW 20JAN45);** -- not on Mstr POW reg by name or SN -- IS listed as MIA in C Co as CPL at Reipertswiller CIB S/SGT in A Co (01/44 - 01Jan44 per CC); GCM PVT in C Co (16/44)	POW 20Jan45
1192. Williams, John W., Jr. 33089663 PCM-C	CPL	C	(Deployed w/the company, is on Pine Camp menu as PFC) MIA 13Sep43 DFR (per MR 24Sep43) **(POW 13Sep43);** Mstr POW reg gives rpt date of 13Sep44, Stalag Luft 3, repatriated CIB FM as CPL in C Co 01Jan44 (14/44)	POW 13Sep43
1193. **Williams,** Johnny L. 38700321	PVT-PFC	C	MOS 745 ASGD fm 71st Repl Bn 09Dec44; promoted to PFC 25Dec44 (per MR 26Dec44); Evac **WIA**, TFRD to DofP 14Jan45 (per MR 14Jan45); RTD fm 71st Reinf Bn 20Apr45 (per MR 21Apr45) CIB 01Jan45 (01/45); GCM (32/45)	WIA 14Jan45
1194. **Willingham,** Dennis E. 6955255	SSG	C	MOS 653 ASGD fm 103rd Inf Div 27Jan45 (per MR 01Feb45); Evac **WIA** 18Mar45 (per MR 18Mar45) CIB 01Mar45 (10/45); GCM (8/45)	WIA 18Mar45

1195.	Willis, Albert L. PCM-C 20829721	PFC	C	(Deployed w/the company, is on the Pine Camp menu) MIA 13Sep43 DFR (per MR 24Sep43) **(POW 01Dec43);** SN given as 20839731, s/b 20829721; Mstr POW reg gives rpt date of 01Dec43 w/o unit ID, Stalag 2B, repatriated CIB FM 01Jan44 (14/44) POW date was 13Sep43	POW 13Dec43
1196.	Wilson, Joe G. PCM-G 34365376	PVT	G, C	On Pine Camp menu as G Co; ASGD fr Co G 28Sep43; evac sk 03Nov43 per MR 06Nov43; RTD fm sk 27Nov43 per MR 29Nov43; evac sk 09Dec43 per MR 14Dec43; already evac sk, TFRD to DofP, DFR per MR 11Jan44 CIB FM 01Jan44 (14/44)	
1197.	**Wilson, Luther R.** 34517303	**PFC**	C	MOS 746 **(Unknown date of assignment, not on Pine Camp menu)** RTD fm 2nd Repl Dep 11Jan44 per MR 13Jan44; MIA 03May44, DFR; change from MIA 31May44 to **KIA** 31May44 (24Jun44) (buried in Sicily-Rome Cemetery);); KIA31May44 per div & 157list; MIA/KIA31MAY44 per ANB; ABMC 31May44, PH CIB (01/44 - 01Jan44 per CC	**KIA 31May44**
1198.	Wilson, Rolland I. 39924727	PVT	C	MOS 745 ASGD fm 71st Repl Bn 09Dec44; evac sk, TFRD to DofP 24Dec44; REASG fm 71st Reinf Bn 14May45 (per MR 15May45) CIB 01Jan45 (01/45); 2nd CIB as PFC eff 01Jan45 (35/45); GCM as PVT (32/45)	
1199.	Wilson, Walter F. (E.) 33634237	PVT- SGT	C	MOS 745/653 ASGD fm 2nd Repl Bn 14Jan44 per MR 18Jan44; Pmtd to Pfc 04Mar44 per MR 12Mar44; **LIA** not-hosp (burns 1st deg hands WP shell) 10May44 (MR 16May44); promoted to CPL (per MR 05Aug44); promoted to SGT MOS 653 07Oct44; promoted to SSG 24Nov44; evac sk, TFRD to DofP 26Nov44 (per MR 28Nov44) CIB (04/44 - 01Feb44 per CC); GCM SGT (16/44)	INJ 10May44
1200.	**Winemaker,** Sylvester S. 33073724	PVT-PFC	C	MOS 745 (Deployed w/the company, is on Pine Camp menu as PVT) **WIA** evac 12Sep43 (per MR 18Sep43); RTD fr DofP 06Mar44 per MR 10Mar44; **WIA** not hosp 10Jun44; **(Missing entry for evac)**; fm evac sk to 5th Army Rest Camp 01Jul44 (MR 07Jul44); RTD fm 5th Army Rest Camp 11Jul44; promoted to PFC 20Nov44 (per MR 27Nov44); Temporary duty to USA 06Dec44 CIB as PVT in C Co 01Jan44 (11/44); GCM (16/44)	WIA 12Sep43 WIA 10Jun44
1201.	Winfrey, Clifford J. SN NA (Delta, CO)	SGT	C	Induction Roster, 16Sep40	
1202.	Wiszowaty, John T. 42133752	PFC	C	GCM (32/45)	
1203.	Woleslagle, Philip M. 33670879	PFC	C, E	MOS 504 **(unknown date of assignment, not on Pine Camp menu) (Missing entry of evac)**; RTD fm 2nd Repl Dep 11Jan44 per MR 13Jan44 CIB DP (07/44) in E Co	

1204.	Wolfe, David H. 36878657	PVT	C, 3HQ	MOS 610 ASGD fr 2nd Repl Dep 29May44 (11Jun44); TFRD to 3HQ (27Jun44) CIB 01Sep44 (11/44) in 3HQ	
1205.	**Wolfe**, Jerry M. 32191515	CPL	L, C	**(Unknown date of assignment, on Pine Camp menu as PFC in L Co) (Missing entry of evac)**; RTD fm sk 30Oct43 per MR 01Nov43; evac **WIA** 12Nov43 per MR 15Nov43; already evac **WIA** TFRD to DofP, DFR per MR 15Dec43 CIB FM as CPL in C Co 01Jan44 (14/44)	WIA 12Nov43
1206.	**Woodruff, Alva H., Jr. 15102845**	**PVT**	C	MOS 745 ASGD fm 71st Repl Bn 09Dec44; promoted to PFC 25Dec44 (per MR 26Dec44); MIA 21Jan45 (per MR 23Jan45) (**KIA** O/A 20JAN45) (buried in USA); MIA21JAN45 per ANB; KIA21Jan45 per div list -- NOT ON 157 LIST; not on ABMC reg CIB 01Jan45 (01/45)	**KIA 20Jan45**
1207.	Woods, Henry L. PCM-B 38006078	SGT-PVT	C	SGT in B Co per Pine Camp menu; ASGD & jd from B Co per MR 16Mar44; evac sk 26Jul44 (27Jul44); already evac sk reclassified limited assignment 28Jul44 GCM in B Co (02/44); CIB FM as PVT in C Co 01Jan44 (14/44)	
1208.	**Worth**, Walter A. 34170178	PFC-CPL-SGT	C	MOS 653 (Deployed w/the company, is on the Pine Camp menu as PFC) Pmtd to CPL per MR 02Dec43; evac sk 27Dec43 per MR 01Jan44; RTD fm sk 17Jan44 per MR 20Jan44; evac sk (oellulitis left foot) 09Feb44; RTD fm sk 02Mar44 per MR 10Mar44; pmtd to SGT 10Apr44 (per MR 11Apr44); evac **WIA** (BC Pen W hand & L knee shell frag) 30May44; already evac **WIA** TFRD to DofP and DFR 02Jun44 (15Jun44); REASG fm DofP 06Aug44; evac sk, TFRD to DofP per MR 16Sep44 CIB as SGT in C Co (03/44); 01Jan44 per CC; GCM (02/44)	WIA 30May44 WIA 02Jun44
1209.	Worthington, Gaylon O. 36562888	CPL	C	MOS 653 ASGD fm 3rd Repl Bn 20Dec44 (per MR 21Dec44); MIA 21Jan45 (per MR 23Jan45) **(POW 20JAN45);** Mstr POW reg gives rpt date of 26Mar45 w/o unit ID, Stalag 5B, repatriated -- check date disparity CIB 01Jan45 (01/45)	POW 20Jan45
1210.	Wozniak, Stanley A. 33330601	CPL	C, E	MOS 653 ASGD fr 2 Repl Dep 04Jun44 (14Jun44); evac sk 03Jul44; TFRD to 2nd Repl Dep but not dptd 19Jul44 ; s/b ATCHD & jnd (MR 23Jul44); RTD fm sk 08Jul44; already attached fm 2nd Repl Det reld fm atchment (per MR 05Aug44); (KIA in E Co w/o date as SSG per div list; KIA01DEC44 per 157 list; MIA/KIA01DEC44 per ANB; ABMC 01Dec44, Epinal Cemetery SS, PH) CIB as SGT in E Co 01Sep44 (13/44	(KIA 01Dec44 in E Co)

1211.	**Wren,** Clyde H. PCM-C 20837751 (Delta, CO)	SGT	C	PVT in C Co per Induction Roster, 16Sep40; SGT in C Co per Pine Camp menu) **(Missing entry of WIA)**; already evac **WIA**, DFR per MR 23Nov43 CIB FM as SGT in C Co 01Jan44 (14/44)	**WIA unk**
1212.	Wright, James I. 33856561	PVT	C	GCM (32/445)	
1213.	**Wright**, Jesse L. 33649143	PVT-PFC	C	MOS 603/504 **(Unknown datge of assignment, not on Pine Camp menu)** Evac **WIA**, TFRD to DofP 23Sep44; RTD fm 2nd Repl Bn 18Dec43 (per MR 22Dec43); evac **WIA** (pen w l foot, shell frag) 02Mar44 per MR 07Mar44; RTD fm **WIA** 18Apr44 (per MR 21Apr44); promoted to PFC (per MR 05Aug44); REASG but not joined fm 2nd Repl Dep 07Oct44; joined 08Oct44; evac sk, TFRD to DofP 25Nov44 (per MR 28Nov44) CIB (03/44 - 01Jan44 per CC); GCM (16/44)	WIA 23Sep44 WIA 02Mar44 WIA 18Apr44
1214.	**Wright**, William E. 36690447	PVT	C	MOS 745 ASGD fr 2 Repl Dep 29May44 (14Jun44); promoted to PFC 07Oct44; **WIA** not hosp 30Oct44 (11Nov44); evac **WIA**, TFRD to DofP 04Nov44; REASG fm 2nd Repl Dep 11Nov44; evac sk, TFRD to DofP 25Nov44 (per MR 28Nov44) CIB 01Sep44 (13/44)	WIA 30Oct44 WIA 04Nov44
1215.	**Wyrostek**, Stanley W. 31445390	PFC	C	MOS 745 ASGD fm 2nd Repl Dep 29Sep44; evac **SWIA**, TFRD to DofP 11Oct44; ASGD fm 3rd Repl Bn 31Jan45 (per MR 31Jan45); Evac INJ, TFRD to DofP 20Mar45 (per MR 20Mar45) CIB FM 01Oct44 (14/44)	WIA 11Oct44
1216.	**Yanulaitis,** Charles G. 33073865 PCM-C	PFC	C	(Deployed w/the company, is on the Pine Camp menu as PFC) **WIA** 14Jul43; already evac **WIA**, DFR (01Aug43) CIB FM as PFC in C Co 01Jan44 (14/44)	WIA 14Jul43
1217.	Yashinsky, John J. 33621132	PVT	C	MOS 521 ASGD fm 2nd Repl Dep per MR 11Dec43; evac sk 19Dec43 per MR 21Dec43; already evac sk TFRD to DofP, DFR per MR 21Jan44; **(Missing entry of RTD)**; **(Missing entry of evac)**; already evac sk, TFRD to 401st Repl Co 05Jun44 CIB FM 01Jan44 (14/44)	
1218.	Young, Ples D. 20418809	PFC	C, E	MOS 604 ASGD & joined 07Feb44; tfr in grade to E Co per MR 05Mar44 CIB (01/44); 01Mar44 per CC **(NOT ON THIS GO IN C OR E)**; GCM (08/44)	
1219.	Yurash, Alfred J. 32918016	PVT-PFC	C	MOS 653 ASGD fm 2nd Repl Bn 14Jan44 per MR 18Jan44; **(Missing entry of promotion to PFC)**; evac sk 18May44 (MR 21May44); RTD fm sk 23May44; evac sk 03Jun44; already evac sk to DofP/DFR 14Jun44 (20Jun44) CIB FM 01Feb44 (14/44)	
1220.	Zamora, Mike L. PCM-C	SGT	C	On Pine Camp menu	

1221.	Zander, Edward H. 36834902	PVT	C	**(Unknown date of assignment)** Evac sk 29Jul44 (30Jul44); already evac sk, TFRD to DofP/DFR 30Jul44 (06Aug44) **(Not on CIB register)** No discovered GO for CIB or GCM	
1222.	**Zankel**, Leonard G. PCM-B O-2011728	2LT	B, A, C	PVT in B Co per Pine Camp menu; ASGD 08Apr45 upon commission 08Apr45 from elsewhere (per MR 11Apr45); **WIA** not hosp (fragment to upper lip) 19Apr45 (per MR 30Apr45 CIB as SSG in A Co (01/44 - 01Jan44 per CC); GCM as 1/SGT (02/44) Lt in C Co at Dachau	WIA 19Apr45
1223.	Zauhar, Donald R. 37598944	PVT-PFC	C	MOS 745 ASGD fm 3rd Repl Bn 24Jan45 (per MR 26Jan45); PMTD to PFC 06Mar45 (per MR 06Mar45); Evac **INJ**, TFRD to DofP 18Mar45 (per MR 18Mar45); REASG but DS to 71st Reinf Bn 07Apr45 (per MR 11Apr45); relieved of DS to 71st Reinf Bn 11Apr45 (per MR 11Apr45) CIB 01Mar45 (10/45); GCM as PFC (32/45)	INJ 18Mar45
1224.	Zelasko (or Zelasto), Emil J. 35065412	PVT	C	MOS 745 ASGD fm 2nd Repl Bn 14Jan44 per MR 18Jan44; evac sk (exhaustion) 20Feb44; already evac to DofP/DFR 29Mar44; RTD 20Apr44 (MR 24Apr44); evac sk 10May44 (MR 15May44); to DofP/DFR 16May44 (MR 24May44) CIB FM 01Feb44 (14/44)	
1225.	**Ziegler,** Dale W. 36446695	PVT- SSG	C	MOS 345 ASGD fm 2nd Repl Dep per MR 11Dec43; attached to 45th Div Mule Train 12Dec43 per MR 13Dec43; attached to 45th Div Mule Train 16Dec43 DUPLICATE ENTRY, SEE MR 12Dec43 (corrected by MR 27Jan44 to delete this entry); RTD fm SD w/Div Mule Train 02Jan44 per MR 06Jan44; erron rptd twice as SD to 45th Div Mule Train on MR 13&16Dec43, rmk on 16Dec43 s/b deleted per MR 27Jan44; Pmtd to Pfc 04Mar44 per MR 12Mar44; pmtd to Cpl **(Unknown date)**; pmtd SGT MOS 653 24May44; pmtd to SSG (01Jul44); evac **WIA** 24Sep44; **(Missing entry for RTD)**; evac sk, TFRD to DofP 25Nov44 (per MR 28Nov44) CIB (03/44 - 01Jan44 per CC); GCM S/SGT (08/44); CIB S/SGT FM 01Jan44 (14/44)	WIA 24Sep44
1226.	**Zielinski**, Stanley J. 33435040	PVT	C	ASGD fr Co G 28Sep43; evac sk 20Dec43 per MR 27Dec43; already evac sk TFRD to DofP, DFR per MR 21Jan44; RTD fm DofP 23Jan44 per MR 27Jan44; evac **WIA** (LW epigastruim r shell frag) 14Feb44; TFRD to DofP & DFR 24Feb44; already evac **WIA**, trfd to DofP and DFR 24Feb44 per MR 15Mar44 CIB FM 01Jan44 (14/44)	WIA 14Feb44

1227.	**Zito, Angelo F.** **31412156**	**PVT-PFC**	C	MOS 745 ASGD fm 3rd Repl Bn 24Jan45 (per MR 26Jan45); PMTD to PFC 06Mar45 (per MR 06Mar45); **KIA** 20Mar45 (per MR 22Mar45) (buried in USA); KIA20Mar45 as PFC per div & 157 list; not on ABMC reg CIB 01Mar45 (10/45)	**KIA 20Mar45**
1228.	**Zuckerman,** Sidney (NMI) 12148825	PVT	C	MOS 745/677 ASGD fr MP Platoon 45th Div 10Aug43; evac **WIA** 13Sep43 (per MR 20Sep43); RTD fm DofP 20Dec43 per MR 24Dec43; evac sk 25Dec43 per MR 28Dec43; already evac sk, TFRD to 2nd Repl Dep per MR 16Jan44 CIB FM 01Jan44 (14/44)	WIA 13Sep43
1229.	**Zurbrugg**, Oscar F. 32680762	SGT-SSG-TSG	C	MOS 652/651 **(Unknown date of assignment, not on Pine Camp menu)** RTD fm 2nd Repl Dep 11Jan44 per MR 13Jan44; pmtd to SSG per MR 25Jan44; evac sk (FUO) 11Jun44 (13Jun44); RTD fm sk (16Jun44); pmtd TSG (24Jun44); evac **WIA** 24Sep44; evac sk, TFRD to DofP 23Nov44 (per MR 27Nov44) – erron entry per MR 01Dec44; REASG fm 2nd Repl Dep 21Nov44 (per MR 22Nov44); entries of 23Nov44 of evac sk and 26Nov44 of TFRD to DofP 23Nov44 are erroneous (per MR 01Dec44); Discharged to accept commission 22Nov44, left company (per MR 04Dec44) CIB (01/44); 01Feb44 per CC; GCM (02/44)	WIA 24Sep44
1230.					
1231.	**Barth, Carl (NMI)** 38006009	T-5	MD	**KIA** 31May44 (MR 05Jul44); per MR 08Jul44 this man s/b rptd on MR of Med Det (buried in USA) (not on ABMC register) **EM NOT INCLUDED IN COMPANY TOTAL, SINCE HE WAS ASSIGNED TO THE MEDICAL DETACHMENT** No discovered GO for CIB or GCM	**KIA 31May44**

Printed in the United States
By Bookmasters